THE LONG WAR

A New History of U.S. National Security Policy Since World War II

Andrew J. Bacevich, *Editor*

Columbia University Press   *New York*

Columbia University Press
Publishers Since 1893
New York   Chichester, West Sussex

Library of Congress Cataloging-in-Publication Data
The long war : a new history of U.S. national security policy since World War II / Andrew J.
Bacevich, editor.
     p. cm.
  Includes index.
  ISBN 978–0–231–13158–2 (cloth : alk. paper) — ISBN 978–0–231–50586–4 (e-book)
  1. National security—United States.   2. United States—Military policy.   3. United
States—Politics and government—1945–1989   4. United States—Politics and government—
1989– I. Bacevich, A. J. II. Title.
  UA23.L685   2007
  355'.033573—dc22   2006037804

CONTENTS

INTRODUCTION

Andrew J. Bacevich

Growing up in the Midwest during the 1950s and early 1960s, I came to understand the narrative of contemporary history and the narrative of the Cold War as one and the same. That the Cold War provided the organizing principle of the age was self-evident, even to a young boy. Catch the headlines on WGN, read the *Chicago Tribune,* flip through an occasional issue of *Time* or *Life,* and the rest was easy: the era's great antagonisms—the United States vs. the Soviet Union, West vs. East, Free World vs. Communist bloc—told you pretty much everything you needed to know.

In this sense, if the Cold War was not without its anxious moments, it also served to impart order and clarity to American life. The anti-Communist crusade provided an authoritative template, equally useful for interpreting events abroad and developments at home. View the world through the Cold War prism, and discriminating between friend and foe, good and evil, important priorities and marginal ones became child's play.

Further enhancing the Cold War's standing was the disparity between what we knew about the way it began and what we were able to project about its likely course and conclusion. Whereas observers fixed the origins of the conflict with reassuring specificity, its scope and duration appeared ominously indefinite. We knew (or thought we knew) exactly when and how the Cold War had come about; we were clueless about when and how it was going to end.

As one consequence, the past became largely irrelevant. When World War II ended, history had (apparently) begun anew, thereby endowing the Cold War with an aura of remarkable singularity: Americans were living in a time the like of which humankind had never before encountered. Although events that had occurred prior to 1946 or 1947 might retain a certain quaint interest, few of them had much to say about the daunting challenges now facing the nation. Munich, Pearl Harbor, Yalta, and Hiroshima were the exceptions that proved the rule: events shorn of historical context and pressed into service as dark parables teaching universal truths.

As a second consequence, crisis became a permanent condition. In Cold War America, urgency, danger, and uncertainty permeated public discourse. Presidents competed with one another in proclaiming states of national emergency that seemingly never got revoked. All of this had a powerful disciplining effect. In 1917, an acerbic Randolph Bourne had observed that "In a time of faith, skepticism is the most intolerable of insults."[1] Americans in the decades after World War II embraced an especially compelling faith; for the great majority of citizens, skepticism became not simply intolerable but unimaginable.

The essence of that faith, to which all but a handful of marginalized contrarians devotedly adhered, was contained in twin convictions. According to the first, the United States was a nation under siege, beset by dire threats, its very survival at risk. According to the second, only the capacity and willingness to assert all of the instruments of hard power, instantly and without hesitation, could keep America's enemies at bay.

These two notions describe the essence of the national security paradigm that has shaped U.S. policy for well over a half-century. From the late 1940s through the 1980s, responding to the threat posed by international communism meant placing a premium on maintaining, threatening, and at times using force. From this imperative there evolved the various components of the national security state: a large standing military establishment scattered around the world; a vast arsenal of strategic weapons kept ready for instant employment; intelligence agencies operating beyond public scrutiny in a "black world"—the entire conglomeration tended by an army of devoted bureaucrats planning, managing, budgeting, and elevating group-think to a fine art. To lend a veneer of rationality to the activities of this sprawling apparatus, successive administrations devised "doctrines" with imposing names. For Harry Truman there was Containment; for Dwight D. Eisenhower, Massive Retaliation; for John F. Kennedy, Flexible Response. With anxious citizens looking to the commander-in-chief to keep them safe, presidents accrued—and exercised—an ever-expanding array of prerogatives. In the process, the legislative branch by-and-large functioned as an enabler and drifted toward irrelevance.

With the Congress deferential if not altogether supine on matters related to national security, politics centered increasingly on the question of
who controlled the Oval Office. More often than not, the key to winning
the White House lay in scare-mongering, successful candidates from
Eisenhower onward letting it be known that in a "dangerous world" elect-
ing their opponent was to invite the barbarians through the gates or risk
the cataclysm of World War III.

Although the social and cultural upheaval associated with the 1960s,
reinforced by the disaster of Vietnam, briefly opened up a window for
skepticism, the overriding requirements of national security soon slammed
that window shut. Americans today remember the Sixties as an era of profound and enduring change. When it came to national security policy,
however, the impact proved to be ephemeral and insignificant.

Within a half-decade after the fall of Saigon, orthodoxy had reasserted itself: with the election of Ronald Reagan to the presidency, America was once
again "standing tall." In the context of domestic politics, the phrase "Jimmy
Carter" took its place alongside "Munich" and "Yalta," warning of the fate
certain to befall any politician insufficiently alive to the imperative of basing
U.S. policy on vigilance, assertiveness, and unassailable military superiority.

The Cold War did eventually end. As far as the cult of national security
was concerned, this ostensibly monumental development hardly mattered:
our security preoccupations survived the passing of the Soviet Union intact.
The symbiotic relationship between the national security state and the imperial presidency endured into the 1990s. As the various alarms of that decade demonstrated, even after the collapse of communism—even when
history itself had "ended"—the drumbeat of ongoing crisis continued.

The aura of insecurity that had enveloped Cold War America persisted—as did the habits, routines, and practices that had evolved over the
previous half-century. In Panama and the Persian Gulf, in Somalia and
Haiti, in the Balkans and the Taiwan Straits, George H. W. Bush and Bill
Clinton acted in accordance with the dictates of the established national
security paradigm. In doing so, and by no means incidentally, they sustained the freedom of presidential action that had evolved during the
postwar era. If Truman could order U.S. forces into Korea, Eisenhower
could overthrow the governments of Iran and Guatemala, and Kennedy
could decide for or against nuclear war in October 1962, then surely
there could be no objection to Clinton bombing Belgrade or Baghdad.

In this sense, George W. Bush's response to 9/11 did not mark some radical departure from the past. Following in the footsteps of his predecessors,

Bush merely exploited the process whereby the imperial presidency and our obsessions with national security feed on one another. The essence of the Bush Doctrine can be distilled into a single phrase: "more still"—more emphasis on accruing military power, more authority to the president to employ that power, more diligent efforts to impose American will on the world beyond our borders.

According to the Bush administration, the threat posed by Islamic radicalism obliged the United States to shed any lingering constraints (and scruples) pertaining to the use of force. In 2002, the president explicitly committed the United States to a doctrine of preventive war, a strategic concept uncomfortably reminiscent of Japan and Germany in the 1930s.[2] Furthermore, consistent with real and manufactured emergencies of the previous sixty years, deciding when and where to employ armed force remained the president's business and his alone. So at least President Bush and his loyal lieutenants have insisted, with neither the Congress nor the Democratic opposition nor the media mounting anything more than half-hearted objections.

The administration marketed this enterprise as the Global War on Terror, a conflict that it likened to the great struggles of the twentieth century. The label stuck. Seeing September 11 as a reprise of December 7, most Americans readily embraced the proposition that only by embarking upon a vast open-ended war could the United States avert an even greater disaster. That in conducting this war President Bush should claim the autonomy that Truman had enjoyed in dealing with Korea or JFK with Cuba was taken for granted.

By early 2006, however, according to statements by senior officials in the Bush administration and in the United States military, the global war on terror had morphed into what they now chose to call "the Long War."[3]

Detached from place, excluding any reference to adversary or purpose, admitting no limits, the Long War reveals only a single aspect of the conflict it purports to describe: its temporal dimension, which is vast. Amorphous, malleable, infinitely expansible, and therefore easily adaptable to changing conditions or requirements that present themselves, the Long War confers on the national security elite unlimited drawing rights on American resources. It is the ultimate blank check.

Yet cast in somewhat different terms, this conception of a Long War is rich with analytical potential. Indeed, as a means to gain some fresh historical perspective on our current national security predicament, this evocative and suggestive phrase is ideal.

Seen from a historian's point of view, America's Long War did not begin with the attack on the World Trade Center. Instead, the conflict dates
from World War II. Ever since that time, despite much talk of peace lying
just around the corner, the people constituting what Bourne referred to as
"the significant classes" have tacitly subscribed to the premise that genuine security is actually unobtainable and that even imperfect, tenuous security requires that the United States engage in perpetual struggle and
accept the necessity of endless exertions.[4]

Far from inaugurating the Long War, the events of 9/11 merely marked the
transition to that war's latest phase. Indeed, on the far side of the immediate
struggle against violent Islamic radicalism lie more threats and new challenges. Some of the those threats even now are becoming visible, with many
in Washington already pointing to China as the inevitable next competitor
with which the United States will be obliged to deal. With the Long War having
already proven to be of far greater duration than most Americans recognize,
it is not hyperbole to suggest that the conflict promises to go on forever.

The aim of this volume is to take stock of that Long War from various
points of view and to argue that a fresh, comprehensive interpretation of
America's response to the insecurities that have plagued the nation since
World War II is an urgent intellectual task. In conceiving this volume, it
was never my intent that those participating in the project would conform to some preconceived interpretive line. Nor did I expect our collective efforts to yield a particular set of conclusions in which all might
concur. As editor, I merely encouraged contributors to take a broad view,
to take into account the latest findings of other scholars, and, if they were
so inclined, to be willing to break some interpretive china. They have not
disappointed me.

Each of the essays that follow stands on its own. Having said that, in my
own judgment at least, the collection as a whole conveys certain larger insights that may have some bearing on the still-evolving Long War.

The first of these has to do with what we might call the enduring
shadow of World War II. Out of the American experience of global war
during the years 1941–1945 came habits, ambitions, and expectations that
left a large and lasting imprint on virtually all subsequent matters related
to national security. As more than a few of the essays in this collection
suggest, World War II ought to be regarded as the Long War's opening
chapter rather than as its prehistory.

The second point offers a variation on the first. As several of the following essays make clear, if it makes no sense, in the context of national

security policy, to draw a sharp line between World War II and the decades that follow, neither does it make any sense to perpetuate the conventional demarcation of those decades into discrete episodes: the Cold War from 1947 to 1989, the brief post–Cold War era from 1990 until September 2001, and the Global War on Terror, from 9/11 onward.

From our present-day perspective, this periodization obscures rather than clarifies. In fact, the so-called Cold War was by no means simply a face-off between East and West; during this period the preliminary rounds of the West's renewed conflict with the Islamic world occurred. For today's undergraduate, the key event of 1948 was not the Berlin Airlift; it was the creation of Israel. The big story of 1956 was not the Hungarian uprising but the crisis over Suez. U.S. support for the Afghan resistance in the 1980s matters less because it helped bring down the Soviet Union than because it produced the Taliban.

As for the so-called post–Cold War period, it was not some dreamy decade during which U.S. policymakers deluded themselves with visions of globalization and free trade. On the contrary, the 1990s saw the United States almost continuously jockeying for advantage in the Persian Gulf, the Horn of Africa, the Balkans, Central Asia, and elsewhere. More often than not, the jockeying entailed violence. Well before September 2001, that is, the locus of the Long War had shifted into Greater Middle East.

The third point relates to the manifest inadequacies of the American foreign policy elite and of the national security apparatus that is their handiwork. My own critical assessment of U.S. civil-military relations since World War II calls attention to a fact that Americans are loath to acknowledge: national security policy has long been the province of a small, self-perpetuating, self-anointed group of specialists. Members of this Power Elite, as C. Wright Mills trenchantly dubbed them a half-century ago, are dedicated to the proposition of excluding democratic influences from the making of national security policy. To the extent that members of the national security apparat have taken public opinion into consideration, they have viewed it as something to manipulate, a charge as true in 1947 when Harry Truman set out to "scare hell" out of the American people about the Soviet menace as it was in 2002 when George W. Bush exaggerated the menace posed by Saddam Hussein. Viewing the average citizen as uninformed, fickle, and provincial, members of this elite imagine themselves to be sophisticated, sagacious, and coolly analytical.

Peppering the essays that follow is evidence calling these claims into question. Although U.S. policymakers have at times evinced prudence and foresight in matters related to national security, the Long War is filled with instances of incompetence, poor judgment, and a callow unwillingness to face the facts. Ignorance, prejudice, and something akin to irrational hysteria have informed decisions.

Time and again, members of the foreign policy elite have misperceived the world and misconstrued American interests, thereby exacerbating rather than alleviating threats. Time and again, they have misunderstood war and the consequences likely to flow from the use of force. The frequency with which senior U.S. officials have disregarded long-term goals in favor of what appears expedient in the short term calls into question the extent to which "strategy" as such actually figures in the making of policy.

Furthermore, the institutions created to assist this elite in managing the Long War have seldom lived up to their advance billing. All too frequently dysfunctional and almost always unaccountable, they have been more attuned to the pursuit of institutional goals and the preservation of bureaucratic privilege than to tending to the national interest. In his brilliant and underappreciated book *The Fifty-Year Wound,* Derek Leebaert tabulated the enormous costs that Americans paid to achieve victory in the Cold War—not only enormous but excessive because of the ineptitude and fecklessness of the national security bureaucracy.[5] The essays collected here carry on with the process of tallying up those costs, material and moral, as they continue to accrue.

The fourth and final point emerges from the third. Because the formulation of national security policy has been undemocratic, public discourse related to those policies has been sterile, formulaic, and unproductive, more posturing than principled debate. The hegemonic status of the national security paradigm has served to squelch any consideration of real alternatives, despite the persistence and sporadic political influence of organized dissent. Habits and routines that became hard-wired during the decades after 1945, but whose relevance to a post-9/11 world has become highly questionable, remain off-limits for critical reexamination. These include the notion that the principal mission of the Department of Defense is not defense but "global power projection;" that the deployment of U.S. forces around the world provides a cost-effective way to maintain stability; and that exerting American power to export American values is good for "them" and good for us.

Whether or not Americans can devise something to take the place of the received wisdom on national security is a very large question indeed. Doing so implies a Great Debate, in Washington but especially among the public at large. Certainly, a precondition for such a debate is to see more clearly exactly how we got where we are today.

In 1917 when the perceived imperatives of national security found two million doughboys crossing the Atlantic to put an end to war while making the world safe for democracy, Randolph Bourne wrote that "There is work to be done to prevent this war of ours from passing into popular mythology as a holy crusade."[6] In our own day, there is similar work to be done: lest it become encrusted with myth and sow confusion as to our own true interests, we must begin seeing the Long War as it really is. We offer this volume in hopes of contributing to that cause.

Notes

1. Randolph Bourne, *The War and the Intellectuals: Collected Essays, 1915–1919* (New York, 1964), 5.
2. "President Bush Delivers Graduation Speech at West Point," (June 1, 2002), http://www.whitehouse.gov/news/releases/2002/06/20020601-3.html, accessed February 11, 2006.
3. Josh White and Ann Scott Tyson, "Rumsfeld Offers Strategies for Current War," *The Washington Post* (February 3, 2006).
4. Bourne, *War and the Intellectuals*, 75.
5. Derek Leebaert, *The Fifty-Year Wound: The True Price of America's Cold War Victory* (Boston, 2002).
6. Bourne, *War and the Intellectuals*, 13.

THE LONG WAR

1. LIBERATION OR DOMINANCE?
THE IDEOLOGY OF U.S. NATIONAL SECURITY POLICY

Arnold A. Offner

In September 2002 President George W. Bush's administration published "The National Security Strategy of the United States" (NSS), an unusually strong ideological statement explaining the U.S. government's intent to combine American principles and power to effect American goals under the rubric of a new "American internationalism."[1] The Bush NSS rests on four concepts. First is the belief that America's unequaled power, sustained by its emphasis on freedom and constitutional government, imposes special responsibility on the United States to move the world toward similar political-economic models. Second is the view that the Cold War security strategies of containment and deterrence of powerful adversaries no longer apply because the new enemies are rogue or failed states that give rise to, or assist, tyrants and terrorists, who make weapons of mass destruction (WMDs) their weapons of first choice. Thus the U.S. must be ready to strike unilaterally and preemptively, i.e., before threats are fully formed.[2] Third is the belief that the "lessons of history" demonstrate that market economies are the best means to prosperity, and the U.S. will press other nations to effect "pro-growth" policies. Fourth, the U.S. will not permit any adversary to pursue a military buildup that equals or surpasses that of this nation.

The Bush NSS has prompted great controversy, especially regarding the concepts of unilateralism, preemption, and hegemony. Some analysts contend that the Bush NSS is consistent with past national security doctrine, including its emphasis on American exceptionalism and mission.[3] Other analysts view the Bush NSS as a radical or revolutionary departure that negates traditional national security principles, especially regarding multilateralism, collective action, equality of nations, and the rule of international law.[4] This essay will explore U.S. national security ideology from the 1940s to the present with a view to assessing the Bush NSS.

I

Ever since John Winthrop admonished his Puritan settlers in 1630 to "be as a city upon a hill," Americans have believed that they were destined to establish an exceptional and model society.[5] Americans have also viewed expansion as a means to prosperity and security. They held that it was their "manifest destiny" to overspread the continent, waged war against Mexico to gain California and facilitate Pacific trade, and took the Philippines after fighting Spain over Cuba. Secretary of State John Hay's Open Door Notes in 1899–1900 calling for equal commercial opportunity for all powers in China sought to advance America's growing "informal empire" over imperial spheres of influence.[6] Thus by 1900 American leaders had forged "a broad definition of national security that would carry the nation toward greatness in the world."[7]

President Woodrow Wilson created the modern ideological framework for global intervention with his call in 1917 for America to make the world safe for democracy and view that American principles were the principles of mankind. His Fourteen Points proposed a program of freer trade, arms limitation, self-determination, and a League of Nations, but resurgent nationalism at home and abroad undermined his grand plans.

Franklin Roosevelt brought pragmatic Wilsonianism to the White House in 1933. Initially he urged a "well ordered neutrality" toward foreign crises. But after the Munich Conference in 1938, he pressed rearmament and then "cash-and-carry" sale of war goods to Britain and France, and following Germany's invasion of Western Europe in 1940 he warned that "old dreams of universal empire are again rampant."[8] He soon stretched his executive authority to exchange "overage" destroyers for British bases in the New World, denounced the "unholy" Axis Alliance, called on America to become the "great arsenal of democracy," and proposed Lend Lease to send war materials to nations deemed vital to U.S. security.[9]

This extraordinary measure drew strong bipartisan support from Kansas Republican newspaper editor William Allen White's broad-based Committee to Defend America by Aiding the Allies, and from the more elite, Atlantic-oriented Century Group, which contended that Nazi Germany's victory would imperil America's world trade and force the United States to become a "garrison state." Strong bipartisan opposition ranged from Socialist leader Norman Thomas to the highly conservative America First Committee, whose leaders wanted the U.S. to build Fortress America behind the security of two oceans. And mainstream conservative leaders, such as Republican Senator Arthur Vandenberg of Michigan, charged that Lend Lease committed the U.S. to spending "*billions upon billions*" and made the White House headquarters for "the world's wars."[10] But Lend Lease carried, propelled by hope that aid to the allies might keep the U.S. out of war.

After Germany attacked the Soviet Union in 1941, FDR extended aid to Moscow, convinced that the Red Army was the best means to defeat Adolf Hitler's forces.[11] Roosevelt and Prime Minister Winston Churchill also issued their Atlantic Charter, a Wilsonian statement of "war aims" that renounced territorial gain and affirmed the right to self-government, freedom of the seas, free trade, and freedom from fear and want.[12] FDR then deceptively used the incident of a German submarine firing torpedoes at the U. S. destroyer *Greer* to order U.S. ships to shoot on sight in the Atlantic, and in a ringing Navy Day address he claimed to have secret German documents (all forgeries, provided by the British intelligence service) showing Nazi intent to carve Central and South America into vassal states and replace "the God of Love and Mercy with the God of Blood."[13]

FDR also sought to contain Japan's war against China by curbing critical exports, including oil, to Tokyo in 1941, but this raised the stakes for Japan. And when negotiations with Japan faltered, U.S. fear of a "Pacific Munich" led it to reject a proposed summit meeting and an interim accord. But even as war seemed imminent, Roosevelt rejected a preemptive strike because "We are a democracy and a peaceful people."[14]

Still, FDR had already forged the ideology and basic systems for the national security state. He had defined the global war in Manichean terms: democratic, freedom loving nations that sought no aggrandizement, spoke for political and commercial rights for all, and represented the God of Mercy, versus the evil Axis of totalitarian states that sought world domination and represented the God of Hate. He had built an immensely powerful presidency, with authority to dispense "billions and billions" of dollars of war goods to nations deemed vital to U.S. security, and he waged undeclared war in the Atlantic and used questionable incidents and spurious documents to rouse the public to national security threats.

During the Second World War, Roosevelt blended Wilsonianism and realism to maintain an alliance of necessity. He made "freedom" the rallying cry of U.S. policy with his pledge in 1942 to Four Freedoms—of speech

and religion, and from fear and want—for all people.[15] But the State Department balked at his proposal to settle with Russia on its historical territorial and security claims as a "Baltic Munich" and violative of the Atlantic
Charter. Military imperatives also complicated the pursuit of freedom.
The delay of the Anglo-American second front in Europe until June 1944
left the Russians to fight their immensely costly "Great Patriotic War" in
the East, but this allowed the Red Army to gain control of Eastern Europe.
Thus at the Yalta Conference in 1945 FDR had to settle for an unenforce-
able commitment to free elections in the Declaration on Liberated Europe. He also agreed to the Soviets' reclaiming their former Czarist
concessions in Manchuria in order to secure Stalin's commitment to enter
the Pacific War and his promise to support Jiang Jieshi's Guomindang
(GMD) regime in China in the looming battle with Mao Zedong's Chinese Communist Party (CCP).

The Roosevelt administration also sought to effect postwar reconstruction, currency stabilization, and a liberal world trading order by creating the
International Bank for Reconstruction and Development and the International Monetary Fund at Bretton Woods in 1944.[16] Further, FDR supported
creation of the United Nations to repulse aggression through collective action, and hoped as well to contain the Soviet Union by incorporating it into
the UN and an evolving, multilateral postwar world order.[17]

II

The Second World War brought massive death and destruction to Europe
and Asia, but the United States emerged relatively unscathed and with a
burgeoning economy.[18] This reinforced Americans' sense of exceptionalism, their duty or destiny to lead the world, and the presumption that all
people aspired to their political-economic system, including representative government, and freedom of speech, press, religion, and enterprise.
Americans also believed that the enduring lesson of the 1930s was that
there could be no more appeasement or "Munichs."

President Harry Truman reflected the nation's outlook. He believed in
America's moral superiority and greatly admired Wilson and his League.
As a Senator during 1934–1945, he had supported FDR on neutrality revision, rearmament, and Lend Lease, and proposed global preparedness to
protect American democracy and resources. Truman blamed international conflict on "outlaws" and "totalitarians," and in 1941 said that the

Germans and Russians should be left to mutual destruction (but added that Germany could not be allowed to win).[19] After succeeding to the presidency in April 1945, he said he wished to keep every agreement with the Soviet Union, but he viewed Russian leaders as akin to "Hitler and Al Capone," deplored those "twin blights—atheism and communism"—and feared that appeasement, lack of military preparedness, and enemies at home and abroad would thwart America's mission (the "Lord's will") to "win the peace" on American terms.[20]

Truman, Secretary of State James Byrnes, and Secretary of War Henry Stimson believed that America's industrial strength and possession of the atomic bomb put the United States in a position to dictate the terms of postwar European and Asian settlements. Although the Potsdam Conference in July 1945 proved a standoff, Truman and Byrnes hoped that use of the atomic bomb might not only bring about Japan's rapid surrender and save American lives, but also minimize Russian gains in Manchuria and deny them occupation rights in Japan.[21] The president regarded the United States as the world's atomic "trustee," and shared in the view that the "genius" of the American mind and technology assured superiority in any arms race. Truman sought to preserve this advantage, and the press hailed his remark in October 1945 that other nations would have to catch up "on their own hook."[22]

Diplomatic pressure brought atomic negotiations in 1946, with Dean Acheson, Undersecretary of State, and David Lilienthal, director of the Tennessee Valley Authority, formulating an innovative plan for international control of all atomic resources and production facilities adaptable to military use. But, after Senate conservatives and military officials objected, Truman named highly conservative financier Bernard Baruch to head the talks. He added terms regarding on-site inspections, sanctions, no use of veto power, and maintenance of the U.S. monopoly that the Soviets predictably rejected. The deadlock allowed the United States to preserve its "winning weapons" monopoly, and Congress soon prohibited exchange of data about atomic weapons or fissionable materials with all nations.[23] The point was unmistakably clear: to the extent that after 1945 "the bomb" had come to define the essence of military power, the United States intended to preserve its unique access to that power, which it presumed would last for a considerable period of time—but proved to be only four years.

Meanwhile Secretary of the Navy James Forrestal, persuaded that Russia was driven by a "religion" devoted to world revolution and the use of force, circulated widely a report on "The Philosophy of Communism" that said America's only recourse was to build an "invincible" defense force.[24] At the same time, Byrnes sought to break the growing ideological-political standoff in late 1945 by going to Moscow to negotiate Yalta-style agreements, recognizing Soviet predominance in Eastern Europe in exchange for U.S. control in China and Japan. But critics in the White House, Congress, and the media cried "appeasement."[25] Truman reacted by dressing down Byrnes over Russian "outrages" in Europe and Iran, and attempts to intimidate Turkey. The president said that Stalin understood only an "iron fist," and that he was tired of "babying" the Russians.[26] Thus Truman, confronted with a choice between Forrestal's militancy and Byrnes's pragmatic willingness to deal, effectively opted for the former.

By early 1946 the "Commanding Idea" of U.S. policy was that the Soviets threatened national security and world peace, and that the United States needed to enhance its military preparedness and integrate industrial capacity to maintain an arsenal of democracy.[27] Stalin's February 1946 speech calling for Russian reindustrialization in the face of alleged renewed encirclement by capitalist nations was taken as a "declaration of World War III."[28] Most notably, George Kennan's "Long Telegram" from Moscow posited that the Kremlin's "neurotic" view of world affairs derived from traditional Russian society, whose rulers knew that their system could not stand contact with advanced Western societies, and who sought only the total destruction of rival power. Marxism was merely a "fig-leaf" that covered their militarism, dictatorship, and intent to destroy America's way of life and its international authority.[29]

Kennan's views, which powerfully fused older American loathing of Russian autocracy and militarism with newer fears about Soviet totalitarianism and communism, were widely circulated and took on extraordinary influence.[30] Similarly, Washington officials were extremely receptive to (and helped to write) Churchill's memorable address in Fulton, Missouri, in March 1946, in which he charged that the Soviets had brought down an "iron curtain" between East and West Europe, and that they wanted not war but "the fruits of war" and indefinite expansion.[31] U.S. officials ignored Churchill's calls for an Anglo-America alliance and negotiations with the Soviets, but his dark view of Soviet ambitions resonated widely.[32]

Shortly, Truman's request to White House aides to assess Soviet aims led to their September 1946 "Russian Report" that combined Kennan's Long Telegram, Churchill's speech, and worst-case scenarios drawn by senior diplomatic-military-intelligence officials. The result depicted a Soviet

Union intent on extending communism throughout Europe, creating "puppet" regimes in Greece and Turkey, and pursuing a strategy of unlimited expansion and world revolution. The Report's authors urged that the United States devise a global foreign policy, build more overseas bases, reject arms limitation, and expand its arsenal of atomic and bacteriological weapons.[33]

Influential public intellectuals endorsed similar conclusions. In 1946–1947 liberals with strong New Deal-Fair Deal political roots formed the Americans for Democratic Action (ADA), whose founders regarded themselves as domestic reformers and strong internationalists who promoted Wilsonianism abroad and opposed communism everywhere.[34] Reinhold Niebuhr, the nation's most prominent Christian theologian, chaired the first ADA meeting, and conceded that original sin and the "will to power" negated American claims of innocence and underlay past U.S. imperial expansion. America's saving grace, however, was its limited and balanced power of government, whereas the Soviet Union had a monstrously centralized regime impervious to change. Worse, the communists' belief in a historical dialectic led them to use power without scruple. Thus Niebuhr argued forcefully that the United States had an inescapable obligation to preserve freedom and oppose communism globally, even if God's ultimate intention was unknown.[35]

Similarly, historian Arthur Schlesinger Jr., recent Pulitzer Prize winner and influenced by Niebuhr, argued that both fascism and communism used the power of the state to suppress freedom, but that recognition of human fallibility—combined with belief in limited government, due process, and individual rights—inoculated American democracy against authoritarianism. He urged that the United States meet its world destiny by sustaining "a vital center," namely, a liberal political philosophy that recognized the primacy of the individual and the benefits of progressive government, was alert to the threat from "the right and the far left," and would battle stagnation and oppression at home and fascism and communism abroad.[36]

In sum, by 1947 an ideological consensus necessary to support the Truman Doctrine had evolved. At a White House meeting called to inform congressional leaders of impending U.S. aid to Greece and Turkey, Acheson said that the world faced the greatest polarization of power since Athens and Sparta, and a choice between American democracy and individual liberty or Soviet dictatorship and absolute conformity.[37] Senator Vandenberg, now chair of the Foreign Relations Committee, held that the Greek crisis was "symbolic of the world-wide ideological clash between eastern Communism and Western Democracy," and he advised the president to "scare hell out of the country" to increase public support.[38] Even this formerly die-hard isolationist had signed on to Cold War internationalism.

In his epochal address to Congress in March, Truman insisted that presently nearly every nation would have to choose between "alternative ways of life": freedom and respect for the will of the majority, or terror, oppression, and submission to the forcible will of the minority. Just as the United States had fought Germany and Japan, now the U.S. had to help free peoples fight totalitarianism.[39] Later Truman would add that "if Russia gets Greece and Turkey," it would also get Italy and France, the iron curtain would extend to Ireland, and the U.S. would have "to come home and prepare for war."[40]

The Truman Doctrine provided an ideological shield to permit U.S. aid to pro-capitalist, and presumably anticommunist, nations.[41] As British ambassador Lord Inverchapel wrote, a "frankly anti-Soviet policy" was being transformed into a "crusade for democracy."[42] Cabinet officers testified to Congress that the United States had to act unilaterally and bypass the UN because that organization was too weak to save Greece. A Republican-led Congress voted overwhelmingly in support of Truman's call for action because, as Massachusetts Senator Henry Cabot Lodge Jr. said, they could not "repudiate the president and throw the flag on the ground and stamp on it."[43] This Republican support for a Democratic president's national security program gave rise to "bipartisanship" which, as Acheson said, allowed the government to mute a critic by alleging that he was "not a true patriot."[44]

Every succeeding administration that sought to intervene in a foreign conflict would cite the Truman Doctrine.[45] But its division of the world into "free" versus "totalitarian" states created an "ideological straitjacket" for U.S. foreign policy and an extremely unfortunate model for later interventions.[46] In fact, Kennan complained that the "sweeping" language of the Truman Doctrine would invite endless military intervention, and he doubted that the Soviets could ever dominate the Muslim Middle East. In summer 1947 his extremely influential essay, "The Sources of Soviet Conduct," published in *Foreign Affairs,* emphasized that the Soviet threat was not military but ideological. He likened Soviet political action to a fluid stream that filled every basin of world power, and urged that the United States avoid threats or bluster and instead follow a long-term, patient, and firm policy of "containment" by applying "counter-force" to deflect

Russian expansive tendencies at shifting geographical and political coun-
terpoints.[47] "Containment" soon became a one-word description of Truman administration policy and that of its successors. To Kennan's chagrin,
however, "counter-force" was interpreted as implying military action, covert as well as overt, with the idea that containment should be implemented
on a global scale.[48] Thus a policy prescription that Kennan conceived as
prudent and circumspect was expanded into a strategy of confrontation
without limits.

The internationally prominent journalist Walter Lippmann was appalled. He dissected the strategy of containment in a series of columns
that were soon published as a book whose title, *The Cold War*, became
the catchphrase for the Soviet-American confrontation.[49] Lippmann
held that the Soviets were heir not just to Marx but to traditional Russian concerns about balance of power and security. He ascribed the
Soviet presence in Eastern Europe not to ideology but to Hitler's aggression and the Second World War. Lippmann said that U.S. policy failed to
recognize the need for increased negotiations between nations with different goals and values, and that the United States should propose joint
troop withdrawals—not try to apply counterforce—to test Kremlin
aims in Europe. He also chided Kennan for not distinguishing between
U.S. vital interests in Europe and Japan and peripheral ones in Eastern
Europe, and warned that containment would militarize American society and foreign policy, and lead to U.S. support for an array of "satellites" and "puppets." For Lippmann, a central concern was that American
power had limits, which a global strategy of containment failed to
recognize.[50]

The Truman administration ignored the Kennan-Lippmann caveats;
officials now held that the postwar era had produced not "one world" but
two—one "free" and one Soviet-dominated. Further, they held that the
United States had to consolidate its sphere in anticipation of a climactic
showdown.[51] Thus, in June 1947, Secretary of State George C. Marshall
made his historic proposal of economic aid for Europe. He insisted that
his proposal was not directed against any nation or doctrine. But the underpinning of the resulting Marshall Plan was the ideologically driven
fear that Europe's declining economic conditions would spur Communist
advances, especially in France and Italy, which would cause these or other
nations to align with the Soviet Union, and thereby threaten the security
of the U.S. by cutting it off from its traditional allies, markets, and resources. Hence, the U.S. imposed economic controls on all recipients of

Marshall Plan aid that virtually assured Soviet refusal to take part, further evidence of the plan's ideological content.[52]

The United States forged a European Recovery Program (ERP) that served multiple purposes: it helped to spur reconstruction and integration of Great Britain and Western Europe, inspired Franco-German rapprochement, and created a stable European political economy that favored American interests. ERP also sought to minimize Communism in Europe, "contain" the Soviet Union, and loosen its hold on Eastern Europe. As Truman said in 1948, "we will raise the Iron Curtain by peaceable means."[53]

The United States also joined NATO in 1949, with intent to establish "a preponderance of power" over the Soviet Union and to increase U.S. influence over allies who might incline toward "neutrality and appeasement," as diplomatist Averell Harriman said.[54] Still, many opponents of NATO, including leading conservatives such as Republican Senator Robert Taft of Ohio—who viewed the Soviet Union and communism as consummate enemies—saw no current Soviet military threat to Europe, and worried that Europeans might use American arms to police their colonies (as France did in Indochina). They also feared that the executive branch would increasingly dominate foreign policy, and be able to make war globally by proxy by dispensing arms to NATO allies.[55]

Truman's announcement in late 1950 that he intended to send U.S. troops to Europe started a "great debate," again led by conservatives, including Taft and former President Herbert Hoover. They challenged the president's prerogative to act without Congressional approval, which would also mean sole power to determine war and peace.[56] Truman denounced his opponents as "isolationists," declared that as commander-in-chief he could send forces "anywhere in the world," and insisted that the defense of Europe was the defense of the "whole free world."[57] This debate culminated in 1951, when a bipartisan sense of the Senate resolution consented to the president's sending the first four divisions to Europe, but requiring Congressional approval for additional forces. The president's right to send troops anywhere in the world remained in dispute, however, at least in theory.[58] More broadly, efforts by Taft, Hoover, and other self-described conservatives to articulate an alternative basis for foreign policy after 1945 failed. The reorientation of U.S. policy undertaken by the Truman administration, subsequently enshrined as "liberal internationalism," took on the appearance of being the received wisdom. As a consequence, at least until the mid-1960s, there were no serious challenges to an

ideologically grounded approach to policy. This was the real meaning of
"bipartisanship."

III

American anxiety about world affairs heightened, however, with the emergence of the People's Republic of China (PRC) in 1949. The triumph of Mao
Zedong undermined the belief that the United States enjoyed a "special relationship" with China, based on missionary and education work there, the
Open Door Policy, and presumed Chinese aspiration to American-style institutions.[59] Above all, U.S. officials saw the GMD–CCP civil war as an integral part of the American–Soviet Cold War. They failed to grasp that
intense nationalistic rivalry, not amity, marked Chinese–Russian relations,
and they believed that a U.S. failure to take a "strong stand" in China
meant Soviet domination of Asia.[60] In Washington, ideological predisposi-
tions blinded policymakers to the actual political dynamics of East Asia.

U.S. officials recognized the GMD's weakness and corruption, and had
long urged it to broaden its political base.[61] But the president and others deplored China's "so-called Commies," or bandits, and insisted that Chinese
society would never adapt to Marxism.[62] Although General Marshall tried
to mediate China's civil war in 1946, the decision to continue aid to the
GMD even if it remained intransigent fatally undermined his efforts.[63]
Truman vetoed any talks with the CCP that might have opened channels of
communication. Even as the GMD withdrew to its bastion on Taiwan, National Security Council officials held that the CCP had not proven its ability to govern, and they threatened to foster "a new revolution," or even a
"test of arms," if the new government in Beijing did not remain independent of Moscow.[64]

The State Department's China White Paper in 1949, elaborating on vast
aid that the U.S. had given to the GMD, was intended to insulate the administration from criticism of having "lost" China to communism. But
Secretary Acheson's letter of transmittal was a diatribe that charged the
CCP with having forsworn its Chinese heritage and chosen subservience
to Moscow. Acheson urged the Chinese people to reassert their "democratic individualism" and to throw off the "foreign yoke" of Russian
imperialism—ideologically charged language that resonated domestically,
but was wildly at variance with reality and served only to further offend
CCP leaders.[65]

The United States refused to recognize the newly proclaimed PRC in October, and Acheson branded the regime "a tool of Russian Imperialism."[66] His National Press Club address in January 1950 conceded that the driving force in Asia was nationalism inspired by "revulsion" against foreign domination. Acheson's "omission" of Taiwan from the U.S. defense perimeter in the Pacific reflected his belief that war over Taiwan would contravene America's "preaching of self-determination in Asia," and JCS views that the island was not vital to U.S. security.[67] But congressional pressure, especially from the Republican-led China bloc in Congress, impelled the administration to continue to aid the GMD, now on Taiwan, and to acquiesce in GMD bombing of China's coastal cities in U.S.-marked airplanes.[68]

Following the signing of the Sino-Soviet pact in early 1950, Acheson charged that the PRC had sold its sovereignty and become a Soviet "dependency." But this overlooked the PRC's need to engage in mutual defense and that Russia now had to return the port and rail concessions in Manchuria it had gained at the Yalta Conference.[69] Similarly, after Mao protested that U.S. movement of the 7th Fleet between China and Taiwan when the Korean War began in June 1950 violated PRC sovereignty over the island, Truman snapped that the PRC was "nothing but a tool of Moscow, just as the North Korean government is."[70] The remark reflected failed U.S. expectations for Sino-American collaboration in Asia, and the widely held belief that a Sino-Soviet monolith threatened U.S. security.

Meanwhile, the State and Defense Departments produced the highly ideological National Security Document 68, "A Report on . . . United States Objectives and Programs for National Security," in April 1950.[71] Written in alarmist language to "bludgeon" the minds of "top government" officials, as Acheson said, NSC 68—a highly classified document kept from public view until 1975—described the current bipolar balance of power as auguring a "continuing crisis" between the "free" and "slave" states, and warned that the Soviets were animated by "a new fanatical faith, antithetical to our own," and an intent to dominate the globe.[72]

NSC 68 held that U.S. survival depended on building a successful political-economic system in the free world, constructing defenses able to deter attack, and fighting limited wars to impose U.S. terms. It disavowed both negotiations with Moscow and preventive war. Instead, it proposed global "affirmative" containment, i.e., development of vast stores of WMD, powerful conventional weapons and forces, a U.S.-led military alliance, psychological warfare, and covert operations. Armed with this "preponderance of power" the United States would seek to reduce Soviet control over its

periphery, and to promote Eastern European independence, national aspirations within the Soviet Union, and change of the Soviet system. Exhort-
ing the public to "unity" and "sacrifice," the administration sought to forge
a permanent Cold War consensus that would allow it to mobilize the resources needed to impel the Soviets to unconditional surrender.

NSC 68 ideology resonated with Truman, although he feared its estimated defense increases—from 5 percent to 20 percent of GNP—would
ruin the economy and create a garrison state. But as Acheson later wrote, the
Russians were "stupid enough" to instigate the Korean War, and the president ordered implementation of NSC 68. A Manichean struggle between an
American-led free world and the "evil men" of the Kremlin became the ideological basis of national security policy for the next four decades.[73]

The sentiments expressed in NSC 68 infused the U.S. response to the
war in Korea, which officials viewed as the "ideological battleground" of
Asia.[74] They perceived North Korean's attack on South Korea as Soviet-
inspired aggression, not escalation of an ongoing civil war. Truman also
likened communist action to that of fascists in the 1930s, insisted that
"Korea is the Greece of the Far East," and predicted that failure to resist
would allow the Soviets to "swallow up" Asia.[75] U.S. intelligence and
European diplomatic reports took a similar view.[76]

Truman acted correctly and boldly to halt the attack on South Korea, a
UN-recognized state. But he refused to seek a war declaration or its
equivalent from Congress to legitimize longer term military action.[77] His
speech in July 1950 escalated this "police action" against "bandits" into
an issue of American security and world peace and stipulated that Korea
was the front line in the global struggle between freedom and tyranny.[78]
As events on the battlefield turned against the North Koreans, American
officials saw an opportunity for the United States to become "the first aggressors for peace" by sending troops across the 38th parallel to destroy
the Communist regime and to unify Korea militarily.[79] This fit with Truman's biblical view that "punishment always followed transgression," and
Acheson's more imperial belief that Korea offered a "stage to prove to the
world what Western Democracy can do to help the underprivileged countries of the world."[80] The policy also countered Republican charges that
the administration had given the Russians a "green light" to grab China,
Korea, and Taiwan.[81]

Thus containment became "roll-back," or "liberation," in October. Dismissing PRC warnings of intervention as "blackmail," the Truman administration left itself open to a massive PRC attack in November and

bitter U.S. retreat. [82] U.S. officials soon determined to settle, but rejected the British view that the China's new leaders might be both Marxist and nationalist and "not bow to Stalin." In January 1951, the Americans got the UN to brand the PRC an "aggressor," effectively ending any prospect of an early cease fire.[83]

Armistice talks began in June 1951, but deadlocked over U.S. insistence on voluntary repatriation of prisoners of war (POWs), although standard military practice and the Geneva Convention of 1949 called for compulsory "all for all" repatriation of POWs.[84] The American demand for voluntary repatriation rested partly on moral grounds, but also reflected a desire to embarrass the Chinese and North Koreans, and a belief that bombing would force them to submit.[85] Thus the war was prolonged until President Dwight Eisenhower's administration forged a favorable compromise in 1953, which sent nonrepatriated POWs to a neutral commission for release as civilians.

Meanwhile, the rearmament induced by the Korean War raised U.S. military spending to NSC 68 levels, and led to U.S. commitments to South Korea, the GMD on Taiwan, and the French in Indochina, with U.S.–PRC relations embittered for decades. Most significantly, the Truman administration had created a powerful and long-enduring national security ideology that depicted democratic America and its free world allies locked in a Manichean struggle against the totalitarian Sino-Soviet communist bloc bent on global conquest. To question this construct was to place oneself beyond the pale of respectable opinion—an ideological straitjacket made to order for Senator Joseph McCarthy of Wisconsin, and others who railed against alleged communists and conspiracies at home and abroad.

IV

Belief in American exceptionalism and the U.S. role as leader of the free world remained undiminished despite Korean War costs. Truman's successors may have differed with him and with one another on the specifics of policy, but they all subscribed to a common view of the world and of America's responsibility to that world. The continuity in the ideological rationale of U.S. policy is striking. Eisenhower insisted in 1953 that "destiny has laid upon our country responsibility for the free world's leadership," and President John Kennedy, in his inaugural address in 1961, said that the torch had been passed to a new generation of Americans who remained committed to human rights at home and abroad and were prepared to "pay any price, bear any burden, meet any hardship, support any friends, oppose any foe to assure the survival and success of liberty."[86] President Lyndon Johnson repeatedly stated that America's cause was the "cause of all mankind," and that the United States was waging war for all who wished to enjoy freedom from political oppression and economic want.[87] And Dean Rusk, Secretary of State under Kennedy and Johnson, said that perhaps the "most significant single factor of the twentieth century" was that the world's most powerful nation sought no aggrandizement but has "committed itself to protecting and promoting freedom for the human race as a whole."[88] One could add to this list nearly identical quotations from a long roster of policymakers, Republicans and Democrats alike.

Serious questions about America's alleged exceptionalism and foreign policy did emerge with growing U.S. military involvement in Vietnam. Early criticism came from pacifist groups, such as the Fellowship of Reconciliation and the War Resisters League, that opposed any war or taking of human life; from the Committee for a Sane Nuclear Policy (SANE), which feared nuclear confrontation with the Soviet Union or PRC; and from students, many of whom were active in the civil rights movement and now joined organizations such as the Students for a Democratic Society (SDS), which sought fundamental change in society.[89]

So, too, did scholars begin to challenge orthodox Cold War tenets. Revisionist, or so-called New Left, historians argued that U.S. foreign policy aimed not to promote freedom so much as to secure open doors for American capital to dominate markets and resources globally, and that the government had always opted for war when facing domestic economic difficulties or another nation's challenge in a crucial region. Thus the United States had fought in more wars on more continents than any other nation in the last 150 years, and appeared committed to perpetual war to maintain America's prosperity and its informal empire that ran from the Caribbean to Cam Ranh Bay.[90]

Most notably, influential congressmen, led by Democratic Senator J. William Fulbright of Arkansas, began to question not just the efficacy of U.S. military policy in Vietnam but its rationale.[91] In 1966 Fulbright chaired Senate hearings on the war, and lectured and wrote publicly about "The Arrogance of Power." In his view, there were "two Americas": that of Abraham Lincoln, which was generous, self-critical, and judicious, and that of Teddy Roosevelt, which was egotistical, self-righteous, and "arrogant in the use of power." Both Americas were driven by moralism,

Fulbright said, but the first was tempered by knowledge of human imperfection, while the second was wholly self-assured and never questioned its right to intervene in the affairs of neighboring nations. In Vietnam, the U.S. had entered into "a growing war against Asian communism, which began and might have ended as civil war if the American intervention had not turned it into a contest of ideologies." In Fulbright's view, that war was disrupting American society and undermining U.S. relations with the rest of the world.[92]

Continued escalation of the Vietnam War led to a growing antiwar movement, now linked with the civil rights movement. Opposition to the war inspired "national mobilizations" and marches in major cities and on Washington and the Pentagon in 1967, and brutal police response to protesters at the Democratic National Convention in Chicago in 1968. Even more chilling were events such as Ohio National Guardsmen killing four students at Kent State University and police killing two students at Jackson State University in Mississippi in May 1970 amidst public outrage over the U.S. incursion into Cambodia. In opposing the war, this broad-based movement implicitly challenged seemingly sacrosanct post-1945 assumptions about American exceptionalism and the motives for U.S. intervention in foreign conflicts.

Despite the upheaval, President Richard Nixon insisted in fall 1969 that the "wheel of destiny" had so turned that survival of peace and freedom in the world depended on the American people having the courage to meet the "challenge of free world leadership." And even after the United States had to exit Vietnam hastily in spring 1975, President Gerald Ford held that America was "unique in the history of nations" because no other country had devoted two centuries to perfecting a "continuing revolution" in a free society.[93]

Similarly President Jimmy Carter believed that America had "exceptional appeal" to other nations because of its dedication to moral principles, while for his part President Ronald Reagan was committed to the proposition that that the U.S. had to be "a light unto the nations of the world—a shining city upon a hill."[94] Even President George H. W. Bush, who shied from "the vision thing," declared in 1989 that America had just begun "our mission of goodness and greatness." And President Bill Clinton held that "only America" could make a difference between war and peace, freedom and repression, and hope and fear because it "stands alone as the world's indispensable nation."[95] In short, at the pinnacle of American politics, the ideological questions raised by the Sixties-era protest made little impact. And presidents in the post-Vietnam era did not retreat from their predecessors' broad assertions about America's providential responsibilities.

V

Meanwhile containment and anticommunism remained the ideological touchstones of national security ideology. The most popular "Cold War axioms" of prominent politicians and foreign policy experts during the 1950s and 1960s were that the free world versus Communism was the central feature of international politics, that the Soviet Union and PRC were monolithic and expansionist, that every communist gain was a free world loss, that the Third World was a new Cold War battleground, and that the United States had to aid any free people resisting communism.[96]

Eisenhower won the presidency in 1952 running on a Republican platform that assailed containment policy as "negative, futile and immoral" for allegedly abandoning countless people to "despotism and godless terrorism."[97] He added that the United States had to be prepared to go to "the far corners of the earth" to protect the resources essential to U.S. defense and industry.[98] John Foster Dulles, who wrote the Republican platform and became secretary of state, proposed "liberation" of "captive peoples" and "massive retaliation" against Russian aggression, and he touted his "brinkmanship," i.e., nearing the brink of war without getting into it.[99]

Eisenhower gave his first major foreign policy speech, "The Chance for Peace," in April 1953, one month after Stalin's death and his successors' hints about "peaceful coexistence." It reflected traditional conservative beliefs that increased military spending and burgeoning bureaucracy would bring a garrison state, and that the arms race would drain the world's "wealth and labor" and leave "humanity hanging from a cross of iron." But his proposal to hold elections to unify Germany and yet allow it to join NATO offered the Russians no incentive to negotiate.[100]

Meanwhile the administration's major national security review, "Operation Solarium," weighed policies that ranged from vigorous containment combined with negotiations with the USSR to drawing a line between the free and communist world and pressing an aggressive military (including nuclear) stance to effect U.S. aims. Eisenhower, however, rejected the idea of preventive war, and his and Dulles' remarks about removing the "taboo" on use of atomic weapons were pushed aside.[101] The result in October 1953 was NSC 162/2: vigorous global containment, an emphasis on nuclear retaliation, and covert action and propaganda to undercut the Soviet bloc. In sum, NSC 161/2 called for the U.S. to remain supreme commander of the free versus communist world struggle.[102]

The president also articulated the "domino theory," perhaps his most lasting contribution to national security ideology. Eisenhower first voiced concern about a "falling domino" in April 1954, a month before the French defeat at Dienbienphu, when he said that the fall of Indochina to communism would cause the loss of other lands—Thailand, the Malay peninsula, Indonesia—and that the U.S. would thereby lose access to essential raw materials and face threats to its Pacific defenses.[103] The "domino theory" soon became the most frequently cited reason for U.S. involvement in Vietnam. At the same time, the administration dismissed "disengagement," Kennan's public proposal in 1957 for mutual Soviet-American troop withdrawals from Germany, as well as Polish Foreign Minister Adam Rapacki's idea to create a nuclear-free zone in Europe.

Eisenhower's eight years in office served to affirm the basic architecture of U.S. national security policy along with the principles employed to justify it. Yet he used the occasion of his Farewell Address in January 1961 not only to assail the global communist menace, but also to warn sternly about the rapid growth of a military-industrial complex and scientific-technological elite that threatened American liberty through their insidious influence on government, business, and universities. The only recourse was "disarmament with mutual honor," a proposition that Eisenhower had done little to advance.[104]

Cold War rhetoric escalated still further under President John F. Kennedy, who had already blamed his own party for the "loss" of China and Eastern Europe, regarded Vietnam as the "cornerstone of the Free World in Southeast Asia," and held that the United States needed to take the initiative against communist regimes.[105] During the 1960 campaign, he charged that Eisenhower had allowed a "missile gap" to grow between the U.S. and the Soviet Union, and he vowed to build "nuclear retaliatory power second to none" and to develop U.S. ability to "intervene effectively and swiftly in any limited war."[106] In fact, the United States enjoyed a substantial strategic superiority over the Soviet Union, but for Kennedy the electoral benefits of promising to bolster ostensibly sagging defenses proved irresistible. JFK also professed to subscribe to the Manichean imagery that had been commonplace since the late 1940s, referring to the

Cold War as a "struggle for supremacy between two conflicting ideologies: Freedom under God versus ruthless, godless tyranny."[107]

Kennedy's inaugural address told Americans never to fear to negotiate, but spoke more dramatically to Cold War challenges, notably that a new generation of Americans would not allow freedom to be undone anywhere in the world. The new president welcomed the summons of the trumpet and the challenge of defending freedom in its hour of "maximum danger."[108] His first State of the Union address warned against believing that the USSR or PRC had "yielded in its ambition for world domination."[109] Kennedy promised not so much to reorient policy as to reinvigorate it.

Vigorous anticommunism led Kennedy to seize the CIA plot, hatched under Eisenhower in 1960, to train Cuban exiles to overthrow Fidel Castro, whose machismo, as well as radical politics, offended the New Frontiersman.[110] But when the Bay of Pigs landing in April 1961 proved a "perfect failure," Kennedy salvaged his public honor by taking full responsibility.[111] He also accepted the building of the Berlin Wall in August 1961 as intended to halt East Germany's "brain drain," and he resisted calls to knock down the Wall, which he said privately was "hell of a lot better than a war."[112] He used the occasion of a visit to Berlin in 1963, however, to proclaim that the Wall marked the difference between "free world" and the "evil" communist one.[113] In public, Kennedy hewed carefully to the ideological line his predecessors laid down; in private he proved to be pragmatic, flexible, and even unprincipled.

Hence, during the Cuban missile crisis in October 1962, Kennedy once having set a deadline for removal of the Soviet missiles, sent his brother, Attorney General Robert Kennedy, to assure the Russians secretly of Cuba's safety and his intent to remove U.S. missiles in Turkey. Khrushchev seized the deal, which earned President Kennedy high praise for his "crisis management," although it was his own earlier recklessness over Cuban policy that had spurred the crisis.[114]

The near miss of nuclear war influenced Kennedy's American University speech in June 1963, which offered a variation on sentiments contained in Eisenhower's Farewell Address. Kennedy deplored the arms race and insisted that although Americans found Communism repugnant, this did not preclude finding virtue in the Russian people and seeking common ground with them.[115] These sentiments were not hypocritical; they paved the way for the 1963 Limited Nuclear Test Ban, a precursor to the 1968 Nuclear Nonproliferation Treaty. But throughout the Kennedy era, containment and anticommunism predominated.

Notably, Kennedy sought to make Vietnam a battleground for free-dom.[116] He increased U.S. military advisers there to 16,000 by late 1963, en-larged South Vietnam's army, and expanded existing "nation-building" efforts by means of a "strategic hamlet" program intended to protect the peasantry from communist reach. Kennedy urged political-economic re-forms on President Ngo Dinh Diem, whose intransigence led the U.S. to ac-cede to a military coup in October 1963. But Kennedy's assassination next month leaves unknown whether he would have his changed course.[117]

Containment continued unabated under President Johnson. He in-sisted he would not lose a war or a country to communism, and subscribed to Rusk's dictum that to lose in Saigon was to lose in Berlin.[118] Johnson also shared the Wilsonian view that "our cause has been the cause of all mankind," and that U.S. reform programs were exportable: if the Viet-namese followed the American way "we can turn the Mekong [River area] into the Tennessee Valley."[119] He also used dubious reports about alleged North Vietnamese attacks on U.S. destroyers *Maddox* and *Turner Joy* in the Gulf of Tonkin in August 1964 to secure a near unanimous congres-sional resolution authorizing all necessary measures to "prevent further aggression" against U.S. forces, portraying U.S. military actions as defen-sive in nature.[120] The Tonkin Gulf resolution served as political cover in the presidential race against the hawkish Republican, Senator Barry Gold-water, and as a virtual blank check for later military escalation.

Goldwater, an arch-conservative from Arizona, proposed to offer Amer-icans "a choice, not an echo" in domestic and foreign policies. His *Why Not Victory?: A Fresh Look at American Foreign Policy* (1962) proffered a radical alternative to the bipartisan consensus that had developed around contain-ment. In sum, he proposed a "primarily offensive" strategy: break relations with the Soviet Union and all other communist states, urge "captive peo-ples" to revolt against their rulers and, if Moscow intervened, send military forces to the scene "armed with nuclear weapons" to "compel compliance," even if this meant war. In a sense, Goldwater—in his view—was calling on Americans to quit temporizing: the time had come to make good on all of the promises to spread freedom that had accumulated since 1945.

But Goldwater's aggressive program, combined with his statement upon accepting the Republican nomination, that "extremism in defense of lib-erty is no vice," enabled the Democrats to depict him as an extremist who would rapidly expand the Vietnam War and provoke a nuclear World War III.[121] Johnson won the 1964 election in a landslide, and in February 1965 initiated massive long-term bombing against North Vietnam, despite the advice of Vice President Hubert Humphrey, a forceful ADA containment advocate, that bombing would not defeat North Vietnam or stabilize South Vietnam. Humphrey predicted that escalating the war in Vietnam would undermine arms control and the Great Society, while failure to provide an acceptable war rationale would turn liberals against Johnson's policy and splinter the Democratic party.[122]

Johnson began to Americanize the war in summer 1965 with major U.S. troop increases. Officials insisted that to withdraw was to ignore the "lessons" of the 1930s, and Defense Department "body count" reports were used to contend that the U.S. was winning the war.[123] But the bold communist Tet (Lunar New Year) offensive in South Vietnam in February 1968 discredited that claim, and the president's "Wise Men," an advisory group of former senior officials, said it was time to disengage. Thus, on March 31, Johnson announced a bombing cutback, a readiness to negotiate, and finished by stating that he would not seek reelection.[124] But a settlement evaded him, largely because South Vietnam looked to better terms from the Republican presidential candidate, Nixon, who narrowly defeated Humphrey in November.

Johnson's continued commitment to war in Vietnam had derived from a host of ideas or principles that were common to his 1930s–World War II– Cold War generation. He feared that failure to support South Vietnam would be viewed as appeasement and would undermine American credibility and its commitment to defending freedom, while other nations in the area would incline to neutralism and accommodation with the PRC. Even worse, the loss of South Vietnam to communism might cause the other nations, or "dominoes," in South East Asia to fall to that evil ideology. At the same time, Johnson, an exceptionally powerful politician accustomed to imposing his will on Congress and the national agenda, believed that American power was too great to be resisted, and that North Vietnam would soon accept a political compromise rather than risk increased U.S. military escalation.

President Nixon, a fervent Cold Warrior since the 1940s, knew that the war was unwinnable, although he had hinted during the campaign at having a secret plan to end it honorably.[125] Similarly, his national security adviser, Henry Kissinger, opposed U.S. withdrawal or a coalition government, but feared that U.S. overcommitment was costing it dominance in world affairs.[126] Thus Nixon announced his Guam Doctrine in July 1969: Asian nations would have to defend themselves, with the U.S. providing only military-economic aid. This constituted a step away from the Truman

Doctrine and Kennedy's pledge to have Americans go anywhere to defend liberty.[127] The Nixon administration also began to Vietnamize the war, i.e., withdraw U.S. forces, provide more military aid to South Vietnam, and increase bombing, including secretly in Cambodia.[128]

The administration did not reach an agreement with North Vietnam until January 1973. Nixon claimed the terms brought "peace with honor," but he and Kissinger really aimed to gain a "decent interval" between U.S. withdrawal and North Vietnam's inevitable victory, which came in 1975.[129] Kissinger later said "Vietnam was a great tragedy. We should not have been there at all."[130] But for twenty-five years the U.S. had been there, bound to a lost cause by the perceived need to defeat communism, contain Russia and/or the PRC, and preserve America's credibility.

Although not overtly rejecting Cold Warrior ideology, Nixon and Kissinger regarded themselves as realists who believed that the United States had to come to grips with long-term changes, such as the passing of U.S. nuclear predominance and Asia's entering the world scene.[131] Kissinger believed that world order was best maintained not by a hegemonic nation but by a concert of powers that balanced one another and contained war, revolution, and smaller, adventuristic states. He believed that nationalism would override ideology, and that conflicting Russian and Chinese national interests would overcome communist solidarity.[132]

Similarly, Nixon, long a leader of the "China Lobby" that sought to make a pariah of the PRC, asserted in an article, "Asia after Vietnam," that he wrote for *Foreign Affairs* in 1967, that ultimately the United States and others would have to incorporate the PRC into "the family of nations," especially before China increased its nuclear capability.[133] Nixon viewed the U.S. less as a "world policeman" and more as an organizer of Asian nations, and he hoped to use the PRC to leverage the Russians and to settle the Vietnam War. And borrowing from FDR's four policeman idea and Kissinger's concert of Europe construct, Nixon stated in 1971 that the world was divided into five power centers: the U.S., the USSR, Europe's Common Market states, Japan, and the PRC—and that these "economic superpowers" had to keep order in their regions and would determine the future of the world.[134]

Nixon and Kissinger thus fostered détente and "linkage"—Kissinger's term calling for the Russians and Chinese to match each U.S. concession—and abandoned the idea of nuclear supremacy in favor of sufficiency.[135] This culminated in 1972 with the signing of a Soviet–American statement of Basic Principles that obliged both nations to seek to avert confrontation, and a Strategic Arms Limitation Treaty (SALT I) that limited each nation's intercontinental and submarine-launched ballistic missiles (ICBMs and SLBMs), and restricted each power to two Anti-Ballistic Missile (ABM) sites.[136] President Gerald Ford extended this in 1974 at Vladivostok with an agreement limiting the total number of missiles and warheads of each side. Finally, at the 1975 Conference on Security and Cooperation at Helsinki, the U.S., USSR, and European nations pledged to continue détente, accepted Europe's post-1945 borders as permanent, and agreed to a list of "human rights" regarding freedom of information and emigration.

Nixon's second initiative was his "opening to China," marked by secret diplomacy and his headline-making trip in 1972 to the PRC. There he signed the Shanghai Communiqué that expressed U.S.-PRC accord on friendship, trade, and PRC membership in the UN. Nixon agreed that there was only "one China," which included Taiwan, and that the United States would reduce its troops there and cut ties with its government, leaving it to the Chinese to settle the Taiwan issue peacefully.[137] Nixon's seven days in China were not, as he claimed, "the week that changed the world," for the U.S. still lost in Vietnam, and the PRC continued atomic development. But his journey opened the way to long overdue U.S. recognition of the PRC and its critical Asian role.[138]

All of this—accepting less than victory in Vietnam, détente with the Soviets, and the opening to China—was sharply at odds with the ideology of U.S. national security that had evolved since World War II. Nixon and Kissinger appeared not to believe that the United States was an exceptional nation. They saw American power as limited, perhaps even in decline, and they seemed to doubt the universality of American ideals. They were willing to accept evil—even, as Nixon's fawning over Mao Zedong suggested, to shake hands with the devil. For observers who were committed to the proposition that America's mission to the world was ultimately a moral one—and that communism was evil—Nixon and Kissinger seemed amoral.

As a consequence, their policies produced a powerful ideological backlash. Although the political left loathed Nixon and Kissinger for their use of bombing in Southeast Asia and assaults on smaller nations, such as Chile, that inclined to the left, the most sharp and perhaps most effective critique of their policies came from disenchanted quarters of the right. This ideology, soon called neoconservatism, was fueled in part by Norman Podhoretz, editor of *Commentary*, which began in 1970 to feature articles by academics and public intellectuals who assailed the antiwar movement as isolationist or appeasement-oriented, argued that détente was American give and Russian take, and insisted that the world depended on U.S. power and leadership. Meanwhile Paul Nitze (author of NSC 68), and Eugene Rostow (Undersecretary of State in the Johnson era), founded the soon highly influential Committee on the Present Danger that depicted the Soviet Union as an expansive empire that threatened U.S. security just as had Nazi Germany. The Committee insisted that the U.S. had to undertake a major arms build up before dealing with Moscow.[139]

By 1976, this backlash had persuaded President Ford to banish the word détente from public discourse and to insist that the U.S. stood for "peace through strength." Ford's highly conservative challenger for that year's GOP presidential nomination, Governor Ronald Reagan of California, charged that the United States had slipped to number two in military power in a world where "it is dangerous—if not fatal—to be second best."[140] Similarly, Ford's Democratic opponent, Governor Jimmy Carter of Georgia, attacked the Vladivostok and Helsinki accords, while Ford's campaign debate gaffe—answering a query about the Helsinki accords by saying that the Poles, Romanians, and Yugoslavs did not think they were dominated by the Soviet Union—may have cost him the election.[141] Although memories of Vietnam were still fresh, assertiveness and muscle-flexing were already returning to political favor.

VI

President Jimmy Carter wasted no time in trying to reinvigorate the ideological content of U.S. foreign policy. Carter shied from the term "realism." He used his inaugural address and a speech at the University of Notre Dame in May 1977 to try to make a global and "absolute" commitment to human rights and moral values the ideological basis of U.S. foreign policy.[142] He appointed Andrew Young, a prominent civil rights associate of Martin Luther King, Ambassador to the UN, created the position of Assistant Secretary for Human Rights, and submitted the 1948 UN Declaration on Human Rights to Congress (where it remained unratified). His Presidential Directive NSC 30 in 1978 committed the United States to promote human rights worldwide, and demarcated three human rights goals: reduction of government violation of individual integrity, ensuring civil and political liberties, and securing basic economic and social rights for all.[143] Carter also corresponded publicly with Soviet dissidents, and imposed aid or trade penalties on nations that violated human rights.

Much to the disappointment of the neoconservatives, however, his administration continued arms control, concluding the 1979 SALT II treaty establishing Soviet-American nuclear parity, and halted production of the very expensive B-1 bomber and the neutron bomb. But JCS pressure forced approval of plans for two hundred huge MX missiles and agreement to provide NATO allies with Pershing II and cruise missiles.[144]

Carter's religiosity—he was a born-again Christian—may also have impelled his diligent pursuit of the proverbial peace in the Middle East, where since formation of the state of Israel in 1948 U.S. policymakers had to balance between helping Israel preserve its independence, securing U.S. access to Arab state oil, and minimizing Soviet influence in the region. But after four wars (in 1948–1949, 1956, 1967, and 1973) not one Arab state had either recognized Israel or signed a peace treaty. And after the 1967 war, Israel occupied Egypt's Sinai and Gaza and Jordan's West Bank, with the latter two areas populated by almost 2 million Arab refugees, represented by the Palestine Liberation Organization (PLO).

After Egyptian President Anwar Sadat's dramatic trip to Jerusalem in 1977, Carter toured the Middle East, and then invited Sadat and Israel's Prime Minister, Menachem Begin, to Camp David in September 1978. The president's intense personal diplomacy inspired a treaty that led to Israel's return of the Sinai to Egypt (which became the only Arab state to recognize Israel), and a "Framework for Peace in the Middle East" that called for a transitional Palestinian authority to govern Gaza and the West Bank, with the final status of the occupied territories, rights of the Palestinian people, and Israel's security to be settled within five years. But Muslim extremists assassinated Sadat in 1981, and Israeli-Palestinian-Arab relations were soon mired in violence, with the "Framework" unfulfilled. Nonetheless, the Camp David accords marked a highly significant development despite continued hostilities and terrorism in the Middle East. Carter's dramatic intercession halted the seemingly endless cycle of Israel–Arab state wars and elevated the concept of peace in the Middle East from that of an American interest to a major component of America's larger mission in the world.

Carter's effort to restore the moral dimension of U.S. foreign policy ran aground in Iran and Afghanistan. Iran had been a client state since a CIA coup in 1953 restored the Shah to power. Revolt against his repressive rule, however, by a rising middle class and the powerful Muslim fundamentalist forces of Ayatollah Ruhollah Khomeini, who branded the U.S. the "Great Satan," forced the Shah to flee in early 1979, with Khomeini's followers taking control.[145] Carter's subsequent decision to allow the Shah to enter the U.S. for medical treatment led angry young Iranians to seize the U.S. embassy and over fifty hostages on November 4, "Day One"—according to the news media's nightly counting—of an ultimately 444 day crisis.[146] Eventually media depiction of the U.S. as a Gulliver held down by Lilliputian Iranians led Carter to accede in April 1980 to a helicopter and commando rescue mission, but it crashed in the desert. After the Shah died, however, the U.S. pledged to repatriate $8 billion in frozen Iranian assets and not to intervene in Iran, which agreed to return the hostages, but delayed this until just after Carter left the presidency.[147] The crisis reinforced U.S. hardliners' view that it was impossible to negotiate with communists or radical Muslims.

Meanwhile after Soviet troops marched into Afghanistan in December 1979 to preserve a Marxist regime under fire from dissident Marxists and Muslims, Carter declared Moscow's action a threat to the U.S. position in the Middle East and access to oil. And in January 1980 he proclaimed his doctrine that the U.S. would resist, including by force, the effort of any nation that tried to "gain control of the Persian Gulf region." He then withdrew the SALT II treaty from the Senate, imposed a grain embargo on the Soviets and a boycott of the Olympics in Moscow, and instituted a military and intelligence operations build-up.[148] Vilified by his critics for being weak, Carter spent the last year of his presidency trying to demonstrate his toughness.

A scant five years after the fall of Saigon had seemingly provided a definitive demonstration of the perils of crusading, the mood of the country was shifting. The Second Round of the Cold War was underway, with neoconservatives such as Jeane Kirkpatrick, a hawkish former Democrat and Humphrey supporter, lambasting Carter's policies. In "Dictatorships and Double Standards" in *Commentary* in 1979, she argued that in seeking to move beyond the Cold War, Carter (and liberals) had wrongly undermined dictatorships on the Right and accepted those on the Left. She urged that the U.S. support "traditional autocracies" (e.g., in Chile, South Korea, or the Shah's Iran) because they were open to liberalization and allowed private enterprise, and oppose "revolutionary ["totalitarian"] autocracies," e.g., Cuba and the PRC, because they denied all personal freedoms, including religion, and they never moderated their repressive rule.[149]

In the presidential election of 1980, growing neconservatism, U.S. conflict with Marxists and Muslims abroad, and an economy battered by rising oil prices and global competition from retooled Germany and Japan brought Ronald Reagan to power. A former movie actor and FDR supporter turned arch conservative and virulent anticommunist after 1945, he held that NSC 68 had it right: the Soviets were intent on world domination. Reagan also called the Vietnam War a "noble cause" that ought to have been won.[150] His national security ideology rested on five assumptions: (1) that the Soviet Union was an illegitimate, godless society, without respect for any law; (2) that the USSR was an expansionist power, or "evil empire," as he said in 1983; (3) that appeasement always led to war, as the 1930s showed; (4) that "Mutually Assured Destruction" was inadequate for security, while "superiority" would protect the U.S.; and (5) that arms control had damaged national security.[151]

Reagan imported into the 1980s the assumptions and assertions that had informed U.S. foreign policy in 1950, when NSC 68 was written. In early 1981 he assailed Soviet leaders as willing to "commit any crime; to lie; to cheat," to advance their cause, and two years later he called the Cold War a "struggle between right and wrong, good and evil."[152] He rejected détente (a "one way street"), and proposed to spend several trillion dollars (the largest peacetime defense budget in history) on major weapons systems to enable the U.S. to fight two and one-half wars at once.[153] In 1983 he gave this emphasis on the imperative of military superiority his own twist by proposing the Strategic Defense Initiative. SDI, or "Star Wars" (as it was called by critics), envisioned the deployment into space of a laser particle beam system allegedly capable of shooting down as many as ten thousand incoming missiles. Eventually staggering costs ($3 to $5 trillion) and scientists' doubts about its feasibility caused SDI to be sidelined, but Reagan clung to the fantasy of a technological "quick fix," providing perfect security.[154]

Reagan also said that if "we purged ourselves of the Vietnam syndrome," the U.S. could uphold world order.[155] His presidency saw the return of American military activism, albeit with mixed results. Hence, he sent Marines to Lebanon in 1982, presumably to support a UN peacekeeping mission—and to back a pro-Western government—but withdrew the forces after terrorists drove a car bomb into the Marine barracks in Beirut in October 1983.[156] Two days later U.S. troops invaded the tiny Caribbean island of Grenada, with Reagan charging that a Marxist coup (against another Marxist regime) endangered eight hundred American medical students, and that Grenada was a "Soviet-Cuban colony being readied for a major military bastion to export terror and undermine democracy. We got there just in time."[157] But the 784 Cubans there were only building a British-Canadian financed airport for tourism, and the students were not under threat. U.S. action did violate Grenada's sovereignty, as even Conservative Prime Minister Margaret Thatcher said, but Reagan persisted he had to preclude the "nightmare of our hostages in Iran."[158]

Reagan also effected Jeane Kirkpatrick's doctrine of support for right-wing over left-wing authoritarians. His National Security Decision Directive (NSDD) 17 instructed the CIA to train and equip Nicaraguan exiles—"Contras"—to fight the Marxist Sandinistas, who had ousted Anastasio Somoza's brutal regime in 1979. With the Contras failing in 1983, the CIA took over illegal covert actions, which Congress discovered and prohibited, including use of government funds.[159] Senior national security officials sought to evade these congressional restrictions by covertly selling arms to Iran's Islamic republic in exchange for its seeking release of U.S. hostages in Lebanon. NSC staff member Lt. Colonel Oliver North subsequently diverted arms sale revenue to aid the Contras. This became public during 1986–1987, and led to grand jury indictments (and later convictions), with the president finally forced to admit to selling arms to Iran to try to gain release of hostages, but denying knowledge of the illegal diversion of funds—an impeachable offense—to the Contras, a denial North later said was hard to believe.[160]

The president's supporters celebrated this so-called Reagan Doctrine as evidence that the United States was becoming more assertive in its support for anticommunist freedom fighters, but the truth was considerably more ambiguous. To be sure, Reagan did ratchet up the program of covert support, inaugurated by Carter, that offered weapons and other assistance to Afghans resisting the Soviet occupation. In Reagan's eyes, these Afghan "freedom fighters" shared in the common cause of opposing Soviet totalitarianism. In fact, the mujahedeen, for the most part Islamic fundamentalists, had little sympathy for democracy or human rights or other Western values. As events would show, they represented a variant of oppression, although the Manichean view to which Reagan subscribed made it impossible for him to see that.

Meanwhile, Reagan modified his Cold War ideology in 1984 to calm fears that his militancy might spur nuclear war, and he won resounding reelection. Next spring Mikhail Gorbachev became General Secretary of the Soviet Communist Party. A younger member of the post-Stalin generation, he worried about his nation's failing economy, and the costs of the Afghanistan war and arms race, and he proposed "new thinking" that included glasnost, or political openness, and perestroika, or restructuring the Soviet economy, and arms control.[161]

This opened the way to a Reagan–Gorbachev meeting in 1985 in Geneva, where they agreed to cut strategic weapons sharply, and then in 1986 at Reykjavik, Iceland, where the Soviet leader pressed to eliminate intermediate range nuclear weapons (INF), and then all nuclear weapons. Reagan initially accepted this stunning idea, but his insistence on continuing to develop SDI stymied it. At a Washington summit in 1987, however, the two leaders signed the landmark INF treaty eliminating all medium- and short-range missiles, with longer range ones to be discussed later.[162] Next spring in Moscow, Reagan declared that the Soviet Union "had changed," and that the "evil empire" and Cold War were gone.[163] His admirers credited this to his military build-up and SDI; others looked to Gorbachev's decisions to reduce nuclear arms, disavow wars of liberation, pull Soviet troops from Afghanistan, and call for a "common European home."[164]

Regardless, Reagan's willingness to deal with the Soviets was not inconsistent with his firm anticommunism, although he had to know that successful arms negotiations would divert attention from the Iran-Contra scandal and provide some budgetary relief in an era of mounting federal deficits. But the president also believed that the worldwide opposition to Marxism-Leninism had caused the Soviets to recognize that their political-economic system was no match for American liberal capitalism, and that they had no choice but to strike a deal before the United States drove them into bankruptcy.

President George Bush's new administration responded cautiously to this shifting political landscape, although in 1989 he said that use of the words "Cold War" did not recognize recent advances in U.S.-Soviet relations, and that it was time to move beyond containment. Bush held out the prospect of "integration of the Soviet Union into the community of nations" provided the Soviets accepted national self-determination and political pluralism and human rights at home. He also insisted that there could not be a common European home unless everyone in it was "free to move from room to room."[165]

Bush was criticized for little new thinking, but in 1989 events moved faster than anyone anticipated. This included free elections in Poland that led to Lech Walesa's Solidarity Workers' party becoming the first noncommunist government in Eastern Europe since 1948, East Germans tearing down the Berlin Wall, the most famous Cold War symbol, and Communist regimes then being swept from power in Bulgaria, Czechoslovakia, and Romania. Then in 1990 the Christian Democrats' electoral victory in

East Germany led to complex negotiations—with the Soviets giving way—that gained the long-held American ambition of Germany reunited within NATO. In short order the Warsaw Pact dissolved.[166]

Meanwhile, the Bush administration proposed to integrate the Soviet Union into the world order through liberal trade relations, and the Russians pledged to align their economy with the world trading system and stay out of third world conflicts.[167] At the same time Gorbachev struggled to steer a middle position between old guard communists who wished to preserve their Soviet system, and younger leaders who sought political pluralism, a market economy, and a decentralized nation. The Bush administration hailed Soviet political-economic transformation, but shied from economic aid, and then pressed a major Strategic Arms Reduction Treaty (START I) in Moscow in July 1991 that sharply cut long range nuclear arsenals. And in Kiev, Bush praised Gorbachev's commitment to democracy and economic liberty, and warned Ukrainians pressing for independence against practicing "suicidal nationalism based upon ethnic hatred."[168]

The U.S. could not save Gorbachev, however. Although he survived a KGB and military coup in August 1991, once the Russian Federation became a "Commonwealth of Independent States" committed to a market economy, he disbanded the Communist Party and resigned as president of the Soviet Union, which ceased to exist on December 31 of that year. No U.S. official had foreseen this monumental event. Indeed, Bush, like Reagan in his second term, had devoted substantial effort to preserving a reformed Soviet Union, anticipating that the Kremlin might become Washington's partner in fostering a stable world order. The failure of that effort did not lead Bush to reflect on the potential limits of American power. It moved him instead to claim that "by the Grace of God, America had won the Cold War," and had cemented its position as the "undisputed leader of the age." This judgment met with considerable favor among the majority of the American people.[169]

Even as the Cold War wound down, the U.S. was engaged in a fresh round of fighting to advance what Bush called "the new world order."[170] Since 1979 Saddam Hussein had ruled Iraq brutally, but he gained Reagan administration support while he waged war against Ayatollah Khomeini's Iran during 1980–1988. This support included restoration in 1984 of full diplomatic relations (broken during the 1967 Arab–Israeli war), $4 billion in agricultural credits, U.S. military advisers and intelligence, and U.S. support for sale by its allies to Iraq of arms, dual-use technology, and material for manufacture of biological and chemical weapons.[171]

As the Iran-Iraq War subsided, the Bush administration weighed closer relations with Iraq. When Saddam began to use a boundary dispute to badger Kuwait, oil-rich and located at the head of the Persian Gulf, American policy wavered. Defense Secretary Richard Cheney warned that the U.S. would defend Kuwait. Ambassador April Glaspie told Saddam in July 1990 that the U.S. had "no opinion" on Arab-Arab conflicts, but hoped that he would resolve this one by "suitable means."[172] Shortly thereafter, Iraqi troops occupied Kuwait.

The president was taken off guard, but urged on by Prime Minister Thatcher, he soon denounced Iraq's "naked aggression," and vowed "this will not stand."[173] In truth, throughout the Cold War, the Middle East had been an ideological dead zone. American policymakers barely maintained the pretense that U.S. actions in the Middle East were intended to support freedom and democracy. Oil, stability, Israel, and determination to keep the Soviets out were the primary factors influencing U.S. policy. But now U.S. policy in the region began to take on an explicitly ideological cast. Thus Bush likened Saddam to Hitler, invoked the Munich analogy, and got UN resolutions imposing severe economic sanctions on Iraq and demanding its withdrawal from Kuwait. Bush also declared Saudi Arabia, with 20 percent of the world's oil reserves, to be a vital U.S. interest, and sent 200,000 troops there. On September 11, the president told Congress that he hailed the coming of a "new world order" free from terror.[174]

Bush did not propose to use force until Saddam annexed Kuwait in August. The president cited the UN Charter's Article 51 ("self defense") to initiate Pentagon planning, forged a coalition (including Saudi Arabia, Egypt, and Syria) of thirty-four nations, and gained a UN resolution setting January 15, 1991, as Iraq's deadline to leave Kuwait. Bush also got Congress to approve the use of force, although the Senate vote was close, and he claimed the right to act as commander-in-chief. Then a bombing campaign against Iraq starting in mid-January 1991, followed by a ground assault from Saudi Arabia, ejected the Iraqi army from Kuwait, and brought a cease-fire in February.[175]

Although the military action was accompanied by a rhetoric of "liberation" that recalled World War II, the United States acted less to create a "new world order" than to preserve traditional rules about equality of states, sanctity of borders, and freedom from external attack. Nor did it try to depose Saddam, because the UN mandate was to liberate Kuwait, not to engage in "regime change," which the Arab states would have opposed. Bush did try "liberation" politics by urging Iraqis to overthrow

Saddam, but his forces crushed dissident Kurds and Shiites, and the U.S. stood aside until public outrage forced support of UN-approved "safe havens" and "no fly" zones to block Saddam's air assaults. Despite the efforts to fit this first major crisis of the post–Cold War era into the ideological framework that had evolved since World War II, the policies of the Bush administration resembled those of a traditional great power rather than those of an "exceptional" nation endowed with a providential mission. For this reason, among others, the victory gained in Operation Desert Storm soon lost its luster. The loose ends left by the war were as much moral as they were practical.[176]

The United States had also not resolved the ideological dilemma of how to respond when states repressed their citizens. Thus in June 1989, when the Chinese government brutally cracked down on student-led forces gathered in Tiananmen Square in Beijing to demand greater political and civil liberties, Bush publicly rebuked the use of force, but he would not go beyond a "prudent, reasoned response." He rejected sanctions, and twice sent his national security adviser, Brent Snowcroft, to reassure the PRC of U.S. intent to maintain good relations and trade ties.[177] By contrast, Bush used invasion forces in late 1989 to oust Panama's president-dictator, General Manuel Noriega, who had aided U.S. covert actions in Central America in the 1980s, but lost favor by dealing with Cuba and Marxist revolutionaries in Colombia, and trafficking in drugs.[178] The U.S. also supported UN sanctions against President Slobodan Milovsevic's regime in Belgrade, which aided the minority Serbs' brutal "ethnic cleansing" campaign in Bosnia against Muslims. But Washington refused to provide troops or air cover (as in Iraq), insistent that Bosnia's case was a civil war, not state against state aggression.[179]

So too did the U.S. resist sending troops to Somalia, where the overthrow in 1991 of U.S.-backed dictator Siad Barre brought chaos and bitter battles for power among armed warlords who blocked food and medical relief in the port city of Mogadishu. Only after losing the 1992 election did Bush send U.S. forces to aid UN relief efforts. Although he commended the military for "doing God's work," he insisted that the "United States alone cannot right the world's wrongs."[180] Then in his last major address, at West Point in January 1993, Bush said that the U.S. had to lead in building a new world order of governments that were democratic, economically free, tolerant at home, and committed to peaceful resolutions abroad. "There is no one else" to do this except the United States, he said, but its role could not be unilateralist or hubristic. Nor could the U.S. be "the world's policeman," or deploy troops unless the stakes warranted doing so and the intervention could be effective.[181]

As the post–World War II–Cold War era came to a close, President Bush could not fully endorse the ideological claims that his predecessors had made; yet neither could he abandon them. By contrast, Defense Secretary Cheney's department promoted a Defense Planning Guidance document (DPG) in 1992 that translated the received ideology of national security into a new set of policy imperatives. That document stated that the U.S. should guarantee its permanent primacy by preventing the emergence of any new rival power, should be prepared to strike first and unilaterally to prevent the proliferation of WMD, should rely less on alliances than on "ad hoc assemblies" to advance its security, and should resurrect plans to build an SDI-style defense system. The draft DPG leaked, Democratic Senator Joseph Biden labeled it a form of Pax Americana, and the Defense Department revised the language.[182] But the ambitions contained in the document gave a hint of what was to come: there would be no backing away from America's ideological claims or intent to maintain global military supremacy.

VI

The demise of communist states in Europe and the rise of the United States to hegemonic status produced a heady American belief that "The End of History" was at hand, as Francis Fukuyama, a former State Department official, stated in an influential essay in 1989 that was soon expanded into an acclaimed book.[183] In his view, history was a struggle of ideas, and it was now clear that Western liberalism had triumphed over fascism and then communism. Thus the "end" of history had come, meaning that there was no halting of the "ideological evolution and universalization of western liberal democracy as the final form of human government." Ultimately all nations would conform to the American model because the globalism of Western liberalism was inevitable.

More somberly, Samuel P. Huntington, a highly prominent political scientist and former NSC official in the Carter administration, soon published in *Foreign Affairs* a challenging essay, "The Clash of Civilizations?"; it, too, was expanded into a celebrated book.[184] In his view, the Cold War marked the end of the world's great ideological competition, but a new divide, or clash between civilizations, or cultures, was now at hand. In this new clash, religion would be a key differential factor. Thus, while states would remain powerful world actors, the new conflict was likely to be a virulent revival of an old one: the West versus the world of Islam, with Islam deeply resentful of the West's far greater military-economic power and presence in crucial regions, e.g., the Persian Gulf, and perhaps looking toward acquiring WMD, the great "equalizer."

Moreover, Huntington said, the idea of a universal civilization was a concept of the West, whose primary political values did not resonate in the non-Western world. Hence, to preserve "Western civilization," Huntington urged an "Atlanticist" policy, namely expansion of its systems across Europe and regions of the former Soviet Union, greater "Westernization" of Latin America, and—above all—avoidance of intervention in other civilizations, which would only produce the most dangerous global conflict.

Fukuyama and Huntington represented opposite poles in a larger debate to define the nature of the post–Cold War international order. Remarkably, Bill Clinton, who in 1993 became the first true post–Cold War president and who viewed himself as a pragmatic Wilsonian, managed to amalgamate, at least for a while, both of these perspectives. Clinton was happy to endorse Fukuyama regarding the triumph of democratic capitalism. But as someone who had won election in 1992 by insisting the key issue was the U.S. economy, he was not keen to induce new conflicts by embarking upon a new round of military interventionism. Clinton held that economic security was the first pillar of U.S. foreign policy; the second and third pillars were streamlining the military and promoting democratic values.[185]

What did this mean in practice? After debate arose over U.S. willingness to intervene in world conflict, national security adviser Anthony Lake declared in September 1993 that the United States had emerged from the Cold War into a "moment of immense democratic and entrepreneurial opportunity." The Clinton administration proposed to replace containment with a new doctrine of "enlargement" aimed at expanding the world's "free community of market democracies."[186] The U.S. would harness globalization—the integration of the world's markets, resources, and financial and investment centers—to rejuvenate its sluggish economy, redress its trade balances, and promote an interlocked, peaceful, and secure world order. In sum, economic enlargement and technological advance would overcome ideological conflict and foster global democracy. The Clinton administration had no intention of forfeiting America's Big Stick, but it expected that nurturing an integrated international economic order would be more important in assuring prosperity at home and stability abroad.

Thus the Clinton administration pushed through Congress in 1993 the North American Free Trade Agreement, negotiated earlier by the Bush administration, that aimed to create a vast U.S.-Canada-Mexico market for investment and production and sale of goods.[187] The United States also increased economic ties with Russia, which it made a charter member of the World Trade Organization (WTO) in 1995, and implemented full trade relations with Vietnam and the PRC.[188] But the use of force, especially in cases of national or ethnic chauvinism, remained problematic. When the UN sought to go beyond humanitarian aid to improve Somalia's political framework in 1993, the Clinton administration sent a battalion of commandos, only to withdraw them after a warlord's forces shot down two helicopters, killed 18 Americans, and dragged a soldier's body through the streets of Mogadishu.[189] The U.S. and UN then stood aside in 1994 in Rwanda, where the predominant Hutus carried out virtual genocide against the minority Tutsis.[190] Closer to home, after the military in Haiti overthrew Jean-Bertrand Aristide's elected government and created a desperate flow of immigrants to the U.S., Clinton sent an invasion force (Operation Restore Democracy) that caused the junta to flee. Aristide returned to power, and the mass flight of Haitians bound for Florida ended, but there was no real democracy. The U.S. rejected nation-building and sharply limited humanitarian intervention.

The administration also initially declared that violence in Bosnia did not affect U.S. national security, but after Muslim Croats got arms from Iran to beat back their Serbian tormentors by 1995, the U.S. joined with NATO to bomb Serbian forces heavily. Then in negotiations in Dayton, Ohio, the U.S. imposed peace terms that created a Muslim-Croat Federation and Serbian Republic, with a NATO force to stabilize conditions.[191] Similarly, Secretary of State Madeleine Albright pressed Clinton in 1999 to undertake a bombing campaign that forced Milosevic to withdraw his Serbian troops from Kosovo, where their brutal ethnic cleansing campaign sought to drive out the majority Albanian population.[192] Thus the U.S. used great force to bring some stability to the Balkans, and extended American influence by promoting free trade and globalization and inviting the Czech Republic, Poland, and Hungary to join NATO.

The administration was fortunate in not having to confront an "evil empire," but starting in February 1993 it had to deal with an increasingly emergent enemy—radical Islamic terrorists—who exploded a car bomb in the basement of the World Trade Center in New York City. Although terrorists with links to Osama bin Laden were soon arrested, officials knew little about him or his organization until 1996. That same year terrorists for Hezbollah ("Party of God")—a radical Islamic group formed after Israel's incursion into Lebanon in 1982—exploded a truck bomb at a housing complex for foreign military personnel in Dhahran, Saudi Arabia, killing nineteen U.S. servicemen and wounding hundreds of other people. Then in August 1998 al-Qaeda terrorists bombed U.S. embassies in Kenya and Tanzania, and in October 2000 they rammed and nearly sank the U.S. destroyer *Cole* in Yemen with an explosives-laden small boat. After the embassy bombings, Clinton ordered cruise missile strikes against al-Qaeda facilities and training camps in the Sudan and Afghanistan, but left the presidency before there was certainty that al-Qaeda was responsible for the *Cole* incident.[193]

In 1999, his administration published "A National Security Strategy for A New Century" that proposed to maintain—and forward deploy—the world's best-trained, best-equipped, and most efficient forces; the United States would also sustain a "robust capability" to determine the source of any attack and to respond effectively, along with a "triad of strategic nuclear forces" to deter potential adversaries who might seek WMD. The U.S. would also "act alone" when necessary, but recognized that objectives could best, and sometimes only, be met by working through international organizations and alliances. The U.S. also wished to modify the ABM treaty to permit building of a limited national missile defense system to defend against nuclear threats from "rogue" states, but the ABM treaty remained "a cornerstone of strategic stability," and the U.S. supported current nuclear limitation and nonproliferation treaties.[194] The Clinton document espoused a strong but mainstream internationalist posture toward national security, although its emphasis on forward deployment of forces and need to build a limited national missile defense system suggested that precepts from the highly controversial DPG of 1992 had begun to insinuate into the conventional wisdom endorsed by Democrats and Republicans alike.

National security ideology was not a key issue in the 2000 election campaign. Vice President Al Gore proposed to continue Clinton's policies and to build bridges to the twenty-first century through greater trade and globalization, and Republican Governor George W. Bush of Texas stated that the United States was overcommitted in world affairs and would gain greater respect by remaining strong but humble. Notably, candidate Bush eschewed anything that smacked of "nation-building."[195]

Initially the Bush administration paid little attention to terrorism, but revealed its highly nationalist and unilateralist ideology by proposing to negate the 1972 ABM treaty and build a national ballistic missile defense system, and by rejecting the Kyoto Treaty on Global Warming, the Comprehensive Test Ban Treaty (CTBT), the International Criminal Court (ICC), and the Treaty on Land Mines (TLM).[196] The September 11 attacks changed the administration's priorities and the president's rhetoric. Bush proclaimed that the United States was engaged in a global war and that he was a war president, which expanded his power. He also said that he wanted Osama bin Laden "dead or alive," and that the U.S. would undertake a "crusade" in Afghanistan, words that had visceral, but short-lived, appeal.[197]

After U.S. forces drove the Taliban from power (with Osama and many of his cohorts escaping), Bush's State of the Union address in January 2002 announced that the "war against terrorism" had just begun, and would include dealing with regimes that threatened the U.S. or its allies directly with WMD or by passing WMD to terrorists. He also branded states seeking WMD capacity, such as Korea, Iran, and Iraq, an "axis of evil," a controversial phrase soon abandoned.[198] But at West Point in June, Bush emphasized that "we are in a conflict between good and evil" in which the Cold War doctrines of deterrence and containment were no longer wholly applicable. Now even "weak states and small groups," with the aid of "unbalanced dictators," could acquire WMD and ballistic missile capability to strike great nations with "catastrophic power." Further, the United States could not accept the word of tyrants who "systematically break" nonproliferation agreements; nor could it win the war on terror on the defensive. Rather the U.S. had to "take the battle to the enemy," and confront the worst threats before they emerge, in short, "be ready for preemptive action," and "maintain strength beyond challenge." The president also claimed universality for American values with his statement that "moral truth is the same in every culture, in every time, and in every place."[199]

This West Point address was precursor to the Bush NSS published in September 2002 in which the president's cover letter insisted that the United States would combine its principles and power to foster the world's organization based on the "exclusive model" of the U.S. system of "freedom, democracy, and free enterprise." The Bush NSS elaborated four points: the U.S. obligation to move the world toward similar political-economic systems; the need to strike unilaterally and preemptively at terrorists and tyrants who might use WMD as their weapons of choice; the "lessons of history" that proved the superiority of America's "pro-growth" economic system; and the imperative of maintaining U.S. military superiority.

The Bush NSS has prompted sharp debate as to whether its ideology and proposed policies are continuous with past American ideas and policy or a radical or revolutionary departure, especially the emphasis on unilateral action, preemption, and hegemony. The Bush doctrine clearly draws on American traditions of exceptionalism and mission, and Cold War containment and deterrence. And U.S. presidents have repeatedly acted unilaterally and preemptively, especially in Latin America, although these actions have been seriously questioned. Further, FDR rejected preemptive strikes against Germany and Japan in 1941 as contrary to American principles, and in 1962 Robert Kennedy counseled the president against a Pearl Harbor type attack on Cuba.[200] Equally important, the Bush NSS, despite its Wilsonian rhetoric, hews more closely to the 1992 Cheney DPG, which proposed to prevent the emergence of any new rival power, brushed off alliances but told America's allies to rely on U.S. protection, and proposed to strike unilaterally and preemptively against anyone seeking WMD.

The Bush doctrine also marks a major shift from the 1999 Clinton doctrine, which accepts U.S. unilateral action if necessary, but emphasizes leveraging U.S. power through alliances or international organizations. The Clinton doctrine does not mention preemptive action, but rather maintaining a "robust triad of nuclear forces" to deter potential adversaries who might seek access to, or use of, WMD. And while the Clinton doctrine talked of building a missile defense system to protect against rogue states with WMD, it affirmed the ABM treaty as the "cornerstone of strategic stability" and U.S. commitment to arms agreements and multilateral accords.

The Bush doctrine pays only lip service to enlisting other nations; it prefers to work with "coalitions of the willing" and, most significantly, cites the need to strike preemptively against "emerging threats before they are fully formed." This transforms internationally accepted doctrine of preemptive action against an imminent threat into a dubious doctrine— without sanction in international law—of "preventive" action against a distant or vague threat.[201] Further, the Bush doctrine's emphasis on maintaining military superiority over every nation or adversary suggests U.S. intent to be not just the world's policeman but its permanently predominant power, a policy likely to inspire resentment from allies and less friendly states.

Finally, the Bush NSS appears to have been written to target Saddam Hussein, given the emphasis on U.S. need to act preventively against "tyrants" or "unbalanced dictators" who possess, or seek to possess, WMD, and who might aid terrorists willing to use these WMD to inflict "catastrophic damage" on even great nations. In fact, the Bush administration began to plan military operations against Iraq shortly after the September 2001 attacks, and throughout 2002 senior officials, especially Vice President Cheney, persisted that Saddam possessed WMD or materials and facilities that would enable him to acquire them soon, and that his regime maintained close operational ties with al-Qaeda.[202]

By July 2002 British intelligence was reporting that U.S. officials regarded war with Iraq as "inevitable," and were "fixing" intelligence and facts to fit policy.[203] On October 10 Bush got Congress to authorize his use of force against Iraq if Saddam did not comply with UN resolutions demanding that he turn over to that body all his WMD and production facilities for them.[204] The next month the UN voted to resume WMD inspections, but before they were completed Secretary of State Colin Powell told the UN in February 2003 that the U.S. had compelling intelligence on Iraq's possession of WMD, although he knew that the evidence was highly dubious.[205] And on March 19, the U.S. and its "coalition of the willing" invaded Iraq, without UN sanction. Bush announced "mission accomplished" on May 1, although Saddam was not captured until December. Even then the mission was not accomplished. The United States soon found itself confronting a major insurgency in Iraq while also trying to contain protracted bitter sectarian conflict. American troops, who the Bush administration said would be welcomed as liberators, are now seen as occupiers, and have suffered over 3000 deaths, while U.S. spending on the war has neared $500 billion, with no end in sight.[206]

Further, UN inspectors subsequently concluded that there were no WMD in Iraq, while the Bush administration, unable to produce any evidence that Saddam's regime had WMD or the ability to produce them, or that Baghdad had meaningful ties to al-Qaeda, shifted its rationale for war by claiming that its purpose had been to free the Iraqi people from a brutal dictator and open the way to democratic government. In effect, Bush embraced the doctrine of nation-building he had originally eschewed, and became, in the eyes of his supporters at least, a successor to crusading predecessors such as Wilson, Truman, Kennedy, and Reagan. His critics charged that his administration had manipulated intelligence in order to deceive the nation into accepting the need to go to war, while also failing to plan for the postwar period, thus leading Americans, once again, into a quagmire.[207]

VII

Ideology matters greatly in the formulation of national security policy. Americans have always been imbued with a sense of exceptionalism and mission, and their leaders have often summoned them to make the world safe for democracy or promote freedom globally. Presidents have also proposed that the United States become the "great arsenal of democracy," establish a permanent preponderance of power, and maintain credibility long after political-military undertakings have been shown to be misguided or hopeless. National leaders have also inclined to exaggerate the nature or cause of military incidents and threats to American security, and to demonize opponents of the U.S. as "evil."

Grandiose plans, rhetorical excess, and deceitfulness may have served to mobilize public support for foreign policy and national security efforts. But they also created the basis for disillusion by establishing unrealizable goals and rigid principles that left little room for changes in position, and made negotiation with opponents subject to charges of appeasement or capitulation. And too often later revelations about hostile incidents or security threats have undercut the credibility of policymakers and their stated reasons for war.

Still, U.S. leaders did try to transform their World War II alliance of necessity into a postwar United Nations that would promote collective security and the rule of international law; they provided economic assistance intended to promote a prosperous and peaceful liberal-capitalist world order free from extremes of left and right; and they built alliances that sought to contain aggressors. Policymakers also learned to negotiate with nations with extremely different, if not antithetical, political-economic systems and beliefs, and to effect multilateral treaties that intended to establish a balance of power and mutually assured survival, and to deal in concert with problems—global warming, poverty, and disease—that created a dangerous environment for all people.

Unfortunately, the demise of the Soviet Union and communism in Europe, and the end of the Cold War, did not bring a new world order so much as heady belief that the "end of history" meant that Western liberal democracy would become the final and universal form of government, and that globalization, and the Clinton administration's doctrine of "enlargement," would produce myriad market democracies and a peaceful world order. And while American power and primacy did remain unrivalled, rising radical Muslim ideology and terrorist assaults on American people and property in the United States and abroad posed a challenge to the nation's security.

During his presidential campaign in 2000, George Bush said the United States had to remain strong but act humbly in foreign affairs, but his administration immediately rekindled intense nationalism and unilateralism in 2001 by rejecting multilateral accords and proposing to negate the 1972 ABM treaty and to build a ballistic missile defense system. And after the 9/11 attacks, the president announced a "crusade" in Afghanistan to kill or capture Osama bin Laden, and soon denounced the so-called "axis of evil" of Iran, Iraq, and North Korea, although these countries had nothing to do with the attacks.

Most important, Bush's NSS of 2002, which draws heavily on the 1992 Cheney DPG that was labeled a Pax Americana, marks a radical, even revolutionary, change in U.S. policy. First, the document seeks to transform the accepted principles of preemptive action against imminent threats into the legally dubious doctrine of preventive action by saying that the United States will act no matter how distant or vague threats might be. Second, the Bush NSS emphasizes military superiority over all other nations, and downplays international organizations and alliances in favor of loosely organized coalitions that the U.S. can easily dominate. Thus the U.S. proposes to be both the world's policeman and its predominant military power. Third, the president's insistence in his cover letter that the twentieth century ended with only one "sustainable model of national success: freedom, democracy, and free enterprise," combined with the NSS emphasis that the "lessons of history" demonstrate that the best means to prosperity are a market economy and "pro-growth" policies, seem aimed more at promoting a conservative Republican agenda than national security. Moreover, the Bush NSS says little about major long-term threats, such as global warming, poverty, disease, and civil, ethnic, or tribal conflicts that often lead to genocide.

Finally it is significant that the Bush administration began to plan military operations against Iraq shortly after the 9/11 attacks, with senior officials, especially Vice President Cheney, repeatedly distorting intelligence information in order to insist that Saddam had WMD or the materials and facilities to produce them soon, and that his regime had close operational ties to al-Qaeda. The Bush administration also readily went to war without sanction from the UN or such close allies as France and Germany.

Simply put, the Bush administration has rejected three principles of international affairs: the long-established Westphalian doctrine of state sovereignty and noninterference in other nation's internal affairs; the UN Charter prohibition on use of force except in self-defense or by Security Council mandate; and the Nuremberg trials judgment that preventive war is a crime. The administration has also repeatedly deceived or lied to its constituents with regard to intelligence, which it has sought to "fix" to fit its actions, and it has disdained the Geneva Conventions and basic legal procedures in dealing with those it has alleged to have posed a threat to the United States. Such behavior does not appear to be a new "American internationalism," as Bush would have it, but rather a revolutionary policy more suited to a "rogue" nation than a world leader.[208] And in that case, Americans need to be concerned that ultimately their nation will find, as have all other imperial powers, that there are limits to the reach and longevity of its power, especially as other people or nations come to perceive the U.S. not as a liberator promoting freedom but as a dominator threatening their beliefs and ways of life, and causes them to join together and to take up arms against America.

Notes

1.   http://www.whitereafter cited as Bush NSSehouse.gov.nsc/nss/html (h).

2.   The Bush NSS uses the generally acceptable term "preemptive strike," i.e., in the face of an imminent threat, and avoids uses of the more controversial concept of a "preventive" strike, i.e., before a threat is fully formed, which international law holds to be illegal.

3.   John Lewis Gaddis, *Surprise, Security, and the American Experience* (Cambridge, MA, 2004); for a more ambivalent view, see Melvyn P. Leffler, "9/11 and American Foreign Policy," *Diplomatic History* 29 (June 2005): 395–413; six critiques of different persuasions follow by Robert Kagan, Walter L. Hixson, Daniel W. Drezner, Arnold A. Offner, and Anna Kasten Nelson, 415–39.

4.   T. D. Allman, *Rogue State: America at War with the World* (New York, 2004); James Bamford, *A Pretext for War: 9/11, Iraq, and the Abuses of America's Intelligence Agencies* (New York, 2004); Chalmers Johnson, *The Sorrows of Empire: Militarism, Secrecy, and the End of the Republic* (New York, 2004); and Michael Mann, *Incoherent Empire* (London and New York, 2003).

5. Winthrop quoted in Thomas G. Paterson, ed., *Major Problems in American Foreign Policy*, 3rd ed., 2 vols. (Lexington, MA, 1989), vol. 1: *To 1914*, 28–29.

6. William Appleman Williams, *The Tragedy of American Diplomacy*, rev. ed. (New York, 1972), 50–57.

7. Michael Hunt, *Ideology and United States Foreign Policy* (New York, 1987), 281–82.

8. Roosevelt Speech, April 15, 1940, in Samuel I. Rosenman, ed., *The Public Papers and Addresses of Franklin Delano Roosevelt*, 13 vols. (New York, 1938–50), 9: 158–164.

9. Roosevelt Fireside Chat, December 29, 1940, in *ibid.*, 633–44.

10. Diary entry for March 8, 1941, Arthur Vandenberg Jr., ed., *The Private Papers of Senator Vandenberg* (Boston, 1952), 10–12.

11. John Lewis Gaddis, *Russia, The Soviet Union, and the United States* (New York, 1990), 146–47.

12. Arnold A. Offner, *The Origins of the Second World War: American Foreign Policy and World Politics, 1917–1941* (New York, 1975), 209–11.

13. Robert Dallek, *Franklin D. Roosevelt and American Foreign Policy, 1932–1945* (New York, 1979), 287–85; John F. Bratzel and Leslie B. Rout, Jr., "'FDR' and the 'Secret Map,'" *The Wilson Quarterly* 9 (New Year's 1985): 167–73

14. Robert E. Sherwood, *Roosevelt and Hopkins: An Intimate History* (New York, 1948), 310.

15. John Fousek, *To Lead the Free World: American Nationalism and the Cultural Roots of the Cold War* (Chapel Hill and London, 2000), 42.

16. Thomas J. McCormick, *America's Half Century: United States Foreign Policy in the Cold War* (Baltimore and London, 1989), 52–53.

17. John Lewis Gaddis, *Strategies of Containment: A Critical Appraisal of Postwar American National Security Policy* (New York, 1982), 9–13.

18. Thomas G. Paterson, *On Every Front: The Making and Unmaking of the Cold War*, rev. ed. (New York and London, 1992), 10–20.

19. Truman quoted in Arnold A. Offner, "'Another Such Victory': President Truman, American Foreign Policy, and the Cold War," *Diplomatic History* 23 (Spring 1999): 132; see also *New York Times*, June 24, 1941.

20. Truman to Bess Truman, December 30, 1941, in Robert H. Ferrell, ed., *Dear Bess: The Letters from Harry to Bess Truman, 1910–1959* (New York, 1983), 471, and Truman to Myron Taylor, May 19, 1946, Box 1, Myron Taylor Papers, Harry S. Truman Library, Independence, MO; Truman Speech, March 27, 1946, in *The Public Papers of the Presidents: Harry S. Truman*, 8 vols. (Washington, 1962), 2: 170–171 (hereafter *PPHST*).

21. Truman to Bess Truman, July 31, 1945, in Ferrell, ed., *Dear Bess*, 522–23; see also Arnold A. Offner, *Another Such Victory: President Truman and the Cold War, 1945–1953* (Stanford, 2002), 96–99.

22. Truman Radio Report, Aug. 9, 1945, *PPHST*, 1: 212–14, and Abe Fortas to Truman, Sept. 26, 1945, Box 112, President Secretary's Files (hereafter PSF), Harry S. Truman Papers, Harry S. Truman Library, Independence, MO; Truman quoted in Greg Herken, *The Winning Weapon: The Atomic Bomb and the Cold War, 1945–1950* (New York, 1982), 146–52.

23. Bernard Baruch quoted on "winning weapons" in Herken, *Winning Weapon, 173;* Offner, *Another Such Victory,* 146–52.

24. Offner, *Another Such Victory,* 127.

25. Daniel Yergin, *Shattered Peace: The Origins of the Cold War and the National Security State* (Boston, 1977), 151–53, 155–57.

26. Truman to Byrnes, January, 5, 1946, PSF, Box 333, Truman Papers.

27. Yergin, *Shattered Peace,* 193–200, 219–20.

28. Supreme Court Justice William O. Douglas quoted in entry for February 17, 1946, in Walter Millis, ed., *The Forrestal Diaries* (New York, 1951), 134–35.

29. Kennan to Byrnes, February 22, 1946, U.S. Department of State, *Foreign Relations of the United States, Diplomatic Papers, 1946,* 11 vols. (Washington, 1969–1972), 6: 696–709 (hereafter *FR,* year, and volume).

30. Offner, *Another Such Victory,* 133–34.

31. *New York Times,* March 6, 1946.

32. Offner, *Another Such Victory,* 136–37.

33. Russian Report in Clifford to Truman, September [24], 1946, Box 15, Clark M. Clifford Papers, Truman Library; the Report is also in Arthur Krock, *Memoirs: Sixty Years on the Firing Line* (New York, 1968), Appendix, 418–82; Clark Clifford, *Counsel to the President: A Memoir* (New York, 1991), 123–24.

34. John Ehrman, *The Rise of Newconservatism: Intellectuals and Foreign Affairs, 1945–1994* (New Haven and London, 1995), 12–13.

35. Reinhold Neibuhr, *The Irony of American History* (New York, 1952), esp. 17–42, and Walter LaFeber, *America, Russia, and the Cold War, 1945–2002,* 9th ed. (New York, 2003), 50–51.

36. Arthur Schlesinger, Jr., *The Vital Center* (New York, 1949), and Alonzo Hamby, *Beyond the New Deal: Harry S. Truman and American Liberalism* (New York, 1973), 280–81.

37. Acheson quoted in Joseph M. Jones, *The Fifteen Weeks (February 21-June 5, 1947)* (New York, 1955), 138–42.

38. Vandenberg quoted in Howard Jones, *"A New Kind of War": American Global Strategy and the Truman Doctrine in Greece* (New York, 1989), 260n.3.

39. Truman Address before a Joint Session of the Senate and House . . . , March 12, 1947, *PPHST,* 3: 176–80.

40. Diary entry for November 4, 1947, in C.L. Sulzberger, *A Long Row of Candles: Memoirs and Diaries, 1934–1954* (New York, 1969), 364–65.

41. Fousek, *To Lead the Free World,* 129.

42. Lord Inverchapel to Foreign Office, March 15, 1947, Records of the British Foreign Office, File 371, Piece 61054, Public Record Office, London, England (hereafter cited by File/Piece).

43. U.S. Senate Committee on Foreign Relations, *Legislative Origins of the Truman Doctrine, Hearings Held in Executive Session . . . on S. 398: A Bill to Provide Assistance to Greece and Turkey* (Washington, 1973), 142.

44. Acheson quoted in Thomas G. Paterson, "Presidential Foreign Policy, Public Opinion, and Congress: The Truman Years," *Diplomatic History* 3 (Winter 1979): 17; for Congress's deference to the Executive branch but occasional assertiveness, see Robert David Johnson, "Congress and the Cold War," *Journal of Cold War Studies* 3 (Spring, 2001): 76–99.

45. Harry S. Truman, *Memoirs*, 2 vols. (Garden City, NY, 1955–1956), vol. 2, *Years of Trial and Hope*, 106, calls the Truman Doctrine the "turning point in American foreign policy."

46. John Lewis Gaddis, *The United States and the Origins of the Cold War, 1941–1947* (New York, 1973), 352; J. William Fulbright, "How the Devil Theory Has Beddeviled U.S. Foreign Policies," *The Times*, January, 17, 1972, says all U.S. foreign policy mistakes abroad stem from the Truman Doctrine.

47. "X," [George F. Kennan] "The Sources of Soviet Conduct," *Foreign Affairs* 25 (July 1947): 566–582.

48. George F. Kennan, *Memoirs, 1925–1963*, 2 vols. (New York, 1967–1972), 1: 357–67.

49. Walter Lippmann, *The Cold War: A Study in U.S. Foreign Policy*, new ed. (New York, [1947] 1972).

50. Ibid., 16; for an analysis of containment that likens it to a demand for Soviet unconditional surrender, see Frederik Lovegall, "A Critique of Containment," *Diplomatic History* 28 (September 2004): 473–95.

51. Charles Bohlen Memorandum, Aug. 30, 1947, *FR 1947*, 1: 762–65.

52. Avery Peterson Memoranda, June 24–June 26, 1947, ibid., 268–93; Michael J. Hogan, *The Marshall Plan: America, Britain, and the Reconstruction of Western Europe, 1947–1952* (New York, 1987), 1–25.

53. Truman Special Conference with Editors of Business Magazines and Newspapers, April 23, 1948, *PPHST*, 1: 231–33.

54. Harriman quoted in LaFeber, *America, Russia, and the Cold War*, 90.

55. Henry W. Berger, "Senator Robert A. Taft Dissents from Military Escalation," in Thomas G. Paterson, *Cold War Critics: Alternatives to American Foreign Policy in the Truman Years* (Chicago, 1971), 183–85.

56. Ibid., 187–88.

57. Offner, *Another Such Victory*, 434; Truman State of the Union Address, Jan. 8, 1951, *PPHST* 7: 6–13.

58. Offner, *Another Such Victory*, 434.

59. David McLean, "American Nationalism, the China Myth, and the Truman Doctrine: The Question of Accommodation with Peking, 1949–1950," *Diplomatic History* 10 (Winter, 1986): 26.

60. Diary entry for November 27, 1945, in John Morton Blum, ed., *The Price of Vision: The Diary of Henry A. Wallace* (Boston, 1973), 519–21.

61. Office of Far Eastern Affairs Memorandum, April 18, 1945, Box 73, PSF, Truman Papers, Truman Library.

62. Truman Memorandum, November [?], 1945, in Robert H. Ferrell, ed., *Off the Record: The Private Papers of Harry S. Truman* (New York, 1980), 74.

63. Marshall Memoranda of Conversations, December 11 and December 14, 1945, *FR 1945*, 7: 767–70.

64. Sidney Souers Notes, February 28, 1949, and NSC 34/2, "U.S. Policy Toward China," *FR 1949*, 9: 491–95.

65. Gordon H. Chang, *Friends and Enemies, The United States, China, and the Soviet Union, 1948–1971* (Stanford, 1990), 36–41, and Acheson Letter of Transmittal, July 30, 1949, in U.S. Department of State, *United States Relations with China, with Special Reference to the Period 1944–1949* (Washington, 1949), iii–xvii.

66. Acheson quoted in McLean, "American Nationalism," *Diplomatic History* 10: 30–31.

67. *New York Times*, January 13, 1950; Acheson Memorandum, January 5, 1950, *FR 1950*, 6: 260–63.

68. Philip Sprouse Memorandum, February 16, 1950, *FR 1950*, 6: 260–264; Acheson Memorandum, March 27, 1950, Box 27, Dean Acheson Papers, Truman Library.

69. Acheson Speech, "United States Policy Toward Asia," March 15, 1950, Department of State, *Bulletin* (March 29, 1950), 469–470.

70. Truman quoted in McLean, "American Nationalism," *Diplomatic History*, 10:40.

71. "A Report to the National Security Council by the Executive Secretary," April 14, 1950, *FR 1950*, 1: 234–92.

72. Dean Acheson, *Present at the Creation: My Years in The State Department* (New York, 1969), 374.

73. Ibid.; Note by Executive Secretary of the NSC, Sept. 30, 1950, *FR 1950*, 1: 400.

74. Edwin Pauley to Truman, June 22, and Truman to Pauley, July 16, 1946, *FR 1946*, 8: 706–9, 713–714.

75. George M. Elsey Notes, June 26 and June 27, 1950, Box 71, George M. Elsey Papers, Truman Library.

76. Offner, *Another Such Victory*, 371–72.

77. Elsey Memorandum, July 16, 1951, Box 76, Elsey Papers, Truman Library.

78. Truman Special Message to Congress, July 19, 1950, *PPHST*, 6: 531–37.

79. *New York Times*, August 18 and August 26, 1950, referring to Navy Secretary Francis Matthews' remarks.

80. Robert H. Ferrell, ed., *The Autobiography of Harry S. Truman* (Boulder, CO, 1980), 33; Acheson quoted in Matthew Connelly Cabinet Notes, Sept. 29, 1950, Box 2, Matthew Connelly Papers, Truman Library.

81. Rosemary Foot, *The Wrong War: American Policy and the Dimensions of the Korean Conflict, 1950–1953* (Ithaca, NY, 1988), 69–70.

82. Truman, *Years of Trial and Hope*, 462–64.

83. U.S. Delegation Minutes of First and Second Meetings of President Truman and Prime Minister Attlee, December 4 and December 5, 1950, *FR 1950*, 7: 1361–74, 1394–1408; *Burton J. Kaufman, The Korean War: Challenge in Crisis, Credibility, and Command* (New York, 1986), 136–38.

84. Barton J. Bernstein, "The Struggle Over the Korean Armistice: Prisoners of Repatriation?" in Bruce Cumings, ed., *Child of Conflict: The Korean-American Relationship, 1945–1953* (Seattle, 1983), 273–75.

85. Connelly Cabinet Notes, September 12, 1952, Box 2, Connelly Papers, Truman Library.

86. Eisenhower and Kennedy quoted in Trevor B. McCrisken, *American Exceptionalism and the Legacy of Vietnam: U.S. Foreign Policy Since 1974* (New York, 2003), 21, 24.

87. Johnson quoted in *New York Times*, June 28, 1967, and LaFeber, *America, Russia, and the Cold War*, 249.

88. U.S. Department of State, *Bulletin* (March 9, 1964), 371.

89. Randall Bennett Woods, *Fulbright: A Biography* (New York, 1995), p. 394.

90. In addition to Williams, *Tragedy of American Diplomacy* (1959, rev. ed., 1962), see Denna Frank Fleming, *The Cold War and its Origins, 1917–1960*, 2 vols. (Garden City, NY, 1960); Gar Alperowitz, *Atomic Diplomacy: Hiroshima and Potsdam* (New York, 1965); and Gabriel Kolko, *The Politics of War: The World and United States Foreign Policy, 1943–1945* (New York, 1968); for a survey of the impact of the Vietnam War on writing about U.S. foreign policy, see Jerold A. Combs, *American Diplomatic History: Two Centuries of Changing Interpretations* (Berkeley, 1986), 322–83.

91. Woods, *Fulbright*, p.402.

92. J. William Fulbright, *The Arrogance of Power* (New York: Vintage Books, 1966), 245–46.

93. Nixon and Ford quoted in McCrisken, *American Exceptionalism*, 35, 42–43.

94. Carter and Reagan quoted in ibid., 57, 85.

95. Bush and Clinton quoted in ibid., 133, 162.

96. Ole R. Holsti and James Rosenau, "Cold War Axioms," in Ole Holsti, Randolf Siverson, and Alexander George, eds., *Change in the International System* (Boulder, CO: 1980), 266–67.

97. Robert R. Bowie and Richard H. Immerman, *Waging Peace: How Eisenhower Shaped the Enduring Cold War Strategy* (New York, 1998), 75–76.

98. LaFeber, *America, Russia, and the Cold War*, 140.

99. Hans J. Morgenthau, "John Foster Dulles," in Norman A. Graebner, *An Uncertain Tradition: American Secretaries of State in the Twentieth Century* (New York, 1961), 293–96.

100. Saki Dockrill, *Eisenhower's New Look National Security Policy, 1953–1961* (London, 1996), 29; cf. Bowie and Immerman, *Waging Peace*, 119–22.

101. Dockrill, *Eisenhower's New Look*, 36–42.

102. Ibid., 43–47; Bowie and Immerman, *Waging Peace*, 139–46.

103. Gary R. Hess, *Vietnam and the United States: Origins and Legacy of War* (Boston, 1990), 45–46.

104. *New York Times*, January 19, 1961.

105. David Burner and Thomas R. West, *The Torch is Passed: the Kennedy Brothers and American Liberalism* (New York, 1984), 71–75; Lawrence Freedman, *Kennedy's Wars: Berlin, Cuba, Laos, and Vietnam* (New York, 2000), 28–31.

106. LaFeber, *America, Russia, and the Cold War*, 219–20, 244.

107. Quoted in Thomas G. Paterson, ed., *Kennedy's Quest for Victory: American Foreign Policy, 1960–1963* (New York, 1989) p. 12.

108. Freedman, *Kennedy's Wars*, 34–35; inaugural address in Edwin H. Judge and John Langdon (eds.), *The Cold War: A History Through Documents* (Upper Saddle River, NJ, 1999), 113–15.

109. Kennedy quoted in Paterson, ed., *Kennedy's Quest*, 9.

110. Thomas G. Paterson, "Fixation with Cuba: The Bay of Pigs, Missile Crisis, and Covert War Against Fidel Castro," in ibid., 124.

111. Freedman, *Kennedy's Wars*, 139–46.

112. Kennedy quoted in Michael R. Beschloss, *The Crisis Years: Kennedy and Khrushchev, 1961–1963* (New York, 1991), 278.

113. Quoted in Robert Dallek, *An Unfinished Life: John F. Kennedy, 1917–1963* (Boston, 2003), 625.

114. Ibid., 260–89.

115. Kennedy Address, June 10, 1963, quoted in Judge and Langdon, *Cold War Documents*, 125–26.

116. LaFeber, *America, Russia, and the Cold War*, 220.

117. Freedman, *Kennedy's Wars*, 324–39, 362–97.

118. Ibid., p.129.

119. Johnson quoted in LaFeber, *America, Russia and the Cold War*, 249–50.

120. George C. Herring, *America's Longest War: The United States and Vietnam*, 4th ed. (New York, 2002), 134–37; reports of the attacks seem to have derived from freak weather effects on radar and sonar systems; further, the administration denied until 1968 that both ships had recently taken part in attacks on North Vietnam; see also Robert Mann, *A Grand Delusion: America's Descent Into Vietnam* (New York, 2001), 346–55.

121. Dallek, *Flawed Giant*, 169–70.

122. Humphrey to Johnson, February 17, 1965, Vice Presidential Files, Box 924, Hubert H. Humphrey Papers, Minnesota State Historical Society, St. Paul, MN.

123. H. W. Brands, *The Wages of Globalism: Lyndon Johnson and the Limits of American Power* (New York, 1995), 241–42; Herring, *America's Longest War*, 171–73.

124. Brands, *Wages of Globalism*, 249–52.

125. Herring, *America's Longest War*, 243–46.

126. Henry Kissinger, *American Foreign Policy: Three Essays* (New York, 1969), 101–35.

127. Lloyd C. Gardner, *A Covenant with Power: America and World Order from Wilson to Reagan* (New York, 1984), 182.

128. Robert Schulzinger, *Henry Kissinger: Doctor of Diplomacy* (New York, 1989) 34–36.

129. Hess, *Vietnam and the United States*, 134–35; on "decent interval," see Jussi Hahnhimaki, "A Prize Winning Performance: Kissinger, Triangular Diplomacy, and the End of the Vietnam War," Nobel Institute Research Paper, April 2001, 17.

130. Kissinger quoted in Hess, *Vietnam and the United States*, 140.

131. Henry A. Kissinger, "Between the Old Left and the New Right," *Foreign Affairs*, 78 (May/June 1999): 99–100.

132. Schulzinger, *Henry Kissinger*, 12–13, 78–79.

133. Richard M. Nixon, "Asia After Vietnam," *Foreign Affairs*, 47 (October 1967), 111–125.

134. Gaddis, *Strategies of Containment*, 280–81.

135. For a critique of linkage, see *ibid.*, 310–20.

136. Ibid., 324–25.

137. Michael Schaller, *The United States and China: Into the Twenty First Century*, 3rd ed. (New York, 2002), 172–76, 180.

138. Nixon quoted in Stephen E. Ambrose, *Nixon: The Triumph of a Politician, 1962–1972* (New York, 1989), 517.

139. Ehrman, *Rise of Neoconservatism*, 42–62, 104–14; H. W. Brands, *The Devil We Knew: Americans and the Cold War* (New York, 1993), 151–56.

140. Ford and Reagan quoted in Francis L. Loewenheim, "From Helsinki to Afghanistan: American Diplomats and Diplomacy, 1975–1979," in Gordon Craig and Francis L. Loewenheim, eds., *The Diplomats, 1939–1979* (Princeton, 1994), 639.

141. Ibid., 641.

142. McCrisken, *American Exceptionalism*, 59.

143. Ibid., 162.

144. Gaddis Smith, *Morality, Reason, and Power: American Diplomacy in the Carter Years* (New York, 1986), 79–83.

145. Smith, *Morality, Reason, and Power*, 188–89.

146. Seyom Brown, *The Faces of Power: United States Foreign Policy from Truman to Clinton*, 2nd ed. (New York, 1994), 361–71.

147. Ibid., 371–76.

148. Smith, *Morality, Reason, and Power*, 218–32.

149. Article reprinted in Jeane J. Kirkpatrick, *Dictatorship and Double Standards: Rationalism and Reason in Politics* (New York, 1992), 23–52.

150. Rose McDermott, "Arms Control and the First Reagan Administration: Belief-Systems and Policy Choices," *Journal of Cold War Studies*, 4 (Fall, 2002): p. 43.

151. Ibid., 37–56.

152. *New York Times*, Jan. 30, 1981; Gardner, *Covenant with Power*, 230.

153. McDermott, "Arms Control and . . . Reagan," *Journal of Cold War Studies*, 4, 499.

154. Brown, *Faces of Power*, 396–402; for a full account, see Frances Fitzgerald, *Way Out There in the Blue: Reagan, Star Wars, and the End of the Cold War* (New York, 2000).

155. Reagan Speech to Chicago Council on Foreign Relations, March 17, 1980, in Kiron K. Skinner, Annelise Anderson, and Martin Anderson, eds., *Reagan in His Own Hand* (New York, 2001), 479.

156. LaFeber, *America, Russia, and the Cold War*, 325.

157. Quoted in Brown, *Faces of Power*, 467–68.

158. Ibid., 467.

159. Ibid., 475; LaFeber, *America, Russia, and the Cold War*, 327–28.

160. Brown, *Faces of Power*, 470–82; Oliver North with William Novak, *Under Fire: An American Story* (New York, 1991), 12, 14.

161. Robert G. Kaiser, *Why Gorbachev Happened: His Triumphs and His Failures* (New York, 1991), and Mikhail Gorbachev, *Perestroika: New Thinking for Our Country and the World* (New York, 1997).

162. Gaddis, *Russia . . . and the United States*, 328–36, and Richard Smoke, *National Security and the Nuclear Dilemma: An Introduction to the American Experience in the Cold War*, 3rd ed. (New York, 1993), 264–72.

163. Reagan quoted in LaFeber, *America, Russia, and the Cold War*, 340.

164. Ibid., 351–57.

165. Brown, *Faces of Power*, 505–6; *New York Times*, May 13, 1989.

166. LaFeber, *America, Russia, and the Cold War*, 355–56.

167. Brown, *Faces of Power*, 516.

168. Bush quoted in *ibid.*, 521–22.

169. *New York Times*, January 29, 1992; LaFeber, *America, Russia, and the Cold War*, 366.

170. *New York Times*, September 12, 1990.

171. Larry Everest, *Oil, Power, and Empire: Iraq and the U.S. Global Agenda* (Monroe, ME, 2004), 100–106; Chalmers Johnson, *The Sorrows of Empire: Militarism, Secrecy, and the End of the Republic* (New York, 2004), 223–25.

172. Brown, *Faces of Power*, 535–36.
173. Ibid., 537.
174. Ibid., 538–40.
175. Ibid., 540–41.
176. Charles, Tripp, *A History of Iraq*, 2nd ed. (Cambridge, 2000), 255–58; Brown, *Faces of Power*, 562–564.
177. *New York Times*, June 6, 1989; Schaller, *U.S. and China*, 201–6.
178. Brown, *Faces of Power*, 526–35, see also Eytan Gilboa, "The Panama Invasion Revisited," *Political Science Quarterly*, 110 (Winter, 1995–1996): 539–62, which argues the U.S. needed to have been clearer with Noriega (and with other dictators, including Saddam Hussein).
179. Brown, *Faces of Power*, 556–68.
180. *New York Times*, December 5, 1992.
181. Ibid., January 6, 1993.
182. The document remains classified, but critical excerpts have appeared in many places, including *New York Times*, May 23, 1992, and David Armstrong, "Dick Cheney's Song of America: Drafting a Plan for Global Dominance," *Harper's Magazine*, 305 (October 2002), 76–78.
183. Francis Fukuyama, "The End of History?," *The National Interest*, 16 (Summer 1989): 3–18; and *The End of History and the Last Man* (New York, 1992).
184. Samuel P. Huntington, "The Clash of Civilizations?," *Foreign Affairs*, 72 (Summer 1989): 3–18, and *The Clash of Civilizations and the Remaking of the World Order* (New York, 1996).
185. Brown, *Faces of Power*, 182; William G. Hyland, *Clinton's World: Remaking American Foreign Policy* (Westport, CT, 1999), 15–26, assesses contending Wilsonian and Realist currents in the administration, and contends that Clinton's focus on domestic matters proved to the detriment of foreign policy.
186. *New York Times*, September 26, 1993; Hyland, *Clinton's World*, 24–25.
187. Hyland, *Clinton's World*, 67–73.
188. Ibid., 113–123. The author notes Clinton's frustration with the U.S. inability to get China to alter its domestic political-human rights policies.
189. Chester A. Crocker, "The Lessons of Somalia: Not Everything Went Wrong," *Foreign Affairs*, 74 (May/June, 1995): 2–8, is a balanced account.
190. LaFeber, *America, Russia, and the Cold War*, 373–74.
191. Ibid., 374–75, and Maud Beeman, "Fingerprints," *New Republic* (October 28, 1996), 26–28.
192. LaFeber, *America, Russia, and the Cold War*, 384–85.
193. Richard A. Clarke, *Against All Enemies: Inside America's War on Terror* (New York, 2004), 135–226.
194. "National Security Policy for a New Century," The White House, December 1999, posted at: http://www.dtic.mil/doctrine/jel/other-pubs/nssr1999.

195. Michael Kinsley, "The Limits of Eloquence," *Washington Post*, November 14, 2003.
196. Clarke, *Against All Enemies*, 227–38; see also "Halting Response to Terror Risk in Summer 2001," *New York Times*, April 4, 2004.
197. Mann, *Incoherent Empire*, 123–27.
198. Bush speech of June 1, 2002, posted at: http://www.whitehouse.gov/news/release/2002/0129–11.html.
199. Bush speech of June 1, 2002, posted at: http://www.whitehouse.gov.news/release/20020601/-3html.
200. Evan Thomas, *Robert Kennedy: His Life* (New York, 2000), 215–16.
201. For a discussion of preemptive and preventive war, see "Beating them to Pre-war," *New York Times*, September 28, 2003, and Fred Kaplan, "Bush at Sea," posted February 9, 2004, at: http://slate.msn.com.id/2095184/e.
202. Philip H. Gordon and Jeremy Shapiro, *Allies at War: America, Europe, and the Crisis Over Iraq* (New York, 2004), 367–77.
203. The reference is to a memorandum of July 23, 2002, written by Matthew Rycroft, a senior foreign policy adviser to Prime Minister Tony Blair, reporting the comments of Sir Richard Dearlove, head of British intelligence, following his conversations with senior Bush advisers. Dearlove is reported as saying that U.S. officials regarded war with Iraq as "inevitable," and were "fixing" facts and intelligence to policy; the memorandum appears in full in Mark Danner, "The Secret Way to War," *New York Review of Books*, June 9, 2005, 71; it first appeared in the *Sunday Times*, May 1, 2005.
204. *New York Times*, October 11, 2002.
205. Ibid., February 6, 2003; for analysis of the highly faulty intelligence claims, see Bamford, *Pretext for War*, 367–377, and Bob Woodward, *Plan of Attack* (New York, 2004), 309–12.
206. For a chronicle of the war, see "2003 Invasion of Iraq," posted at http://www.wordiq.com./definition
207. Paul R. Pillar, "Intelligence Policy and the War in Iraq," *Foreign Affairs*, 85 (March/April 2006): 15–27; Lewis H. Lapham, "The Case for Impeachment," *Harper's Magazine*, 312 (March 2006), 27–35.
208. Clyde Prestowitz, *Rogue Nation: American Unilateralism and the Failure of Good Intentions* (New York, 2003), esp. 23.

2. VARIATIONS ON THE AMERICAN WAY OF WAR

James Kurth

During the last third of the twentieth century, military strategists and historians developed the idea that there was a distinctive American strategic culture or "way of war." There was general agreement that the American way of war was characterized by a reliance upon such American advantages as (1) overwhelming mass, i.e., a pronounced advantage in men and material; (2) wide-ranging mobility, i.e., a pronounced advantage in transportation and communication; and (3) high-technology weapons systems, i.e., a comparative advantage in capital investment versus manpower.[1]

Parallel to these three military qualities were a political feature and an international one. The political feature was well-known. Underlying and sustaining U.S. success in wars, writers generally agreed, was a reliance upon high public support for the war effort—the advantage that came when an aroused democracy was mobilized behind a popular cause. The international feature, in contrast, was little discussed, even though it had actually been an integral part of the way that the United States had really fought its recent wars. This was a reliance upon allied countries, who were also fighting America's enemies and who provided a good deal of the necessary mass—the men and material—themselves. The real secret of America's advantage in mass was that some ally was always there to bring even more mass to America's side. This had been the case with the French and British armies in World War I and, most momentously (but largely unrecognized), with the Soviet army in World War II. Among other things, the American way of war was a coalition way of war.

The archetypal expression of the American way of war had of course been the greatest of all American foreign wars, World War II, in which all five of these advantages contributed to the epic U.S. victory. In turn, the heroic age of World War II created and established a U.S. military paradigm that has persisted in many ways down to the present day. The history of U.S. national security policy since World War II can be seen largely as a series of successive foreign challenges to this classical paradigm, which in turn have produced a series of successive responses or even major transformations within the American way of war. In particular there have been four such major transformations since 1945. As it happens, and as we shall see, they have occurred roughly every twenty years, coming along in the mid-1940s, the early 1960s, the early 1980s, and most recently, the early 2000s.

THE U.S. MILITARY SERVICES AND THE AMERICAN WAY OF WAR

Each of the U.S. military services has claimed to represent and combine most of the elements of the American way of war. In general, however, the U.S. Army has focused most on the element of mass; the U.S. Navy, as well as "the Navy's army," the U.S. Marines, have focused most on the element of mobility; and the U.S. Air Force has focused most on the element of high technology. During the course of World War II, however, the Air Force (then officially the U.S. Army Air Force) combined the elements of mass, mobility, and high technology into an especially destructive and terrible synthesis—the strategic bombing offensive, which combined mass destruction of enemy civilians, unprecedented mobility of offensive power, and the highest development of military technologies and which culminated in the atomic bombing of Hiroshima and Nagasaki.[2] The Air Force's peculiar synthesis of these elements of the American way of war made it the dominant military service in U.S. national security policy during much of the Cold War.

Each of the U.S. military services has also claimed to be representing the fourth element of the American way of war, the will of the American people. In practice, however, only the Army has operated in a way and on a scale that has necessitated high and sustained public support for its combat operations. Naval, marine, and air force operations have often been conducted without large numbers of American casualties, which means that the president has been able to carry them out without having to build extensive support among the public.

Conversely, none of the U.S. military services has wanted to say much about the fifth element, the reliance upon allied countries. And in practice,

only the Army has operated in a way and in theaters which have necessitated extensive cooperation with allied counterparts for its combat operations. The double reliance of the Army upon public support and allied
cooperation has made it, for the most part, the most politically and diplomatically sophisticated of all the U.S. military services.

The Origins of the American Way of War

The apotheosis of the American way of war was World War II, but its origins lie in the greatest American war of all, the Civil War. The use of overwhelming mass, exemplified by the strategy of Ulysses S. Grant, was
crucial to the final victory of the North. Conversely, the use of wide-
ranging mobility, exemplified by the strategy of Robert E. Lee, was crucial
to the initial victories of the South. The mass destruction of civilian resources, exemplified by the strategy of William Tecumseh Sherman, was
also part of the final victory of the North. (Sherman, however, targeted
property, rather than persons.) [3]

Although the U.S. Navy certainly used wide-ranging mobility in the
Spanish-American War, and the U.S. Army tried to use overwhelming
mass during World War I, for the most part there was little evidence of a
distinctive American way of war during the eighty years between the Civil
War and World War II.[4] Indeed, for much of this period, the model for the
U.S. Navy seemed to be the British Navy, and the model for the U.S. Army
seemed to be the German Army. But underneath this indistinctive, and
undistinguished, military surface, profound geographical and economic
realities were beginning to shape the future wars of America.

The emerging American way of war was a product of the distinctive
geographical and economic features of the United States: a vast continental territory, which was endowed with ample natural resources, and a population larger than that of most European powers. This meant that up
through World War II, the United States always had a pronounced advantage in men and material, i.e., mass. Only the Soviet Union during the
Cold War could surpass the United States in these respects.

In turn, the vast continental area and widespread population created a
need for a correspondingly extensive transportation and communication
network, and the large industry and advanced technology of the U.S.
economy provided the means with which to build it. Furthermore, the
United States was bordered by two vast oceans. This also created

demand for a transportation and communication network that extended
to other continents. This meant that the United States always had a pronounced advantage in the rapid movement of people and products in
peace and of men and material in war, i.e., mobility. No power has ever
surpassed the U.S. in this respect. The conjunction of a pronounced advantage in both mass and mobility made the United States the most successful military power of the twentieth century and thereby made the
twentieth century the American century. No other military power could
excel on both dimensions.

The First Great Challenge: Soviet Mass

Immediately after its epic validation with the U.S. victory in World War
II, the first dimension of the American way of war was trumped by America's new adversary in Europe, the Soviet Union, which could surpass the
United States in both men and material. It quickly became clear to U.S.
policymakers that this would require a major revision or even transformation of the strategy that had just proven itself so successful against Nazi
Germany and Imperial Japan.

It was natural that policymakers would try to build upon the remaining
advantages of the American way of war. Although the United States had lost
its advantage in mass, it still retained its advantage in mobility. Indeed, because the U.S. was the dominant naval power (it possessed more major ships
than all of the other navies of the world combined), and the Soviet Union
was at first hardly a naval power at all, the U.S. could expect to retain this
advantage in mobility far into the future. It was the U.S. advantage in naval
power and mobility that provided the underlying military foundation for
the new national strategy of containment. Although the Soviet Union occupied the vast central landmass of Eurasia, what Halford Mackinder had
called "the Heartland" of "the World Island,"[5] the United States had allies
and bases around most of the Eurasian periphery, and these could be reached
from the oceans that encompassed the world island. Of course, if the Soviet
Union ever flung its great advantage in mass against the U.S. allies and
bases, Soviet mass would overwhelm American mobility. Something else
was needed to trump, or at least contain, the Soviet advantage in mass.

Initially, there was some discussion among U.S. military leaders, particularly in the U.S. Army, about the possibility of restoring the classical
U.S. advantage in men and material through such proposals as "Universal

Military Training," i.e., conscription and a period of military service for all males, as well as economic mobilization or "preparedness" during peacetime, or more accurately during the "national emergencies" that had become permanent since the 1930s.[6] However, these proposals to restore the first element of the American way of war were aborted by the constraints imposed by the fourth element, the necessity for high public support. Elected officials understood that there was no public support for a truly universal military draft and for a permanently mobilized economy. In addition, some of these officials also understood that, if these measures were enacted on a permanent basis, they might transform the United States into something like a "garrison state."[7]

THE FIRST GREAT TRANSFORMATION: NUCLEAR DETERRENCE

With the first element (mass) blocked by the fourth (public support), and with the second element (mobility) not in itself sufficient, the only remaining alternative was the third element, high technology. And of course, the way that World War II had ended, with the atomic bomb (A-bomb) and the big bang over Hiroshima and Nagasaki, seemed to make it blindingly evident that this was the way to go. Thus, very quickly, U.S. policymakers developed the military strategy of nuclear deterrence, which they thought would provide an additional military foundation, and one more substantial than naval power, for the new national strategy of containment.

By 1949, the new U.S. strategy for the new challenge posed by the Soviet Union seemed to be securely in place. The new American way of war for the Cold War represented a shift of weight among the four elements of the classical American way of war, which had been exemplified in World War II. The roles of mobility (particularly the Navy) and high technology (particularly the Air Force) were enhanced and combined into the national strategy of containment and the military strategy of nuclear deterrence. The role of mass (particularly the Army) was diminished to the point that it became something of a symbolic presence (developing by the late 1950s into a nuclear tripwire), which would provide reassurance to U.S. allies while their economies and societies were restored with U.S. economic aid, particularly with the Marshall Plan. And because the costs in men and material of this national strategy seemed to be rather low (only 3 percent of GNP in 1949), it seemed very likely that the American public would support it.[8]

This new strategic equilibrium was upset almost immediately, however, by two great events, which permanently changed the strategic landscape and posed two new, interrelated challenges to the United States. In September 1949, the Soviet Union had tested its own atomic bomb. Then, a month later, the Chinese Communist armies completed their conquest of the Chinese mainland. These two events came together in a third when, in January 1950, the Soviet Union and Communist China signed a long-term treaty of friendship and cooperation.

The Soviet Bomb and More Nuclear Deterrence

One response of U.S. policymakers to the most shocking of these events, the Soviets acquiring the atomic bomb, was the famous NSC 68, which is discussed in detail elsewhere in this volume. In terms of our analytical framework, however, the central U.S. response was the decision to develop a new and much more powerful kind of nuclear weapon, the hydrogen bomb (H-bomb), and also new and faster kinds of delivery systems, jet bombers (the B-47).[9] In essence, having already chosen in 1945–1946 to trump Soviet mass with American high technology, the United States in 1949–1950 continued to advance down this path. Indeed, for the next forty years, the United States and the Soviet Union would engage in an arms race with respect to nuclear weapons. Sometimes the competition focused upon the nuclear warheads: during the 1950s and early 1960s, the effort was to produce warheads with greater destructive energy; From the later 1960s through the 1980s, the effort was to produce smaller, multiple warheads. Sometimes the competition focused upon the delivery systems; at first this meant bombers and then, after the mid-1950s, it meant missiles. During most decades of the Cold War, at least until the 1970s, there was competition in regard to both quantity and quality, as both the United States and the Soviet Union sought to achieve both greater numbers and higher technology in regard to both warheads and missiles.

The Chinese Revolution and Appeasement

The new U.S. strategy of containment and nuclear deterrence had been designed to check the threat of a Soviet invasion of Western Europe. The U.S. decision to extend nuclear deterrence into more and bigger bombs (the H-bomb) and more and better delivery systems (the B-47) seemed a logical way to preserve this strategy in the face of the challenge of the Soviet A-bomb and bomber, their version of the American B-29. But how should the United States respond to the other new challenge of the fall and winter of 1949–1950, the Communist victory in China and the subsequent Sino-Soviet alliance?

The initial response of U.S. policymakers to the Communist challenge in Asia was precisely the opposite of their response to the challenge in Europe. Instead of confronting Communist China, they essentially wrote off two Chinese neighbors, which remained anti-Communist, Taiwan (then called Formosa) and South Korea. U.S. policymakers thought that, "when the dust settled," China's natural antipathy to Russia (and presumed natural friendship with America) would reassert itself, and that this natural development would be facilitated if the United States did not contest China's traditional extension of its influence over Taiwan and Korea.[10] Given the largely domestic origins of the Chinese revolution, and especially given the natural tendency of policymakers to deny the nightmarish prospects of a Sino-Soviet alliance, which would control one-third of the world's population and most of the Eurasian landmass, this approach seemed to be a reasonable and realistic one. It was not, however, containment; it was essentially appeasement.

Given the U.S. perceptions of the Sino-Soviet bloc at the time, no one could imagine that small communist states (then termed "Soviet satellites") could take aggressive action by themselves. Then, in June 1950, the armies of Communist North Korea suddenly thrust across the 38th parallel and into this conceptual void.

THE NORTH KOREAN INVASION AND THE CLASSICAL AMERICAN WAY OF WAR

Given the earlier U.S. decision to write off South Korea, the most logical U.S. response to the North Korean invasion might have been to "let the dust settle" there too. Instead, U.S. policymakers surprised the Communist powers (and perhaps even surprised themselves) by deciding to use U.S. military forces to stop and repel the invasion. When President Truman later explained this turnabout of U.S. policy, he emphasized the analogies between the North Korean armed aggression and the earlier armed aggressions of Imperial Japan, Fascist Italy, and Nazi Germany in the 1930s and his resulting belief that the sooner the U.S. stopped such aggressions, the better it would be. If so, this suggests that the United States would not have intervened if North Korea had instead employed a strategy of guerrilla war against the South Korean regime, rather than one of conventional invasion.[11]

However, it is also important to note that U.S. domestic politics had undergone a major change in the first half of 1950. The Republican Party in general, and Wisconsin Senator Joseph McCarthy in particular, had begun to attack the Democratic administration for its failure to prevent the Communist victory in China. There was a growing belief in America that Communism had to be contained (or perhaps even rolled back) in Asia, as well as in Europe. And so the Truman administration decided upon military intervention in Korea. But how should that intervention be carried out?

In accordance with the recent emphasis on U.S. naval and air power, and the related de-emphasis of U.S. ground forces, policymakers initially tried to stop the North Korean invasion with naval and air strikes alone. (This practice would later be repeated in the Vietnam War in 1965 and the Persian Gulf War in 1991.) Within a few days, however, it became clear that the United States would have to send in ground forces as well.

After an initial period of chaos and retreat, the U.S. commander, General Douglas MacArthur, in September 1950 executed a brilliant and audacious amphibious landing at the port of Inchon, combined with a breakout from the U.S. redoubt around the port of Pusan. This particular operation was a masterful combination of the classical U.S. strengths of mass (the counterattack from Pusan), mobility (the invasion at Inchon), and high technology (the bombing of North Korean forces). It immediately reversed the course of the war, and the U.S. quickly drove the North Korean forces back across the 38th parallel. Up to this point, the Korean War could be seen as a brilliant, although smaller and faster, recapitulation of the successful U.S. strategies in World War II, and as a dramatic and convincing validation of the classical American way of war. It would have been very fitting if the Korean War had stopped there.

The Chinese Intervention and a Stalemated War

The reason that it did not was that U.S. ground forces did not stop at the 38th parallel or, alternatively, stop at the "narrow neck" of North Korea, which was north of its capital of Pyongyang but substantially south of the

Chinese border along the Yalu river.[12] The U.S. drive toward the Chinese frontier activated China's own intervention in the war, and in November 1950 its own ground forces poured across the Yalu. Chinese mass immediately trumped all of the American advantages, and U.S. forces had to retreat once again, not only across the 38th parallel but even south of the South Korean capital of Seoul. The result was, as U.S. policymakers immediately understood, "a whole new war."

How should the U.S. fight this new war? Unfortunately, neither the classical (conventional) American way of war or the new (nuclear) version had any obvious and convincing answers. The conventional methods had brilliantly succeeded against a small enemy, North Korea, but they had manifestly been inadequate against one, China, which possessed an overwhelming advantage in mass, at least in numbers of men. The nuclear method, with its truly massive firepower, could conceivably trump China's massive manpower, but it seemed that China had come under the umbrella of the Soviet Union's own nuclear deterrence with the Sino-Soviet alliance of January 1950. The United States, the creator of the strategy of containment and nuclear deterrence, was itself now contained and deterred by the Soviet counterpart of that strategy.

The United States never did develop a *satisfying* solution to the Chinese challenge in Korea (although, since it ultimately succeeded in restoring the independence and territory of South Korea, it did develop a *satisfactory* one). The Korean War of 1951–1953 became a grinding stalemate between Chinese manpower and U.S. firepower, which had little in common with World War II (with the exception of the dreary U.S. campaign in Italy during 1943–1945), but which had a great deal in common with the Western Front during World War I. During this time, the U.S. strategy was one of attrition, and it relied greatly upon building up the army of its South Korean ally, which provided a good deal of useful manpower. The wartime stalemate came to an end in July 1953 only because of an unusual conjunction of circumstances: the inauguration of a new U.S. president, Dwight Eisenhower, in January 1953; the death of the old Soviet leader, Josef Stalin, in March 1953; and the discreet but distinct threat by Eisenhower to use nuclear weapons, if that were what it would take to break the stalemate on the battlefield.[13] An armistice or peacetime statement ensued, which largely continued for fifty years until 2003, when North Korea's development of its own nuclear weapons created a new and dangerous reality on the Korean peninsula.

The Korean War, or more accurately the Chinese war within the Korean War, thus did not fit into the classical paradigm of the American way of war. This is one reason why, for many Americans, it became "the forgotten war"; they simply did not know how to think about it. However, for a number of U.S. national security policymakers and specialists, and in particular for three different groups of them, there were important lessons to be learned from the Korean War—lessons they thought should shape the U.S. national security policy of the future. These three groups were (1) the Eisenhower administration and more generally the Republican Party; (2) the U.S. Army; and (3) a new kind of thinker about military matters, civilian "defense intellectuals."

THE EISENHOWER ADMINISTRATION AND THE REPUBLICAN PARTY: "THE NEW LOOK"

The new Eisenhower administration understood clearly that it should avoid anything like the Korean War in the future. The reasons for this were political, economic, and strategic.

First, the Eisenhower administration itself, and more generally the Republican Party, had been elected in 1952 in large part because of the American public's frustration with the stalemated war in Korea and with the inability of the Democratic Party to offer a convincing solution. The Republicans did not want to become the future victims of the same kind of political issue they had used so successfully against the Democrats. Second, the Republicans, as the party most representative of business interests, were appalled by the economic costs of the Korean war, which had led to a massive increase in government spending and an initial surge in inflation, followed by the imposition of wage and price controls. Business interests did not want to become the future victims of the same kind of economic disruptions and restrictions they had just suffered. Third, by 1953 the earlier decisions of the Truman administration to acquire large numbers of bombs and bombers made it possible for the United States to produce vast amounts of nuclear weapons at a cost substantially lower than that for conventional forces; nuclear weapons now appeared to offer "more bang for the buck." The United States no longer possessed a nuclear monopoly, but it certainly could possess nuclear plenty; and this seemed to promise a great strategic advantage over the Soviet Union.

The Eisenhower administration therefore undertook what it called its "new look" at U.S. national security policy; the resulting new strategy represented a synthesis of these political, economic, and strategic considerations.[14] The "new look" strategy was designed to address the political problem with "no more Koreas," the economic problem with "more bang for the buck," and the strategic problem with a new doctrine known as "massive retaliation," which was supposed to be executed "by means and at places of our own choosing." The threat of new armed aggressions by Communist powers (such as had occurred in Korea) would be met by the threat of massive retaliation by the United States (which would include the use of U.S. nuclear weapons). In other words, any Communist advantage in masses of men and material would be trumped by U.S. advantages in massive retaliatory firepower, in mobility ("means and places of our own choosing"), and in high technology (advanced nuclear weapons and delivery systems). The United States would not get bogged down in the future in local, conventional wars, where its strategic advantages could not be deployed and where Communist mass could trump U.S. mass.[15]

Although the Eisenhower administration claimed that its new strategy was the result of a "new look," it was actually a recapitulation of the once-new strategy of containment and deterrence the Truman administration had developed in 1947–1949, in order to confront the first great challenge to the U.S. after World War II—that of Soviet mass. The difference now was that the original strategy was being extended from the Soviet Union to Communist China and even to any other Communist state (such as North Korea). This extension of containment and deterrence was accompanied by the extension of formal alliances, boundary lines, and nuclear thresholds around the frontiers of the Communist powers—from NATO in Europe to METO (later CENTO) in the Middle East, to SEATO in Southeast Asia, and to bilateral defense treaties with Taiwan, South Korea, and Japan in East Asia. Critics within the Democratic Party referred to this part of the administration's strategy as "pactomania." It was, however, a logical and elegant (if not always practical and robust) deduction not only from the "new look" of the Eisenhower administration, but from the genuinely new strategy of containment and deterrence of the Truman administration as well.

Thus, by 1955, the Eisenhower administration could think that it had created and established a new strategic equilibrium, solidly based upon the advantages of the new—and nuclear—American way of war, which would prevent both global wars like World War II and dismal aberrations like the Korean War, and which conformed to the underlying political and economic realities of America.

The U.S. Army: "No More Land Wars in Asia"

The U.S. Army had been the central military service fighting the Korean War, receiving the bulk of the costs and casualties, and so it was essential that it also draw lessons from the war. However satisfactory the war might have been in achieving its primary objective of preserving the independence and territory of South Korea, it was deeply unsatisfying in the way it contradicted the classical American way of war and the Army's definition of how it should fight and win America's wars. The Korean War, particularly the obstacles produced by China's massive advantage in manpower, was an experience that the Army wanted never to repeat. Indeed, the Army leadership extended the lessons of Korea into a general rule: "No more land wars in Asia."

It is noteworthy that this formula did not simply reject and exclude particular kinds of future wars, most obviously a war with China like the recent war within Korea. It also approved and included particular kinds of future wars, such as those which might recapitulate the legendary Army campaigns in World War II, i.e., the land war in Europe and the island war in the Pacific. But since there was little prospect that the Army would be centrally involved in Pacific wars in the future (these would be under the command of the U.S. Navy and would emphasize the U.S. Marines), in practice the Army's formula meant that its focus would be on Europe, which had always been its preferred theater anyway.[16]

The Army recognized, of course, that the Soviet Union could deploy in Europe a massive advantage in manpower and indeed in much of material as well. Its strategy to trump, and at least contain, this Soviet advantage was composed of two parts. First, the Army planned to use recent developments in nuclear-weapons technology—i.e., smaller warheads that could be used on the scale of the battlefield ("tactical" nuclear weapons)—so that the Soviet advantage in manpower could be overcome with a U.S. advantage in firepower. Second, the Army saw itself as the most powerful and advanced, and therefore the leading, ground force in a grand alliance of other armies within Europe, especially the British, French, and West German armies, all organized within NATO and under a top U.S. general, the Supreme Allied Commander, Europe (SACEUR). Although this Army strategy incorporated nuclear weapons, these appeared to be merely "just another weapon" to be used on the battlefield, and overall the new strategy seemed to be a logical and practical updating of the classical American way of war, which the Army knew and loved so well.[17]

The end of the war in Korea had created a situation along the armistice line near the 38th parallel that was structurally and operationally similar to the situation along the inter-German border in Europe, with Communist mass on one side being contained and deterred by U.S. firepower (tactical nuclear weapons) and allied armies on the other side. Consequently, the U.S. Army was willing to apply its new strategy for the European Central Front to its new responsibilities for South Korea, even if this might one day mean a "land war in Asia." That kind of prospective land war, however, would really be fought like the prospective war in Europe, rather than like the past war in Korea during 1950–1953. As for the rest of the world, the Army was largely willing to leave responsibility for that to the other U.S. military services, or to other, allied armies.

It soon became clear that the Army's notion that battlefield nuclear weapons were just another weapon was naïve, particularly after the Soviet Army acquired its own extensive stock of such weapons. If both sides were to use tactical nuclear weapons, there was a very high probability not only that both armies would be destroyed on the battlefield but that local allied nations (particularly West Germany and East Germany) would be destroyed also and, indeed, that the nuclear war would escalate until it reached the cities of both the United States and the Soviet Union themselves. Eventually (but not until the early 1980s), the Army would build upon a very different kind of high technology (the "Revolution in Military Affairs" or RMA, which focused upon advances in precision-guided munitions, telecommunications, and computers) to develop a wholly new strategy (the "Air-Land Battle Doctrine"). This creatively used U.S. advantages in mobility and technology to trump the Soviet advantage in mass. But for more than two decades, from the mid-1950s to the late 1970s, Army strategy incorporated the dubious element of tactical nuclear weapons.

Although the Army was naïve about the nature of nuclear weapons, it was very realistic about the nature of itself. World War II had taught the Army that there were certain kinds of wars it could fight and win, and the Korean War had taught it that there were those it could not. The latter could be summed up by "no more land wars in Asia," a formula that appeared simple-minded, but that actually and accurately captured the essence, the strengths, and the limitations of the Army.

If there had been some vital U.S. national interest that could be preserved only by a land war in Asia, the Army's conception of its identity and its strategy would have been not only dangerous, but disgraceful as well. However, by the mid-1950s, a good deal of the dust had indeed settled on the Asian land mass. There was no longer any realistic prospect of invading and rolling back the Communist parts of that land mass (the Soviet Union, China, North Korea, and the recently created North Vietnam). Conversely, it seemed to be a relatively simple task to contain and deter the Communist powers with respect to Japan, South Korea, Taiwan, the Philippines, and even Malaysia, which were actually islands or peninsulas. The only remaining problematic area in Asia was the land mass of Southeast Asia, particularly the successor states to French Indochina. But the Eisenhower administration never made the case that this was so vital a U.S. national interest that it should be defended with the U.S. Army. Rather it had written off North Vietnam to the Communists in 1954, and it relied upon a flimsy combination of military and economic aid and advisors, along with an ambiguous commitment from SEATO, to defend South Vietnam, Cambodia, and Laos. It was reasonable for the Army to think that, if these measures should ever prove insufficient against Communist attacks, the U.S. government would write off the rest of Indochina as well, and certainly that it would not send the Army itself into a war there.

SOVIET NUCLEAR DEVELOPMENT AND COMMUNIST MASS ARMIES

By the late 1950s, however, it was becoming clear that the Soviet Union was determined to match—and that it was capable of doing so—every technological and quantitative advance that the United States was making in regard to nuclear weapons. The Soviets, therefore, could now effectively deter the U.S., just as the U.S. had deterred the Soviets before. Consequently, the distinct strategies of the Eisenhower administration and of the U.S. Army each had an inherent weakness or Achilles' heel. The United States could not credibly threaten massive, nuclear retaliation against Communist aggression, if the Soviet Union could credibly threaten massive, nuclear retaliation against the U.S. in response. Similarly, the U.S. Army could not effectively employ tactical nuclear weapons on the battlefield, if the Soviet army could effectively employ them against the U.S.

Army in response. At both the strategic and the tactical levels, therefore, a point was approaching where the U.S. nuclear weapons and the Soviet ones would deter each other. This would not be a symmetrical situation, however, because the Soviets and the other Communist powers would be left with their advantage in mass with respect to conventional forces. The entire non-Communist periphery, which bordered the Communist bloc of the Eurasian land mass, could be in danger of invasion and conquest by Communist armies.[18]

Neither the Eisenhower administration nor the U.S. Army were able to propose a convincing solution to the emerging dilemma posed by Soviet nuclear development. This created a void which a new kind of thinker about military strategy—civilians who were called "defense intellectuals" and who were often associated with the Democratic Party—sought to fill. Thus began a great effort to find some clever way to contain and deter Communist conventional forces with the conventional forces of the United States and its allies.

THE CIVILIAN DEFENSE INTELLECTUALS: "LIMITED WAR"

The most consequential result of this effort was a reconstruction, a sort of new look, at the Korean War itself. Whereas both the Eisenhower administration and the U.S. Army had seen this war as something so bad that it should never be repeated, the new defense intellectuals (most of whom had never fought in Korea) discovered the good side of the war. The United States had, after all, achieved its main political objective (preserving the independence and territory of South Korea), while avoiding either the escalation of the war into nuclear weapons or the expansion of the war into China or the Soviet Union. The Korean War was, in other words, a *limited* war—indeed one limited in a double sense—and that was its distinctive, and very impressive, virtue.[19] Indeed, the war was so good that the United States should expect to repeat it in the future. Of course, the United States might not be able to fight a limited war against Soviet forces (now both massive and nuclear) or Chinese forces (now even more massive than before), but it should expect to fight and prevail against the forces of a smaller Communist power, whoever and wherever it might be. The last time it was North Korea in Northeast Asia. Although the limited-war theorists did not specify it then, the next time it would be North Vietnam in Southeast Asia.

The defense intellectuals normally did not describe just how the United States would trump the large numbers of men even small Communist powers would deploy, but the answer was implicit in the Korean War, which was their model, i.e., U.S. conventional firepower (artillery and bombs) would trump, or at least contain, Communist manpower (infantry and irregular forces). As in the Korean War, the U.S. strategy would be one of attrition.

Whatever the strengths of an attrition strategy might be under some circumstances (e.g., Ulysses S. Grant's campaigns in Northern Virginia in 1864), it does not normally draw upon any advantages in mobility. More fundamentally, an attrition strategy does not represent the classical American way of war. Nor does it represent the U.S. Army's normal view of how it should fight and win America's wars.

THE KENNEDY ADMINISTRATION AND THE DEMOCRATIC PARTY: THE SECOND GREAT TRANSFORMATION

Given the way that the concept of limited war, Korean-style, so contradicted the American way of war and the U.S. Army's organizational essence, it would take a radical transformation in national security policy to establish it as the new U.S. strategy. This could only come about the way any radical transformation does, with a new political regime coming to power and with its civilian leadership determined to impose its radical views, by a purge if necessary, upon old bureaucratic institutions.

The Kennedy administration and the Democratic Party came to power in 1961 determined to implement a new U.S. national security policy, which would better meet the new challenges—particularly Soviet nuclear development and also Maoist revolutionary warfare strategy—which were posed by the Communist world. The new policy included many elements invented by civilian defense intellectuals, including the concept of limited war. The new administration, particularly Secretary of Defense Robert McNamara, was perfectly willing to impose its new views upon the old Army. Indeed, within a year, it retired (purged) many of the Army's top generals. The "never-again club," generals who represented the attitude of "no more land wars in Asia," was replaced with the "can-do club," generals who were willing to adopt and implement the new limited-war doctrine.[20] By 1963, the radical transformation in the Army's high command and military doctrine was complete. It was just in time

for the next challenge from one of the lesser Communist powers. This
was, of course, North Vietnam.

The Vietnam War: The Ordeal of an
Un-American Strategy

North Vietnam was providing ample support and even direction to Communist insurgents in South Vietnam. At first, during 1961–1964, the United
States tried to defeat this insurgency merely by providing military aid and
advisers to the forces of the South Vietnamese government. But by late
1964, this effort was manifestly insufficient, and so in early 1965, the Johnson administration sent regular U.S. military forces into the war.

Following a common U.S. tendency, the initial U.S. military strategy in
Vietnam was to rely on air power alone. The bombing of North Vietnam,
an operation termed "Rolling Thunder," was supposed to deter and attrit
the North's support of the Communist insurgents in the South. But these
air strikes were limited to the small, southern part of North Vietnam, and
they soon proved insufficient to stop the growth of Communist strength
in South Vietnam. Within a few months, therefore, the Johnson administration decided to deploy large numbers of ground forces to South Vietnam, and the full-scale U.S. war in Vietnam began.

The U.S. strategy for this war was largely shaped by the lessons which
the Johnson administration and the defense intellectuals had drawn from
the Korean War. As we have seen, the civilian strategists had already decided that a conventional war of attrition, one in which U.S. firepower
ground down Communist manpower, was a perfectly rational way for the
U.S. to fight a war; the war could and should be limited to conventional
weapons, without any specter of escalation to nuclear ones.[21]

However, the Korean War had also been limited with respect to territory, and not just weaponry. The Korean War had taught the lesson that, if
U.S. forces approached a Chinese border or, more subtly, sought to completely destroy a Chinese buffer state, then China would intervene with its
armies and its advantage in mass. The Johnson administration, therefore,
decided that U.S. military operations in Vietnam would have to be limited
with respect to territory as well. In particular, U.S. air operations would
avoid the northern part of North Vietnam, and U.S. ground operations
would avoid North Vietnam in its entirety. The fear of Chinese intervention effectively deterred the United States, imposing fundamental

constraints upon U.S. strategy. In a sense, the most important battle shaping the Vietnam War was not fought in Vietnam or during that war at all; it had been fought in Korea near the Yalu River in 1950, years before.

Thus, like the Truman administration before it, the Johnson administration was condemned to a long, grueling, and, it appeared by early 1968, stalemated war. Once again, as it approached the next election, the Democratic Party could offer no convincing solution, and thus once again, the Republican Party won control of the Presidency.

The new Nixon administration lacked some of the advantages that had earlier benefited the Eisenhower administration. In particular, it could not credibly threaten the use of nuclear weapons to break the military stalemate. It had to find some other way to draw upon traditional American advantages, particularly the use of allied manpower and U.S. airpower. The United States did build up the army of South Vietnam to the point that it could successfully handle most counterinsurgency operations. However, the ultimate solution would be to credibly threaten North Vietnam with the destruction by conventional bombers of its vital centers, i.e., its capital of Hanoi and its port of Haiphong. But before this could happen, the United States would have to persuade the Soviets and the Chinese to withdraw their protective umbrellas over North Vietnam, which were deterring a U.S. bombing assault.[22]

It would take three years of preparation and negotiation, but by early 1972 the Nixon administration had bought off the Soviets with an arms control treaty and the Chinese with U.S. diplomatic acceptance, if not yet full recognition. Therefore, in spring 1972 and then in December, the United States did engage in major bombing of Hanoi and Haiphong, and this greatly contributed to the Vietnam Peace Accords of January 1973, which provided for a sort of armistice in Vietnam, one with some similarities to that in Korea twenty years before. The underlying basis of the armistice was the credible threat that the U.S. would, if necessary, engage in even more bombing of North Vietnam in the future. In a sense, the Nixon administration, like the Eisenhower administration before it, had won its land war in Asia, or at least it appeared to have achieved its main political objective of preserving the independence and territory of its client, South Vietnam. (The condition of the neighboring clients, Cambodia and Laos, was more problematic.)

Two years later in early 1975, however, North Vietnam broke this armistice agreement and launched a full-scale invasion of South Vietnam. It could do so because Nixon was no longer president (he had resigned because of the Watergate scandal), and the Democratic majority in Congress prevented the new Ford administration from carrying out the bombing threat. And so South Vietnam, along with Cambodia and Laos, fell decisively to the Communist military forces. It was the only true defeat for the United States in the long history of American wars. A major reason for this defeat was that, for much of the course of the Vietnam War, U.S. military operations had been in clear violation of the American way of war.

The Vietnam War was so prolonged, so divisive, and so much a debacle that there was no chance that it would become a "forgotten war" like Korea. The memory, even the trauma, of the war lasted so long and was so deep that it became a powerful influence upon U.S. national security policy for many years to come, an influence which was even given its own name, "the Vietnam Syndrome." However, once again and as after the Korean War, three different groups of national security policymakers and specialists drew lessons from the war. They were (1) the Carter administration and more generally the Democratic Party, which provided a rather simple case of the Vietnam Syndrome; (2) the U.S. Army, which represented a thoughtful and sophisticated version of it; and (3) a new kind of civilian defense intellectual, one who would become known as a "neoconservative," determined to overcome the Vietnam Syndrome (and therefore, in a way, to forget the Vietnam War) as soon as possible.

THE CARTER ADMINISTRATION AND THE
DEMOCRATIC PARTY: "NO MORE VIETNAMS"

The Democratic Party won the Presidency in 1976, more because of the effects of the Watergate scandal than the effects of the Vietnam War. After all, it had been the Democrats who had begun the war in the first place. However, the new Carter administration understood clearly that it should avoid anything like the Vietnam War in the future, and once again the reasons for this were political, economic, and strategic. The political costs (massive protests) and economic costs (pervasive inflation) of the war were obvious to everyone. The strategic costs of America's first loss of a war were a dramatic decline in U.S. military and political credibility around the world. Unlike after Korea, however, this time the United States could not rely upon its nuclear weapons to provide the base for a new U.S. strategy; by now the Soviet nuclear arsenal largely matched the U.S. one, both in the quantity and the quality of the weapons.

The Carter administration therefore drew a rather simple lesson from the Vietnam War—"no more Vietnams." By this, it meant not only no more land wars in Asia, but also no more land wars against revolutionary guerrilla movements anywhere. As it happened, the administration was fortunate enough not to be challenged by these, except in Nicaragua in 1979 and in El Salvador in 1980, and so it could avoid the potential negative consequences of its new negative strategy. But the Democrats in Congress continued to adhere to this position throughout the 1980s, whenever the question of intervention with U.S. ground forces arose. Indeed, the Democrats generally would not favor such interventions until the 1990s, when the Clinton administration deployed ground forces within several countries in the name of human rights. Even then, as we will see below, the Democrats were quite hesitant and half-hearted in their use of ground forces.

THE U.S. ARMY: THE AIR-LAND BATTLE DOCTRINE AND THE POWELL DOCTRINE

As in the Korean War, the U.S. Army had been the central military service fighting the Vietnam War. It received the bulk of the costs and casualties, to the point that it came close to a collapse of service morale, and so once again it was critical for the Army to draw lessons from the war. Since the United States had not achieved its primary objective of preserving the independence and territory of South Vietnam, and since the conduct of the Vietnam War had clearly contradicted the classical American way of war, the war had been deeply disorienting in every way. The Vietnam War, particularly the grueling ordeal of counterinsurgency operations, was an experience that the Army never wanted to repeat. Like the Carter administration and the Democratic Party, the U.S. Army was seeking a version of the lesson "no more Vietnams," particularly no more land wars against guerrilla forces—revolutionary or otherwise.[23]

Like the formula the Army had adopted after the Korean War—"no more land wars in Asia"—the post-Vietnam formula had not only its obvious negative side but also an implied positive side. There certainly remained a kind of war the Army was very willing to fight, and that was once again a land war in Europe. In addition, the earlier analogy between the inter-German border and the Korean armistice line still obtained, and so the Army was prepared to fight in Korea as well.

The Army recognized, of course, that the Soviet Union could employ in Europe a massive advantage in manpower and material. Indeed, the Soviet advantage in mass was even greater after the Vietnam War than it had been after the Korean War. So once again the Army had to come up with a strategy to trump, or at least contain, this Soviet advantage.

More tactical nuclear weapons. There were a few attempts by the Army to merely come up with a new version of the old, obviously inadequate, strategies based upon tactical nuclear weapons. One proposal was the "neutron bomb," a nuclear weapon that, by working primarily through an expanded radiation effect rather than through the blast effect, would kill people while leaving buildings and other structures intact. This proposal did not really eliminate the flaws in the older nuclear strategies. Moreover, since it would have entailed the deaths of large numbers of civilians as well as soldiers, the neutron bomb was immediately rejected by the very allies (especially West Germany) it was supposed to protect and upon whose territory it would have to be based.

A second proposal was to add to the existing land-based, Army-controlled nuclear missiles in Europe (named Pershing 1), a new nuclear missile with a much larger range (Pershing 2). But whereas Pershing 1 had a range of 150 kilometers and was seen as a battlefield weapon, Pershing 2 had a range of 2,000 kilometers and was clearly a theater weapon. Indeed, since it could reach Soviet cities and even Moscow, it was really not a tactical nuclear weapon at all, but rather a strategic one. It had more in common with the intercontinental ballistic missiles (ICBMs) of the Air Force and the submarine-launched ballistic missiles (SLBMs) of the Navy than with anything else in the Army. As such, Pershing 2 did nothing to solve the central strategic dilemma of the Army itself. Although Pershing 2s were actually deployed in Europe in the mid-1980s (despite widespread opposition among European populations), the real strategic thinkers in the Army were developing something much more innovative and creative, and much more in keeping with the classical American way of war.

The Air-Land Battle Doctrine. These Army's strategic innovators sought to use recent developments in non-nuclear technologies—i.e., greatly improved capabilities in battlefield command, control, communication, and information (C^3I) and precision-guided munitions (PGMs)—so that the Soviet advantage in mass could be overcome with a U.S. advantage in both technology and mobility. By the early 1980s, these new technological developments were together termed ET (emerging technologies), and by the mid-1980s there was a widespread belief among military analysts that together they had brought about a "revolution in military affairs" (RMA). In the early Reagan administration, the Army built upon these new technologies and concepts and produced a new battlefield strategy, the Air-Land Battle Doctrine, which coherently integrated C^3I, PGMs, air power, and land power. The Army made a convincing case that this new strategy enabled it to fight and win a conventional (non-nuclear) war with the Soviet Union in Europe.[24] Indeed, the Army's case was so convincing that it seems to have persuaded the high command of the general staff of the Soviet army, particularly its chief, Marshal Nikolai V. Ogarkov, who soon directed his own army to try to catch up with the new RMA.[25]

The Powell Doctrine. Because the damaging effects of the Vietnam War upon the Army had been so profound and so prolonged, any new post-Vietnam formula had to be much more profound and elaborate than the old post-Korea one. "No more land wars in Asia" had meant no more wars against Asian Communist mass armies, which were protected by Soviet nuclear deterrence. "No more Vietnams" added to this specific stricture the new specific one of no more wars against guerrilla forces anywhere. But because of the profound impact of the Vietnam War, thoughtful Army leaders saw the need to make the new strictures much more general and fundamental. Instead of being cast merely in terms of specific adversaries, they should be cast in terms of general rules. Various Army think-tanks, including the Army War College, turned their attention to this task, and the result was a new, explicit, and comprehensive formula stating the conditions under which the nation, and particularly the Army, should or should not go to war. The Secretary of Defense in the Reagan administration, Caspar Weinberger, publicly announced the new formula in 1984, causing it to become known first as the Weinberger Doctrine. Then, the Chairman of the Joint Chiefs of Staff in the administration of the first President Bush, General Colin Powell, elaborated upon and developed the doctrine, causing it to become known as the Weinberger-Powell Doctrine or simply as the Powell Doctrine (the term we shall hereafter use).[26]

As is well known, the Powell Doctrine specified a series of conditions or tests that had to be met before U.S. policymakers should commit the nation to war (and to send the Army into one). There was supposed to be (1) a clear U.S. national interest at stake; (2) a clear, realizable objective for U.S. military forces to achieve; (3) a coherent military strategy for achieving that objective; including (4) the use of overwhelming military force and (5) a plan for bringing an end to the war, i.e., an "exit strategy;" and (6) the clearly expressed support of the American people for the war.[27] It was also clear that the Powell Doctrine was very consistent with the classical American way of war, which the Army had long thought was the only right way of war, at least for itself.

THE NEOCONSERVATIVE INTELLECTUALS: NUCLEAR SUPREMACY AND PREEMPTIVE ATTACK

After the Korean War, a new kind of national security specialist, the defense intellectual, had reinterpreted that war, arguing that it was actually a sort of success for the United States and that, even more, it was a sort of model for the future. Defense intellectuals went on to develop an entire theory of limited war in the nuclear age. Since the result of this thinking was the U.S. debacle in Vietnam, and since that debacle was so pervasive and profound, there was no way that a similar kind of revisionism would develop after the Vietnam War. Nor at the time was anyone prepared to develop a new theory of counterinsurgency war, analogous to the earlier theory of limited war. Nevertheless, not long after the Vietnam War, there did emerge a new kind of defense intellectual; they would become known as "neoconservatives" (although given their strategic views, "offense intellectuals" would have been a more accurate term). They were determined to overcome the Vietnam Syndrome as soon as possible (even though none of them had fought in Vietnam); their way of doing this, however, was not so much to reinterpret the Vietnam War as to forget it, particularly by changing the subject of the national security debate.

Their new subject, the growing Soviet threat, was of course really just a new version of the old subject that had been around since the beginning of the Cold War. Traditional conservatives and "realists," such as Richard Nixon and Henry Kissinger, viewed the Soviet Union as being generally a normal great power whose foreign and military policies were largely determined by its rational calculation of its national interests. This led them to promote a sober and prudent ("realistic") form of the policy of "détente."[28] In contrast, the neoconservatives viewed the Soviet Union as an aggressive, even reckless, great power driven more by ideological compulsions than by interest calculations. This led them to promote a large-scale build-up of the U.S. nuclear arsenal so that the United States would always have nuclear supremacy. They wanted to ensure that the U.S. could, if necessary, destroy the Soviet nuclear forces in a preemptive

attack or "first strike." As such, the apparently new strategic proposals of
the neoconservatives largely recapitulated what was the actual longstanding strategic doctrine of the U.S. Air Force. Other than also providing support for the deployment of Pershing 2s in Europe, however, the
neoconservative strategic proposals at this time had little to do directly
with the Army and its own developing strategy.[29]

Why were the neoconservatives so focused upon the Soviet threat and
so opposed to the détente policy? Since some neoconservatives were former Communists, or at least former Trotskyites, they had become, like many
people swept up in a conversion experience, especially anti-Communist.
Moreover, since many neoconservatives were Jewish, they were especially
concerned about the Soviet persecution of Jews within the Soviet Union
and about the Soviet support of Arab states which were enemies of Israel.
In any event, the neoconservatives were persistent advocates for building
up the U.S. military, particularly U.S. nuclear forces, from the late 1970s
right down until the collapse of the Soviet Union in 1991. Indeed, they
have often claimed credit for the Soviet collapse.

The Reagan Administration and the
Republican Party: The Third Great Transformation

The Republican Party returned to power in 1981, and the new Reagan administration was determined to build up U.S. military forces. It was especially concerned about the growing Soviet threat, and it also wanted to
eliminate the Vietnam Syndrome. As such, it held much the same views
as the neoconservatives, and indeed neoconservatives held some third-
tier national-security positions within the administration.[30] However, the
sources of the administration's strategic views went beyond a mere cadre of
defense intellectuals. They included such formidable interests as the aerospace industry, the military services, and the traditional anti-Communism
of the Republican Party. As such, the strategic program of the administration also went beyond that of the neoconservatives. It was a comprehensive
and coherent integration of the main strategies of each of the military services, and it sought not only to fight and win a war with the Soviet Union,
if this should become necessary, but to produce an economic crisis and
collapse within the Soviet Union even without war. With respect to this
latter strategic objective, which seemed audacious and illusory to most

national security professionals at the time, the Reagan administration was ultimately and resoundingly successful.[31]

The administration's strategic program was basically composed of five elements, which were essentially drawn from the strategic programs of each of the three major military services: (1) a large increase in the U.S. defense budget in order to provide the resources for the weapons systems desired by the services and to send a clear signal to the Soviet Union that the United States was able and willing to engage in a serious military competition; (2) a build-up of nuclear forces capable of a pre-emptive attack upon Soviet nuclear forces, i.e., the first-strike program of the Air Force; (3) a build-up of land forces, which could fight and defeat the Soviet army in Europe in a conventional war, i.e., the Air-Land Battle Doctrine of the Army; (4) a build-up of naval forces, which could fight and defeat not only the Soviet navy but also other Soviet forces in coastal regions around the Soviet periphery and in a conventional war, i.e., the Maritime Strategy of the Navy; and (5) the Strategic Defense Initiative (SDI), a new vision for a high-technology, anti-ballistic missile system, portions of which would be assigned to each of the three military services but with the principal role being given to the Air Force.[32] Taken together, these five elements constituted a third great transformation in U.S. national security policy since 1945. For the most part, they were also consistent with the classical American way of war.

This comprehensive and integrated strategic program, which was based upon the U.S. advantages in an immense economy and in high technology, was designed to get the Soviets' attention, and it did. The chiefs of the KGB, Yuri Andropov, and the Soviet general staff, Marshal Nikolai V. Ogarkov, took very seriously the U.S. economic and technological lead (indeed, they saw the United States being even stronger in these dimensions than it actually was), and they believed in the reality of the revolution in military affairs. They thus initiated a chain of decisions which, inadvertently but ultimately, would lead to the collapse of the Soviet Union itself.

THE SOVIET RESPONSE AND COLLAPSE:
PERESTROIKA AND GLASNOST

Andropov and Ogarkov concluded that the Soviet military would have to match the U.S. military in the RMA. Furthermore, it realized that in order to do so the Soviet Union would also have to match U.S. high technology;

and in order to do that, it would also have to reform and even restructure (*perestroika*) the Soviet economy; and in order to do that, it would also have to reform and even open up (*glasnost*) the Soviet bureaucracy. Andropov died before his reform program could be put in place, but in 1985 his protégé, Mikhail Gorbachev, came to power and proceeded to carry out *perestroika* and *glasnost*. As it turned out, of course, the old Soviet system was incapable of absorbing this new kind of reform. Within half a decade, the system had disintegrated and collapsed, and in the end, in 1991, the Soviet Union even as a country and a state was abolished.[33]

After more than four decades, the United States had decisively won the Cold War. Its original national strategy of containment and military strategy of nuclear deterrence, composed during the first great strategic transformation so long before and extended and amended at certain points in the years since, had at last prevailed. Moreover, although the Cold War had been punctuated by two damaging local and limited hot wars—that in Korea and in Vietnam—and by an extraordinarily dangerous nuclear crisis—that over Cuba in 1962—the United States and the Soviet Union had never engaged in a hot war with each other. Surely, the U.S. victory over the Soviet Union was one of the greatest strategic successes in history.

OLD ANTI-SOVIET STRATEGIES IN NEW POST-SOVIET CONDITIONS

And so the Soviet Union collapsed and the Cold War ended without the United States having had to fire a shot in the long struggle's final years. The creative and innovative strategies of the Reagan administration never had to be employed against the Soviet Union in an actual war. But since preemptive first strike, the Maritime Strategy, and SDI had all been designed against military threats specific to the Soviet Union, these strategies now immediately became obsolete. Consequently, the Air Force and the Navy found themselves in a strategic void and in a search for a new strategic purpose.

The situation was very different for the Army. The Air-Land Battle Doctrine had certainly been designed with the Soviet army in mind, but in fact it could be directed against any substantial conventional army that might become an enemy. Even with the Cold War nearing its end, there were still several such armies around, in particular those of North Korea and perhaps China, along with Iraq and perhaps Iran.

For old and familiar reasons, the Army was not interested in a land war with China. It was also reluctant to contemplate an invasion of a country as large and as populous as Iran. However, the Army could easily find an appropriate and fitting purpose in being prepared to fight North Korea or Iraq. In particular, the Air-Land Battle Doctrine could be applied against these two armies, all the more so since each had been organized according to the Soviet model. Indeed, the Army claimed that it would be able to fight both the North Korean and the Iraqi armies simultaneously, if need be. This was the new concrete meaning of the "two-war capability," which was the official, declared U.S. military policy. The idea was that the U.S. military should have the capability of fighting two separate wars in two different regions (most probably East Asia and the Middle East) at the same time.[34]

The Persian Gulf War and the Two Army Doctrines

Consequently, when Iraq invaded Kuwait in August 1990, the Army was prepared, and it was so in a double sense. First, it had available the Powell Doctrine, which told it how U.S. policymakers should go to war. Second, it had available the Air-Land Battle Doctrine, which told it how the Army should fight the war. And, although there were some anomalies and frictions along the way, the U.S. conduct of the Persian Gulf War largely conformed to both doctrines. The administration of the first President Bush defined the war in terms of (1) clear U.S. national interests (secure access to Gulf oil and the international law against military aggression); (2) a clear and realizable military objective (the expulsion of Iraqi forces from Kuwait and the restoration of Kuwait's territorial integrity); (3) a coherent military strategy (designed by the Army and based upon its Air-Land Battle Doctrine), including (4) the use of overwhelming force and (5) an "exit strategy" (the decisive defeat of the Iraqi army but no effort to conquer Baghdad or to occupy Iraq itself); and (6) the clearly expressed support of the American people (expressed through the Congressional resolution authorizing the war). For its part, the Army employed the major features of the Air-Land Battle Doctrine, particularly the extraordinary mobility of U.S. army forces, concentration of mass at the enemy's weak flanks, and surprise and flexibility, all facilitated by high technology in C^3I.[35]

Since the U.S. conduct of the Gulf War largely conformed to both the Powell Doctrine and the Air-Land Battle Doctrine, it also largely conformed to the classical American way of war, in particular (1) overwhelming mass, (2) wide-ranging mobility, (3) high-technology weapons systems; and (4) high public support for the war effort. And, although the United States did not rely upon allied countries to provide much in the way of actual soldiers (the fifth classical element), it did rely upon them to provide international legitimacy for the war (by voting for it in the U.N. and by providing some military forces) and also to provide much of the war's financing.

The Persian Gulf War in National-Security History: Looking Backward and Looking Forward

The Persian Gulf War stood in a very meaningful contrast to the Vietnam War. Whereas the Vietnam War had been the longest war in American history (eight years, counting from 1965 to 1973), the Gulf War was the shortest (five weeks). Whereas the Vietnam War had been America's fourth most costly war in terms of U.S. deaths (more than 55,000), the Gulf War was the least costly up to its time (less than 250). And whereas the Vietnam War had been a demoralizing defeat, the Gulf War was seen as a dramatic victory. The contrast between the two wars was all the more meaningful because the United States had won the Gulf War by applying the lessons so painfully taught by the Vietnam War. At least, this was the confirmed view of the Army. The Vietnam Syndrome may not have been fully eliminated (as President Bush exclaimed at the time), but the post-Vietnam strategies of the Army had certainly been vindicated.

The Gulf War was also an important milestone and turning point in the history of U.S. national security policy since World War II. On the one side, it was one of the very last acts of the old era of the Cold War. Iraq had been a Soviet ally, and its army had been modeled after the Soviet army. The Air-Land Battle Doctrine that defeated the Iraqi army in the Iraqi desert had originally been designed to defeat the Soviet army on the North German plain. In some respects, the Gulf War was the last limited and lo-cal hot war of the Cold War.

On the other side, the Gulf War also looked to the new era to come in national security policy. For many years after the end of the Cold War, national security professionals would debate what to name this new era. A case can be made that a good name for the period from 1991 (the Gulf War and the end of the Soviet Union) to 2001 (9/11 and the Islamist terrorists

attacks upon New York and Washington) is the era of globalization.[36] And
a case can also be made that a new era in national security policy began after 9/11 and that a good name for it is the era of Islamist terrorism, which
is now developing and expanding into a global Islamist insurgency. If so,
the Gulf War was one of the very first acts of the new era or eras that lay
ahead. Iraq's invasion of Kuwait represented a threat to secure access to
Gulf oil, a core component of the global economy. And the way that the
United States dealt with Iraq in the decade after the Gulf War (imposing
U.N. economic sanctions upon it and stationing U.S. military forces
within Saudi Arabia) soon became grievances that Islamist extremists,
such as Osama bin Laden and al-Qaeda, would point to as they recruited
for their terrorist operations. In some respects, the Gulf War was the first
war of the globalization era, and it was also the first limited and local war
in the much longer and more global war with Islamist terrorists.

The Clinton Administration and the
Democratic Party: An Array of Choices

The Clinton administration which took power in 1993, near the beginning
of the new era of globalization, therefore was faced with an array of choices
and with a degree of freedom with respect to national security policy that
were almost unprecedented. The last administration to enter office with
so few foreign threats to U.S. security was probably that of Herbert Hoover
in 1929, and even he would shortly have to deal with the world-wide effects
of The Great Depression.[37]

What were the national security policy options at the beginning of the
Clinton administration? They depended upon what was perceived to be a
foreign threat.

The no-threat option. One option was to perceive that there was no longer any substantial foreign threat at all. This would have been a reasonable
conclusion at the time, although looking back years later, especially after
al-Qaeda's attacks on 9/11, it became clear that the seeds of the Islamist
terrorist threat were already germinating in 1993. After forty-five years of
Cold War and after sixty years of "national emergencies," however, the
United States was not ready to believe that it could return to an era of
"normalcy," like the 1920s. Too many U.S. institutions and interests now
depended upon some kind of continuing foreign threat. These included

the U.S. military services. Furthermore, the U.S. economy in the 1920s had largely been a *national* economy, with its interests and investments largely within the United States itself. In contrast, the U.S. economy in the 1990s was now a *global* economy, with its interests and investments spread world-wide—hence the great interest, and indeed obsession, of American businesses in globalization. Given the intense interest of the U.S. military services in preservation and given the equally intense interest of American business enterprises in not only preservation but also expansion, the no-threat option was a nonstarter, and it was never seriously considered.

The humanitarian-intervention option. One of the important activist elements in the Democratic Party was composed of people concerned about universal human rights. In part growing out of the Wilsonian conception that American ideals were universal ones and in part growing out of the civil-rights movement of the 1960s, the human-rights movement had played an important role in the Carter administration. Now, in the new era of globalization, human-rights activists saw the opportunity to make their project truly universal.[38]

By themselves, the human-rights activists would have had little influence with practical public officials, who naturally focus upon serving substantial interests, particularly those which provide substantial campaign contributions. However, there did indeed now exist very substantial interests with a global, and therefore a universal, perspective, i.e., American multinational corporations and financial institutions. The project of universal human rights, with its emphasis upon open societies and international enforcement of individual rights against repressive national governments, provided a useful legitimacy and a compelling ideology for global corporate and financial interests. Consequently, global business people (most notably, George Soros) provided substantial funds for the human-rights organizations, as well as for the Democratic Party. This in turn enabled the former to have substantial power within the latter. The human-rights activists were a persistent pressure pushing the Clinton administration to in turn push the U.S. military into "humanitarian interventions."[39]

The new-enemy option. Another option was to look for some new version of the now-vanished Soviet Union, and each of the U.S. military services had its preferred candidate. The Army, as we have noted, was already focused upon particular smaller states that had Soviet-style regimes and Soviet-style armies, i.e., North Korea and, even after its defeat in the Gulf War, Iraq. Unfortunately for the Army, although it understood that these two rogue states by themselves could justify maintaining a large Army, this was not so evident to civilian officials, especially those in the new Clinton administration or in the Democratic Party more generally. Instead, these officials started looking for ways either to reduce the Army and spend the savings on domestic programs ("the peace dividend") or, alternatively, to maintain the Army and send it into foreign countries to further some kind of liberal project, especially the protection or promotion of human rights through humanitarian interventions.

Conversely, the Navy was already focused upon China, which still had a Communist regime as well as a very long coastline bordering the Pacific, which made it a large maritime theater where a large navy could be deployed (and therefore justified). As for the Air Force, it could focus upon the still-remaining vast nuclear arsenal of Russia, and it could also find a role for air power in any war with the other candidate states, that is, Iraq, North Korea, and China. But being able to fly to any place around the globe—and to fly over and bomb any particular country—the Air Force began to advance the idea that it, through air power alone, could coerce any nation that might pose a threat to U.S. interests, whatever they might be, and that it was the only truly global U.S. military service, one especially well-fitted for the new era of globalization.

As it happened, the Clinton administration largely accepted each of these service definitions and justifications, and each of the three services was largely maintained throughout the 1990s. But with the Army, the administration added to the Army's conception of its national mission—the protection of clear national interests (and possible wars with North Korea and Iraq)—its own conception of a liberal mission—the protection of universal human rights. This expanded mission soon grew into Army interventions in Somalia and Haiti and (after U.S. air power brought about Serbian acquiescence) Army occupations in Bosnia and Kosovo. Each of these four Army operations violated the tenets of the Army's two strategic pillars, the Powell Doctrine and the Air-Land Battle Doctrine.

The Navy and the Air Force did not have to suffer any such distortions of their chosen missions and doctrines. The Navy was able to do what it wanted to in the Pacific, which was to focus upon the rising power and potential threat of China. In addition, naval aircraft and cruise missiles joined with the Air Force in several military operations during the 1990s. The Air Force itself was even able to move further toward its preferred identity and ideology of victory through air power alone, both in Bosnia and in Kosovo. The Air Force achievement in the latter seemed especially impressive. At the end of the Kosovo war in June 1999, it appeared that precision bombing alone had forced the Milosovic regime in Serbia to end resistance and to accept the U.S. and NATO terms, and this was without a single U.S. fatality.[40] (Later evidence indicated that the U.S. threat to send in ground forces also played an important role.) It looked as if the Air Force might become the premier U.S. military service in the coming twenty-first century, as it had been during much of the Cold War.

THE NEOCONSERVATIVE INTELLECTUALS IN THE GLOBALIZATION ERA

The collapse of the Soviet Union did not mean that the neoconservatives would turn their attention to domestic affairs. To the contrary, they became even more focused upon what they saw to be foreign threats to the United States. These happened to be the same Arab states (e.g., Iraq and Syria), Islamic movements (e.g., Hamas and Hezbollah), and Islamic states (Iran) which were the enemies of Israel. By the mid-1990s, the neoconservatives were already arguing that all of these entities were also enemies of the United States.[41]

It was at this point that the views and projects of the neoconservatives began to impinge upon the interests and doctrines of the U.S. Army. The Powell Doctrine specified that the United States should go to war only in defense of clear U.S. national interests and with the clear support of the American public. When the issue had been the defense of Western Europe against a Soviet nuclear or conventional attack, it was very likely that these conditions would obtain. However, when the issue was the defense of ambiguous U.S. interests in the Middle East against this or that entity, one remote or unfamiliar to the American public, it was much less likely that the necessary conditions would be met.

While the Army was learning its lesson from Vietnam and composing its new doctrine on going to war, it had not stopped with merely a geographical definition. It had gone on to develop general and fundamental rules, one of which was the support of the American public, which was to be achieved through the democratic political process. At the base of the Powell Doctrine was the sovereignty of American democracy at home. Now that the neoconservatives were composing their own new strategy on going to war, they analogously did not stop with merely a geographical definition, such as the defense of America's political interests (Israel) and economic interests (oil) in the Middle East. They went on to develop general and fundamental values, one of which was the universal applicability of the American version of liberal democracy. At the base of the neoconservative strategy was the spread of American democracy abroad. However, as successive public opinion polls often demonstrated, most Americans did not want to go to war—and they certainly did not want to expend many American lives—to bring democracy to other countries. In other words, when American democracy was truly functioning well at home, there was little likelihood that it would choose to go to war to spread American democracy abroad. This contradiction between the domestic functioning of American democracy and the foreign spread of it was well understood by both the Army and by the neoconservatives. Since the Army considered strong public support of any war to be fundamental, it was inclined to oppose wars whose main purpose was to spread democracy. Conversely, since the neoconservatives considered the spread of democracy to be fundamental, they were inclined to outflank (and at times to belittle) both the public and the Army. They argued for the superiority of elite opinion (their own) over public opinion and, with respect to Republican administrations, for the superiority of civilian political appointees (which they hoped would be themselves or their friends) over career military officers.

THE BUSH ADMINISTRATION AND THE REPUBLICAN PARTY: THE FOURTH GREAT TRANSFORMATION

In 2001, the Republican Party regained the Presidency. The new administration of George W. Bush was very different in its national security policy than the administrations of both his father, George H.W. Bush, and Bill Clinton. The new Secretary of Defense, Donald Rumsfeld, immediately began to work vigorously and systematically to overthrow the classical American way of war and the Powell Doctrine and to replace them with a new program of military "transformation." He reduced the role of heavy weapons systems (armor and artillery) and large combat divisions in the U.S. Army and increased the role of lighter and smaller forces (airborne and special operations); in effect, he sought to reduce the role of mass and to accentuate the role of mobility. In implementing this transformation, he canceled the Crusader heavy artillery system, and he appointed a retired Special Forces general to be the new Army Chief of

Staff. Most importantly, however, Rumsfeld saw a war with Iraq to be the pilot plant and exemplary case of his grand project of transformation. If the U.S. could win a war in Iraq with a transformed military and a transformed doctrine, it would also be a decisive victory in Washington for a thoroughly new American way of war, in its bureaucratic struggles with the old, classical one.[42]

The Rumsfeld transformation project gained credibility because there were indeed some serious problems with the classical American way of war—particularly with its implication that the U.S. Army should fight only another army. The most obvious difficulty was that, with the exceptions of the rogue states of Iraq and North Korea, there no longer seemed to be any other real armies to fight. However, the United States still had other kinds of enemies, particularly transnational networks of Islamist terrorists, and this became even more obvious after 9/11. Both the rogue states and the terrorist networks, however, will seek to attack the United States not with conventional military forces or an American-style way of war, but with "asymmetrical warfare." At the upper end of the war spectrum, this will be weapons of mass destruction (WMD), particularly nuclear ones (e.g., North Korea). At the lower end of the spectrum will be terrorist operations (e.g., al-Qaeda) and guerrilla warfare (with the Iraqi insurgents being the current exemplar). Of course, the most ominous threat comes from a diabolical synthesis of the upper end and the lower end—weapons of mass destruction in the hands of transnational terrorist networks. For all of these unconventional or asymmetrical threats, the classical American way of war seemed to have no credible strategy or solution.

However, neither did the notions of Secretary Rumsfeld. The Rumsfeld transformation project (along with the concurrent Bush Doctrine of unilateral preemption, which was promulgated in 2002) did not really address the challenge of North Korea, i.e., of rogue states that have already acquired nuclear weapons. Hypothetically, some combination of highly accurate intelligence and highly effective weapons (e.g., nuclear "bunker bombs") could destroy an enemy's stock of WMD. However, the failure to find any such weapons in Iraq certainly cast doubt on the accuracy of U.S. intelligence. And even highly effective weapons systems would have a hard time destroying widely dispersed stocks of nuclear or biological weapons. The only way that the two strategic innovations of the Bush administration—the Bush Doctrine and the Rumsfeld project—could deal with the WMD threat would be when a rogue state has not yet acquired such weapons and a U.S. military operation could destroy the rogue regime before it does so. But this would really be a preventive war, not a preemptive one. This was the case with Iraq. Some advocates of the Bush Doctrine and the Rumsfeld project, particularly neoconservatives, also thought that it could next become the case with Iran.

Nor did the Rumsfeld transformation project really address the challenge of transnational terrorist networks, such as al-Qaeda. This threat is better dealt with by a multidimensional array of agencies and instruments (intelligence, security, and financial) working with their counterparts in other countries that face similar threats, particularly those in Europe. The war in Iraq certainly did not help to enhance these counterterrorist capabilities, and it made the necessary international trust and cooperation more difficult.

The Rumsfeld Army and Imperial Wars

Other than dealing with non-nuclear rogue states, the only task the new Rumsfeld army—with its lighter, more mobile configuration—could arguably have performed better than the old classical army—with its heavy armor and artillery configuration—was operations against an enemy that was even more light and mobile, i.e., guerrillas and insurgents. It appears that the new Rumsfeld army was really designed to engage in colonial kinds of war—with the U.S. Army putting down rogue states and insurgent movements who are resisting American hegemony or empire and the local regimes allied to the United States—rather than a national kind of war—with the U.S. Army fighting another nation's army. The Rumsfeld project can also be seen as providing the military dimension of the globalization project, the imperial stick that must go along with the global carrot. The promoters of globalization (who are often called neoliberals) and the promoters of American hegemony or empire (who are usually neoconservatives) both know that the classical American way of war, with its large numbers of troops or mass, requires the sustained support of the American public, and they know also that the American public is unlikely to give that support to wars for their global and imperial purposes. These purposes can be achieved only with a new American way of war and with an American military that is so light and mobile that it doesn't need the support of the American public at all.[43]

There were, however, several ironies attending the Rumsfeld transformation project. First, the origins of the Powell Doctrine lay in the lessons learned from the Vietnam War, and its basic impetus was "no more Vietnams." Among other things, this meant that the Army would fight no more counterinsurgency wars. The Rumsfeld transformation project amounted to a radical overthrow of the Powell Doctrine, and it sought to return the Army to the period at the beginning of the Vietnam War—the era when Secretary of Defense Robert McNamara was engaged in his own radical program of military transformation, and when other political appointees of the Kennedy and Johnson administrations were enthusiastic advocates of some major combination of high technology and counterinsurgency as the new way that the United States would fight its future wars.

Second, even before Rumsfeld began his construction of his new army and his deconstruction of the old one, the United States already had a long-established, lighter, and more mobile ground force, and that was the U.S. Marines ("the Navy's army"). During the first half of the twentieth century, the Marines had far more experience and success with light and mobile operations than did the Army. This included many operations against insurgents in the Caribbean basin and in Central America.[44] With only minor modifications and some modest expansion, the Marines by themselves could perform many of the colonial tasks that Rumsfeld's lighter, more mobile, transformed army was supposed to perform (although not an invasion and conquest of large rogue states, such as Iraq or Iran). But this new army may not be able to perform some of the tasks that the old army could perform so well, e.g., quickly overwhelming another large army, if one should ever come into being again and pose a threat to the vital national interests of the United States.

Third, it was not until the United States invaded Iraq and imposed a military occupation upon it that the U.S. faced any guerrilla or insurgent threat that needed to be dealt with by regular U.S. military forces. (Almost everyone agreed that the guerrilla forces in Afghanistan and in Colombia would be better dealt with by a combination of U.S. Special Forces and local military forces.) The U.S. occupation of Iraq created, for the first time since the Vietnam War, the very problem that the Rumsfeld transformation project was supposed to solve.

THE RUMSFELD ARMY AND THE IRAQ WAR

When it invaded Iraq in March 2003, the new Rumsfeld army was spectacularly successful against the army of Saddam Hussein. (Of course, the old,

American-way-of-war army had been similarly successful against Saddam
Hussein's army back in 1991.) The "shock-and-awe" tactics of the U.S. Air
Force and the fluid and flexible tactics of the unusually light and highly
mobile U.S. Army and Marines quickly won the conventional war, so that
President Bush on May 1, 2003, famously (and as it turned out, fatuously)
declared "mission accomplished" and the end of "major combat operations." But it soon became clear that the real war, the counterinsurgency
war, had just begun.[45]

The Army had actually anticipated that its real challenge in Iraq
would come *after* its defeat of Saddam Hussein's conventional forces.
The Army had conducted a series of studies of previous U.S. military occupations, and these had produced some sophisticated conclusions.[46]
One simple ground rule for occupations was that, in order to establish
security and deter insurgency, it was necessary to have a ratio of about
20 soldiers for every 1,000 civilians within the occupied population.
These soldiers could include collaborating units drawn from the occupied country, but of course the core forces had to be provided by the U.S.
military. Given that Iraq had a population of about 25 million, the number of occupation troops would have to be about 500,000. This is why
the Chief of Staff of the Army, General Eric Shinseki, had stated on the
eve of the war that the forces required for establishing the peace would
have to consist of "several hundred thousand" soldiers for several years.
For this, he was publicly rebuked and ridiculed by Rumsfeld and Deputy
Secretary of Defense Paul Wolfowitz, as being "wildly off the mark." The
conclusions of the Army studies and the statement of Shinseki did not
conform to the Rumsfeld transformation project's notion of a light and
lean U.S. Army.[47]

The United States invaded Iraq with about 140,000 troops (not all of
them combat personnel), and allied units—especially British forces—
added another 40,000. These numbers were enough to defeat Iraq's conventional forces, but they were obviously not enough to establish security
and deter insurgency. Now began the damaging consequences of Rumsfeld's violation of the Powell Doctrine's tenet of overwhelming force. An
interregnum, or rather an anarchy, of looting, sabotage, kidnappings, and
murders ensued. This in turn provided the conditions for the beginning
and growth of a vigorous and organized insurgency. Moreover, since the
U.S. military had too few forces to secure or destroy the vast stores of arms
and ammunition the old regime had distributed around Iraq, the insurgents had easy access to all the weapons that they needed.

The Iraqi Insurgency and the U.S. Incapacity

The insurgents quickly moved to confirm the isolation of U.S. occupation forces by attacking the few allies that they had. Using an array of classical insurgent tactics—bombings, ambushes, kidnappings, and beheadings—they repeatedly attacked the military units, civilian organizations, and simple individuals from every nation that was providing support to the occupation. In most cases, the governments of these nations had provided their support without mobilizing their own publics behind it, and in some cases they had done so despite the clear opposition of public opinion. The insurgents' attacks upon exposed allied personnel also exposed the gap between the allied governments and their publics, which had hardly been a robust example of democracy in action. Of even more fundamental and fatal importance were the insurgents' attacks upon Iraqis who were working with the occupation. A particularly crucial target was the U.S. effort to recruit and organize new Iraqi security forces (e.g., repeated insurgent bombings of recruiting centers and police stations).

The U.S. military soon found that it had no good options for putting down the insurgency. If the U.S. ground forces engaged in direct assaults upon urban areas sheltering the insurgents (e.g., Fallujah and other cities in the "Sunni Triangle"), the resulting fatalities among U.S. forces would arouse the opposition of American public opinion, while the fatalities among local civilians would arouse the opposition of the Iraqi and allied publics. Similarly, U.S. air strikes upon these urban areas would inflame Iraqi and allied public opinion. Finally, if the U.S. military simply tried to maintain a defensible position in Iraq, it would suffer a slow but steady stream of fatalities, which would eventually arouse the opposition of the American public (the specter of the Vietnam War). More fundamentally, the new American way of war, which Rumsfeld sought to establish with his transformation project, had no effective answer to the challenge posed by the insurgency in Iraq.

Any proposals for any new U.S. wars will be greatly constrained by the effects of the Iraq War upon the U.S. Army and the U.S. Marines. The post-Vietnam military was a volunteer military, and underlying and ensuring a steady and sufficient stream of volunteers was the classical American way of war. At some level, the recruits to the U.S. military assumed that they would be defending the vital national interests of the United States, or at least that they would be sent into war according to some sort of reasonable principles (like those articulated by the Powell Doctrine). The Iraq War violated these assumptions, and the consequence was a decline in Army and Marine recruitment and retention, a decline that made it exceedingly difficult to launch a new war in some other country. This military reality was evident for all to see, including the enemies of the United States, and this greatly diminished the U.S. ability to deter its enemies with the threat to invade and occupy their country with U.S. ground forces.

The Global Islamist Challenge and the American Way of War

Six decades ago, the United States was challenged by a new and grave threat to its national security, which was the Soviet Union and its Communist allies around the world. The classical American way of war, which had reached its apotheosis in World War II, was not in itself able to provide a satisfactory answer to this new challenge. It had to undergo a great transformation—creating the national strategy of containment and the military strategy of nuclear deterrence—before it could do so. But, in the end, this transformed version of the American way of war defeated the Soviet threat and won the Cold War.

Today, the United States is challenged by a new and very different grave threat to its national security, and that is the global Islamist insurgency and particularly the transnational networks of Islamist terrorists. At present, it seems that neither the classical American way of war nor the various transformed versions that have appeared over the past sixty years have a satisfactory answer to this new challenge. Can the American way of war be transformed again in some way to deal with the Islamist threat?

Despite the visions of Donald Rumsfeld, the neoconservatives, or the protagonists of the RMA, the answer will not lie this time, as it did six decades ago, in rearranging the weights between the first three elements of the American way of war, i.e., mass, mobility, and technology. This might have been a satisfactory way to deter nuclear states or to defeat conventional armies; however, as the American experience in Vietnam and now Iraq demonstrates, it is not the way to defeat local insurgent movements. Nor is there any evidence that it will be the way to defeat or deter transnational terrorist networks, who have no state of their own that they have to defend and which, being a precious possession and lucrative target, would make them susceptible to deterrence. Rather, any promise for the American way of war will lie in some new variation of its fourth and fifth elements, i.e., the support of the American public and the contribution of U.S. allies.

The Fifth Element: Local Security Forces

The simplest transformation would involve the fifth element, the contribution of U.S. allies. The historical record shows that local insurgent forces have never been defeated by foreign military forces operating by themselves alone. The foreign power—be it the United States in South Vietnam or earlier (the 1910s–1920s) in the Caribbean basin and Central America or the British in Malaya or earlier (the 1920s) in Iraq—always needs to rely upon security forces drawn from the local population and, in some sense at least, serving a local regime (even if it is an ally or even a puppet of the foreign power). Indeed, in practice, the local security forces have to provide the bulk of the counterinsurgency manpower, with the foreign power mainly providing material support, elite advisers, and special forces who are expert professionals in counterinsurgency. (By 1971, even the South Vietnamese army had progressed to this point and was operating as an effective counterinsurgency force.)[48]

The Bush administration committed a large number of errors when it went to war in Iraq. Most of these were clear violations of elements of the classical American way of war. Among the most consequential of these errors was a violation of the fifth element, i.e., to have no realistic plan whatsoever for relying upon local security forces drawn from the Iraqi population. At the beginning of the U.S. occupation in 2003, the only options—all of them bad—were (1) elements of the security forces of the old, Saddam Hussein regime, which were dominated by the Baath Party and the Sunni minority; (2) the militias, already highly organized and effective, of the Kurdish minority; and (3) the militias, then merely embryonic but with great potential, of the Shiite majority. The Bush administration chose none of these, which meant that for the first two years of the occupation, it could rely upon no local forces at all. Given this degree of strategic delusion and incompetence, it is not surprising that the insurgency in Iraq—composed principally of Sunnis—grew so quickly and became so large and effective. The clear lesson of the U.S. debacle in Iraq is that if the United States should ever again undertake a counterinsurgency war—be it in a Muslim country or elsewhere—it must have a realistic plan to rely upon local security forces, i.e., it must abide by the fifth element of the American way of war.

The Fourth Element: The Support of the American Public

A more fundamental transformation of the American way of war—really a restoration of it—would involve its fourth element, the support of the American public. In this regard, it is useful to consider a kind of counterfactual or "what if?" history of U.S. national security policy since 1945. Imagine if, on the eve of every war during this sixty-year period, the President had actually sought to obtain the American public's support for the war, as expressed through the once-traditional constitutional provision of a Congressional declaration of war, or at least through the President making an honest and truthful case to Congress and Congress passing a fully informed and fully debated resolution for war. In other words, imagine that the U.S. decision to go to war had actually been arrived at by an authentic democratic process.

The results of this counterfactual inquiry could be instructive. In the case of the Korean War, Congress, after considerable debate, might well have provided the necessary resolution or declaration to go to war and perhaps even to cross the 38th Parallel, given the clear armed aggression by North Korea and given the potential Communist threat to Japan. Consequently, the Korean War might have taken its same dismal military course, although the devisive political conflict at home might have been lessened.

In the case of the Vietnam War, however, it is likely that Congress would never have authorized this war with an honestly-arrived-at resolution or declaration. (The Gulf of Tonkin Resolution of August 1964 was the product of stealthy tactics and deliberate deception by President Johnson). Consequently, North Vietnam probably would have taken over South Vietnam (and Cambodia and Laos as well) sometime in 1965 or 1966. However, the U.S. military debacle and defeat in Vietnam would never have occurred.

In the case of the Persian Gulf War, which largely conformed to the elements of the American way of war, the counterfactual history is largely the same as the actual one. And whatever the eventual consequences of the aftermath of the war—Saddam Hussein being defeated but also re-maining in power—at the time the United States seemed to have achieved a clear and decisive military victory. Conversely, in the case of the four U.S. humanitarian interventions in the 1990s (Somalia, Haiti, Bosnia, and Kosovo), the human-rights activists in the Democratic Party were influential enough to cause President Clinton to engage in them, in his hesitant and fitful way. However, it is doubtful that they would have been influential enough to obtain a full and formal resolution from Congress, especially after the Republicans took control of that body in 1995. Conse-quently, murder and mayhem would have continued in each of these four countries, and overall the counterfactual history would have been more dismal than the actual one. However, in the actual event, the murder and mayhem did continue in the old way in Somalia, it reemerged in a new form in Haiti, and it has only been prevented by a prolonged, and perhaps permanent, military occupation and international protectorate in Bosnia and in Kosovo.

In the case of the Afghan War, which was certainly supported by Con-gress and the American people because of the clear and convincing con-nection between the 9/11 terrorist attacks and the war, the counterfactual history is again largely the same as the actual one. Indeed, Congress and the public would probably have been even more willing than the Bush ad-ministration to use U.S. military forces all the way to the point that they would have succeeded in capturing Osama bin Laden or at least in devas-tating the support base for the Taliban among the Pashtun tribes in east-ern Afghanistan.

Finally, in the case of the Iraq War, which has so many similarities with the Vietnam War, it is again likely that Congress would never have autho-rized the war with an honestly-arrived-at resolution or declaration (the actual Iraq war resolution of October 2002 was the product of false argu-ments about the existence of Iraqi WMDs and about links between al-Qaeda and Saddam Hussein's regime). Consequently, Saddam Hussein would have remained in power. However, the U.S. military and political debacle in Iraq would never have occurred.

Overall then, it appears that the United States and the American people would have been much better off if the counterfactual history had oc-curred, rather than the actual one. And this suggests that they would be better off in the future if they conform to an authentic democratic process in arriving at the decision to go to war, i.e., if they restore the fourth ele-ment of the American way of war.

Let America's Way of War Be American

The classical American way of war was an authentic product of the American nation, as it really was and with all its strengths and limitations. It was designed to defend American national interests, i.e., interests that were both American and national. It was not designed to serve interests that were global rather than American or imperial rather than national. For that, there would have to be a new and different way of war. The strategic transformation projects of the Kennedy and Johnson administrations and Robert McNamara in the early 1960s and of the Bush administration and Donald Rumsfeld in the early 2000s were efforts to construct such new and different ways of war. Whatever expansive interests these projects and their wars might have served, they were not truly American. That is why those administrations never dared to honestly seek the support of the American people when it came to going to war. And that is also why those two transformation projects and their wars failed. As for the future, the national security policy for America that will be most sound and most successful will be the policy that will be most national and most American.

Notes

1.   Russell F. Weigley, *The American Way of War: A History of United States Military Strategy and Policy* (Bloomington: Indiana University Press, 1973).

2.   Michael S. Sherry, *The Rise of American Air Power: The Creation of Armageddon* (New Haven: Yale University Press, 1987).

3.   Weigley, *American Way of War*, chs. 6–7.

4.   Allan R. Millett and Peter Maslowski, *For the Common Defense: A Military History of the United States of America*, revised and expanded edition (New York: The Free Press, 1994), chs. 8–12.

5.   Halford Mackinder, *Democratic Ideals and Reality: A Study in the Politics of Reconstruction* (Washington, D.C.: National Defense University Press, 1996) (contents originally published between 1897 and 1943).

6.   Michael S. Sherry, *In the Shadow of War: The United States Since the 1930s* (New Haven: Yale University Press, 1995); David E. Johnson, *Modern U.S. Civil-Military Relations: Wielding the Terrible Swift Sword*, (Washington, D.C.: Institute for National Strategic Studies, National Defense University, 1997); Samuel P. Huntington, *The Common Defense: Strategic Programs in National Politics* (New York: Columbia University Press, 1961), ch. 4; Weigley, *The American Way of War*, ch. 15.

7.   Aaron L. Friedberg, *In the Shadow of the Garrison State: America's Anti-Statism and Its Cold War Grand Strategy* (Princeton: Princeton University Press, 2000); Michael J. Hogan, *A Cross of Iron: Harry S. Truman and the Origins of the National Security State* (New York: Cambridge University Press, 1998); Samuel P. Huntington, *The Soldier and the State: The Theory and Politics of Civil-Military Relations* (Cambridge: Belknap Press of Harvard University Press, 1957).

8.   Warner R. Schilling, "The Politics of National Defense: Fiscal 1950," in Warner R. Schilling, Paul Y. Hammond, and Glenn H. Snyder, *Strategy, Politics, and Defense Budgets* (New York: Columbia University Press, 1962); Huntington, *The Common Defense*, ch. 4.

9.   Paul Y. Hammond, "NSC-68: Prologue to Rearmament," in Schilling, Hammond, and Snyder, *Strategy, Politics, and Defense Budgets*; David Alan Rosenberg, "The Origins of Overkill: Nuclear Weapons and American Strategy, 1945–1960," *International Security* (Spring 1983): 3–71; Huntington, *The Common Defense*, ch. 5; Weigley, *The American Way of War*, chs. 15–16.

10. Walter LaFeber, *America, Russia, and the Cold War, 1945–2002*, updated 9th edition (New York: McGraw Hill, 2002), ch. 4.

11. Bruce Cumings, *The Origins of the Korean War*, vol. 1, *Liberation and the Emergence of Separate Regimes, 1945–1947* (Princeton: Princeton University Press, 1981).

12. Bruce Cumings, *The Origins of the Korean War*, vol. 2, *The Roaring of the Cataract, 1947–1950* (Princeton: Princeton University Press, 1990); LaFeber, *America, Russia, and the Cold War*, ch. 5.

13. LaFeber, *America, Russia, and the Cold War*, ch. 7.

14. Robert R. Bowie and Richard H. Immerman, *Waging Peace: How Eisenhower Shaped an Enduring Cold War Strategy* (New York: Oxford University Press, 1998); Glenn H. Snyder, "The 'New Look' of 1953," in Schilling, Hammond, and Snyder, *Strategy, Politics, and Defense Budgets*; Huntington, *The Common Defense*, ch. 6.

15. Weigley, *The American Way of War*, ch. 17; Millett and Maslowski, *For the Common Defense*, ch. 16.

16. Huntington, *The Common Defense*, 341–53.

17. Millett and Maslowski, *For the Common Defense*, ch. 16; A. J. Bacevich, *The Pentomic Era: The U.S. Army Between Korea and Vietnam* (Washington, D.C.: National Defense University Press, 1986).

18. Henry A. Kissinger, *Nuclear Weapons and Foreign Policy* (New York: Harper and Row, 1957); also his *The Necessity for Choice: Prospects of American Foreign Policy* (New York: Harper and Row, 1961); Weigley, *The American Way of War*, ch. 17.

19. Robert E. Osgood, *Limited War: The Challenge to American Strategy* (Chicago: University of Chicago Press, 1957); Morton H. Halperin, *Limited War in the Nuclear Age* (New York: Wiley, 1963).

20. Weigley, *The American Way of War*, ch. 18; Millett and Maslowski, *For the Common Defense*, ch. 16.

21. Harry G. Summers Jr., *On Strategy: A Critical Analysis of the Vietnam War* (Novato, California: Presidio Press, 1982); Millett and Maslowski, *For the Common Defense*, ch. 17.

22. Max Boot, *The Savage Wars of Peace: Small Wars and the Rise of American Power* (New York: Basic Books, 2002), ch. 13; Millett and Maslowski, *For the Common Defense*, ch. 17.

23. Boot, *The Savage Wars of Peace*, ch. 14.

24. Harry G. Summers Jr., *On Strategy II: A Critical Analysis of the Gulf War* (New York: Dell, 1992).

25. Peter Schweizer, *Victory: The Reagan Administration's Secret Strategy That Hastened the Collapse of the Soviet Union* (New York: Atlantic Monthly Press, 1994), ch. 13.

26. Andrew J. Bacevich, *The New American Militarism: How Americans Are Seduced by War* (New York: Oxford University Press, 2005), ch. 2.

27. Ibid; Boot, *Savage Wars of Peace*, ch. 14.

28. LaFeber, *America, Russia, and the Cold War*, ch. 11.

29. Bacevich, *The New American Militarism*, ch. 3; Fred Kaplan, *The Wizards of Armageddon* (New York: Simon and Schuster, 1983); Daniel Ford, *The Button: The Pentagon's Command and Control System* (New York: Simon and Schuster, 1985).

30. Jay Winik, *On the Brink: The Dramatic Behind-the-Scenes Saga of the Reagan Era, and the Men and Women Who Won the Cold War* (New York: Simon and Schuster, 1996).

31. Schweizer, *Victory*; Daniel Wirls, *Buildup: The Politics of Defense in the Reagan Era* (Ithaca: Cornell University Press, 1992).

32. Summers, *On Strategy II: A Critical Analysis of the Gulf War*.

33. Stephen Kotkin, *Armageddon Averted: The Soviet Collapse 1970–2000* (New York: Oxford University Press, 2001).

34. James Kurth, "Clausewitz and the Two Contemporary Military Revolutions," in Bradford A. Lee and Karl F. Walling, eds., *Strategic Logic and Political Rationality* (London: Frank Cass, 2003), 286–290.

35. Summers, *On Strategy II*; Michael R. Gordon and Bernard E. Trainor, *The Generals' War: The Inside Story of the Conflict in the Gulf* (Boston: Little, Brown, 1995).

36. James Kurth, "First War of the Global Era: Kosovo and U.S. Grand Strategy," in Andrew J. Bacevich and Eliot A. Cohen, eds., *War Over Kosovo: Politics and Strategy in a Global Age* (New York: Columbia University Press, 2001), 63–96.

37. David Halberstam, *War in a Time of Peace: Bush, Clinton, and the Generals* (New York: Scribner's, 2001).

38. Ibid; David Reiff, *A Bed for the Night: Humanitarianism in Crisis* (New York: Simon and Schuster, 2002); Gary T. Dempsey with Roger W. Fontaine, *Fool's Errands: America's Recent Encounters with Nation Building* (Washington, D.C.: Cato Institute, 2001) ch. 1.

39. Dempsey with Fontaine, *Fool's Errands*, chs. 2–6.

40. William M. Arkin, "Operation Allied Force: 'The Most Precise Application of Air Power in History,' " in Bacevich and Cohen, *War Over Kosovo*, ch. 1.

41. Bacevich, *The New American Militarism*, chs. 3, 7; Stefan Halper and Jonathan Clarke, *America Alone: The Neo-Conservatives and the Global Order* (New York: Cambridge University Press, 2004).

42. Peter J. Boyer, "The New War Machine," *The New Yorker*, June 30, 2003, 55–71.

43. James Kurth, "Iraq: Losing the American Way," in Royce Flippin, ed., *The Best Political Writings 2004* (New York: Thunder's Mouth Press, 2004), 378–90.

44. Boot, *Savage Wars of Peace*.

45. Michael R. Gordon and General Bernard E. Trainor, *Cobra II: The Inside Story of the Invasion and Occupation of Iraq* (New York: Pantheon Books, 2006).

46. James Fallows, "Blind into Baghdad," *The Atlantic Monthly*, January/February 2004, 53–74.

47. Ibid.

48. Summers, *On Strategy: A Critical Analysis of the Vietnam War*.

3. THE POLITICS OF CONVENTIONAL WARFARE IN AN UNCONVENTIONAL AGE

GEORGE H. QUESTER

World War II set the stage for the evolution of American conventional war thinking in two very different ways. The first was the way in which it had been fought, with an unprecedented reliance on air power and on amphibious operations, with each of these innovations inevitably changing how Americans and anyone else thought about normal or "conventional" war.[1] The second was the way it was so abruptly ended, when in August of 1945 American atomic bombs fell on Hiroshima and Nagasaki, producing a surrender that most had not have expected until 1947 at the earliest.[2]

The very phrase "conventional war" may indeed owe most of its meaning to the introduction of nuclear weapons; when anyone was asked to speculate about a war after 1945 in which nuclear weapons would *not* be used, the phrase for this often came to be "conventional" war. In later decades, the "conventional" phrase also sometimes has been used more narrowly to refer to something other than terrorism, or something other than guerrilla war, but for much of the Cold War, it referred simply to any war fought as it had been before Hiroshima.

The United States military establishment before World War II had still been directed by two separate cabinet-level Departments, somewhat illogically named the War Department and the Department of the Navy. While the two obviously had a great deal of necessary interaction in this time, this might not have felt qualitatively different from the interactions of the Department of Justice and Treasury, or between Agriculture and Interior.[3]

One general lesson extracted from the World War II experience was thus that this degree of autonomy and loose coordination could not be retained, for at least two major reasons. The necessity for amphibious operations was one obvious factor. In the Pacific, many were conducted by the Marine Corps, which had grown much larger in the process of preparing for this specialty, and then in having to engage the Japanese across the Central Pacific. The Marine Corps was closely tied to the Navy, under the Secretary of the Navy, with many of its officers being Naval Academy graduates, which eased the problems of land-sea coordination. But all the amphibious operations in the Atlantic, and even many of those in the Pacific, involved U.S. Army units.

The problems of coordination between the Army and Navy were overcome successfully, with the Allied landing at Normandy being a great achievement. Yet Normandy seemed a precursor to even more complex operations to come. For example, the final invasion and defeat of Japan was expected to entail an operation four times the size of the Normandy landings. Even closer integration between naval and ground forces, on training, equipment, and tactics, appeared essential to achieve maximum operational effectiveness.[4]

The role of aircraft in warfare also loomed much larger in the experience of World War II, as the aircraft carrier almost totally replaced the battleship as the capital ship for naval combat, and as air power advocates in the U.S. Army Air Force envisaged winning the war by aerial attack alone. Advocates of air power within the Army had been pressing for a separate U.S. Air Force ever since World War I, with the separate Royal Air Force in Britain being a model. While most naval aviators did not favor joining such a separate air force (although the RAF had for a time incorporated carrier-based aircraft), a few saw this as the only way to secure recognition of the paramount role of airpower in future combat at sea, as well as for the coordination of land-based and carrier-based aircraft.[5]

It is fair to say that the U.S. Navy and its affiliated Marine Corps were the most reluctant to see tighter integration or unification of the American defense establishment at the end of World War II. The Marine Corps feared that it would simply be merged into the U.S. Army, while the Navy and Marine Corps both feared that they would lose their aviation to a newly created and independent Air Force.[6] Yet the general sense of the American public and the Congress, drawing on the lessons of how the war had been fought before Hiroshima, was that some unification was now "of course" required. Rather than conventional war being fought mostly separately in two distinct theaters, land and water, it would now have to be fought in three, land, water, and air, and very often along the interfaces of these theaters.

When military traditionalists resisted such unification and reassignment, this could have been dismissed as the simple inertia of nostalgia and tradition, or it could be made to seem more formidable when dressed up with theories of "bureaucratic politics" subsequently espoused by political scientists. Yet in another sense, the final chapter of the Pacific War might justify skepticism about the supposed imperative of unification. When World War II ended before any amphibious invasion greater than Normandy had to be launched, amphibious operations would soon appear to be all but obsolete. Skeptics about the air power theories promulgated by the U.S. Army Air Force might note that the conventional bombings of Germany had not induced Hitler to surrender, and that similar attacks on Japan prior to August 1945 had not noticeably weakened Japanese resolve; but the ability of a single B-29 to inflict surrender-inducing destruction seemed qualitatively different.[7]

"LIMITED WAR"

If nuclear weapons were now to be the "absolute weapon," in Bernard Brodie's phrase,[8] there would be a question about whether any more ordinary warfare or "conventional warfare" was to be fought. One possible consequence of the introduction of nuclear weapons was that war would now be so horrible that it would never be fought again. A very different possibility was that the next war would end human life as we know it. Air power enthusiasts might see nuclear weapons as finally realizing what they had predicted all along, that airplanes had become so dominant that other weapons might hardly matter.

If these initial reactions to the introduction of nuclear weapons, "weapons of mass destruction," had been correct, the issues of integration of Army and Marine Corps ground combat capabilities would have been largely irrelevant, as would preparations for amphibious warfare, and the bulk of the defense budget ought to have been directed to the newly independent and nuclear-equipped Air Force. If the Soviet Union now retained much larger conventional forces than the United States, and was in a geopolitical position from which it could threaten to occupy Western Europe, it was presumably American nuclear forces that deterred Moscow from launching such an invasion. For as long as the United States was the sole possessor of nuclear weapons, these would offset and outweigh the Soviet advantage in traditional military force. Just as the atomic bomb had been

used to force Japanese soldiers to leave China two years earlier than anyone would have predicted, they could be counted on to keep Russian soldiers from rolling into Frankfurt and Paris.

But the American nuclear monopoly would last for only four years, and
the phrase "conventional war" would soon become synonymous with a
somewhat heretical concept of "limited war," a possibility that might have
been foreseen as a probability if the Soviet Union or another adversary
were able to acquire nuclear weapons of its own. In June 1950, when the
Korean War broke out, that probability became reality. A "limited" war
was one in which each side—fearing for the safety of its cities—held back
its own nuclear weapons, as long as the other side did not use theirs. As the
two nuclear forces deterred each other, they might then not be usable to
deter the tank forces of the opposing side. The implications of Korea
seemed clear: the same Russian-made T-34 tanks that rolled into Seoul in
1950 might soon enough be rolling toward Paris, unless American and allied conventional forces were strengthened to rebut them.

"Limited war" was a strange concept for most Americans. It imposed a
new set of rules by which one used only part of one's arsenal against an enemy in a war.[9] Such constraints were manifestly unpopular in the Korean
War when President Truman relieved Douglas MacArthur from command,[10] and they were still unpopular at the time of the Vietnam War. Unlike Europeans, who had often seen wars fought in the past because their
monarchs were competing for the ownership of one province or another, the
citizens of the American democracy had tended to see war as something
that one treated as a holy fight against evil, or otherwise stayed out of.

"Limited war" thus brought "conventional war" back into relevance, as
nuclear air power might not be able to do much more than deter itself. For
some logical perspectives, this was bad news, and for others it was good.
For those in 1945 who had thought that war would never be fought again,
because of its sheer nuclear horror, this was *bad* news: peace was not inevitable; wars would break out again. For those who in 1945 had thought that
the next war would see the destruction of every city and an end to civilized
human life, "limited war" (and "conventional war") were *good* news: even
if war were still inevitable, the result would fall short of Armageddon.

Politically, for those who were status quo-oriented, like most Americans
content to hold the line of containment, not really aspiring to any military
liberation of Communist-controlled Eastern Europe, limited war was bad
news, for an aggressive enemy could launch wars on the Korean model, trying to expand the Communist empire one small bite at a time. For those

opposed to the status quo, such as the Communist leaders in Moscow and Beijing, limited war was good news, as the Chinese openly endorsed this phenomenon as the means to what they called "liberation."[11]

Within the U.S. armed services, the Strategic Air Command of the U.S. Air Force understandably regarded the notion of limited war as bad news, because it suggested that nuclear weapons would not suffice to solve the entire American defense problem. "Conventional war" had returned to significance. The Army, Navy, and the Marine Corps, and the tactical portions of the Air Force, conversely welcomed the concept of limited war, because it meant that their role in the defense of the United States was safe. No one would claim that any military leader or any service would look forward to actual conventional wars, any more than Americans in general looked forward to being attacked. Rather, these portions of the U.S. defense establishment could aspire to deter such wars by being *prepared* for them.

Overall, the advent of "limited war" suggested that American strategic nuclear forces alone could not effectively deter a Soviet bloc tank attack. If so, it might take American ground forces to forestall such an attack, deterring it by the prospect of "denial," denying the enemy battlefield success, rather than by the prospect of "punishment," the prospect of the nuclear destruction of Soviet cities.[12]

Extended Nuclear Deterrence

The prospect of limited war, illustrated so painfully in the Korean War, initiated a long debate that would last for the rest of the Cold War as to whether "conventional" defense preparations were really the only way to deter Communist conventional attacks. The extreme version of such an analysis argued that the only role for American nuclear weapons was to keep the Soviets from using theirs, and that "extended nuclear deterrence," threatening American nuclear escalation to deter Soviet armored attacks, was always too dangerous, and perhaps inherently undoable. This was basically the argument offered by Secretary of Defense McNamara within the Kennedy administration, stated publicly by him afterward in the 1980s.[13]

But many West European leaders, and also the American strategic planners of the Eisenhower administration, had been reluctant to accept such a wide-ranging shift back to conventional warfare preparations, if only because of the enormous economic cost of matching the Soviets tank-for-tank. Since the days of the Czar, as Mackinder describes, Moscow had the advantage of a central geopolitical position. The power at the center can direct its forces in any direction, into any of the peninsulas sticking out from the Eurasian land mass, into Korea (as in 1950), into Turkey, into South Asia, or into Western Europe. Although the Soviets could attack in any of these places, the United States could not afford to defend them all simultaneously with strong conventional forces. So the possibility of American nuclear escalation was thus never renounced, even in the Kennedy administration. Even today, long after the Cold War has ended, the United States has not relinquished the option of employing nuclear weapons to defend valuable areas such as the NATO countries of Western Europe or South Korea.

But such policies of exploiting the American nuclear arsenal to protect American allies always ran a double risk, a risk that explained why McNamara and many others advocated enhancing U.S. capabilities for conventional warfare. First, there was the fear that the United States might be bluffing about being willing to escalate to nuclear war if, say, West Germany came under conventional attack. If the Soviets called that bluff, the territory attacked would quickly have come under Communist rule, and the United States would suffer a global humiliation, calling into question its commitments everywhere else.

Second, there was the fear that the United States might *not* have been bluffing, but might not have been credible enough in its statements of commitment. In this case, if the Soviets foolishly called the bluff, the result would be a thermonuclear World War III.[14]

The alternative, proposed by some, would have been for the United States to renounce extended nuclear deterrence altogether, to endorse Soviet and other proposals for a policy of "no first use" of nuclear weapons, and instead to take conventional war very seriously, massively expanding the resources assigned to preparing for a Soviet attack. It is easy to belittle the argument against this—that maintaining an army big enough to defeat the Soviet army using conventional weapons alone would have cost too much—for it suggests risking a nuclear holocaust simply to lower American and West European tax rates. Yet it has to be noted that Western economic prosperity was a major factor in the ultimate winning of the Cold War, and that a great deal of the West's quality of life today is the result of having avoided excessive military spending during the Cold War. If the United States had renounced nuclear escalation on behalf of NATO and of South Korea, many more young men would have spent much longer periods of time in military service. Much more of Western steel would have gone to constructing tanks, rather than automobiles; preparations for conventional warfare would have slowed down the capital growth central to the expansion of the Western economies.[15]

Indeed, it can even be argued that U.S. acceptance of Soviet proposals for nuclear-free zones, as in the Rapacki Plan, and of a no-first-use policy, would have forced an increase in *Soviet* defense spending as well; larger arrays of NATO tanks might have called forth larger arrays of Warsaw Pact tanks, as perhaps neither side could have felt secure if the other side were secure. Deterrence without nuclear weapons would have been a far costlier proposition all around.

"Preparations" for Conventional Warfare

For all the years of the Cold War, the years of "extended nuclear deterrence," the question of how one made such deterrence credible remained central. How could Washington convince the Kremlin that the United States would escalate to the nuclear level, with the prospect of an all-out World War III thereafter, if Moscow merely rolled forward its conventional armored forces and advanced into West Germany?

One way to make the linkage more believable was to issue declarations, "jawboning," that dismissed the option of limited war and spoke instead of "defending our allies with every weapon we have." The Eisenhower administration regularly issued statements of this genre, and later years saw NATO alliance declarations of "flexible response" amounting to the same warning: the United States and its allies might rely on conventional defenses initially, but if such defenses did not hold, nuclear escalation would follow.

A related link was the deployment into the prospective battle area of "tactical" or "theater" nuclear weapons. Such "battlefield" nuclear weapons were nominally intended to blunt the Soviet armored advance by destroying advancing tank columns. Whether or not they would have actually achieved this result, however, their employment would certainly have crossed the nuclear/conventional line, with the prospect of massive damage to the surroundings. Again, there was the larger prospect of escalation to all-out nuclear war.[16]

A third way to establish this linkage was to deploy *some* conventional forces, along the front, not with an eye toward repulsing the massive arrays of Warsaw pact armor, but to irrevocably engage the United States and therefore make the prospect of all-out war real. To be sure, the "conventional forces" deployed on the European central front were never told that they were merely to be a "tripwire" or "plate-glass window" triggering nuclear escalation (the shoulder-patch that was never designed or worn would have included the Latin for "plate-glass window"). Their assigned mission was to stop a Soviet conventional advance—a mission that they would most probably not have been able to accomplish. In the process of their being overrun and killed or captured, however, American opinion would have been sufficiently outraged to have made a nuclear response plausible. Furthermore, in the process of being overrun, these forces would have employed their "tactical" nuclear weapons consistent with the artillery tradition that ammunition be expended to prevent its capture by the enemy.

The sum total of these nuclear-conventional linkages made it extremely difficult for war planners in Moscow to conceive of ways for Soviet armored forces to "liberate" Western Europe without inducing World War III in the process. It was most probably not the prospect of a conventional defeat that deterred the Kremlin from exploiting its advantage in geography and in conventional forces, but the prospect of a nuclear escalation.

Inconsistent Conventional War Aims

If the prospect of U.S. nuclear escalation thereby underwrote the security of NATO and South Korea, it followed that plans for conventional defense were not entirely serious. The "conventional" forces deployed on the European central front genuinely believed that they were there to do battle. This conviction actually increased their effectiveness as a tripwire. The nuclear weapons deployed to South Korea and NATO may have been labeled as intended for the "battlefield," but they were more surely a link to all-out escalation.

If the Truman administration had not achieved real integration in war planning, neither did the Eisenhower administration. Eisenhower reduced the defense spending levels that the Truman administration had approved after the outbreak of the Korean War, shifting back to a greater reliance on threats of nuclear escalation while investing less in conventional capabilities. As part of an effort to assuage the separate military services, which were naturally unhappy about budget reductions, he allowed them autonomy again in their war planning. Indeed, it was a common criticism of defense-planning in the Eisenhower years that the various services were structuring themselves for very different versions of any future (conventional) war. The Army was investing substantially in airborne units, although the Air Force was not doing so in regard to the troop carrier aircraft to transport them. The Navy and the Marine Corps were planning for still other forms of a new conventional war.[17] If one accepts the argument, however, that allied security depended on extended nuclear deterrence rather than on a genuinely effective conventional defense, then such mismatches of American military planning were not so much of a problem. At least through the 1950s, the United States, for the most important parts of the world, was not seriously planning for a conventional defense. An Army unit mismatched with an Air Force unit in West Germany might still work very well as a tripwire.

THE ROLE OF CIVILIAN PLANNERS

If war after 1945 was always to lie in the shadow of the possibility of all-out *nuclear* war, it followed, for various reasons, that civilians would be much more involved in the shaping of strategy than before. When asked why civilians played such a large role in writing on post–World War II military strategy, today's military officers often cite the United States Constitution and its stipulation that the civilian President of the United States is the Commander-in-Chief. Yet most of the American writing on strategy and the conduct of war before 1939 was done by people who were or had been military officers, with the man-on-the-street being reluctant to read a book on this subject that was not authored by a "professional." After World War II this changed, quickly and dramatically. A good illustration is the title of Bernard Brodie's first book. During World War II, Brodie, a young civilian political scientist, published an apologetically titled *Layman's Guide to Naval Strategy*.[18] Some years later, after the nuclear age had begun and after Brodie's pathbreaking *The Absolute Weapon* had vaulted him to prominence as a defense intellectual, his first book reappeared, updated and now called simply *A Guide to Naval Strategy*.[19]

The post-1945 intrusion of civilians into what had been the professional domain of Army and Navy officers came about not just because of the U.S. Constitution, but also for at least three other reasons. First, the scientists who had developed nuclear weapons in the Manhattan Project felt a certain amount of guilt and responsibility for what they had unleashed on the world. As every issue of military policy and strategy now had to take the nuclear factor into account, they became active participants in seminars on campus and in many other entry points to the policy process.[20]

Second, the entire issue of escalation and limitation, of guessing whether one's adversary would be deterred or not, brought into play the special insights of psychology, of political science, and of economics and game theory, as military strategy overall had become an exercise of not simply defeating an enemy on the battlefield, but also of bargaining and negotiating with that enemy at the same time, lest unnecessary escalation produce disaster for all concerned.[21]

Third, even where war could be contemplated and planned in its more traditional "conventional" form, the application of new technologies, as amphibious and aerial and other techniques were brought to bear, might require special expertise not commonly found among career military officers.

To summarize, even if nuclear weapons had never been invented, there would have been a greater civilian input into planning for a "conventional war." But Hiroshima and Nagasaki had ordained that no war in the future could be thought of only as a "conventional" war, since the possibility of a nuclear escalation was always with us. This brought in the physicists, since they had invented the big bombs. And it brought in the social scientists with relevant insights on managing the interface between the "conventional" and the "nuclear."

CHANGES UNDER KENNEDY AND MCNAMARA

The United States had fought a major conventional war against Germany and Japan in World War II, ended abruptly by the beginning of the nuclear age. It fought another conventional war in Korea, shortly after the Soviet Union had acquired its own nuclear arsenal, with the big question being posed thereafter on whether Korea was to be the model for many more "limited" conventional wars in the future. As noted, the Eisenhower goal (criticized, but never totally abandoned by the Kennedy administration and those that followed) was to prevent any recurrence of Korean-model conventional wars. As it happened, no such wars occurred.

During the Kennedy era, Defense Secretary McNamara assigned a lot of attention to enhancing preparations for conventional war, in face of great resistance among the European NATO allies, reluctant to shift away from extended nuclear deterrence.[22] The Kennedy administration's increased emphasis on conventional combat, which entailed a 20 percent increase in the defense budget, soon enough found a war. But the action instigating the employment of U.S. forces turned out to be not a conventional armored attack on the 1950 pattern of Korea, but a Communist guerrilla offensive in South Vietnam.

If all one means by "conventional war" after 1945 is non-nuclear, then the phrase is almost synonymous with "limited war." Guerrilla war and terrorism and even MOOTW ("military operations other than war") might be included. Some analysts prefer to distinguish among these categories and define them separately, of course, but it is fair to note that the enhanced preparations for conventional war launched by Secretary McNamara in the Kennedy administration found their most extensive employment in the guerrilla war in Vietnam.

Why did American preparations for a war on the style of World War II or of the Korean War remain untested after 1953? Most probably it was because the devices of extended nuclear deterrence proved effective and plausible enough. Or perhaps it might have been because conventional preparations themselves posed some plausible capability for repulsing a Communist armored attack, so that what held back Moscow and Beijing was a "deterrence by denial" rather than a "deterrence by punishment." Even with the opening of Soviet archives and the interviewing of former Soviet leaders, it may always be difficult to tell which factor accounted for the military success of containment—a "soft" conclusion that emphasizes the uncertainty inherent in strategies of deterrence.[23]

GUERRILLA WAR

If containment showed signs of failing in the latter stages of the Cold War, it was not because Soviet-built tanks were plunging into new territories to "liberate" the workers and peasants of the world, but because the techniques of guerrilla war were enjoying some success in Southeast Asia, and then in Africa and in Latin America. Guerrilla war, and the "counterinsurgency techniques" designed to oppose such guerrilla attacks, constitute a variant of "conventional" war, of course, because nuclear weapons are not involved on either side, and because the same American ground, air, and naval forces originally designed for more ordinary warfare are employed in fighting against the guerrillas.[24]

Yet guerrilla warfare differs in several important ways, so much so that Americans tended to regard such conflicts as other than "conventional."

Despite the historical blindness of a few military analysts, who saw guerrilla warfare somehow as an invention of the Chinese Communists under the leadership of Mao Zedong, this kind of warfare had been around for a much longer time, winning its name in the Spanish resistance to Napoleon's armies at the beginning of the nineteenth century, but having already been used by the American patriots at times in the American revolution.[25]

The Spanish phrase "guerrilla" might seem to be the diminutive of "guerra," implying that guerrilla warfare was simply a "small" version of ordinary warfare. Yet this would be quite misleading, for some guerrilla wars have involved very large forces on each side, and some ordinary wars have been fought without committing large numbers of forces. What the phrase really addressed was a technique of not holding a line and not wearing uniforms. Instead of declaring "They shall not pass!" one lets the enemy pass, and then ambushes him afterward.

The advantage of such an approach was that it denied the "conventional" enemy information on who to shoot at. The disadvantage, of course, was that one could not protect one's hinterland against invasion, one could not maintain a national capital, schools and hospitals, and other trappings of a normal country.

To give Mao his due, his analysis and advocacy of guerrilla war did include at least two crucial innovations.[26] First, Marxists and other advocates of guerrilla war asserted a correlation between success in guerrilla war and popular support, with the most-quoted phrase from Mao being "the guerrilla is to the people as a fish is to water." One could find here the basis of a sound counterinsurgent strategy: If you want to defeat a guerrilla uprising, you must prevent the people from going over to the guerrillas' side. But the elementary logic possessed a broader political significance, for by implication a victory by any guerrilla, by Mao in China, or Ho in Vietnam, or Castro in Cuba, *proved* that the people were on that guerrilla leader's side. The logic here was very upsetting for most Americans, who wanted always to be on the side of democracy and the people's will in the conflicts of the world.

If A is *required* to achieve B, then B *proves* that A existed, and this amounted to a major logical trap for many Americans, for guerrilla wars came to look like a plebiscite, like a free election, an election where it would be unnerving to have American support on the wrong side, on the side of the minority rather than the majority.

The ties of warfare to mass support are an old subject in the analysis of military history. The armies of revolutionary France made up for their lower professional military competence by being able to mobilize larger fractions of the total population in a *levée en masse*, and by presumably harnessing revolutionary fervor in big battles and contests of endurance. The large popular armies of World War I and World War II similarly reflected the more total mobilizations of an entire nation at war.

Yet even where wars after 1789 were no longer fought by smaller bands of mercenaries and professionals, it would have been absurd to claim that battlefield victory in a tank versus tank encounter reflected European popular will, or that the outcome of the Battle of Britain proved that the British cared more for democracy than the Germans cared for Nazism. Popular involvement in warfare is relevant on many dimensions, including the willingness to pay costs in warfare, the issues of military subordination to civilian control, the balance between human and material inputs in combat, and the more general questions of military competence; but none of these quite make the outcome of a campaign seem somehow equivalent to an election contest.

Mao's second contribution, in addition to the alleged ties to popular support, was to project a *dialectical* analysis of guerrilla warfare, somewhat parallel to Marx's original dialectical vision of Communist revolution. According to Mao, what might have seemed a conventional battlefield victory for the ordinary armed forces in the initial stages of a guerrilla encounter was only the sure sign of their ultimate defeat, and what might have seemed to be a total defeat for the guerrillas, as they had to flee the battlefield, was a sure sign of their ultimate victory. This certainly was a great morale-booster for Communist guerrillas at the outset of a war. And it was also a great morale-sapper for Americans and others enmeshed in a long, drawn-out guerrilla onslaught. To drive the enemy from the field and to claim a great victory was seemingly to fall into a trap; once dispersed, the guerrillas planned new ambushes, thereby drawing U.S. forces deeper into the morass and ever closer to exhaustion and defeat.

The two parts of the Maoist interpretation of guerilla war were thus very demoralizing for any typical American. This was the kind of war where an initial success was not a sign of ultimate victory, but instead of ultimate defeat. This was the kind of war which by its very outbreak suggested that the opposing side had the people behind it.

Some analysts of guerrilla war saw all of the above as merely adding some important caveats to the means employed for conventional warfare. In addition to deploying better tanks and helicopters, one had to "win the hearts and minds" of the people. This surely was good advice, in that one always presumably does better in a ground war if the local people are friendlier to our side than to theirs. Yet, if one ever concluded that this popular support was *decisive* in such a contest, one had rounded the corner to a point where the entire political *legitimacy* of one's campaign became open to question.

Other analysts, standing a little further back from the problem, questioned the entire Maoist premise that popular support determined the outcome of guerrilla wars as if such a war simply amounted to a violent form of democratic election. The advice given to President Johnson by W. W. Rostow, as the United States persisted in the Vietnam War, was an example of such a counter-analysis. Rostow argued that guerrilla tactics are in effect alternative methods for waging ordinary warfare, effective here and ineffective there, just like armored warfare or amphibious warfare, in no sense proving the wishes of the people.[27] Supporting such an analysis, one could cite the cases of two opposing sides engaging successfully in guerrilla tactics in the same territory, each disrupting normal life, each ambushing the other. One example would come from the Arab underground and Jewish Haganah taking turns attacking British forces at the end of the British mandate in Palestine, and another would come with the IRA facing off against the Protestant Ulster underground in Northern Ireland. Even with the "new math," it was not possible that both sides had the majority of the people behind it.

Yet such a skeptical analysis of the popular validity of guerrilla attacks did not carry the day in Vietnam, as a large slice of Americans came to conclude that the war was imposing too many casualties (guerrilla war is almost always an endurance contest, a contest of who can stand the pain longer with the more stubborn side prevailing), *and* that we had backed the wrong side, the unpopular side.[28]

The United States did not hold on in the Vietnam endurance contest, but rather lost as students and others rallied to oppose the war, as the morale and military effectiveness of Army units fell, as draftees sometimes threw fragmentation grenades at their officers, and as the professional military more generally felt betrayed by a political establishment that had radiated an enthusiasm for "counter-insurgency" as the key to enhancing U.S. conventional warfare capabilities.

Democrats had criticized the Eisenhower administration and the Republicans for being too reliant on extended nuclear deterrence, and not taking conventional warfare seriously enough. When many of the same Democrats then turned to denouncing Vietnam, and to blaming the military for the damage that a protracted guerrilla war inevitably entailed, the military's feeling of betrayal laid the groundwork for a substantial identification in the future with the Republican Party.[29]

THE ALL-VOLUNTEER FORCE

As a related consequence of the Vietnam War, the draft was terminated, in favor of the All-Volunteer Force (AVF) system that has governed military recruitment ever since. The shift to the AVF drew the support of a very unlikely coalition, drawing together people like Milton Friedman on the right and Noam Chomsky on the left—people who would never have had a cause in common otherwise.

After Vietnam, leftists tended to condemn *all* military preparations as evil. A great deal of campus opposition to the Vietnam War had indeed been tied to the prospect of being drafted to fight in that war, or to the guilt of having evaded being drafted (as someone else was then forced to go), with student deferments being key to escaping the war.

American rightists were what the rest of the world would style "liberals" (a term that has a very different meaning within the United States), people who favor voluntarism over coercion for all social decisions, who trust free choice and markets over government "command-economy" decisions at every bend of the road. Someone like Milton Friedman would qualify as a "liberal" almost anywhere outside of the United States, while being called a "conservative" at home.[30] When Americans speak of a "conservative" approach to military-manning issues, they thus sometimes draw together two extremely different analytic viewpoints, the free-choice backers of the AVF system, and "social conservatives" (Charles Moskos might be one example) who see a military service (and perhaps other forms of "national service) as a "duty," something that young Americans "*should*" take on.[31]

The ending of the draft made sense by many arguments, but was debatable on others. For the shorter term, as conceived by the Nixon administration, it might have been the only chance the president had for maintaining an American willingness to stay in Vietnam. Opinion polls showed that student and other opposition to the war correlated closely with the answer given to the question "do you expect to be drafted to fight in Vietnam?" As positive answers to that question diminished, the vehemence of the opposition to the war also decreased. If the war were henceforth to be fought by volunteers, by people who had *chosen* to serve rather than being coerced into the military, the immediate felt-cost of the war for the American public declined. If the Navy and Air Force could now assume the main burden of sustaining the American commitment, punishing Hanoi with air attacks, while the Vietnamese themselves handled the bulk of the ground fighting, there might be a chance of maintaining some resistance to the Communist guerrilla offensive—at least so Nixon calculated. Until Watergate brought an end to the Nixon presidency, the calculation was not a preposterous one.

When the final collapse of the Saigon regime came, it was hardly then an episode of guerrilla war. As Soviet-built tanks smashed through the gates of the Presidential Palace in Saigon, they marked the culmination of a classic conventional offensive, complete with pincer attacks and armored breakthroughs, with U.S. aircraft unable to punish Hanoi as before, and unable to meaningfully reinforce the South Vietnamese defenders. If the Vietnam War began as something that U.S. policymakers chose to see as something other than a conventional war, it certainly ended in a conventional victory for the North Vietnamese communists.

American popular involvement in warfare, in terms of economic sacrifice and in terms of personal risk in exposure to combat, had been an important variable for the entire twentieth century. World War I and World War II had both required mass mobilization and compulsory military service—for a time seemingly hallmarks of the American way of war. The shift to the AVF *might* have reflected some positive hopes now that newer technologies might yield a new way of war, thereby reducing the need to expose large numbers of young men to the hazards of combat. But in the near term it also reflected a sense that, at least so far as an ambiguous guerrilla war was concerned, Americans were simply *unwilling* to pay such a price.

CHANGES UNDER REAGAN

The end of the Vietnam War thus gave rise to widespread doubt about whether the United States was willing to accept the casualties and other costs of any future wars, and whether it could compete effectively in contests of resolve with Communist opponents. The immediate aftermath of the fall of Saigon in 1975 suggested falling dominoes around the world, with Communism spreading, containment not holding, and the United States losing rather than winning the Cold War.[32]

If the election of Ronald Reagan as President in 1980 reversed this perception, it was hardly because Americans had suddenly gotten over their
aversion to casualties, or their reluctance to commit forces to conventional
combat. The Reagan Republicans continued the Nixon experiment with
AVF. Although U.S. defense spending increased under Reagan, and although, in a manner that no one really predicted, the Communist hold on
Eastern Europe collapsed leading to the eventual the breakup of the Soviet
Union and the termination of Communist rule in Moscow, the effects of
the so-called "Vietnam Syndrome" lingered. Under the terms of the Weinberger and Powell "doctrines" even the discussion of a prospective intervention needed to be accompanied by an agreed upon "exit strategy."

Fearing that the Soviets were gaining a decisive edge in strategic weapons, the Reagan administration had responded with the Strategic Defense
Initiative, which proposed to be able to protect American cities against ballistic missile attack, but could probably never have done so. What SDI did
deliver, however, was a tremendous enhancement of high technology—
especially information technology—applicable to all manners of warfare,
including conventional warfare. As the Soviets sought to keep pace with
this technological competition, their economy basically cracked under the
strain.

Reagan might thus well be credited with rallying the West after its post-
Vietnam malaise, leading to a surprising Western victory in the Cold War,
a mere fourteen years after what had seemed like such a colossal defeat.
But the victory was achieved in terms of technology and economic resources, rather than by enduring the horrors of combat. For Americans, it
was a bloodless victory—and all the more welcome for that. When it came
to conventional war, Americans remained committed to approaches that
promised to minimize the number of their young men and women likely
to be killed or wounded.[33]

Desert Storm

The immediate aftermath of the surprising Western victory in the Cold
War saw another surprise, as Saddam Hussein's regime in Iraq invaded
Kuwait. Saddam probably expected that a world celebrating the end of the
Cold War and the presumed end of threats of thermonuclear war would
shrug this off as a simple rectification of a historical injustice. In a sense,
the challenge to international law and order posed by the invasion of

Kuwait very much recalled what the League of Nations had faced in the actions of Mussolini and Hitler during the 1930s. A world committed to peace
is very vulnerable to an aggressor that claims to be beset with grievances
and demands their rectification, through any means necessary. If the alleged perpetrator of injustice does not resist the aggression, the common
sense intuition of the world is that war has not yet broken out, as when the
Kuwaitis did not resist the Iraqi invasion, or as when the Czechs in 1939 did
not resist the German occupation of Prague. To defend the peace, truly
peace-loving nations must thus paradoxically choose to go to war.

Clausewitz captured the essence of the logical problem best in his comment that "the aggressor is always peace-loving."[34] President George H. W.
Bush very effectively maneuvered around the paradox here, in mobilizing
American and global resistance to the Iraqi invasion. And the advanced
technologies that had been developed in the previous decade—precision-
guided munitions, greatly improved reconnaissance and intelligence capabilities, and "stealthy" aircraft chief among them—allowed the United
States and its allies to win a conventional war quickly and at a very low
cost in casualties.

Defeat in Vietnam, the surprisingly swift turnabout that produced victory in the Cold War, the startling challenge by Saddam Hussein, and the
surprisingly quick and effective solution in Desert Storm: all of these
combined to transform American thinking about conventional war. A
new American way of war had emerged, based on several expectations:
that future conventional wars would not require the mass mobilization of
the younger population; that wars would be fought by volunteers and
would entail low casualties; and that they would emphasize the application of high technology. If this new way of war allowed many American
warriors in uniform to remain more remote from the battlefield, all the
better. If it allowed all of the American public to feel remote from that battlefield, this is what Americans felt they needed.

CONVENTIONAL WAR AT SEA

The naval component of conventional warfare has had an interesting evolution of its own over the years since World War II. The United States
Navy after the defeat of Japan was larger than all the other fleets of the
world combined, a measure of saliency comparable to what the Royal

Navy had accomplished after Trafalgar. For a considerable portion of the Cold War, this American superiority was so established that little discussion had to be assigned to naval strategy. The Soviet Navy seemed a minor adversary, expected mainly to be confined to supporting the flanks of the advancing Soviet ground forces, as it had during World War II.

The years from 1945 to the end of the Cold War, and indeed to the present, saw almost no conventional warfare at sea, even while the U.S. Navy at times was heavily engaged in supporting warfare ashore, in the Korean War, and in Vietnam. With the interesting exception of the South Atlantic War between Britain and Argentina over the Falklands, there would be no attacks on warships on the high seas. The largest ship sunk in combat since the end of World War II was the Argentine cruiser *General Belgrano*, a former U.S. Navy vessel and survivor of Pearl Harbor given to the Argentines after World War II. [35]

"Conventional war" involving naval vessels, and naval aircraft flying from these vessels, was confined to land and in the immediate coastal waters, perhaps out to the twelve-mile limit on sovereignty. But on the high seas and over the high seas, a bizarre peace prevailed throughout the Cold War, even as Soviet and American warships would circle around each other, and as Soviet and American aircraft would fly past each other.

Anyone predicting this absence of war on the high seas in 1944 would have been dismissed as wildly out of touch with reality. Throughout history, when warships have historically been built and deployed, they have come into use. Moreover, when conventional wars have been fought on the land, the antagonists have typically carried their quarrel onto the high seas.

One could explain this *absence* of conventional conflict on the high seas in a variety of ways. One obvious explanation was the postwar U.S. monopoly of naval power (although that monopoly did not extend under the seas: the Soviets in 1945 already had a considerably larger number of submarines than the Germans had possessed in 1914 or in 1939). In any event, this explanation became less persuasive by the 1960s and 1970s, as the Soviet Union invested heavily in surface combatants, and after a time, even in aircraft carriers. [36]

A different explanation might cite the "tactical" nuclear weapons deployed on warships of the United States Navy, and also the Soviet Navy. Attacks on such ships carried the risk of "going nuclear," just as with "tactical" nuclear artillery on land, with a risk then of all-out escalation to a nuclear holocaust. In this sense, the presence of nuclear weapons onboard may have inhibited attacks on U.S. warships. Notably, even when lucrative targets such as American aircraft carriers were regularly conducting air operations against Communist forces during the Korean War or during the Vietnam War, none came under attack.

Yet another explanation might note that the *entire* process of fighting "limited" conventional wars after 1945 was counter to all of military tradition and intuition. Once engaged, limited wars established their own rules, with adversaries on opposing sides learning how they could be fought again, what weapons the other side would use, and what they would not use. This was the process of "tacit bargaining" described so well by Thomas Schelling.[37]

It might thus simply be a major historical accident that the antagonists in the Cold War learned how to fight limited conventional wars with each other on land, without very much risking World War III in the process, and did *not* learn how to do this at sea. As an interesting counter-factual, one can imagine a post-1945 world in which just the reverse pattern of accidents had occurred, where all the wars between the opposing sides would be fought at sea, as a pattern tried out once could be reused again with less risk of all-out escalation, and where none of such fighting would have occurred on land.

As things actually happened, the Navy's experience with conventional war since 1945 has not been comparable to the battles against the Japanese Navy or German submarines in World War II, but has entailed a partnership in the conventional wars fought on land and over the land, and perhaps just off-shore or in inland waterways. This remained true even after the United States ceased to hold the degree of naval superiority it had attained in 1945, and beginning in the 1970s faced a burgeoning Soviet naval presence in every ocean of the world.

U.S. Navy spokesmen utilized the mid–Cold War growth of the Soviet Navy to conjure up scenarios of naval battles on the high seas, thereby bolstering their call for renewal and enhancement of American naval capabilities after Vietnam. As always, such preparations for contingencies were entirely plausible, but no such battles occurred. As a consequence, some of the theories of naval warfare and technical preparations remained untested. Navy officers took fire when flying missions over the land, or when taking small "riverine" boats up channels in combat with an enemy ashore. But they could sleep well at night when they back on board the major ships of their fleet.

BUREAUCRATIC POLITICS

In the agony and the aftermath of the Vietnam War, many political scientists in the United States became quite attracted to theories of "bureaucratic politics," and to analyses of the defense policy process that made the interplay of the separate armed services look pathological and wasteful, rather than an attempt to genuinely serve the national interest. By some of such theories, each of the military services was inclined mainly to look for increases in its budget, and for accompanying increases in mandate, with this explaining the procurement of unnecessary weapons and the otherwise seemingly irrational plunge into Vietnam. According to other versions of such theories, the services were simply wedded to their own traditional ways of doing things, their own "standard operating procedures," clinging to outdated fighting platforms—strategic bombers, tanks, large aircraft carriers—in ways that conflicted with the true national interest.[38]

Such theories of bureaucratic behavior, of course, found application in the civilian side of government as well. Indeed, they could be employed to explain the infighting among academic departments at any state university or even a private university. Yet the enthusiasm for such theories stemmed heavily from military examples, including many examples from the Vietnam War.

On an ad hominem basis, one could discount these theories by noting that their proponents tended to be people who regarded John F. Kennedy as their favorite president since Franklin Roosevelt, and who at the same time hated the Vietnam War,[39] in part because many of them had feared having to fight in it. Reconciling one's love of Kennedy, and one's loathing for the disastrous war that had loomed up on his watch, was no easy task; one solution was to devise theories by which the bureaucracy was actually functionally insubordinate, pushing its own ventures, refusing to give the president real advice on options, but only options that suited the services' purposes, and leaking information to the press whenever the elected president ruled against service interests. Theories of bureaucratic politics let the president off the hook. Some of the motivation imputed to the lower-level policymakers was inevitably true, and not such a new story. An expanding budget or agency usually increases the prospects of promotion and produces more gratification. In the private sector, it is similarly well understood in micro-economics that individual firms wish to pursue profits, and serve the consumer only because the workings of a competitive market force them to take consumer preferences into account, as the way to make this profit.

The real question for the military, or for the entire government, was always whether generals or admirals and bureaucrats were really so free to pursue their private or parochial goals and therefore to ignore the national interest. Although the "command economy" of government could most probably not address consumer demand as effectively as the market does for the private sector, the processes of the executive branch and the oversight of the legislative branch nonetheless provided many mechanisms by which the wishes of the voters, the will of the people, and the national interest, could still be implemented.

Most of the examples chosen by bureaucratic politics theorists came from the military, and indeed from the *American* military. There were a number of possible explanations for this. First, anecdotes were easier to obtain in American examples than in foreign countries, because the entire defense policy process in the United States has always been leakier and less respectful of the classification rules of secrecy. Related to this, it was easier to pick up stories told in English, rather than in some foreign tongue.

Another explanation is a bit more complicated, however. It was entirely possible that bureaucratic politics theories also explained the behavior of *enemy* military services, as the Soviet navy or the Chinese Communist navy would be looking for excuses to build ships, or purchase anti-ship missiles, etc. But if such potentially adverse navies were thus for no good reason augmenting their war-fighting capabilities, the United States Navy would then be facing a *real* threat, and not just an imaginary one. For bureaucratic politics theorists to be illustrating their analyses with adversary examples would thus have been to undercut their basic argument, that American defense spending was higher than it needed to be, that there was no real threat that the U.S. armed services were responding to.

Bureaucratic politics analyses thus probably captured more attention than they really deserved, in large part because they reflected personal feelings about the Vietnam War and the prospect of having to fight in that war. The arguments made were certainly fair, that military bureaucrats (and other bureaucrats) might *want* to serve personal agendas rather than the national interest; but what was left out were all the counter-levers that can be applied, in any government around the world, to steer results back toward the national interest.

FURTHER INTEGRATION

Theorists of bureaucratic politics were hardly the only opponents of the Vietnam War who shared the view that the separate military services preparing for conventional war were too concerned for their own independence and separate agendas. This criticism had been voiced before, during, and right after World War II. Its revival after Vietnam became a major driver for the congressional intervention in the Goldwater-Nichols Act.

As noted from the very outset of this chapter, the United States came out of its victory in World War II believing that a major problem of future conventional warfare was likely to be one of coordination—drawing together the Navy and Army, and the very much expanded Marine Corps that had emerged during that war, and the various component air forces. Some of such problems of coordination are the inevitable concomitant of exploiting specialties. For a navy or an air force to be most effective at what it does, it inevitably must offer less than the maximum of coordination with another military service doing what it does, and this is no different from the inherent problems of coordination between the Department of Justice and the Department of Agriculture, or at a university, the departments of English and Economics.

To paint all insufficiencies of coordination as selfish bureaucratic intrigues or mindless "organizational process" is to make the entire process look too pathological. Yet, as noted at the outset, the revolutionary lesson of *most* of World War II (before Hiroshima and Nagasaki seemed to impart a very new and different lesson) was that the conventional warfare balance between coordination and specialization had to shift, that more coordination was now becoming essential.

Whether insufficient progress in this direction was a major explanation for the American failure in Vietnam is debatable. As noted, the special feelings of political scientists about Vietnam may taint their perspective on that war.

Yet, to pick a much smaller example, the 1983 American intervention into Grenada showed very glaring examples of excessive autonomy in the four American military services participating in the operation.[40] In what seemed almost analogous to the Soviet–American lines drawn across 1945 Germany to avoid friendly-fire casualties as the last Nazi resistance was being overcome, the Pentagon had to draw a line across the tiny island of Grenada, a country smaller geographically than the District of Columbia,

to separate the Navy and Marine Corps sector to the north from the Air
Force-Army sector to the south. The lack of interoperability was so bad
that it at one point required that telephone calls be patched through ATT
switchboards back in New York to allow communications between the
two halves of the American effort.

Senator Barry Goldwater (R, AZ) was neither a dove nor a radical. He
had never doubted the justice of the American cause in Vietnam. He had a
well-deserved reputation for being generally quite sympathetic to the
American military. But after Grenada, he reflected the feelings of many
Americans: the time had come for legislative action to require greater coordination and "jointness" across the armed services.

The services resisted this effort. It is a fair statement that services will
always seem to be resisting pressures for coordination and integration.
Some of this will reflect nothing more than the fact that coordination can
always be overdone, that the benefits of specialization can be lost in the
process. Where resistance reflects more than this elementary caution,
where it is the product of bureaucratic turf-protection or simple inertia, it
is more easily condemned. But some of the accusations of such motiva-
tions may indeed be misplaced.

The Goldwater-Nichols Act was a major legislative attempt to overcome
the barriers to interservice coordination noted above. At the very top of
the structure, it added to the powers of the Chairman of the Joint Chiefs of
Staff, as compared with the separate service chiefs, adding the post of Vice
Chairman, and designating the Chairman as the principal source of military advice to the Secretary of Defense and to the President. At lower levels, it imposed requirements of joint-service experience for the promotion
of officers to higher rank. Analysts would generally agree that the Act contributed to the goal of "jointness" and integration, while they would at the
same time agree that the problems of separation have not been totally
solved.

THE "REVOLUTION IN MILITARY AFFAIRS"

Some of the demand for greater operational coordination of the military
services in conventional warfare stemmed from a demonstrable need for
such coordination, evident ever since World War II and affirmed in subsequent conflicts. By the 1980s, the emphasis on ever greater coordination—
the need to integrate and synchronize—took on a somewhat different

rationale. In the eyes of some military theorists, the greater *possibility* of
such coordination, emphasizing the use of computers and remote sensors
and enhanced communication systems, held the promise of reducing—
almost to the point of eliminating—the inherent confusion of the "fog of
war." Much of the enthusiasm for what became known as the "revolution
in military affairs" (RMA)[41] stemmed from the calculations of the future
of conventional war produced by both sides during the last decade of the
Cold War.

In fact, the Soviets were out in front of the Americans in *theorizing*
about the RMA, the concept of a "military revolution" stemming from
their apprehensions of what might be available to the United States and
its NATO allies, as the Reagan administration invested heavily in the
electronics and other technologies of what was labeled the Strategic Defense Initiative (SDI). If the chance of successfully defending American
cities against Soviet nuclear missiles was indeed very slim, Soviet military
leaders envisioned that the application of these technologies to the conventional battlefield in central Europe might provide the West with a
quantum leap in its conventional capabilities, tilting the military balance
decisively in favor of the U.S. and its allies. The fears outlined by Soviet
Marshal Nikolai Ogarkov, once translated into English, became a source
of instruction for American defense planners. In 1991, some of these Soviet fears then seemed to be realized—and the full potential of RMA was
seemingly demonstrated—as the American-led coalition in Operation
Desert Storm easily defeated the Soviet-equipped Iraqi tank forces of
Saddam Hussein.

Bringing to bear virtually real-time knowledge of the battlefield, in
precisely targeted attacks coordinating missiles, aircraft, and ground
forces, the RMA promised to transform conventional warfare. To begin
with, the United States and its allies (but especially the United States
since, in addition to being far ahead of the Soviets and Chinese in the battlefield application of information technology, it was also far ahead of
Britain, France, or Germany) might now actually have a clear edge in conventional warfare, after all the Cold War decades where this advantage
had been conceded to the Soviet bloc (because of the sheer numbers of
tanks and troops that the Communists could deploy, and because of the
central geopolitical position they held). All the earlier reasoning had required the addition of threats of nuclear escalation as a compensating
equalizer to respond to the supposed Communist advantage in conventional war. But now with the introduction of the RMA in the 1980s, or

124

especially in the 1990s after the dissolution of the Warsaw Pact and the breakup of the Soviet Union, it appeared that U.S. conventional forces held the advantage.

Second, closely related to this, the concomitant logic was that the United States might thus want to move away from the postures of "flexible response" involving an implicit threat of nuclear escalation, with the Russians conversely backing away from their endorsement of "no first use" of nuclear weapons. The side with the conventional disadvantage was necessarily reluctant to forfeit the nuclear card, while the side with the conventional advantage might wish to exclude nuclear weapons from the game.[42] After Desert Storm, for the first time since 1945, the United States found itself in a position where—viewed from an American perspective—nuclear weapons were losing their rationale.

The United States did not totally shift to an endorsement of "no first use" of nuclear weapons or formally renounce all threats of nuclear escalation threats, even though many American analysts contended that it was high time to do so. For some (like former Secretary of Defense McNamara), the inherent risks of an all-out escalation to a thermonuclear war had always seemed to outweigh any benefits; now the RMA seemingly made such risks altogether unnecessary, since U.S. conventional forces had become so dominant.

In actual practice, even after the Cold War, the United States, perhaps because of sheer inertia, or because of the inherent uncertainties of predicting conventional war outcomes, retained the nuclear escalation option. But the shift in emphasis within the military services was unmistakable: conventional war was once again the track to promotion; nuclear warfare assignments were not. If this had always been true for the Marine Corps and the Army, it was now similarly true for the Air Force, where duty with the Strategic Air Command, renamed Strategic Command, lost most of its luster, compared with involvement in tactical support for the conventional wars of the future. As confidence in achieving a decisive conventional victory increased, the Army and Navy were quite happy to shed themselves of "tactical" nuclear weapons.

Evolving American Popular Attitudes

As a third major consequence of the RMA, the promise of elegantly applied information technology, as demonstrated so aptly in Desert Storm, reinforced the general American leaning to low-cost war. The American *desire* to avoid casualties had been evidenced already in the protests against the Vietnam War, and in the elimination of compulsory military service. The advent of the RMA now seemingly endowed the United States with a greater *ability* to avoid such casualties.

It is very hard to be opposed to lowering casualties in warfare, since all our humane instincts support this. Our sense of morality may be troubled a bit more, however, when the *other* side suffers casualties, as the retreating Iraq Army was decimated on the "highway of death" in 1991, as only we and our allies escaped the human costs of war; the aftermath of Desert Storm thus induced a fair amount of speculation about possibilities of nonlethal warfare.

More broadly, the new technological possibilities embodied in the RMA made all of warfare seem a bit more remote, reducing the involvement of American human beings generally, raising issues and concern of a moral detachment, as Americans could have their country fight wars without becoming very much involved themselves, except as spectators.[43]

There are many moral and practical reasons for sparing one's population the horrors of being involved in war. But there are some political and moral problems that may emerge when, because of a reliance on a smaller number of professionals rather than a larger sample drawn from the entire country, and because of a reliance on the latest in technology, a country can go to war without the bulk of the population having their lives disrupted in the process.

A fourth consequence of the breakthroughs of the RMA, and the resulting enhancement of American conventional military capabilities, was to reinforce older American prejudices against multilateralism, against international organizations like the United Nations, and against allies in Europe or elsewhere. If American ground and air forces were now more than a match for the former Soviet Union, or anyone else for that matter, then the assistance of allies like France or Germany was no longer necessary. If the governments in Paris or Berlin were not inclined to go along with American policies in some crisis, so be it. From the 1950s through the 1970s, the United States might have needed allied help to hold back a Warsaw Pact onslaught. But in the post–Cold War world, with the application of breakthroughs in information technology, many Americans began to feel much less need for the support of such allies.[44] After 9/11, this resurgent unilateralism emerged in full form.

"MOOTW"

In the aftermath of the Cold War, military planners in the United States saw some risk of conventional war along the lines of Saddam Hussein's aggression into Kuwait. But the logic of "collective security" was that a resolute resistance to aggression ought to deter such actions in the future. America's apparently unprecedented conventional dominance raised the prospect that the Pentagon's vast conventional military capabilities might remain unused for longer periods of time. After Operation Desert Storm, who would presume to mount a direct military challenge to the United States?

An armed force that thus has to be ready for conventional war, but does not fight them much of the time, must always concern itself, if for no other reason than to serve the public well, about *other* missions it can perform. This concern to demonstrate the utility of conventional U.S. forces manifested itself during the last decade of the twentieth century with "military operations other than war" (MOOTW).[45]

The end of the Cold War, and the breakup of the Soviet Union, promoted a great deal of speculation about whether wars and military preparations in general might become a thing of the past. As the threat of a thermonuclear holocaust had been largely lifted from the world, so presumably was the prospect of tank battles and amphibious invasions, with some analysts seeing a much reduced role for the sovereign state more generally, and thus a much reduced role for military forces.

A debate about whether the end of the Westphalian system of separate sovereignties was at hand promoted speculation that "soft power" was about to transcend "hard power" in importance, with trans-boundary economic interactions and cultural interactions becoming more important than military power, just as "people power" was ostensibly becoming more important than the decisions made by states.

These post–Cold War expectations were challenged immediately, of course, by the example of Saddam Hussein's invading Kuwait. The resolute world response to this invasion had demonstrated that military forces were still required to fend off the aggressors of the world, and one saw the bizarre spectacle of the Pentagon reducing the size of conventional forces in 1990 even while it had to work overtime to prepare the counter to Iraqi aggression. If the precedent set by George H. W. Bush's "New World Order" was established well enough, however (the precedent that Woodrow Wilson's League of Nations had been designed—unsuccessfully—to maintain), the actual punishment for aggression would rarely have to be imposed, and the conventional military would still be a lot less in play than before.

Facing budget cuts and such predictions of a diminished relevance of military force, the search for "military operations other than war" would have seemed entirely predictable to anyone familiar with theories of "bureaucratic politics" by which every agency scrambles to maintain its budget and mandate, even when the real need for its services is diminishing.

In fact, however, the proposed new array of missions was not simply the result of the Pentagon's looking for an excuse to stay in existence. The array of real problems and issues emerging with the end of the Cold War indeed suggested a number of new functions that uniform forces alone could accomplish. Many of the material preparations for conventional war turned out to have great value in the other roles proposed now for the military. Beyond these warfighting capabilities were other qualities inherent in a competent military organization, not least of all the ability to receive an order dictating that people "be there at 0400" and to have everyone show up, possessing the right kit, and ready to move out in unison.

So the end of the Cold War did not render U.S. conventional forces obsolete. Instead it confronted them with a host of new tasks. The various missions here were sometimes all collected under the broad label of "peacekeeping," as many of them were conducted under the auspices of the United Nations Security Council. "Peacekeeping" in its narrower sense, as first practiced in the Suez Canal zone in 1956, had involved the use of conventional forces for interposition. Bringing along very little in the way of armament, but exercising their ability to move in unison and establishing a visible uniformed presence, battalions offered from the armies of nine UN members deployed between the opposing sides in the 1956 war of Egypt against France, Britain and Israel. The aim of this unique gambit was to make it difficult for the opposing sides to continue fighting a war, for fear of hitting the symbols of the world community.[46]

Unlike the model of collective security, international military forces did not align with either side, did not defend a "victim" against an "aggressor," but instead merely made war difficult or impossible by getting in the way. Rather than wearing a maximum of camouflage for effectiveness in combat, "peacekeeping" units altogether abjured camouflage by wearing United Nations light blue headgear and patrolling in vehicles that were painted white. Rather than achieving their mission by shooting (this would indeed have been the sign of the failure of the mission), they would achieve it by remaining in place.

While no United States forces (and no Soviet forces either) were to be so deployed during the years of the Cold War, NATO forces from Canada, Norway, Denmark and the Netherlands participated in such missions. Behind the scenes, the United States military's capacity for conventional war did play a substantial role, as the logistical requirements of such "peacekeeping" missions were handled in large part by the United States Air Force.

"Collective security" had amounted to a continuation of conventional warfare, with the important difference that the missions would be launched by an international mandate in response to an aggressor whose identity could not be identified in advance. But "peacekeeping" (a very useful misnomer) had amounted to something very different, the interruption of a conventional war that was already underway, by the internationally sanctioned deployment of a third "army" between the two that were at war, a third army not very prepared to fight, but symbolizing the world's desire for peace. A glance at color photographs of participants in these new missions would presumably tell which was which. The "peacekeepers" would wear blue hats or blue helmets. The participants in collective security would be in full camouflage and helmets for battle.

Other new missions for U.S. conventional forces in the aftermath of the Cold War exploited unique American logistical and command and control capabilities. In the wake of earthquakes or typhoons, "humanitarian assistance" frequently benefited from the nearby presence of an American aircraft carrier or air base. U.S. forces were employed to rush food and water to large numbers of people. Few governments or people objected to this use of American military forces.

But some of the new problems in the world after 1990 were more manmade. Ethnic strife erupted in many of the areas freed from Communist rule, destroying any illusions that Marxist indoctrination might somehow have eradicated the rivalries of the past. Ethnic conflict, most notably resulting from the breakup of Yugoslavia, produced new responsibilities for outside military forces, including those of the United States. The result would be labeled as "humanitarian intervention" rather than humanitarian assistance. The aim was to prevent one group from massacring another, to shelter minorities and escort them to safety, and, if the only way to end ethnic strife was through ethnic separation, to police the plebiscites held to determine whether a majority of any particular district wanted to belong to one country or to the other. Some of these new missions required an ability to engage in conventional violence when international authority was challenged, while others still depended heavily on the military's capacity for concerted movement and efficient logistics. Some entailed functions at such a small and local scale that they would have been better handled by military police rather than armored units, or by normal police instead of the military.

All in all, the attention paid to MOOTW in the 1990s thus reflected real needs, as well as bureaucratic searches for mission. The collapse of the Warsaw Pact and the Soviet Union had indeed made tank battles less likely in general. The needs of collective security nonetheless dictated that some conventional warfare capability be maintained. In truth with many traditional U.S. allies eager to trim their military budgets after the Cold War, being prepared for any large-scale conventional war fell more and more on the United States. But day-to-day business lay elsewhere—in addressing the disappointments to which the end of the Cold War gave rise and which kept the world in considerable turmoil.

RESPONDING TO 9/11

The persistence of terrorism qualified as one of those disappointments. During the 1990s, U.S. conventional forces were already finding use in the preliminary skirmishing with violent radical Islam—one thinks of the cruise missile attacks on al-Qaeda training camps in Afghanistan in 1996. But these operations remained peripheral, not even rising to the magnitude of normal guerrilla war. In efforts to thwart terrorists, military units would always be of some value, for example in guarding sensitive targets, but few analysts saw anti-terror as a *major* mission for conventional forces before 2001.

Before the al-Qaeda attack on New York and Washington, the dominant view was that terrorists would never wreak mass destruction. Their presumed purpose was to win sympathy for their causes, or to become governments themselves. Employing chemical or biological weapons, or nuclear weapons, against innocents seemed unlikely to advance such aims.

When confronting such non-WMD terrorist attacks, states put some considerable effort into locking up the weak spots, in making it more difficult for terrorists to highjack airliners. As noted, these protective efforts might generate some work for the "conventional" military as well. But until 9/11, the preferred solution was to ignore the discomfort imposed by such terrorism as much as possible, i.e., to frustrate the terrorist attempt to win attention and sympathy.

This all seemed a little analogous to the problem many parents face when their children are being bullied in the schoolyard. One advises the child not to break into tears when harassed by the bully, but to pretend not to be bothered, which, after a time, will lead the bully to shift to someone else as a target. If all the students behave this way, the bully may give up his sadistic inclinations, and perhaps do something useful like trying out for the football team. One's child will protest that it is difficult to hide the pain when being bullied, but one coaches the child on the importance of not giving away one's true feelings in the world of politics and strategy.

Societies were imperfectly capable of minimizing the visible discomfort they felt in face of terrorism, just as they were imperfectly capable of locking up all entry points at which terrorists could inflict pain, but, prior to September 11, 2001, the consensus might well have been that the problem was manageable, that terrorism was losing its ability to influence the flow of politics, and that no great military effort would be entailed here.

All of this changed drastically, of course, with the attack on the World Trade Center and on the Pentagon. Airplanes were hijacked here not to hold passengers hostage in order to get attention for one political grievance or another, but to employ such airliners as guided missiles to destroy major buildings, taking thousands of lives. Any notion that there was an inherent upper limit to the damage terrorists were willing to inflict was now disproved in a matter of minutes.

The terrorists now seemed immune to the normal deterrence of retaliation, with this being underscored by the fact that actual skyjackers all committed suicide by crashing the hijacked airliners directly into buildings. If terrorists could not be *totally* stopped by defenses (the previous assumptions about the terrorist challenge had assumed that skyjackers would, once in a great while, be able to bypass airport checks and seize an airliner), and if they could not be deterred, the concomitant was that the United States might have to initiate conventional warfare to penetrate the country from which they were launching their attacks, so as to root out their bases. If the outside world was later to question the American prerogative of launching preventive wars and preemptive attacks, the shock of the 9/11 attack had actually seen most of the world backing the American right to invade Afghanistan, since the Taliban regime in Afghanistan was openly hosting Osama bin Laden and the al-Qaeda organization.

Rather than entailing "military operations other than war," the terrorist menace, once it had moved to this higher scale of mass destruction and casualties imposed, thus substantially reactivated the primary mission of conventional forces: once again, as had been the case in World War II, the object of the exercise was to seize territory and terminate political threats to the American homeland. The subsequent debate on whether Iraq was also a part of the "war on terrorism," about whether the launching of a preventive war by the United States was *again* justified, did not address the general question of whether or not after 9/11 the U.S. conventional forces needed to be configured to engage in such invade-and-occupy missions. The only question was whether Iraq was really in this category of necessary target.

Some analysts of international politics had seen the rise of terrorism as one more illustration of the weakening of the state and by extension of the declining relevance of preparations for war. After all, the argument went, terrorism reflected the same social injustices and sense of deprivation that also drove forward the popular demonstrations of "people power." As transnational forces weakened and marginalized the prerogatives of Westphalian sovereignty, the same processes of economic interdependence that made separate countries less able to deal with economic issues also made the world more vulnerable to terrorist attacks.

But, when the terrorist attacks began to threaten the lives of tens of thousands of citizens, the response of the American government, or indeed of any other government so threatened, became very traditional again: it was to "rediscover" *conventional* war. What was new about much of the response to 9/11 was not the form it took, a use of air and ground forces, with support from the sea, in conventional warfare. What was new was the provocation, not conventional aggression by the armed forces of an opposing country, but a major terrorist attack. What was new, for Americans, was that United States conventional forces henceforth would have to *initiate* a conventional war, rather than responding in such a war. The political novelty of this might impose a major strain on how Americans see themselves, and on how the world sees the United States, but it did not really change the mission of conventional forces, for it was indeed a return to traditional military operations.[47]

In what is labeled as the "global war on terrorism," the phraseology was not as metaphorical or hyperbolic as in "war on poverty." In fact, the exercise of warfare as more narrowly understood was back.

SOME SUMMARY COMMENTS

To summarize some of the tendencies outlined here, conventional war has become much more complicated, in its interactions of weaponry, than it was before World War II, with the application of information technology eventually emerging as the preferred means of addressing such complications. During most of the Cold War, the deterrent implications of nuclear war overshadowed conventional warfare. As a consequence, such wars were fought much less frequently than they would otherwise have been— the period becoming, at least in some respects, the "Long Peace." Yet it was the mere preparations for the contingency of such wars that played a large role in sorting out the political confrontation between Communism and liberal democracy.

As the Cold War ended, the risks of nuclear war seemingly declined, but predicting the likelihood of conventional war proved elusive. According to some analyses, the physical capabilities for such warfare could find use in missions other than war. The struggle against guerrilla war and against more minor terrorism had already demonstrated the potential for such adaptations, even as the Cold War continued. Yet in Vietnam especially such demonstrations had come at a very high political cost. Because of the pain and frustration of guerrilla war, and for other reasons, Americans by the latter part of the Cold War had developed a fixed preference for minimizing the human exposure to combat and casualties that had traditionally characterized conventional warfare. At the end of this trail, the sudden increase in the level of destruction that terrorists were willing to inflict brought conventional warfare back to center stage, rather than being something that seemed as outmoded as Westphalian sovereignty.

The response to the new threats of terrorism thus hardly amounted to a marginalization of conventional armed forces, or of the traditional governments commanding them. Instead, the international organizations and nongovernmental organizations that had been touted to be such a major factor in the post–Cold War world became marginalized. Terrorism may indeed be one more transnational factor, but eliminating al-Qaeda's ability to launch strikes from Afghanistan entailed a *national* exercise in conventional warfare by the armed forces of the United States.

Notes

1. The new needs of interservice coordination emerging from World War II are discussed in Russell F. Weigley, *The American Way of War* (Bloomington: Indiana University Press, 1973), ch. 15.

2. On the surprising end of the war in 1945, see John Ray Skates, *The Invasion of Japan: Alternative to the Bomb* (Columbia: University of South Carolina Press, 1994).

3. On the transition from the old pattern of interaction between the War and Navy Departments, see Mark A. Stoler, *Adversaries and Allies: The U.S. Joint Chiefs of Staff, The Grand Alliance and U.S. Strategy in World War II* (Chapel Hill: University of North Carolina Press, 2000).

4. Some of the lessons learned by 1945 are outlined in Samuel Huntington, *The Common Defense* (New York: Columbia University Press, 1961), chs. 1–4.

5. Air Force thinking for the years after World War II is outlined in Perry McCoy Smith, *The Air Force Plans for Peace* (Baltimore: Johns Hopkins University Press, 1970).

6. Navy and Marine Corps resistance to unification is discussed at length in Townsend Hoopes and Douglas Brinkley, *Driven Patriot: The Life and Times of James Forrestal* (New York: Knopf, 1992), Vincent Davis, *Post-war Defense and the U.S. Navy* (Chapel Hill: University of North Carolina Press, 1966, and Paolo Coletta, *The United States Navy and Defense Unification* (Newark: University of Delaware Press, 1981.

7. On the World War II strategic bombing campaigns, see Robert Pape, *Bombing to Win* (Ithaca: Cornell University Press, 1996).

8. Bernard Brodie, *The Absolute Weapon* (New York: Harcourt Brace, 1946).

9. A very useful overview of the emergence of limited-war thinking can be found in Morton Halperin, *Limited War in the Nuclear Age* (New York: John Wiley, 1962).

10. See John Spanier, *The Truman-MacArthur Controversy and the Korean War* (New York: Norton, 1965).

11. On the Chinese communist statements welcoming the possibility of limited war, see Alice Langley Hsieh, *Communist China's Strategy in the Nuclear Age* (Englewood Cliffs, New Jersey: Prentice-Hall, 1962).

12. This distinction is well-developed in Glenn Snyder, *Deterrence and Defense* (Princeton, New Jersey: Princeton University Press, 1961).

13. Robert S. McNamara," The Military Role of Nuclear Weapons," *Foreign Affairs* 62, no. 1 (Fall 1983): 57–80.

14. On the risks of a thermonuclear holocaust, and whether they were worth running, see Scott Sagan, *The Limits of Safety* (Princeton: Princeton University

Press, 1993, and Bruce Blair, *The Logic of Accidental Nuclear War* (Washington: Brookings, 1993).

15. For arguments against accepting the high costs of a purely conventional defense, see Bernard Brodie, *Escalation and the Nuclear Option* (Princeton: Princeton University Press, 1966).

16. On the linkages here, see Ivo Daalder, *The Nature and Practice of Flexible Response* (New York: Columbia University Press, 1991).

17. For such criticisms of the substance of defense policy under Eisenhower, see William Kaufmann, *The McNamara Strategy* (New York: Harper and Row, 1964).

18. Bernard Brodie, *A Layman's Guide to Naval Strategy* (Princeton: Princeton University Press, 1942).

19. Brodie, *A Guide to Naval Strategy* (New York: Praeger, 1965)

20. On the role of scientists who had been involved in the Manhattan Project, see Herbert York, *The Advisors* (San Francisco: W. H. Freeman, 1976).

21. The role of the various social science brought to bear here is discussed at some length in Fred Kaplan, *Wizards of Armageddon* (New York: Simon and Schuster, 1983).

22. On West European reluctance to go along with MacNamara's preference for a wholly conventional defense, see Henry Kissinger, *The Troubled Partnership* (New York: McGraw-Hill, 1965).

23. Very useful on these issues are the works of John Lewis Gaddis, *We Now Know* (New York: Oxford University Press, 1998) and *The Long Peace* (New York: Oxford University Press, 1987).

24. Useful discussions of guerrilla war can be found in Sir Robert Thompson, *Defeating Communist Insurgency* (New York: Praeger, 1966), Nathan Leites and Charles Wolfe, *Rebellion and Authority* (New York: Markham, 1970), and Stephen Walt, *Revolution and War* (New York: Columbia University Press, 1996).

25. On the historical evolution of guerrilla warfare, see L. H. Gann, *Guerrillas in History* (Stanford, California: Hoover Institute Press, 1971).

26. The special role of Mao's theories on guerrilla warfare are discussed in Mark Elliott-Bateman, *Defeat in the East: The Mark of Mao Tse-Tung on War* (New York: Oxford University Press, 1967).

27. See W. W. Rostow, "Guerrilla War in the Underdeveloped Areas," *Department of State Bulletin*, August 7, 1971, pp. 233–238.

28. A useful review of the real nature of the Vietnam War can be found in Guenther Lewy, *America in Vietnam* (New York: Oxford University Press, 1978).

29. On the impact of memories of Vietnam on today's feelings in the U.S. military about the two political parties, see Charles E. Neu, *After Vietnam: Legacies of a Lost War* (Baltimore: Johns Hopkins University Press, 2000), Peter Feaver, *Armed Servants* (Cambridge: Harvard University Press, 2003) and David E.

Johnson, *Modern U.S. Civil-Military Relations* (Washington: National Defense University Press, 1997).

30. For a good example of such basically libertarian arguments, see the chapters by Walter Oi and Bruce Chapman in William M Evers, ed., *National Service: Pro and Con* (Stanford, California: Hoover Institution Press, 1990), 81–103, 133–144.

31. See Charles Moskos, *A Call to Civic Service: National Service for Country and Community* (New York: Free Press, 1988).

32. On the post-Vietnam malaise, see Robert Lieber, ed., *Eagle Entangled* (New York: Longman, 1979).

33. The American aversion to casualties is discussed in Steven Kull, "What the Public Knows that Washington Doesn't" *Foreign Policy* no. 101 (Winter, 1995–1996): 107–15, and Jeremy Rosner, "The Know-Nothings Know Something," *Foreign Policy* no. 101 (Winter 1995–1996): 116–29.

34. Karl Von Clausewitz, *On War* (Princeton: Princeton University Press translation, 1976), 370.

35. On the Falklands war, see Max Hasting and Simon Jenkins, *The Battle for the Falklands* (New York: Norton, 1983).

36. Alarmed views of the growth of the Soviet Navy can be found in Richard Fieldhouse, ed., *Security at Sea* (New York: Oxford University Press, 1989).

37. See Thomas C. Schelling, *The Strategy of Conflict* (Cambridge: Harvard University Press, 1960).

38. Some major examples of "bureaucratic politics" reasoning would include Graham Allison, *Essence of Decision* (Boston: Little Brown, 1971), Morton Halperin, *Bureaucratic Politics and Foreign Policy* (Washington: Brookings, 1973) and Richard Neustadt, *Presidential Power* (New York: New American Library, 1964).

39. A criticism of these theories can be found in Stephen Krasner, "Are Bureaucracies Important? (or Allison Wonderland)," *Foreign Policy* no. 7 (Summer 1972): 159–79.

40. For accounts of the Grenada intervention, see Mark Adkin, *Urgent Fury: The Battle for Grenada* (New York: Lexington Books, 1989).

41. On the "revolution in military affairs" or the "military-technological revolution," see Ron Matthews and John Treddenick, eds., *Managing the Revolution in Military Affairs* (New York: Palgrave, 2001).

42. On the shift to "flexible response" in today's Russian military doctrine, see Celester Wallander, "Russia's Strategic Priorities" *Arms Control Today* 73, no. 1 (January/February 2002): 4–6.

43. The escape from direct involvement in combat here is discussed in Edward Luttwak, "Where Are the Great Powers?" *Foreign Affairs* 73, no. 4 (July/August 1994): 23–29.

44. On the new American trend toward unilateralism, see Ivo Daalder and James N. Lindsay, *America Unbound* (Washington: Brookings, 2003).

45. A useful survey of "military operations other than war" can be found in Keith Earle Bonn, *A Guide to Military Operations Other than War* (Mechanicsburg, Penn: Stackpole Books, 2000).

46. The original strategic logic of "peace-keeping" is laid out in Larry Fabian, *Soldiers Without Enemies* (Washington: Brookings, 1971).

47. On the novelty of the United States initiating wars, see Betty Glad and Chris Dolan, eds., *Striking First* (New York: Palgrave Macmillan, 2004).

4. SHIELD AND SWORD
U.S. STRATEGIC FORCES AND DOCTRINE SINCE 1945

TAMI DAVIS BIDDLE

The Second World War ineluctably altered the position of the United States in the world. At the time of the attack on Pearl Harbor in 1941, the United States was still a careful and often reluctant player in international politics; by 1945 the Americans had taken a major role in the defeat of Germany, had brought Japan to its knees, and had developed the most daunting military arsenal the world had ever seen. The preeminent symbol of America's new role was the long-range bomber coupled with the atomic bomb. This pairing, which enabled monstrous destructive power to be delivered anywhere on the globe, was the nucleus of what would become the American postwar strategic force—poised to deter aggression or, in case of war, to inflict prompt and massive damage upon vital enemy assets. This essay will examine the evolution of that force over time, and the assumptions, influences, and bureaucratic dynamics shaping it.

The phrase "strategic forces" has not always been defined consistently and, especially since the end of the Cold War, has been the subject of debate. But perhaps the best way to bring clarity to the category is to place it in the context of Thomas Schelling's pioneering analysis of the use of force, and define it as "coercive force" that can be applied directly and promptly over long distances.[1] In other words, strategic forces offer their owners the power to hold at risk—from standoff distances—highly valued enemy assets. In the era predating heavier-than-air flight, powerful navies could sometimes attain this kind of coercive power through blockade (or the threat of blockade). The advent of long-range aircraft, however, created a new class of weapon that held the promise of threatening, directly and immediately, an enemy's most dearly held and important assets.

During the First World War, air power advocates touted the possibilities inherent in the "strategic bombing" of enemy "vital centers" (Americans at first called it "strategical bombing") in order to inflict direct pain on an enemy and induce his surrender via the threat of further pain.[2] The phrase "vital centers" was principally a euphemism for "cities," since modern conurbations held the valuable populations, factories, and communications/transport nets of industrial societies. In the Second World War the Anglo-Americans in particular utilized large strategic bombing fleets to batter enemy assets in an effort to induce the Germans and the Japanese to surrender.

After World War II, American strategic forces became synonymous with nuclear forces. Facing a daunting Soviet army that appeared to threaten Western Europe, and a growing Soviet arsenal that soon contained nuclear weapons, American decisionmakers countered by holding Soviet assets hostage to American nuclear forces. As the Soviets developed their own nuclear arsenal, the Americans had to respond in terms of targeting and doctrine. But even purely counterforce nuclear weapons (those aimed at Soviet nuclear weapons) were designed to ensure that the United States could continue to offer a credible, direct coercive threat to the Soviet enemy. Once the Soviet Union collapsed, American strategic forces were no longer associated principally with nuclear weapons. But there was—and is—no need to change the label, since the definitional underpinning remains: present-day strategic forces are those with the ability to threaten highly valued enemy assets, and to do so promptly, directly, and from long range. Indeed, United States Strategic Command (STRAT-COM), the post–Cold War successor to Strategic Air Command (SAC), has been invested with the responsibility for developing and overseeing a Global Strike Plan, including both nuclear and non-nuclear assets, "to deliver rapid, extended range, precision kinetic [nuclear and conventional] and non-kinetic [elements of space and information operations] effects in support of theater and national objectives."[3]

*   *   *

The nature of the predominant threat to American interests has, of course, been the principal factor determining the shape of American strategic forces. From the end of the Second World War through the fall of the Berlin Wall in 1989, that threat was perceived to be the Soviet Union and its communist ideology. The U.S.-Soviet rivalry became the focal point of American grand strategy, and the catalyst for the expansion and consolidation of American military might. Once that expansion commenced, it took on its own dynamic and was driven by domestic influences as well as external ones. The size and structure of American strategic forces was, and continues to be, influenced by prevailing ideas about the employment of military force, the development of science and technology, economic considerations, institutional preferences, bureaucratic momentum and conservatism, and interservice rivalries. These various elements have combined in different ways over time, but they have always been operative in setting parameters and shaping outcomes.

For American statesmen, a deep-seated desire to find stability and rationality in the American relationship with the Soviet Union was paralleled by an equally deep-seated mistrust of the closed, autocratic, "Godless" system of governance that took hold behind the Iron Curtain. This mistrust of the intentions of Soviet leaders, coupled with nagging anxiety about whether the Soviets might steal a march on the United States and gain an exploitable advantage in weaponry, was as much a driver in the Cold War arms competition as the actual size, shape, and nature of Soviet forces.

Over time, the U.S.-Soviet competition in strategic arms gained momentum and took on a life of its own, developing its own language and grammar, and its own self-sustaining elements. As time passed, this competition had less to do with the weapons themselves than with the larger political context around them. In other words, the weapons became a primary medium through which a grand narrative of intense political competition was played out. But this led to paradox and irony. If the internal logic of nuclear deterrence theory remained operative—if it remained the paradigm within which defense analysts and planners functioned—its connection to actual warfighting scenarios (and their political underpinnings) grew more tenuous over time, and ultimately became quite strained.[4] The more powerful and deadly the weapons became, the less useful they became, as weapons of war, to those who might have been inclined to use them. Yet the cost of developing, fielding, and updating this arsenal counted to mount and reached breathtaking heights. Between 1940 and 1996, the U.S. alone spent an estimated $5.5 trillion on nuclear weapons and their related delivery systems.[5]

In the United States, concerted efforts were made to provide for "limited strike" scenarios that would preserve options for the president in the event of a crisis, but these efforts were only partly successful at best. And, all through the Cold War, critics of nuclear policy understood not only the disconnect between rhetoric and reality, but also the crisis instability inherent in the structure of the nuclear arsenal. Fears of another 1914—the miscommunication, the reflexive mobilization, and the descent into disaster—weighed heavily on many minds. But none of this, however sobering, could rein in a competition that had gained so much momentum as to be unstoppable.

As the weapons lost value as weapons, per se, they continued to have value as symbols: of prestige, of technological prowess, of national power and identity. They implied "greatness" and thereby reinforced an identity of greatness for populations on both sides of the U.S.–Soviet divide. They reassured allies (even as they sometimes unnerved them), and they influenced domestic politics as the size of one's arsenal was read as evidence of "being ahead" or "falling behind." The overall political influence that was achieved by the possession of a vast nuclear arsenal is difficult to measure, but neither the existence of that arsenal nor the use of modern strategic bombers in non-nuclear roles prevented the United States from enduring a long and unpopular war in Korea in the 1950s, or from suffering a humiliating withdrawal, in 1975, from a war in Vietnam in which it had been directly involved for more than a decade.

From the earliest days of long range bombing, its advocates were inclined to assert or imply that it would be capable of winning wars on its own. But as recent history has shown, modern warfare is an immensely complex endeavor, and no single instrument of power on its own—either military or nonmilitary—is as effective in bringing about resolution as is an intelligent combination of several military and nonmilitary instruments. The "precision era" of strategic weaponry, which had its initial test during the 1991 Gulf War, renewed hopes that long range strike might become an omnipotent tool in war. Surely, conventional precision strike is proving to be infinitely more usable than nuclear weapons ever were, but the early returns—from the Gulf War, Kosovo, Afghanistan, and Iraq—introduce problems and complications into the idea that even an updated, high-tech form of strategic air power can be an independent war winner. It is too soon to say that the argument has been settled, though, and the more strident advocates of strategic air power surely will continue to work hard to prove their case, even as the U.S. Air Force continues to adjust to the joint warfighting environment facilitated by the 1986 Goldwater-Nichols Act.

Though we will never know if nuclear weapons were responsible for putting a boundary around the U.S.–Soviet antagonism, we must acknowledge that the United States and the Soviet Union never fought one another directly during the long years of the Cold War. As instruments of deterrence, U.S. nuclear systems had value. But this came at a cost, not only in terms of opportunities forgone but also in terms of domestic and international anxiety. Managing the U.S.–Soviet nuclear relationship was never easy, and at times—especially in moments of crisis—the beast seemed dangerously liable to escape its cage.

The sudden unraveling of the Soviet empire, commencing in 1989, necessitated a rethinking of the purpose, nature, and shape of American strategic forces. That process of rethinking and restructuring was only partially underway when a new, aggressive threat to American security emerged in the form of al-Qaeda–sponsored terrorism—terrorism animated by an opposition to modern Western ideals and American global influence. As this essay is being written, the work of transforming American grand strategy and strategic forces to meet this new threat is still in its early stages. Like the policymakers who struggled to understand the real nature of the Soviet threat in the immediate postwar years, American decisionmakers today are struggling to comprehend an enemy that is—in its motives and methods—alien and confounding. But understanding the enemy is the essential foundation of strategy, and is thus central to the shaping of future strategic forces.

Early Postwar Strategic Choices, 1945–1948

By the time the United Nations conference convened in April 1945, the United States was already in the midst of a brewing conflict with the Soviet Union. The Soviets had been wary allies of the Anglo-Americans: while the urgent threat of fascism had pushed Stalin into a marriage with the world's leading capitalists, there were few shared interests to hold the relationship together once the crisis had passed.

During the war, American military planners had identified their Soviet ally as the next likely threat to American security, but, in 1945–1946, hope still existed for a reasonable U.S.–Soviet relationship, and for a functioning, effective United Nations.[6] As the war in the Far East drew to a close, Americans at home longed for nothing so much as the return of troops still overseas, and the restoration of a normal, peacetime economy. Concerned about the stability of that economy, President Harry S Truman cut the defense budget radically. From a high of $81.6 billion in 1945, U.S. defense spending declined to $44.7 billion in 1946, and to $13.1 billion in 1947.[7] The demobilization reflected domestic political pressures and echoed past practice in a nation that still had large moats guarding its flanks. And the drastic paring back of the defense budget bespoke fears of recession in a nation whose memories were, understandably, still fixed on the recent experience of searing economic depression.

But these drastic cuts unnerved a military establishment that saw an ever-expanding array of international responsibilities falling into U.S. hands, especially as the British withdrew from a leading role in international affairs. The vast gap between funds and obligations led to fierce fights among the service chiefs for military resources. Debates over the size and strength of the military continued through the early interwar years, and events such as the crises in Greece and Turkey, the Czech coup, and the Soviet blockade of Berlin gave them added urgency. This clear evidence of a troubled and ever-deteriorating relationship with the Soviet Union placed an unusual focus on the U.S. nuclear deterrent. Although the Soviets had maintained a large postwar Soviet army (much of it for occupation duty), which was worrisome to postwar planners who assumed it might readily be redirected toward Western Europe, American strategists banked on the idea that this standing force might be offset to some degree by the existence of the U.S. atomic arsenal.[8]

Prior to 1948, however, that arsenal was small. The production of atomic weapons was extremely laborious and resource-intensive, and the meager output of such bombs was held as the nation's most closely guarded secret. In fact, the U.S. had only two atomic weapons in its stockpile at the end of 1945, nine in July 1946, thirteen in July 1947, and fifty in July 1948. These were bulky, 10,000 pound implosion bombs that were inefficient to deploy since they took thirty-nine men more than two days to assemble. They required a special pit and hoist for loading into aircraft that had been specially modified to carry them. Through 1948 the number of such modified craft was merely thirty—all based at Roswell Air Force Base in New Mexico.[9]

In a nation that was unwilling for political and economic reasons to maintain a large standing army, the strategic air force took on particular significance: it offered a way to trade American technological prowess for manpower. The idea of influencing events and fighting wars from the air was immensely appealing to a nation that had no armies on its borders and had great bodies of water to its east and west. To many Americans, air power seemed to offer a more efficient and effective way to fight (or deter) a war than the slower, more cumbersome (and more bloody) style of ground armies. And air forces seemed to come with few of the political risks and economic costs associated with large standing forces. All of this worked to the advantage of the U.S. Air Force, created in 1947, as it fought for influence—and for scarce dollars—in the late 1940s.

Strategic thinkers wasted no time in exploring and explaining the ways that both military planning and the use of force would be affected and indeed permanently changed by the advent of atomic weapons and long-range bombers. Bernard Brodie, an analyst at the newly born RAND Corporation, was one of the first to articulate the larger meaning of what he termed the "absolute weapon." The primary purpose of military forces would no longer be to win wars, Brodie argued, but rather to deter them. The old principles would have to be rethought and recast into a doctrine of nuclear deterrence.[10] But deterrence had to rest upon a credible threat of use. And forces had to be structured, as well, to accommodate the possibility that deterrence might fail. The military services knew well that the baton would be passed to them if the work of the diplomats and politicians came to naught, or if the enemy struck without warning. The lessons of the failed appeasement and tardy rearmament policies of the interwar years had not been lost on the leaders of the postwar world. All this meant that crucial decisions were required about the future structure, organization, and equipping of the American armed forces.

The Roles and Missions Debate

The new technologies of the twentieth century, and the additional ones on the horizon, caused heated competition for primacy with regard to the "roles and missions" of postwar armed services. Compromises were hard to reach, and nerves were easily frayed. Air Force leaders believed that they had established a firm hold on the strategic bombing role during World War II, and they had no desire to give it up or share it. After the test explosions of atomic bombs at Bikini Atoll in 1946, naval engineers concluded that they would need to construct new "flush deck" aircraft carriers that would minimize damage from the high winds of an atomic blast. The first flush deck was to be in a class by itself: a "supercarrier" bigger than any ship afloat, with the ability to launch aircraft weighing up to 100,000 pounds.[11] To the young Air Force, this looked like a potential encroachment into its own realm of responsibility. And, indeed, the Navy's most aggressive spokesman on the issue, Rear Admiral Daniel V. Gallery, wanted to prove that the Navy could become "the principal offensive branch of the national defense system, the one that will actually deliver the knock-out blows."[12] In the end the Navy did not manage to wrest the strategic bombing role from the Air Force, but if the Air Force remained the premier nuclear service during the early Cold War years, the Navy retained access to nuclear weapons for missions of special importance to sea warfare—and these missions would grow in the coming years.

In the nuclear age the Air Force rose quickly from a subordinate branch of the Army to the focal point of the American defense posture. Like the other services, it suffered from the rapid demobilization and decommissioning of equipment after 1945, but it began its climb to prominence in 1948 when the Berlin airlift brought it attention, and when, later that year, General Curtis LeMay took over the leadership of Strategic Air Command (SAC), the long-range bomber arm of the Air Force and home of the American nuclear deterrent. LeMay, who had been a prominent World War II field commander and then had overseen the Berlin airlift, transformed SAC from its desultory "hollow force" posture of the early postwar years into a highly capable organization with outstanding operational readiness.[13]

The notable prominence of SAC in the years after 1948 was suggestive of how Americans expected future wars to be conducted: they wanted their wars fought efficiently—exploiting American technological strength—and at a distance. As historian Lawrence Freedman has noted: "The requirements for effective punishment of an aggressor also pointed to an unambiguous and certain sanction capable of disabling any offender, inflicted with ease and at minimal cost to the forces of law and order. For both of these purposes airpower, combined with the added strength of atomic weapons, seemed eminently suitable."[14] As LeMay developed the capability of the U.S. nuclear deterrent, academic strategic thinkers, including Bernard Brodie, Herman Kahn, and Thomas Schelling, continued to work out the foundations of a full theory of nuclear deterrence and nuclear warfighting.[15]

By the autumn of 1947 nuclear planning had started in earnest; about a hundred urban centers in the Soviet Union were identified by military planners as potentially viable targets. Had air crews been asked to implement these early plans, however, they would have faced a host of difficulties. Intelligence was poor and maps of the vast Soviet territory were out of date. Crews would have had to fly into Soviet territory under cover of darkness and bad weather; they would have lacked weather data and would have faced featureless stretches of snow-covered tundra. Cities were the only targets that air crews would have had any hope of finding and striking.[16] In 1949 an ad hoc committee headed by Air Force Lieutenant General H. R. Harmon reported to the Joint Chiefs of Staff that even if all the bombs in the plan detonated on their aim points, it would not destroy the roots of communism, weaken Soviet leadership, or seriously impair the ability of the Soviet Union to take "selected areas" of Europe, the Middle East, and the Far East. Nonetheless, the Harmon Committee concluded that since this was the only available way of "inflicting shock and serious damage to vital elements of the Soviet war making capacity . . . the utility of its early use would be transcending."[17] LeMay understood what he was up against, and he sought to find every possible way to improve the readiness of his force, the intelligence element of war-planning, and, generally, the odds for his bomber crews.[18] If his SAC force was first and foremost to be a deterrent, it had to be a credible one. And it had to be an operational force in the event of war.

THE SOVIET ATOMIC BOMB, NSC 68, AND THE KOREAN WAR

Deep budget cuts and the heavy emphasis placed on nuclear weapons assured that when the Soviet Union exploded its own nuclear device in the late summer of 1949, the event would be viewed by Americans as a particularly pressing crisis. So long as the Americans had been able to hold a rough balance between their own nuclear arsenal and the large Soviet army, there was some hope for uneasy accommodation in Europe. But the Soviet A-bomb seemed to endanger not only that tenuous balance of power, but also American territorial integrity and homeland security. In the summer of 1950 the Joint Chiefs would add a new, first priority target set to its planning: "the destruction of known targets affecting the Soviet capability to deliver atomic bombs."[19]

The Soviet bomb, which made its appearance sooner than most Americans had anticipated, came in the wake of high tensions over Berlin and the failure of a final political settlement for Germany. It was followed, in short order, by the fall of the Chiang Kai-shek government in China, and the ascendance of Mao's communists. In the United States, this succession of deeply unsettling events led not only to domestic instability in the form of McCarthyism, but also to the creation of an extraordinary document—National Security Council paper number 68—which would set the terms of American participation in the ever colder Cold War.

The tone of NSC 68 was grave. State Department planner Paul Nitze, the document's principal author, argued that the United States was in the midst of an unavoidable and profoundly consequential struggle against an implacable, omnivorous foe. The opening section, titled "Background of the Present Crisis," noted ominously, "The issues that face us are momentous, involving the fulfillment or destruction not only of this Republic but of civilization itself. They are issues which will not await our deliberations. With conscience and resolution this Government and the people it represents must now take new and fateful decisions."[20]

The solution proposed in NSC 68 was a major expansion of American strength, in terms not only of nuclear weapons, but of conventional weapons as well. In his summary, Nitze wrote: "we must, by means of a rapid and sustained build-up of the political, economic, and military strength of the free world, and by means of an affirmative program intended to wrest the initiative from the Soviet Union, confront it with convincing evidence of the determination and ability of the free world to frustrate the Kremlin design of a world dominated by its will." He added: "Such evidence is the only means short of war which eventually may force the Kremlin to abandon its present course of action and to negotiate acceptable agreements on issues of major importance."[21] Interpreting the famous document, historian Marc Trachtenberg has explained: "The policy of NSC 68 was, in its own terms, a "policy of calculated and gradual coercion"; the aim was "to check and to roll back the Kremlin's drive for world domination." To support such a policy, it was important to go beyond merely balancing Soviet power and build up "clearly superior overall power in its most inclusive sense."[22]

The Korean War, which began in June 1950, seemed to confirm American fears of Soviet influence around the globe, as well as the picture NSC 68 had painted of an aggressive Soviet foe. At the outset of the war, SAC bombers were moved overseas to reinforce the Far Eastern Air Force (FEAF), under the overall control of General Douglas MacArthur. The commander of SAC's Fifteenth Air Force, Major General Emmett O'Donnell, requested MacArthur's permission to firebomb the industrial centers of northern Korea. He thought MacArthur should announce that the communists had forced him, against his wishes, to use "the means which brought Japan to its knees."[23] This approach reflected traditional air force warfighting concepts, as well the experience of the World War II Army Air Forces in the Far East: fire raids would undermine the enemy's will and capacity to fight, and waging them immediately would intensify their psychological effect.[24]

But MacArthur chose not to escalate so dramatically, and O'Donnell chafed under orders that "diverted" his bombers to tactical support of ground troops. In late summer of 1950, bomber missions were expanded to include interdiction strikes, and attacks on North Korean industry. Following the Chinese entry into the war in November, MacArthur permitted attacks on a wide range of targets—including fire raids on North Korean cities—in order to do everything possible to stem the tide of Chinese advance. Incendiary attacks on Pyongyang in early January 1951 burned out 35 percent of the city. Training for atomic missions went forward, but authority for actual use of A-bombs was withheld.[25] The wider use of bombers, however, did not translate into discernible progress toward victory, and as time passed American B-29s became increasingly vulnerable to North Korean air defenses.[26]

Airmen were frustrated by the constraints and politics of the limited war, which kept enemy supply sources outside North Korea (in China and the Soviet Union) permanently off the target lists. After the war LeMay would argue, "We never did hit a strategic target."[27] Though MacArthur's successor, General Matthew Ridgway, generally restrained the use of bombers, he continued to use them to maintain pressure on Chinese troops. But negotiations made little headway, and in the meantime overworked air crews began to suffer morale problems and high abort rates.[28] LeMay's lament highlighted a development that would occur over and over for airmen: weapons designed for strategic missions would be repeatedly pulled into battlefield use in American wars of the late twentieth and early twenty-first centuries.

In May 1952 Ridgway was replaced by General Mark Clark, who was interested in using aircraft to compel movement in the negotiations. Clark authorized a FEAF-designed "air pressure" campaign designed to destroy military targets so situated as to have a "deleterious effect upon the morale of the civilian population actively engaged in the logistic support of enemy forces."[29] The first targets were the North Korean hydroelectric power plants; FEAF destroyed 90 percent of North Korea's hydroelectric potential in less than a week. Still, however, negotiations dragged on, with little apparent change in the enemy's determination to hold out.

The campaign's last phase was particularly dramatic. In March 1953 FEAF targeters began to study North Korea's irrigation system. His patience exhausted, Clark told the Joint Chiefs that he was prepared to breach twenty dams, which would flood areas producing approximately 250,000 tons of rice. In the event, the campaign went forward more modestly, with mid-May attacks on three dams situated near railway lines. (Officially, these could be designated "interdiction" attacks against those railway lines—although neither FEAF planners nor the communists perceived them that way.) The raids flooded nearby villages and rice fields. The North Koreans worked vigorously to repair the Toksan dam site in particular. Two more dams were struck in June, and planners anticipated further strikes. These, however, were delayed pending the outcome of armistice negotiations. Those talks resulted, shortly thereafter, in a truce.[30]

There has been no consensus on the dam raids' actual impact on the conclusion of the war. If the impact of the raids was hard to specify, however, its effect on Korean civilians was not. In 1954 Brigadier General Don Z. Zimmerman, FEAF Deputy for Intelligence, argued, "The degree of destruction suffered by North Korea, in relation to its resources, was greater than that which the Japanese islands suffered in World War II." He believed that "these pressures brought the enemy to terms."[31] But the events bearing on North Korea's eventual acceptance of armistice terms have been debated at length by historians and political scientists. Many have been inclined—both at the time and afterward—to interpret President Dwight Eisenhower's implied nuclear threat to North Korea as the key to war termination. But other historians have argued that the impact of the threat has been exaggerated, and that it was more likely the death of Stalin in March 1953 that ultimately cleared the way for an accommodation between the North Koreans, the Chinese, and the United Nations.[32]

USAF planners wished to put the experience of the Korean War, which they viewed as an aberration, behind them. FEAF's 1954 final *Report on the Korean War* argued that the Korean conflict contained so many unusual factors as to make it a poor model for planning. In particular, the USAF wished to distance itself from the close air support operations that had been a main a feature of the war. The report stated: "Because FEAF provided UN ground forces lavish close air support in Korea is no reason to assume this condition will exist in future wars."[33]

The Korean War had served to make manifest many of the recommendations called for in NSC 68. This meant not only a build-up of American military forces across the board, but an institutionalization of them—including a formalization of the bureaucracy for running them.[34] At the same time, the American nuclear arsenal continued to develop in important ways. After President Truman had concluded, finally, that the prospects for the international control of nuclear weapons (embodied in the failed Baruch Plan) were negligible at best, he decided that the alternative lay in a strong nuclear arsenal. By the autumn of 1949 he had approved a first round of significant increases in the size of the arsenal; a year later, in the early stages of the Korean War, he approved a second increase. In January 1952 Truman approved yet another increase, "amounting to a 50 percent increase in plutonium production and 150% in uranium 235."[35]

Prior to the war, and in response to the Soviet test of an atomic bomb, Truman had ordered work to proceed on a potentially much more powerful "hydrogen" bomb. This decision was made despite the protests of some prominent scientists, including Robert Oppenheimer, the principal architect of the first atomic bomb. But Truman felt that since he could not prevent the Soviets from going ahead on such a project, he had to ensure that the United States would keep pace. The Americans exploded their first hydrogen device in the Pacific in 1952.

Hydrogen bombs introduced a revolutionary change into the U.S. weapons arsenal, since "fusion" allowed for the creation of far larger bombs than did the "fission" principle of plutonium and uranium weapons. What Oppenheimer considered a dangerous and unnecessary ramp-up in the early nuclear arms race, Truman found politically necessary. Even if it was difficult to conceive of political stakes that would justify the use of such massive and destructive bombs, Truman felt he could not afford to place the United States in the psychologically disadvantageous position of *not* having them if the Soviets did. The logic and internal dynamics of nuclear deterrence thus began to take on their own momentum—a momentum that would be increasingly at odds with objective, Clausewitzian analyses of interests and stakes in war.[36]

Not wishing to be left out of the nuclear revolution, the U.S. Army devoted considerable effort and funding to guided missile research and atomic energy programs; in particular, the Army was interested in tactical surface-to-surface missiles capable of carrying nuclear weapons.[37] Indeed, there was no small amount of competition between the services over who would own ballistic missile programs. While the Navy poured its attention and resources into the Polaris submarine project, the Army focused on a liquid-propelled intermediate range missile called the Jupiter. Because of the constant and sometimes heated arguments between the Army and Air Force over ballistic missile ownership, Secretary of Defense Charles Wilson would impose, in 1956, a range limit of 200 miles on future Army-based missile systems.[38]

Critiquing the Truman Administration's willingness to open the floodgates by late 1950, Cold War historian John Lewis Gaddis has observed: "There was in the administration very much a sense of direction without destination—of marching forthrightly forward into unknown areas, without any clear sense of what the ultimate objective was, how long it would take to achieve it, or what it would cost."[39] Dwight D. Eisenhower would bring a different mindset to the creation of U.S. national security policy, and the structuring of national military forces.

STRATEGIC FORCES IN THE EISENHOWER ERA

Eisenhower had been deeply displeased by the radical swings—from severe austerity to overindulgence—in the Truman Administration's defense budgets, and he was determined that, during his tenure, national security would be placed on a more predictable and consistent foundation. Eisenhower's key concern was that the nation might divert so much of its economic might and attention to defense as to turn itself into a "garrison state"; ultimately this would corrode and undermine the very wellspring of American robustness and success. To avoid this outcome, Eisenhower opted for a "New Look" in defense: a policy that would place heavy reliance on a combination of nuclear strength, strong intelligence, and covert operations against American enemies.[40]

Eisenhower's Secretary of State, John Foster Dulles, articulated the nature of the new defense posture in a speech to the Council on Foreign Relations in 1954. He argued that the best way to deter aggression was to "depend primarily upon a great capacity to retaliate instantly by means and at places of our own choosing."[41] The press began to refer to the Eisenhower policy as one of "Massive Retaliation." This was the administration's means of coping with a serious threat while watching the fiscal bottom line—the latter being a task that Eisenhower believed his predecessor had signally failed to do.

In the early 1950s the Soviet threat was considered so dangerous that the administration, the Joint Chiefs, and the Air Force all examined—on several occasions—the possibility of waging preventive war against the Soviets.[42] The weighty concern underlying such deliberations was the fear that the Soviets would, as soon as it was feasible, attack the United States with nuclear arms. And this fear was itself derived from the ideological rhetoric of the Soviet Union, which preached that the dynamics of class conflict would force a battle between communism and capitalism—a battle that was inevitable and unavoidable. In the end, though, the

Eisenhower Administration rejected all preventive war options. It did not, however, rule out *preemptive* attack against the Soviets. Indeed, NSC 68 had condoned preemption, arguing that it was the only feasible way of reliably deterring nuclear war or fighting it in such a way as to preserve— to the greatest extent possible—American territory and the American people. A March 1955 National Security Council report would offer a list of indicators that were to be interpreted as specific evidence that a Soviet attack on the United States was "certain or imminent." President Eisenhower repeatedly made clear that Russia must not be allowed to strike the first blow.[43]

Technological prowess would allow for a reduction of expensive manpower-oriented defenses. Eisenhower's predilection stemmed from an instinctive fiscal conservatism, and a faith in his own abilities as military commander and political leader. The Eisenhower defense budgets remained steady at about 9 percent of GNP throughout the president's two terms, much of the funding going to the Air Force—and SAC in particular.[44] As political scientist and defense analyst Scott Sagan has pointed out, "SAC's capability to strike rapidly—preempting Soviet nuclear attacks against the United States and Western Europe—was absolutely critical" to the successful implementation of the 1955 nuclear war plan.[45]

After Korea, Air Force leaders were anxious to reassert their priority: preparing for strategic air war against the USSR. The funding allotted to the services as a result of the Korean War had greatly increased SAC's size and strength; now, more than ever, SAC's mission reigned supreme in the USAF. General LeMay was appointed Vice Chief of Staff in 1957 and Chief of Staff in 1961; in 1964 three-quarters of the Air Staff's upper echelon came from SAC. Between 1954 and 1962 the United States' total nuclear arsenal underwent phenomenal growth, from 1,750 to 26,500 weapons. SAC, which controlled the majority of them, planned to deliver them in a "massive pre-emptive bomber assault." Other contingencies received little attention. Despite the political upheaval in Southeast Asia in the 1950s, the *Air University Quarterly Review* published (in the whole of the decade) only two articles relating air power to insurgency movements there.[46]

Especially because many planners feared, initially, that the aggression in Korea in 1950 might be a feint or a prelude to a Soviet move in Europe, the Korean War had the effect of galvanizing and institutionalizing the North Atlantic Treaty Organization. The Eisenhower administration also expanded the number of nuclear weapons available to NATO commanders: between 1952 and 1958 that number grew from 80 to more than 3,500.

In 1956, Secretary of Defense Charles Wilson directed that the Joint Chiefs should plan that, "in a general war, regardless of the manner of initiation, atomic weapons will be used from the outset." A year later, President Eisenhower had begun the process of providing for "predelegation": pre-authorization for theater commanders to employ nuclear weapons under a range of emergency conditions. Eisenhower believed that deterrence would be bolstered by maintaining the threat of unconstrained nuclear war, and by leaving to the imagination of Soviet policymakers the kinds of situations that might prompt such a response from the Americans.[47] In preparation for possible nuclear war in Europe, the U.S. Army reorganized itself into "pentomic divisions" designed for greater dispersal on the battlefield. The U.S. Army in Europe focused on a single goal: to fight off any advance by the Soviets beyond the limits of the Iron Curtain. The tactical and operational guidance for carrying out that task would occasionally shift over the years, but the goal itself would remain steady and unquestioned.

Domestically, the Army took on a major responsibility for homeland defense through the NIKE air defense program. The technology for this grew out of the air defense systems developed during the Second World War. By the early 1950s the Army was fielding the NIKE AJAX missile, but concerns about whether this would provide adequate protection against a massed Soviet attack led to the authorization of a new missile, the NIKE HERCULES, in 1953. By 1958 the Army was fielding the new system. At the height of this air defense program in the 1960s, the Army deployed 145 NIKE HERCULES batteries, which were run by both Regular Army and National Guard units. These sites were phased out as the system was inactivated in the 1970s.[48]

Once the Soviets had achieved their own nuclear capability, the central problem for American defense planners was to make the U.S. defense posture as credible and robust as possible. The development of a Soviet strategic air force and intercontinental ballistic missile (ICBM) program posed increasingly complex challenges to U.S. defense planners. From the first, the Soviets had expressed deep interest in the science of ballistic missiles; indeed, the Soviets had been close observers of German rocketry during World War II.[49]

In the early Cold War years the Soviets sought to catch up as quickly as possible in the realm of atomic weapons, and to master the technology that would allow such weapons to be placed on powerful long range missiles. They had no wish to find themselves held hostage to the Americans, politically, because of the American nuclear arsenal. They desired a force capable of deterring American aggression, and they spared no effort or expense to achieve it. Soviet spies penetrated the Manhattan project, thus providing vital information that would speed the production of a Soviet bomb. In addition, the Soviets worked hard to master the science of the hydrogen bomb.[50]

In the absence of any trust between the two superpowers of the postwar era, the situation quickly evolved into a classic "security dilemma," wherein any action taken by one party to improve its defensive posture is perceived by the other party as provocative, aggressive, and offensive in nature.[51] As the Soviets developed their arsenal, the Americans felt it necessary to prevent them from achieving a "first-strike" capability by maintaining a credible "second-strike" force able to survive an incoming Soviet attack and deliver a retaliatory blow. This meant preventing the Soviets from being able to launch an attack on American strategic forces that would be so devastating as to preclude the possibility of equally devastating return fire. This posture, which the Soviets naturally sought as well, became the bedrock of nuclear age deterrence. But the inescapable dynamic in this situation—the ongoing need to prevent an enemy first-strike capability in an environment defined by the instability inherent in the "security dilemma"—was bound to create pressure for continual advances and improvements in weapons and capabilities. And this would establish a spiral bounded only by technological limits and economic constraints.

Two major U.S. studies done in the 1950s, the Killian Report of 1955 and the Gaither Report of 1957, both focused on the need for a robust, survivable nuclear deterrent. Dispersal of bombers, alert systems, acceleration of ballistic missile programs, and overlapping responsibilities through the emerging "strategic triad" all helped to accomplish this aim.[52] In general, Eisenhower and his advisers were convinced that the Americans had strategic superiority over the Soviets. Others in the strategic community were not so sanguine about that, however. The Killian report, named for its chairman, Massachusetts Institute of Technology President James R. Killian, was the work of the Technological Capabilities Panel (of the President's Scientific Advisory Committee). It warned in February 1955 of a potential weapons gap between the U.S. and the USSR, and drew attention to the increasing Soviet ICBM program.[53] In response, in August 1955, the National Security Council recommended that the ICBM be identified as a "research program of the highest national priority, second to no others unless modified by future decision of the President."[54] The report also helped to spur the creation of a sophisticated spy plane, the U-2; in just eighty days, twenty-three Lockheed design engineers had created a high-altitude reconnaissance plane that would be invulnerable to Soviet anti-aircraft fire.[55]

The Gaither Report of 1957 was set in motion by the president's desire to assess the strategic situation. Early in the year, the Soviets had added two bombers to their inventory, the Bison and the Bear; in addition, the general dynamic of the tense Cold War struggle seemed to call for ongoing assessment. Chaired initially by H. Rowan Gaither of the Ford Foundation, the panel's work was completed under Robert Sprague, a veteran of the Killian panel. The distinguished scientists participating predicted that if the situation were not addressed, the Soviets might bring themselves into a position to achieve a first-strike capability through their ICBM program. They recommended increased missile development, research into defensive programs, and a campaign to provide fallout shelters and increased public awareness of the nuclear threat.[56]

Both of these reports made it more difficult than it otherwise would have been for Eisenhower to hold diligently to his own instincts in the nuclear realm, and to expand American forces at a careful and deliberate pace. And it was surely the case that the Soviet launch, in October 1957, of the Sputnik satellite provoked a domestic outcry in the US that resulted in the acceleration of a great number of defense, and defense-related, programs. Historian Walter McDougall has observed astutely: "Sputnik challenged the assumptions of American military and fiscal policy, and thus seemed to have scary implications for American security and prosperity. It involved a romantic but eerie enterprise—space travel—that Americans had come to associate, thanks to Hollywood science fiction, with sudden and irresistible horrors." He added, "Therefore, the response to Sputnik was not just random clamor, or a manipulated panic, but the chaotic product of several waves, their crests and troughs overlapping to reinforce alarm one week and confused inertia the next."[57]

There is no question that the events of the 1950s—and, more importantly, the interpretation of them by American policymakers—created responses that would have a long lasting effect. Writing in the early 1980s, the authors of the Harvard Nuclear Study Group would observe: "These shocks prompted momentous and rapid changes in U.S. nuclear forces and strategy. Twenty years later U.S. nuclear forces and strategy remain largely in the mold set in the early 1960s."[58]

By the late 1950s, the U.S. investment in intercontinental ballistic missiles had begun to pay dividends. Despite technical challenges (including some spectacular flight-test failures), halting progress was made—fueled by the fear that the Soviets might otherwise gain a disproportionate advantage in this realm. The final years of the Eisenhower administration saw the extensive undertaking that was the ICBM launch-site construction program. During the second week of September 1959, after a SAC crew had successfully launched an Atlas training missile—the Air Force declared the ICBM program operational, and one of the three missiles then located at Vandenberg Air Force Base in California was placed on strategic alert.[59] The administration proceeded apace with its long-range missiles, even if that pace was never quite as quick as the public, the media, and the Congress would have preferred. Although the U-2 flights were "irregular and spotty" in their photographic coverage of Soviet territory, they indicated no deployed Soviet ICBMs at all.[60] Even so, the pressure of events in the 1950s meant that the general trajectory charted by Paul Nitze in NSC 68 would be followed, even if Eisenhower had taken issue with aspects of that crucial report. The tendency for Americans to seek security through the possession of arms—especially strategic arms—would be reinforced, expanded, and intensified.

In the 1950s, the Navy felt that it had to pay attention to the ever-expanding Soviet submarine threat to the sea lanes between the U.S. and Europe in particular. A brilliant naval engineer named Hyman Rickover led the way to an increasingly nuclear-powered U.S. Navy. In 1952 the keel of the first nuclear powered submarine, the U.S.S. *Nautilus* was laid; she went to sea in January 1955. By the end of the decade the Navy was working on the Polaris system for submarine-launched ballistic missiles. The first Polaris vessel, the *George Washington*, set out on her first operational deployment in November 1960. By the summer of 1962, Congress had authorized construction of more than forty ballistic-missile launching submarines. The initial program was the precursor to the equally successful Poseidon and Trident missile systems.[61] Though the submarine fleet certainly broke with the traditional set of naval functions, submarine-based ballistic missiles gave robustness to the American nuclear deterrent. Since they were very hard to detect and hit, they guaranteed that the United States would retain a strong second-strike nuclear capability even if the Soviets proved able to launch a successful first strike against land-based U.S. bombers and missiles.

As time passed, strategic planners sought to field increasing capabilities for "blunting" Soviet nuclear systems so as to reduce the ability of the Soviets to damage or destroy American nuclear assets. In light of improved intelligence, SAC targeting was, by the mid-1950s, increasingly oriented to "counterforce" targets—specific military and industrial installations, as opposed to "countervalue" targets—enemy cities. But it was not until the end of the decade that SAC had all the technology and intelligence necessary to implement a true counterforce strike. Until then, SAC targeting combined a concentration on critical counterforce targets with important industrial and governmental centers. Planners believed that holding these assets at risk would deter the Soviets and, in the event of war, the destruction of these targets would undermine the enemy's ability and will to fight. LeMay sought to find a warfighting doctrine that would allow him to do the maximum amount of damage to the Soviet military-industrial complex in the shortest possible time, thus maximizing both surprise and shock.[62]

Some of LeMay's critics have suggested that he was so determined to keep SAC from being caught on the ground in war, and so distrustful of civilian authorities, that he was prepared—in a crisis—to take into his own hands the decision to launch his force. Some have even asserted that he was looking for an excuse to go to war, and was deliberately provocative with SAC overflights of Soviet territory.[63] These criticisms stem from concerns that are not wholly unfounded. LeMay did worry a great deal about the ability of his force to react instantly to a Soviet launch, and he did have antagonistic relationships with some civilian authorities. In addition, U.S. overflights of Soviet territory were a source of profound irritation and anxiety to the Soviet Union. LeMay was surely prepared to be aggressive with the Soviets, and to accept as much responsibility as the national command authorities were willing to give him. But it is useful to remember, too, that LeMay respected the principle of civilian control of the military, and that he had, as a World War II field commander, sent constant letters of condolence back home to grieving parents. A desire to avoid being surprised by war is not the same thing as a desire to start a war. LeMay was faced with a profound challenge: he had to maintain a strike force on the tiptoe of readiness, and yet keep it reined in—well inside the political constraints on national strategy. This tension made his job the most demanding and difficult one in the U.S., save for that carried out by the U.S. president.[64]

By 1955, when the U.S. nuclear stockpile was 2,280 bombs, an American atomic attack was expected to cause the loss of 118 out of 134 Soviet cities, and to kill 60 million people. In the late summer of 1960, the Eisenhower administration created the Joint Strategic Target Planning Staff (JSTPS) to consolidate the military services' nuclear war-planning efforts. The Staff's Single Integrated Operational Plan (SIOP) was completed in December. It called for a massive strike using some 2,244 bombers and missiles, carrying 3,267 weapons yielding more than 7,800 megatons. Execution of the plan would have killed approximately 285 million people in the Soviet Union and the People's Republic of China.[65] As historian David Rosenberg has pointed out, "SIOP-62 represented a technical triumph in the history of war-planning. In less than fifteen years the United States had mastered a variety of complex technologies and acquired the ability to destroy most of an enemy's military capability and much of the human habitation of a continent in a single-day. SIOP-62 incorporated operational choices that aimed to reduce the friction of war, coordinate and protect bomber forces, and integrate bomber and missile forces at the cusp of two eras in warfare." But, Rosenberg added, it was also inflexible, and "with little basis in political and military realities."[66]

SIOP-62 was a manifestation and culmination of the principles that LeMay had inculcated into SAC, and that had come to guide U.S. nuclear planning. It was designed to ensure effective deterrence, and to provide for a prompt and massive assault on the Soviet Union in the event that a war did come. LeMay had been asked to prepare to fight and win a nuclear war if necessary, and this was how he planned to do it. He was determined that his crews would not be caught on the ground, and that they would successfully find their way to as many Soviet targets as possible. But if the plan looked daunting to the Soviets, it very likely would have proven unwieldy and "self-deterring" to American policymakers in a moment of crisis. The dynamics that drove the SAC planning process took nuclear war-planning in a direction that gave statesmen few options other than a massive strike—a strike that would have had grave consequences for all the world's peoples.

From 1945 to 1974 the United States had no detailed national nuclear weapons employment policy. NSC 30, the 1948 U.S. guidance on atomic warfare, concluded that, "in the event of hostilities, the National Military Establishment must be ready to utilize promptly and effectively all appropriate means available, including atomic weapons, in the interest of national security and must plan accordingly." It pointed out that the "decision as to the employment of atomic weapons in the event of war is to be made by the Chief Executive when he considers such decision to be required."[67] This very general guidance gave the military the authority to plan for nuclear war—planning that was embodied in a special annex to what became the annual Joint Strategic Capabilities Plan (JSCP). Under President Eisenhower, guidance remained general and vague; indeed, the Eisenhower administration discouraged the development of constraints on nuclear war-planning.[68] General LeMay was happy to take advantage of the leeway that his commander-in-chief was willing to give him.[69]

As plans for nuclear war grew more complex and more dependent on the timing of attacks and bomber routes to targets, any assumption that presidential control could be fully maintained grew less and less robust. There is no doubt that, even under the best circumstances, launch procedures would have been liable to confusion brought on by the need to make profoundly consequential decisions under exceptionally tight time constraints. It is surely not inconceivable that events might quickly have slipped from the control of politicians and into the hands of the military—just as they had during the First World War under the demands of complex mobilization schedules. The operational details of the war plan would have affected its execution. This circumstance, which did indeed allow LeMay to concentrate authority in his own hands, was unsettling in that it pulled war-planning further and further from the political realities that shape the way states actually enter into wars. SAC's desire to prevail led to war plans that were large and unwieldy, and contained few options for limited strikes.

Defense analysts, policymakers, and military officers became increasingly concerned that enemy states might be able to slide underneath the nuclear threshold and compromise American interests and security. Indeed, three prominent Army officers, Generals Matthew Ridgway and Maxwell Taylor (both former heads of the Eighth Army in Korea and, later, Chiefs of Staff), and Lieutenant General James Gavin, a talented officer serving as the Army's director of research and development, expressed their disagreement with Eisenhower's strategic policy in books they wrote.[70] Other analysts raised their voices as well; of Henry Kissinger's widely read 1957 book, *Nuclear Weapons and Foreign Policy*, Gordon Dean wrote, "the book was perhaps the first to examine the postwar world comprehensively, applying an understanding of nuclear technology and military strategy to political questions and showing the interrelationship between force and diplomacy."[71]

As it was, Eisenhower had in fact begun to bolster American forces across the board by the end of his presidency. But the shift did not prevent John F. Kennedy from making defense an important campaign issue in 1960, or from arguing, ultimately, that the U.S. required a program of "Flexible Response" in order to continue to deter the Soviets effectively and indefinitely.

Kennedy also was able to argue that the U.S. was facing a "missile gap" with respect to the Soviets, who, as we have noted, had invested heavily in ballistic missiles as a delivery system for nuclear weapons. Soviet claims to have outpaced the U.S. in this realm were an attempt, through blustery rhetoric, to try to close the frustrating distance between themselves and the Americans with respect to nuclear arms production. But Eisenhower would not contradict the missile gap thesis in any detail because he did not wish to reveal the extent of his knowledge about the Soviet nuclear systems—to do so would have been to compromise the valuable, highly-secret U-2 reconnaissance overflights of the Soviet Union. Indeed, it was the protection of this secret that prompted Eisenhower to insist, initially, that the U-2 aircraft shot down over the Soviet Union in May 1960 was merely a "weather plane."[72]

Kennedy was able to capitalize on the missile gap issue, as well as growing concern about the credibility of a "Massive Retaliation" strategy in a complex strategic environment, including scenarios where the use of nuclear weapons would have been unwarranted and irrational. Eisenhower's critics made several key points. First, they argued that a stable deterrent balance was emerging between the Soviet Union and the United States (and its NATO allies), and that this stability should be accepted and promoted to the greatest extent possible. Second, they argued that at the level below nuclear weapons, a similar sort of balance should be kept: the U.S. should maintain substantial conventional forces in being to deter the use of Soviet conventional forces—and also to cope with threats to U.S. interests clearly below the nuclear threshold. The latter would preclude the president having to make a choice between resorting to nuclear weapons or doing nothing at all. This call for a spectrum of forces was designed to give U.S. policymakers the widest possible range of tools for deterring enemies and defending American interests.[73]

Strategic Forces in the Kennedy Era

When President John F. Kennedy entered the White House in January 1961, he wanted to introduce some important changes to American policy making. One of the realms he sought to reform was the Pentagon. He brought into his cabinet, as Secretary of Defense, the young Robert McNamara—a former chief executive at Ford Motors who had applied sophisticated managerial skills to bring success to that company. The bright and energetic

McNamara plunged into the pressing issues of American security, and, in line with the premises of Flexible Response, he sought a nuclear deterrent that would be credible and robust without being destabilizing. In addition, he sought to develop the kinds of forces that could operate beneath the nuclear threshold, and thereby prevent the Soviets from gaining influence through limited wars, intimidation, or blackmail of American allies.[74]

McNamara was discomfited by the nuclear war plans presented to him early in his tenure. The growing Soviet weapons arsenal, the increased ability to locate specific targets in the Soviet Union, and the expanding array of American technologies and delivery systems all had combined to produce nuclear war plans that guaranteed large strikes against the Soviet Union and China. McNamara found the result unsettling, and he set out to impose some changes. He sought, first of all, to improve the national command and control system that linked national authorities to the forces in the field. Specifically, he sought a strategic force "to be of a character which will permit its use, in event of attack, in a cool and deliberate fashion and always under the complete control of the constituted authority."[75] If the terms "cool and deliberate" were overly optimistic regarding what was possible in the throes of crisis, they nonetheless highlighted what McNamara believed was a pressing problem inside the world of war-planning. His initial efforts in this regard would find echoes later as subsequent secretaries of defense would try to develop similarly controlled options for the presidents they served.

In addition, McNamara sought to pull the United States and the Soviet Union out of their increasingly deadly nuclear escalation. He announced, in June 1962, a policy of "city-avoidance." He argued that planning for nuclear war ought to be approached in the same manner as would planning for conventional war, and that, to the greatest extent possible, the targeting of the enemy's civilian population ought to be avoided. The Kennedy Administration hoped this would give the Soviets an incentive to avoid targeting American cities. The Pentagon estimated that U.S. casualties could be reduced by a factor of ten if the Soviets could be persuaded to avoid cities in the event of a nuclear exchange.[76] McNamara also revealed a strong early interest in "damage limitation"—an interest that led him to advocate, initially at least, civil defense measures, continental air defense, and ballistic missile defenses.[77]

Ultimately, McNamara's attempt to bring the planning and execution of nuclear war closer to that of conventional war was a failure—however

well-intentioned it may have been. Some critics feared that it might lower
the threshold for the use of nuclear arms in crisis. And the Soviets, who remained deeply wary of U.S. intentions, suspected it might be a strategy for
a "first strike." One Soviet strategist argued: "A strategy which contemplated attaining victory through the destruction of the armed forces cannot stem from the idea of a 'retaliatory' blow; it stems from preventive
action and the achievement of surprise."[78] The co-location of military bases
and cities further confounded the problem. An additional headache to Mc-
Namara was, ironically, the Air Force's embrace of the new strategy. They
had wanted, on their own, to move away from a city-oriented posture to
one that held a very wide array of Soviet targets at risk; the endorsement of
"no cities" by the Secretary of Defense seemed like a green light for the
funding of a range of new (and expensive) "counterforce" programs.[79]

McNamara remained intent on giving the chief executive some options
in the event of nuclear war, even as he backed slowly away from the "no-
cities" rhetoric. During his tenure he also lost much of his early tendency
to emphasize strategic defenses.[80] Instead, he increasingly stressed the
mutually-deterring element of a situation in which two super-powers possessed nuclear weapons. He argued that nuclear parity, however rough,
was a stabilizing element in the relationship between the United States
and the Soviet Union. McNamara thus sought to place an emphasis on
avoiding nuclear war entirely, rather than avoiding cities in the event of
nuclear war. As historian Lawrence Freedman has pointed out, the new
emphasis on "assured destruction" was embraced "to warn of the dangers
of nuclear war rather than to describe how a nuclear war should be
fought." Just as importantly, McNamara would come to use the concept as
a standard—a measurement of sufficiency—through which he might
bring the escalation of the arms race under some degree of control within
the Pentagon and the wider defense community.[81]

"Mutual Assured Destruction" (with the disturbingly ironic acronym
MAD) is perhaps the strategic idea most strongly associated with the Mc-
Namara era—even though the conditions leading to MAD had developed
prior to McNamara's tenure at the Pentagon, and would remain there after
he had left. After the Cuban missile crisis of October 1962, McNamara recognized that the very prospect of mutual suicide had done the most to ensure a peaceful outcome for this most dangerous of Cold War crises: the
stakes were high, but the imperative to avoid nuclear war was even higher.[82]

Soviet Premier Nikita Khrushchev had placed intermediate-range nuclear weapons in the Soviet satellite state of Cuba in an attempt to redress

the imbalance of forces between the U.S. and the Soviet Union—particularly the embarrassment of U.S. Jupiter intermediate range ballistic missiles (IRBMs) on the Soviet doorstep, in Turkey, and the ongoing American threat to the communist, pro-Soviet regime of Fidel Castro. (The latter had been highlighted dramatically the previous year with the failed "Bay of Pigs" Operation.) IRBMs just off the coast of Florida would, Khrushchev assumed, make Castro largely invulnerable to U.S. hostility and threats, and would help to compensate for the Jupiters. Khrushchev's plan was to slip the missiles into Cuba under the nose of U.S. reconnaissance and make them operational before they were discovered. It was a bold and risky plan, but one that appealed to Khrushchev's propensity for high-stakes gambles. The gamble failed, however, as American intelligence officials discovered the Soviet plan through U-2 overflights.[83]

Without question, the thirteen-day "Cuban Missile Crisis" was the most serious and dangerous face-off between the two superpowers during the long years of the Cold War. While the divided city of Berlin had been and would remain a serious irritant to the Soviets, and the cause of much East-West tension throughout the Cold War, U.S. strategic forces would be raised only once to the second-highest level on the "Defense Condition" scale (DEFCON 2)—and that was in October of 1962 in the midst of the Cuban crisis. Both sides sought a peaceful way out of the situation—but both needed to avoid capitulation, embarrassment, and loss of face. After intensive debate, Kennedy Administration officials chose to cope with the situation by imposing a naval "quarantine" on Soviet ships bound for Cuba. This sober approach, while hardly risk-free, was far more manageable than the air strike option that General LeMay and some other Kennedy advisers urged.

The sensible choice of a quarantine proved an enlightened response. That, and some important back-channel diplomacy promising the withdrawal of the Jupiters and a U.S. pledge not to attack Cuba in the future, brought a peaceful end to the crisis.[84] The fact that it could be resolved without shots being fired was a tribute to clear-headed statesmanship, ingenuity, good luck, and the sobering effect of worst-case scenarios. The episode highlighted the need for an overhaul of the U.S. command and control system for strategic forces, including improved communication with the Soviet Union. The establishment of a National Military Command Center in June 1962 was followed, after the October crisis, by an updating of the White House Situation Room's command and control capabilities, including a direct link to the National Security Agency (the nation's principal collector of communications and electronic intelligence) at Fort Meade, Maryland. Both the expansion of U.S. listening posts overseas and the advent of reliable satellite reconnaissance led to the coordination and enhancement of both intelligence and warning information.[85]

If some of the consequences of this daunting crisis were salutary, some would contribute to further instability. The outcome was widely perceived as a "victory" for the United States; the Soviets saw it as unfavorable to themselves, and they emerged from it determined to make an exceptional effort to meet and even exceed U.S. levels of weapons development, procurement, and deployment: "Soviet leaders became determined never to let a humiliation like the Cuban Missile Crisis happen to them again. They began a substantial (3%-4% a year) and sustained increase in defense spending, strengthening their military capabilities across the board. In the late 1960s the Soviets carried out a dramatic increase in their nuclear forces comparable to what the U.S. had undertaken in the first half of the decade."[86]

For the Americans, maintaining a viable, credible second-strike force would continue to be the principal aim of U.S. nuclear strategy throughout much of the 1960s. Placing an emphasis on Assured Destruction enabled McNamara to try to bound the spiral of weapons procurement: he believed that once the Soviets and the Americans had reached a point where they could impose catastrophic damage on one another, large numbers of additional forces made little sense in terms of logic or strategy. Outside of McNamara's attempts to keep nuclear planning grounded in logic and linked to a broader conception of strategy, however, were all the other imperatives that seemed to impel momentum in the U.S.–Soviet arms race. These included mistrust, misperception and cognitive error, competitive rivalry, cultural identity, domestic politics, the dynamics of the U.S. military industrial complex, the pace of technological change, and the paradoxical internal dynamic of nuclear deterrence theory. No work of history of the era has ever been able to capture these elements so brilliantly as filmmaker Stanley Kubrick did in 1964, with his silver-screen parody of the nuclear dilemma, *Dr. Strangelove, Or How I Learned to Stop Worrying and Love the Bomb*.

McNamara, who stayed on as Secretary of Defense after President Kennedy's death in 1963, was able to persuade President Lyndon Johnson to cap U.S. strategic forces at a thousand Minuteman ICBM launchers and forty-one missile submarines. He canceled the Skybolt air-to-surface missile, resisted Navy proposals to develop a system to track and destroy Soviet Submarine-Launched Ballistic Missiles (SLBMs), and denied the Air

Force authorization to proceed with a new, advanced, manned strategic bomber. On the other hand, McNamara authorized work on multiple independently targetable reentry vehicles, (MIRVS) for some ICBMs and SLBMs, and agreed to keep some 600 of SAC's B-52 bombers on active duty.[87] The Americans pursued MIRVs for essentially the same reasons that Truman had pursued a hydrogen bomb: to attempt to keep the United States ahead in the strategic arms race, and to preclude the possibility that U.S. strategic forces would be left in a disadvantageous position if the Soviets sought out the new technology on their own. With mutual distrust between the superpowers so entrenched, and with the Soviets consistently refusing to countenance domestic verification of any arms control arrangement, the scope for meaningful progress in this realm remained limited. Still, many critics have lamented the fact that the Americans never sought a comprehensive prohibition of MIRVs, arguing that the Soviets might have honored it since the effort to keep up with the U.S. technologically was costing them heavily.

Though the Kennedy-Khrushchev relationship was initially very blustery, some progress was made on a few fronts. In 1961 President Kennedy had established the Arms Control and Disarmament Agency to give a point of focus to efforts scattered across a variety of government offices. In August of 1963, following a famous speech by Kennedy (in June) on the need to find ways to cope with the arms race, the Limited Test Ban Treaty was signed. It outlawed nuclear explosions in the atmosphere, under water, or in outer space (underground testing was still permitted).[88]

Back to Asia: Kennedy, Johnson and the War in Vietnam

In the summer of 1964 President Johnson engaged U.S. forces directly in the Vietnamese civil war, fearing that a failure to do so would signal to allies and domestic political challengers that he was "weak on communism." Johnson and his advisers counted on being able to quell the insurgency principally through the use of coercive air power. Thus, between 1965 and 1968 the "Rolling Thunder" bombing campaign worked in tandem with an increasing commitment of American ground troops. But sophisticated efforts to coerce and to punish through air power had little discernible impact, and the efforts of American ground troops to search for and destroy insurgency forces proved slow, costly, and frustrating. An ideological battle that pitted North Vietnamese communists and South Vietnamese insurgents against South Vietnam's indigenous army and the American forces supporting that army, the war was, until its late stages, unconventional in nature—even though the Americans tried hard to fight it as a conventional war. The enemy did not rely on sophisticated industrial power, or on an advanced, mechanized army to achieve its aims. In addition, key enemy sources of supply came from the Soviet Union and China, both of which were off-limits to U.S. target planners, since Johnson had no wish to fight the war in a way that would risk expanding it into a direct conflict with the major communist powers.[89]

If the Vietnam War was ultimately a losing cause for the Americans, it nonetheless tested American force projection capabilities, and placed heavy demands on American conventional forces. New technologies for precision bombing were honed. By 1972 the Air Force was in a position to use new precision-guided munitions, including electro-optically guided bombs and laser guided bombs. This development would profoundly affect future use of air power. These new munitions greatly increased accuracy, and, during the Linebacker I air campaign (from May to October 1972), they were used to attack bridges and other pinpoint targets. The Air Force also implemented an effective long range navigation system (LORAN) for North Vietnam. Like its precursor, the SHORAN system used in Korea, it enabled aircraft to determine their position with a high degree of accuracy. It was not, however, as effective as its Korean War predecessor since the distances from its transmitters in South Vietnam were longer than the distances covered by SHORAN in Korea.

Fighting an able and increasingly sophisticated opponent in the skies over Vietnam also pushed the Air Force to constantly refine its tactics and technology for penetration and survivability. Sophisticated jamming equipment helped neutralize the effect of improved North Vietnamese radar; and agile evasion tactics helped Air Force and Navy pilots evade SA-2 Surface-to-Air missiles (SAMs). Developments in electronic warfare, including the use of EC-121 aircraft and Navy ships, enabled U.S. forces to track Russian-supplied MiG fighters and alert pilots to their presence. Command and control, routing, and escort and support tactics evolved constantly.[90]

But Vietnam's bitter lesson was that technological overmatch does not always guarantee military and political victory. As was the case in Korea, the Air Force saw its most sophisticated aircraft, including strategic bombers, drawn down into the tactical fight. In North Vietnam there was no true "center of gravity" that American forces could readily attack and destroy. And interdiction against an enemy that needed little more than a few days' supply of rice was an exercise in frustration and futility.[91] The insurgents could control the pace of conflict: when the pressure was raised on them, they could simply merge back into the social fabric and wait for an opportune moment to resume their struggle. By late 1967 most of the targets on the Joint Chiefs of Staff's target list had been destroyed; by the end of the war the U.S. Air Force had dropped some 6,162,000 tons of bombs on Vietnam—vastly more than had been dropped by the Allies in all of the Second World War. None of this caused the insurgents to stop their efforts, or to modify their aims in ways that would have been politically acceptable to the United States.[92]

JOHNSON, NIXON, AND ARMS CONTROL

Though preoccupied by the Vietnam War, the Johnson Administration nonetheless oversaw the 1967 Outer Space Treaty, which obligated the U.S. and the Soviet Union to refrain from placing weapons of mass destruction into earth orbit, on the moon, or on other celestial bodies. (The Seabed Treaty of 1971 would set up a similar proscription against placing weapons on the ocean floor.) In addition, the Johnson Administration was able to celebrate the Nonproliferation Treaty of 1968. This was an initial, high-priority attempt to gain some control over the worldwide spread of nuclear weapons. Non-nuclear signatories agreed not to obtain nuclear weapons, and nuclear signatories committed themselves to not providing them. Non-nuclear powers were promised help, however, in the development of nuclear power for peaceful purposes. A number of states chose not to sign the NPT, including France, China, Israel, Brazil, India, and Pakistan.[93]

As the war in Vietnam progressed, the Soviets took advantage of American preoccupation to accelerate their own nuclear build-up, mentioned above. To address this, and to extend McNamara's desire to impose some ceiling on the nuclear weapons spiral, President Johnson initiated a process that would pay dividends in the realm of arms control. For just a few hours in late June 1967, Johnson met with Soviet Premier Alexsei Kosygin, who was to address the United Nations. Meeting in New Jersey, the two men took the opportunity to discuss the issue of the strategic arms race.

This brief "summit" put in place the initial groundwork for what would later become the Strategic Arms Limitation Talks (SALT).[94]

Johnson had helped to lay a foundation in arms control that the administration of President Richard Nixon would build upon during its tenure in office. In 1972 an international convention was signed prohibiting the development, production, and stockpiling of biological weapons. Two years later the U.S. Senate ratified the convention and finally ratified the 1925 Geneva convention outlawing the use of (but not production or stockpiling of) chemical weapons.[95] The most important treaty of 1972, however, was one resulting from the initiative taken by President Johnson in 1967. In late May 1972, President Nixon met with his Soviet counterpart, Leonid Brezhnev, to sign the first treaty resulting from SALT.

What became known as "SALT I" had several parts. It prohibited the deployment of antiballistic missile systems except at two sites, each containing no more than 100 intercepter missiles. And for a period of five years it limited the U.S. to 1,054 ICBMs and 44 SLBM boats. The Soviets were likewise limited to 1,618 ICBMs and 62 SLBM boats. The tradeoff for the higher limits afforded the Soviets was that there would be no limit placed upon U.S. bombers or forward-based systems. Within these constraints, each side was allowed to substitute newer weapons for older ones, and was able to mix weapons (SLBMs for ICBMs, for instance) within constraints. SALT I was perhaps more meaningful as an initial step in an important direction than as a detailed agenda for serious constraint. But a wary U.S. Senate, concerned that the Nixon Administration had been too generous, ratified SALT I only after Senator Henry Jackson (D, Washington) introduced an amendment demanding that in follow-on agreements the two sides would have to adhere to the principle of "essential equivalence."[96]

Many commentators have argued that the United States missed a key opportunity to impose meaningful limitations on nuclear weapons at this point by failing to prioritize and push for a ban on MIRV tests at the time of the first SALT agreement. While Richard Smoke acknowledges that it was not clear how interested the Soviets were in this, he has argued that they had expressed *some* interest in MIRV limitation, and that therefore it might have been possible to hammer out a "package agreement, restricting ABMs and halting MIRV tests." He has explained too, though, that the nature of the U.S. military industrial complex would have made this an uphill climb because the Poseidon and Minuteman III test programs were by then underway: "Thousands of people, billions of dollars, and huge organizations were committed to pushing them as rapidly as possible."[97]

The Ongoing Evolution of Nuclear Strategy in the 1970s

NATO never seriously attempted to match the Soviet conventional threat in terms of manpower. Instead, it relied on the U.S.-provided "nuclear umbrella" to deter the Soviets by threatening the security of their homeland. Worried that the Soviets would not find a U.S. nuclear threat credible in all contingencies, the Americans lobbied for European acceptance of "Flexible Response." After determined efforts by Robert McNamara, NATO adopted this as its strategic posture in 1967, although only reluctantly, since members feared doing so might lower the bar to war. NATO and the Warsaw Pact engaged in "Mutual and Balanced Force Reduction" (MBFR) talks through the 1970s, but to little useful end. Enhanced technologies were envisioned as a potential solution to imbalance; some of these were embraced, including a new generation of anti-tank guided missiles, but others, like the "enhanced radiation weapon," ("neutron bomb") were not.[98]

As the Vietnam War drew to a close, Nixon understood that the public mood gave him little scope to argue successfully for the maintenance of clear nuclear superiority. As a result, he opted for what he termed "strategic sufficiency," which, as historian Steven Rearden has pointed out, was "an elastic term that strategic planners in the Pentagon interpreted as including all the elements required to achieve their basic objective of assured destruction."[99] Like Kennedy, Nixon did not want to be left in a position in which large attacks on Soviet cities (and the resulting mass casualties) would be his only strategic option if faced with a serious nuclear challenge. Even though McNamara had sought to provide the president with a range of options, there remained none below the level of a major counterforce attack, and such an attack would itself have been massive. Nixon also wished to address a number of other concerns he had with nuclear strategy, in particular the maintenance of credible "extended nuclear deterrence" to NATO partners in Europe, and the possibility that Assured Destruction might ultimately be threatened if the Soviets combined strategic defenses with highly potent offensive forces.[100] Some of this was folded into the SALT process. But the issues needed to be addressed doctrinally, and through force modernization as well.

All of this resulted, ultimately, in National Security Decision Memorandum 242 (NSDM 242) of January 1974, presented by Secretary of Defense James R. Schlesinger and thus known as the "Schlesinger Doctrine." It offered "a series of measured responses to aggression which bear some relation to the provocation, have prospects of terminating hostilities before general nuclear war breaks out, and leave some possibility for restoring deterrence."[101] In the fashion of McNamara, Schlesinger was making another attempt to bring real options—in the form of planned, limited nuclear strikes—to the President. If NATO partners largely accepted the Schlesinger Doctrine as a necessary updating of extended deterrence, some in the United States argued that the further development of limited options would be destabilizing and would lower the threshold to nuclear war. But Schlesinger countered that nuclear deterrence would remain robust only if the forces involved were actually *usable* forces; if the U.S. nuclear posture remained so large and unwieldy as to be unusable, its value as a deterrent would be unacceptably undermined. He argued further that his doctrine was not destabilizing because it did not offer meaningful "damage limitation"—the kind that would raise Soviet suspicions that the Americans were seeking a first-strike capability.[102]

Once again like McNamara, Schlesinger moved forward with the U.S. MIRV program, extending it to large portions of the ICBM and SLBM forces. This was tied in part to another pillar of Schlesinger's thinking: the attack on Soviet industrial assets, and, concomitantly, the prevention of Soviet economic recovery in the aftermath of an attack. As Scott Sagan has pointed out, the "counter-recovery" strategy provided clear guidance to planners: the capability to destroy 70 percent of the Soviet industry that would be needed to achieve economic recovery after a nuclear exchange. It would, for the next six years, remain the "highest priority" for war planners.[103]

NSDM-242's quest for a secure deterrent that would also provide options for control in the event of a nuclear exchange would be updated again in 1980, as Presidential Directive 59 (PD-59) drawn up by Secretary of Defense Harold Brown for President Jimmy Carter. Like NSDM-242 before it, this new directive sought to offer a range of options for the "controlled" application of nuclear power against a "broad spectrum of targets." If, privately, Brown was not entirely convinced that nuclear war could be controlled once it had been unleashed, he nonetheless felt—like those before him—that he had an obligation to provide the president with options that fell somewhere between capitulation and all-out countercity warfare. PD-59 also attempted to incorporate into nuclear targeting an increased focus on Soviet perspectives and political vulnerabilities, in particular the Soviet command and control infrastructure central to the coherence and cohesion of the regime.[104]

When President Nixon left office following the Watergate scandal, President Gerald Ford took up the set of international responsibilities that included arms control. In November 1974 he met with Brezhnev to sign the Vladivostok accord, pledging numerical ceilings (to be specified in accordance with future negotiations) for all strategic launch vehicles and vehicles carrying MIRVs. The ceilings were disappointingly high, but the two leaders felt they had set the foundation for a new accord, in particular because they reached a compromise allowing the inclusion of heavy bombers in exchange for the exclusion of forward-based systems (U.S. nuclear systems based in NATO nations). But the good intentions of the Vladivostok accords did not, however, translate into prompt progress at the negotiating table: U.S.-Soviet negotiations stumbled and stalled, and the plan for a second SALT accord, which would be in force until 1985, receded into the distance.[105] In the end, an accord was not signed until June of 1979— and then was never ratified by the U.S. Senate. Cruise missile technology, a new Soviet bomber (the "Backfire" bomber), and the Soviet deployment of MIRVs placed hurdles in the path of the negotiators. Despite the "détente" of the early 1970s, mistrust and competitiveness continued to hinder the U.S.–Soviet relationship. Equally frustrating was the failure to put any qualitative constraints on the arms race, so new weapons simply became faster, more accurate, more lethal, and more numerous. As Richard Smoke has pointed out: "Thanks to MIRVS, the number of separate nuclear warheads that each side could rain down on the other side increased from between one and two thousand as SALT was getting underway to approximately ten thousand in the 1980s."[106]

Gerald Ford, who had pardoned Richard Nixon and thus still seemed to have a faint air of Watergate about him, lost his bid for the presidency in 1976. The new President, Jimmy Carter, was committed to arms control and gave his new Secretary of State, Cyrus Vance, full rein to engage in talks with the Soviets with renewed energy and vigor. But Vance's intensified efforts were unable to move the SALT process forward quickly. SALT II was finally submitted to the Senate in the summer of 1979; it was a long and complicated accord that seemed to fully satisfy no one. Its main provision limited the U.S. and the Soviet Union to an aggregate of 2,400 launch vehicles each (bombers, ICBMs, and SLBMs) to the end of 1981. Thereafter they would be limited, to 1985, to 2,250 each.[107] American liberals felt that it was only a half-hearted effort, while conservatives complained that it conceded far too much to the Soviet Union. A group of moderates in between was prepared to fight for the treaty, but their prospects were hurt by the Soviet invasion of Afghanistan in late December 1979. Early the next year, the administration withdrew the treaty from Senate consideration, and forbade American athletes from competing in the Moscow Olympic games, scheduled for July. Carter, however, announced that he would honor the terms of the agreement. When the new U.S. president, Ronald Reagan, came into office in January 1981, he also announced that he would uphold the terms of the treaty (even though he had pledged, during his campaign, that he would not resubmit it to the Senate).

The fate of the SALT II treaty was due largely to the growing concerns in the American defense analytic community about the Soviet strategic weapons build-up through the 1970s. Even though the Soviets had participated faithfully in the SALT process, they had—within the wide bounds of the initial treaty—continued a process of weapons expansion and modernization that had commenced in the aftermath of the Cuban Missile Crisis. At the time SALT I was signed, the U.S. and the USSR had rough parity in strategic systems. As the decade wore on, though, that began to change. First, the Soviets produced four new ICBM models, three of which were deployed in number. One of these, the SS-18, was immense: it carried eight MIRVs (as opposed to the three carried by U.S. Minuteman missiles). The Soviets had not yet mastered miniaturization technology, and so they needed large warheads, and a large vehicle ("bus") for carrying them. Second, the Soviets built and deployed two classes of sophisticated submarines (Delta and Typhoon) that were capable of carrying advanced warheads—the latter MIRVed. In addition, the Soviets deployed the long-range "Backfire" bomber, and by the end of the decade they were producing nearly double the number of tactical aircraft as the USAF. Finally, the Soviets began super-hardening some of their missile silos, and continuing with the kinds of civil defense preparedness programs that the U.S. had abandoned long ago.[108]

NATO planners remained concerned by what they perceived as an ongoing imbalance between their forces and those of the Warsaw Pact. Western anxiety increased in 1976 when the Soviets deployed the SS-20 intermediate range missile. It could reach any target in Western Europe (in minutes) with accurate, MIRVed warheads. The European-based Pershing I missiles belonging to the United States did not have the range or quick-launch features of the SS-20. In response to divided opinion within the Alliance, NATO members opted to pursue a two-track decision on IRBMs: they would seek an arms control agreement, but if such negotiations failed, they would deploy a new, highly accurate and longer range Pershing II missile, along with newly developing ground-launched cruise missiles (GLCMs).[109]

Many explanations were proffered for the Soviet behavior, including increased tensions with the Chinese. But conservatives focused on worst-case scenarios and demanded a bolder response than either the Ford or Carter administrations had offered. The conclusions of the "Committee on the Present Danger" (headed by Paul Nitze, the principal author of NSC 68) were a major cause of opposition to SALT II inside the Senate. Richard Pipes, a Sovietologist who would later become a high-ranking official inside the government, published (in 1977) a high-profile article titled: "Why the Soviet Union Thinks It Could Fight and Win a Nuclear War."[110]

The Soviet humiliation in the aftermath of the Cuban Missile Crisis had led to a build-up that, by the late 1970s, had given American conservatives an apparent reason to beat an alarmist drum. The result was a domestic political debate that could be interpreted, generously, as more evidence of the inescapable "security dilemma," or, instead, as further evidence of a need within the collective American psyche to appear more powerful and formidable—in every realm—than the Soviets. And this need, all the more apparent following the undignified U.S. exit from Vietnam, was manifested in the enthusiastic response to the tough-talking rhetoric of 1980 presidential contender Ronald Reagan.

The hardening of the Soviet ICBM force and their lead in the number of launchers also created deep unease among many close observers of U.S. national security policy. According to the Committee on the Present Danger, this situation left open a "window of vulnerability" that the Soviets might exploit before an improved U.S. missile system could be put in place. But it was not at all clear how the Soviets might exploit this "window," since any attempt to do so would have brought down upon them a devastating response that would far outweigh any potential gain they might have achieved. Indeed, the U.S. second-strike capability had only increased in the 1960s and 1970s.[111]

Writing at the time of Reagan's election, defense analyst Warner Schilling argued that the United States "has already built the forces it needs to deter attacks or threats by the Soviet Union and to deny the Soviet Union any meaningful advantage . . . from a nuclear exchange. But Washington is nonetheless seized with the worry that the Soviet Union or other states might be led to contrary judgments by examining the charts and graphs (all supplied by the United States) that compare the forces of the superpowers in terms of various static and dynamic measures: numbers of warheads, delivery vehicles, equivalent megatons, countermilitary potential, or the ratio of post-exchange warheads, or megatons, etc."[112] Language itself, and methods of measurement, provided a platform on which to build a debate that had become, in many ways, a social construction of the defense analytic community. And this platform was seized once again by those who mistrusted the Soviets so much as to deny them a margin in any category of strategic forces.

Their rhetoric was politically resonant in the United States and, when elected, President Reagan would pursue an across the board built-up of weapons that was not unlike the one begun by the Truman administration in the early 1950s. In their search for a way to close the "window of vulnerability," defense planners sought to come up with a new basing mode that would foil Soviet efforts to target it with certainty. It would be designed to convince the Soviets that they simply could not achieve their aims in a nuclear war. This meant, in the end, a mobile basing. But how would the mobility be provided? All kinds of options were examined by the services and the defense analytic community, including moving the missiles around by truck on interstate highways, and even moving them by airships (blimps).

When first elected, President Carter had deferred approval of a mobile "MX" (Missile Experimental) system pending further study and research; he had hoped that the SALT negotiations might make the system unnecessary. The Air Force preferred a "racetrack" basing system that would have allowed missiles to move around at random (from one hardened shelter to another) on a specially built highway system in Nevada and Utah. Under increasing pressure from conservatives, and in an ultimately failed effort to win Senate approval of SALT II, the Carter Administration sanctioned the future construction and deployment of the MX system. Disillusioned with the SALT process, and disturbed by the Soviet invasion of Afghanistan, President Carter took an increasingly hard line with the Soviets by the end of his presidency.[113]

PD-59 (outlined above) was a major statement of declaratory policy regarding nuclear weapons. Impelled by the same perspective as NSDM-242, PD-59 sought a continuum of options against a wide array of targets. It also included a close look at Soviet nuclear doctrine, which resulted in a new target category, designed to reflect Soviet priorities (and vulnerabilities): "counterpolitical" targets, sometimes called "counterleadership" targets. These included top-tier elements of the Soviet command and control system, such as governmental and Communist Party headquarters, and military command posts. If these targets were not new to U.S. nuclear policy, the heightened emphasis on them was, along with a sense that specific Soviet efforts to shelter political leaders in wartime were revealing of their centrality to Soviet will and cohesion. What Brown would call the "countervailing strategy" would require upgrades in the U.S. command, control, communications, and intelligence system in order to be fully implemented. It also placed a renewed emphasis on counterforce targeting—of Soviet nuclear *and* conventional forces, and favored the direct and specific targeting of key industries, instead of NSDM-242's more general guidance designed to inhibit Soviet economic recovery following a war.[114]

But Carter's harder line came too late in the eyes of most Americans. Critics of the administration who sounded alarms over the Soviet build-up had begun to have a significant impact, and a severe downturn in the economy—including high fuel prices, inflation, and high energy costs—demoralized the American people. All of this heightened the sense that the United States had slipped to second place status vis-à-vis the Soviet Union. The final blow to the Carter presidency came late in 1979 when the Iranian revolution created a hostage crisis that intensified the sense of American demoralization. President Carter allowed the Shah to enter the country in October for cancer treatment, and this enraged the Iranians. Militants stormed the U.S. Embassy in Tehran and took sixty-nine Americans hostage (ultimately they kept fifty-nine).[115]

THE ERA OF RONALD REAGAN

Ronald Reagan brought with him an assertive approach to rivalry with the Soviet Union. Since there had been no accommodation on intermediate range missiles and the threat posed by the Soviet SS-20, Reagan decided to go forward with the Pershing II/GLCM deployment that had been part of NATO's previous dual-track decision. In March 1983 he announced that he wanted the United States to pursue a "Strategic Defense Initiative" (SDI) that would result, ultimately, in the creation of a ballistic missile shield over U.S. air space. To many liberals, Reagan's rhetoric—and apparent

challenge to the stable logic of MAD—seemed like gratuitous antagonism
of a dangerous enemy. They worried that his words and his ideas might
bring about a return to the anxious, frosty environment of the days before
SALT and détente.[116]

The Europeans were especially outspoken about Reagan's unapologetic
anti-communist rhetoric, which they worried might raise the prospect of
a clash—perhaps even a nuclear war—with the Soviet Union. Vast popular protests cropped up across Western Europe on the eve of the Pershing
II deployment, while back home critics derided SDI as a fanciful and irre-
sponsible leap toward an unproven set of technologies that would provide
little real protection while costing billions in research and development
funds. They also worried that it would signal U.S. rejection of Mutual Assured Destruction and thus set in train a major new arms race. But Reagan
remained firm.

The Reagan Administration's response to the Soviet arms build-up had
been to open up the coffers and spend extensively on defense. This was the
major pillar of Reagan's larger attempt to restore a sense of optimism and
pride to Americans in the aftermath of Vietnam. In addition to unlimited
investment in the SDI program, the Reagan Administration reversed an
earlier Carter decision and went ahead with the B-1 strategic bomber for
the Air Force as well as investing heavily in cruise missiles and the Trident
nuclear submarine program, which received a bigger and more accurate
reentry vehicle, the D-5 RV. Though it abandoned the controversial racetrack system, the Reagan Administration (following the findings of a commission led by retired Air Force Lieutenant General Brent Scowcroft)
decided to deploy one hundred MX missiles in existing Minuteman silos.
The administration reengineered the KC-135A aerial tanker force and deployed four National Emergency Airborne Command Post (NEACP) aircraft
for use by the National Command Authorities. The Reagan administration
raised the defense budget's rate of growth from five percent to over eight
percent annually; much of the increase went to conventional forces, but
strategic forces were increased as well.[117]

In addition to the restoration of American primacy following Vietnam,
Reagan seems to have been driven by two overriding aims—neither of
which was completely apparent at the time, and neither of which was easily accommodated by the more simplistic portraits of him sometimes
painted by his critics. First, Reagan's willingness to spend lavishly on defense programs appears to have been part of a calculated effort to further
stretch the threadbare fabric of the Soviet economy by forcing the Soviets

to keep up with a new round of American weapons systems. The idea was not a new one; its provenance could be traced all the way back to NSC 68, and elements of it—outspending and outbuilding the Soviets in both offensive and defensive systems—had been suggested by Earle J. Wheeler, Chairman of the Joint Chiefs of Staff, in his statement to the Senate Armed Services Committee regarding military procurement for fiscal year 1968. But the budgetary demands of the Vietnam War had made it impossible for President Johnson or his successors to entertain this idea.[118]

Second, Reagan genuinely loathed the nuclear dilemma that defined the Cold War world, and hoped to use the Strategic Defense Initiative as a mechanism for forcing both serious dialogue and a paradigm shift in the U.S.-Soviet arms negotiations. As Paul Lettow has recently argued, "Reagan's nuclear abolitionism, which grew out of his deeply-rooted beliefs and religious views, resulted in some of the most significant—and least understood—aspects of his presidency."[119]

The members of the Reagan Administration did not continue the specific language of the countervailing strategy, but in most respects they cleaved to it with few significant changes. The administration continued to place a heavy emphasis on targeting the Soviet leadership and key industrial facilities. Naturally this required a continued focus on acquiring the C^3I capabilities that would make such targeting realistic.[120] Though the Reagan administration held initially to the terms of the SALT II agreement, they did not resubmit it to the Senate, or consider any new arms control plans for a year after entering office. In the spring of 1982 the President announced a new initiative: moving away from the tainted acronym SALT, he proposed new "Strategic Arms Reduction Talks," or START. As an opening gambit he proposed that the Soviets and the Americans each cut their number of ballistic missile warheads to 5,000, with no more than 2,500 on land-based missiles. The Soviets agreed to recommence arms control talks, but dismissed Reagan's plan as disproportionately advantageous to the United States, which had the bulk of its ballistic missiles on submarines. The START process got underway in Geneva, but the Soviets walked out of the talks in November in protest of Reagan's resolve to deploy Pershing IIs and GLCMs after the Soviets turned down the "zero-zero" option calling on them to remove their SS-20s in exchange for a promise that the Americans would not deploy the new generation intermediate range missiles in Europe.

Following the death of Leonid Brezhnev in November 1982, the Soviets went through a leadership crisis. Throughout this tumultuous period,

Reagan pushed hard regarding SDI, START, and nuclear arms in Europe. Upon Reagan's reelection in 1984, the Soviets accommodated themselves to a new attempt at arms control. Beginning in March 1985, this new round of talks addressed European, strategic, and ballistic missile defense issues. At this point Reagan surprised his critics: he changed course and met with his Soviet opposite number five times in three years. Mikhail Gorbachev, the new Communist Party chairman, was a compelling, dynamic individual interested in interaction with the West, and a revitalization of the moribund Soviet economy; he and Reagan would develop a useful working relationship, and a genuine mutual respect.[121]

At a summit held in Reykjavik, Iceland, in the autumn of 1986, Gorbachev and Reagan went well beyond the expectations of their advisers by seriously discussing the possibility of significant weapons reductions, including the prospect of removing Soviet and U.S. intermediate range weapons from Europe. A deal in the offing ultimately was killed by Gorbachev's insistence that the United States give up its SDI program. But Reykjavik offered clear evidence that these two men—for their own individual reasons—might be prepared to enact sweeping changes, and to place the U.S.–Soviet relationship on a whole new footing.

The changes foreshadowed in Iceland came increasingly to pass. In December 1987, Gorbachev and Reagan signed the INF treaty in Washington, D.C., and the U.S. Senate ratified it quickly. The treaty provided that both sides would eliminate all ground-launched and cruise missiles (deployed and not-yet deployed) with a range of 500 to 5,500 kilometers. This did not mean that the Soviets and Americans had no capacity to use nuclear weapons in Europe: nuclear-capable aircraft remained, and strategic systems on both sides could be retargeted for the European theater. Nonetheless, it was the first treaty ever to eliminate an entire class of weapons, and it was the first U.S.–Soviet treaty ever to embrace thorough verification measures for each side. The willingness of Soviet officials to agree to these terms revealed the extent to which Gorbachev had already instigated a revolution in Soviet domestic affairs.[122]

A Brave New World

The issues surrounding the long-range nuclear systems were every bit as complex as those in Europe. Increased Soviet investment in long range systems yielded important fruit in the 1980s when the Soviets began deploying two new ICBMs (in the West called, SS-24s and SS-25s). The former carried ten MIRVed warheads, and could be moved by special railroad cars. By July 1991 the Soviets had deployed nearly one hundred SS-24s, and over three hundred smaller SS-25s. The earlier improvements to the Soviet bomber and submarine forces, noted above, also created hurdles to progress in arms control.[123]

The alarmist language of the early Reagan administration had been partly countered, in April 1983, when a blue ribbon commission under General Scowcroft had downplayed the "window of vulnerability" rhetoric that had held such a central place in the President Reagan's first electoral campaign. But this dismissal of the highly publicized worries of the Committee on the Present Danger had not led to stagnation in U.S. strategic systems. As noted above, American submarines were equipped with highly accurate Trident II D-5 missiles, and upgraded MX ("Peacekeeper") missiles were deployed in existing silos as the U.S. debate over a mobile system continued, unresolved. And the Scowcroft Commission's preferred, single-warhead "Midgetman" missile system—an alternative solution to the problem of hard-target kill against land-based systems—went forward too, ultimately with the support of presidential administration of George H. W. Bush in the late 1980s.[124]

At the end of the day it would be the winding down of the Cold War that would lead to genuine progress in limiting long range nuclear systems. If the arms competition had gained a life of its own, it was nonetheless an extension of Cold War politics. The reforms that Gorbachev had introduced took hold and gained momentum—leading, in the end, to an unraveling of the old Soviet political system. Increasingly confident that Gorbachev would not intervene and support the forces of conservatism, proponents of change in Eastern Europe began to stir their respective political pots. In early 1989 the Solidarity trade union movement in Poland regained its legal status and helped to frame a new representative constitution; in June it won control of the new parliament, and two months later installed the first noncommunist prime minister in the state since 1940. Also in June 1989 the Hungarians celebrated the reburial of their hero from the 1956 revolt, Imre Nagy. In early November the Berlin Wall came down, and later in the month five hundred Czech students marched toward Wenceslas Square in Prague, calling for the rights of free speech and assembly.[125]

The speed and sweep of these changes left statesmen on both sides of the Iron Curtain breathless. Even as the revolution gained early momentum, no one anticipated the range and the degree of the changes that would so quickly transform the strategic landscape both outside and inside the Soviet Union. In the United States, planners and analysts were left reeling as the context—the Cold War paradigm—in which they had worked for decades transformed itself, seemingly overnight.

THE PERSIAN GULF WAR

In light of the changing nature of the international environment, SAC had begun planning, by early 1987, for a dual role: strategic operations that would include nuclear and/or conventional operations. By January 1989, when Ronald Reagan turned the White House over to his former vice president, George H. W. Bush, the world of the old Cold War Strategic Air Command was gone for good. But new challenges lay ahead.

On August 2, 1990, armies under Saddam Hussein of Iraq invaded the neighboring, oil-rich state of Kuwait. With the strong support of Britain's Prime Minister Margaret Thatcher, President Bush froze Iraqi assets, promised to send troops to Saudi Arabia, and demanded that Iraq withdraw unconditionally from Kuwait. Days later, U.S. aircraft began arriving in Saudi Arabia; they were the first American assets deployed in what would become a massive commitment (Operation Desert Shield) to protect Saudi Arabia and its vast oil reserves. When diplomatic and economic pressure failed to eject Saddam, Operation Desert Shield became, for the Americans, Operation Desert Storm. American troops made up the great bulk of what became a vast multinational effort to liberate Kuwait.[126]

The "Persian Gulf War," as it came to be called, saw the first extensive use of post–Vietnam era U.S. troops and equipment. U.S. Army General Norman Schwarzkopf, who led the military operation, envisioned it in four phases: (1) a strategic air campaign against Iraq; (2) an air campaign against Iraqi forces in Kuwait; (3) an attrition phase to neutralize the Republican Guard forces and isolate the Kuwaiti battlefield; (4) a ground attack to drive Iraqi forces out of Kuwait. The first three would be carried out by coalition air forces, and the final phase would be conducted by ground forces.[127] The strategic air campaign over Iraq was designed to directly pressure and coerce Saddam's regime.

A primary intellectual influence on the strategic air campaign was Colonel John A. Warden III, USAF, who had been in charge of the Deputy Directorate for Warfighting Concepts within the Air Staff Directorate of

Plans. A strong advocate of independent air operations, Warden had conceived of a targeting theory based on five principal categories, envisioned
as five concentric rings (like the rings in a bull's eye) that increase in value
as they approach the center. The focal point—his designated "center of
gravity"—was the enemy leadership. Just outside of that, in the position of
second priority, was the enemy state's energy sources, advanced research
facilities, and key war-supporting industries. Beyond that, in the third
ring, was enemy infrastructure, such as transportation systems. The
fourth ring contained the enemy's population, and the fifth ring designated the enemy's fielded military forces. Warden's ideas, which he promulgated effectively and energetically, brought back to the surface some
heated service debates over the primacy that should be accorded to independent air operations.[128]

The plan that Warden and his staff developed for the crisis in the Middle East focused on strategic air attacks on Iraqi centers of gravity; it was
designed to pit American strengths against Iraqi weaknesses while minimizing U.S. casualties, collateral damage, and civilian deaths. Warden
sought to target the heart of Saddam's regime—the key structures, institutions, and resources that facilitated his control of the state. Though
modified somewhat before implementation, the main objectives of Warden's plan remained, and these "continued to emphasize leadership; electrical, nuclear, biological, and chemical facilities; and the other target sets
derived from the five rings."[129]

Following in the tradition of some of the World War II air power advocates who believed that strategic bombing might preclude the need for a
ground campaign, Warden believed that his plan could stand alone.
Schwarzkopf, following in the tradition of World War II ground commanders, saw the air plan as the first phase of a larger, integrated air-
ground liberation of Kuwait. The seven hundred aircraft that were ready
on the eve of war, would, Warden hoped, achieve Coalition political aims
essentially on their own. But even though the aircraft coming into the
theater comprised the vast majority of the USAF's precision delivery capability at the time, the force was not ideally suited to the task Warden had
set for it. Technological evolution throughout the Vietnam War had
yielded some promising results in highly precise, guided bomb technology, but the USAF had been leisurely in appropriating it and integrating it
into doctrine and mission statements: most of the combat aircraft pro-
cured between 1972 and 1990 (the F-15C, F-16, and A-10 series) did not include guided bomb unit-delivery capability.[130] Still, the USAF had the

capacity to employ air-delivered precision-guided munitions, and this would become a centerpiece of its war effort. A dramatic new delivery system in the U.S. arsenal was the F-117A "Stealth" fighter, introduced to the public in late 1988.

The air war plan underwent updating right through the opening hours of the war on January 17, 1991. Many hours before bombs began falling over Baghdad, seven hulking B-52Gs took off from Barksdale Air Force Base, Louisiana, to begin a 14,000 mile round-trip delivery of air-launched cruise missiles into Iraq. The Air Force, anxious to prove its "Global Reach," did not wish to be overshadowed by the Navy's ship-based Tomahawk missiles about to launch from the Persian Gulf and the Red Sea. Thoughout Iraq, coalition forces struck command and control targets (including Baath Party headquarters), electrical facilities, and Scud missile launchers. Anti-radiation missiles homed in on radar facilities and anti-aircraft defenses while both British and American planes cratered the runways on Iraqi airfields. Iraqi oil refineries and storage facilities came under attack as well. At the end of only two nights, coalition aircraft had struck nearly half of 298 identified strategic targets. The stealth fighter-bombers proved their worth early on: one F-117A with two bombs could do the same work as more than 100 World War II-era B-17 bombers carrying nearly 650 bombs.[131]

But the aerial pounding alone did not deliver the coalition war aims, and the ground campaign, which had been planned all along as the final phase of major combat operations, finally kicked off on February 23.[132] Simultaneously, coalition aircraft struck Iraqi airfields, aircraft, and bridges near the front. Strategic raids continued to target leadership, and industrial facilities in Iraq. Newly developed GBU-28 penetrator bombs were used against high-priority targets, including the Al Taji command bunker. Iraq, which had fought a long and draining war with Iran, owned the fourth largest army in the world. In the United States there had been much hand-wringing over the idea that the ground war might be bloody. But the well-trained and well-equipped Americans were able to overwhelm the opposition in a matter of days.

In a turn of events that would have seemed ironic to the old SAC bomber hands, B-52s were used primarily to hit Iraqi ground forces in Kuwait, while the F-117A fighter-bombers took on strategic targets in Iraq proper. The B-52s proved to be the real workhorses of the campaign, dropping nearly a third of the coalition's total tonnage (although they made up only three percent of its total aircraft) and contributing mightily to the unraveling of Iraqi ground troops. But the stealth fighters and the other precision bombing platforms garnered most of the attention and acclaim. The Air Force liked the results of high precision, and subsequently accelerated its investment in the systems and weapons that could provide it.

THE POST–COLD WAR U.S. NUCLEAR ARSENAL

The central role that SAC had once played in the U.S. strategic construct had been eroding for some time. Missiles had long overtaken bombers as the core of the U.S. deterrent threat, and submarine-launched ballistic missiles were the most robust and invulnerable weapon in the arsenal; over time, the latter had become increasingly accurate. Other trends pushed toward change. As it became clear that the Soviet threat really had receded, and that it would not reemerge, Americans began to look forward to a reduction in defense expenditure and the "peace dividend" that it would yield. On June 1, 1992, the Air Force inactivated SAC; a new "Air Combat Command," headquartered in Langley, Virginia, received SAC's bombers and missiles, and fighter aircraft belonging to the former Tactical Air Command (also inactivated). Also on that date, a new joint command, the United States Strategic Command (STRATCOM) took wartime responsibility for nuclear deterrence functions. STRATCOM was headquartered at the old home of SAC, Offutt Air Force Base in Omaha, Nebraska.[133]

The nuclear arsenals of the United States and the Soviet Union had developed their own momentum and their own logic over the long years of the Cold War, and this momentum continued on, even as world politics changed, albeit more slowly than in the past. As noted above, the Soviets had deployed some 300 SS-25s and nearly 100 SS-24s by mid 1991, and they had retired old missiles to keep their overall numbers within the SALT II ceilings. (The Reagan administration had ignored the SALT II ceilings once the five-year term of the unratified treaty had expired.) President George H. W. Bush had come into office interested in deploying a mobile ICBM system, and the first rail system infrastructure was delivered to a Wyoming site in 1990. A year later, though, as the Cold War continued to wind down, Congress backed away from any elaborate mobile system, and the expensive Midgetman program was canceled. The American Trident SLBM program continued to receive steady support and funding from Congress, however, and the Soviet Navy, likewise, continued to build submarines for purposes of nuclear deterrence. Moreover, the Soviets deployed a new, high-yield, accurate SLBM. Both sides also had growing inventories of air- and sea-launched cruise missiles, and tactical aircraft capable of delivering nuclear weapons.[134]

The U.S. SDI program had been the main barrier to any real progress in arms control during the Reagan administration: the Soviets tried to link every arms control initiative to slowing or halting American work on SDI, and the president had consistently refused.[135] SDI's relationship to the ABM treaty was unclear, even within the administration, and the confusion surrounding the issue surely heightened the domestic debate over the expensive and highly experimental program. After the dramatic events at Reykjavik and the breakthrough of the INF treaty, it seemed the time was right for deep cuts in intercontinental systems. But Reagan left office still committed to the construction of a space defense system. His successor, however, did not feel so strongly, and some guarded progress was made in this realm.

U.S. Secretary of State James Baker met with Soviet Foreign Minister Eduard Shevardnadze in the autumn of 1989, in Jackson Hole, Wyoming; the latter agreed to talk about missile reductions even while research on SDI continued. (Shevardnadze knew, by this time, that Bush held a different level of commitment to SDI than his predecessor.) He also acknowledged that the Soviet radar at Krasnoyarsk—long a sticking point with the Reagan Administration—had been a violation of the ABM treaty. Later in the year, Bush and Gorbachev met at Malta and agreed to prioritize progress on strategic arms control. The commitment led ultimately to the START treaty, signed in Moscow in late July 1991.[136]

The START treaty put some broad boundaries around permissible numbers of strategic nuclear weapons; it was designed to begin a process of overall drawdown. It allowed each side 1,600 strategic delivery vehicles and up to 6,000 accountable warheads; up to 4,900 of the latter could be placed on ballistic missiles—and of those only 1,540 on heavy ICBMs and 1,100 on mobile missiles. In two separate documents (not part of the treaty but nonetheless considered binding), the two parties agreed that "Backfire" bombers would not have intercontinental range, and that both sides would limit submarine-launched cruise missiles to 880. These numbers represented a roughly 25 percent cut in the total strategic nuclear forces of the two powers at that time. This was substantial progress compared to what had been achieved in the past, and it was the first ever *reduction* in superpower strategic nuclear forces. In light of the changed political circumstances, however, it was more modest than it might have been. And, as it turned out, the treaty drew little sustained attention from the public.[137]

More important than the START treaty's numbers were its elaborate provisions for inspection and verification. These arms control elements had stymied superpower progress throughout the Cold War, because of the powerful, mutual lack of trust between the United States and the Soviet Union. In 1991, however, both sides agreed to inspection provisions more intrusive than those developed for the INF treaty. President Bush followed this initiative with unilateral cuts, the removal of all bombers (and all ICBMs scheduled to be decommissioned) from "alert" status; and the removal of all short-range nuclear weapons from abroad, and from Navy ships.[138] Gorbachev accepted President Bush's invitation to follow suit, but the precise details of Soviet progress were muddied by internal political unraveling in what was soon to be the "former" USSR.

In the meantime, a young Democrat named Bill Clinton swept Bush out of office in the November 1992 U.S. presidential election. But the new administration continued to proceed carefully; it kept the START framework intact, carefully observed the Russian Federation's attempts to structure its own post–Cold War nuclear posture, and sought to track fissile materials in the midst of rapid political change behind the old Iron Curtain. Clinton and Russian Federation president Boris Yeltsin signed START II in 1993, which had as one of its goals the limitation of both sides to between 3,000 and 3,500 warheads by January 2003. In May 1995 the U.S. and Russia agreed to a "Joint Statement on Transparency and Irreversibility" intended to lock in the reductions of START I and II.[139]

Though the U.S. Senate ratified START II in 1996, the Russian Duma refrained from doing so. This reluctance was fueled in part by new concerns over the ABM treaty, and hostility toward the expansion of NATO. In 1997 a START II protocol was signed, which delayed the completion of phases I and II of force reductions (to 2004 and 2007, respectively) in order to ease the cost to Russia of dismantling weapons. In addition the U.S. agreed to commence START III as soon as START II entered into force— the overall aim being to bring the total number of warheads down to 2,000–2,5000 by 2007.[140]

Political disarray in the former Soviet Union and the war in Chechnya became obstacles to continued arms control progress in Europe, following the Conventional Forces in Europe treaty of the early 1990s. Indeed, it was not until November 1999 that an agreement came into existence on the

"Adaptation of the Treaty on Conventional Armed Forces in Europe." One of the biggest problems facing the Clinton administration through the 1990s was the political deterioration inside the former Soviet Union, and the challenges this posed for securing and destroying nuclear material. The nuclear arsenals that had been bought at such great cost and that were so highly valued were now a physical liability: nuclear sites had to be guarded, material had to be safely destroyed, and the environmental impact had to be responsibly considered. Economic strain put the Russian scientific community into a state of "protracted crisis" that "gave Russian scientists both greater incentives and greater opportunities to sell their knowledge to governments or terrorist organizations that harbor hostile intentions toward the United States and other Western democracies."[141]

In 1991 Senators Richard Lugar (R-Indiana) and Sam Nunn (D-Georgia) developed the Nunn-Lugar Cooperative Threat Reduction Program to lessen the nuclear threat at its source by deactivating and destroying weapons of mass destruction (WMD) in the former Soviet Union, and to help former Soviet weapons scientists retrain and work for peace. Since that time, resources provided by Nunn-Lugar have helped to deactivate or destroy more than 6,700 nuclear warheads. In 2003 Congress adopted the Nunn-Lugar Expansion Act, which authorized work outside the Soviet Union to address proliferation and WMD security threats. And in November 2005 Senators Lugar and Barak Obama (D-Illinois) introduced legislation to find and secure vulnerable stockpiles of conventional weapons, and also to aid U.S. allies in finding and interdicting WMD.[142] Despite U.S. efforts to address these problems, however, the issues of weapons proliferation, technology transfer, and, especially, "loose nukes" are likely to remain high on the national security agenda; indeed, they are a principal concern of scientists, diplomats, and statesmen.[143]

In general, the 1990s saw both progress and frustration in arms control. Though the Nonproliferation Treaty was extended indefinitely in 1995, nuclear and non-nuclear states continued to spar over the pace of disarmament. In addition, the Indian and Pakistani nuclear tests of 1998 aroused considerable discomfort around the world, and revealed problems in the global nonproliferation regime. In 1999 the U.S. Senate refused to ratify the Comprehensive Test Ban Treaty. The Biological Weapons Convention (BWC) lacked a binding verification and compliance agreement. Finally, the Chemical Weapons Convention (CWC) of 1997 had a bumpy reception around the world, with several key Middle Eastern states choosing to remain outside its reach.[144]

STRATEGIC AIR POWER AT THE START
OF A NEW CENTURY

As the Cold War drew to a close, several policy analysts argued that the
global political landscape might now include more tension, strife, and war
than had been the case during the Cold War years. Events proved them
correct, as troubles erupted in a range of locations around the globe, including the ethnically mixed regions of what had been the nation of Yugoslavia. Tensions boiled over into conflict, and on two occasions the Western
powers intervened with air strikes, using them in an effort to change the
behavior of ethnic Serbians toward Bosnian Muslims, and later Kosovar
Albanians. In the former case air power was used (in 1995) as a lever with
which to help bring recalcitrant forces to the negotiating table. In the latter case—the brief but troubled Kosovo War of 1999—NATO used strategic air power to try to stop the Serbian ethnic cleansing campaign being
waged against Kosovar Albanians. The Kosovo War will not be remembered as one of the landmark events of the late twentieth century: the war
that had started in March was over by June, and NATO was able claim victory in its first-ever test in actual battle against a far weaker opponent.
Nonetheless, this odd little war, which may garner only a couple of para-
graphs in as yet unwritten general histories, may well be studied in detail
by those who seek to understand strategic bombing as a tool of war.

The success of precision bombing in the Gulf War of 1991 had prompted
the Air Force to shape its future with an eye fixed upon precision capability. By the end of the decade the service had developed a bombing force of
unprecedented accuracy. The United States had no true strategic stake in
Kosovo, but the very existence of the air power tool may have tempted the
Clinton administration to intervene—and to do so in a way that would
minimize the risk to U.S. combatants (and thus, so it was assumed, minimize the potential domestic opposition to war). In the event, the air campaign did not halt the ethnic cleansing, and, indeed, probably accelerated
it. But Serbian leader Slobodan Milosevic finally capitulated—and did so
prior to any NATO ground forces being deployed. The outcome naturally
enabled air advocates to claim that air power had won a war on its own.
But the course of the war raised difficult questions about the use of coercive force from high altitude.[145]

Serbian troops were able to offset the power of U.S. precision weapons
by using cover, concealment, and deception; after many weeks of heavy

bombing, the Serb forces (including infantry and tanks) had endured only minimal damage. Frustrated by the lack of progress, NATO planners increasingly targeted Serbian industrial and economic infrastructure in order to raise the level of public pressure on Milosevic. Naturally this meant attacking locations frequented by noncombatants. And the results of these attacks—including such things as the collapse of the electrical power grid—involved suffering for noncombatants, especially among those who are most vulnerable in such situations: children, the infirm, and the elderly.[146] In addition, the reasons for Milosevic's capitulation remain unclear, and the course of the war suggests that it would be unwise to draw a simple straight line from bombing to victory.[147]

In 1999 and 2000 George W. Bush had run a presidential campaign that emphasized reorienting American foreign policy away from humanitarian intervention, and, especially, away from nation-building. Instead, the administration was interested in developing a ballistic missile defense system to help cope with threats posed by a wide array of potential adversaries, and leveraging new technologies for security. In particular, the new Secretary of Defense, Donald Rumsfeld, was prepared to pit himself against entrenched Pentagon interests to create a smaller, lighter, and more nimble American military centered on high technology. But the administration barely had had enough time to move the nation in a new direction when a handful of al-Qaeda terrorists redirected the entire U.S. national security agenda by flying airliners into the twin towers of the World Trade Center on the morning of September 11, 2001.

Shortly thereafter the administration sent troops to Afghanistan to take down the Taliban regime that had been harboring al-Qaeda operatives within its borders. While the administration felt compelled to strike at al-Qaeda right away, it chose to do so using the force structure preferences emphasized by Rumsfeld. His insistence on a slimmed-down, high-tech use of military means meant reliance on long range, precision stand-off weapons employed with the aid of U.S. Special Operations Forces (SOF) for the support of indigenous ground troops (the Northern Alliance) operating against al-Qaeda and the Taliban. Because of the shadowy nature of al-Qaeda, targeting information was slim. The U.S. Air Force struck such infrastructure as there was in Afghanistan. When this did not coerce the various elements of the Taliban (including al-Qaeda), the USAF joined the effort to use ground-based SOF—working in conjunction with indigenous friendly forces in Afghanistan—to attack elements of the enemy dispersed through various regions of the country.

The operation in Afghanistan was generally considered a success, and was surely interpreted that way by the Office of the Secretary of Defense, even though some key al-Qaeda leaders escaped across the Afghan border into Pakistan.

While the Afghanistan campaign was ongoing, the Bush Administration was at work modifying and updating the formal, written "National Security Strategy" (NSS) of the United States. The September 2002 document acknowledged the "profound transformation" of the security environment for the United States following the collapse of the Soviet Union, but pointed to the "deadly challenges" emerging from rogue states and terrorists. While recognizing that the new threats did not control the same overall destructive power as the Soviets did, the NSS authors argued that the "greater likelihood" of terrorists and rogue states to use weapons of mass destruction made the existing security environment "more complex and dangerous."[148]

Significantly, the new NSS argued that since "deterrence based only on the threat of retaliation" was unlikely to work in the new security environment, the United States would have to reserve for itself the right to take preemptive action against imminent threats. This was not new; as we have seen, NSC 68 reserved the same right. But the "preemption" passages in the new NSS drew a lot of attention, and made many observers— especially foreign observers—uneasy, since it was not clear how Americans would define "preemption" in the post 9/11 world. This kind of speculation grew more voluble as it became clear that many in the Bush Administration were increasingly intent upon bringing down the regime of Saddam Hussein in Iraq. For a variety of reasons—including, most prominently, the widespread assumption that Saddam possessed WMD and was likely to transfer them to terrorists—the momentum toward a preemptive attack on Iraq grew, facilitated in part by the emphasis given to it by Bush's powerful vice president, Richard Cheney. An invasion of the country was launched in March 2003.[149]

The invasion plan integrated air, ground, and naval attacks. The opening stages of the battle, however, saw aerial pyrotechnics over Baghdad—a display of American precision bombing that seemed like a made-for-TV event, right down to its oft-repeated media moniker: "shock and awe." At the same time the Air Force waged an attack on the Dora Farms complex when real time intelligence indicated that Saddam Hussein might be located there. But Saddam was neither killed nor, apparently, shocked, and the war moved into its next phase, which saw the Air Force cripple enemy air defenses, and degrade enemy communications. Due to American strength and preponderance, the USAF was able to attack a wide range of targets simultaneously, and was able to continue to hammer enemy forces, even as weather halted the ground offensive for a time.[150]

One of the major ongoing debates about the future use of strategic air power pits proponents of the Warden systems approach (with its heavy emphasis on leadership) against proponents of battlefield effects. In his recent book, *Air Power*, Stephen Budiansky has argued that operations in Afghanistan and in Iraq (2003) have largely discredited the Warden theory, or any "shock and awe" approach, and have instead validated the idea that air power's greatest contribution is to be made on the battlefield against fielded forces.[151]

This debate has taken place alongside another one that examines the use of overwhelming military force against enemies that choose to fight via guerrilla and terrorist tactics. This discussion has shadowed the unfolding of events in Iraq following the brief and successful invasion phase of the war. High hopes for the emergence of a model democracy have been slowly trampled by a low-intensity but ever-expanding civil war that has seen resistance by a Sunni minority against the Shi'ite and Kurdish populations—and, more recently, a split within the Shi'ite community that has further aggravated a deteriorating situation.

U.S. NUCLEAR FORCES IN THE TWENTY-FIRST CENTURY

The American nuclear arsenal—a structure built and repeatedly remodeled during the Cold War—was in place so long that it became part of the strategic landscape. The assumptions and mechanisms for operating it became so embedded that they have been resistant to change; only slowly and carefully have analysts and operators begun to pull themselves away from the familiar tropes and routines that were designed to provide stability in the bipolar world of the post-1945 era. Careful steps and a policy of watchful waiting characterized the approach taken by both the Bush (1989–1993) and Clinton (1993–2001) administrations. Even today the U.S. and Russia maintain launch-ready arsenals of more than seven thousand nuclear warheads; when both nations pare back to the 2,000-weapon goal of the Strategic Offensive Reductions Treaty (SORT) of 2002, the result will be little more than a scaled-down version of the former paradigm.[152] And SORT, as one nuclear analyst has pointed out, allows for large non-deployed reserves of nuclear weapons, "some of which could be re-deployed in hours."[153]

These most recent reductions, agreed to by Presidents Vladimir Putin and George W. Bush, should continue; indeed, keeping them on track is a worthwhile goal. But provisions to merely dismantle the weapons rather than destroy them speaks to a kind of psychological dependence that is more about habit than about the strategic realities of the twenty-first century. Arguments for deep cuts in the arsenal have been presented by a wide array of politicians and strategic thinkers, including—among other members of the military—General Lee Butler, a former head of Strategic Air Command. These arguments rest on several assumptions about the potential effect of deep cuts: (1) they would not adversely affect U.S. security; (2) they would eliminate weapons that have little military use and have been stigmatized by the international community; and (3) they would reduce the risk of accident, and the built-in instability of "launch on warning" policies.[154]

The Bush Administration's "Nuclear Posture Review" (NPR) of January 2002 responded to the events of 9/11 by asserting a new blueprint designed to integrate nuclear and non-nuclear forces for the purpose of deterring a wide range of future threats.[155] Animated by a sense of urgency, Bush Administration planners began seeking out ways in which the existing arsenal (and a modified future arsenal) might be used to bolster deterrence against two classes of enemies: (1) adversaries who have acquired or are attempting to acquire nuclear weapons; and (2) adversaries who have the capability (or potential capability) to produce and use chemical and biological weapons. The NPR sought to translate into the nuclear realm the shift—articulated earlier in the 2001 Quadrennial Defense Review—from "threat-based planning" to "capabilities-based planning." In its style, intent, and tone it remained squarely within the American tradition, articulated clearly in NSC 68, of seeking to deter and manage enemies by outgunning and overwhelming them. In addition, the Bush administration went forward with the creation of a ballistic missile defense system. Though the system currently deployed is designed to meet a limited, near-term ballistic missile threat, the administration envisions expansion and evolution of the program as the technologies develop to support a more elaborate defensive shield.[156]

The NPR asserted a "new strategic triad" of offensive strike systems (nuclear and non-nuclear), passive and active defenses, and a revitalized infrastructure including improved command, control, and intelligence. It promised doctrinal innovation, most prominently the integration of nuclear and non-nuclear strike forces in order to deter a wide range of threats. Going beyond the well-established concept of deterring nuclear attacks by threatening nuclear retaliation (potentially massive in scale), the NPR's authors argued that the United States should be prepared to use nuclear weapons in a wide range of scenarios, including conflicts with "emerging threats," to include Iran and North Korea. While the available portions of the NPR do not outline the details of any probable employment of nuclear weapons, they surely retain the option of nuclear strikes (either preemptive or retaliatory) against enemy weapons of mass destruction (WMD), including chemical and biological weapons (CBW).

By asserting that the United States would use nuclear retaliation against chemical or biological attacks, the authors of the NPR hoped to preserve and indeed bolster the strategic ambiguity that aids deterrence. NPR authors and supporters took the view that adversaries might be deterred from creating or using CBW if they believe that such use might bring nuclear retaliation. NPR critics, however, have argued vigorously in another direction, pointing out that threatening the use of nuclear weapons against enemy CBW would provide little or no additional deterrent effect, and—by emphasizing the military utility of nuclear weapons— would compromise nonproliferation conventions that the U.S. has championed over the years. Critics have insisted that the U.S. instead can deter CBW attacks (and strike CBW arsenals) with its formidable existing array of conventional weapons. Other commentators, however, have distinguished between retaliatory use and preemptive use of nuclear weapons, arguing that to own a capability and threaten to use it is *not* equivalent to condoning the use of that capability *preemptively*. While the latter would violate international norms, and perhaps encourage proliferation, the former would do neither.[157]

Another controversial element of the NPR document has been its focus on precision strike capabilities, including the construction of low-yield, highly accurate nuclear weapons designed to destroy heavily hardened and deeply buried targets, including CBW arsenals and command and control bunkers. Those envisioning the new earth-penetrating weapons (EPW) believe that they would enhance deterrence against emerging threats, and that, if employed, they would be able to attack buried targets with more limited fallout than traditional nuclear weapons. Critics have decried the prospect of the United States getting back into the realm of nuclear testing in order to design a new generation weapon with specialized properties;

they fear that such activity would undermine the prevailing moratorium on testing. Other commentators, while seriously questioning whether EPWs would in fact produce less fallout, have argued that it would be possible to construct them based on existing warhead designs, thus sidestepping the requirement for a resumption of nuclear testing.[158]

Even before 9/11 the Air Force had begun to assimilate and consolidate the most productive developments and adaptations emerging from the first Gulf War and the conflicts in the Balkans. At the top of the priority list were: time-critical targeting, all-weather precision, restrictive rules of engagement (ROE), collateral damage control, and access to enemy air space. In addition, the USAF took particular note of the utility of integrating air and space operations—a lesson made widely apparent in both the Gulf War and Balkan operations.[159] In 1985 the Joint Chiefs had established U.S. Space Command as a new unified command; this move recognized and confirmed the increasing utility of space assets for military operations. Over the next fifteen years, the Air Force continued to draw linkages between air warfare and space assets. With a particular focus on guaranteeing access to enemy airspace, the USAF inaugurated the Global Strike Task Force (GSTF) as the service's contribution to the nation's "kick-down-the door-force." In 2001 Air Force Chief of Staff, General John Jumper argued that "GSTF will rapidly establish air dominance and subsequently guarantee that joint aerospace, land, and sea forces will enjoy freedom from attack and freedom to attack. It will combine stealth and advanced weapons with a horizontally integrated command, control, control, intelligence, surveillance, and reconnaissance (C^2ISR) constellation that provides lethal joint battle-space capability."[160]

After 9/11 the "Global Strike" concept gave teeth and operational planning support to both deterrence and long-range strike options, including the preemptive attack concepts outlined in the declaratory policy asserted in both the 2002 NPR and NSS. In October 2002, the Department of Defense merged U.S. Space Command with STRATCOM; this produced what was functionally (if not in name) a new command "intended to synergize the best of both previous commands to yield a flexible, globally focused command with a disciplined planning underpinning."[161] In January 2003 President Bush asked STRATCOM to take on four new responsibilities: global strike, missile defense integration, Department of Defense Information Operations, and C^4ISR (command, control, communications, computers, intelligence, surveillance, and reconnaissance).[162] Earlier in the year, Secretary of Defense Donald Rumsfeld had issued updated planning guidance that directed the military to prepare to undertake "unwarned strikes . . . from a position of forward deterrence." This evolution of the Global Strike concept, analyst William Arkin explains, "was partly in response to the realization that the military had no plans for certain situations. The possibility that some nations would acquire the ability to attack the United States directly with a WMD, for example, had clearly fallen between the command structure's cracks." It resulted in CONPLAN 8022–02, for "imminent" threats from such states as North Korea and Iran.[163]

An updated National Security Strategy of March 2006 reaffirmed the Bush Administration's commitment to preemption. In light of history, this should not be surprising; after all, the right to preemption claimed by the Bush Administration is one that Americans claimed in NSC 68, and retained (if sometimes in low profile), thereafter. And the rhetoric of the Global Strike concept ("a rapid-reaction, leading edge, power-projection concept that will deliver massive around the clock firepower") is of a piece with the overwhelming dominance ideas articulated in NSC 68—ideas that are resonant with Americans, and that have come to define U.S. responses to national security threats. But to recognize that these ideas are inside a preferred American paradigm is not to condone them. In writing about "Global Strike," William Arkin has called for a national debate on it, not only because public articulation of the plan might enhance its deterrent aspects, but also because the plan in general—in particular the nuclear component—deserves to be thoroughly examined, for all the reasons that past U.S. nuclear doctrine was examined in the public realm. "Though CONPLAN 8022 suggests a clean, short-duration strike intended to protect American security," Arkin wrote, "a preemptive surprise attack (let alone one involving a nuclear weapon option) would unleash a multitude of additional and unanticipated consequences. So, on both counts, why aren't we talking about it?"

CONCLUSION

In the years right after the Second World War, the United States and the Soviet Union circled one another warily. American atomic weapons and an expanding basing program for strategic forces worried the Soviets, just as the large Soviet ground army and expansionist, ideological Soviet rhetoric worried the Americans. The Czech crisis of 1948, and the Berlin Crisis of the same year signaled a worsening relationship. Following the shocks of the Soviet atomic bomb and the fall of China in 1949, Paul Nitze of the State Department's Policy Planning Staff found that the time was right to articulate and argue for an aggressive U.S. national security policy that called for a major commitment to defense spending, and to the development of large conventional and nuclear forces. The following summer the war in Korea prompted a reluctant President Truman to begin implementing this blueprint.

In many ways, the United States has never departed from NSC 68's call for across-the-board dominance as a means of providing for national security. Once the incentives and institutions were in place to support and undergird the architecture of the plan, they became difficult to modify—even when modification was warranted. And once the rhetoric of an aggressive, dominance-seeking Soviet Union had taken hold in the American mind, it became very easy, politically, to trumpet new calls to arms to ward off weakness, or second-class status in the superpower clash of the titans. Given the reality of the particularly pernicious security dilemma produced by postwar bipolarity, a dramatically different outcome may not have been possible. But one must wonder, nonetheless, if the Americans did not manage to give a self-sustaining quality to the competition—and the arms race born of that competition—because of the particular nature of our political and economic systems. And one must wonder, as well, if our own elaborate charts, graphs, and equations did not help to paint our fears in bright colors—and thus make them seem more vivid and more daunting. In 1981 Warner Schilling speculated that, "Given the complexities involved, it is plausible that the actual military capabilities which the United States has maintained during the past decade in the name of strategic equality owe more to the end products of the bureaucratic and Executive-Congressional politics of acquisition policy than they do to the formal guidelines for employment policy that have been associated with the strategic doctrines of sufficiency, equivalence, or countervailing power."[164] It was a prescient observation.

The nature of the nuclear arms race took a particularly unusual and ironic direction. The dynamics that caused both sides to continue to build up arms in response to one another, led—ultimately—to weapon systems that were so absurdly powerful as to have no utility outside the role of deterrence. There was no political stake for which superpower nuclear warfare was a suitable or reasonable instrument of attainment. And yet the race—and the arms build-up—continued, obtuse to reason beyond its own internal logic. We are fortunate that the potential consequences of nuclear war did not escape policymakers on either side of the Iron Curtain. Though there were surely tense times and some close calls, decision-makers picked their way through a decades-long minefield—perhaps with the heightened sensory awareness that comes when one knows that a single false step could be one's last.

But as we breathe a sigh of relief at having survived the most tense moments of the Cold War, we must acknowledge the general failure of efforts to provide the commander-in-chief with more genuinely limited nuclear warfighting options—and more comprehensive forms of command and control—than those produced by the bureaucratized war-planning mechanisms of the various military services. The dilemma that so troubled Secretary McNamara in the early 1960s never went away entirely; should war have come, this monstrous problem would have been exacerbated by the inherent limits to rationality posed by the problem of having to respond within an absurdly short decision cycle, and in the environment of imperfect information that always characterizes wartime. The latter has not changed, despite the "information revolution" of recent decades. Ever-improving command and control capabilities, including space assets, are likely to tempt future presidents toward the direct control of the U.S. strategic arsenal. But the Dora Farms strike in the opening phase of the 2003 Iraq War might serve as a cautionary tale in this regard. The ability to attain information is not a guarantee that the information will be reliable.

Clearly, a case can and should be made for maintaining a capacity to hold enemy assets at risk through strategic weapons that can be employed immediately and from a long distance. And a case can be made, as well, for retaining some portion of the U.S. nuclear arsenal. Several regional powers, including North Korea and Iran, have nuclear ambitions and interests opposed to those of the United States, and China surely has the potential to pose a major threat to U.S. interests in the future. Deterrence against enemies with no return address is more difficult, but the Bush Administration's efforts to leverage what it can against these enemies is hardly misplaced. What is essential, though, is that the strategic arsenal—including the chemical and biological arsenal—be tailored to the requirements of deterring a new kind of enemy while not furthering trends toward proliferation, or creating regional or crisis instability. If the Americans managed to pick their way through the many hazards of the Cold War, they did so by constantly debating their choices and revisiting their assumptions. The contemporary threats posed to U.S. security deserve the same priority; the discussion about them needs to be open and wide-ranging—and it should command the attention of the best minds in the nation.[165]

In addition, the record—since 1945—of the warfighting use of strategic air forces (armed with conventional weapons) should provide guidance and insight to administrations tempted to use this tool in the future. In the realm of air warfare there has always been a propensity to discount the past as any sort of guide to the future. Airmen were, after all, a self-selected population who kept their focus forward on the horizon.[166] But if ongoing improvements in precision, intelligence, target acquisition, and strike capability continue to refine and empower the strategic air mission, they cannot—of themselves—force warfare to become a less complex and confusing business, immune to human emotion and calculations that fall entirely outside the realm of rationality. The lessons that Carl von Clausewitz taught in the nineteenth century still hold, even for the high-tech strategic warriors of the new millennium.

Notes

1. See Thomas Schelling's analysis of "coercion" and "brute force" (and also the distinctions and overlap between them) in *Arms and Influence* (New Haven: Yale University Press, 1962), esp. pp. 1–34 ("The Diplomacy of Violence"). Coercion is the use (by a state or political actor) of a threat in order to achieve an aim. The threat to inflict pain operates like blackmail; it exploits an enemy's fears and needs. It operates best when it is held in reserve, but the power to hurt—to inflict harm on enemy assets—can also be communicated by some performance of it. By contrast, "brute force" involves taking what one wants by sheer force. It operates best when it is used, can be directly measured, and is associated principally with armies. There is no clear divide between coercion and brute force in war (the act of long range bombardment involves both coercion and brute force, for instance), but the two operate by distinct mechanisms. Strategic forces, by threatening to inflict prompt and direct pain on an enemy, can structure an enemy's motives and thus influence its political behavior.

2. For an excellent analysis of American thinking about long range bombardment in World War I, see George K. Williams, "The Shank of the Drill: Americans and Strategical Aviation in the Great War," *Journal of Strategic Studies* 19, no. 3 (September 1996): 381–431.

3. Declassified portions of the Global Strike Plan can be read on the Web site of the Federation of American Scientists: *www.fas.org*. For an excellent overview, see William Arkin, "Not Just a Last Resort," *Washington Post*, May 15, 2005, B01.

4. Two seminal books addressing the problems of deterrence and nuclear strategy are: Robert Jervis, *The Illogic of American Nuclear Strategy* (Ithaca: Cornell Unversity Press, 1984); Robert Jervis, Richard Ned Lebow, and Janice Gross Stein, *Psychology and Deterrence* (Baltimore: Johns Hopkins University Press, 1985).

5. www.brook.edu/fp/projects/nucwcost/schwartz.htm

6. See Michael Sherry, *Preparing for the Next War* (New Haven: Yale University Press, 1977).

7. See James T. Patterson, *Grand Expectations: The United States, 1945–1974* (New York: Oxford, 1996), 121–22. And, in line with past practice, Truman demobilized the wartime military quickly. On V-J day U.S. armed forces consisted of 91 Army and 6 Marine divisions (combat ready), a vast array of aircraft organized into 213 combat groups, and 1,166 combat vessels in the Navy. Twenty-two months later, the armed forces had shrunk down to ten under-strength Army divisions (only two of which were combat ready), two under-strength Marine divisions, an air service with only eleven operational groups (out of 63 total), and a Navy of 343 combat ships.

8. See Gregg Herken, *The Winning Weapon: The Atomic Bomb in the Cold War, 1945–1950* (New York: Random House, 1981). For an excellent general history of this period, see Melvin Leffler, *A Preponderance of Power* (Stanford: Stanford University Press, 1992).

9. See David A. Rosenberg, "The Origins of Overkill: Nuclear Weapons and American Strategy, 1945–1950," in Steven Miller, ed., *Strategy and Nuclear Deterrence* (Princeton: Princeton University Press, 1984), 113–82.

10. Bernard Brodie, *The Absolute Weapon: Atomic Power and World Order* (New York: Harcourt Brace, 1946); see also generally, Fred Kaplan, *The Wizards of Armageddon* (New York: Simon and Schuster, 1983).

11. Steven L. Rearden, *The Formative Years, 1947–1950*, History of the Office of the Secretary of Defense, vol. 1 (Washington, D.C.: OSD Historical Office, 1984), 389–90.

12. Gallery quoted in Rearden, *The Formative Years*, 390.

13. See generally, Walton Moody, *Building a Strategic Air Force* (Washington, D.C.: GPO, 1996).

14. Lawrence Freedman, *The Evolution of Nuclear Strategy* (New York: St. Martin's, 1981), 48.

15. On this community of scholars see Kaplan, *The Wizards of Armageddon*.

16. Rosenberg, "The Origins of Overkill," 125.

17. The Harmon Committee report quoted in Rosenberg, "The Origins of Overkill," 126.

18. See Curtis E. LeMay with MacKinley Cantor, *Mission with LeMay* (New York: Doubleday, 1965).

19. Rosenberg, "The Origins of Overkill," 126–27.
20. National Security Council Paper no. 68 reprinted in Ernest May, ed., *American Cold War Strategy: Interpreting NSC 68* (Boston: St. Martin's Press, 1993), 26. See also May's very useful introductory chapter.
21. NCS 68, reprinted in May, ed. *American Cold War Strategy*, 80–81.
22. Marc Trachtenberg, "A 'Wasting Asset': American Strategy and the Shifting Nuclear Balance, 1949–1954," in Trachtenberg, *History and Strategy* (Princeton: Princeton University Press, 1991), 109–10.
23. O'Donnell quoted in Conrad C. Crane, "Raiding the Beggar's Pantry: The Search for Air Power Strategy in the Korean War," in *The Journal of Military History* 63, no. 4 (October 1999): 889. See also, generally, Crane, *American Air Power Strategy in Korea, 1950–1953* (Lawrence: University Press of Kansas, 2000).
24. See Michael Sherry, *In the Shadow of War* (New Haven: Yale University Press, 1995), 181–82.
25. Crane, "Raiding the Beggar's Pantry," 893–903.
26. Mark Clodfelter, *The Limits of Air Power* (New York: The Free Press, 1989), 21.
27. LeMay quoted in Thomas Hone, "Strategic Bombardment Constrained: Korea and Vietnam" in R. Cargill Hall, ed. *Case Studies in Strategic Bombardment* (Washington, D.C.: Air Force History and Museums Program, 1998), 517.
28. Crane, "Raiding the Beggar's Pantry," 905.
29. Ibid., 912.
30. Clodfelter, *Limits of Air Power*, 18–20l; Crane, "Rading the Beggar's Pantry," 918.
31. Zimmerman quoted in Robert Frank Futrell, *Ideas, Concepts, Doctrine: A History of Basic Thinking in the United States Air Force* (Maxwell Air Force Base, AL, 1971), 177.
32. See in particular McGeorge Bundy, *Danger and Survival* (New York: Random House, 1988), 238–45.
33. Futrell, *Ideas, Concepts, Doctrine*, 177, and 180–81.
34. The militarization of American foreign policy, American politics, and American life generally is traced brilliantly in Sherry's *In the Shadow of War*. On the early Cold War see in particular, 123–87 (and, on the impact of the Korean war, 183–87). For a continuation of this argument in a more recent context, see Andrew Bacevich, *The New American Militarism: How Americans Are Seduced by War* (New York: Oxford University Press, 2005).
35. Rosenberg, "The Origins of Overkill," 131–33.
36. On the hydrogen bomb, see Bundy, *Danger and Survival*, 197–235; David Holloway, *The Soviet Union and the Arms Race* (New Haven: Yale University Press, 1983), esp. pp. 23–27; Kai Bird and Martin Sherwin, *American Prometheus: The Triumph and Tragedy of J. Robert Oppenheimer* (New York: Knopf, 2005).
37. William W. Epley, *America's First Cold War Army, 1945–1950* (Arlington, VA: Association of the U.S. Army, 1993), 23.

38. Steven Rearden, "U.S. Strategic Bombardment Doctrine Since 1945," in R. Cargill Hall, ed., *Case Studies in Strategic Bombardment* (Washington, D.C.: Air Force History and Museums Program, 1998), 414.

39. John Lewis Gaddis, *Strategies of Containment: A Critical Appraisal of Postwar American National Security Policy* (New York: Oxford University Press, 1982), 126.

40. Gaddis offers an expert analysis of Eisenhower's perspective in, *Strategies of Containment*, 127–36; see also McGeorge Bundy, *Danger and Survival*, 236–318; Scott D. Sagan, *Moving Targets: Nuclear Strategy and National Security* (Princeton: Princeton University Press, 1989), 18–24; Richard Immerman and Robert Bowie, *Waging Peace: How Eisenhower Shaped an Enduring Cold War Strategy* (New York: Oxford University Press, 1998); Aaron Friedberg, *In the Shadow of the Garrison State* (Princeton: Princeton University Press, 2000).

41. Dulles quoted in Sagan, *Moving Targets*, 23.

42. See generally Trachtenberg, "A 'Wasting Asset?'"; Tami Davis Biddle, "Handing the Soviet Threat: 'Project Control' and the Debate on American Strategy in the Early Cold War Years," *The Journal of Strategic Studies* 12, no. 3 (September 1989); Sagan, *Moving Targets*, 19–24.

43. See Sagan, *Moving Targets*, 19–23; quoted material on 22.

44. See appendix "National Security Expenditures as a Percentage of Total Government Expenditures and Gross National Product, 1945–1980," in Gaddis, *Strategies of Containment*, 359.

45. Sagan, *Moving Targets*, 24.

46. See Crane, "Raiding the Beggar's Pantry," 920; and generally, Dennis M. Drew, "Air Theory, Air Force, and Low Intensity Conflict: A Short Journey to Confusion," in Phillip Meilinger, ed., *The Paths of Heaven: The Evolution of Airpower Theory*" (Maxwell Air Force Base: Air University Press, 1997), 321–55.

47. Rosenberg, "Nuclear War Planning," in Michael Howard, et al, eds. *The Laws of War* (New Haven: Yale University Press, 1994), 171–73.

48. See www.redstone.army.mil/history/nikesite

49. Walter McDougall, . . .*The Heavens and the Earth: A Political History of the Space Age* (Baltimore: Johns Hopkins University Press, 1985), 42–43; Holloway, *The Soviet Union and the Arms Race*, 20–23.

50. See generally, David Holloway, *Stalin and the Bomb* (New Haven: Yale University Press, 1996).

51. On the fundamental ideas shaping the political environment of Cold War era deterrence, see Robert Jervis, *International Politics: Enduring Concepts and Contemporary Issues*, 6th ed. (New York: Longman, 2002).

52. On the Killian and Gaither Reports, see Rearden, "U.S. Strategic Bombardment Doctrine," 412–20.

53. McDougall adds insightful detail to the story of the Killian report. See *The Heavens and the Earth*, 116–117.

54. Cited in Jacob Neufeld, *Ballistic Missiles in the United States Air Force 1945–1960* (Washington, DC: Office of Air Force History, 1990), 135. See also 132.

55. McDougall, *The Heavens and the Earth*, 117.

56. See ibid., 151.

57. Ibid., 142. On 145 he adds: "A national primer on the mechanics of spaceflight arrived on millions of doorsteps two weeks after the fact [of Sputnik] in the pages of *Life* magazine. But among the scientific stories and charts was editorial material that *instructed* the American people to panic and told them that their wiser neighbors already had." (Italics in original.)

58. Albert Carnesale, et al, *Living with Nuclear Weapons* (New York: Bantam, 1983), 83.

59. Neufeld, *Ballistic Missiles*, 208.

60. McDougall, *The Heavens and the Earth*, 219.

61. Kenneth Hagan, *This People's Navy* (New York: The Free Press, 1991), 346–54. On Polaris see also George Baer, *One Hundred Years of Sea Power* (Stanford: Stanford University Press, 1994), 352–59.

62. Rearden, "U.S. Strategic Bombardment Doctrine," 408–9.

63. See for instance, Richard Rhodes, "The General and World War II" in *The New Yorker*, June 19, 1995, 47–59.

64. See Tami Davis Biddle, "Curtis E. LeMay and the Ascent of American Strategic Airpower," in *Realizing the Dream of Flight*, Virginia P. Dawson and Mark D. Bowles, eds. (Washington, DC: National Aeronautics and Space Administration, 2005), esp. pp. 145–50.

65. David A. Rosenberg, "Nuclear War Planning," in Michael Howard et al, eds., *The Laws of War*, 169. See also a fascinating study by Lynn Eden, *Whole World on Fire: Organizations, Knowledge, and Nuclear Weapons Devastation* (Ithaca: Cornell University Press, 2004).

66. Rosenberg, "Nuclear War Planning," 174–75; Sagan, *Moving Targets*, 24–26.

67. NSC 30 quoted in Rosenberg, "Nuclear War Planning," 169.

68. Rosenberg, "Nuclear War Planning," 169–71.

69. On command and control issues generally, see Paul Bracken, *The Command and Control of Nuclear Forces* (New Haven: Yale University Press, 1983); Bruce G. Blair, *Strategic Command and Control: Redefining the Nuclear Threat* (Washington, D.C.: The Brookings Institution, 1985); Peter D. Feaver, *Guarding the Guardians* (Ithaca: Cornell University Press, 1992).

70. Russell Weigley, *History of the United States Army* (New York: MacMillan, 1967) p. 526.

71. See Dean's introduction to the 1958 edition of Henry Kissinger's *Nuclear Weapons and Foreign Policy*, first published by the Council on Foreign Relations in 1957.

72. McDougall, *The Heavens and the Earth*, 220.

73. Kennedy's defense policy, and its many points of contrast with "Massive Retaliation," is explained well in Gaddis, *Strategies of Containment*, esp. pp. 198–273.

74. Another useful and readable description of Kennedy Adminstration thinking is offered by Richard Smoke, *National Security and the Nuclear Dilemma*, 3rd ed. (New York: McGraw-Hill, 1993), 101–124.

75. McNamara cited in Freedman, *The Evolution of U.S. Nuclear Strategy*, 232.

76. Ibid., 238.

77. Sagan, *Moving Targets*, 36.

78. Quoted in Freedman, *Evolution*, 239.

79. Ibid., 243.

80. This was due to the cost of these systems, the increasing Soviet emphasis on ballistic missiles, and studies that revealed the USSR could readily overwhelm U.S. defenses through cost-effective, offensive countermeasures. See Sagan, *Moving Targets*, 36

81. Freedman, *Evolution*, 246–47; quoted material on 246. See also Rearden, "U.S. Strategic Bombardment Doctrine," 429; and Sagan, *Moving Targets*, 33–34.

82. On this point see Rearden, "U.S. Strategic Bombardment Doctrine," 429.

83. The literature on the Cuban Missile Crisis is very large. A very readable, informative, and comprehensive recent account is offered by Aleksandr Fursenko and Timothy Naftali, *"One Hell of a Gamble": Khrushchev, Castro, and Kennedy, 1958–1964* (New York: Norton, 1998).

84. See *The Cuban Missile Crisis 1962: A National Security Archive Documents Reader*, Laurence Chang and Peter Kornbluh, eds. (New York: The New Press, 1992), esp. pp. 389.

85. See Paul Bracken, *The Command and Control of Nuclear Forces* (New Haven: Yale University Press, 1983), 25–27.

86. Carnesale, et al, *Living with Nuclear Weapons*, 88.

87. Rearden, "U.S. Strategic Bombardment Doctrine Since 1945," 430.

88. See Richard Smoke, *National Security and the Nuclear Dilemma*, 125–47.

89. An excellent overview of the war is offered in George Herring, *America's Longest War*, 3rd ed. (New York: McGraw-Hill, 1996); on bombing in the war generally, see Clodfelter, *The Limits of Air Power*.

90. Hone, "Strategic Bombardment Constrained," 509–10; Richard Davis, "Strategic Bombing in the Gulf War," in Hall, *Case Studies*, 529.

91. On the reasons for U.S. failure in Vietnam, see Robert Pape, *Bombing to Win: Air Power and Coercion in War* (Ithaca: Cornell University Press, 1996); Andrew Krepenevich, *The Army in Vietnam* (Baltimore: Johns Hopkins University Press, 1986); and Clodfelter, *The Limits of Air Power*.

92. See Earl Tilford, "Setup: Why and How the U.S. Air Force Lost in Vietnam," in *Armed Forces and Society* 17, no. 3 (1991): 327. See also, Robert Pape, "Coercive Air Power in the Vietnam War" *International Security* 15, no. 2 (Fall 1990): 103–46; and Pape, *Bombing to Win*, 174–210.

93. See Smoke, *National Security and the Nuclear Dilemma*, 139–147.

94. Ibid., 149.

95. Ibid., 140–141.

96. Ibid., 149–174; Carnesale et al, *Living with Nuclear Weapons*, 86–95; John Baylis, "Arms Control and Disarmament," in *Strategy in the Contemporary World*, John Baylis et al., eds. (New York: Oxford University Press, 183–207). Also, generally, John Newhouse, *Cold Dawn: The Story of SALT* (New York: Holt, Rinehart and Winston, 1973).

97. Smoke *National Security and the Nuclear Dilemma*, 159–160.

98. See, generally, David Schwarz, *NATO's Nuclear Dilemmas* (Washington, DC: Brookings, 1982).

99. Steven Rearden, "U.S. Strategic Bombardment Doctrine Since 1945," 434–39, with quoted material on 434.

100. Sagan, *Moving Targets*, 39–48.

101. Steven Rearden, "U.S. Strategic Bombardment Doctrine Since 1945," 434–439, with quoted material on 439.

102. See Sagan, *Moving Targets*, 43–44.

103. Ibid., 44–45.

104. On PD 59 see Rearden, "U.S. Strategic Bombardment Doctrine," 440–43.

105. For a full account of the story from an insider's perspective, see Strobe Talbott, *Endgame: The Inside Story of SALT II* (New York: Harper and Row, 1979).

106. Smoke *National Security and the Nuclear Dilemma*, 159. He argues that the United States missed another opportunity to place serious constraints on MIRVs, right as SALT I was being signed. On nuclear issues in the 1970s, see also Warner Schilling, "U.S. Strategic Nuclear Concepts in the 1970s" *International Security* 6 no. 2 (Fall 1981) reprinted in Steven E. Miller ed., *Strategy and Nuclear Deterrence* (Princeton: Princeton University Press, 1984), 183–214; also, generally, Jerome H. Kahan, *Security in the Nuclear Age* (Washington, D.C.: The Brookings Institution, 1975).

107. The treaty is printed in full in an appendix to Talbott's *Endgame*.

108. For a good overview of the Soviet build-up, see Smoke, *National Security and the Nuclear Dilemma*, 175–81.

109. See Ibid., 188–91.

110. Richard Pipes, "Why the Soviet Union Thinks It Could Fight and Win a Nuclear War," *Commentary* 64, no. 1 (July 1977).

111. Warner Schilling notes that "the second strike capacity of the United States was larger in 1980 than it was in 1964, when the Soviet build-up began." Schilling, "U.S. Strategic Concepts in the 1970s," 185.

112. Ibid., 201.

113. For a comprehensive but concise overview of Carter's national security policy, see Gaddis, *Strategies of Containment*, 345–57. On MX see Smoke, 207–9.

114. Rearden, "U.S. Strategic Bombardment Doctrine," 442–43: Sagan, *Moving Targets*, 48–54.

115. The events of the Iranian revolution are summarized in Robert Schulzinger, *American Diplomacy in the Twentieth Century*, 3rd ed. (New York: Oxford University Press, 1994), 328–31.

116. See John Lewis Gaddis, "The Unexpected Ronald Reagan," in *The United States and the End of the Cold War* (New York: Oxford University Press, 1992), 119–32; and generally, Gil Troy, *Morning in America: How Ronald Reagan Invented the 1980s* (Princeton: Princeton University Press, 2005).

117. Smoke, *National Security and the Nuclear Dilemma*, 211–12; Rearden, "U.S. Strategic Bombardment Doctrine" p. 445. Allan Millett and Peter Maslowski have written: "Reagan understood that his strategic grand design required grand budgets. Communicating his proposals with a relaxed, jocular militancy that soothed his constituents and frightened the rest of the world, the President proposed and Congress accepted—without major alteration—six years (FY 1980–FY 1985) of increased defense spending, the longest sustained peacetime investment in the armed forces in the twentieth century." See Millett and Maslowski, *For the Common Defense: A Military History of the United States of America*, rev. ed. (New York: The Free Press, 1994), 615–16.

118. On the Wheeler statement, see Schilling, "U.S. Strategic Concepts," 190. See also, generally, Paul Lettow, *Ronald Reagan and His Quest to Abolish Nuclear Weapons* (New York: Random House, 2005).

119. In his robustly argued book, which is based in part on extensive interviews with Reagan's advisors, Lettow adds: "He intended that SDI would catalyze the total elimination of nuclear weapons. An effective missile defense, he believed, would make not just ballistic missiles but all nuclear arms negotiable." See Lettow's introduction, esp. ix–x (quoted material at x).

120. Sagan, *Moving Targets*, 52–54.

121. On the Reagan-Gorbachev relationship, see Gaddis, "The Unexpected Ronald Reagan," 126–130.

122. The terms of the INF treaty can be found in Smoke, *National Security*, 269.

123. Ibid., 289.

124. Ibid., 288–91, and Rearden, "U.S. Strategic Bombardment Doctrine," 445–46.

125. These events are summarized in Thomas G. Paterson and J. Gary Clifford, *America Ascendant: U.S. Foreign Relations Since 1939* (Lexington, MA: D.C. Heath, 1995), 286–87.

126. Perhaps the best general history of the 1991 Gulf War is Michael Gordon and Bernard Trainor, *The General's War* (Boston: Little, Brown and Co., 1995).

127. Richard G. Davis, *Decisive Force: Strategic Bombing in the Gulf War* (Washington, D.C.: Air Force Museums and History Program, 1996), 20. For the most

comprehensive treatment of the air campaign, see Thomas Keaney and Eliot Cohen, *Gulf War Air Power Survey*, 5 vols. (Washington, D.C.: GPO, 1993).

128. Davis, *Decisive Force*, 9–12; on Warden see also John Andreas Olson, "Col. John A. Warden, III: Smasher of Paradigms?" in Peter W. Gray and Sebastian Cox, eds. *Air Power Leadership: Theory and Practice* (London: HMSO, 2002), 129–59.

129. Davis, *Decisive Force*, 19.

130. Ibid., 2.

131. Richard G. Davis, "Strategic Bombardment in the Gulf War," in Hall, ed. *Case Studies in Strategic Bombardment*, 573–575; and Davis, *Decisive Force*, 42–43.

132. For a critique of coercive air power in the Gulf War, see Pape, *Bombing to Win*, 211–53.

133. Daniel Haulman, *One Hundred Years of Flight: USAF Chronology of Significant Air and Space Events* (Washington, D.C.: Air Force History and Museums Program, 2003), 141. By 1998 the USAF was in the midst of further change, moving toward implementation of a plan that would divide its combat strength, and the elements supporting that strength, into ten "Aerospace Expeditionary Forces" (AEFs). This shift was undertaken in order to enhance joint operations, and to make the service more responsive to the international environment and changing national strategy. See Richard G. Davis, *Anatomy of a Reform: The Expeditionary Aerospace Force* (Washington, D.C.: The Air Force History and Museums Program, 2003).

134. Smoke, *National Security*, 293–95. His discussion of Midgetman runs from 292–94.

135. On Reagan's SDI initiative, see Sagan, *Moving Targets*, 98–134; and generally, Lettow *Ronald Reagan*.

136. Smoke, *National Security*, 300–305.

137. The details of START I are listed in Ibid., 305–9. The treaty can be accessed on line through the Carnegie Endowment for International Peace: www.ceip.org/files/projects/mpp/resources/start1text.htm.

138. Smoke, *National Security*, 305–7.

139. John Baylis, "Arms Control and Disarmament," in Baylis et al, *Strategy in the Contemporary World* (New York: Oxford University Press), 2002, 194.

140. Ibid., 195.

141. Deborah Yarsike Ball and Theodore P. Gerber, "Russian Scientists and Rogue States: Does Western Assistance Reduce the Proliferation Threat?" *International Security* 29, no. 4 (Spring 2005): 50.

142. See http://lugar.senate.gov/nunnlugar.html.

143. Up to date and ongoing information about these and related problems can be found at the Web site of the Federation of American Scientists: www.fas.org.

144. Baylis, "Arms Control and Disarmament," 196.

145. Many of the most important questions are addressed in Andrew J. Bacevich and Eliot Cohen, eds. *War Over Kosovo: Politics and Strategy in a Global Age*

(New York: Columbia University Press, 2001). For an overview of the air war, see the essay by William Arkin "Operation Allied Force" (pp. 1–37); on the political appeal of precision bombing, see the essay by Eliot Cohen, "Kosovo and the New American Way of War" (pp. 38–62).

146. On the ethical issues raised by the war, see Alberto Coll, "Kosovo and the Moral Burdens of Power," in Bacevich and Cohen, *War Over Kosovo*, 124–54.

147. More work remains to be undertaken on this issue, but a start has been made by: Ivo Daalder and Michael O'Hanlon, *Winning Ugly: NATO's War to Save Kosovo* (Washington, D.C.: Brookings Institution, 2000); Benjamin Lambeth, *NATO's Air War for Kosovo* (Santa Monica, CA: RAND, 2001); and Stephen Hosmer, *Why Milosevic Decided to Settle When He Did* (Santa Monica, CA: RAND, 2001).

148. *The National Security Strategy of the United States of America*, The White House, Washington, D.C., 2002, 13.

149. The best account to date of the march to war is George Packer, *The Assassin's Gate* (New York: Farrar, Strauss, and Giroux, 2005).

150. For an overview of the Iraq War (2003), see Michael Gordon and Bernard Trainor, *Cobra II: The Inside Story of the Invasion and Occupation of Iraq* (New York: Pantheon, 2006).

151. Stephen Budiansky, *Air Power* (New York: Viking, 2004), 441.

152. See Ivan Oelrich, *Missions for Nuclear Weapons after the Cold War*, Occasional Paper no. 3, Federation of American Scientists, January 2005, 12–13.

153. Ivan Oelrich, *Missions*, 13.

154. See Bruce Jentleson, *American Foreign Policy: The Dynamics of Choice in the 21st Century*, 2nd ed. (New York: Norton, 2004), 390–91.

155. Excerpts of the NPR can be found at http://www.globalsecurity.org/wmd/library/policy/dod/npr.htm. See also J. D. Crouch, Special Briefing on the Nuclear Posture Review, 9 January 2002, http://www.defenselink.mil/transcripts/2002/t01092002_t0109npr.html.

156. See the web site of the U.S. Missile Defense Agency: http://www.mda.mil.

157. While he critiques some of the provisions of the NPR, Richard Sokolsky takes this view. See Sokolsky, "Demystifying the Nuclear Posture Review," *Survival* (Autumn 2002).

158. Charles Glaser and Steve Fetter, "Counterforce Revisited: Assessing the Nuclear Posture Review's New Missions," *International Security* 30, no. 2 (Fall 2005): 84–126.

159. Gen. John P. Jumper, USAF, "Global Strike Task Force: A Transforming Concept, Forged by Experience," *Aerospace Power Journal*, Spring 2001, available at: www.airpower.maxwell.af.mil/airchronicles/apj/apj01/spr01/jumper.htm

160. Ibid., quoted material on pp. 5–6.

161. See Maj. Gen. William L. Shelton, "This is Not Your Father's US Strategic Command," *High Frontier: The Journal for Space and Missile Professionals*, vol. 1, no. 4 (June 2005): 2; also "About USSTRATCOM" at http://www.stratcom.mil.

162. Ibid., 2.

163. Arkin, "Not Just a Last Resort?," *Washington Post*, May 15, 2005, B01.

164. Schilling, 200–201.

165. For a useful primer on this topic, see Rensselaer Lee, "Rethinking Nuclear Security Strategy" at the Web site of the Foreign Policy Research Institute, fpri.org/enotes.

166. The motto of the interwar U.S. Air Corps Tactical School was *"Proficumus More Irretenti,"* (We progress unhindered by tradition). See Tami Davis Biddle, *Rhetoric and Reality in Air Warfare* (Princeton: Princeton University Press, 2002), 138.

5. ELUSIVE BARGAIN
THE PATTERN OF U.S. CIVIL-MILITARY RELATIONS SINCE WORLD WAR II

Andrew J. Bacevich

I

History, the American statesman Henry L. Stimson once observed, "is often not what actually happened but what is recorded as such." This difference between reality and record does not emerge by accident. It reflects the interests of those in a position to influence the recording.

When it comes to the history of U.S. civil-military relations since the end of World War II, the gap between actual events and the story woven from those events looms especially large. It does so because that gap has served and continues to serve an important function. What we might term the approved interpretation of U.S. civil-military relations offers a sanitized version of the past designed to affirm and reassure.

According to that interpretation, there is really not much of a story to tell. Assessing the health of civil-military interaction according to a single criterion—the propensity of soldiers to overthrow the government—the approved version of events finds those relations to be beyond reproach. Notably, since the United States emerged as a global power during World War II, there is no evidence—none—suggesting that the American officer corps has ever plotted a coup or even contemplated the possibility of doing so. As for the "man on horseback," the general bent on seizing power illegally, he exists only in the fevered imagination of pulp fiction writers and sensation-flogging filmmakers. In practice, the otherwise highly permeable world of modern American politics has never accommodated an American Caesar. Indeed, observed James Bryce over a century ago, "Caesarism is the last danger likely to menace America"—a judgment that remains true in the present day.[1]

Granted, from time-to-time, evidence of civil-military tension, even animosity, erupts into public view, General Douglas MacArthur's clash with President Harry S Truman during the Korean War being the most notorious example. But these incidents are explained away as anomalies, unwelcome perhaps, but mere temporary departures from the norm that prove nothing. Besides, wasn't MacArthur fired for his insubordination? Didn't the civilian commander-in-chief prevail over his willful field commander?

In a formal sense, therefore, civilian control of the military, ever since 1945, as it had been before that date, has remained sacrosanct. The constitutional order is secure. According to proponents of the conventional view, the conclusion is axiomatic: no coup, no problem, and, with regard to the history of U.S. civil-military relations more generally, no real story.

Who benefits from this benign interpretation?

The answer to that question lies first in appreciating the extent to which the vast realm of programs and activities encompassing what Americans refer to as "national security policy" has since World War II become the particular preserve of a self-contained, self-perpetuating elite.

The impact of democratic processes on basic issues related to U.S. national security is negligible. Decisions to forge alliances, to go to war, to expand, contract, or reconfigure U.S. forces, to deploy them abroad, to acquire new weapons, or to arm other countries: these fall within the purview of a small civil-military directorate consisting of high-ranking civilian officials, both elected and appointed, and senior military officers, along with a handful of legislators, corporate executives, policy-oriented academics, and insider journalists. In deciding such matters, members of this elite neither seek nor seriously consider the views of the larger public, whom they are inclined to see as inherently suspect anyway. For their part, conditioned by habits developed during the protracted emergency of the Cold War, most citizens even today dutifully accept their exclusion from such matters.

For members of the national security elite, perpetuating this deference and their own monopoly over policy ranks as an objective of paramount importance. Toward that end, a reading of history that describes relations between civil and military authorities as reliably harmonious and that credits American soldiers with being reliably submissive to their civilian masters is eminently useful.

Such an interpretation does several things. First, it seemingly demonstrates that the "very improbable supposition that any people can long remain free, with a strong military power in the very heart of their country" is not so improbable after all. The words are those of Samuel Adams, urging in 1768 that "a wise and prudent people will always have a watchful and jealous eye" on the soldiers in their midst. But the sentiment is one that remained a central tenet of American republican ideology long after Adams had passed from the scene.[2] Portraying the dealings between the brass and "the frocks" as uneventful helps to sustain the notion that such concerns have long since outlived their day.

Furthermore, by ostensibly showing that liberty and military power are not incompatible, the benign view of U.S. civil-military relations helps make palatable the maintenance of an immensely powerful and permanent military establishment—for members of the national security elite the wellspring of careers, riches, fame, and the ultimate narcotic, namely, access to the innermost circle of power and the concomitant opportunity to participate in decisions affecting the course of world history and the life and death of thousands.

Above all, this prevailing view of U.S. civil-military relations reassures the American people that they have nothing to worry about—there is no need for that watchful and jealous eye—and, hence, they may attend to other, more mundane considerations. By extension, it deflects any inclination ordinary citizens may have of prying into matters over which the national security elite has become accustomed to enjoying exclusive oversight.

II

All of which might be fine were it not for the fact that the interpretation of U.S. civil-military relations to which Americans habitually pay homage is wildly misleading, where not simply dead wrong. Further, the very persistence of that interpretation conceals the pernicious implications of actually existing arrangements and practices. The counsel offered by Samuel Adams, meanwhile, has lost little of its relevance.

To begin with, the absence of coups or coup attempts alone does not qualify as proof of effective civilian control, any more than the absence of fistfights on the floor of the Congress qualifies as evidence of legislative bipartisanship or the absence of blatant fraud and stock manipulation is proof of corporate responsibility. Genuine civilian control has a positive as well as a negative aspect—that is, in addition to shielding the constitutional order from the danger of a military takeover, it also creates a framework within which soldiers and civilians collaborate to advance the national interest.

The "unequal dialogue" forming the nexus of this collaboration will inevitably produce much heat as well as light—weighty issues relating to war, strategy, the management of military campaigns, and the fate of cherished institutions being fraught with uncertainty and emotion.[3] In other words, real dialogue involves more than civilian leaders dictating instructions to compliant warriors. It implies give-and-take, candid and at times even contentious. But the principle of civilian control (along with the parallel principle establishing the absolute primacy of politics in war) mandates that the dialogue proceed consistent with the common understanding that, whatever the issue, at the end of the day, civilian masters will prevail and soldiers will abide by their decisions.

But even this more expansive understanding of civilian control does not suffice to define a "healthy" civil-military relationship. Ultimately, it is not simply the tenor of discourse that counts but the quality of the decisions that result. Even if the norms of civilian control are honored, civil-military interaction that yields defective policies—resulting in waste, needless loss, and even defeat or effects harmful to the practice of democracy—is inherently flawed.

Based on these criteria—open and honest dialogue consistent with the imperatives of civilian supremacy *and* effective policy outcomes—the historical record of U.S. civil-military relations since 1945 is at best mixed.

Indeed, to consider what actually happened rather than what has been recorded as such is to realize that civilian control of the military during the postwar era was frequently contested, at times highly contingent, and on a few occasions downright precarious. To be sure, with rare exceptions, the principal actors in and out of uniform carefully observed the formal conventions of proper behavior. But beneath the surface a different reality prevailed, in which the operative mechanism was not dialogue informed by mutual respect and a recognition of civilian supremacy, but hard bargaining and mutual manipulation informed by suspicion and mistrust and driven as often by narrow self-interest as by concern for the common good.

In other words, in the years following 1945 "civilian control" not infrequently became little more than a slogan, a useful fiction concealing a reality that was far more fractious, combative, and problematic. Just as the meatpacker is loath to invite consumers to tour his slaughterhouse, so too members of the national security elite are loath to permit mere citizens to glimpse the unedifying truth about civil-military interaction in the upper reaches of the United States government. In both cases, the likelihood that a hitherto pliant clientele will recoil in disgust and begin to ask awkward questions is just too great to contemplate.

Furthermore, on numerous occasions, this spurious dialogue gave birth to policies contrary to the national interest, for which the American people paid heavily. To cite just one example, among the many explanations for the debacle of Vietnam, the atmosphere of civil-military dishonesty and mistrust prevailing throughout that war deserves a place of honor.

In short, while it is true that the United States military has never since 1945 posed a threat to the constitutional order, that truth—noteworthy in its own right—obscures other hardly less important truths about the reality of U.S. civil-military interaction, a story too long neglected and in our own time richly deserving to be told.

III

Viewed as an episode in the history of U.S. civil-military relations, World War II qualifies as a singular triumph. The architects of the American war effort, led by President Franklin D. Roosevelt, cobbled together a system that melded reigning liberal democratic principles with the imperatives of waging total war on a global scale. The result was decisive victory. But victory created new circumstances and set in motion developments that in short order ensured that system's demise.

World War II became the ultimate expression of a longstanding American penchant for approaching armed conflict as an industrial enterprise. In waging war, U.S. policymakers have preferred to expend material, not men, providing the wherewithal to defeat the enemy—optimally by equipping others to do the actual fighting—while shielding the home front from sacrifice and tampering as little as possible with existing arrangements encompassing "the American way of life."

Thus did President Roosevelt in December 1940—a full year before formal U.S. entry into the war—indicate clearly what role he intended America to play. The United States, he proclaimed during the course of one of his famous fireside chats, was to serve as "the great arsenal of democracy."

So the nation became, although the arsenal's actual purpose was less to promote the spread of democratic ideals abroad than to advance the concrete interests of America's own actually existing, if imperfect democracy.

Thus, reflecting the president's intention, and with American industry and American agriculture performing prodigious feats of production, the Roosevelt administration fought World War II as a war of abundance.[4]

This characterization applies in two respects. On the one hand, the United States mobilized vast resources to support the war effort, making it possible to raise, deploy, and sustain massive land, sea, and air forces that became renowned for the lavish style in which they subsisted and fought.[5]

In addition, through its policy of "lend-lease," the United States shared the bounty of its fields and factories with its allies, some of them not even remotely democratic.[6] As a direct consequence, although the United States spent more on the war than any other nation, it suffered the fewest casualties of any major belligerent.[7]

On the other hand, mobilization for total war pulled the United States out of the economic doldrums in which it had languished throughout the 1930s. With much of the population of war-torn Europe and Asia living hand-to mouth, and despite a shortage of consumer goods and the annoyance of rationing, life for the average American improved, thanks to the military Keynsianism of the early 1940s. Indeed, the U.S. gross domestic product doubled in just four years. By 1945, this war-induced boom had catapulted the United States to a position of unquestioned global economic preeminence that it would not soon relinquish.[8]

To be sure, prosperity did not provide an antidote to old pathologies. Massive violations of civil rights, racial hysteria and tensions, labor unrest, and social dislocation: all these formed part of life on the home front.[9] But on balance the Roosevelt administration hewed to a course that suited most Americans, content as a result to let the president and his generals decide how best to wage the war.

Central to that task was the problem of creating the forces needed to fight. The German invasion of Poland in September 1939 found the U.S. armed services unprepared for war. The United States Army (which also included America's air forces) consisted of fewer than 200,000 ill-equipped regulars. The Navy's total strength was 125,200 and that of the Marine Corps 20,000.[10] By the time the war ended, twelve million Americans were serving in uniform. With regard to civil-military relations, there are two points to be made about how the Roosevelt administration raised and organized this force.

First, relatively few among those twelve million were volunteers. Already in the summer of 1940, with an eye toward distributing manpower among the services without depriving industry of essential workers, preparedness-minded members of Congress had persuaded a majority of their colleagues to institute a draft. After December 7, 1941, limited peacetime conscription gave way to a much larger wartime program lasting for the duration. By war's end, over forty-nine million Americans had registered, nineteen million had been selected, and ten million were actually inducted, a process that met with minimal obstruction, dissent, or evasion.[11]

Second, federal authorities implemented the draft, and more broadly established terms of military service, consistent with prevailing American notions of democracy. When it came to determining eligibility for service, the principle of equality applied. Class, color, race, or creed did not provide the basis for claiming special exemptions. Nor did they offer an allowable pretext for discrimination. Rich and poor, famous and obscure, white and black: all stood equal in the eyes of their local draft board.[12]

At the same time, local draft boards evinced little interest in using conscription as a vehicle for overturning the existing social order. Most Americans saw the war as an effort not to rethink democracy, but to preserve it: the object of the exercise was to defeat the enemy and restore the status quo ante. Franklin Roosevelt—proclaiming that reform-minded Dr. New Deal had given way to the more focused Dr. Win-the-War—endorsed this view.

But the norms of American democracy prevailing in the 1940s included a profound and pervasive racism. Although African Americans were called to the colors in proportion to their population as a whole, they served in segregated units, relegated for the most part to noncombat roles behind the front lines. In a Jim Crow era, the armed services adhered faithfully to Jim Crow practices.[13]

Americans in the 1940s took it for granted that the battlefield was an exclusively male preserve. Women were thus by definition ill-suited for combat and by extension were ineligible for the draft. The limited numbers serving during World War II did so as volunteers, organized, trained, and housed separately from men and consigned to medical and administrative tasks. There would be no women warriors and no tampering with entrenched gender roles.

Furthermore, a rapidly industrializing, increasingly urban American society in the 1940s habitually permitted farmers to wield outsized political clout—reflecting a lingering nostalgia for a fast-fading agrarian ideal—and it accorded a privileged place to the role of father as breadwinner—reflecting an endorsement of the nuclear family. Each of these preferences made its imprint on how the Roosevelt administration implemented conscription. When it came to establishing guidelines to determine which

eligible males to induct, federal regulations were notably generous in granting deferments to farm workers and married men claiming dependents.

From the point of view of sheer military expediency, none of these provisions made much sense. But each accorded nicely with the will of the
majority and in the context of the times qualified as democratic. Each illustrates the terms of the government's implicit wartime contract with the
public, a civil-military bargain designed to win broad public support for
the war and to secure for Roosevelt and his generals a free hand in determining how to fight it.

Managing a conflict fought on a truly global scale against multiple adversaries posed challenges for which the executive branch in its prewar
configuration was ill-prepared. As was his wont, Roosevelt's response was
to improvise, devising new institutions and procedures that suited his
own operating style and his determination to concentrate ultimate authority in his own hands.

Largely excluding the civilian heads of the War and Navy Departments from operational matters, the president chose to deal directly and
routinely with the service's uniformed leaders, now constituted in the
executive office of the president (but not established by statute) as the
Joint Chiefs of Staff. In addition to the chief of staff of the Army and the
chief of naval operations, the wartime Joint Chiefs included the commanding general of U.S. Army Air Forces—an acknowledgment of the
growing importance of air power at a time when an independent air service did not yet exist. To coordinate the activities of the Joint Chiefs and
serve as de facto chairman, Roosevelt recalled to active duty a retired
admiral and installed him in the White House as chief of staff to the
president. But Roosevelt left no doubt about who was in charge: as commander-in-chief, he was.[14]

Consulting with (and on occasion overriding) his military chiefs, Roo-
sevelt personally laid down the basic lines of U.S. wartime policy. But
World War II was a war of coalitions. To coordinate coalition strategy,
FDR relied on summit meetings, periodic face-to-face negotiations with
allied leaders such as Winston Churchill and Josef Stalin. At each of these
famous wartime conferences, beginning with Argentia, Newfoundland, in
August 1941, the American president made a point of including the Joint
Chiefs in his entourage, thereby ensuring that the consideration of grand
strategy did not occur in a military vacuum.

To implement agreements resulting from these summits, the United
States mounted simultaneous large-scale operations on several fronts,

each designated a "theater of operations" and each the responsibility of its own "supreme commander." Acting at the president's behest, the Joint Chiefs issued guidance to these commanders and allocated to each a mix of units appropriate to the theater. When it came to the actual employment of combat forces, however, commanders like General Dwight D. Eisenhower in Europe or MacArthur in the Southwest Pacific enjoyed considerable latitude. That is, although at the level of strategy senior officers remained firmly subordinate to civilian authority, the actual direction of combat operations tended to reinforce traditional military assertions of professional autonomy. In the field, supreme commanders reigned supreme.

There was a further complication. Although the modern battlefield required a hitherto unprecedented degree of collaboration among land, air, and naval forces, World War II planted the seeds for future interservice rivalry.

Even during the war itself this became apparent. The vast wartime expansion of U.S. forces, an essentially limitless defense budget, and the several military technologies reaching maturity during the war gave rise to large dreams. Learning from the Germans, the United States Army mastered the art of combined arms mechanized operations and affirmed, to its own satisfaction at least, the primacy of war on land. Spurred by the Japanese, the United States Navy rebuilt itself around the carrier task force and developed the capability to project power around the world. For its part, the United States Marine Corps not only solved the riddle of amphibious operations, but also evolved into a full-fledged army in its own right, complete with its own supporting air arm. Even more significantly, air power advocates cited wartime advances in strategic bombing to validate their calls for creating an independent air force and to argue that the air weapon alone would decide the outcome of future wars. Each service evolved its own distinctive paradigm of armed conflict that it intended should provide the template for designing the postwar defense establishment.[15]

In the spring of 1945, Roosevelt died. That summer, the atomic bomb revolutionized warfare yet again, with implications that seemed mindboggling. With Japan's final surrender in September, many of FDR's most gifted lieutenants, both military and civilian, departed public life. As hostilities ended, strategic clarity gave way to confusion. Bitter internecine conflict erupted among the services. As one result, the edifice of civilmilitary cooperation and control that Roosevelt had erected and that had served the nation well throughout the world war began to crumble.

IV

Whatever the public's hopes of restoring normalcy to the home front once the war ended, few observers expected the United States to revert to its prewar "isolationism." Members of the American elite were as one in their determination to avoid the "mistakes" committed in the aftermath of the previous world war. This time the United States would remain engaged internationally. It would shoulder the burdens of global leadership. By extension, America's armed forces would take on permanent new responsibilities. Henceforth, even in peacetime, the United States would maintain great military power.

But agreement on these general points did not translate into agreement on specifics. In the realm of military policy—after 1945 referred to as national security policy—the war's immediate aftermath brought to the fore a host of contentious issues relating to recruitment, organization, service roles and missions, the level of the defense spending, and the control of nuclear weapons.

Each of these issues was important in its own right. But the controversies that they provoked unfolded against the backdrop of an even more fundamental, if seldom explicitly acknowledged, dispute. At the heart of this dispute lay a disagreement between soldiers and civilian authorities over whether and how to adapt existing civil-military arrangements— both precepts enshrined in tradition and wartime expedients devised by Roosevelt—in light of the radically new circumstances to which World War II had given rise.

Underlying the dispute were three distinct clusters of questions:

- Was war as traditionally conceived still feasible? After Hiroshima, was it possible any longer to see war as in Clausewitz's definition, simply the continuation of politics by other means? Or had war itself become absurd?
- Did a distinctive sphere of military competence and autonomy still exist? In an age when war had obscured the distinction between combatants and noncombatants, pitting peoples against peoples rather than armies against one another, did the traditional model of military professionalism retain any relevance? Or had war and military affairs generally become, once and for all, too important to be left to the generals?

- Would America be able to wield great military power without for-feiting American freedom? Could the United States maintain a large permanent military establishment—in the old ideology of republi-canism, a "standing army"—without succumbing to militarism or becoming a garrison state?

The postwar emergence of the Soviet Union as a threat to U.S. national security, raising the specter of a third world war, imparted added urgency to these questions. The ensuing Cold War provided the specific context in which the battle was joined.

Widely divergent service views about the changing nature of warfare complicated efforts by postwar uniformed leaders to bring a consistent and coherent military perspective to that battle. But in general, the officer corps rejected suggestions that armed conflict was becoming obsolete, viewed the advent of nuclear weapons as simply continuing the evolution toward ever more powerful arms, and resisted civilian intrusion into in-ternal service affairs, war planning, and especially the conduct of opera-tions. When facing defeat on an issue that they considered vital to service interests, officers exploited the public's heightened Cold War era preoccu-pation with national security to court sympathy and support, played off the legislative and executive branches against one another, and did not hesitate to challenge or even defy the president himself.

For their part, successive presidents during the early Cold War, differ-ing less on matters of basic national security policy than partisan politi-cal considerations obliged them to pretend, each had to expend time and energy fending off attempts by uniformed officers to subvert elements of that policy. Over the course of their times in office, Harry S Truman, Dwight D. Eisenhower, and John F. Kennedy each evinced frustration with the perceived recalcitrance, insularity, and parochialism among se-nior military leaders. Each came to question the utility of professional military advice. Each worried about the extent to which he was actually able to exercise effective civilian control.

V

President Truman, although credited by a subordinate with being "the most rocklike example of civilian control the world has ever witnessed," found it particularly difficult to keep his admirals and generals in check.[16]

For the officers who ran the armed forces and for the service secretaries that they diligently labored to co-opt, obedience during the Truman era became selective.[17] Through a series of audacious challenges to civilian authority, military leaders effectively renegotiated the basic terms of the civil-military compact. The revised arrangement, which greatly enhanced the military's leverage vis-à-vis civilian authorities, endured long after Truman himself left office.

Truman's troubles began when he announced his intention to reorganize the military establishment in light of the lessons from the just-concluded war, lessons he lumped together under the rubric of unification. Declaring that the war had demonstrated "beyond question the need for a unified department," the president on December 20, 1945, sent a message to Congress calling for legislative action to combine the existing services (along with a new air force) into a single entity.[18]

In essence, Truman sought to amalgamate the armed forces into an integrated corporate structure over which a single civilian cabinet officer would preside as chief operating officer, reporting in turn to the president in the role of CEO. A unified defense establishment promised to reduce waste and redundancy, facilitate unity of effort, clarify lines of authority, and sharpen the quality of military advice provided to civilian decisionmakers.

But unification did not necessarily suit each of the armed services. Opposition from the Navy, intent on preserving its traditional independence and worrying it might lose control of its air arm, and from the United States Marine Corps, fearing absorption into the Army, was especially vociferous.[19] As a result, Truman's call for unification touched off a fierce and protracted imbroglio, pitting the services against one another and against the White House.

In the course of this dispute, the services employed tactics that soon became standard in subsequent civil-military controversies. To discredit the concept of unification, naval officers and Marines, along with their civilian allies, orchestrated elaborate disinformation campaigns, leaking sensitive information to sympathetic (or merely scandal-mongering) journalists. They roused veterans groups and like-minded civic organizations to protect them from an ostensibly predatory U.S. Army. They lobbied the Congress and testified in opposition to the president's position, "hiding their defiance behind congressional coattails."[20]

In this particular case, opponents of unification justified their defiance as an expression of a determination to prevent any weakening of civilian control. Thus, for example, did Fleet Admiral Ernest King profess to worry that consolidating the military services might give rise to a Prussian-style general staff responding to the orders of a single supreme military commander, thereby increasing the risk of a man on horseback. Viewed in this light, King instructed Congress, unification was "incompatible with our concept of democracy."[21] The argument was completely disingenuous, disguising motives that were in fact thoroughly parochial. But coming from such a respected figure—King had been chief of naval operations during World War II—it carried weight.

The fight over unification educated Truman regarding the limits of his writ as commander-in-chief: in practice, short of ordering a wholesale purge of the officer corps, there was little he could do to enforce his will. By the spring of 1946, the president himself recognized that and "reduced to a supplicant, pleading with the Army and the Navy for support" was ready to throw in the towel.[22] So the posturing ended and the serious work began: the president's men, led by White House operative Clark Clifford, agreed to sit down with representatives of the service chiefs to work out a face-saving deal.

Hidden from the public's prying eyes, the ensuing negotiations established precedents that recurred in the years and decades to follow. In effect, the dispute over unification set the terms of subsequent civil-military elite interaction. That resolving that dispute entailed negotiations itself amounted to a tacit acknowledgment that military deference to civilian authority could no longer be taken for granted. By reducing the president to the status of supplicant on matters related to national security, the services demonstrated that they possessed—and on matters that they considered vital to their own interests intended to wield—the power to obstruct, frustrate, and even veto. Henceforth, when it came to controversial issues, securing the consent of senior uniformed leaders would oblige the commander-in-chief to engage in horse-trading and compromise.

Having said that, all parties recognized their common interest in preserving the appearance of civilian supremacy. As a result, brokering deals was not the business of the president and his most senior generals and admirals, but of proxies like Clifford working behind the scenes. When these agents had completed their task, ratification came with the president endorsing the prearranged bargain as if it were his own creation, while the service chiefs ceremoniously paid obeisance to the rituals of civilian control. Truman pretended that his authority remained intact and unquestioned and senior officers pretended that they were dutiful subordinates loyally doing the bidding of their commander-in-chief.[23]

Thus, in ending the unification controversy, the substance of the deal that Clifford negotiated with his military interlocutors gave the Navy and Marine Corps everything they wanted while conceding to the president a figleaf: the creation of a nominally unified military establishment where as a practical matter the individual services—now including a fully independent air force—retained the bulk of their traditional prerogatives. A civilian secretary presided over that establishment but lacked either the staff or the authority to direct its activities. To provide the secretary and commander-in-chief with professional advice, the deal also included the creation in law of a new Joint Chiefs of Staff, the uniformed heads of each service conceived as a committee of co-equals, destined like any committee so-conceived to be ineffective.

In effect, the Navy and Marine Corps won, but the nation lost. The upshot of military obstructionism was bad policy. Reformers spent the next several decades trying to correct the defects enshrined in the resulting National Security Act of 1947.[24]

Thus concluded the "the first of many challenges that eventually established for the military a new degree of independence from presidential control."[25] Others followed in short order.

For Truman, just persuading the Joint Chiefs to abide by budgetary guidance issued by the White House proved to be a daunting problem. To be sure, the problem was one to which the president himself contributed. Even as he was insisting that the Soviet Union posed a dire threat to U.S. national security, Truman remained firmly committed to a policy of fiscal austerity and a balanced federal budget. Apart from the politically unpalatable option of raising taxes, the only way to put an end to the deficits that had occurred during the war years was to cut defense spending.[26] This, the JCS, unwilling or unable to reconcile the costly ambitions nursed by each service, fiercely resisted.[27]

For instance, in planning for fiscal year 1947, the White House established a ceiling on peacetime defense spending of $13 billion, down from $44.7 billion in fiscal year 1946 and $81.6 billion the year prior.[28] From the perspective of the military services this figure was manifestly inadequate, so the JCS blithely chose to disregard it and submitted budgetary requirements far in excess. When orders from the White House insisted that the services produce a budget proposal in line with Truman's guidance, the chiefs simply refused to comply. Until the outbreak of the war in Korea in 1950 paved the way for a large-scale rearmament program, each annual budget cycle provoked a similarly ugly row pitting the White House against the senior leadership of the armed services. Caught in the middle of this recurring fight was James Forrestal, the first secretary of defense. Tormented by his inability either to control the Joint Chiefs, his nominal subordinates, or to satisfy the president, his immediate boss, Forrestal suffered a nervous breakdown and committed suicide in May 1949, soon after leaving office.[29]

Truman's efforts to lay down basic policies relating to nuclear weapons elicited similar obstreperousness. As long as United States enjoyed a nuclear monopoly, more than a few senior U.S. military officers flirted with the idea of preventive war as a way to deal with the Soviet threat.[30] As a matter of principle, Truman intended to keep the development, production, and control of such weapons firmly in civilian hands. The military's role was to be a limited one: it would employ "the bomb" if and when the commander-in-chief so directed.

This did not jibe with the services' own preferences. That nuclear weapons would exercise a decisive influence in determining the outcome of future wars appeared certain. Whoever controlled the bomb could expect, therefore, to have a large say in the actual conduct of those wars. In peacetime, meanwhile, ownership of the bomb would confer prestige, clout, and in all likelihood, a claim to greater resources. But there was also a larger principle at stake: controlling America's arsenal had always been a military prerogative, integral to the notion that war was the province of warriors; for the Truman administration to make an exception of this new class of weapons undermined that claim. To forfeit control of weapons to a civilian agency would constitute an unprecedented civilian intrusion into what soldiers regarded as an exclusively military sphere of activity.

So when Truman announced his intention to entrust the development, production, and storage of nuclear weapons to a new Atomic Energy Commission (AEC), the services fought him tooth and nail. Frustrated in its efforts to dominate the AEC upon its creation in August 1946, the Pentagon thereafter agitated to circumscribe its authority, an effort that included making common cause with conservatives in Congress who smeared David Lilienthal, appointed by Truman to head the AEC, for being soft on communism.

Months of skirmishing ensued, with Lilienthal describing the military at one juncture as "hopelessly out of control." Even when Truman himself declared publicly and definitively in July 1948 that just as "a free society places the civil authority above the military power," so too "the control of atomic energy belongs in civilian hands," serving officers continued to lobby their allies on Capitol Hill in an effort to overturn the president's decision. Only in 1949 did the military finally relent and begin to work with rather than against the AEC.[31]

By that time yet another civil-military crisis was in full swing. In April 1949, Louis A. Johnson, Forrestal's successor as secretary of defense, cancelled construction of the aircraft carrier *United States*. The first of a new class of supercarriers designed to carry planes large enough to deliver atomic bombs against land targets, this ship was key to efforts by naval officers to claim for their service a part of the atomic mission. But, in a time of fiscal stringency, Johnson viewed the carrier as unaffordable and unnecessary; in his view, the Air Force, with its new long-range B36 bomber, could handle strategic bombing contingencies.[32]

The Navy's response, in the words of General Omar Bradley, was tantamount to "a complete breakdown of discipline." According to Bradley, "never in our military history had there been anything comparable" to what ensued: an open revolt led by "insubordinate, mutinous" senior naval officers.[33] Determined to reverse Johnson's verdict, these officers orchestrated a secret campaign of press leaks and disinformation depicting the B-36 as a "billion dollar blunder" and implying that the secretary of defense had a financial interest in ensuring its production.[34] Only with the dismissal of the chief of naval operations and the disciplining of several other perpetrators did this "revolt of the admirals" subside—although the outcome did not by any means persuade the Navy to acquiesce in the Air Force's monopoly over nuclear weapons.

Professing shock at the Navy's defiance of civilian authority, General Bradley was himself not above stiffing the president on matters he considered important. Race was one such matter. When Truman on July 26, 1948, issued Executive Order 9981, directing the armed forces to end their practice of racial segregation, Bradley as Army chief of staff signaled that his service had no intention of complying. "The Army is not out to make any social reforms," he declared in remarks reported in the *Washington Post* on July 28. "The Army will put men of different races in different companies. It will change that policy when the Nation as a whole changes it."[35]

Truman's action signified an unacceptable breach in the longstanding tradition of permitting the military to govern its own internal affairs. Thus, rather than integrating, the Army instituted a policy of "equality of opportunity on the basis of segregation"—essentially a variant of the doctrine of separate but equal that formed the basis for Jim Crow. This reflected not just Bradley's preference but that of the senior Army leadership more generally. As a consequence, when the Korean War began in the summer of 1950, 98 percent of black soldiers were still serving in segregated units.[36]

When during the course of that conflict the Army did begin to integrate it did so neither in response to the commander-in-chief's directive issued nearly three years earlier nor out of any commitment to racial equality per se, but strictly out of pragmatic considerations: observing the niceties of racial separation when the service was expanding rapidly while simultaneously fighting a large-scale war was becoming unmanageable. Even so, when General Matthew Ridgway decided in 1951 to desegregate the combat formations in Korea, he did so only after *first* requesting the Army chief of staff's concurrence.[37] When a year later the commanding general of U.S. Army Europe announced an end to segregation in his command he justified this step by noting that "The Department of the Army has directed this command to initiate a . . . program of racial integration."[38] By implication, the authority that really counted was not the president's but that of the service's own leadership.[39]

Taking this wider context into account, Truman's showdown in the spring of 1951 with the officer whom he described privately as "Mr. Prima Donna, Brass Hat, Five Star MacArthur" deserves to be seen not as a unique event but as the culmination of a sustained military assault on civilian control that since the end of the world war had altered the terms of the basic civil-military compact in ways both profound and troubling.[40] Indeed, the report of the Commission on Organization of the Executive Branch of the Government, popularly known as the Hoover Commission, was already warning in 1949—that is, well *before* Korea—that the cumulative impact of postwar developments had "resulted in a failure to assert clear civilian control over the armed forces."[41]

General of the Army Douglas MacArthur was a living, breathing affirmation of that judgment. Whatever the traditional strictures defining professionally correct behavior, MacArthur had long since concluded that he was one soldier to whom they did not apply. Gaudy, imperious, and puffed up with self-regard, a general officer for over three decades before the Korean War broke out in June 1950, MacArthur had spent the previous five years ruling occupied Japan like some Oriental potentate. His own lengthy and highly-visible flirtation with the Republican Party having hinted at his own presidential ambitions, the general viewed Harry Truman as at best a near equal and at worst an upstart and pretender.

In its initial stages, MacArthur's management of the Korean War, especially in conceiving the daring amphibious invasion at Inchon that broke the back of the North Korean invaders, added further luster to his glittering reputation. But his ill-considered decision to press the attack beyond the 38th Parallel, endorsed by Washington in large part because MacArthur insisted the risks of doing so were minimal, produced disaster. The general had predicted publicly that the troops would be home by Christmas. That holiday instead found his command on the verge of defeat at the hands of Chinese forces that MacArthur had assured Truman posed no threat.

By January 1951, MacArthur was telling the JCS that the war was all but lost and began preparations to evacuate the peninsula. But Ridgway, having arrived the previous month to assume command of allied forces in the field, rallied his troops and soon stopped the Chinese offensive, thereby further calling into question MacArthur's grasp of the situation.

To divert attention from his own egregious errors in judgment, MacArthur now concocted a fresh explanation for the twists and turns that the war had taken following the Chinese decision to intervene. The problem all along, it turned out, was the president: Truman had denied his theater commander the tools necessary to win and was continuing to do so, most notably in refusing to allow MacArthur to carry the war directly to China itself, if need be employing the atomic bomb. To make this case, the general employed techniques that had by now become standard: leaking his complaints to favored journalists, rousing veterans groups in opposition to administration policy, and making an end run to sympathetic members of Congress.

But in this case, insubordination—carrying with it the danger of world war—was intolerable. On April 10, having first taken care to secure the backing of his Joint Chiefs, Truman sacked MacArthur and named Ridgway as his successor.

Truman thereby delineated the outer limits of permissible military dissent. But doing so cost him dearly. MacArthur returned home to a tumultuous hero's welcome. The senior serving officer on active duty publicly declared that "No proposition could be more dangerous" than for soldiers to confuse loyalty to the country with allegiance "to those who temporarily exercise the authority of the executive branch." Others might "cower before the threat of reprisal if the truth be expressed in criticism of those in higher political authority," but he, MacArthur, would not.[42]

For his part, Truman found himself denounced, derided, accused of treason, and burned in effigy.[43] Dissatisfaction with his administration, already widespread, mushroomed. The Truman-MacArthur controversy ended in a draw. It cost the general his job. But as the increasingly unpopular

Korean War dragged on, firing a renowned soldier who promised victory also helped kill any chance of the president winning another term in the White House.

VI

As Truman's antagonist in that controversy no doubt hoped, the presidential election of 1952 installed a five-star general in the Oval Office. But the general's name turned out to be Eisenhower rather than MacArthur.

One might have expected the ascent of a widely respected career soldier to the presidency to affirm civilian control and restore a modicum of civil-military harmony. Such, however, did not prove to be the case. As one historian has aptly observed, the situation Eisenhower inherited upon becoming president in January 1953 was one in which "military leaders could no longer be counted on to bow before the principle of civilian supremacy." The several civil-military controversies of the Truman era institutionalized a new, more contentious relationship. As a result, the generals now "demanded a greater voice in decision making, resisted decisions they did not like, and in some cases openly defied civilian authority, including the authority of the president."[44] This continued to be the case during the Eisenhower presidency even though one of the new president's first acts was to purge the Joint Chiefs—seen by many Republicans as tainted by Truman's policies—and install his own team.[45]

On Ike's watch, the issues prompting military challenges to civilian control changed, reflecting changes in the new president's approach to national security strategy. But the reality of those challenges persisted. For his part, Eisenhower, perhaps because of his own long service as a professional officer of the old school, found this new civil-military reality even more disconcerting than his predecessor had. Over the course of his eight years in office, he also developed an acute concern about the danger inherent in the continuing militarization of national policy.

By the time he became president Eisenhower himself had concluded that the advent of nuclear weapons had made war all but senseless. As early as 1946 he had remarked that "to discuss war as a means of advancing peace . . . is a contradiction in terms." To resort to armed conflict in a nuclear age was "completely futile" and "stupid."[46]

The essential dilemma facing the United States, therefore, was to avoid war while still containing communism and also maintaining American freedom and prosperity. Viewing the Cold War as an ideological struggle of indeterminate duration and determined to equip the United States for what he called "the long haul," Eisenhower found his answer to that dilemma in a new strategy of Massive Retaliation. The logic of this strategy, capitalizing on the existing U.S. nuclear supremacy, was simplicity itself: the threat of an all-out response to aggression would deter the Soviet Union and permit Americans at home to pursue a course conducive to their own economic and political well-being, to wit, the familiar Republican Party agenda of small government, low taxes, a balanced budget, and an end to extravagant and wasteful expenditures, not least of all on the machines of war.[47]

In the realm of civil-military relations, adopting this strategy had two adverse effects, neither of which Eisenhower anticipated. First, it sent the U.S. Army into opposition; the president's old service mounted a sustained campaign to discredit and overturn his policies. Second, by establishing nuclear war as the centerpiece of national security strategy, it shifted the balance of power among the services. This, in turn, raised up a new military elite devoted not to averting World War III as Eisenhower intended, but to fighting and winning it.

Since the strategy of Massive Retaliation did not envision the repeat of anything like Korea, the advent of the Eisenhower presidency saw the Army, the chief instrument of conventional warfare, falling on hard times. From 1953 onward, relative to the other services, the Army endured a precipitous loss of end strength, budget share, and prestige.[48]

In response, the Army's leadership, led by Ridgway, Eisenhower's handpicked candidate to serve as Army chief of staff, developed and promoted a vigorous critique of the president's strategy. Initially within the councils of government but soon employing the usual outlets for military dissent, the Army leadership faulted the concept of massive retaliation for being illogical, unrealistic, unprincipled, immoral, and contrary to the traditional canons of soldierly honor. Although willing to indulge a degree of internal disagreement, by the end of 1954 the president had had enough: in an Oval Office meeting called for the purpose, he told the JCS that the time for compliance was at hand. Even with that, Ridgway, having convinced himself that the military profession's very survival hung in the balance, refused to comply. The Army's campaign to subvert Massive Retaliation did not abate.[49]

Frustrated, the president in 1955 eased his Army chief of staff into early retirement. To succeed Ridgway, Eisenhower appointed General Maxwell

D. Taylor, but not before first securing Taylor's pledge that he would "accept and carry out orders of civilian superiors," a matter about which Taylor sniffed he "would not have expected to be questioned."[50] Once confirmed, Taylor proceeded to disregard that pledge. Organized resistance continued, reaching a point that by 1956 the *New York Times* was featuring front-page stories of a "Colonel's Revolt."[51]

When Taylor himself went into unhappy retirement in 1959, he unleashed one final salvo of protest, a book attacking the national security policy in the Eisenhower era just drawing to a close.[52] Among Democrats with an eye on the next year's presidential election, Taylor's scathing critique met with great favor, as did the author himself.

Once upon a time, retired generals with literary inclinations had contented themselves with penning memoirs in which they recounted past campaigns and battles. That by the 1950s soldiers astute in the ways of Washington viewed departure from active duty as an opportune moment for attacking the policies of the commander-in-chief they had served—and that doing so might (and in Taylor's case did) win points with the political opposition—was another indicator of how developments since the end of World War II had redrawn the boundaries of civil-military propriety.

Yet in some respects Eisenhower's troubles with the Army paled in comparison with those he faced with the Air Force. The Army's challenge to civilian control was overt and unambiguous. The challenge posed by the Air Force—and in particular by the Strategic Air Command (SAC), the nation's chief nuclear strike force—was shrouded in secrecy, doubletalk, and obfuscation. Even as they professed their full support for the concept of Massive Retaliation, Air Force leaders, above all General Curtis LeMay as SAC commander, twisted the strategy's declared purpose in order to pursue their own institutional agenda. In the Truman era, propagandists for air power, often abetted by friends in the media, had vastly overstated not only the Soviet threat, but also the potential effectiveness of strategic bombing.[53] Now under Eisenhower, the Air Force hijacked Massive Retaliation. Its leaders converted a strategy devised to avert war and curb military spending into a justification for continuously expanding the nation's nuclear arsenal even as they sought to remove obstacles and inhibitions to that arsenal's employment—developments that Eisenhower found himself powerless to prevent. By the end of the 1950s, SAC had become a "cocked weapon" of enormous destructive capacity. But it was not entirely clear whose finger rested on the trigger.

A partial explanation for LeMay's success lies with his driving personality and ruthless insistence on results.[54] But more important still was the fact that during his long tenure at SAC from 1948 to 1957 his command asserted exclusive control of nuclear war planning and enjoyed a predominant role in intelligence collection.[55] SAC alone identified the targets that the United States would attack in the event of war with the Soviet Union. That target list determined the number of weapons required to execute the war plan and by extension the number of aircraft (eventually supplemented with ballistic missiles) needed to deliver those weapons. When it came to allocating resources among the various services, the overriding importance assigned to the nuclear mission put the Air Force clearly in the driver's seat: throughout the Eisenhower era, when it came to appropriations, the Air Force (and especially SAC) got what it asked for, even if the result in terms of the overall level of defense spending and the size of the force bore scant resemblance to what the commander-in-chief actually intended.

As a practical matter, SAC's target list expanded consistent with the nation's nuclear weapons production capacity. In the early 1950s, the command's air offensive called for striking some 70 targets in the Soviet Union. By 1956, with the age of nuclear plenty now at hand, the target list jumped to 2,997. A year later it grew to 3,261. Two years later, SAC was estimating that by 1963 it would need to destroy 8,400 targets and, by 1970, 10,400.[56] These requirements, in turn, provided the rationale for a vast expansion of the nation's nuclear stockpile. When Eisenhower became president in 1953, that stockpile consisted of 1,169 warheads. By 1960, his last full year in office, it had swollen to 18,638.[57] As a further consequence, and to the dismay of the other services, the U.S. Air Force's share of the defense budget had increased accordingly so that it roughly equaled that of the Army and Navy combined.[58]

From his headquarters in Omaha, the commander-in-chief of Strategic Air Command ruled over a vast fiefdom of bases at home and abroad with hundreds of B-47, B-52, and B-58 bombers supported by reconnaissance aircraft and jet tankers for airborne refueling. By the end of the 1950s, a new land-based intercontinental ballistic missile force was taking shape. Wrestling with the considerable problems inherent in defeating the Soviet Union in a third world war while preserving the United States from nuclear devastation, he and his staff continuously refined their plans for penetrating Soviet air defenses and in a single, comprehensive stroke laying waste to the enemy's military forces, political apparatus, and industrial infrastructure—a goal that not only generated ever greater requirements for more bombs on more targets but also led inexorably to the consideration of preemptive if not preventive attack. The political, economic, environmental, or moral consequences of engaging in such a war—the very event Eisenhower's strategy was intended to preclude—did not receive comparable attention. Indeed, supremely confident that the United States maintained a clear strategic edge throughout the 1950s and into the 1960s, SAC generals tended to cultivate a positively cavalier attitude about a prospective nuclear showdown with the Soviet Union.[59]

By the end of the Eisenhower era, the logic of overkill had prevailed. Planning and preparing for nuclear war had taken on a life of its own. In establishing the parameters within which those efforts proceeded, Omaha, not the Oval Office, had gained the upper hand.[60] Although Eisenhower repeatedly spoke of placing limits on SAC's proposed offensive, he proved unable to do so.[61] Adept at currying favor on Capitol Hill, the Air Force found ways of persuading the Congress to underwrite the design and production of more planes and more weapons, regardless of the preferences expressed by the White House.

Eisenhower found himself unable even to reclaim control of the war-planning process: after all, a credible deterrent required that the president appear *always* to be fully in charge with his military commanders fully and reliably subordinate; for Eisenhower to acknowledge publicly the existence of a far more complex and ambiguous reality would call into question the viability of Massive Retaliation itself.

So Eisenhower, although disgusted with the persistence of interservice rivalry, angered by scare-mongering generals, appalled by the prospect of an unnecessary arms race, and deeply worried by evidence of domestic militarization, remained silent. Or at least he did so until the very eve of his departure from office.[62]

On January 17, 1961, in nationally televised remarks, the general-turned-president offered what the White House advertised as his farewell address to the nation. Apart from adding a single phrase—"military-industrial complex"—to the lexicon of American politics, the speech itself was quickly forgotten, swept aside by the excitement marking the inauguration of his successor. But Eisenhower's farewell address was, in fact, a remarkable presentation—remarkable, that is, as a description of the precarious state of existing civil-military arrangements and as a striking, if oblique admission of the president's own failure to remedy the situation.

The previous decade, Ike observed, had seen the wholesale transformation of U.S. military policy. The result was an entirely new circumstance, one that "bears little relation to that known by any of my predecessors in peace time." The central elements of that new reality were an immense arms industry and a large standing military establishment, each without precedent in American history. Eisenhower did not question the necessity of these changes. But he noted that arms merchants, generals, and legislators eager to provide jobs for their constituents shared certain interests in common. And he rejected out of hand any assumption that those interests necessarily coincided with those of the republic as a whole. "We must never let the weight of this combination endanger our liberties or democratic processes," he warned. "We should take nothing for granted. Only an alert and knowledgeable citizenry can compel the proper meshing of huge industrial and military machinery of defense with our peaceful methods and goals, so that security and liberty may prosper together."

In his own dealings with the military's senior leadership throughout eight years as president, Eisenhower had experienced at first hand the difficulty of meshing that machinery so as to reconcile security and liberty. Now with this veiled admonition, he surrendered the task of managing the fractious American military to the young John F. Kennedy.

VII

Priding himself in harboring few illusions, John Kennedy held none at all about the brass. During World War II, as a young officer serving in the Pacific, he had developed a distinctly jaundiced view of senior officers.[63] As a rising member of Congress following the war, he came to appreciate the extent to which horse-trading and mutual manipulation had become institutionalized as central to the interaction of civilian and military elites.

Yet Kennedy also understood that as president he could ill afford to alienate the Joint Chiefs of Staff. If anything, his comparative youth and inexperience made it all the more essential to keep the chiefs on board. United, they could effectively veto any initiative related to national security. Determined (despite the overheated rhetoric he employed on public occasions) to ease tensions with the Soviet Union, the new president needed the chiefs' acquiescence in that effort, if only by serving as willing props at White House ceremonies and offering supportive remarks to congressional committees. But Kennedy entertained few expectations of actually benefiting from their counsel. On that score at least the Joint Chiefs did not disappoint him.

When the JCS offered up direct, unvarnished advice—for example, urging full-scale U.S. intervention, including the likely use of nuclear weapons and the bombing of cities in China and North Vietnam, to prevent a communist takeover of Laos—Kennedy blanched at their recklessness and inability to grasp the implications of such an action.[64]

When, as was more frequently the case, the chiefs shrouded their views in bureaucratic, slightly evasive language—as with their guarded endorsement of the CIA-sponsored invasion at the Bay of Pigs in April 1961—the president found their efforts singularly unhelpful. When that operation subsequently ended in spectacularly embarrassing failure, Kennedy included the uniformed military among those sharing the blame. "Those sons-of-bitches with all the fruit salad just sat there nodding, saying it would work," he complained.[65]

Kennedy's suspicion that the Joint Chiefs rather than accepting responsibility sought instead to dodge it by surreptitiously pointing fingers at the Oval Office infuriated him.[66] It was bad enough that the chiefs had already branded themselves as stupid; for a Kennedy, the one truly unforgivable sin was disloyalty. In an administration that fancied itself to be sophisticated, quick, and brainy, Kennedy's senior military advisers managed to come across as crude, unimaginative plodders and as untrustworthy to boot.

In the complicated bureaucratic maneuvering surrounding the question of Vietnam, Kennedy viewed the JCS less as a source of counsel than as vehicle offering political cover. The central issue facing the Kennedy administration over South Vietnam was whether to escalate efforts to prop up the regime of Ngo Dinh Diem or to cut U.S. losses, with a communist takeover of South Vietnam a near certain result. The Joint Chiefs and other administration hawks were pressing to increase the level of American effort, deploying U.S. combat troops if need be. Despite his promises to pay any price for liberty, the president was not eager to fight a major land war in Asia. Indeed, he wanted to reduce the U.S. military profile in Southeast Asia. Determined to protect himself from charges of being "soft" on communism, Kennedy tasked the chiefs to develop a contingency plan for a scheduled withdrawal of U.S. advisers. If the time came to pull the plug on South Vietnam, the president wanted the military implicated in the decision, so that he alone would not be held accountable. Notwithstanding the appearances maintained on public occasions, at the very top suspicion and mistrust had now entrenched themselves as core themes of U.S. civil-military relations.[67]

By the time of the Cuban missile crisis of October 1962, relations between the president and his generals had grown so poisoned that the president's overriding concern was to minimize military involvement in the
deliberations of the so-called ExCom, the group JFK convened to devise a
response to the Soviet build-up in Cuba. Throughout the thirteen days of
the crisis, Kennedy met with his senior military advisers just once.[68]

Debate as it evolved within the ExCom was complex and fluid. But by
the time he met with the JCS at mid-morning on October 19, the president
himself—framing the issue as primarily political rather than military—
had already indicated his preference for imposing a naval blockade on
Cuba rather than using force. The Joint Chiefs unanimously rejected this
approach and pressed Kennedy to order a massive, surprise air attack to
destroy Soviet military facilities in Cuba with a full-scale invasion of the
island to follow. In advancing their argument, the chiefs strayed far afield
from their supposed military expertise. General LeMay, now Air Force
chief of staff, told the president that a blockade would be "almost as bad as
the appeasement at Munich." Admiral George W. Anderson, the chief of
naval operations, opined that "It's the same thing as Korea all over again,
only on a grander scale." All the chiefs insisted on the absolute imperative
of a direct military response. None matched LeMay in his willingness to
goad his commander-in-chief into more forceful action. "I think that a
blockade, and political talk, would be considered by a lot of our friends
and neutrals as being a pretty weak response to this," he told Kennedy.
"And I'm sure that a lot of our own citizens would feel that way, too. You're
in a pretty bad fix, Mr. President."[69]

Unpersuaded but having gone through the motions of consultation,
Kennedy concluded the interview and departed, leaving the chiefs—
unaware that the entire session was being tape recorded—to express their
contempt for what they perceived as the shilly-shallying of their commander-in-chief.[70] For his part, the president was soon thereafter telling a
friendly journalist, "The first advice I'm going to give to my successor is to
watch the generals and to avoid feeling that just because they were military men their opinions on military matters were worth a damn."[71]

Kennedy's dealings with the military in the various crises of his brief
presidency affirmed the extent to which postwar efforts to renegotiate the
bargain between civilian and military elites had produced something approaching dysfunction. In the realm of personnel appointments, Kennedy
himself took two actions aimed at least in part to work around this civil-
military problem. Although the president himself did not live to see the

full results, the impact of these two fateful appointments—restoring General Maxwell Taylor to active duty and selecting Robert McNamara to be secretary of defense—transformed dysfunction into complete paralysis and paved the way for outright collapse.

Taylor was Kennedy's kind of general, possessed of a distinguished war record, but also bright, smooth, and politically adept—"a cool man in a cool era."[72] Following the Bay of Pigs and reflecting his disenchantment with the service chiefs that he had inherited from Eisenhower, Kennedy called Taylor out of retirement, first installing him in the White House as Military Representative of the President and then in October 1962 appointing him to be JCS chairman.

The other chiefs understood the resurrection of Maxwell Taylor for what it was: an effort to circumscribe their own influence by installing the president's own man at the top of the military hierarchy. By overtly politicizing the uppermost echelon of uniformed leadership Kennedy was in effect abandoning any pretense that the JCS constituted a source of apolitical, disinterested advice. For their part, the chiefs viewed Taylor no longer as one of their own but as a Kennedy loyalist.[73] As such, they could not depend on Taylor either to reflect their own views accurately or to represent the military's own interests and agenda. In short, Taylor's appointment further corroded a relationship already based to a large extent on pretense and double-dealing.[74]

Initially, the chiefs did not know what to make of McNamara, the former Eagle Scout and Harvard MBA who had made his reputation as one of the Whiz Kids who saved Ford Motor Company following World War II and who was a mere forty-four when Kennedy selected him to run the Pentagon.[75] They soon learned.

Arguably both the most brilliant man ever to serve as secretary of defense and also the most disastrously unsuccessful, McNamara was in no doubt about the propriety of civilians asserting ultimate responsibility for national security policy. Legislation passed in 1949, 1953, and 1958 had substantially increased the authority inherent in the office to which Kennedy had appointed him.[76] McNamara accepted the appointment intent on bolstering civilian control while also bringing to the formulation and execution of defense policy greater rationality, efficiency, and coherence.[77]

In pursuit of those worthy goals, neither he nor the new generation of Whiz Kids he recruited to join his staff showed any particular regard for professional military expertise. Indeed, they treated serving officers with barely concealed disdain. "Their initial position," recalled one observer, "was that military people were border-line literate at best and communicated by animal noises."[78]

Intent on imposing a managerial revolution from above, McNamara set about transforming the way the Pentagon operated. Weapons design and procurement, force structure, budgeting, nuclear strategy and war planning, contingency operations: in each of these areas and more, McNamara inserted himself far more deeply and forcefully than had any of his predecessors.[79] Relentless, intensely energetic, and supremely confident, the new secretary prodded, probed, and questioned—and then rendered judgments he declared to be definitive.

In making his revolution, he came to view the Joint Chiefs not so much as collaborators but as obstacles to be bypassed. To his new questions, they offered only tired, old answers, carefully calibrated to satisfy various service interests but of tenuous relevance to the matter at hand. McNamara demanded reasoned analysis supported by data; the chiefs offered opinion informed by tradition and experience. After one especially painful encounter with the JCS in 1961, an angry McNamara was heard wondering "Do they think I'm a fool? Don't they have ideas?"[80]

For their part, senior military leaders bitterly resented the high-handedness with which they were treated.[81] They resented too the fact that in McNamara's Pentagon a young number cruncher out of MIT or RAND, fluent in the language of systems analysis, wielded more clout than a three- or four-star veteran of combat command in World War II or Korea.[82] A contemptuous LeMay labeled the new Whiz Kids "self-appointed military savants," amateurs who presumed to know more about war and military affairs than did seasoned professionals.[83] General Thomas D. White, upon retiring as Air Force chief of staff, blasted "the pipe-smoking, tree-full-of-owls type of so-called 'defense intellectuals'" that McNamara had imported, dismissing them as overconfident, arrogant, and lacking "sufficient worldliness or motivation to stand up to the kind of enemy we face."[84]

Perhaps even more destructive to the possibility of effective civil-military collaboration was McNamara's hypocrisy, an exasperating blend of moral sanctimony and blatant dishonesty. Second only to the president as the official most directly responsible for decisions relating to America's nuclear arsenal, McNamara viewed the prospective use of such weapons with outright horror. As a consequence, he found SAC's approach to war planning—in 1961, a single orgasmic attack designed to incinerate the entire communist world several times over—to be morally indefensible.[85] And he was hardly less offended by the casual willingness of senior officers to treat the bomb as a readily available trump card, to be played whenever lesser measures failed to produce a desired outcome.[86] Such cavalier prattle violated the secretary's own humane sensibilities. By implication, the sources of such prattle stood condemned as heartless and morally inert.

Yet when military officers measured the secretary of defense against their own moral code, he was the one found wanting. As they saw it, McNamara lacked integrity. To advance his policy agenda and to protect himself or the president, he routinely deceived, dissembled, and misled. In his dealings with the Congress, the press, and his own subordinates, McNamara thus showed himself to be—like Taylor—unworthy of trust.[87]

Thus by the time John Kennedy's assassination in November 1963 thrust Lyndon Baines Johnson into the presidency, problems with the interaction of civilian and military elites that had festered across three administrations were reaching crisis proportions. Efforts inside Washington to manage those problems—typically through legislative tinkering or the sacrifice of some especially irksome officer or civilian official—had just about exhausted their utility.

To be sure, outside of Washington, the American people remained largely oblivious to the existence of any such crisis. Ritualistic expressions of civil-military harmony, intended for public consumption, continued to issue from the lips of high officials. Indeed, although tested by the unpopular war in Korea, the terms of the broader liberal democratic compact that FDR had forged between the nation as a whole and its military remained into the early 1960s largely intact. Americans continued to find the terms of that arrangement agreeable: hence, their unquestioning deference to Washington on matters of national security, their willing support— evident even on the campuses of the nation's best universities—for a large, far flung military establishment, and their acquiescence in a peacetime draft that had become an accepted part of the postwar landscape.

Before the decade concluded, all that had changed. With the advent of war in Vietnam, the liberal democratic civil-military compact dissolved.

VIII

The debacle that became Vietnam had many architects. From a civil-military perspective, however, the war was largely the handiwork of McNamara, abetted by Taylor, first as JCS chairman and then from July 1964 as

U.S. ambassador to South Vietnam, and by General William C. West-moreland, the senior field commander from 1964 to 1968.

Whether the United States could have won the war or whether it should have fought the war at all is, for present purposes, moot. The facts perti-nent to the case at hand are these. First, in order to help Johnson win the presidential election of 1964, McNamara and Taylor intentionally con-cealed from the public the depth of the problem posed by Vietnam and deepening U.S. involvement there. Second, when the United States inter-vened the following year, McNamara—with an eye toward preventing the conflict from undermining LBJ's domestic reform agenda—devised a strategy of "gradual escalation" derived from a radically new reading of war's essential nature. Third, in support of this strategy, Taylor and West-moreland committed U.S. forces in South Vietnam to "search and de-stroy" tactics, counting on massive American firepower to persuade the enemy eventually to call it quits. Fourth, as the defects of this approach became manifest, Westmoreland kept calling for more troops while Mc-Namara lied to the Congress and the American people, forecasting even-tual success he himself had concluded was not in the offing.[88] Throughout, basic questions of strategy went not only unanswered but even unasked.

Each and every element of this formula turned out to be, as McNamara wrote in his famously self-exculpatory memoir, "wrong, terribly wrong."[89] The result was to mire the United States in a protracted and immensely destructive stalemate dragging on from one year to the next with over a half-million U.S. troops eventually committed and an ever-mounting toll of casualties.

What role did the Joint Chiefs of Staff play in this unhappy sequence of events? In their statutory capacity as the president's senior military advis-ers they proved to be remarkably ineffectual. To be fair, their advice was not especially welcome. As far as McNamara was concerned, the JCS rec-ommendations for how to fight the Vietnam War pointed directly to a nu-clear showdown with the Soviet Union and China. Decades later he remained completely unapologetic for having "held the lid on unleashing the military."[90]

Having dealt with a progression of military senior military leaders over the course of his long career in politics, President Johnson himself had long since come to view them with considerable suspicion. "The generals know only two words," he complained, "spend and bomb."[91] But LBJ knew that generals who became disgruntled—like MacArthur in Korea—could cause trouble. Thus, although Johnson the commander-in-chief had scant regard for professional military judgment, Johnson the student of politics had thoroughly assimilated the key lesson of postwar civil-military relations, namely, in wartime keep the generals on the team.[92]

This perspective informed the role Johnson and McNamara allotted to the chiefs regarding Vietnam: pro forma consultation combined with exclusion from the actual decisionmaking process, while the administration projected a reassuring façade of civil-military unity.[93] Johnson, a hard and devious man, browbeat the JCS into submission.[94] McNamara summarized the real object of the exercise: "we decide what we want and impose it on them."[95] In essence, through a series of clashes with civilian authorities, the military's senior leaders by the early 1960s had frittered away their claim to being masters of the art of war and devoted servants of the state. When it came time to make the crucial decisions on Vietnam, they no longer possessed the credibility to command a serious hearing.

For their part, apart from the usual leaks to the press, the Joint Chiefs acquiesced. They did so in part because persistent internal disagreement along service lines complicated their efforts to articulate a unified, authoritative position. But they acquiesced too because, as one distinguished historian has observed, "they had learned how to play the game, soft-pedaling their disappointment with the president's decisions, perhaps assuming that once the United States was committed they could maneuver him into doing what they wanted."[96] In other words, encouraged by General Earle Wheeler, the skillful military bureaucrat who succeeded Taylor as chairman, the chiefs signed off on policies with which they disagreed—such as LBJ's refusal to mobilize the reserves and the restrictions placed on the air campaign directed against North Vietnam—because they counted on the pressure of events to force Johnson and McNamara ultimately to fight the war their way.

In this regard, they miscalculated badly. In fact, events, culminating in the Tet Offensive of 1968, destroyed the Johnson presidency and thoroughly discredited McNamara, Taylor, and Westmoreland. When Wheeler connived to use Tet to maneuver LBJ into widening the war, calling up reserves, and sending an *additional* 200,000 reinforcements to the war zone, the ploy backfired and served only to demonstrate the poverty of the chiefs' thinking.[97]

McNamara left office in early 1968. For generations of soldiers, his name remained a synonym for civilian meddling and malfeasance. But his departure from the Pentagon did nothing to repair the civil-military dysfunction to which he had contributed?. Even as the new Nixon

administration took office in January 1969, antagonism and suspicion remained the order of the day. At one point the chiefs actually installed
their own spy—a Navy yeoman—on the staff of National Security Adviser Henry Kissinger in order to pilfer sensitive documents forbidden
them by the White House.[98]

Meanwhile, the war rolled on, dividing the country, wrecking the economy, and sweeping away the last remnants of the civil-military compact
that had prevailed since 1945. The antiwar movement gave birth to antimilitarism, producing a deep cleavage between soldiers and influential
segments of American society. In progressive quarters, the avoidance of
military service became a mark of enlightenment. Elsewhere, disdain for
those who did serve became something like a socially acceptable form of
bigotry. For their part, the armed services themselves—rife with careerism and beset with indiscipline, rampant drug abuse, racial polarization,
and plummeting morale—teetered on the brink of disintegration.[99]

IX

The civil-military rupture induced by Vietnam manifested itself in three
specific ways. All three figured prominently among the problems that preoccupied military and, to a lesser extent, civilian leaders determined to restore American power after Vietnam.

The first manifestation was a deep-seated resentment harbored by serving officers and directed at those they held responsible for the humiliation
and defeat they had suffered in Vietnam. In a peculiarly American variant
of the "stab in the back" thesis, the officer corps singled out for blame
members of the media and the professoriate, but above all politicians. As
one senior general counseled his fellow officers in the war's aftermath,
"Remember one lesson from the Vietnam era: Those who ordered the
meal were not there when the waiter brought the check."[100] Angered at
having been stuck with footing the bill for an ill-advised and ill-managed
war, the officer corps had no intention of being snookered again.

The second manifestation was a radical change in American thinking
about war and the use of force, adversely affecting the standing of the
armed services within American society and (by no means incidentally)
the prestige and status to which senior officers since 1945 had become accustomed. War, in the aftermath of Vietnam, came to be seen as an exercise in futility, pointing inexorably toward quagmire and costly failure.

Amidst the continuing cultural upheaval triggered by the 1960s, military institutions seemed at the very least retrograde, if not repressive. In the eyes of many, to be a soldier was to be either a callous incompetent or, perhaps worse, a dupe. By the war's end, William Calley, notorious for his role in the My Lai massacre, had displaced figures like Alvin York and Audie Murphy as the embodiment of the American fighting man. The postwar moral authority of the generals—some of whom had actively conspired to cover up Calley's crime—wasted away. Defeat and dishonesty debased the currency of professional military expertise.

Finally, there was the Great Divorce, the abandonment of the military by the American elite—symbolized by the decision of universities such as Harvard and Yale to terminate their support for ROTC and ratified by President Richard M. Nixon when he ended the draft in 1973, declaring that henceforth all the services would rely on volunteers to fill their ranks. No one seriously expected very many graduates of Harvard or Yale to be among those volunteering.

Recovering from Vietnam required due attention to each of these problems. The result—in essence, an attempt to restore in modified form the liberal-democratic civil-military compact the war had demolished—became central to the military reform agenda through the end of the Cold War.

The military's effort to ensure that it would never again be left holding the check for a war it had not ordered up took two forms. First, in reconfiguring U.S. forces after Vietnam senior military leaders did so with an eye toward preventing any future commander-in-chief from doing what Lyndon Johnson had done—through outright lies and half-truths camouflaging from the American people the fact that he was taking the United States into a major war. That reconfiguration assigned to the reserves certain functions essential for the conduct of large-scale combat operations. Henceforth, going to war would require prior mobilization of these reserves, and by extension, the explicit endorsement of the Congress and the American people. In slamming shut the backdoor to war, the creation of this so-called "Total Force" represented a bold effort by U.S. military leaders to tie the hands of their civilian masters.[101]

Second, when it came to deciphering the "lessons of Vietnam"—a veritable cottage industry even before the war ended—the officer corps intended to ensure that *its* version of those lessons emerged as authoritative to serve as guidance for future policy.[102] From the military's perspective, failure in Vietnam stemmed from a simple fact: the United States did not fight the war as it needed to be fought. Beguiled by clever academic theories, the same civilian officials who permitted the United States to be dragged into Vietnam insisted that the ensuing struggle there was *sui generis*, a conflict in which the time-honored principles of war did not apply. They had prevented soldiers from applying those principles—in essence, denying them the means to win. Meddling civilians: that was the problem. Investing authority for the war's conduct in "appointive civilian officials lacking military experience and knowledge of military history" had been a "mistake," wrote Westmoreland in his memoir. "Overall civilian control of the military is one thing," he observed; "shackling professional military men with restrictions in professional matters imposed by civilians who lack military understanding is another."[103] Although this interpretation was at best a vast oversimplification if not simply wrongheaded, it offered the benefit of letting the officer corps itself off the hook—hence, its appeal to the leadership of the armed services.[104]

By 1984, this interpretation had matured sufficiently to provide the basis for new guidelines for when and how the United States would fight. Although known as the Weinberger Doctrine after Secretary of Defense Caspar Weinberger, the official who articulated its terms in a speech at the National Press Club in November 1984, the guidelines deserve to be read as the military's attempt to codify its own conclusions about Vietnam and to establish parameters governing the future use of force. Weinberger's role was to legitimate the military's conclusions and give them the weight of policy.

The Weinberger Doctrine did two things. First, it imposed a set of stiff preconditions to any use of force, permitting intervention *only* on behalf of vital national interests, *only* in pursuit of "clearly defined political and military objectives," *only* with the prior assurance of public and congressional support, and, *only* as a last resort. Second, it insisted that once civilians decided on war, it became incumbent upon them to allow soldiers a free hand in fighting it. "If we decide it is necessary to put combat troops into a given situation," Weinberger declared, "we should do so wholeheartedly and with the clear intention of winning. If we are unwilling to commit the forces or resources necessary to achieve our objectives, we should not commit them at all."[105]

Under the terms of the Weinberger Doctrine, wars would occur infrequently and end quickly and neatly. This was the marker that an obliging Weinberger laid down on behalf of an officer corps badly burned by Vietnam and determined to exert a large say in future decisions regarding the use of force.

To restore the standing of the armed services in the eyes of American society and to refurbish the legitimacy (and authority) of the military profession, uniformed leaders in the wake of Vietnam set out to reinvent warfare. Or, more accurately, they returned to the style of warfare with which they were most comfortable and which played to traditional American strengths, namely, conventional operations against armies organized and equipped along conventional lines. Having lost its taste for people's war—protracted, ambiguous, saturated with political complexity—the officer corps after Vietnam rediscovered a conception of warfare based on the clash of opposing armies, where campaigns and battles directed by military elites (not bothersome civilians) determined the outcome.

Lending political plausibility to this initiative was the existence of a ready-made threat—the large, well-equipped legions of the Soviet empire apparently poised to assault the West—and thus serving the U.S. military's institutional needs.[106] There existed as well a ready-made theater of operations, the expanse of industrialized and democratic Europe stretching from Denmark south to Switzerland, from the Iron Curtain west to the Atlantic ports. By establishing as its true *raison d'être* the defense of NATO Europe against a prospective a Warsaw Pact attack, the American armed services might begin to undo the effects of Vietnam. Even without fighting, military professionals could recover the stature and legitimacy they lost in Southeast Asia.

Thus beginning in the mid-1970s and continuing through the 1980s, this rediscovery of the Soviet "other" provided both focus and sense of urgency to efforts to revitalize American military power. Leaving few parts of the armed forces untouched, this effort manifested itself most prominently in the realm of doctrine, particularly in the AirLand Battle Doctrine unveiled by the Army in 1982 and formally endorsed by the Air Force as well. AirLand Battle provided the blueprint according to which outnumbered U.S. forces would turn back a full-scale, non-nuclear Warsaw Pact attack, relying on superior technology, superior training, and superior personnel to compensate for the enemy's greater numbers.[107]

The object of the exercise was not to court World War III. Rather it was to make the case for war's continued utility—defending Europe might be *necessary*; AirLand Battle asserted that it would also be *possible*. By extension, the object of the exercise was to reclaim war as the special preserve of a distinctive warrior caste deserving the respect of society and some amount of deference on the part of civilian elites. In short, to the extent that the prospect of a war to defend Europe loomed large, the opinions of the generals might once again matter.

Defending Western Europe against the large, mechanized formations of the Soviet Union and its satellites also provided a rationale for lifting Vietnam-induced limits on defense spending. Implementing AirLand Battle required new weapons based on the latest technology. It required new approaches to training and higher standards of readiness. All of these cost money.

Ronald Reagan's ascent to the presidency in January 1981 opened the nation's coffers to provide that money.[108] Reagan's professed coolness toward détente and his apparent eagerness for a decisive showdown with the Soviet "evil empire" provided the strategic rationale for a massive defense build-up. Meanwhile, whether out of genuine affection or political expediency, the president known as the Great Communicator routinely paid tribute to soldiers, past and present, as the nation's best and brightest—directly contradicting the conventional wisdom of the Vietnam era, when dodging military service had been a mark of virtue and intelligence. Reagan's generosity, financial and rhetorical, won the hearts of the officer corps, which became in the 1980s self-consciously conservative and which began to identify its fortunes with those of the Republican Party. However politicized ranking generals might have become, throughout the twentieth century, the officer corps as a whole had viewed itself as above politics; now that apolitical model of officership fell out of favor. Although few observers in or out of uniform were willing to acknowledge the fact openly, the officer corps increasingly was becoming an interest group.[109]

Finally, there was the matter of the Great Divorce and the challenge of making the All Volunteer Force (AVF) a success, despite the absence of levers such as the draft to induce the sons of the affluent and privileged classes to serve. This too was at its core a civil-military issue. To persuade able-bodied young Americans to volunteer in numbers sufficient to meet the needs of the armed forces meant changing the minds of young people raised on the myths and realities of World War II, Korea, and Vietnam about what military service entailed. Doing that required the Pentagon first to rethink the very concept of enlisted service. This, in turn, meant jettisoning habits of mind derived from the longstanding tendency to see enlisted soldiers as a pool of cheap labor—transitory, largely unskilled, and available for discharging menial housekeeping chores having little to do with readiness or warfighting.

Toward this end, each of the services and the Department of Defense as a whole instituted policies that moved in a direction of incorporating enlisted members fully into the military profession. Pay improved. Barracks life became more congenial. With the presumption that a volunteer was likely to stay on for a career, the services began paying more attention to enlisted career development and to family needs such as housing and childcare services. Training for war received more attention. Fatigue details like cutting grass, painting rocks, and pulling KP (kitchen duty) were jettisoned or contracted out to a civilian work force.[110]

Of equal importance, the Great Divorce obliged the services to reevaluate their relations with two hitherto undervalued constituencies, namely African-Americans and women. Both proved crucial to the prospects of the All Volunteer Force. Pentagon planners expected that with the advent of the AVF black Americans would volunteer for service in disproportionate numbers, seizing an opportunity for upward mobility not necessarily available elsewhere in American society. The complexion of the armed services was about to change. That assumption proved correct. Yet if African-Americans promised to be a welcome source of new recruits, a large infusion of black enlisted volunteers combined with a continuing underrepresentation of blacks in the commissioned ranks risked the possibility of creating a quasi-apartheid force of black soldiers led by white officers.[111] The delicate state of race relations within the military after Vietnam and in the nation as a whole made that prospect untenable.

Thus, it was the end of the draft that finally induced in the military a genuine and wholehearted commitment to racial equality. Embracing the concept of affirmative action with a will, the services, led by the Army where the enlisted force soon became over 30 percent African American, abandoned the practice of de facto racial tokenism in the officer ranks. The number of blacks admitted to the service academies increased significantly. To make up for the loss of ROTC programs in elite universities, the services expanded the ROTC presence in historically black institutions of higher education.[112] The presence of African Americans on the uppermost rungs of the military hierarchy—culminating in the appointment of General Colin Powell to be JCS chairman in 1989—became commonplace.[113]

For service chiefs searching for a formula to fill the ranks with volunteers, women represented a great, virtually untapped resource. In 1948, just days before Truman issued Executive Order 9981 starting the process of racial desegregation in the armed forces, Congress had passed the Women's Armed Services Integration Act, giving women permanent regular status in the armed forces. But through the end of the Vietnam War, that status remained a marginal one, with women still restricted to a limited range of noncombat specialties and constituting less than 1 percent of the total force. Real soldiering remained an exclusively male preserve.

With the advent of the AVF that began to change. Each of the services, albeit in different ways, began expanding the opportunities available for women, while still excluding them from combat. As a practical matter, this relegated female soldiers, whatever their numbers, to the status of second-class citizens. To those for whom the link between masculinity and the warrior's calling seemed immutable—not only most male soldiers but also in all likelihood the majority of American citizens—this made sense. But in the post-Vietnam political climate, in which the drive for women's rights acquired fresh momentum, the proposition soon proved to be unsustainable.

There ensued a protracted struggle, pitting the services, eager to recruit more women but intent on dictating the terms of their service, against advocates of gender equality, determined to exploit the military's need for women to advance the larger cause of women's rights.[114] The key milestone in this struggle—prefiguring its eventual outcome—came in 1976 with the admission of women into the hitherto exclusively male precincts of the service academies. Other barriers continued to fall. By the end of the century, women were captaining warships on the high seas and piloting fighter jets in combat. Female officers reaching the rank of general or admiral no longer qualified as newsworthy. Women were killed in action, wounded, and taken prisoner. Although a handful of specialties such as the infantry remained off-limits, and although no woman had yet risen to senior combat command or to occupy a seat on the Joint Chiefs, the nation's attitude regarding the relationship between women and war and military service had—for better or for worse—undergone a sea change. And with the armed services approximately 15 percent female, the AVF became irreversibly dependent upon the continued willingness of American women to serve.

Some observers interpreted all of this as evidence that the post-Vietnam military was becoming more progressive, leading rather than trailing the rest of the nation on important social issues. Whatever the merits of that argument—and events of the 1990s were to provide abundant contrary

evidence—the relevant point here is that the military establishment responded to the civil-military rupture caused by Vietnam by dramatically
changing the face it presented to young Americans generally and by recali-
brating its relationship with two segments of society it previously took for
granted.

As measured by the ability of the services to maintain a steady stream
of willing volunteers, this effort by the mid-1980s largely succeeded. But
no success is without costs. Accommodations made along the way—especially with regard to women—steadily chipped away at claims connecting
military effectiveness to the preservation of a distinctive military way of
life. Making the AVF work set in motion a cultural convergence between
the armed services and American society as a whole. Even for the career-
minded, military service became less of a calling and more of an occupation, with consequences impossible to foresee.[115]

The years immediately following Vietnam saw one additional reform
initiative with large implications for relations between civilian and military elites. This initiative, pursued by members of Congress and imposed
on an unreceptive Pentagon, aimed at addressing one of the Vietnam
War's "lessons" to which the officer corps did not subscribe, namely, the
conviction that persistent flaws in the national security structure created
in 1947 made it next to impossible for the Joint Chiefs to render sound
and timely professional advice. The outcome of this initiative—the Department of Defense Reorganization Act of 1986, more commonly known
as Goldwater-Nichols—attempted to legislate an end to the interservice
rivalry that had undermined the JSC system from its beginnings. The
proposed antidote to service parochialism was "jointness," which in
practice meant centralization. Thus, among other things, Goldwater-
Nichols greatly enhanced the authority of the JCS chairman, designating
the chairman (rather than the chiefs collectively) as sole military adviser
to the president and secretary of defense. As a result, the service chiefs fell
from the inner ring of power, their influence drastically diminished.
Henceforth, policymakers need only consult, persuade, cajole, or maneuver around one single officer.[116]

By the end of the 1980s, post-Vietnam military reforms, made possible
by the largesse of Reagan-era defense budgets and reinforced by President Reagan's politically popular empathy for the American soldier, the
restoration of domestic economic prosperity, and the end of the Cold
War—for the United States a historic victory won without further shots

being fired—restored a semblance of civility to relations between soldiers and civilians. It remained for events to show whether this amounted to genuine reconciliation or whether old grudges and suspicions lurked beneath the surface.

X

At the outset of the 1990s, the American military establishment—led by the charismatic and politically savvy Powell, easily the most influential soldier of his generation—was determined above all to consolidate and preserve the gains that it had achieved during the recovery of the previous fifteen years.[117] But the Cold War itself provided the rationale for that recovery. The passing of the Cold War transformed the political and strategic landscape and, in doing so, necessarily raised new questions about America's purpose and the role of U.S. military power in achieving that purpose. Powell's determination to deflect these questions—to freeze the late-Cold War military (and civil-military arrangements) in amber—produced renewed and persistent friction between civilian and military leaders. As a result, the early 1990s saw the most explicit challenges to civilian control since the late 1940s, with consequences only intermittently conducive to sound policy.[118]

Little of this was visible as the Cold War gave way to a new era. In a military sense, that new era began on a note of apparent triumph as the U.S. forces led (and totally outclassed) a broad military coalition that in early 1991 liberated Kuwait, occupied the previous summer by the Iraqi dictator Saddam Hussein.[119] In the years following, Operation Desert Storm lost much of its luster.[120] But the civil-military implications of the war remain considerable.

For President George Herbert Walker Bush, the Persian Gulf War of 1990–1991 offered an opportunity to demonstrate that he for one had fully assimilated the lessons of Vietnam. With that in mind, the president went to great lengths to show that his own approach to civilian leadership in wartime bore no comparison to that of the bungling Johnson and the execrable McNamara. According to Bush, the commander-in-chief's job was simply to identify clear and realistic objectives and to provide the military with whatever it needed to get the job done—and then to get out of the way. There would be no meddling or micromanagement on his watch.[121]

As a rendering of actually existing relations between the president and his generals during the brief war, this picture was egregiously misleading.

Behind the scenes, civilians scrutinized and (by no means inappropri-
ately) put their imprint on just about everything. They ordered the wholesale revision of campaign plans, scheduled the coalition attack, and
decided how to respond to Iraqi Scuds launched against Israel. To the extent that the hands-off account was true—for example, when the White
House allowed General H. Norman Schwarzkopf, the theater commander,
a free hand in negotiating the terms of the cease fire ending hostilities—
the results were disastrous. Schwarzkopf's unnecessary and ill-advised
concessions to the Iraqis enabled Saddam Hussein to maintain himself in
power and foreclosed the possibility of a neat and tidy "exit strategy." Despite what the Bush administration advertised as a triumph of historic
proportions, the Persian Gulf became a new quagmire from which the
United States could not extricate itself.[122]

But all of that lay in the future. For Powell—indeed, for a nation made
giddy by a spectacular demonstration of American military might—the
war appeared for moment to be an unvarnished success.[123] Operation
Desert Storm seemingly demonstrated the wisdom of the military's entire post-Vietnam recovery project. It validated the Weinberger Doctrine,
now amended with the addition of so-called Powell Doctrine emphasizing "overwhelming force" to achieve U.S. objectives quickly and efficiently. It seemed also to bury any lingering antagonism between the
military and society. According to Powell, the war provided the occasion
when "the American people fell in love again with their armed forces."[124]
Finally, Operation Desert Storm restored the credibility of the American
military profession to something akin to what it had been in the immediate aftermath of World War II. Powell and Schwarzkopf emerged (briefly)
as demigods.

As JCS chairman, Powell wasted no time in capitalizing on the boost
Desert Storm had given to the military's stature. The Gulf War had mo-
mentarily postponed key decisions about the size and role of the post–
Cold War military establishment. Victory now put the generals, and
especially Powell himself, in a better position to shape those decisions. "I
was determined to have the Joint Chiefs drive the military strategy train,"
he later recalled, "rather than have military reorganization schemes shoved
down our throat."[125]

The 1992 presidential election held large implications for who Powell
would be shoving against. Bush and the reliably pro-military Republicans were out. Bill Clinton—who had actively solicited the endorsement of retired senior military officers to offset the fact that during the

Vietnam era he had adroitly maneuvered to avoid serving and as a young man had written that he "loathed the military"—was in.[126] With him came a coterie of liberal Democrats.[127] The military's dislike of the incoming commander-in-chief and his lieutenants was immediate and visceral. Whatever the new team might intend with regard to policy, it represented the very antithesis of the values for which Powell's rejuvenated military claimed to stand.[128]

With Clinton's unwitting assistance, Powell and the other Joint Chiefs launched a preemptive strike aimed at schooling the new president regarding the limits of his authority. What Harry Truman learned over the course of the many long months of the unification controversy, Clinton learned, however painfully, in the very first few weeks of his administration.

On the campaign trail, candidate Clinton had promised if elected to issue an executive order lifting existing prohibitions on homosexuals and lesbians serving in the military. Laboring under the misimpression that as commander-in-chief his role was to decide and the military's role was to execute, Clinton indicated after his election that this was one campaign promise that he intended to keep.

With the question of gay rights a major battleground in the ongoing culture war, Clinton's plan was bound to provoke controversy. Senior military leaders led by Powell exploited that potential for controversy by publicly declaring their own adamant opposition to allowing gays to serve. Homosexuality, in their view, was incompatible with military service. The presence of large numbers of gays in the ranks would severely damage the cohesion essential to combat readiness. Allow homosexuals to serve openly, Schwarzkopf told a congressional committee, and American soldiers "will be just like so many of the Iraqi troops who sat in the deserts of Kuwait, forced to execute orders they don't believe in."[129] In other words, the presence of gays in their midst would convert American military men and women into a bunch of demoralized losers.

Thus did "gays in the military" emerge as a full-blown crisis, one threatening to cripple the Clinton administration before it even left the gate. With newly emboldened senior military leaders tacitly aligning themselves with enraged cultural conservatives, the crisis was one where the commander-in-chief had little chance of prevailing. As the Joint Chiefs hinted at the possibility of resigning in protest, Clinton—in the manner of several of his postwar predecessors—decided to cut the best deal that he could. Congressional Democrats obligingly negotiated the necessary compromise: there would be no executive order—no dramatic redress of a grave injustice with a single stroke of the presidential pen. Instead, in a policy subsequently known as "don't ask, don't tell," new regulations prohibited commanders from inquiring as to a serviceman or woman's sexual orientation; but any overt evidence of homosexuality continued to provide the basis for immediate discharge. In essence, closeted gays could serve, as they had been doing all along.[130]

Clinton's humiliation over gays—along with the collapse in October 1993 of the U.S. intervention in Somalia, where the JCS deftly maneuvered the White House and especially Secretary of Defense Les Aspin into taking the fall—established the parameters of the civil-military relationship that prevailed throughout the two terms of the Clinton presidency.[131] In essence, these two events laid the basis for a larger deal. For the duration of his presidency Clinton carefully respected the military's red lines: he refrained from pressing military leaders to assume risks, take on responsibilities, or make changes with which they were less than comfortable. Within those red lines, uniformed leaders tried wherever possible to be as obliging as possible. But whenever Clinton showed any inclination to stray over those lines—for example, in aggressively pursuing Balkan war criminals or Middle Eastern terrorists—the generals, according to one senior White House official, "made it almost impossible for the President to overcome their objections."[132]

On the surface—with only occasional exceptions—the appearance of civilian control prevailed.[133] That is, Clinton pretended to give orders and the military pretended to obey. Beneath the surface, a complex process of give-and-take preceded and informed policy decisions, affecting everything from progress toward "military transformation" (despite much talk, almost nonexistent) to the use of force (increasingly frequent, but largely ineffective).[134]

In one sense, then, the story of civil-military relations in the 1990s is one of military clout restored, with the generals once again able to exercise something like a veto power over issues related to national security. Indeed, the officers charged with presiding over U.S. military activities abroad—in the jargon of the 1990s, the regional "CINCs"—assumed new prerogatives for actually making U.S. policy, emerging as major powerbrokers.[135] Yet that was by no means the entire story. A parallel, but contrary theme related to the military's relationship to society as a whole. Here the story was more complex.

While Powell's observation that the Persian Gulf War of 1990–1991 sent the U.S. military's stock with the American people sky high is correct, in the years following the services seemed hell-bent on throwing away those gains. In the aftermath of Operation Desert Storm, too many commentators—usually those with an axe to grind in the ongoing culture wars—attributed the undoubted competence of America's armed forces to the ostensible moral superiority of the individual American soldier. This hypothesis proved difficult to sustain.

On the Right, depicting the armed services as bastions of sturdy patriotism and traditional values in a vast sea of craven, self-absorbed liberalism had a certain political appeal. Among other things, such pandering might help ensure that the military remained a reliable constituency of the Republican Party, as it had by now become.

Lending the notion a superficial plausibility was the accumulation of evidence suggesting that the post-Vietnam military existed in something of a cocoon, set apart from the rest of America. By the 1990s, the old concept of citizen-soldier had become largely obsolete; Americans under arms were now long-service professionals. Even the "weekend warriors" serving in the reserves and the National Guard, as social types, had more in common with the Redcoats of 1776 than with the Minutemen. In a moral context, to be different, in the eyes of some observers, carried with it a suggestion of being better.[136]

A seemingly never-ending series of embarrassing incidents suggested otherwise, not only exposing as false claims of superior soldierly virtue but also casting doubt on the claim that on social issues the armed forces might serve as a beacon for the rest of the country. Each of these incidents centered on sex and the military's treatment of women.

The first and most egregious came to be known as Tailhook. Created to promote the interests and celebrate the accomplishments of naval aviation, the Tailhook Association, like many other such organizations, each year hosted an annual meeting that combined professional and social aims. The Tailhook tradition tended to emphasize the latter over the former, a fact well-known to the Navy's senior leadership. The 1991 version of that event, convening in Las Vegas just months after Operation Desert Storm, turned out to be an especially wild, not to say debauched, affair. In its aftermath, a female naval officer in attendance complained that she had been sexually assaulted. Although her superiors tried to brush off those complaints, she persisted, her efforts eventually giving rise to a lurid and highly public scandal, replete with sensationalistic press coverage, pathetically futile efforts to cover up or dodge responsibility, multiple investigations, and the summary relief or resignation under pressure of various high-ranking officials starting with the civilian head of the Navy.[137]

The essential verdict was immediate and incontrovertible: Tailhook showed that the Navy was unacceptably out of step with the rest of American society. When it came to women, the Navy didn't "get it." Rather than bolstering martial virtue, traditional service culture provided a convenient pretext for an atavistic yet officially tolerated machismo that delighted in the humiliation and abuse of women.

With almost numbing regularity, similar scandals followed, sullying the reputations of each of the other services: drill sergeants found guilty of offering favorable treatment to female trainees in exchange for sexual favors; the Army's senior noncommissioned officer court-martialed for sexually harassing his subordinates; a female general complaining of being pawed in her Pentagon office by a male counterpart; recurring reports of senior officers being disciplined for sexual misconduct; at the U.S. Air Force Academy charges that the academy leadership had routinely turned a blind eye to sexual assault and rape victimizing female cadets.

By the end of the century, these scandals shredded military pretensions to moral superiority. Yet even their cumulative impact left the military's overall standing with the American people largely unaffected. Indeed, in polls assessing public confidence in major national institutions, the armed forces routinely came out on top.[138]

When it came to sexual shenanigans, as with Bill Clinton so too with the United States military: misbehavior produced outrage, but left popularity apparently intact. Why?

As never before in their history, the American people by the 1990s were enthralled with military power. But if they professed warm admiration for the soldiers who wielded that power on their behalf, they preferred to do so from a safe distance.[139] For the vast majority, actually serving in the military was now something that other people did, no longer, as was the case from World War II through Vietnam, a shared obligation linked (for males at least) to claims of citizenship. The individual who chose to volunteer might be called upon to sacrifice. But under the terms of the civil-military bargain that evolved out of Vietnam, Americans generally were spared that prospect. As long as the armed services upheld their end of that bargain—which entailed the avoidance of anything remotely approaching another Vietnam—periodic transgressions by the odd military institution, if not likely to garner explicit approval, could be tolerated.

XI

The election to choose Clinton's successor turned out to be the closest and most controversial in at least a century. Both parties had recruited retired military officers to endorse their candidate, although the Republicans were more explicit in identifying themselves as the pro-military party.

The outcome of the 2000 race between Vice President Al Gore and Texas Governor George W. Bush hung on Florida. Political operatives in Bush's camp rejoiced that Florida had an unusually large number of absentee voters, many of them military personnel serving outside of the state. They did so because they expected soldiers as a matter of course to vote Republican and give him the necessary edge—an expectation fully shared although less happily so by the Gore campaign. The allegiance of most serving soldiers to one particular party was now all but taken for granted.[140]

 In the end, Bush prevailed. But the return of the Republicans to power did not immediately repair the uneasy civil-military relations of the Clinton years. In terms of self-confidence, style, and ambition, Bush's choice to head the Defense Department, Donald Rumsfeld, came across as a somewhat crustier version of Robert McNamara. In his dealings with the top brass, the new secretary was anything but deferential. Determined to curb the military's incursions into matters traditionally beyond its purview, he could be brusque to the point of being abusive. Intent on transforming everything from the way that services were organized and equipped to the way that they fought, Rumsfeld had no patience for foot-dragging. He wanted things done his way and he wanted them done now. The military fired back with the usual leaks about unwelcome intrusions into matters best left to the professionals and fresh warnings of "a strong sense of alienation between the uniformed leadership and the civilians."[141] Within a matter of months, press speculation about Rumsfeld's imminent departure was rife.

Then came 9/11 and the war on terror—the public's ready endorsement of an open-ended war waged on a global scale affirming a now reflexive American inclination to view force as the preferred response to any international problem. Having failed either to anticipate or foil the most devastating attack in the nation's history, Bush's national security team cited that failure as the basis for claiming a blank check for future action. The Bush Doctrine of preventive war, promulgated in the aftermath of 9/11, consigned the old reticence of the Weinberger Doctrine permanently to the waste bin. While terrorists frightened Americans, it appeared that war no longer did, perhaps because the average citizen had lost his ability to calculate the costs of war, which he expected, in any case, someone else to pay.

Certainly, popular support for the war on terror did not translate into any particular willingness to enlist in the ranks of those called upon to fight it. Instead, Americans were content to cheer lustily from their living rooms as U.S. troops occupied Afghanistan and then in the spring of 2003 followed up with an invasion of Iraq that quickly toppled the Baathist regime of Saddam Hussein.

At first glance, each of these victories appeared to be decisive—Desert Storm all over again. Credited with having conceived them, Rumsfeld saw his reputation briefly rebound. From having been dismissed as a grumpy has-been, he became overnight a steady hand on the tiller of national security policy—the masterful "Secretary of War." With each apparent success, popular confidence in American arms grew apace. "The U.S. armed services may be the one truly functional major institution in American life," gushed one observer, expressing a view that in the first years of the twenty-first century had become commonplace.[142] Any lingering inclination to question the administration's response to 9/11 diminished accordingly. Indeed, to express skepticism about how Bush and Rumsfeld were managing the nation's several wars was to invite the charge of failing to support the troops, which had become tantamount to treason.

Meanwhile, reassuring images—of Rumsfeld sharing a podium with appropriately respectful senior military officers or of worshipful young sailors surrounding their commander-in-chief on the deck of an aircraft carrier—conveyed the impression that in the civil-military realm all was well.

But this too proved to be an illusion. When the Iraq occupation turned into a protracted and brutal insurgency, both senior retired officers and some active soldiers quickly resumed their sniping at the Pentagon's senior leadership. During the run-up to the Iraq War, the Army chief of staff had predicted that the occupation was likely to prove difficult and to require a very large number of U.S. troops. For having the temerity to speak up, the general found himself rebuked by Rumsfeld's deputy—a public humiliation that the services did not soon forget.[143]

By the spring of 2006, as the Iraq War entered its fourth year, officers unhappy with the civilian leadership's handling of the conflict were focusing their ire on Secretary Rumsfeld, whom they described as an arrogant micromanager. A growing chorus of recently retired generals, including several Iraq veterans, called for his ouster.[144] Lieutenant General Greg Newbold, who had occupied a senior position on the Joint Staff after 9/11, offered an even wider indictment, chiding the civilians he had served for committing U.S. forces to war "with a casualness and swagger that are the special province of those who have never had to execute these missions—or bury the results." Newbold revived the discredited MacArthur Doctrine of 1951, claiming that a senior officer's allegiance was "not to a person but to the Constitution." He offered "a challenge to those still in uniform" to resist policies they found objectionable.[145] In the eyes of some observers, the resulting confrontation amounted to a "military revolt."[146]

The grumbling of those in uniform along with growing recruiting difficulties that promoted talk of reviving the draft seemed to suggest that the civil-military compact forged in the wake of Vietnam was close to unraveling. Certainly, it suggested that the officer corps was rethinking its alliance with the Republican Party.[147] Senior leaders had entered that alliance with two expectations: not only that the GOP would support high levels of military spending, but that it could be counted on to protect the armed services from abuse and misuse. This had been the promise implicit in the Weinberger Doctrine, a promise that the Bush administration once and for all discarded as it set about waging its war against terror on a genuinely global scale.

With U.S. military commitments stretching existing resources to the limit, with the prospect of more war stretching to the far horizon, and with the implications of an increasingly militarized conception of policy simply ignored, national security nonetheless remained after 9/11—as it had been since World War II—the one arena of American life from which democratic processes were persistently excluded.

Thus did the civil-military reality that that had pertained throughout the Cold War persist during the new global war on terror: as factions of the national security elite, both civilian and military, vied with each other behind closed doors to control this or that aspect of policy, all remained united in their collective determination to keep the people—assumed to be ill-informed, vacillating, and untrustworthy—out.

In this sense more than any other it is possible to argue that the system of civil-military relations in existence since 1945 has achieved its intended purpose.

Acknowledgment

I am grateful for critical comments offered by Eliot A. Cohen, Peter Feaver, Benjamin Fordham, Christopher M. Gray, Richard H. Kohn, Adrian R. Lewis, Arnold Offner, and William O'Neill, and Alex Roland. I alone am responsible for the views expressed.

Notes

1.   James Bryce, *The American Commonwealth* (New York, 1899), 2:444.

2.   Samuel Adams, *The Writings of Samuel Adams*, Harry A. Cushing, ed. (New York, 1904), 1: 264–65.

3.   Eliot A. Cohen, *Supreme Command: Soldiers, Statesmen, and Leadership in Wartime* (New York, 2002), 208–24.

4.   By way of example, between July 1940 and July 1945, American factories churned out over 300,000 military aircraft, 71,000 ships, 86,000 tanks, and almost 2.5 million trucks, not to mention the components for two atomic bombs. Alan L. Gropman, *Mobilizing U.S. Industry in World War II.* McNair Paper 50 (Washington, D.C., 1996), 141–45.

5.   Williamson Murray and Allan R. Millett, *A War To Be Won: Fighting the Second World War* (Cambridge, Massachusetts, 2000), 530.

6.   Under the terms of lend-lease, the United States provided over $42 billion dollars of materials to its wartime allies. Murray and Millett, *War To Be Won*, 534.

7.   Allan R. Millett and Peter Maslowski, *For the Common Defense: A Military History of the United States of America* (New York, 1984), 408. This is not to imply that for America the conflict was bloodless. Far from it: from 1941 to 1945 the United States sustained some 400,000 military deaths from all causes. But in comparison with the cataclysmic toll suffered by the other major belligerents— for example, total Soviet losses, civilian and military, amounted to some twenty million—U.S. casualties were relatively modest.

8.   James L. Abrahamson, *The American Home Front* (Washington, 1983), 139, 148

9.   As the war grows more distant, the literature examining the sins of the home front grows. But one of the most thoughtful accounts remains John Morton Blum, *V Was for Victory: Politics and American Culture in World War II* (New York, 1976).

10. Gropman, *Mobilizing U.S. Industry*, 3.

11. For a comprehensive account of World War II conscription policy, see George Q. Flynn, *The Draft, 1940–1973* (Lawrence, Kansas, 1993), 9–87.

12. Not all who appeared before their local draft board were eager to serve. On the contrary: individuals exploited available loopholes to stay out of uniform. Still, present-day Americans, accustomed to the rich and famous arrogating to themselves special privileges, should contemplate the roster of those who did their duty when Uncle Sam called in World War II: athletes like Ted Williams, Joe DiMaggio, and Joe Louis, movie stars like Jimmy Stewart and Clark Gable, and moguls like William McChesney Martin, president of the New York Stock Exchange. Flynn, *The Draft*, 27.

13. This is not intended to slight the accomplishments of the relative handful of African Americans organized into combat units nor to discount the significance of their achievements as a milestone in the civil rights movement. But that was tokenism, not representative of the overall black military experience in World War II.

14. The authoritative account of the Joint Chiefs in World War II is Mark A. Stoler, *Adversaries and Allies: The Joint Chiefs of Staff, The Grand Alliance, and U.S. Strategy in World War II* (Chapel Hill, North Carolina, 2000).

15. David E. Johnson, *Modern U.S. Civil-Military Relations: Wielding the Terrible Swift Sword* (Washington, D.C., 1997), 13.

16. James Forrestal quoted in Michael S. Sherry, *In the Shadow of War: The United States Since the 1930s* (New Haven, Connecticut, 1995), 137.

17. The Navy was particularly adept at reducing civilian secretaries to the status of figureheads. "Rarely challenging the principle of civilian supremacy frontally, the uniformed navy worked assiduously to wrap its Secretaries in flattery and perquisites, to give them plenty of nineteen-gun salutes, side boys, and a yacht for cruising the Potomac River, while yielding little information, authority, or control." As a result, "genuine civilian control of the navy was a fragile, ephemeral condition." Townsend Hoopes and Douglas Brinkley, *Driven Patriot: The Life and Times of James Forrestal* (New York, 1992), 138.

18. Hoopes and Brinkley, *Driven Patriot*, 327.

19. On the latter, see Gordon W. Keiser, *The U.S. Marine Corps and Defense Unification, 1944–1947: The Politics of Survival* (Washington, 1982).

20. Michael J. Hogan, *A Cross of Iron: Harry S. Truman and the Origins of the National Security State, 1945-1954* (Cambridge, UK, 1998), 42.

21. Quoted in Hogan, *Cross of Iron*, 35.

22. Hogan, *Cross of Iron*, 47.

23. For a vivid illustration of the process, see Hoopes and Brinkley, *Driven Patriot*, 349.

24. For a political scientist's perspective on the deficiencies of the resulting national security establishment, see Amy B. Zegart, *Flawed by Design: The Evolution of the CIA, JCS, and NSC* (Stanford, California, 1999).

25. Hogan, *Cross of Iron*, 42.

26. Hogan, *Cross of Iron*, 69–72, 102.

27. For example, the Navy's initial plans for a peacetime fleet included thirty-seven aircraft carriers, seventy-nine escort carriers, eighteen battleships, and nearly eight hundred other surface combatant ships. By way of comparison, the United States Navy in 2006 had twelve aircraft carriers and no battleships. Hogan, *Cross of Iron*, 74.

28. Hogan, *Cross of Iron*, 75.

29. Hoopes and Brinkley, *Driven Patriot*, 422–66.

30. Russell D. Buhite and Wm. Christopher Hamel, "War for Peace: The Question of an American Preventive War Against the Soviet Union, 1945–1955," *Diplomatic History* 14 (Summer 1990): 372–74.

31. Hogan, *Cross of Iron*, 234–52.

32. A comprehensive account, sympathetic to the Navy, is Jeffrey G. Barlow, *Revolt of the Admirals: The Fight for Naval Aviation, 1945–1950* (Washington, 1994).

33. Omar N. Bradley with Clay Blair, *A General's Life* (New York, 1983), 507, 510.

34. Barlow, *Revolt of the Admirals*, 208.

35. Quoted in Michael R. Gardner, *Harry Truman and Civil Rights: Moral Courage and Political Risks* (Carbondale, Illinois, 2002), 113.

36. Alan L. Gropman, "The Korean War and Armed Forces Racial Integration," in William J. Williams, ed., *A Revolutionary War: Korea and the Transformation of the Postwar World* (Chicago, 1993), 92.

37. Gropman, "The Korean War and Armed Forces Racial Integration," 83.

38. Jack D. Foner, *Blacks and the Military in American History* (New York, 1974), 192.

39. The United States Marine Corps also defied Truman's order to desegregate until the onset of Korea. The Navy responded with token reforms while maintaining a substantially segregated force through the 1950s. Even before Truman issued EO 9981, the Air Force had decided on its own to desegregate—again for pragmatic reasons. For a concise account on how each service responded to Truman's directive, see Gropman, "The Korean War and Armed Forces Racial Integration," pp. 83–107.

40. Quoted in Robert Donovan, *Conflict and Crisis: The Presidency of Harry S Truman, 1945–1948* (New York, 1977), 141. According to Truman, MacArthur was "worse than the Cabots and the Lodges—they at least talked with one another before they told God what to do. Mac tells God right off." *Ibid.*

41. Quoted in C. Wright Mills, *The Power Elite* (New York, 2000, original edition published 1956), 187–88.

42. D. Clayton James, *The Years of MacArthur: Triumph and Disaster, 1945–1964* (Boston, 1985), 644. The quotations come from MacArthur's speech to the Massachusetts state legislature in Boston, July 25, 1951.

43. For a vivid contemporaneous account, see Richard H. Rovere and Arthur M. Schlesinger, Jr., *The General and the President* (New York, 1951), 3–17. The best

overall account of the controversy is Roy K. Flint, "The Truman-MacArthur Conflict: Dilemmas of Civil-Military Relations in a Nuclear Age," in Richard H. Kohn, ed., *The United States Military Under the Constitution of the United States* (New York, 1991), 223–67.

44. Hogan, *Cross of Iron*, 469.

45. Eisenhower spared only the commandant of the Marine Corps. Even Ike's West Point classmate Omar Bradley, by 1953 serving as JCS chairman, was given his walking papers.

46. Quoted in Robert R. Bowie and Richard H. Immerman, *Waging Peace: How Eisenhower Shaped an Enduring Cold War Strategy* (New York, 1998), 48.

47. Ibid., 43–52.

48. A. J. Bacevich, *The Pentomic Era: The U.S. Army Between Korea and Vietnam* (Washington, 1986), 15–21.

49. A. J. Bacevich. "The Paradox of Professionalism: Eisenhower, Ridgway, and the Challenge to Civilian Control, 1953–1955," *The Journal of Military History* 61 (April 1997): 303–33.

50. Maxwell D. Taylor, *Swords and Plowshares* (New York, 1972), 156.

51. Bacevich, *Pentomic Era*, 44–46.

52. Taylor called for "a thorough housecleaning to throw out many outmoded concepts, illusions, shibboleths, and fallacies." Maxwell D. Taylor, *The Uncertain Trumpet* (New York, 1959), 165.

53. Arlene Lazarowitz, "Promoting Air Power: The Influence of the U.S. Air Force on the Creation of the National Security State," *The Independent Review* 9 (Spring 2005): 483–88.

54. The key principle informing LeMay's own theory of civil-military relations was that civilians should give him what he wanted and stay out of his way. He described his favorite members of Congress as those who were "keen and knowledgeable, yet pliant." Curtis E. LeMay with MacKinlay Kantor, *Mission with LeMay* (New York, 1965), 454.

55. Citing security concerns, SAC refused to allow even the JCS to review its war plans! David Alan Rosenberg, "The Origins of Overkill: Nuclear Weapons and American Strategy, 1945–1960," *International Security* 7 (Spring 1983): 37.

56. Rosenberg, "Origins of Overkill," pp. 50, 55.

57. Robert J. Watson, *Into the Missile Age, 1956–1960* (History of the Office of the Secretary of Defense, Volume IV) (Washington, 1997) p. 457.

58. *Annual Report of the Secretary of Defense* (July 1, 1959, to June 30, 1960) (Washington, D.C., 1961), 34.

59. Richard H. Kohn and Joseph P. Harahan, eds., *Strategic Air Warfare: An Interview with Generals Curtis E. LeMay, Leon W. Johnson, David A. Burchinal, and Jack J. Catton* (Washington, D.C., 1988), 95–96, 112–19.

60. Eisenhower had managed to kill SAC's planned next-generation long-range bomber, the B-70. But this presidential action had provoked a military backlash

that Ike privately characterized as "damn near treason." Quoted in George C. Herring, *LBJ and Vietnam: A Different Kind of War* (Austin, Texas, 1994), 27.

61. Rosenberg, "Origins of Overkill," 44.

62. On Eisenhower and the dangers of militarization, see Sherry, *In the Shadow of War*, 190–205, 214–20.

63. Robert Dallek, *An Unfinished Life: John F. Kennedy, 1917–1963* (Boston, 2003), 93–94.

64. Ibid., 352–53.

65. Ernest R. May and Philip D. Zelikow, eds., *The Kennedy Tapes: Inside the White House During the Cuban Missile Crisis* (Cambridge, Massachusetts, 1997), 28.

66. Dallek, *An Unfinished Life*, 367; Lawrence Freedman, *Kennedy's Wars: Berlin, Cuba, Laos, and Vietnam* (New York, 2000), 297–303.

67. Gareth Porter, *Perils of Dominance: Imbalance of Power and the Road to War in Vietnam* (Berkeley, California, 2005), 165–79.

68. May and Zelikow, eds., *The Kennedy Tapes*, 11.

69. Ibid., 177–82.

70. Ibid., 188. When following the conclusion of the crisis, Kennedy summoned the Joint Chiefs to the White House to thank them for their assistance, LeMay told the president that thanks were inappropriate. "We lost!" he told the president. "We ought to just go in there today and knock'em off." Quoted in Richard Reeves, *President Kennedy: Profile of Power* (New York, 1993), 425. Elsewhere, LeMay described the outcome of the crisis as "the greatest defeat in our history." Quoted in Donald Kagan, *On the Origins of War and the Preservation of Peace* (New York, 1995), 546.

71. Benjamin C. Bradlee, *Conversations with Kennedy* (New York, 1975), 122.

72. David Halberstam, *The Best and the Brightest* (New York, 1972), 465.

73. The chiefs' reading was a correct one. In his memoirs, Taylor stated his conviction that the chairman of the JCS "should be a true believer in the foreign policy and military strategy of the administration which he serves." Maxwell D. Taylor, *Swords and Plowshares* (New York, 1972), 252.

74. H.R. McMaster, *Dereliction of Duty: Lyndon Johnson, Robert McNamara, The Joint Chiefs of Staff and The Lies That Led To Vietnam*, (New York, 1997), 11–17, 22–23.

75. For a competent biography, see Deborah Shapley, *Promise and Power: The Life and Times of Robert McNamara* (Boston, 1993).

76. For a useful review that highlights the importance of the Defense Reorganization Act of 1958, see Watson, *Into the Missile Age*, 243–75.

77. Robert S. McNamara with Brian VanDeMark, *In Retrospect: The Tragedy and Lessons of Vietnam* (New York, 1995), 22–24.

78. Quoted in Freedman, *Kennedy's Wars*, 45.

79. For a description of McNamara's managerial style see Shapley, *Promise and Power*, 96–111.

80. Ibid., 99.

81. The most storied example during the Kennedy years occurred during the Cuban Missile Crisis, when he invaded the inner sanctum of the Navy's high command to instruct the chief of naval operations on how to implement the blockade of Cuba. Of McNamara's confrontation with Anderson, Deborah Shapley writes, "the Flag Plot episode would mark McNamara as the most heavy-handed civilian boss in the military's long and unforgiving memory since Truman fired Douglas MacArthur." Ibid., 177.

82. Johnson, *Modern U.S. Civil-Military Relations*, 24.

83. LeMay, *Mission with LeMay*, 506.

84. Quoted in Bernard Brodie, *War and Politics* (New York, 1973), 466. White's comments appeared in an article that he published in the May 4, 1963 issue of *The Saturday Evening Post*.

85. McNamara, *In Retrospect*, 160.

86. Shapley, *Promise and Power*, 160.

87. Ibid., xi, 230, 294–95, 359–60.

88. On the dishonesty of McNamara and Taylor, see McMaster, *Dereliction of Duty*, especially pp. 57, 77, 100–106, 301, and Lewis Sorely, *Honorable Warrior: General Harold K. Johnson and the Ethics of Command* (Lawrence, Kansas, 1998), 152–57, 222, 284.

89. McNamara, *In Retrospect*, xvi.

90. "I Sweated Blood at Night," *Newsweek* 125 (April 17, 1995): 53. The article reprints an interview with McNamara by Jonathan Alter.

91. Quoted in Rowland Evans and Robert Novak, *Lyndon B. Johnson: The Exercise of Power* (New York, 1966), 539.

92. Johnson was explicit on this point, warning Westmoreland in 1966 "not to pull a MacArthur on me." Quoted in Herring, *LBJ and Vietnam*, 25.

93. Not until October 1967 did the chairman of the JCS begin attending the small "Tuesday Lunch" that was Johnson's primary venue for managing the war effort. Herring, *LBJ and Vietnam*, 40.

94. For one account of LBJ subjecting the Joint Chiefs to "the Johnson treatment," see Charles G. Cooper, "The Day It Became the Longest War," *U.S. Naval Institute Proceedings* (May 1996), 77–80.

95. Herring, *LBJ and Vietnam*, 42.

96. Ibid., 36.

97. Ibid., 155–60.

98. Robert Buzzanco, *Masters of War: Military Dissent and Politics in the Vietnam Era* (New York, 1996), 354–55.

99. Johnson, *Modern U.S. Civil-Military Relations*, 64; Robert J. Heinl, Jr., "The Collapse of the Armed Forces," in Marvin E. Gettleman et al., eds., *Vietnam and America* (2nd ed., New York, 1995), 326–35. Heinl's essay appeared originally in the June 7, 1971 issue of *Armed Forces Journal*.

100. Johnson, *Modern U.S. Civil-Military Relations*, 56. The speaker was General William Knowlton addressing the U.S. Army War College class of 1984.

101. For more on this point, see Lewis Sorley, *Thunderbolt: General Creighton Abrams and the Army of His Times* (New York, 1992), 361–62.

102. The intellectual centerpiece of this effort was a seriously flawed, but profoundly influential analysis of the war by a career military officer, Colonel Harry G. Summers Jr. Written while Colonel Summers was serving on the faculty of the U.S. Army War College, the book was published to considerable acclaim as *On Strategy: The Vietnam War in Context* (Carlisle Barracks, Pennsylvania, 1981). The then army chief of staff, General Edward Meyer, directed that copies of the book be sent to all serving army generals and to the White House. Johnson, *Modern U.S. Civil-Military Relations*, 58.

103. William C. Westmoreland, *A Soldier Reports* (Garden City, New York, 1976), 121.

104. On the inadequacy of the "meddling civilians" thesis and the military's own shared accountability for Vietnam, see Cohen, *Supreme Command*, 175–84.

105. "Excerpts From Address Of Weinberger," *The New York Times* (November 29, 1994), A5.

106. Johnson, *Modern U.S. Civil-Military Relations*, 78, fn. 73.

107. For further elaboration, see A. J. Bacevich, "The Use of Force in Our Time," *The Wilson Quarterly* 19 (Winter 1995): 50–63.

108. The massive defense build-up of the 1980s actually began in the last year of the Carter administration, but Jimmy Carter got no credit on that score.

109. By 1984, a *Newsweek* poll reported that 85 percent of active duty admirals and generals queried described themselves as political conservatives. Anne C. Loveland, *American Evangelicals and the U.S. Military, 1942–1993* (Baton Rouge, Louisiana, 1996), 272.

110. Robert K. Griffith, Jr., *The U.S. Army's Transition to the All-Volunteer Force, 1968–1974* (Washington, D.C., 1997), 70, 76.

111. Ibid., 235.

112. Charles C. Moskos and John Sibley Butler, *All That We Can Be: Black Leadership and Racial Integration the Army Way* (New York, 1996), 48.

113. For a breakdown of the racial composition of the services by the mid-1990s, see Moskos and Butler, *All That We Can Be*, 7.

114. Griffith, *U.S. Army's Transition*, 188–94.

115. Charles C. Moskos, Jr. "The All-Volunteer Military: Calling, Profession, or Occupation?" *Parameters* no. 1 (1977): 2–9; James Burk, "The Military's Presence in American Society," in Peter D. Feaver and Richard H. Kohn, eds., *Soldiers and Civilians: The Civil-Military Gap and American National Security* (Cambridge, Massachusetts, 2001), 247–75.

116. James R. Locher, III, *Victory on the Potomac: The Goldwater-Nichols Act Unifies the Pentagon* (College Station, Texas, 2002).

117. Colin L. Powell, *My American Journey* (New York, 1995), 437.

118. For further discussion of U.S. civil-military relations in the 1990s, see Andrew
J. Bacevich, "Neglected Trinity: Kosovo and the Crisis in U.S. Civil-Military
Relations," in Andrew J. Bacevich and Eliot A. Cohen, eds., *War Over Kosovo:
Politics and Strategy in a Global Age* (New York, 2001), 155–88.

119. One could argue that the military history of the post–Cold War era actually
began with U.S. invasion of Panama in December 1989. But military intervention in and around the Caribbean had been a staple of U.S. policy, predating
the Cold War by several decades. Operation Just Cause merely continued that
tradition.

120. Andrew J. Bacevich, "A Less Than Splendid Little War," *The Wilson Quarterly*
25 (Winter 2001): 83–94.

121. George H.W. Bush and Brent Scowcroft, *A World Transformed* (New York,
1998), 354.

122. Cohen, *Supreme Command*, 188–99.

123. Ironically, Powell himself had been a reluctant warrior, arguing against the use
of force to liberate Kuwait. With the apparent intent of establishing a record of
his opposition to the war in the event that things went awry, he had made himself available for extensive prewar interviews with an accommodating journalist. See Bob Woodward, *The Commanders* (New York, 1991).

124. Colin Powell, *My American Journey* (New York, 1995), 532.

125. Ibid., 437.

126. Clinton used the phrase in a December 3, 1969, letter to Colonel Eugene Hol-
mes, who headed the ROTC program at the University of Arkansas.

127. Most prominent among the officers endorsing Clinton was Admiral William
Crowe, who had served both Reagan and George H.W. Bush as JCS chairman.
President Clinton subsequently appointed Crowe to be his ambassador to
Great Britain.

128. On Clinton's postinaugural introduction to the troops, a visit to a U.S. Navy
aircraft carrier, the crew greeted their new commander-in-chief with boos.
One U.S. Air Force major general chose a public occasion to denounce Clinton
as a "dope-smoking, skirt-changing, draft-dodging" ne'er do well. See Andrew
J. Bacevich, *American Empire: The Realities and Consequences of American Diplomacy* (Cambridge, Massachusetts, 2002), 170.

129. Quoted in A.J. Bacevich, "Military Culture and Effectiveness," *Society* 31 (November / December 1993): 44.

130. Bacevich, *American Empire*, 170–71.

131. Aspin was forced to resign over the incident.

132. Richard A. Clarke, *Against All Enemies: Inside America's War on Terror* (New
York, 2004), 145. Clarke was the Clinton administration's anti-terrorism czar.
For specific examples of military obstructionism during the Clinton era, see
David Halberstam, *War in a Time of Peace* (New York, 2001), 35–36, 276–77.

133. At times even the appearance was strained. The Clinton years saw the Pentagon issuing periodic reminders to the troops that public expressions of disrespect for the commander-in-chief violated military law. See for example, Steven Lee Myers, "Military Warns Soldiers of Failure to Hail Chief," *The New York Times* (October 21, 1998), A22.

134. Bacevich, *American Empire*, 130–40, 143–66. Evidence in the early 1990s that the bonds of civilian control were becoming strained provoked a lively response from concerned scholars, beginning, most famously, with Richard H. Kohn, "Out of Control: The Crisis in Civil-Military Relations," *The National Interest* 35 (Spring 1994): 3–17; but see also, Charles J. Dunlap, Jr., "Welcome to the Junta: The Erosion of Civilian Control of the U.S. Military," *Wake Forest Law Review* 29 (1994): 341–92.

135. Dana Priest, *The Mission: Waging War and Keeping Peace with America's Military* (New York, 2003).

136. On the inordinate sense of moral superiority pervading the U.S. military after the Persian Gulf War, see Thomas E. Ricks, *Making the Corps* (New York, 1997).

137. For a comprehensive journalistic account, see Gregory L. Vistica, *Fall From Glory: The Men Who Sank the Navy* (New York, 1995). Among the victims that the scandal claimed was Admiral Mike Boorda, the chief of naval operations, who committed suicide in May 1996. For more on Boorda, see Peter J. Boyer, "Admiral Boorda's War," *The New Yorker* 72 (September 16, 1996): 68–86.

138. See, for example, Leslie McAneny, "Military on Top, HMOs Last in Public Confidence Poll," (July 14, 1999), *www.gallup.com*, accessed August 3, 2004.

139. On the restoration of public confidence in the U.S. military after Vietnam, see David C. King and Zachary Karabell, *The Generation of Trust* (Washington, D.C., 2003).

140. As David Halberstam has noted, this military identification with Republicans expressed itself in a "double standard." Serving officers "were hard on Democrats who had not gone to Vietnam but paid little attention if it was a friendly Republican politician who had somehow avoided the draft." Halberstam, *War in a Time of Peace*, 417.

141. Quoted in Bacevich, *American Empire*, 212.

142. Daniel Henninger, "Troops in Fallujah Are the Best Since World War II," *Wall Street Journal*, (November 10, 2004), A16.

143. Eric Schmitt, "Pentagon Contradicts General on Iraq Occupation Force's Size," *New York Times*, (February 28, 2003), 1.

144. For one example, see Paul D. Eaton, "For His Failures, Rumsfeld Must Go," *International Herald Tribune*, (March 20, 2006). Major General Eaton had spent a year in Iraq charged with training Iraqi security forces.

145. Greg Newbold, "Why Iraq Was a Mistake," *Time* (April 17, 2006), 42. Newbold had been director of operations on the Joint Staff from 2000 to 2002.

146. Richard Holbrooke, "Behind the Military Revolt," *Washington Post*, (April 16, 2006), B7.

147. Hanna Rosin, "A Shrinking Base," *The Washington Post* (July 21, 2004), C1; Peggy Fikac, "Military Vote Gap Might Be Closing," *San Antonio Express-News* (July 9, 2004), 1B.

6. THE EVOLUTION OF THE NATIONAL SECURITY STATE
UBIQUITOUS AND ENDLESS

ANNA KASTEN NELSON

The national security state was created by the Cold War, sustained
and enlarged by that war, and further refined by the Gulf War in the Middle East. It is now the handmaiden of the "war" on terrorism, using the
structure created by the Cold War more than fifty years ago to fight terrorism. The national security state has grown even more pervasive in recent years, tainting our republican institutions, defying congressional
oversight, and alienating our former allies.

In the national security state the perceived need for security from the
nation's enemies, known or unknown, influences every part of national
life. Built on secrecy, it increases the power of the president exponentially
while calling upon every American to put their blind trust into government actions, including those about which they know nothing. In the
name of national security, laws, rules and regulations can be enhanced,
stretched, or even broken. It thrives in time of war, even a "Cold War," because military budgets fuel the economy as the president assumes the
powers of the commander-in-chief.

Other aspects of life reflect the militarization that results from the national security state, which is not just accepted but cherished by parts of
the country where the manufacture of armaments creates jobs and prosperity. It also has brought to our vocabulary the language of war. "Battle-
grounds" describe school board disagreements; "armies" of cicadas
invade; "battalions of ants" follow; and with a code we activate our home
"security" systems. Films and television magnify the view of the White
House as the hub of the universe. Spies chase America's enemies, using
the arcane words of intelligence organizations. Few Americans remember

a different time—a time when Americans watched *I Love Lucy*, rather than 24.

Since 1950 there has been little public discussion about the nature of national security or its effect on American government and culture. The national security state does not encourage discussion of its premises. In the name of security, we are asked to bury our questions.

After World War II there was both public discussion and disagreement in Congress and the press about the future course of this nation. As Michael Hogan notes, there were two dynamics at work after 1945, "one associated with an older political culture" fearful of the effects of militarization of America, "and the other with the new ideology of national security."[1] The "new ideology" prevailed.

This essay will concentrate on the evolution and expansion of the national security state from its creation in 1947 to the present. Its evolution was marked by a national security structure that slowly moved from diversity to greater exclusivity, that used and misused secrecy, and that failed to compel coordination in the face of many "turf wars" between agencies. Policymakers, generally free from the oversight of Congress and the judiciary, enlarged that structure until it became a ubiquitous part of American life.

The tools of war are many. First among equals are the military services, which supply the logistics as well as foot soldiers. But no recent war in the United States has been fought just because the military wanted to go to war. Presidents, advised by hand-picked assistants, including the Director of Central Intelligence (DCI), decide whether to lead the country into war or to keep the peace. Because we no longer "declare war" in the constitutional sense, the public has no influence over these decisions, another pernicious example of the growth of the national security state.

From its very beginning, the hub of the national security state was in the office of the president. From that vantage point the instruments of policy were managed and manipulated to suit the policy goals. Not every president was equipped for his responsibility, but each president used to their fullest capacity the powers given to him by the instruments of the state. This essay will concentrate on the domination and control of national security policy by the White House and its most important tool, the secrecy surrounding the intelligence agencies. The role of the military is discussed in another essay in this book.

Organizing for National Security

The United States became an economic power during the first quarter of the twentieth century, and demonstrated its ability to mobilize a world-class fighting force in 1917. But foreign policy remained the domain of the Secretary of State, the president he advised, and a personal assistant he could trust. The necessity for change became clear, however during World War II. There was little coordination among the burgeoning departments such as State, War, and Navy in spite of efforts of the State-War-Navy Co-ordinating Committee (SWNCC) and the informal organization of the Joint Chiefs of Staff (JCS). The unwieldy executive branch of the federal government Harry Truman inherited in 1945 was poorly equipped to organize itself into an effective entity either in time of war or peace. Certainly it did not answer the needs of a great power. Throughout World War II men as different as General George Marshall and Secretary of the Navy James Forrestal advocated structural changes to assure a more orderly conduct of foreign policy. To Forrestal, for example, changes became even more critical after the inexperienced Truman found himself behind the desk in the Oval Office. Yet, faced by the postwar perception of a menacing Soviet Union actively promoting world communism, there was little agreement on the nature of those changes.[2]

No one knew how to "fight" a Cold War, just as today there is little agreement on fighting the threat of terrorism. How do you formulate a cohesive policy when the definition of a victory is so ambiguous, and how do you implement this policy in a decentralized executive branch? The solution that emerged in 1947 was the creation of a national security system that was benign in its devotion to procedure. Its components were part military and part foreign policy, leavened with an intrusive intelligence agency and internal domestic surveillance. In the course of time it became the core of the national security state, evolving over three decades into an ever more powerful component of the American republic.

The National Security Act, which President Harry Truman signed on July 26, 1947, reflected the chaotic conduct of World War II and the admiration of the military leaders for the orderliness of the British system with its Chiefs of Staff and Committee of Imperial Defense. The authors of the act sought to emulate the British system but succeeded only in part. The father of the National Security Act was Secretary of the Navy

James Forrestal, although the organizing event was Truman's desire to unify the armed services.

Since the early days of the republic the War Department and Navy Department had been separate entities. Military forces were further fragmented as the Army, Navy, and Marines fought the air war in World War II with three separate air forces. From his experience in the Senate as chairman of a special committee to investigate the national defense program, Truman was convinced that the armed services must unify, and shortly after becoming president he turned his attention to this knotty and controversial issue.[3]

Meanwhile Forrestal, who was convinced that the militarily powerful Soviet Union would be a dangerous antagonist, was eager to add a military component to American foreign policy. He was also concerned that unification would mean the preponderance of the Army to the detriment of the Navy. Most of all he did not want any new cabinet secretary to intervene between himself and the president.

Seeking a way to answer these challenges and forestall the Army plan under discussion, Forrestal asked his friend Ferdinand Eberstadt to study the effect of unification and to recommend an effective process for protecting the country. Specifically answering Forrestal's concerns, Eberstadt proposed a national security council that would advise the president and whose membership would include representatives from the Departments of State, Army, and Navy. The council was a crucial component, since it would automatically provide equal access to the president by both the Navy and the Army and would allow the military services to rely on interdepartmental committees for cooperation rather than unification.[4]

Truman's proposal, which he sent to Congress in December 1945, unified the services into a single department under a chief of staff. He opposed an advisory council and saw no need for a coordinating agency. But, perhaps because of Forrestal's personality and the influence of the Navy, the proposal of the Subcommittee of the Senate Armed Services Committee, and all those that followed, included the idea of a coordinating advisory council.

For eighteen months unification was studied, debated, attacked, and revised.[5] Finally, in order to achieve unification, Truman accepted the idea of a council, although it was not the entity imagined by Eberstadt or Forrestal. The council that was originally adopted in the Senate bill was rather precisely defined, given statutory power, and required Senate confirmation of its executive-director. Truman's advisers warned that such a council would undermine the president's unique position in the decisionmaking process. While working to redraft the proposal, they turned this advisory group with well-defined functions into a group with no statutory authoritative functions and a staff appointed at the sole discretion of the president. Unwittingly, Truman's staff created a unique body that flourished over the years because it had no clear parameters. Unlike all other agencies in the Executive Office of the President, the NSC does not report to the Congress and its staff is chosen entirely at the discretion of the president.

The National Security Act of 1947, which set the basic organizational structure for fighting the Cold War, created four coordinating bodies—new agencies to coordinate old ones: The National Military Establishment, the Central Intelligence Agency (CIA), the National Security Council (NSC), and the National Security Resources Board (NSRB). Each was designed to correct problems faced during World War II, while simultaneously answering the perceived needs of the Cold War. One of those agencies, NSRB, disappeared in 1953. None of the others ever actually worked in the manner foreseen by the authors of the legislation. Instead of coordinating existing agencies, they each grew into central components of the national security state, overwhelming the agencies and departments they were meant to coordinate.

The NSC was designed to be the link between all other national security agencies. Its lack of specificity has made it the ideal agency for presidents to use or not use, to manipulate or trust. The statute stated that the council was "to advise the President with respect to the integration of domestic, foreign, and military policies relating to the national security. . . ." To do this, the council is to "assess and appraise the objectives, commitments and risks of the United States in relation to our actual and potential military power. . . ." (P.L.253) The Council had no other statutory function, and was unique in its relation to the Congress.

Given the NSC's future prominence, it should be noted that the Senate Armed Services Committee, which examined and approved the National Security Act, did not regard the NSC as an important component of the act and paid very little attention to it. The Committee had been concerned with the issue of unification, after which it turned its attention to the creation of the CIA. Forrestal continued to see the Council as a part of the defense establishment. It was to be housed in the Pentagon, where he would chair the group in the president's absence. The White House, however, saw the situation quite differently, and the first NSC executive-secretary quickly moved his small administrative staff into the White House.[6]

When discussing the early years of the NSC, it is usually noted that President Truman rarely attended NSC meetings before the outbreak of the the Korean War made it useful as a war-making body.[7] The original purpose of the Council was to coordinate the views of the departments and agencies so that the president could receive a coherent set of policy recommendations. His presence was not deemed essential. What *was* essential was the support of the State Department, whose officials quickly indicated their disregard for this time-consuming, paper-oriented group. The statute required State to participate in NSC meetings and with the various interagency staffs writing the policy papers discussed in these meetings, but throughout the Truman Administration the State Department refused to recognize the NSC as an important policymaking group.

Secretary of State Marshall sent his Under Secretary to NSC meetings. Secretary of State Dean Acheson ignored the Council until Truman started attending meetings in 1950. He then took control by ensuring that the State Department would chair all the various committees. The State Department did not even agree with the principal premise behind the creation of the NSC: that it would provide a mechanism for the military establishment to influence foreign policy decisions. As the Director of Policy Planning in the State Department, George Kennan's views were representative of the State Department when he wrote that the NSC was there to provide "guidance *to* the military for its military strategic planning."[8] Paul Nitze, who followed Kennan as Director of Policy Planning, shared these views. The disdain felt by these policymakers, who left office in 1953 when Republican President Dwight D. Eisenhower was elected, would bear fruit in another ten years and irrevocably change the structure of the NSC.

As noted, the most contentious coordinating agency created by the 1947 Act was the National Military Establishment, whose very name indicates the reluctance to have a unified department under the direction of a Secretary of Defense. The months of discussion, disagreement, and compromise had weakened the mechanisms designed to promote unity and given little authority to the Secretary of Defense. The military services were still intact as executive departments. The Navy and Marine Corps even kept their aviation components, although the act created a separate Air Force. The act did give the JCS a statutory base and stated that the chiefs would be the principal military advisers to the president.

It was not until the National Security Act was amended in 1949 that a Department of Defense (DOD) was established and the authority of the Secretary of Defense strengthened. The military services were downgraded to military departments and the service secretaries were removed from the NSC, further enhancing the position of the Secretary of Defense. On the other hand, the legislation also established the position of JCS chairman, who had direct access to the President. This made it possible for the JCS to openly disagree with the Secretary.

President Eisenhower reorganized DOD in June 1953, further enlarging the size of the Office of the Secretary and giving the Chairman of the JCS more authority over the Joint Staff which served to give the chiefs independent information. The next reorganization in 1958 further subordinated the military departments to the Secretary.[10] Reorganization of DOD is never finished, however. Every president or Secretary of Defense in the last half century has tried to gain some control over the behemoth housed in the Pentagon. In spite of these efforts, interservice rivalry, duplication of resources, and the exploitation of congressional connections by individual services persist.

The National Security Act appeared to be an organizational blueprint. The objections to its passage were largely devoted to protecting turf. It is the now forgotten United Military Training Act (UMT) that stimulated a substantive discussion on the "garrison state" and the future character of the United States. UMT required every young man in the country to serve a fixed term with one of the military services. Active duty would be followed by a set time in the active reserves. To its greatest supporter, George Marshall, it was a typically American act, far more egalitarian and cost effective than Selective Service. To its detractors it had all the earmarks of government coercion. Its very universality stimulated the fears of militarization that would result from exposing the entire male population to military service.

This debate, nominally about UMT, was actually about the very nature of the country as it faced a war without end. It marked the public suspicion of the coercive power of the "garrison state."[11] To UMT supporters, the future security of the country depended on trained citizens, since a standing army large enough to defend the United States would not be feasible. Supporters, including Marshall and Truman, never doubted the need for such an army, whereas the opponents rejected that view. Since the public acceptance of UMT would have required a very radical change in the historic view of conscription, UMT was discarded.

Discarded at the same time was public discourse on the future of the American state. After 1950 and the Korean War, debate on the possibility of militarism or "garrison state" came to a halt. We were at war. Although dissidents remained, their views never again entered the mainstream of public discussion.

President Truman and his advisers, particularly Secretary of State Dean Acheson, made uneven use of the provisions of the National Security Act. Budget constraints were placed on the Defense Department, for example. Both Truman and Acheson were convinced that the Soviet Union was an expansive, dangerous country whose primary plan was to undercut democracy in the West through subversion.

It was the Korean War and the perception that the Soviet Union was turning from subversion to military action that brought radical change to the concept of national security and the first hint that the country would soon be dominated by national security considerations. The combination of events as 1949 came to an end, including the USSR's detonation of a nuclear bomb and the "loss" of China to the communists, led to a new paradigm that was reinforced when the North Koreans moved South. Ignoring his personally imposed budget ceilings, Truman allowed the money to flow into the coffers of defense and intelligence.[12] The CIA managed to grow and flourish in spite of its spectacular intelligence failures during the Korean War. After a series of weak leaders, the CIA also finally gained a strong minded DCI in the person of Walter Bedell Smith and was thus prepared for the halcyon years ahead.

President Dwight D. Eisenhower entered office promising a "new look" to national security policy. While his Secretary of State, John Foster Dulles, was implementing that look by proposing "massive retaliation" and forming regional alliances to contain communism, the former general was clearing away the procedures he inherited so that he could preside over a White House with orderly processes. In particular, he enhanced the role of the National Security Council. Under Eisenhower's direction, the NSC developed a complicated three-part structure and met regularly. Guided by a small staff under the direction of the newly appointed national security assistant, the NSC produced a series of planning papers and thrived during Eisenhower's two presidential terms, though even he knew that it moved at a slow, ponderous pace.[13]

Eisenhower religiously attended NSC meetings, whose attendees went well beyond the statutory members, and fully participated in the discussions. Usually briefed before the NSC met, he spent an inordinate amount of time in NSC meetings listening to the repetition of that information. To Eisenhower, this was time well spent, since he believed that a major purpose of the NSC was to resolve disagreements and fully inform lower level officials in cabinet agencies and the White House. Giving these officials a sense of participation would, in turn, lead to better policy implementation. Many of the meetings were intentionally informational (Dulles reporting on a NATO meeting, the science adviser explaining the workings of the intercontinental ballistic missile).

This NSC system put policy-planning into slow motion. It was a system designed to reiterate the status quo and make sure there were no rocking boats. Meanwhile, policy was made in the Oval Office, although the sparring in NSC meetings between the parsimonious Secretary of Treasury and the internationalist Secretary of State must have had an impact on that policy.

Perhaps in an effort to distance the president from potentially unsuccessful foreign policy, Eisenhower and his national security assistants continued to insist that policy was made in the NSC. His first national security assistant, Robert Cutler, referred to the NSC as the "top of policy hill."[14] Policy was aired, discussed, and disseminated by NSC meetings, but decisions continued to be made in the Oval Office and Eisenhower's principal adviser continued to be the Secretary of State, John Foster Dulles. The picture of "government by committee," was persuasive. As a result, Eisenhower defeated his own desire to set a pattern for future presidents.

Since Eisenhower's White House was so benign that no president chose it as a model, it would seem that the growing national security state was on hold for a decade. But the appearance was misleading. Along with his DCI, Allen Dulles, he unleashed the CIA.

In the final weeks of his presidency Truman also handed down to Eisenhower a new intelligence agency, so secret that few knew of its existence.[15] The National Security Agency (NSA), created on November 4, 1952, brought together all of the signals intelligence work scattered among other agencies. It assumed the duties of the Armed Forces Security Agency, other military components, and the signals intelligence responsibilities of the CIA. Perhaps because of its earlier tie to the military, Truman made the fateful decision to place NSA under the direction of the Secretary of Defense, separating its information and analysis from the CIA. This act proved to be only the first of many to encourage the proliferating intelligence agencies until by the 2004, the total had grown to fifteen.

Eisenhower was an internationalist who actively promoted the Cold War paradigm; any Soviet loss was a U.S gain and any American loss was an automatic Soviet gain. But he was also a leader of the Republican Party, a party of low budgets and low taxes. Large armies and navies were very expensive, hence the doctrine of "massive retaliation," which relied upon nuclear bombs to stop the Soviet tanks parked at the edge of Western Europe.

But bombs and missiles did not solve the problem of communist infiltration, which was perceived to be the major threat to national security. In particular, Eisenhower and Dulles were concerned about countries with left of center governments in sensitive areas. Sending the Marines was no longer feasible and not very cost effective. Covert action to prevent or overthrow unfriendly governments was much cheaper and more effective. It kept the figleaf over U.S. involvement, and since it was secret, it could proceed without open debate or congressional input. Best of all, the structure for covert action was in place as Eisenhower took office.

The Evolution of the Central Intelligence Agency

The CIA, like the Defense Department, was the product of a rocky past and ultimately evolved into an unrecognizable agency. In the post 9/11 effort to restructure the intelligence organizations, it is important to learn about the early attempts to organize and the inherent problem of control.

The military services had intelligence agencies, but unlike our wartime allies the United States had no agency specifically devoted to intelligence-gathering until the CIA was created in 1947. The Office of Strategic Services (OSS), which had carried out covert actions and assisted resistance groups in Europe during World War II, was quickly disbanded after the conclusion of the war.[16] Intelligence was once more an ancillary function of the State Department as well as each of the military services.

Increasing tensions between the United States and the Soviet Union clearly demanded a greater commitment toward a coordinated intelligence program. But the various intelligence agencies were unwilling to share their information. Naval intelligence had a long history of gathering information from around the world, the Army had its own intelligence service (G-2) and foreign service officers traditionally sent information back to the State Department. In an effort to appease everyone, the Truman administration created the unwieldy, unworkable Central Intelligence Group in 1946. Funded and staffed by State, War, and Navy, it was under the direction of a Director of Central Intelligence (DCI), who was advised by an Intelligence Advisory Board, and answered to a National Intelligence Authority. But each of these entities comprised representatives of the same departments who preferred dominance to coordination. The CIG was a completely inadequate solution.

The National Security Act, therefore, not only created the Central Intelligence Agency, it specifically provided that the DCI coordinate all intelligence information from the various intelligence agencies. Under the provisions of the 1947 Act, the new agency absorbed the major tasks of its predecessors, including the overt and clandestine collection of information. Vague provisions also instructed the agency to "perform such other functions and duties related to intelligence affecting the national security as the NSC will from time to time direct." In addition, it was to advise the NSC, recommend ways to coordinate intelligence activities in the various agencies, and prepare national intelligence estimates based upon the information it coordinated.[17]

It would seem that Congress foresaw an agency that would prepare intelligence estimates and engage in the kind of covert psychological warfare already established in the U.S. arsenal of reactions to the Soviet threat. It would, of course, necessarily include spies to gather the kind of information held closely by the enemy.

Meanwhile, the DCI would gather the information from elsewhere in the intelligence world, and place it together with CIA information for presentation to the policymakers. But the directors of intelligence soon learned the parameters of their power; the military services and even the State Department were unwilling to share their knowledge with another agency. By 1950, it became clear that the Director of Central Intelligence was the director of an agency, not coordinator of the field of intelligence. Numerous studies since 1950 have recommended that the DCI return to the coordination of all intelligence agencies but all proposals have been unsuccessful. No other intelligence agency would give up its control to another agency [18]

Ultimately, unwittingly helped along by President Truman, the CIA became increasingly independent and the DCI the intelligence Czar. Rather than receive numerous intelligence reports, Truman asked the DCI (or his designate) to brief him each morning. Briefing the president gave the CIA the unequaled ability to push their own views. Truman's request became the handle for the CIA to determine what presidents should know.

As noted above, the National Security Act of 1947 stipulated that the CIA perform its duties "under the direction of the National Security Council." It was to advise the NSC concerning intelligence activities and make recommendations for the coordination of these activities. This arrangement was either remarkably naïve or remarkably clever. The NSC could not direct CIA activities unless the CIA told them what they were and made recommendations. The only power the NSC really had over the CIA was to accept or reject its recommendations, but since these were often based upon top-secret information, the NSC largely received verbal intelligence from the DCI at Council Meetings.

Nevertheless, from its very first meeting on September 26, 1947, the members of the NSC had turned their attention to the question of counteracting Soviet activities in Europe through psychological warfare. For more than a year, a joint State, Army, Navy, and Air Force group had been studying the issue of psychological warfare, covert warfare under a more acceptable name. This report endorsed an organization to influence public attitudes in foreign countries, turn them toward the objectives of the United States, and counter anti-American propaganda. The organization would be directed by the Secretary of State with advice from the CIA and military services.[19]

The report and comments were referred to the NSC staff (an interdepartmental body) for revision. The resulting paper that emerged on December 9, 1947 was NSC 4 and the closely held NSC 4a. These were papers that clearly gave the CIA a mandate to carry out covert operations. The DCI was given the task of initiating and conducting covert psychological operations and ensuring they were consistent with American foreign policy. Even though the DCI, Admiral Roscoe H. Hillenkoetter, quickly established an Office of Special Operations within the CIA to conduct psychological operations, he was criticized for his caution and failed to gain the respect of the policymakers in State and Defense. He preferred being at sea and quickly departed Washington at the outbreak of the Korean War.

In January 1948, less than four months after the first NSC meeting, a restive Forrestal suggested that the NSC prepare a new study of the CIA. The report of the three-member NSC Survey Committee had a profound effect on the structure and role of the CIA.[20] It also led to a revision of NSC 4a. There is no question that former DCI Hillenkoetter was reluctant to follow the more active and intrusive policy desired by State and Defense. At the root of the problem was the fact that he did not believe that the legislation establishing the CIA gave him the authority to indulge in the psychological warfare activities usually associated with "black propaganda"—activities that comprised confusion, subversion, and political involvement. The General Counsel of the CIA confirmed to his satisfaction that Congress was primarily interested in the coordination of intelligence and specifically rejected a mandate for "overseas collection" when considering the National Security Act. But like all good lawyers, when it became necessary, the CIA Counsel, Lawrence Houston, found a loophole. The statute did provide that the CIA had the duty "to perform *for the benefit of existing intelligence agencies,*" and for the NSC, such additional services that can be completed only by a central agency. This provision, although taken completely out of context, could provide unlimited interpretation, noted Huston.[21] It was a flimsy foundation upon which the CIA managed to build a castle.

The obsessive desire for an immediate and more active clandestine program was as much a product of external influences as internal ones. The overriding issue before the new NSC was the Italian elections. NSC 1 was a response to the growing influence of the Italian Communist party and other parties of the left and expressed the fear that the relatively moderate Christian Democratic party would lose the election. All stops were pulled out to help the Christian Democratic Party maintain control of the Italian government: food provisions, a larger dollar credit line, favorable trade policies. In addition, in March 1948, with the April elections around the corner, the NSC had approved an outline of covert political action. The Christian Democratic Party won the election.

The lessons learned in 1948 seemed to prove the need for an organization devoted to covert activities. Since the impetus came from the State Department, questions concerning the control of psychological warfare were raised once again. In a Policy Planning Memorandum of May 4, 1948, George Kennan made his own position (and probably that of Secretary Marshall) absolutely clear. There are two kinds of political warfare, he wrote, "Both, from their basic nature should be directed and coordinated by the Department of State." Ad hoc or "impromptu" covert actions (such as those in Italy) will no longer be enough. Political warfare, he continued, means that a nation may use "any means short of war, to achieve national objectives. While the US has carried out some political warfare," it has "operated on the concept that there is a basic difference between war and peace."[22] The implicit message here was that this distinction was no longer viable. But Kennan's plan for an agency under the NSC with a director answering to State ended up as a division of the CIA with a director nominated by State but approved by the NSC and the DCI.

During the brief life of the Office of Policy Coordination (OPC) it became a particularly active participant in the war against communism. For example, it sponsored the National Committee for Free Europe and its sibling, Radio Free Europe and sent radios to dissidents behind the Iron Curtain. By the end of 1952, OPC had 47 overseas stations under its control, a staff of over 2,800 and a budget 17 times larger than in 1949.[23]

The work of this office reflected a turning point in national security policy and the impact of the Cold War on the secret and seamy side of foreign policy. NSC 10 (which superseded NSC 4) clearly defines covert operations as those "so planned and executed" that the responsibility of the U.S. government is not known, or if uncovered can be plausibly denied. They include sabotage, anti-sabotage, demolition and evacuation measures; subversion against hostile states, including aid to underground resistance and guerrilla movements, refugee liberation groups, and support of indigenous anti-communist elements in threatened countries of the "free world."[24] Clearly, as early as 1948, both the State and Defense Departments, as well as the White House, came to regard covert action as a normal part of foreign policy.

The core attribute of covert action is secrecy, but secrecy designed for the enemy soon developed into a "culture of secrecy" at home. The obsession with national security secrets deprived citizens of the right to know. Even fellow security specialists with the need to know were kept in the dark about policies they were expected to uphold. As the years passed almost every foreign policy decision or act had a covert component. Control of information thus became a hallmark of the national security state. Ten to twenty years later, as past covert activities were revealed, public imagination took hold and conspiracy theories proliferated.[25] By the end of the Nixon administration, obsessive secrecy began to corrode the support for government policy. The roots of disaffection that destroyed the foreign policy consensus and government credibility during the Vietnam War are embedded in these initial attempts to undercut the perceived Russian subversion of countries in the "free world."

President Dwight D. Eisenhower, placed his foreign policy into the hands of both Dulles brothers, John Foster at State and Allen at the CIA. As individuals, they were as different as night and day, but they shared the view that no country could be "lost" to communism. While Foster Dulles traveled the world and created multinational treaties designed to support

American interests, Allen returned to his glory days in the OSS and promoted covert actions. With the acquiescence of the president, these were
blatant, if still covert, attempts to influence political developments in other
countries. Sending radios to dissidents or parachuting émigrés into satellite countries were no longer enough. Overturning governments that included communists or even leaned too far to the left was now the preferred
action. In the two best known of these interventions, Iran and Guatemala,
popular will was ignored and a elected government overturned. Not all
Eisenhower-era actions were as successful as those in Iran and Guatemala,
and even today we do not know the extent of the failed operations. But like
those in the previous administration, they carried the support of the president and his Secretary of State and expressed the goals of American foreign
policy. Covert actions had one big advantage. They did not involve Marines
pouring out of amphibious landing vessels or armies of occupation and
hence could remain mostly invisible to the American people.

President Eisenhower is often praised for his efforts to keep the peace
and bring the military budget under control. But he did so at great cost.
Although his countrymen were pleased that he fought no wars, the countries suffering the effects of U.S. covert action and those who owed their
corrupt (but anticommunist) governments to the United States, hardly
thought of him as a man of peace. In any case, the national security state
took a remarkable leap forward in the 1950s.

As Eisenhower entered the final phase of his eight years in office, the
Democratic Party began planning for victory in the 1960 election. Among
the Democratic Senators seeking national recognition for a potential run
for the presidency was Henry Jackson from Washington. "Scoop" Jackson
was among the group of Cold War liberals who, throughout his years in
the Senate, combined support for a progressive domestic policy with a
militant approach to national security affairs. Jackson decided to use his
position on the Government Operations Committee to investigate "national policy machinery" as a way of critiquing the Eisenhower administration. He launched his Subcommittee on National Policy Machinery in
1959 under a set of guidelines limiting the subcommittee to the study of
organization and procedure, since current officials could not discuss secret national security policy. He and his able staff, held well-publicized
hearings in 1960 and issued a lengthy report.[26]

The hearings featured testimony from officials in the Truman and
Eisenhower administration as well as other members of the foreign policy
establishment. Remembering their own frustrations with the system that

had been imposed upon the State Department, the Democrats who had served under President Truman, including George Kennan and Paul Nitze, uniformly criticized the NSC system. But the enthusiastic testimony of members of Eisenhower's staff may have been more damaging and hence more important in the long run. Once again by emphasizing the importance of the NSC they convinced their listeners that national security policy was the product of the NSC. None mentioned the importance of the Oval Office or the relationship between the president and Secretary of State Dulles before his death. Instead, the Jackson Subcommittee, under the assumption that Eisenhower's NSC made policy, promoted the view that a change in policy could come only with a change in the NSC system.[27]

John F. Kennedy and his advisers paid close attention to the criticism heaped upon the Eisenhower system and the resulting policy. They were convinced that the stolid, paper based structure of that NSC system was responsible for the timid foreign policy that in their view marked the Eisenhower years.

THE 1960S: SYSTEMIC CHANGES IN NATIONAL SECURITY

Guided by the advice of Richard Neustadt, a former member of the Truman Administration as well as the Jackson Subcommittee, Kennedy irrevocably changed the system. Immediately after taking office, he quickly dismembered the Eisenhower NSC structure and placed his National Security Adviser, McGeorge Bundy, in the basement. After the debacle at the Bay of Pigs, the adviser and his staff quickly returned to the world of windows and Bundy became a critical focal point for information. But the NSC as such was not restored.

Kennedy made substantive changes that marked a turning point in the further development of the national security state. First, as noted, he turned the national security assistant into a National Security Adviser. The significance of that change went far beyond the change of a word since it implied a change of function, although its impact was not immediately apparent. Bundy kept a low profile, forgoing interviews and only rarely being mentioned in newspapers during his years with Kennedy.

Next, at the president's request, Bundy broke from the tradition of a small administrative staff and assembled a policy staff who served him and by extension the president. A policy staff in the White House greatly increased the power of the president and his control over foreign policy. This expanded White House control would lead inexorably to an enlargement of the national security state, since power and influence were no longer diffused. If the president has few precise powers, he also has few limitations.[28]

Because of the lessons he presumably learned from the Bay of Pigs, Kennedy chose new leaders for the CIA but did not in any way diminish its influence. He not only put it in charge of remaking the government in Cuba, a plan that included assassinating Fidel Castro, but also increased its influence in Southeast Asia as the Vietnam War threatened to become intractable. Historians are still uncovering the scope of covert operations carried out in the 1960s. While less obvious than Guatemala, they were far greater in number and more insidious. The CIA along with other intelligence agencies burrowed even further into the foreign policy process. From the Congo to Cuba and Indochina, the CIA used all the rabbits hidden within its hat, although often unsuccessfully.

Meanwhile, another intelligence agency was created by Secretary of Defense Robert McNamara. In an attempt to coordinate the production of intelligence analysis by each of the military services, McNamara sought to alleviate their parochialism. The Defense Intelligence Agency (DIA) also provided support for the Secretary, the JCS, and their staffs. Quite separate from the CIA, McNamara had quietly given the Pentagon its own ability to analyze intelligence information, and further expanded its reach.

Kennedy also created the White House Situation Room, allowing the NSC staff to obtain the international "traffic" between the various diplomatic, military and intelligence missions abroad without any agency filters. Forty years later a torrent of information flows into the White House while the twenty-five-person round-the-clock staff provides the president with whatever level of information he desires. Although some messages and reports are sent between agencies, only the White House sees them all. It is hard to exaggerate the importance of this communication hub in the White House to presidential control of foreign policy.[29]

Kennedy basically functioned with a different configuration of advisers and preferred to form ad hoc groups to solve particular problems. Presidents Truman and Eisenhower had unalloyed confidence in their Secretaries of State. Kennedy, however, hardly knew his Secretary of State and increasingly regarded the secretary and his department as stodgy, slow-moving, and ineffectual. An impatient, energetic man, Kennedy did not have time for the State bureaucracy to write policy papers or even vet policy positions. Instead, the State Department became an important source of information for the White House national security staff. Previous national security staffs required policy papers and recommendations from interdepartmental groups, but they were usually chaired by State and projected its influence. As other presidents followed the Kennedy model, the State Department never regained its former supremacy within the policymaking machinery of the government. Supremacy now rested with the National Security Adviser and his policy staff.

Kennedy was unusual among recent presidents in his reliance on Secretary of Defense Robert McNamara. He was far more attuned to his dynamic Secretary of Defense who was busy remaking the Defense Department than to the quiet, calm Secretary of State, Dean Rusk. Through force of intellect and boundless energy, McNamara became a powerful figure in the administrations of both Kennedy and President Lyndon Johnson. With McNamara at the helm, the Kennedy administration set about replacing massive retaliation—handy for large world wars—with conventional forces backed by ICBMs and other sophisticated technology, better suited for small wars to counter leftist/communist insurgencies. General Maxwell Taylor, who headed the JCS, reinforced this position, since he had been vocally critical of the Eisenhower administration's defense policy. An unanticipated result of these changes was to encourage American intervention into the underdeveloped world, since the tools were at hand.

In addition to establishing a policy staff for a National Security Adviser in the White House, establishing a White House situation room, and restoring the conventional military forces, Kennedy brought his brother, Attorney General Robert Kennedy, into the inner circle of policymakers. The Attorney General handled tasks of particular sensitivity. Among his other duties, he appeared to be the person responsible for the underside of national security. For example, he presided over Operation Mongoose to rid Cuba of Castro. Robert protected his brother's "deniability," but no one in an official capacity ever doubted that Robert Kennedy spoke for his brother, as he served as the eyes and ears of the Oval Office. A brother in the cabinet was an aberration, of course; but in helping JFK watch over the FBI and intelligence agencies, "Bobby" expanded the reach of the White House even further.

The growth and importance of the national security state took a giant leap during the Kennedy Administration as the White House took more and more control over all facets of international policy, including matters traditionally in the hands of Treasury and State, such as all international

financial and economic matters excluding aid programs, as well as problems of alliance politics in Western Europe. Within a year of taking office,
the Kennedy White House was in charge of the national security state. No
president has since relinquished that hold, although several have not managed to control it.

Kennedy leavened the impact of his changes through his charisma and
his use of rhetoric. The national security state had its critics, but Kennedy
disarmed them. By 1960, most Americans had accepted the Cold War paradigm, were willing for the national security state to subsume the resources of the country, and saw no harm in handing the president the
power of a commander-in-chief. Liberals, uncomfortable with the military side of the national security state, were pleased with Kennedy's innovative policies like the Peace Corps and the Alliance for Progress. So they
did not challenge the budgets prepared by Secretary of Defense McNamara. As the new and more frightful Cold War culture penetrated the
films Americans saw, the books they read, and the news they received on
their TV screens, the national security state became increasingly immune
to criticism.

For the first few years of his presidency, Lyndon B. Johnson left in
place both the Kennedy national security system and its principal actors.
When then-Senator Johnson had served on the Senate Armed Services
Committee, his interest was in efficiency and the toll of waste in the Pentagon rather than military policy. Not incidentally, he also represented
the interest of Texas in obtaining military installations. As vice president,
Johnson traveled widely, met world leaders, and was not so uneducated in
the ways of the world as his detractors assumed. Nevertheless, he never
seemed as comfortable with international affairs as his three predecessors. Much of his domestic policy was based upon personal experience
and, as he once noted, other people in the world were not raised like
Americans.

Johnson ran his White House in much the same way he had run the
Senate while Majority Leader. However important, the staff were no longer filtering all the president's information. When Lyndon Johnson wanted
to know something, he just picked up the telephone. On the other hand,
he had a close working relationship with Secretary of State Dean Rusk, a
fellow Southerner, and indicated his respect for both McGeorge Bundy
and Robert McNamara, both of whom served his administration until
1966 and 1968 respectively. But Johnson was as impatient with NSC meetings as Kennedy.

The position of the National Security Adviser marked the end of the Council side of the NSC, although, rather than dying a quick death, it just shriveled to nothing. Kennedy and Johnson held meetings at the beginning of their administrations but quickly found them time-consuming and repetitive. When responding to a crisis, both presidents would publicly call for an NSC meeting, but this was largely for show, assuring Americans that the president was at work with his advisers.

After Johnson won reelection and sent the first combat troops to Vietnam, he obsessively turned his attention to that conflict and began the systematic process of further shrinking the size of his national security policy meetings.[30] Feeling himself under siege, his formal meetings with advisers soon consisted of the number who could sit around a table for lunch each Tuesday. In attendance were the secretaries of state and defense and the National Security Adviser. The director of the CIA and Chief of the JCS also attended. Whatever the impact on Vietnam, the usual subject of these meetings, these discussions further narrowed the advisory nature of the national security system. Ameliorating this situation was Johnson's dependence on his telephone. Instrument in hand, he sought the advice of old Senate colleagues such as Mike Mansfield, who was opposed to Johnson's Vietnam policy, and old, trusted friends such as Abe Fortas and Clark Clifford, who did not always tell him what he wanted to know.

Johnson made no great structural changes that influenced the further development of the national security state, but the war in Vietnam accomplished that task in unforeseen ways. The CIA as well as military intelligence became an integral part of the American wars in Asia. During the war the CIA had one of its largest stations in Saigon and grew in influence accordingly. Counterinsurgency occupied all intelligence agencies whether military or CIA. Intelligence agents, often acting independently in Southeast Asia, dealt directly with heads of state and other governmental officials. Their actions muddied diplomatic and military planning. Curiously, while the president and his generals shared blame for the Vietnam disaster, the intelligence agencies were barely scarred.

Johnson's reluctance to face defeat in Vietnam caused a credibility gap not only with the public, but also for government analysts who sensed that no one in authority was listening. Even though the record shows that Johnson received advice and warnings from personal friends opposed to the war, none provided an acceptable way out of Vietnam. Thus his response to the quandary presented by the war was to further tighten the small circle of policymakers and isolate himself from protesting crowds. The Sixties came to be defined by Lyndon Johnson's war.

The somewhat neglected story of the 1960s may be the burgeoning intelligence community. Kennedy and Johnson both relied on the CIA and rarely provided any means of monitoring their activities. The oversight exercised by the NSC disappeared with the virtual abandonment of a formal NSC system. The result was the shocking exposure in 1974 by the Senate Subcommittee on Intelligence chaired by Frank Church (D–ID) of the misdeeds of the CIA, including assassination attempts on foreign leaders. Senator Church announced that the CIA had become a "rogue elephant." In fact, the CIA rarely carried out such operations without the knowledge and permission of the president.

The long war in Vietnam expanded the influence of the intelligence and military organizations over foreign policy and also contracted the number of presidential advisers. It also solidified the role of the president as commander-in-chief, a position President Richard Nixon would readily assume when he took office.

THE NIXON/KISSINGER WHITE HOUSE: A TURNING POINT

In a recent interview, General Andrew Goodpaster, Staff Secretary to President Eisenhower and an adviser to Nixon's transition team, commented that quite unlike Eisenhower, Nixon believed in going beyond the control of policy. "He was going to *do* policy. And he was going to direct it, he was going to engage himself in it."[31] Nevertheless, he could not "do" policy alone. He needed a National Security Adviser and staff.

Henry Kissinger seemed a curious choice for National Security Adviser, given Nixon's negative view of eastern intellectuals. However, they agreed on common goals: détente with the Soviets, a new China policy, curtailment of the arms race through a Strategic Arms Limitation Treaty (SALT I), and, last but not least, unambiguous White House domination of foreign policy.

Kissinger implemented Nixon's desire to dominate foreign policy. He did this with a large and talented NSC staff under his control in the White House. Whereas McGeorge Bundy had a handful of staff members, by the end of 1972, Kissinger's national security staff officially numbered around 142. As a result, the White House further supplanted traditional State Department functions. Kissinger now chaired interdepartmental committees, met with foreign officials, and made more important official trips abroad than the Secretary of State.

Richard Nixon's circle of foreign policy advisers narrowed even further than Johnson's. He rarely seemed to receive advice from associates or even specialists within the federal government. It was Kissinger who was in contact with agency officials and received information from them.

Unlike most presidents, Nixon also did not receive firsthand information from other members of the national security staff, since Kissinger never brought them along to meetings with the president. Most members of the Kissinger's staff met the president the day they shook his hand and departed.[32]

Nixon and Kissinger achieved their policy successes through secrecy, deceit, and even disdain for democratic institutions. It was not difficult to deceive a public accustomed to secrecy as an important component of national security. Nixon's trip to China is an example of the secrecy that permeated policy. It was "a one man show." Deceit was the hallmark of Kissinger's use of the "back channel" for negotiating behind the back of appointed officials. Kissinger also met with the press, leaking choice tidbits to them from time to time. Finally, Kissinger met with individual congressmen, but the secret negotiations precluded congressional discussion or input.

However much they tried, neither Nixon nor Kissinger could control the situation in Vietnam or the backlash at home. Nixon's tendencies toward paranoia, combined with Kissinger's willingness to use all the tools at his disposal to control the situation and the American public's growing vocal opposition to war in Vietnam, were a deadly mixture. National security as defined by Kissinger and Nixon gave them the right to misuse the legitimate functions of the FBI, wiretap White House employees, and curtail the civil liberties of any person or organization that opposed their policies. Finally, the president went too far. The Watergate scandal brought the administration to an end, but not before President Nixon had illustrated the dangers inherent in the national security state. Under the rubric of security and the secrecy it required, the president and his staff assumed unlimited power over policy while disregarding the rule of law.

The Nixon-Kissinger years were another turning point in the evolution of the national security state. Control from the White House was now complete. None of the presidents who followed cut back on the national security staff or on the power of the National Security Adviser. The assistant who began as a facilitator for the president now occupied the top rung of the policymaking hierarchy.

As the inexperienced President Jimmy Carter struggled with his foreign policy, the dissension within his administration finally drew attention to the question of the National Security Adviser's accountability. President Carter entered the Oval Office with plans to change both the foreign policy of Nixon and Kissinger and the secrecy that characterized it.[33] He wanted his foreign policy to emphasize human rights, control of armaments, and his "conviction that the world could be redeemed by faith and [good] works."[34] In particular, Carter wanted to move away from the obsession with communism and the Soviet Union. He came to the office at what should have been a propitious time: the long Vietnam War was over and contentious dissent was in the past.

Except for his membership in the Trilateral Commission, which was established in 1973 to foster better international relations between the United States, Europe, and Japan, Carter had no experience in the world of national security policy. Zbigniew Brzezinski, an academic and analyst who, along with David Rockefeller, was responsible for the birth of the Commission, befriended Carter and began advising him. It was no surprise that Carter named him to the post of National Security Adviser. If Brzezinski had a role model as he joined the administration it was that of Henry Kissinger, whose power and influence he wished to mirror.

Carter was only slightly acquainted with his Secretary of State. But in Cyrus Vance he found an experienced public official who had served in both the Kennedy and Johnson administrations. Unfortunately, Vance and Brzezinski had strong policy differences. Vance shared the president's "principled approach" to foreign policy.[35] Brzezinski, on the other hand, while willing to defend human rights, thought in terms of geopolitical and strategic power. Soviet power still had to be contained and the spread of communism halted. Carter was convinced he could ensure a balance between Vance and Brzezinski, but he immediately gave Brzezinski the edge. He created two committees under the NSC. Vance chaired the group that dealt with diplomacy, while Brzezinski chaired the committee with oversight over matters pertaining to intelligence, arms control, and crisis management. Thus Vance was at a disadvantage from the very beginning of the administration.[36] The president often found Brzezinski more persuasive and his physical proximity to the president gave him the "inside track" shared by all National Security Advisers.

Even when a president is both knowledgeable and decisive, tensions develop between policymakers vying for his attention and approval. Carter was not experienced and exacerbated the problem by choosing two men who disagreed on fundamental policy assumptions. Dissension between Vance and Brzezinski began with their different views of the Soviet menace and touched almost every policy issue, including those concerned with Somalia, SALT II, and Soviet intentions.[37] Brzezinski deliberately undercut Vance's position as he publicly commented on issues in contradiction of administration policy and used the "back channel" to maneuver behind Vance's back. The Iranian hostage crisis brought the dissension to a head. Without Vance's concurrence, Carter and Brzezinski decided to try to liberate the American hostages by sending helicopters to Iran. Vance submitted his resignation.

The dissension between Vance and Brzezinski was an open secret. Richard Burt, writing in the *New York Times*, reported on July 20, 1979 that Brzezinski had finally won the power battle and was the dominant force in the making of national security policy. The domination of policy by Kissinger, and the attempts by Brzezinski to dominate the Carter administration finally came to the attention of Congress. Senator Edward Zorinsky (D-NE) offered an amendment requiring that the National Security Adviser and his deputy be subject to Senate confirmation. For the first time since passage of the National Security Act in 1947, Congress turned its attention to the unanticipated power of the NSC and the presidential adviser. The Senate Foreign Relations Committee held a series of hearings on "The National Security Adviser: Role and Accountability," in response to the Zorinsky amendment. The underlying issue throughout the hearings was the lack of accountability to Congress by this powerful White House adviser. The hearing was brief (although the appendix to the transcript is long). Witnesses before the committee included the Deputy Secretary of State Warren Christopher representing the administration, former adviser Brent Scowcroft, a lawyer to discuss constitutional procedures, and a policy analyst critical of the current status quo.[38] Christopher's testimony was bloodless and most additional information was equally deficient in describing the theoretical position of the president's adviser as opposed to reality. No present or past member of a presidential administration approved the amendment, even as newspaper stories proliferated about the disagreements between the State Department and the Carter White House. Zorinski's amendment died, Carter was defeated in the election of 1980, and no Senate Committee would ever again raise the issue of Senate confirmation of the National Security Adviser. Nevertheless, the hearings did highlight the absolute power of the president's chief adviser, whose position was entirely outside the purview of Congress.

Ronald Reagan had six National Security Advisers during his eight years in office, a clear indication of the weakness of his national security system. Reagan entered office with little understanding of the intricate diplomatic problems faced by the country, or the technological changes influencing the military preparedness he promoted. His world view was based upon the ideology that had influenced him over a lifetime: Communism was evil and democracies at risk. But ideology is no substitute for policy, so notwithstanding his firm views, Reagan was a weak manager of the White House national security process.

Memoirs of his administration describe Reagan as a delegator. He set the big picture—anti-communism and a military buildup to accompany it—and delegated the policy details to others. Elliott Abrams, who served as Assistant Secretary of State for Inter-American Affairs noted that Reagan was a great president but "not a terrific prime minister." Reagan was not a very good executive, Abrams continued, and did not feel the presidency required that talent. Reagan, he thought, saw the presidency as an "inspirational position." [39]

Paul Nitze, noting the president's firm conviction and eloquent speeches on the superiority of the democratic system, added that Reagan had "all kinds of defects." He failed to master details, had a poor sense of organization, and was not skillful in selecting people.[40] Policy and the policy process both suffered in the first Reagan administration from great inconsistency and unwieldy organization. Reagan's White House was organized around a triumvirate of three assistants, Mike Deaver, James Baker, and Ed Meese. The first National Security Adviser, Richard Allen, answered to Ed Meese, not to the president. The second adviser, William Clark, was a former California associate of the president and managed to cut away the middle person so that he and future advisers could meet with the president without an intervening figure. Robert McFarlane, Clark's deputy, who followed him, was the first adviser who had extensive experience with the foreign policy issues; he had served on the NSC staff during the administrations of Nixon and Ford. McFarlane was destined never to be a close adviser to a president who had little interest in the details of policy. While he briefed the president every morning, he was generally allotted only about fifteen minutes.[41] Meanwhile, success as a coordinator of policy eluded him since Secretary of State George Shultz and Secretary of Defense Caspar Weinberger rarely agreed.

As governor of California, Reagan had always operated with a small group of handpicked advisers. Evidently he, too, regarded the NSC meetings as encompassing too large a group, since it often included the deputies or assistant secretaries of the agencies. In August 1981, the president established an "informal" body, the National Security Planning Group (NSPG). Participants were the president, vice president, secretaries of state and defense, the National Security Adviser, William Casey, the DCI, and Ed Meese, who attended in his capacity as Counselor to the president. Except for Meese, this was the same combination of advisers used by all presidents. This group was reportedly split into two camps. Shultz and McFarlane with the support of Vice President Bush agreed with the general proposal for military buildup but thought that the buildup should be combined with an effort to deal with the Soviets, especially on arms control agreements.

Weinberger and Casey, joined by Meese, were opposed to any compromises or pragmatic arrangements with an untrustworthy Soviet Union committed to Communist ideology and seeking global dominance. To them, strong military force was essential to counter the expansive communists. This meant that the president's chief advisers were deeply divided on very basic policy concerns. The dangers created by a national security system based on ideological views and delegation of power bore fruit in the Iran-Contra scandal. The president was determined to defeat the Sandinistas in Nicaragua and free hostages in Lebanon. Urging his NSC staff to find a solution while disassociating himself from the specifics led to an out of control, operational NSC in the White House covertly trading arms for hostages and independently financing the "contras" who opposed the government in Nicaragua. Both McFarland and John Poindexter, the next National Security Adviser, were discredited and departed. Although Reagan pled innocence, he was not just a bystander to this subversion of legislative intent and constitutional limitation.[42] Meanwhile, during his second term, Reagan's policy shifted as much as his stream of National Security Advisers. Forgotten was the "evil empire," as he met with the new Soviet leader, Mikhail Gorbachev, took a radical new stance on arms control, and sought a place in history as a peacemaker.

Ronald Reagan remains an enigmatic man whose chosen biographer could not fathom his thoughts.[43] In some ways he was transparent—a genial man who was politically adept and persuasive through his ability to communicate to the public. On the other hand, Reagan's thoughts largely remain unknown and the reasons for his mistakes as well as victories remain mysterious. His lack of detailed knowledge about foreign affairs made him appear indifferent to enlarging the mandate of the national security state. Yet, like Eisenhower, because he supported and encouraged the Director of Central Intelligence, the expansion of the national security state continued.

There is some question as to whether the DCI has ever been totally above politics, but William Casey politicized the position as no other director before him. Not only did Iran-Contra bear his unseen hand, but he also greatly expanded American arms shipments for the Afghani mujahedeen fighting the Soviet invasion of Afghanistan, an action that continues to haunt the United States. To Casey, who set out to create an alliance between the CIA, Saudi intelligence, and the Pakistani army, the Afghan jihad was "an important front in a worldwide struggle between communist atheism and God's community of believers."[44] With the acquiescence of Congress, Casey and his partners spent huge sums on the Afghanistan operation. Independence of Afghanistan now became his personal goal, although this was not the goal of the presidential finding of 1980 that sanctioned CIA involvement in that country.

Casey was willing to send US/CIA money around the world to support any noncommunist groups. Aside from Nicaragua and Afghanistan, money went to Angola, Ethiopia, and Cambodia. He saw all these communist resistance groups as a unit and did not hesitate to extend the U.S. influence around the world, since he saw each country as a great threat to American national security.[45] Casey took the United States into uncharted country but the sudden end of the Cold War masked its importance for a decade.

One of the striking aspects of the Reagan administration's national security policy was the complete failure to see the coming disintegration of the Soviet Union. Weinberger consistently urged an arms buildup, noting the possibility of Soviet tanks crossing Central Europe. Reagan was convinced that the Soviets had made significant gains during the Carter years in countries such as Nicaragua, Afghanistan, and Angola. For the Reagan administration the observable problems in the Soviet Union seemed not to matter. The failure to foresee the rapid dissolution of the Soviet Union was either a triumph of ideology over observation or a massive failure of intelligence.[46]

The Berlin Wall collapsed just as George H.W. Bush assumed the presidency. Forty years of the Cold War finally came to an end. The events and fears that so dominated the world were history. Russian leaders became our friends, former Soviet satellites sought to join the North Atlantic Treaty Organization (NATO), and the United States found itself facing a changed world. But even though the enemy disappeared, the national security state created to fight the Cold War remained in place, ready to be exploited for a new world facing new wars.

President Bush set out to restore the NSC structure after the Reagan debacle. As a first step he ordered that NSC meetings be limited to the statutory members. He also set up the requisite national security process. Beneath the NSC was a principals committee, which met without the president and vice president, a deputies committee, and eight new policy coordinating agencies. The purpose of this structure, like others before and after, was to incorporate information from State, Defense, and the CIA while maintaining an independence from their conclusions. Except for the principals meetings, no policy emerged from this structure. Instead, policy continued to be the prerogative of the president and his National Security Adviser.

The Clinton White House adapted the Bush structure, including the idea of meetings without the president. The absence of the president and vice president from the principals meeting marked an unusual turn. Although the original National Security Act had envisioned NSC meetings without the president, for almost forty years the president attended the NSC meetings, even as their frequency diminished. The return to meetings by the members of the NSC plus the National Security Adviser and DCI (basically the principals) did not mark a new beginning for the council but rather furthered its demise. The NSC staff prepared papers for these meetings and presumably they discussed and refined ideas before presenting them to the president.[47]

Old Cold War habits were hard to break. Military intervention, covert operations, secrecy, and presidential control of foreign policy persisted. First, President Bush intervened in Panama (Operation Just Cause). Then, gathering together thirty allies, the U.S. used a forbidding array of military forces to turn back Saddam Hussein's invasion of Kuwait (Operation Desert Storm).

Manuel Noriega, who gained control of Panama in 1979, was deeply involved in the drug trafficking that made him millions and had angered North Americans, who held him responsible for the drug addiction prevalent in American society. Bush invaded with 22,500 troops, and his venture was a rousing success. Unknown to the public, Noriega had received regular sums of money from the CIA in the 1960s and had been pressed into duty by the Reagan administration to help the contras.

Similarly, throughout the 1980s, Saddam Hussein had quietly received U.S. support in his war against Iran. Baghdad received arms, intelligence data, and agricultural credits. No one stopped Hussein from receiving illegal bank loans in order to buy Western technology for his weapons programs. All of this help was deemed necessary in order to defeat the mullahs running Iran. These actions were surely known to Vice President Bush who, since leaving the position of DCI, had taken a special interest in the work of the intelligence agency. When Iraq invaded Kuwait, President Bush, with the support of American allies, began bombing the country in January 1991. The military invasion followed. After Iraq was defeated, the UN imposed peace terms that guaranteed the boundary of Kuwait and demanded that Iraq give up its research on deadly weapons and nuclear bombs, comply with UN inspectors, and submit to other restrictions on its sovereignty.[48]

Had the earlier delivery of CIA money influenced Noriega to ignore the warnings the U.S. delivered to Panama? Did Saddam Hussein misunderstand the help he received? Did it make him feel free to move into Kuwait? These provocative questions illustrate how easy it was for secret, covert action to spread in the name of U.S. national security and how hard it was for the national security state to control the events that ensued.

These wars further illustrate that the tenets and attributes of the Cold War were still at hand. The tools of the national security state were not allowed to disintegrate with disuse. As the world's sole military power, the United States could use new wars to extend its reach. These tools reaffirmed the ability of the president to conduct wars, overt and covert, without congressional permission. But with the monolithic enemy gone, policymakers failed to adjust their thinking. It was a new age of nationalism and ethnic struggle, a new era for the CIA.

President Clinton, unlike his predecessor, entered office primarily concerned with the economy. Whereas Bush, the former DCI, had a deep interest in his intelligence briefings, Clinton was indifferent when the CIA briefer appeared each morning with the President's Daily Brief and he rarely met with his DCI,[49] since he was skeptical of covert action and was inherently suspicious of the CIA. During his first years in office, his economic advisers occupied his time while his national security team had far less access to him. Unlike his predecessor, however, whose decision-making process was described as limited and "highly" secretive, Clinton's NSC staff was more open to Congress and even included a speech writer.[50]

Nevertheless, David Gergen, who had worked in a number of White Houses, estimated that most presidents spent about 60 percent or more of their time on foreign policy. In his first years as president Gergen believed that Clinton spent no more than 25 percent of his time on foreign policy. Indeed, it often appeared that international policy was being made by the

Secretary of the Treasury, Robert Rubin, rather than the Secretary of State, Warren Christopher.

Ultimately the world intruded upon Clinton and he, too, faced difficult challenges abroad. Terrorism was a continuing threat. Since 1980, while Reagan and Casey were preoccupied with world communism, terrorist attacks began to draw the attention of the American government and people. The U.S. Embassy in Lebanon was struck in 1983. A truck loaded with explosives struck the U.S. Marine Barracks in Beirut, killing 241 marines. TWA flight 847 was hijacked and Leon Klinghoffer, an elderly man in a wheelchair was murdered on the cruise ship *Achille Lauro*.

The CIA opened its first Counterterrorism Center in 1986, but found it difficult to infiltrate the Islamic organizations in the Middle East. Still concerned with the Afghani jihad, the news that Osama Bin Laden, a wealthy Saudi, was spreading money around the Pakistan–Afghanistan border was welcomed. In 1998, the Clinton administration escalated the response to terrorism by establishing a new counterterrorism czar in the White House. Frightening messages emanated from this office as "Czar" Richard Clarke warned against biological warfare, truck bombs, and every terrorist tool in between. But terrorism was still something to read about, not experience, and Clarke's warnings began to sound like the little boy who cried wolf too many times.

Before he left office, President Clinton had followed his predecessors in moving away from domestic policy, learning bitter lessons along the way. The president, however, was probably reflecting the desire of most Americans when he withdrew from Somalia after the death of nineteen U.S. Army Rangers in 1993 and hesitated to intervene in Haiti. Americans had answered the aggression in the Gulf, but with the end of the Cold War, they seemed otherwise content to let the world solve its own problems.

By the time Clinton left office, the last vestiges of the original National Security Council had disappeared into the person of the National Security Adviser and his staff. The policy structure was not radically changed, but White House control was absolute. In both the Bush and Clinton administrations, Interdepartmental Working Groups were usually chaired by an NSC senior director, not a representative of the State Department; meetings were held in the White House; papers were directed to the deputies meetings chaired by a deputy assistant of the NSC before being sent to the meeting of principals, chaired by the National Security Adviser. Clinton himself was not a man who cared much about structure. He appointed a congenial group of cabinet members, relied on his National Security

Adviser, and simply reacted to events as they occurred. His policies were often criticized because there seemed to be neither vision nor strategy, but as his first National Security Adviser, Anthony Lake, pointed out, the Clinton Administration was the first since Truman to lack a defining issue. It did not concede any of the powers gained by their predecessors, however.[51]

Meanwhile, technology continued to promote the control of national security policy by the White House. Under the Bush and Clinton administrations, interdepartmental meetings were often done by video conferences. While this was a more efficient approach, it also was more private and secretive. Reporters could no longer even "count the cars driving into West Executive Avenue," or wonder about the issues bringing so many VIPs to the White House.[52]

As the information age produced newer and newer technology, the situation room, established by President Kennedy in the basement of the White House, became increasingly important as it moved the electronic traffic into the Oval Office far faster than ever imagined by John F. Kennedy. Cabinet agencies involved in national security had traditionally had their own operation centers for obtaining and decrypting messages, the most important of which were then sent to the White House. Although State, Defense, and the CIA all collect data in their own centers, none of them see all the messages. Only the president gets the full story. With new techniques, these agencies can now "skim off" important national security information so that the president's advisers are immediately informed electronically. The ramifications are clear. The president and his National Security Adviser now have more knowledge quicker than anyone else in the government. This attribute further solidified the power of the National Security Adviser and the president.[53]

Although President George W. Bush, a former governor of Texas, also had no foreign policy experience, he chose quite different advisers than Clinton. The Cold War marked the careers of his foreign policy advisers, including Vice President Richard Cheney, Secretary of Defense Donald Rumsfeld, and Secretary of State Colin Powell. The only new face was Condoleezza Rice, who wrote her Ph.D. thesis on the Soviet Union and Czechoslovakia during the Cold War and was regarded as a Russian expert. Bush was necessarily dependent on advisers, but his style as president was to depend on a chosen few.

His administration was marked from the beginning by contentious disagreements among his advisers. Rumsfeld and Powell, supported by their deputies, Paul Wolfowitz and Richard Armitage, were largely at odds with each other over basic national security decisions. Powell generally found himself overruled by Cheney, who had his own national security staff, and Rumsfeld. Rice, who was unusually close to the president and served as an early tutor, was rarely able to broker an agreement.[54] Perhaps this was because she tended to accept the views of Cheney and Rumsfeld.

The fearful and tragic events of September 11, 2001, transformed the presidency of George Bush. They unleashed forces in domestic and foreign policy that harkened back fifty years to the early Cold War. In a defining statement soon after 9/11, Bush announced, "We are at war." These four words were fraught with meaning. Once again, the president morphed into the commander-in-chief, with all its additional powers. Declaring a war means changes in society. Domestic programs are sacrificed as money is siphoned into the coffers of the Defense Department and secrecy gains legitimacy.

Bush was not just marking the U.S. move into Afghanistan to remove al-Qaeda; he had declared war on terrorism. The threat posed by Iraq, he assured Americans, was part of this war, although Iraq was not responsible for September 11 and had no interest in the fundamentalist views of Bin Laden. The United States, said the president, would now adopt a policy of preemption to replace containment. The United States would seek out enemies before they threatened.

But there is no way to fight a "war" on terrorism. Terrorism has no specific enemy; it is the use of violence to gain certain political objectives. Terrorists bedeviled our European allies for decades, but they never went to "war." As noted above, terrorism has been on the U.S. agenda for more than twenty years, troops have been sent and wars were fought, but not against terrorism. Perhaps, no one declared a "war" because a war against terrorism is a war without end.

Meanwhile, Bush opened a new front, against Iraq, ostensibly because its ruler was tied to terrorism. The regime of Saddam Hussein unquestionably terrorized the Shi'a and Kurds in his own country, but there was no evidence that he supported the terrorists that devastated the World Trade Center and destroyed so much of the Pentagon.

In spite of public references to the NSC, Bush has fought these wars with a small circle of advisers. Recently departed members of his cabinet refer to these advisers as the "palace guard." Bush described his management style to a golfing friend in one sentence. "I'm not afraid to make decisions, and I hire good people and then listen to them." He relies so heavily on those "good people" that they even pick the newspaper articles he should read. Those around him acknowledge that he lacks both curiosity and patience. His critics point to his failure to consider alternatives or look for complexity when making decisions. Certainly these traits led him into the morass in Iraq with its complicated and varied ethnic population and weak institutions.[55]

The Bush wars reflect the lack of differentiation between peace and war that characterizes the national security state. Whether preemptive war, as in Iraq, or war without end against terrorists, he has at hand two great advantages: one, the large superstructure of the national security process created fifty years ago for the Cold War and never dismantled; second, a public now accustomed to the perception of perpetual crisis, the president as commander-in-chief, a wealthy Pentagon, and an impoverished public sector. In the name of national security, Americans have spent more than fifty years rallying to the flag.

But, as this essay illustrates, the structure surrounding President Bush is quite different from the one conceived in 1947. Forrestal was determined to widen the circle of presidential advisers through coordinating agencies and the NSC. President Kennedy abandoned this approach in 1961 when he appointed a National Security *Adviser*, rather than an assistant. Soon, the Adviser and his staff supplanted the NSC. Although the formal NSC continued to meet occasionally, it was never again the widely attended Council familiar to Truman and Eisenhower. The circle of advisers began to close with the administration of Lyndon Johnson. Kissinger's schedule often included NSC meetings but these were no more than the interdepartmental "committees" that constituted his NSC. Presidents that followed tended to sit around a table with two cabinet secretaries, the DCI, and the National Security Adviser. Jimmy Carter added the vice president.

As the CIA has grown, it has loomed larger and larger in the decision-making process. As the NSC has faded from view, presidents have relied on smaller and smaller groups of advisers. Meanwhile, policymaking became highly centralized in the White House. The result was the shrinking ability of the State Department to influence policy.

In one sense, however, those who fashioned the system did foresee its most important function. The National Security Act, including the NSC, provided a perfect blueprint for preparing for war. Over the years, war and peace began to merge as the omnipresent Cold War further stimulated national fears from real and imagined threats from abroad.

The national security state is now in the hands of a generation stunned by the events of September 11, 2001. They are more secretive, more arrogant in their assumptions, more committed to flexing the muscles of the world's only military superpower. There is every reason to assume that the national security state will grow only more pervasive in the future.

Ironically, it is doubtful that the national security state has ever made the American people feel safer as they faced its enemies. A nation obsessed with national security necessarily must continue to promote crises and incite fear. After all, that is its *raison d'être*.

Notes

1. Michael J. Hogan, *A Cross of Iron: Harry S. Truman and the Origins of the National Security State, 1945–1954*. (New York: Cambridge University Press, 1998), 463.
2. Alfred D. Sander, "Truman and the National Security Council: 1945–1947," *Journal of American History* 59 (September 1972).
3. Demetrios Caraley, *The Politics of Military Unification: A Study of Conflict and the Policy Process* (New York: Columbia University Press, 1966).
4. Jeffery M. Dorwart, *Eberstadt and Forrestal: A National Security Partnership, 1909–1949* (College Station: Texas A&M University Press, 1991), 90–130.
5. This interesting story unfolds in the National Defense Unification folders, George M. Elsey Papers (Harry S Truman Library, Independence, MO.).
6. Anna Kasten Nelson, "President Truman and the Evolution of the National Security Council," *Journal of American History* 72, no.1 (September 1985): 360–78.
7. See for example, Keith C. Clark and Laurence Legere, eds. *The President and the Management of National Security: A Report by the Institute for Defense Analyses* (New York: Praeger, 1969), 58–59.
8. Memorandum, Under Secretary Meetings on the National Security Council, May 2, 1949, Policy Planning Staff (PPS), Department of State (DS)RG 59, National Archives; Correspondence between George F. Kennan and Mr. Saltzman, February 17, 18, 1949, PPS, DS. FOIA document in possession of the author.
9. Steven L. Rearden, *History of the Office of the Secretary of Defense, Vol.1, The Formative Years 1947–1950* (Washington, D.C.: Department of Defense, 1984), 23–55.
10. The Department of Defense, Documents on Establishment and Organization, 1944–1978 (Washington: Historical Office, Office of the Secretary of Defense, 1978), Sec. 111.
11. Aaron L. Friedberg, *In the Shadow of the Garrison State* (Princeton: Princeton University Press, 2000).
12. NSC 68 provided the blueprint for Truman's actions.

13. Anna K. Nelson, "The Importance of Foreign Policy Process: Eisenhower and the National Security Council," in Gunter Bischof and Stephen E. Ambrose, eds., *Eisenhower: A Centenary Assessment* (Baton Rouge, Louisiana State University Press, 1995), 112–25. Also see Fred I. Greenstein, *The Hidden-Hand Presidency* (New York: Basic Books, 1982).

14. Robert Cutler, "The Development of the National Security Council," *Foreign Affairs* (April 1956): 448–49.

15. James Bamford, *The Puzzle Palace* (New York: Penguin Books, 1982), 15–19.

16. Arthur B. Darling, *The Central Intelligence Agency: An Instrument of Government to 1950* (University Park: Pennsylvania State University Press, 1990), 3–41.

17. Ibid., 187.

18. The Final Report of the National Commission on Terrorist Attacks Upon the United States, (New York: Norton, 2004). Known as The 9/11 Commission Report gave up on the position of DCI and recommended a Director of Intelligence who would supersede both the CIA and all Defense intelligence agencies, not only by directing the intelligence, but through control of the total intelligence budget.

19. This section is based upon the Department of State, *Foreign Relations of the United States 1945–1950, Emergence of the Intelligence Establishment* (Washington: Government Printing Office, 1996). Hereafter *FRUS*.

20. The three were Allen Dulles, Matthew Corea, and William Jackson.

21. *FRUS*, 622–23. Emphasis added.

22. *FRUS*, 669.

23. Michael Warner, "The CIA's Office of Policy Coordination from NSC 10/2 to NSC 68," unpublished paper presented at a Society for Historians of American Foreign Relations, June 1998.

24. *FRUS*, 713–15.

25. That the CIA conspired to kill John F. Kennedy is a theory that never dies. Another was the suggestion that the CIA deliberately spread drugs through the Oakland, California, African American community.

26. U.S. Congress, 86th Congress, 2nd Sess., Senate, Subcommittee on National Policy Machinery of the Committee on Government Operations, *Report* (Washington, D.C., 1960).

27. U.S. Congress, Senate, Subcommittee on National Policy Machinery of the Committee on Government Operations, *Hearings on Organizing for National Security* (Washington, D.C., 1960), Testimony of Kennan and Nitze, 801–75; Testimony of Eisenhower officials, 577–608, 696–721.

28. Arthur M. Schlesinger Jr., *A Thousand Days: John F. Kennedy in the White House* (Boston: Houghton, Mifflin, 1965).

29. Bradley H. Patterson Jr., *The White House Staff: Inside the West Wing and Beyond* (Washington, D.C.: Brookings Institution Press, 2000), 50–52.

30. Emmette S. Redford and Richard T. McCulley, *White House Operations: The Johnson Presidency* (Austin: University of Texas Press, 1986), 99–111. Johnson often called the White House Situation Room in the middle of the night to talk about the events in Vietnam. See for example, Recordings of Conversations, WH6504.05, 3:30 A.M.; WH 6504.05, 2:43 A.M. Lyndon B. Johnson Library, Austin Texas.

31. *The National Security Council Project.* Oral History Roundtables, "The Nixon Administration National Security Council," December 8, 1998, Center for International and Security Studies at Maryland School of Public Affairs, University of Maryland. Hereafter Roundtables and Title.

32. Roundtables, *The Nixon Administration National Security Council,* December 8, 1998.

33. William Stueck, "Placing Jimmy Carter's Foreign Policy," in Gary M. Fink and Hugh Davis Graham, eds., *The Carter Presidency: Policy Choices in the Post-New Deal Era* (Lawrence: University Press of Kansas, 1998).

34. David S. McLellan, *Cyrus Vance* (Totowa, New Jersey: Rowman & Allanheld, 1985) 26.

35. Ibid., 25.

36. I. M. Destler, Leslie H.Gelb, and Anthony Lake, *Our Own Worst Enemy, The Unmaking of American Foreign Policy* (New York: Simon and Schuster, 1984), 217–18.

37. McClellan, *Vance*, 39, 45, 115. The Panama Canal Treaty was an exception.

38. U.S. Senate, Hearing before the Committee on Foreign Relations, "The National Security Adviser: Role and Accountability," April 17, 1980, 96th Congress, 2nd Session (Washington, D.C., 1980). The two additional panel members were Thomas M. Franck and I. M. Destler.

39. Kenneth W. Thompson, ed., *The Reagan Presidency: Ten Intimate Perspectives of Ronald Reagan* (Lanham, MD: University Press of America, 1997), 96.

40. Ibid., 22–23.

41. Reagan also exhibited very little interest in his intelligence briefing. John L. Helgerson, *Getting to Know the President: CIA Briefings of Presidential Candidates, 1952–1992* (Washington, D.C.: Center for the Study of Intelligence, Central Intelligence Agency, 1996) or *http://www.cia.gov/csi/books/briefing/cia-8.htm.* Chapter 6.

42. Frank Carlucci and Colin Powell were the final national security advisers.

43. Edmund Morris, *Dutch, a Memoir of Ronald Reagan* (New York: Random House, 1999).

44. Steve Coll, *Ghost Wars: The Secret Histry of the CIA, Afghanistan, and Bin Laden, from the Soviet Invasion to September 10, 2001.* (New York: Penguin Press, 2004), 93.

45. Bob Woodward, *Veil: The Secret Wars of the CIA 1981–1987* (New York: Simon and Schuster, 1987), 373.

46. Donald T. Regan, *For the Record, From Wall Street to Washington* (New York: Harcourt Brace Jovanovich, 1988); Beth A. Fischer, *The Reagan Reversal: Foreign Policy and the End of the Cold War* (Columbia: University of Missouri Press, 1997).

47. Patterson, *The White House Staff*, 50–51.

48. Thomas Powers, "The Perils of Covert Policy," *Los Angeles Times*, October 29, 1989; Woodward, *Veil*, 439, 480.

49. Helgerson, *Getting to Know the President*, ch. 1

50. Adam Pertman, "Bush Moves Reveal Strengths and Flaws of a One-Man Show," *The Boston Globe*, January 7, 1990; *Roundtables*, The Clinton Administration National Security Council.

51. Thomas L. Friedman, "Clinton's Foreign Policy: Top Adviser Speaks Up," *New York Times*, October 30, 1993.

52. Patterson, *The White House Staff*, 52.

53. Ibid., 50–52.

54. Elisabeth Bumiller, "A Partner in Shaping an Assertive Foreign Policy," *New York Times*, January 7, 2004.

55. The above description of Bush's management style is based upon Mike Allen and David S. Broder, "Bush's Leadership Style: Decisive or Simplistic?" *The Washington Post*, August 30, 2004.

7. INTELLIGENCE FOR EMPIRE

JOHN PRADOS

Americans today take it for granted that the United States maintains a vast array of agencies and entities that collect, process, and disseminate information, and carry out such other activities as are ordered by the president. In fact, the origins of this so-called "intelligence community" are relatively recent. It grew like topsy under pressure of war—World War II that is. Many analysts trace the beginnings of the U.S. intelligence community to the Japanese attack on Pearl Harbor, to our determination never again to be taken by surprise as we were on that Sunday morning in December 1941. Another school believes that the community originated with William J. ("Wild Bill") Donovan, whom President Franklin D. Roosevelt dispatched on special missions to Europe, observing in particular the British intelligence service, and who got FDR to approve the creation of the Office of the Coordinator of Information in July 1941. This entity soon became the Office of Strategic Services (OSS), a full-spectrum intelligence agency. Yet another view points to the existence of intelligence units within the War and Navy Departments from the nineteenth century, and at the State Department since 1915.

No matter how the origins of U.S. intelligence are traced, World War II marked a key passage in its evolution. That conflict proved that intelligence could contribute importantly both to military operations and to diplomacy, that technological development could make intelligence even more capable, and that these new pillars of intelligence could support methods of analyzing information that enabled intelligence for the first time to supply comprehensive estimates of secret foreign capabilities. The war also demonstrated that intelligence agencies could carry out operations that amounted to an ancillary form of military action. This is not to say that intelligence techniques had not existed previously—spying is often called the second-oldest profession—but rather that the war brought exponential changes to intelligence.

These advances might have been lost in the postwar era and that, really, is where Pearl Harbor comes in. As World War II drew to a close in 1945, Harry S Truman, Roosevelt's successor, seeing little need for an independent intelligence agency in peacetime, terminated the OSS. Its clandestine service component was absorbed into the War Department and its intelligence analytical unit into the State Department. But in the months following the end of the war the United States Congress formed a joint committee to investigate the Pearl Harbor attack, and one of its main concerns was the quality of prewar U.S. intelligence. Reinforcing this concern was a series of studies regarding how the United States should organize itself for the postwar era. Among the most prominent of these was the Eberstadt report, which advocated the creation of a unified Department of Defense as well as a centralized intelligence service. While President Truman has left no record of what his private thinking may have been, the Pearl Harbor investigation nevertheless made intelligence a politically sensitive issue, and Truman's timing in moving to create a new supervisory mechanism, the National Intelligence Authority (NIA), in January 1946 strongly suggests the connection.

Under the NIA, Truman in effect reestablished an independent intelligence agency called the Central Intelligence Group (CIG) to boil down the information from the other spy units and furnish him with consolidated reports on key subjects. The CIG prepared short memoranda whenever necessary, often daily, and was responsible for weekly and monthly intelligence "products" as well. The Director of Central Intelligence (DCI), headed the group. Truman first assigned the job to his trusted associate Rear Admiral Sidney W. Souers. Although Souers began with a crew of people committed to preparing analyses, his CIG quickly ran into the problem of not having the right set of data for what it needed to fulfill its role. U.S. military agencies, primarily the Army through its G-2 intelligence staff, its Strategic Services Unit (SSU)—the rump of the old Office of Strategic Services—and its Counterintelligence Corps, controlled the bulk of overseas stations that were engaged in espionage. The armed services were loathe to share their data, arguing that the CIG had no business in the military field. The Group also needed political, economic, and other intelligence the military did not collect. The State Department, which was interested in these other areas, did not see itself as an intelligence collection

agency. Truman's January 1946 decision was to give overt collection responsibility to the CIG. Since the new unit was to draw its budget and personnel from the existing agencies, it soon became a haven for former OSS
personnel who had been languishing at SSU or in the State Department.

The onset of the Cold War lent great impetus to this entire process, one
that seemed to put the Pearl Harbor precedent at the center. When wartime cooperation between the Western powers and the Soviet Union disintegrated quickly after the defeat of Germany and Japan, Russian moves
in Eastern Europe and the Near East posed an apparent threat; and there
were real questions as to whether the Soviets might be ready to fight to secure their goals in Europe and elsewhere. At the same time, it was not
clear if U.S. intelligence had the capability to warn of an impending attack. All this made it urgent that the U.S. house be set in order on intelligence matters. In addition, the political-military competition against the
Soviet Union that formed the core of the Cold War seemed to require intelligence operations of a more active character, similar to those military
covert operations that had been useful in World War II.

The basic framework for defense organization in the United States
would finally be set in the fall of 1947 with the passage of the National
Security Act, one major provision of which created a unified Office of the
Secretary of Defense to supervise all the armed services, an independent
Air Force, a specified Marine Corps, all under the National Security Council (NSC), the president's central tool for policy decision, which would
work out of the White House. The act also established an independent
Central Intelligence Agency (CIA). The CIA would quickly assume the
mantle of America's premier Cold War agency.[1]

PATTERNS AND LADDERS

The events of 1945–1947, which led to the creation of the CIA, exhibit a pattern that repeated itself time and again throughout the Cold War era and
into the twenty-first century. The pattern works like this: external influences changing the shape of world events combine with an internally generated expectation of new technological or analytical opportunities to
produce perceptions of a need for intelligence reform. Over time, this has
produced a steady increase in U.S. investment in intelligence and in the
organizational breadth of the community itself. Among the periods of
major change are 1950–1952, which witnessed creation of the National

Security Agency (NSA) and revamping of the CIA; 1958–1962, which saw creation of the National Reconnaissance Office (NRO) and Defense Intelligence Agency (DIA) along with the beginnings of an intelligence community structure; 1992–1995, which brought the advent of the National Imagery and Mapping Agency (NIMA, subsequently renamed the National Geospatial Intelligence Agency); and 2002–2004, in which we see creation of the Department of Homeland Security (DHS) and Terrorist Threat Intelligence Center (TTIC).

From 1945 to 1947, when this pattern first emerged, the experience of World War II had left a clear understanding of a need for transformation in national security as a whole, and that included intelligence. The Pearl Harbor factor and the onset of the Cold War functioned as twin catalysts. The wartime achievements of U.S. intelligence analysis, which had included unprecedented sophistication in strategic analysis, high-level economic analysis, and operational, tactical, and basic intelligence of great accuracy and scope, had been spurred by technological developments applied to intelligence. The war had brought about considerable advances in cryptography, the first precision use of overhead photography, and huge advances in scientific intelligence. All of these were now amenable to consolidation in fresh organizational entities. The clandestine warfare function, which had figured importantly in the global conflict, also had no obvious location within the existing U.S. organizations that were conducting intelligence work. Creation of the CIA would be the logical result.

During the second period, 1950–1952, the Korean War acted as the external catalyst. That event seemed to threaten escalation to general war if the Soviets should take advantage of the Korea situation to attack in Europe, making the need for intelligence all the more acute. In addition, there were specific controversies similar to those that had surrounded Pearl Harbor, connected to the June 1950 North Korean invasion of South Korea as well as the Chinese intervention that followed some months later, both of which surprised U.S. officials. Although some research indicates that U.S. communications intelligence had an inkling of the impending attacks,[2] the truth is that separate cryptographic units of the several armed services lacked any central coordinating mechanism. In addition, computers were now beginning to have practical applications for communications interception and codebreaking, although they were still so expensive that they could be best exploited by a national-level organization. Again the logical result would be a new entity, the National Security Agency (NSA).

Meanwhile, on the CIA side, Cold War incidents had created dysfunction within the agency. The pressure to carry out covert operations against the Russians had left the CIA with what amounted to two clandestine services. One, the Office of Policy Coordination (created in 1948), responded to the desire for operations. The second, the original unit, the Office of Special Operations, was supposed to do the spying. But espionage was necessary in support of covert operations, and both units often ended up in competition for the same agents, networks, and apparatus.[3] When General Walter Bedell Smith took over as DCI in 1950 he determined to merge these units, creating the Deputy Directorate for Plans (DDP, today known as the Directorate of Operations), which became the CIA's active overseas arm. General Smith also responded to doubts regarding CIA analysis by establishing a new category of high-level intelligence reports, the National Intelligence Estimates (NIEs), together with an organization for producing them.

In the third period of substantial transformation (1958–1962) the space race would provide the catalyst. At that time space exploration had an overt Cold War political content—the fact that the Soviet Union was the first to launch a space satellite (Sputnik) on top of a rocket that was essentially an intercontinental ballistic missile (ICBM) seemed to suggest Russia had surpassed the United States in scientific and technical progress. From an intelligence standpoint, the November 1957 Sputnik launch had come as a surprise to the United States (again the Pearl Harbor factor) and there was the immediate problem of evaluating the Soviet ICBM threat. In addition to this overseas catalyst, harnessing scientific progress in the service of intelligence promised immediate benefits although it was difficult to achieve. Early developments like the U-2 spyplane (designed in 1955 and operational by 1957) could be handled on an ad hoc basis, but its successors required sustained engineering effort and real organization. The Eisenhower administration, actively engaged in developing reconnaissance satellites and the supersonic SR-71 aircraft, carried out a policy review on intelligence organization. That led to the creation of the National Reconnaissance Office (NRO) in 1960. Aware of the growing importance of technology issues for intelligence, the CIA, under DCI John McCone, finally established a directorate for these matters in 1962 (initially called the Directorate for Research, it was retitled Directorate for Science and Technology in 1963).

In the meantime, the military intelligence branches of the armed services, especially in the Air Force, had played a leading role in most controversial predictive miscalculations of the era, especially the "bomber gap" and the "missile gap" of the 1950s. Bluntly, the services had profoundly

overestimated Soviet strategic strike capabilities. When Robert S. Mc-
Namara became Secretary of Defense in the Kennedy administration, he
was determined to improve the analytical rigor of the Pentagon's military
estimates. This meshed neatly with bureaucratic concerns among military
officers that the CIA had come to overshadow the Department of Defense
even in their own areas of expertise. The solution was to create a consolidated military intelligence organization, the Defense Intelligence Agency
(DIA), which McNamara devised in 1961.

As intelligence organizations blossomed and grew, the DCI, presump-
tively the head of the entire community, began to understand that he
lacked the capacity to actually lead it. Most of the agencies that existed by
1962, including DIA, NRO, NSA, the armed services components of NSA,
and the armed services intelligence branches, were extensions of the Department of Defense. This is the origin of the frequent observation that
the Secretary of Defense controls more of the intelligence budget than the
Director of Central Intelligence. In 1962, DCI McCone, who was aware of
this issue, established a unit called the National Intelligence Programs
Evaluation (NIPE) staff, forerunner of the Intelligence Community Staff
that exists today. McCone's action marked the beginning of repeated—
and largely unsuccessful—efforts by the Directors of Central Intelligence
to exert stronger unified control over the community as a whole.

The next round of transformation did not occur until 1992–1995, after
the end of the Cold War. Again the Pearl Harbor factor was in play (although this time the surprise was a favorable one) with the shocking fall
of the Berlin Wall (and the Soviet satrapies of Eastern Europe) followed by
the disintegration of the Soviet Union itself. The breakup formed an international catalyst, after which there could be no doubt of the need for
change, in intelligence as everywhere else.

In the early years of the Clinton Administration, a presidential commission was entrusted with a major reassessment of intelligence capabilities. Led by two former secretaries of defense, Les Aspin and Dr. Harold
Brown, who had served presidents Bill Clinton and Jimmy Carter respectively, the report, named for the commission's co-chairs, eschewed
the most radical proposals (such as eliminating the CIA), but advocated
formation of a central service to consolidate work on interpretation of
overhead imagery and mapping. This led to creation of the National Imagery and Mapping Agency, more recently renamed the National Geospatial Intelligence Agency. After 9/11, it has been charged that reductions
in U.S. intelligence in the wake of the Cold War had emasculated the

community; but this argument is greatly oversimplified. The problem was not one of overall capabilities but of strategic priorities. At all times over the decade 1991–2001, intelligence budgets in real dollars remained greater than they had been in 1980, 1970, 1960, or 1950, and raw collection capability remained larger as well.

The terrorist attacks on the United States that took place on September 11, 2001, again an external catalyst, one widely compared to Pearl Harbor, ushered in a fresh transformational period that has yet to run its course. So far this new era has featured establishment of the Department of Homeland Security, an interagency Terrorist Threat Intelligence Center (TTIC), and a reorganization of the Federal Bureau of Investigation. Repeated proposals for a domestic intelligence service equivalent to the CIA (along the lines of the British service MI-5), remains on the table at this writing. Congress also approved President George W. Bush's initiative to create a new post of National Intelligence Director along the lines of the chairman of the Joint Chiefs of Staff, and a new national counterterrorism center reporting to the director.

In addition to these periods of major transformation there have been numerous instances of lesser reorganization. Within the CIA there are three key directorates, operations (DO), intelligence analysis (DI), and science and technology (DS&T). The DO, although its exact organizational structure is classified, is known to have been organized as a set of regional and functional divisions that changed with political understanding (for example, the Soviet Division became the Soviet Bloc Division as Eastern Europe gained greater prominence in the Cold War, then the Soviet and East European Division, then with the collapse of the Soviet Union, the Eurasian Division). The DI has also existed as a collection of regional offices, functional ones, or a combination of both. The DS&T has had offices centered around distinct analytical or technological activities, for example, the Office of Technical Services to develop spy equipment or the Office of Scientific Intelligence, long the premier center for intelligence analysis on complex scientific subjects. The biggest change took place in the late 1980s and 1990s with the community's growing fascination with "fusion," the notion that significant advantage might accrue by drawing on the CIA and other intelligence orgnizations to create teams of analysts, technicians, and operations officers and focusing their efforts on a given (functional) subject. The fusion units are supposed to bring together information from all sources, combine it with clandestine intelligence, and carry out field operations in their areas of concern. The Counterterrorism

Center, the Counternarcotics Center, and the Weapons Intelligence and Arms Control Center are all fusion activities of this sort.

There have also been patterns in the style and structure for oversight of the intelligence community, whose tendency has been to resist this. Because the community has always existed as a world apart, answering only to presidential authority, demands for reform have been less effective catalysts than blatant intelligence failures. In fact, White House monitoring of the intelligence community was strengthened precisely to head off congressional oversight. This was certainly the case in the mid-1950s, when President Eisenhower created the President's Board of Consultants on Foreign Intelligence Activities precisely when Congress was considering establishing a joint congressional oversight committee for intelligence. President Kennedy briefly abolished the unit, but re-created it as the President's Foreign Intelligence Advisory Board (PFIAB) after the CIA's failed paramilitary invasion of Cuba at the Bay of Pigs in April 1961.[4] Throughout the decades of the 1950s and 1960s monitoring intelligence remained almost exclusively a prerogative of the executive branch. Congressional oversight, what there was of it, was limited to small subcommittees (five members in each house) located within their armed services committees.

Pundits in the press and elsewhere dubbed 1975 the "Year of Intelligence" because of the extensive investigations of U.S. intelligence that year by special committees of both the Senate (Church Committee) and House (Pike Committee). Even here President Gerald R. Ford attempted to head off a congressional investigation by establishing a commission chaired by Vice-President Nelson A. Rockefeller to conduct a similar, more limited, inquiry. The CIA's role had become increasingly controversial over time, not only because there had never been a public review of intelligence activity, but also as a result of the Vietnam war, which had thrown up questions as to possible U.S. intelligence participation in assassination programs, inhumane interrogation techniques, and questionable covert activities. In addition, the CIA had been involved in the overthrow of the government of Chile in 1973. The direct catalyst, however, was the revelation that the agency had carried out extensive domestic activities against Americans in the course of both the Cold War and Vietnam. The legal context was that domestic activity was specifically prohibited in the National Security Act of 1947, which had created the CIA. The high-profile congressional investigations, while they greatly increased public awareness of U.S. intelligence and resulted in certain administrative reforms, nevertheless failed to build momentum for a legislative charter governing

U.S. intelligence that could supersede the 1947 Act. The major change would come with the establishment of formal intelligence oversight committees in both houses of Congress. That legislation also codified a 1974 law, the Hughes-Ryan Amendment, which had required that a number of congressional leaders be formally notified of U.S. covert operations, a proviso that led to the practice of issuing "presidential findings" (memoranda of notification) for significant covert operations. Again President Ford attempted to blunt the drive for legislative oversight by executive branch action, including the creation of an Intelligence Oversight Board (IOB) alongside the PFIAB to review certain covert intelligence activities, and issuing an executive order that authorized some activities and constrained others.

Executive actions following the Ford administration shaved away at the new oversight system. The Carter administration not only opposed an intelligence community charter, which would have defined precise intelligence responsibilities and roles, but also supported a much narrower provision for covert operations notification, restricting findings essentially to the intelligence committees. This arrangement replaced Hughes-Ryan in 1980. During the first Reagan administration an Intelligence Identities Protection Act became law in 1982, following charges that public identification of a CIA officer had led to his murder, making it illegal to reveal the names of CIA covert officers except under certain circumstances.[5] Legislation requested by DCI Bill Casey in 1984 exempted a huge fraction of CIA files from the Freedom of Information Act. In effect, although the Church and Pike revelations had seemingly heralded significant change in the management of intelligence activities, efforts by subsequent presidential administrations, Republican and Democratic alike, went far toward maintaining the status quo.

Indeed, by the Reagan era, effective oversight by the legislative branch was once again negligible. Director Casey misled Congress by providing very sparse information on CIA covert operations, especially in Nicaragua, which led to controversy (also in 1984) when it became apparent the CIA was being cagey with information on the mining of Nicaraguan harbors. Congress remained quiescent, however, until a fresh catalyst emerged in the form of the Iran-Contra Affair, in which White House staffers combined with Casey and a small number of CIA personnel to continue covert support to Nicaraguan rebels, including the diversion of money earned from illegal arms sales in the Middle East, at a time when CIA support to the Nicaraguans had been prohibited by Congress as a result of the 1984 mining. The Iran-Contra affair played out in 1986–1988, and in it the Reagan administration asserted the right to justify actions by means of retroactive findings, "mental" findings (an artifact of attorney general Edwin Meese), and simply refusing to inform Congress of sensitive covert operations in progress. In addition, the affair revealed that the White House's internal oversight mechanisms, such as the IOB, had been essentially moribund. The controversy led to new efforts to define the scope and content of presidential findings. A requirement for notification to Congress within forty-eight hours was not ultimately enacted until 1991, however.

Time and again, evidence of oversight failures appeared long after the fact, embarrassing the CIA and reviving demands that it be more closely supervised. In the mid-1990s, for example, it was revealed that the CIA had carried on its payroll agents who had actually participated in the torture of American citizens. There were also allegations that the agency had been directly involved in such activities during the 1980s, part of the Reagan administration's campaign to defeat leftist insurgents in Central America. Once again the call arose for improved legislative oversight. Again the executive branch—now controlled by Democrats—deflected such demands. DCI John Deutsch issued internal regulations restricting CIA employment of "bad" individuals and requiring pre-hiring background checks of prospective agents.

One effect of the 9/11 attacks was to roll back restrictions, even though the CIA had repeatedly reported to Congress that its collection efforts had never been hampered by the strictures on hiring. Another consequence of 9/11 was that President George W. Bush further limited the flow of intelligence to Congress, threatening at one point to restrict it to just a handful of senior legislators. This occurred despite the provision in U.S. law, in the Intelligence Oversight Act of 1980, that "Nothing in this Act shall be construed as authority to withhold information from the intelligence committees on the grounds that providing the information . . . would constitute the unauthorized disclosure of classified information or information related to intelligence sources and methods."[6] The general impact of 9/11 has been to reduce, not extend, congressional oversight of U.S. intelligence. For example, the report by a presidential-congressional commission to investigate the 9/11 terrorist attacks observed that U.S. homeland security officials were required to respond to a broad array of congressional authorities with overlapping jurisdictions. The Bush administration, in agreement with that criticism, then exempted the CIA from this requirement.[7] Most recently, the first Director of National Intelligence, John

Negroponte, instructed agency heads to use their discretion in reporting activities to Congress.

Over time the pattern of oversight of the U.S. intelligence community has been one of episodic intervention. Regardless of the party that happens to be in power, the White House places a premium on ensuring the flexibility and efficiency of intelligence. When it comes to these activities, presidents want maximum freedom of action. Congressional authorities have demonstrated complacency—in a sense, endorsing presidential preferences—until obvious failures or major scandals demand action. But the attention span of Congress tends to be limited; as a consequence, loudly touted "reforms" deliver less than promised. This combines with large-scale intelligence failures leading to expansion of the community or increase in investment rather than the reverse. The net effect is that, except for minor fluctuations (such as that following the end of the Cold War), the intelligence community has exhibited a steady and gradual expansion from the end of World War II to the present.

REDUCTIONS RECONSIDERED

The CIA's defenders typically respond to charges of intelligence failures by complaining that the government has denied the resources needed to get the job done. The complaint most frequently heard is that economizing staffing reductions have emasculated the CIA and the larger American intelligence community, undermining its ability to identify and anticipate emerging threats. This is a plausible argument. Logic suggests that in the aftermath of a war, whether cold or hot, at least some existing capabilities become superfluous and, no longer necessary, may end up on the chopping block. The basic charge is that economizers ought to be held accountable when the dismantling of intelligence agencies produces subsequent intelligence failures. This blame-the-budget-cutters argument was especially evident in two specific cases: first, in the aftermath of the Vietnam war, when a "Reduction-in-Force" (RIF) took place under DCIs James Schlesinger, William Colby, and Stansfield Turner; and second, during the interregnum following the end of the Cold War, when as many as a quarter of all CIA personnel were ostensibly let go.

One way to analyze these claims is to view them in the context of the post–World War II experience, when a similar RIF followed the abolition of the Office of Strategic Services. At its peak strength near the end of 1944 the OSS had had almost 13,000 personnel (including 4,500 women). At the end of 1946 the nascent CIA, then still known as the Central Intelligence Group, had 1,816 total employees. Rounding that number to 2,000 for comparative purposes the overall reduction amounted to almost 85 percent.

The RIF that followed the U.S. withdrawal from the Vietnam war was of nothing like that magnitude. At the time the CIA's personnel was estimated (actual numbers remain classified) at between 14,000 and 17,000.[8] James R. Schlesinger is reported to have furloughed or ended the contracts of approximately 1,000 men and women from the Directorate of Operations plus up to half as many from other parts of the agency, a RIF executed primarily during William E. Colby's tenure, since Schlesinger held the position of DCI for only nine months. Stansfield Turner, who followed Colby, reduced the agency by another 820 positions. Turner recounts that a Directorate of Operations management study carried out while George H. W. Bush was DCI in 1976 had recommended a reduction of 1,350 over five years. In fact, Turner limited the cut to slightly more than half that number, and accomplished it mostly through retirements and a hiring freeze. Admiral Turner records that only 17 persons were fired and 147 forced into early retirement.[9] A special CIA retirement act passed during this period gave the DCI authority to grant favorable early retirement bonuses to up to 2,000 employees. Taking the highest figures for reductions, adding the Schlesinger RIF, and using the lowest estimate for CIA personnel equates to an overall post-Vietnam reduction of slightly more than 21 percent. Other estimates range from 7 to 11 percent. This pales in comparison to post–World War II experience. In fact, the end number for CIA personnel *after* the reductions compares favorably to the peak wartime strength of the OSS. In addition, a comparison between the CIA and other U.S. intelligence agencies shows that the Defense Intelligence Agency's post-Vietnam reductions took the organization from a peak strength of about 7,500 to a final personnel strength of 4,500, which it maintained through the 1980s.

Upon assuming office, President Reagan's DCI, Bill Casey, immediately began to build back the strength of the CIA, and the agency would eventually attaining staffing levels greater than at the height of the Vietnam war. The increase has been estimated as a third. These levels prevailed throughout the Reagan and (first) Bush administrations. Walter Pincus, a reporter for *The Washington Post* with excellent connections in the intelligence community, reported a precise peak strength for the 1980s: 20,481.[10] However, in

July 1994 the Clinton administration's DCI of that time, R. James Woolsey, proposed to reduce the CIA once again, speaking of a target of a 25 percent reduction by 1997.[11] That would have led to an end-strength of roughly 15,400, *larger* than the *peak* for the Office of Strategic Services, about equal to CIA personnel serving at the height of the Cold War in the mid-1950s, and almost comparable to Vietnam in the 1960s and 1970s. Actually, a substantial portion of the reduction was achieved by the wholesale transfer of the National Photographic Interpretation Center, which the CIA had run as a service of common concern for the community and which had had more than 1,300 employees, to the new entity known today as the National Geospatial Intelligence Agency, formed in 1996 as a result of the Aspin-Brown commission recommendations. In sum, an analysis of total staffing indicates not only that subsequent cutbacks were far short of the magnitude of the post–World War II reductions in intelligence, but also that later RIFs left the CIA with substantial capability, not the crippled derelict suggested by proponents of massive expansion. When George Tenet became DCI in 1998, the CIA resumed its buildup and its strength today is estimated to be about 24,000 men and women.

An examination of staffing levels within the Directorate of Operations (DO), the locus of the CIA's covert action, paramilitary, and espionage capability, produces similar conclusions. In the early 1970s, its size was reliably reported at 6,000.[12] Of these some 1,800 were paramilitary officers, men and women who carry out special operations or organize indigenous partisan movements or quasi-military militias. The post-Vietnam cutbacks zeroed in on the paramilitary staff, not the spies. Nor was the CIA alone in losing most of its paramilitary cadre. For example, Army Special Forces personnel declined from their 1969 level of 13,000 to just 3,000 by 1980.[13] The Iran Hostage Crisis proved a turning point, with the failure at Desert One revealing weaknesses in U.S. unconventional warfare capability, and once again a buildup began. Anecdotal evidence from the CIA's secret wars in Nicaragua and Afghanistan in the 1980s indicates that the agency retained sufficient paramilitary assets to conduct its covert operations of that era. In fact, with the military expansion of special operations forces during the 1980s, overall U.S. paramilitary capability grew substantially. By the mid-1990s the Pentagon had about 45,000 special forces personnel—and at that time the CIA began to reconstitute an independent paramilitary capability in a new Special Activities Division.

Spies among the clandestine service were hit hardest by the intelligence reductions of the post–Cold War round. The anecdotal evidence of the

1990s is one of the Directorate of Operations (DO) in disarray, with widespread dissatisfaction, resignations, atrophied language skills, and more. But the story told by the numbers is somewhat different. Cuts in DO during the decade totaled 20 percent, according to testimony under oath at the 9/11 Commission hearings by CIA's then-deputy director for operations, James L. Pavitt.[14] That amounted to less than the agency-wide reductions (20 vs. 25 percent). To extrapolate from these numbers, if the DO retained the same size relative to the full CIA as it had had in the 1960s, it would still have had approximately 7,500 officers, and the reduction in the 1990s would have amounted to about 1,500.[15] That would have left 6,000 men and women in the clandestine service, which equates to the DO's full strength during the Vietnam era.

None of this is to deny that the Directorate of Operations has had problems in the recent past. Agency officers complain of over-bureaucratization, micromanagement from headquarters, excessive reliance on official cover, insufficient language capability, or a general uninterest in clandestine service. Nevertheless, the point is that the standard critique emphasizes short-term over long-term trends. The truth is that the history of the CIA, much like that of the intelligence community as a whole, has been one of growth, not retrenchment. This holds for both the agency and the DO. Indeed, by 1998, DCI George J. Tenet was already crusading to resurrect the Directorate of Operations, speaking in public about the losses among case officers and the need to rebuild the organization. Director Tenet began seeking money for this in the following year's intelligence budget. When Tenet told the 9/11 Commission in 2004 that the CIA needed another five years to get the Directorate to where it needed to be, the agency had just completed training the largest class of clandestine services officers in its history. The following class would again set a record. In fact, the rebuilding process was well on its way. Tenet was not restoring the organization to where it had been, but rather sending its capability toward new heights. Today the problem is more one of masses of inexperienced officers rather than a lack of personnel.

In the swirling arguments about capabilities of the clandestine services, most recently framed in the context of their ability to spy on terrorist groups such as al-Qaeda, proponents of DO expansion have frequently overlooked the roots of the problem. In the 1940s and 1950s the focus was on Russia, in the 1960s and 1970s it shifted to Vietnam, and then back again to Russia. The claim was *always* that CIA needed more clandestine capability and was unable to penetrate the lairs of the current opponent. That was true of the Doolittle Report in 1953, the Cunningham Report in 1967 (whose overall theme was that the U.S. collects too much intelligence), various congressional intelligence committee investigations, the Aspin-Brown commission (1995), the Bremer commission on terrorism (2000), the Hart-Rudman national security study for the twenty-first century (2000), and every known management study of the intelligence community. In effect, the persistent calls for more agents in the field stand as a tribute to the inherent difficulty of espionage. The notion that higher personnel numbers and monetary resources in the DO will result in greater acquisition of data through espionage is more an article of faith than an analytical finding.

The actual pattern of CIA investments—in both human and financial resources—shows that the agency itself understands the inherent difficulty of spying. That is, faced with the choice between the marginal budget dollar put into the clandestine service or one or another form of technical intelligence collection, the U.S. intelligence community has shown a consistent preference for machines. There are a number of reasons for this, among them that machine spies can be precisely targeted, that collection item-for-the-dollar can be measured more easily, that such programs can be conducted unilaterally and are not dependent upon the vagaries of agent recruitment, and that the harnessing of science for intelligence purposes has yielded amazing results in the past.

Too often commentaries on intelligence themes assume that reductions equate to inadequate capability across the board, and fail to take into account how capacity has been shaped by the organizational developments that have occurred. A better way of assessing the evolution of U.S. intelligence over the Cold War era is to consider specific aspects of intelligence work—the "disciplines" in recently coined CIA argot. From this kind of evaluation a different picture will emerge.

THE ANALYTIC ELEMENT

In many ways intelligence analysis was the CIA's founding raison d'être. It has been often said about Pearl Harbor that the surprise might have been averted had there been a government agency to put together all the disparate reports from military and diplomatic intelligence sources. This very essence of "central" intelligence, embodied in the CIA's very name, had been incorporated into the National Security Act in 1947 that created the agency. In fact, in contrast to other types of CIA's activity, the reporting function is explicitly discussed in the Act, which states that the agency's purpose is "to correlate and evaluate intelligence relating to the national security, and provide for the dissemination of such intelligence within the Government."[16] Spying, influence peddling, covert operations, and the rest of the panoply of CIA's "disciplines" exist in the law only as "services of common concern" provided by the agency or as "such other functions and duties related to intelligence . . . as the National Security Council may from time to time direct."

In the early days of the Central Intelligence Group, the reporting function was the province of what was called the Office of Reports and Estimates (ORE). Reporting required the preparation of various kinds of documents, which were termed "products"—a term that continues to be applied to intelligence reporting to this day. The ORE products were of a variety of types, among them short memoranda that presented spot reports to the president, often daily (the origins of the contemporary *President's Daily Brief*), analytical papers called special estimates, and the flagship product which was the weekly "Estimate of the World Situation." By 1949 there were eleven kinds of regular ORE reports. The organizational principles that would dominate the CIA were also in evidence at the outset, with ORE consisting of an array of branches, each of which relied upon area experts to produce intelligence on a region of the world, feeding material to a staff of editors who selected items for the different intelligence products.

The establishment of standard procedures for ORE products also meant that intelligence analysts were producing their reports for a level of managers interposed between the substantive experts and the final output rather than directly for consumers. As will be seen, the relationship between analysts and managers has been a key stumbling block to the efficient processing of raw intelligence into reporting useful to consumers. Another constant has been the pressure to be "relevant," which not only exacerbated tensions between analysts and managers, but also created a tendency to emphasize current events–type reporting as opposed to longer-term inquiries.

Beyond these constants lay other nagging issues. Two were of particular importance. The first addressed the question of whether the CIA should be permitted a voice on military intelligence, a field zealously guarded by the military agencies. The second dealt with the question of "estimates" and their formulation.

From the outset, the CIA was careful to hire as analysts a number of former military officers, and later, in establishing its estimates organization, made sure some of the personnel slots were filled by senior military officers on active duty or recently retired. Armed services resistance to CIA's military reporting gradually ebbed and disappeared almost completely by the time of the Korean War, when the military were glad to share with CIA some of the fault for having been taken by surprise by the June 1950 outbreak of the conflict and the October–November 1950 Chinese intervention.

It was also during Korea that the estimates process was regularized. In the specialized vocabulary of intelligence, estimates are a category of intelligence reports crafted by agreement among different offices to represent the consensus of the entire intelligence community. In early 1949, an outside review of CIA organization, the Dulles-Jackson-Correa Report, had noted that estimates were still not well-established in U.S. intelligence.[17] Later that year an internal study in ORE found that current intelligence was eclipsing the CIA's efforts at predictive, longer-range estimates. But little was done until the Korean War galvanized action in this area. In October 1950, General Walter Bedell Smith became DCI. General Smith had been chief of staff to allied supreme commander Dwight D. Eisenhower in World War II and was familiar with both British Joint Intelligence Committee appreciations, which were estimative in nature, and products from the OSS. When DCI Smith came on board he discovered that U.S. intelligence had no coordinated estimate on the situation in Korea. To rectify that he created an Office of National Estimates (ONE) and ordered it to quickly produce a set of reports whose contents would be coordinated with other agencies on subjects ranging from Korea to the probability of war with the Soviet Union. Composed of analysts expert in particular subjects or regions, this staff sought contributions from other intelligence agencies and drafted a text that would be revised by a Board of National Estimates (BNE) composed of the most senior analysts at CIA. The BNE then briefed the draft estimate to DCI Smith and the Intelligence Advisory Committee (IAC), a board comprising the directors of all U.S. intelligence agencies. The BNE and IAC both had the authority to revise the draft, while agencies that disagreed with some point could register their dissent by inserting a footnote stating their view.[18] The finished reports became known as National Intelligence Estimates (NIEs) reflecting their status as coordinated overall views on broad subjects of the U.S. intelligence community. A separate series of Special National Intelligence

Estimates (SNIEs) evolved in the later 1950s to consider narrower issues. Typically, the NIEs were long-term predictive papers and the SNIEs focused on shorter-term matters such as foreign responses to given U.S. actions. For example, in November 1956 the community produced an SNIE on Sino-Soviet intentions in the Suez crisis. In either case, these estimates became the intelligence community's premier product—and, hence, the focus of intense controversy, internal wrangling, and frequent criticism.

Without an estimative function the old ORE lacked its previous coherence and became a source for reports on all subjects excepting science, which had been handled since 1949 by an Office of Scientific Intelligence. The ORE was broken up in early 1951, but it became the basis for a fresh constellation of units starting with the Office of Research and Reports and the Office of Current Intelligence. There was also an Office of Operations to mine open-source data, and an Office of Collection and Dissemination responsible for storing data and distributing reports. In January 1952, these units were grouped into a Directorate for Intelligence, the entity that has continuously handled CIA's analytical work to the present day.

With the establishment of the Directorate of Intelligence (DI) this side of the CIA assumed primacy on reporting. The unit responsible for NIEs has been located at times within the DCI's own office or at others in the DI. Today it belongs to the Director of National Intelligence. As the CIA began to engage in more scientific work, especially with the great volume of research and development effort put into overhead reconnaissance beginning in the late 1950s, the Office of Scientific Intelligence was relocated in a new Directorate for Science and Technology (in 1963). Other offices were added or subtracted as well. The Office of Research and Reports became the Office of Economic Research in the 1960s, when the Office for Strategic Research and the Office for Political Research were added to the DI. Later the Office of Strategic Research moved to the Directorate for Science and Technology. In the Carter administration, the entire directorate became the National Foreign Assessment Center, with a new office devoted to global issues, but it reverted to its previous identity during the Reagan years. By then the office structure included units for Soviet Analysis, European Analysis, Near East and South Asia, East Asia, Africa and Latin America, Global Issues, Scientific and Weapons Research, Current Production and Analytic Support, Imagery Analysis, and Central Reference. There were also staffs for collection requirements and management, a senior review panel, and special assistants for community interests and for nuclear proliferation.

It is not the purpose of this review to analyze all the specific intelligence disputes that have consumed the community over the decades, but enumerating some of them suggests the breadth of the work in which the community has engaged. During the Cold War many of these disputes concerned U.S. perceptions of the Soviet Union. At the very outset, analysts differed over when the Russians would perfect an atomic bomb. In the 1950s two huge controversies revolved around Soviet capabilities to strike the United States, first the "Bomber Gap," then the "Missile Gap," in both of which the intelligence community initially overestimated Russian military power. At the same time, and continuing into the 1960s, there was a dispute over the significance of the Sino-Soviet split. During the 1960s, there were differences over Soviet development of antiballistic missile defenses, multiple warhead missiles, the pace and scope of the Soviet missile buildup, the size and characteristics of forces ranged against the U.S. in the Vietnam war, the dangers of nuclear proliferation, the intentions and capabilities of the People's Republic of China, and more. In the 1970s followed controversies over Soviet military spending and Soviet intentions, as well as Soviet naval developments and actions in Africa. Beginning then and extending into the 1980s were more disputes over the Russian economy, the reality and purpose of the Gorbachev reforms in Russia, and Soviet military modernization. New issues included ones over Soviet intentions in Central America and South Asia. In the 1990s, there were controversies over the collapse of the Soviet Union, the consequences of that collapse for Europe, foreign development of ballistic missiles, and so on. Most recently there has developed a controversy over the intelligence preceding the 2003 U.S. war with Iraq.

Career advancement in the DI involves moving from the work of line analyst to that of manager, resulting in ever more editors poring over the intelligence reporting. The analyst versus manager problem grew during the 1980s and 1990s, when the DI had become even larger and with more functional units, while several of the old regional offices were consolidated after the collapse of the Soviet Union and end of the Cold War. In 1998, when U.S. intelligence failed to predict India and Pakistan's nuclear weapons tests, a review panel under Admiral David Jeremiah attributed the failure in part to a lack of enough available analysts to review the reams of data collected on the subject. Too many line analysts had been moved up to managers, and thus removed from the basic mission of interpreting data.

Back in 1973, Director William E. Colby had changed the process for creating NIEs. There were already complaints that the process worked to reduce intelligence opinions to their lowest common denominator, so that the estimates that were published smoothed over the sharp differences. Colby abolished the ONE and BNE and substituted a National Intelligence Council (NIC) on which national intelligence officers hold portfolios for specific subject areas and are the lead drafters for an NIE. The officers have limited help from an assistant and from personnel drawn from an Analytic Group that supports the NIC, but the latter are essentially writers. However, the National Intelligence Council system, which is the standard organization today, is open to a different objection: the NIC lacks the corporate strength of the BNE. Estimates can be more easily compromised by pressures from other parts of, or even from outside, the intelligence community. The defective NIE on Iraqi weapons of mass destruction done in 2002 in advance of the U.S. war on that country illustrates the problems of this system.

During the 1990s there was also a push to make NIEs more relevant, shorter, and more responsive to consumer requests. This led to estimates becoming more like current intelligence—less predictive, shorter-term, and less capable of appreciating nuance. There also developed a contrary thrust in which the NIC responded by casting its net over subjects so broad and amorphous—such as "Global Trends 2015"—that prediction amounted to little more than punditry. In part this was a consequence of new issues on NIC's plate, such as predicting the consequences of AIDs for internecine warfare in Africa, but the movement also testifies to the deterioration of the NIE as a source of authoritative intelligence projection.

Under the 1947 National Security Act, the CIA was also tasked with carrying out "services of common concern" for the full intelligence community. Fulfilling this mission required a unit, first created in 1953, to interpret overhead photography, and another engaged in the translation and dissemination of texts of radio broadcasts, press articles, and speeches from overseas (but open) sources. The first of these, the National Photographic Interpretation Center, at first independent, was absorbed into the Directorate for Science and Technology (DS&T) in 1974, and then moved to the National Geospatial Intelligence Agency in the late 1990s. The second was the Foreign Broadcast Information Service. It too went to DS&T, in 1977.

The Foreign Broadcast Information Service was one of the few elements of U.S. intelligence that dealt in information not born secret. This "open source" data constituted then, and still does, the large majority of the information utilized by intelligence analysts. Despite special interest in the 1990s in providing for better exploitation of open source information this category remains a poor sister among the pillars of intelligence.

In keeping with the increasing focus on overhead reconnaissance, technical intelligence, and electronic intelligence on the part of U.S. authorities, the Directorate of Science and Technology has been the most dynamically expanding part of the CIA since the 1960s. The DS&T made notable contributions to intelligence analysis on nuclear weapons issues, on Russian and Chinese strategic weapons systems, and on photographic and foreign language analysis as already suggested. It would have a direct role in collection in places like the U.S. embassies in Nicaragua and Afghanistan during the secret wars in those countries. Most important DS&T developed an enormous role in technological development, for satellite systems, for collection methods, in ground intelligence collection stations in Iran and China, in unmanned aerial vehicles (such as the current Predator system), and for innovations in the use of information technology.

Among the most promising developments of the 1990s was a dedicated-user computer network called "Intel-Link." This was a sort of classified internet project—the CIA called it an information "architecture"—and enabled intelligence consumers to connect directly with the analysts. An NSC staffer, for example, could communicate directly with the national intelligence officer in a certain field, or even a working-level analyst, and pull up the latest information and analyses, or even ask for some analysis done to his or her own specifications. However, the Intel-Link network also threatened to cut managers of intelligence analysis out of the loop, and issues regarding the system's circulation of "finished" intelligence products versus raw data are not known to have been worked out. It also further accentuated the tendency to focus on current events rather than estimative reporting. Judging from the paucity of commentary on this system, Intel-Link may have succumbed to bureaucratic wrangling or technology woes, or the ambitious project may have degenerated into a sort of data-base program; in any case, it is in place and secret. A similar dedicated network to support intelligence operations against terrorism was initiated with the creation of the Terrorist Threat Integration Center. Testimony at hearings of the 9/11 Commission indicated that after two years of work the network had yet to become fully interactive, which further underlines the difficulties of the original Intel-Link.

CLANDESTINE SERVICES VERSUS
TECHNICAL COLLECTION

Although the CIA was conceived chiefly as an intelligence-coordinating mechanism and analytical unit, within months of its inception it found itself, at the request of President Truman's National Security Council, in the business of spying and covert operations. Espionage followed naturally from the need to collect information. At the time, the military was not much interested in the Strategic Services Unit, the rump OSS leftover that had been doing this work. Even though the unit had extensive semi-overt collection activities in place in Europe and the Far East, and true clandestine operations underway in seven nations of the Near East and four in North Africa, this made little difference. Later that year SSU would be moved to the Central Intelligence Group, eventually reconstituted at the CIA as the Office of Special Operations (OSO), which was given the mission of "the conduct, under the direct supervision of the Director [DCI], of all organized Federal espionage and counterespionage operations outside the United States and its possessions for the collection of foreign intelligence information."[19]

This was the classic clandestine service, its forward elements, called stations, attached to American embassies overseas, where case officers posing as diplomats liaised with friendly intelligence services, recruited agents, and built espionage networks to gather secret data. A survey of some of the daily spot reports sent to President Truman indicates that the OSO enjoyed a fair degree of success on subjects ranging from detecting secret arms shipments to the nascent Israeli military to indications of Russian activity in East Germany. Espionage work became and remained a staple of CIA activity.

Covert operations were another matter. By late 1946 Pentagon officials were already pressing the DCI to consider using tactics that had been employed by the Resistance movements in Europe and elsewhere during World War II. In 1947, executive branch discussions became more serious. Within weeks of the passage of the National Security Act in 1947, the DCI of that time, Vice Admiral Roscoe Hillenkoetter, was recommending psychological warfare operations (though he would have placed them under the auspices of the Joint Chiefs of Staff). Instead, on December 14, 1947,

Truman approved NSC Directive No. 4–A, assigning this function to the CIA, which created a Special Procedures Group to carry out such psychological operations. A few of these kinds of activities ensued over the following months, but far more important was the ad hoc intervention the CIA carried out in Italy in early 1948 in an effort to prevent an election victory by the Italian Communist Party in the voting scheduled for the spring. The CIA used American dollars to fund pro-Western Italian politicians, while CIA officers helped to create anticommunist groups and discredit the communists. Their efforts seem to have borne fruit: the Communist Party was defeated.

President Truman was impressed with the results and decided to regularize this kind of activity. In June 1948, he approved another order, NSC Directive 10–2, which provided for an Office of Policy Coordination (OPC) within the CIA but under the joint direction of the DCI, the secretary of state, and the secretary of defense. The NSC directive set up a 10–2 Panel to oversee OPC operations. By 1949, the OPC, an embryonic covert action unit, had a personnel strength of 302 and a $4.7 million budget. It expanded rapidly: by 1952 the OPC had a staff of almost 6,000 members (among them 3,100 served overseas in 82 stations) and a budget of $82 million. The OPC carried out the operations that made the CIA America's primary Cold War agency. It engaged in operations in France and again in Italy, similar to the Italian intervention on 1948; it attempted, through paramilitary operations, to incite revolt against communist governments in Albania and Russia; it engaged in "cultural warfare" across Europe— funding labor movements, youth groups, student organizations, journals, and radio stations. The CIA also enjoyed some success in recruiting Europeans in several Western countries to participate in embryonic resistance movements or espionage networks to be activated in case of a Soviet takeover of their nations.

Both OPC and OSO had stations in many embassies, which led to confusion as to just who represented the CIA, while both used similar tradecraft, the same tactics, and in many countries competed to recruit the same people. The DCI's problem was further complicated because OPC also responded to direction from the secretaries of state and defense. Within a week of taking over the CIA in late 1950 General Walter Bedell Smith assumed full control over OPC and had the Pentagon and State Departments submit instructions through him. DCI Smith ultimately eliminated OPC–OSO conflict by establishing a single Directorate of Operations responsible for both espionage and covert action. With the advent of the

Eisenhower administration in January 1953, Allen Dulles, who had been the CIA's first deputy director for operations, moved up to become DCI. His successor in his former position was Frank Wisner, who had formerly been the chief of OPC. The Dulles-Wisner era at the DO marked a phase of tremendous CIA activism. In 1953, the CIA (with British assistance) ousted the government of Iran. The following year it repeated this feat in Guatamala. But the list did not stop there. The CIA carried out covert paramilitary actions in the Korean War, in the Philippines until about 1953, in northern Vietnam in 1954 and after, in southern Vietnam in 1955, on mainland China after 1952, in Tibet from 1956 on, in Indonesia in 1957–58, in Syria in 1956–57, in Lebanon and Iraq in 1958, and others. Most of these involved attempts to mobilize resistance against communist governments or to overthrow governments considered too friendly to Moscow. With the exception of Tibet, where the CIA supported a nationalist resistance that sputtered on for years, most of these operations failed. In Lebanon President Eisenhower averted a complete failure in covert action only by dispatching regular military troops as an occupation force.

Nor is this list complete: Political actions were carried out in Austria, Egypt, Indonesia, Japan, and the Philippines. As in Italy in 1948, these involved subsidizing political parties, politicians, and media outlets in efforts to affect opinion. Political action proved successful in Japan and the Philippines, moderately successful in Europe, and failed in Indonesia and Egypt.

A formal NSC-level approval process for covert actions through what was called the 5412 Committee (the successor of the 10–2 Panel) was created in 1955. Investigations of the CIA carried out by the Church committee in 1975 established that between 1953 and 1961 clandestine collection and covert action absorbed 54 percent of the CIA's annual budgets. During that period the DO added 1,000 staff slots, and the CIA recruited another 1,000 persons to support DO activities.

The clandestine service's other function, espionage, produced mixed results during the Dulles era. Against the Soviets the major resource was line-crossers of one sort or another—that is, persons who crossed the Iron Curtain in either direction. The main sources included displaced persons left over from World War II, German scientists and prisoners returning from Russia, persons fleeing East Germany and Hungary, tourists who visited Russia and permitted the CIA to debrief them afterwards, and Soviet defectors. The CIA also became fairly adept at recruiting agents. Most of them were not Russians, but West Europeans, South Asians, Japanese and Koreans, Latin Americans, or from the Middle East. Most of CIA's successes with Russians came when the latter were stationed abroad. In Vienna, for example, the agency recruited a couple of Russians who worked for the U.S. for awhile and then defected, and also the most significant U.S. spy of the 1950s, the Russian military intelligence officer Pyotr Popov. The latter furnished the CIA with its first authentic data on Soviet military organization. Vienna too became the locale for an early U.S. technical collection program. Implemented by the DO in 1949, it involved the tapping of Soviet telephone cables out of the city. This formula was repeated in Berlin with even greater success, becoming the DO's biggest operation in the period 1954–1956, and spectacularly again, now utilizing high technology, against Russia itself in the 1970s and 1980s.

The Vienna and Berlin wiretaps provide an early suggestion of the attractiveness of technical collection as compared to espionage. Technical programs did not depend on spies' reliability or their access. Overhead reconnaissance was especially seductive, not being dependent at all on clandestine means but rather on scientific talent and investments in technology. Imagery and communications intelligence collection built on a solid foundation of development in World War II. Beginning in 1954 the CIA threw itself into the development of three successive overhead reconnaissance systems, the U-2 spyplane, the SR-71, a highly advanced supersonic aircraft, and the CORONA reconnaissance satellite. All of these were managed by a special assistant to Allen Dulles, but later transferred to the Directorate of Science and Technology. The transition of the overhead programs from development and special missions status to major intelligence component similarly fueled the expansion of the community with the establishment of the National Reconnaissance Office (NRO). Like the OPC, the NRO originated as a polyglot union of people from the CIA, the Air Force, and the Pentagon research establishment. It eventually matured into an independent service within the Department of Defense, which shared in the development of reconnaissance satellites and controlled their operation.

Technical collection can be said to have reached maturity in 1962 with the Cuban Missile Crisis, in which the key intelligence upon which the U.S. relied derived primarily from these systems. CORONA and successor imaging satellite systems also furnished the intelligence that in 1961 laid to rest the contentious "Missile Gap." Several subsequent intelligence disputes, such as those surrounding Soviet ballistic missile defenses, multiple warhead missiles, ballistic missile submarine systems, manned bombers,

and missile accuracy, were also analyzed in the 1960s and 1970s, principally on the basis of data collected by technical intelligence.

Espionage specialists could reasonably argue that their craft provided
data that was key in understanding the intelligence derived from technical
means. For example, the most significant U.S. agent of the 1960s, Russian
military intelligence officer Oleg Penkovskiy, gave the CIA material that
included field manuals on Soviet missile and antiaircraft units which
proved vital in identifying the surface-to-air-missile and long-range missile installations in Cuba during the 1962 crisis. Espionage reports also
cued the CIA to mount the U-2 flights that identified the missiles in Cuba.
Dmitri Polyakov, another Soviet military intelligence official, recruited in
about 1962, became the longest-running successful spy, not apprehended
by the Russians until the mid-80s, though his specific contributions remain unknown. Later in the decade Soviet economic data from spies enabled the CIA to better calibrate its estimates of Russian agricultural
production and the overall size of the Soviet economy.

Clandestine service agent recruitment in the 1960s was probably even
more significant in terms of acquiring political influence in foreign countries. The CIA's influence was also felt on general foreign policy questions.
For example, in South Vietnam and in the Congo, places where major covert operations occurred during the 1960s, key officials of both governments were on the CIA payroll or were aligned with the agency.[20] Former
DO officer Phillip Agee is regarded as a turncoat by erstwhile colleagues for
a memoir of his service in Ecuador in the late 1960s that named names of
agency people, but what emerges equally clearly from Agee's account is that
the CIA had the Ecuadoran government essentially in its hip pocket.[21]

The 1950s can be seen as the era when the CIA extended to other parts
of the globe the kind of effort it had first focused on the Soviet Union. The
trend increased in the 1960s. To some degree this reflected the Kennedy
administration's desire to counter Cuban efforts in Latin America and Africa, as well as those of Russia and China, but expansion was also sparked
by the knowledge that the CIA had been weak in these areas. For example,
in the 1960s the agency was less well-established in Argentina but had
good liaison relations with local intelligence agencies, and DCI Richard
Helms considered that performance good enough that the chief of station
in Buenos Aires was promoted to become the last CIA station chief in
South Vietnam. In Uruguay and Bolivia during the 1960s the CIA maintained close ties with security services fighting Marxist guerrilla movements. In fact, when the revolutionary Che Guevara perished in Bolivia in

1967, a CIA contract officer sat at his side.[22] Mexico had been a well-established CIA post, but the decade brought new initiatives there and elsewhere. Indeed, the DO's Western Hemisphere Division grew by 40 percent between 1960 and 1965, and its Africa Division by 55.5 percent between 1959 and 1963.

The Bay of Pigs failure did not end CIA actions against Cuba. The renewed projects not only involved the CIA in other Central American nations, but also left the agency feeling itself to be at war against Cuban attempts to export revolution to Latin America, requiring greater CIA efforts to counter Cuba throughout the hemisphere.

Similarly, the Congo proved to be a baby step followed by greater CIA penetration into Africa. The agency supported counterinsurgency by Portugal in that nation's African colonies, and tried to harness governments in Ethiopia, the Sudan, and Somalia, as well as newly independent states such as Ghana and Tanzania. South Asia had long been important to the agency, especially in the context of its Tibetan operations, but the Pakistani tilt to China and India's move to friendlier ties with the Soviet Union in the late 1960s accentuated CIA efforts there as well. Southeast Asia during the Vietnam war, of course, was a major operational theater—the Saigon station became the largest in the DO, just as Germany had been (for action against Russia) in the early 1950s, and Miami (for Cuba) in 1961–1963. The Church Committee concluded later that paramilitary action had become the dominant form of CIA clandestine activity, surpassing covert psychological and political initiatives in budgetary allocations by 1967, and that "the combination of the paramilitary surge and self-sustaining operations made the period 1964 to 1967 the most active for the execution of covert activities."[23]

Under the circumstances, it is not surprising that the CIA staff reductions made in the wake of the Vietnam War centered on the agency's paramilitary contingent. It is also understandable that the post-Vietnam 1970s would be a low point for CIA paramilitary action. An operation in the former Portugese colony of Angola became the major paramilitary endeavor of the mid-1970s, but that was ended by congressional intervention before the end of the Ford administration.

Meanwhile the tension between espionage and technical collection persisted. From about 1962 to 1973 CIA clandestine collection had been greatly hobbled by allegations from some defectors that the agency had been penetrated by "moles"—agents recruited by the Soviets to serve as agents in place. Counterintelligence investigations of a number of CIA officers made others wary to attempt recruitments of spies. None of the agency officers investigated were shown to be moles, but all of their careers were ruined. Reacting to this, CIA directors, beginning with William E. Colby, deemphasized counterintelligence in an attempt to jump start the recruiting of fresh Soviet spies. During the 1970s, the CIA recruited some excellent Soviet Bloc spies. Arkady Shevchenko was a senior Soviet diplomat assigned to the United Nations secretariat. Ryszard Kuklinski had been a colonel on the Polish army general staff, which afforded the CIA access to much Warsaw Pact military planning, as well as preparations for military (and Soviet military) intervention in the Solidarity crisis in Poland in 1979–1981. In the 1980s espionage successes abounded. In Russia, Adolph Tolkachev, an aeronautical designer, furnished hard data on the characteristics of Soviet aircraft and electronic systems. There were also a number of spies located within the Russian intelligence services.

Even major spies, plus a legion of minor agents, had stiff competition from the technical collectors. By the 1970s and 1980s third-generation satellites for both overhead imagery and communications–electronic signal reception had the ability to remain in orbit for very long periods of time, and even to maneuver in space to bring new targets under observation. The National Reconnaissance Office was fully occupied. There were ships and sophisticated ground stations to monitor Soviet missile tests, as well as land-based and sea-based communications interception stations. There were even new versions of telephone wiretapping technology that were coupled underwater to Soviet trunk-line cables, which became major boons for the National Security Agency. The take of communications intercepts already copied but still awaiting analysis, alone, was said to have filled entire boxcars on railroad sidings outside NSA headquarters.

But as technical collection thrust ahead, in the game of spy versus spy the CIA's clandestine services suffered major losses beginning in the mid-1980s. The reduced emphasis on counterintelligence opened the way for true moles. Aldrich Ames at the CIA and Robert Hanssen at the FBI essentially gave the Russians enough data to identify and arrest all the CIA's key sources. Ronald Pelton at the NSA gave away the submarine-cable monitoring program. Larry Wu-tai Chin provided important data to the Chinese. American code systems were compromised by the Walker brothers beginning in the late 1960s. Both served in the U.S. Navy and were not uncovered until the 1980s. Starting with the Russian arrests of American spies identified by Ames, from the mid-1980s there was renewed focus on domestic counterintelligence and the beginning of another mole hunt

(1985, when Pelton and two other spies were arrested, would be called the "Year of the Spy" in U.S. intelligence circles). But Aldrich Ames would not actually be uncovered until 1995, and Robert Hanssen not until 2001. Meanwhile, the technical collection programs remained strong.

One other point should be made about the spy game. To a very great degree the competition between Soviet and American spies has been about espionage itself. That is, throughout the Cold War period, spies revealed far more about the spy services on the other side than they did about the adversaries' intentions or capabilities. For every Penkovsky or Tolkachev there were a dozen valued agents whose intelligence pertained mostly to the enemy's agents. For the Soviets, the primary value of Ames and Hanssen, for example, was their ability to identify CIA agents in Russia. While understandable, this also calls into question the theory and practice of espionage as a valuable tool for intelligence collection. When William J. Casey took over U.S. intelligence with the advent of the Reagan administration, emphasis shifted back to covert operations, which Casey was determined to invigorate. Casey greatly accelerated a nascent paramilitary campaign against the Soviets in Afghanistan, revived a dormant operation in Angola, and started new ones in Nicaragua and Cambodia. The relative ease with which CIA could mount these projects demonstrates that agency paramilitary capabilities after Vietnam had not, in fact, been completely eliminated, and also that CIA cooperation with U.S. special operations forces, which provided the bulk of field officers in the new campaigns, was smooth and certain. Casey himself, and President Reagan, with their contempt for congressional oversight and tenuous arguments for the goals of these activities, ended up producing a domestic backlash against these operations. Mounting congressional opposition forced DCI Casey into extra-legal avenues from 1984 on with respect to Nicaragua. President Reagan's credulousness and his permitting the NSC staff to meld the Casey operation into Middle East efforts, to free U.S. hostages taken by terrorists, led directly to the Iran-Contra affair, which came close to igniting a constitutional crisis in the United States. Where it did end was in the imposition of new congressional restrictions on U.S. covert operations.

Then, in 1991, came the fall of the Soviet Union and the end of the Cold War. The conventional wisdom, which sees the malaise in CIA's Directorate of Operations as a consequence of staff and budget cuts at the agency, is a vast oversimplification. In truth, there were at least four other streams of experience contributing to DO's problems. The first was the continued

strength of the Directorate of Science and Technology and technical collection programs in general. Outside the agency the dominance of the
National Security Agency and National Reconnaissance Office underlined
that strength. The DO saw itself as outclassed by the technologists. Second
was the knowledge that moles were at work at the agency's heart, with obvious implications for DO's effectiveness. The third was the diversion of
DO resources into the novel device of "fusion" intelligence centers for counterintelligence, counterterrorism, narcotics, and so on, a DCI-mandated
initiative. Fourth was the sensitivity attached to covert operations in the
wake of the Iran-Contra affair. This was further accentuated in the mid-
1990s when it emerged that agents on the CIA's payroll in Guatemala were
participants in the torture of American citizens. New recruitment regulations initiated by DCI John Deutsch in the wake of the Guatemala fiasco
were a logical result, but only contributed further to the perception the
DO had become "risk-averse." Staff and budget reductions, a consequence
of the end of the Cold War, added to the perception of problems at the Directorate of Operations but were not the only or even the primary cause.
As already noted, moreover, the DO was protected from the deepest cuts
of the CIA reduction scalpel.

None of this reduced the tension between technical collection and human intelligence. Meanwhile, policy reviews like that by the Aspin-Brown
Commission uniformly recommended reinvesting in the Directorate of
Operations. Within months of becoming DCI, George J. Tenet had accepted the challenge of resuscitating the clandestine service. Wary DO
officers worried that Tenet, with his congressional and NSC staff background, might be a risk-averse DCI, but in fact the new director spoke
out publicly on increasing the clandestine service before the end of 1998.
The rising focus on international terrorism also drove the DO reinvigo-
ration. Tenet declared war on terrorism in late 1998, formed a Special Activities Division within the DO as a new paramilitary unit, and requested
budget increases for training and personnel. Suddenly technologies like
unmanned aerial vehicles (such as the Predator) were being adapted specifically for DO purposes. Much of this was done while the Clinton administration was still in office; much more would be accomplished after
the September 11 attacks.

Meanwhile, development of technical collection systems continued. The
DS&T still contributes to research and development, and the National
Reconnaissance Office, which gained its own headquarters complex and
base in the mid-1990s, is stronger than ever. The next-generation satellite

imaging system remains a headache for both the DS&T and NRO, but cost overruns and delays have been endemic to the technical collection side of intelligence. The odd thing is that DS&T–NRO failures rarely result in adverse consequences for those units whereas DO failures at the CIA frequently do. Perhaps that is because failures in technical collection remain shrouded in secrecy while espionage and covert action gaffes often lead to public scandal.

Viewed across the long sweep of Cold War history, the CIA's Directorate of Operations has led a cyclical existence. In contrast, the Directorate of Science and Technology and the technical collection agencies, though they treaded water on a few occasions, have sustained an upward trend of growth. How the two collection methods will play out against each other in the coming years remains an open question, but in the near-term post-September 11 budget increases will provide for growth across the board. Observers should also expect to see a significant increase in CIA covert operations.

Conclusion

The Cold War marked an important passage for America and a key event for U.S. intelligence. The Cold War resulted in the creation of a centralized, peacetime intelligence community in the United States. The CIA and its brethren achieved remarkable advances in estimating and predicting foreign behavior, in analyzing intelligence data, in collecting huge amounts of information, in scientific and technological advances, and in the traditional tradecraft of espionage. Those developments certainly furnish a basis for a move into a new world. Whether that world will feature an American empire or a brief moment of U.S. supremacy hangs today in the balance. Meanwhile, U.S. intelligence continues to move away from its Cold War origins.

Notes

1.   David F. Rudgers, *Creating the Secret State: The Origins of the Central Intelligence Agency, 1943–1947* (Lawrence: University of Kansas Press, 2000), passim.

2.   Matthew M. Aid, "US Humint and Comint in the Korean War: From the Approach of War to the Chinese Intervention," *Intelligence and National Security* 14, no. 4, (Winter 1999): 17–63.

3. On this point see Lyman B. Kirkpatrick, *The Real CIA* (New York: Random House, 1968).

4. The PFIAB has been in continuous existence since then even as other mechanisms for oversight have evolved.

5. The charges were aimed at anti-CIA activists and their publications in the United States, and concerned the murder of CIA station chief Richard Welch in Greece in 1975. The charges were never substantiated, and in fact, when the Greek terrorists involved in this plot were on trial in Athens in 2002–3, they reported having had no access to, and had never heard of, the activists and publications. Ironically, the first grand jury investigation of Americans under the Act would be of White House operatives for revealing the identity of a CIA officer in the course of political in-fighting over the Iraq war in 2003 (popularly known as the Plame case).

6. 50 U.S.C. 413 Section 501(e).

7. President George W. Bush remarks, The White House, August 2, 2004.

8. Victor Marchetti and John D. Marks in their book *The CIA and the Cult of Intelligence* (New York: Dell Books, 1975, 74), which the CIA attempted to classify, and then gutted with numerous security deletions, reported in their tabulation of agency strength that the number of personnel was approximately 16,500. (The CIA attempted to suppress this tabulation, but was prevented by the courts.)

9. Admiral Stansfield Turner, *Secrecy and Democracy: The CIA in Transition* (Boston: Houghton Mifflin, 1985), 196–97.

10. Walter Pincus, "CIA Struggles to Find Identity in a New World," *The Washington Post*, May 9, 1994, A9.

11. R. James Woolsey, "The Future Direction of Intelligence," Speech at the Center for Strategic and International Studies, Washington, DC, July 18, 1994.

12. Marchetti and Marks, *The CIA*, table, 77.

13. Thomas K. Adams, *US Special Operations Forces in Action: The Challenge of Unconventional Warfare* (London: Frank Cass Ltd., 1998), 172.

14. James L. Pavitt, Written Statement for the Record, National Commission on Terrorist Attacks Upon the United States, April 14, 2004, 4 (http://www.cia .gov/cia/public_affairs/speeches/2004/pavitt_testimony_...).

15. In his July 1994 speech referred to earlier, James Woolsey had put the number 700 forward as the target for reductions in the DO by 1997. It is reasonable to suppose that actual personnel losses from the clandestine service ranged somewhere between Woolsey's 700 and our estimated 1,500.

16. National Security Act of 1947 (Public Law 253–79), July 26, 1947. 50 U.S.C. 403 Section 103 (d) (3).

17. The report was solicited by the National Security Council and the study was done by Allen W. Dulles, William Jackson, and Matthias Correa. It was most

notable for its recommendations on consolidation of the clandestine service, as shall be seen below, but it also had a strong impact on the analytical side of the CIA. Both Dulles and Jackson would subsequently become CIA officials.

18. The practice of dissenting from an estimate thus became known as "taking a footnote" even though in practice such dissents were reflected in different ways over time, including the footnote method described, writing dissents directly into the text of estimates, or presenting them in text parallel to the main text of the report.

19. DCI Hoyt Vandenberg, Memorandum to Assistant Director for Special Operations, October 25, 1946; in Michael Warner, ed., *CIA Cold War Records: The CIA Under Harry Truman* (Washington: CIA History Staff: Center for the Study of Intelligence), 1994.

20. For South Vietnam see John Prados, *The Blood Road: The Ho Chi Minh Trail and the Vietnam War* (New York: Wiley, 2000). For the Congo see, most recently, David W. Doyle, *True Men and Traitors: From the OSS to the CIA, My Life in the Shadows* (New York: Wiley, 2001).

21. Philip Agee, *Inside the Company: CIA Diary* (London: Allen Lane, 1975).

22. Felix Rodriguez and John Weisman, *Shadow Warrior: The CIA Hero of a Hundred Unknown Battles* (New York: Simon & Schuster, 1989).

23. Anne Karalekas, "History of the Central Intelligence Agency" (a supplementary staff study by the Church Committee) in William M. Leary, ed., *The Central Intelligence Agency: History and Documents.* (Tuscaloosa: University of Alabama Press, 1984), 79.

8. THE MILITARY-INDUSTRIAL COMPLEX
LOBBY AND TROPE

Alex Roland

The military-industrial complex was both a historical phenomenon and a political trope. The phenomenon was a lobby that campaigned intensely in the United States to promote increased military spending and arms production. It flourished for a quarter of a century during the Cold War. The trope gained currency in the antiwar movement of the Vietnam era. It, too, is best understood in a Cold-War context.[1]

Both meanings of the term are captured by the *Oxford English Dictionary*. It defines "military industrial" as

> (orig. U.S.), of or relating to a nation's armed forces and to its industries (esp. those producing military equipment); esp. in military-industrial complex (orig. and chiefly U.S.), these resources as a whole, regarded as a powerful vested interest and a strong influence on government.

The fourth edition of the *American Heritage Dictionary of the English Language* presents another meaning that has grown up around the term:

> the aggregate of a nation's armed forces and the industries that supply their equipment, materials, and armaments.

It is in this guise that military-industrial complexes have been sighted on every continent and as far back in history as the Middle Ages. This essay will focus on the first two meanings, a lobby and a trope, which reflect America's experience of the Cold War.

The Warning

President Dwight Eisenhower introduced the "military-industrial complex" in his farewell address to the nation on January 17, 1961. His speechwriter, Malcom Moos, coined the term to capture what Eisenhower called in private the "delta of power."[2] The President included Congress in a triangular nexus with the armed services and industry. Collaboration among these three powerful institutions pressured him relentlessly to expand the armed forces and their budgets. Particularly galling to Eisenhower was the mindless pursuit of new and often redundant weapons systems, devices through which the services contended with each other for roles and missions and laid the groundwork for increased budgets and force levels to match their new equipment.

Ironically, Eisenhower was lamenting an institution he had once advocated. In a 1928 paper at the Army War College and again in a 1932 paper at the Army Industrial College, Eisenhower had called for closer cooperation in peacetime between industry and the military, so that when war came they would be prepared to work in harmony.[3] The military had to communicate its needs to industry; industry had to meet those needs on short notice and under stress.[4] Again in 1946, Eisenhower, then Chief of Staff of the U.S. Army, called for even more "cooperation with science and industry" than the country had achieved in World War II.[5] This wish had been fulfilled by 1961. "We have been compelled," Eisenhower said in his address to the nation, "to create a permanent armaments industry of vast proportions." When combined with "an immense military establishment," the complex's "total influence—economic, political, even spiritual—is felt in every city, every Statehouse, every office of the Federal government." While recognizing the need for this development, he worried about its "grave implications." In the most quoted passage of his address Eisenhower warned:

> In the councils of government, we must guard against the acquisition of unwarranted influence, whether sought or unsought, by the military-industrial complex. The potential for the disastrous rise of misplaced power exists and will persist. . . . Only an alert and knowledgeable citizenry can compel the proper meshing of this huge industrial and military machinery of defense with our peaceful methods and goals.[6]

He was equally alarmed by the transformation of science and technology. This danger ran in two directions. "Big science" was displacing the "lone inventor" and the "free university."[7] "The prospect of domination of the nation's scholars by Federal employment, project allocations, and the power of money is ever present," he warned, "and is gravely to be regarded." So too was the power of science and technology. "In holding scientific research and discovery in respect," he said, "we must also be alert to the equal and opposite danger that public policy itself become the captive of a scientific-technological elite."

The clarity of the language did not prevent scholars from arguing about exactly what the President meant by the "military-industrial complex" and the "scientific-technological elite." Eisenhower's science advisers, for example, were surprised and aggrieved by his reference to their community. Eisenhower assured one of them that he did not have them in mind, but they nonetheless felt tarred by the brush.[8] Others believed that Congress should have been included as part of the military-industrial complex, and still others would have added academia as well.

Years later, Eisenhower would clarify his meaning in a classified speech he gave at the Naval War College in 1969. As reported in the *New York Times*, he spoke of "the Congressman who sees a new defense establishment in his district; the company in Los Angeles, Denver, or Baltimore that wants an order for more airplanes; the services which want them; the armies of scientists who want so terribly to test out their newest view. . . . Put all these together," he continued, "and you have a lobby."[9]

Eisenhower's aversion to lobbies appears to have been deeply rooted in his military experience. He embraced the American tradition that serving officers should eschew politics. His mentor and benefactor, General George C. Marshall, who went on to be Secretary of Defense and Secretary of State, claimed proudly that he had never voted in an election.[10] An officer's duty, he and Eisenhower believed, was to carry out the orders of the commander-in-chief, the president. Civilian control of the military was a sacred constitutional principle. It was not their place to shape national policy either through electoral politics or through intervention in the political process in Washington. The unprecedented power of the military in shaping national strategy in World War II was bestowed on them by the president, not seized by them in the halls of Congress or other corridors of power. Other military leaders of World War II, such as Chief of Naval Operations Admiral Ernest King, might manipulate the political system for the benefit of their service,[11] but Marshall and Eisenhower played it

straight. When Ike became president, he expected his senior military officers to do the same. He deeply resented the role of the military in undermining his authority as commander-in-chief by conspiring with industry
and Congress to shape his administration's policies.

On the surface, at least, President Eisenhower's aversion to lobbies appeared to resonate with the sociologist C. Wright Mills's influential book,
The Power Elite, which appeared in 1956. Mills argued that power in the
United States was concentrated in the hands of a few hundred government
officials, corporate executives, and military officers. He did not include
scientists, even though Eisenhower had labeled them elites. Nor did Mills
suggest that this power elite operated conspiratorially to subvert the will
of the people. Rather, he believed that the elites developed among themselves a shared worldview that bred consensus among them on the fundamental policies guiding American life. In the case of the Cold War, for
example, Mills's elite embraced the Marshall Plan, containment, and NSC
68, the foundations of America's Cold War policy. Once members of the
elite had concluded that the Soviet Union posed a continuing threat to the
United States—one that warranted a standing military establishment—
then the great outline of American policy quickly took shape and thereafter remained fixed. Force structure, weapons procurement, and deployment
decisions simply filled in the details of a grand canvas. The power elite
might contend with one another over these details, but their real influence
lay in forging the grand consensus.

To Eisenhower, who endorsed the grand consensus, these details mattered a great deal. In spite of his public image as an avuncular old soldier
slightly out of touch with the demands of the presidency, Eisenhower was
an astute and accomplished government executive and politician. Like Sovietologist George Kennan, he believed that the greatest risk posed by the
Cold War was the temptation to imitate the enemy, to allow the United
States to slip into a Soviet-style command economy, bent disproportionately to the production of armaments and the maintenance of a large,
standing military establishment.[12] He doubted that the Cold War would
turn hot. Rather, he anticipated a long standoff between competing economic and political systems. Eisenhower believed it crucial that the United
States not bankrupt itself in an arms race with the Soviets. Pressure from
the military-industrial complex to increase defense spending undermined
his consistent efforts to balance the budget and promote a sound economy
unburdened by excessive taxation.

Despite its apparent similarities to Mills's power elite, Eisenhower's farewell address was rooted in a very different framework. In both public and private statements, the president had often expressed his concern about the United States becoming a "garrison state."[13] In 1941, political scientist Harold Lasswell had warned about "the garrison state, . . . a world in which the specialists on violence are the most powerful group in society."[14] This possibility had suggested itself to Lasswell when he learned of the Japanese bombing of China in 1937. He wondered if the subjection of civilians to military attack, what he called the "socialization of danger," would not empower the military to permanently organize society for war. The "specialist on violence," he suggested, might displace the businessman, the bureaucrat, and the politician atop "the power pyramid." C. Wright Mills' "power elite" might be militarized, paradoxically,

> by specialists on violence [who] are more preoccupied with the skills and attitudes judged characteristic of nonviolence. We anticipate the merging of skills, starting from the traditional accouterments of the professional soldier, moving toward the manager and promoter of large-scale civilian enterprise.[15]

Two trends converged in Lasswell's garrison state. On the one hand, a conventional militarization of society allowed uniformed officers and military considerations to gain purchase in the formulation of national policy. Those given to such fears could see the appointment of General George C. Marshall as Secretary of State in the Truman administration as evidence of this trend, to say nothing of the election of General Eisenhower. On the other hand, civilian leaders elected and appointed to oversee the military were themselves imbued with many of the values Lasswell dreaded. Secretary of State John Foster Dulles, who envisioned a moral crusade against godless communism and was prepared to take the United States to the brink of Armageddon in defense of security, exemplified these "militarized civilians."[16]

Before he introduced the term "military-industrial complex," Eisenhower spoke of a garrison state as shorthand for the related problems of the arms race, escalating costs, and economic crisis. "If we let defense spending run wild," he said, "you get inflation . . . then controls . . . then a garrison state . . . and *then* we've lost the very values we were trying to defend."[17] "Total mobilization," he said on another occasion, "would mean . . . all the grim paraphernalia of the garrison state."[18] His most dramatic and eloquent plea to rein in the excesses of arms development and procurement came in an address on April 16, 1953. The arms race, he told the American Society of Newspaper Editors, promised

> a life of perpetual fear and tension; a burden of arms draining the wealth and labor of all peoples. . . . Every gun that is made, every warship launched, every rocket fired signifies, in the final sense, a theft from those who hunger and are not fed, those who are cold and not clothed. This world in arms is not spending money alone. It is spending the sweat of its laborers, the genius of its scientists, the hopes of its children. . . . This is not a way of life at all, in any true sense. Under the cloud of threatening war, it is humanity hanging from a cross of iron.[19]

For Eisenhower, then, the power elite and the garrison state formed complementary images for his conceptualization of the military-industrial complex, or what he sometimes called in private the "delta of power." He had a clear vision of the need to sustain America's core values, as he saw them: constitutional, democratic government and free-enterprise capitalism. The Cold War was a contest of political and economic systems. The U.S. system would win if it were not undermined by the interest groups bent on accelerating the arms race, expanding a provocative and excessive American arsenal, and subordinating America's economic vitality to a command economy that supplanted prudence with fear.

Furthermore, the military-industrial complex bred inefficiencies and waste that further undermined his attempts to restrain government spending. Special interests championed policies and acquisitions that benefited them more than the country at large. Cozy relationships between the military services and their leading contractors invited corruption and mismanagement. And a revolving door admitted executives from arms manufacturers to senior civilian posts in the Pentagon, while retiring officers passed out the other side to join the companies whose contracts they had administered in office. The close cooperation that Eisenhower had once advocated between the military and industry had turned into an incestuous and counterproductive cronyism.

Three examples of the military-industrial complex at work in the Eisenhower administration will suggest the kinds of pressure that Eisenhower felt and the complexity of the issues. All three are drawn from the aerospace sector, the realm cited by Eisenhower in his 1969 speech at the Naval War College as the largest and most powerful component of the MIC.

The first, and perhaps most notorious, tale is that of TRW. Simon Ramo and Dean Wooldridge were scientists turned engineers in the Electronics Division of Hughes Aircraft. In 1953, Trevor Gardner, the Special Assistant to the Secretary of the Air Force for Research and Development, became enamored of their "excellent leadership" of Hughes's Falcon air-to-air missile program, which he considered to be "a model for the rest of the military technology industry."[20] When Gardner sought staff support for a blue-ribbon Strategic Missiles Evaluation Committee, known by its code name of Teapot Committee, he gave a letter contract to Ramo-Wooldridge Corporation, which the two engineers left their Hughes jobs to create just in time to be of service to Gardner. The new corporation provided technical services to the Teapot Committee and drafted its report. The Teapot Committee recommended that the Atlas intercontinental ballistic missile program be accelerated on a crash basis. But the Air Force, newly created in 1947—and lacking the staff, facilities, or expertise to run a program on the scale envisioned by the Teapot Committee— hired Ramo-Wooldridge to assume "technical responsibility" for Atlas.

Itself lacking capital and personnel, Ramo-Wooldridge merged with Thompson Products Company of Cleveland, which put up half a million dollars. For their part, Ramo and Wooldridge retained 51 percent control of their firm for an investment of $6,750 each. The company's fee for its initial contract with the Air Force was 14.3 percent of the contract cost, more than twice the average fee for research-and-development contracts in the Department of Defense. By the time the company reorganized again in 1958, to become Thompson-Ramo-Wooldridge, Inc. (TRW), the young engineers had parlayed their initial investments of $6,750 into $3,150,000 each. The Atlas program succeeded, but at the price of high salaries and alarming profits for TRW.

The facts of the Ramo-Wooldridge story are not in doubt; most of them came out during the course of a 1959 congressional investigation into the company's relationship with the Air Force.[21] But what do they mean? Ramo-Wooldridge Corporation may be seen as a product of privilege and favoritism, exacting unwarranted profits from an indecent conflict of interest. But the Atlas missile may be seen as a technological marvel resulting from a unique alliance of free-enterprise capitalism and government sponsorship. Eschewing the socialist model of many other industrialized states, such as Japan and France, to say nothing of the command economy of the Soviet Union, the United States linked the public and private sectors in a cooperative scheme that retained strong aspects of both: the government would make enormous capital investments in long-term projects essential to national security, while industry would mobilize the private sector for discrete undertakings. Still, Ramo-Wooldridge represented the kind of collusion between the military and industry that troubled Eisenhower.

The "bomber gap" of 1955 provides another example. In that year, observers at the Soviet May Day parade in Red Square counted more strategic bombers flying overhead than U.S. intelligence had predicted. A group of senior American military officials invited to witness the Soviet Union's annual Air Day in July of the same year also saw waves of Soviet Bison bombers fly by. These planes had the theoretical capability to deliver nuclear weapons on targets in the United States. Denizens of the military-industrial complex raised a public alarm, and Congress convened hearings. Air Force General Curtis LeMay testified that the Soviets would have a larger bomber fleet than the United States by 1959. A great hue-and-cry ensued, with demands that the administration do something to prevent the United States from falling behind. In fact, when 1959 came, reconnaissance by the new U-2 spy plane disproved the theory of a bomber gap. In retrospect it appears that the Soviets had duped the American observers by flying the same planes past them in multiple waves. In the meantime, however, pressure from Congress and the Air Force, enthusiastically supported by defense contractors, had obliged President Eisenhower to accelerate production of American B-52 bombers and fund a massive air defense program that continued long after the bomber gap was discredited.[22]

A third and related incident revolved around the so-called "missile mess." In the inter-service scramble for roles and missions, and the funding that went with them, the services often duplicated each other's programs. The Army and the Air Force, for example, launched similar programs in the mid-1950s to build intermediate-range ballistic missiles, those that flew between roughly 1,700 and 3,500 miles. The Army claimed that this was long-range artillery. The Air Force claimed that the missile offered a variation on strategic bombing. Repeated attempts within the Department of Defense to rein in the services proved unavailing. Spending on intermediate-range and intercontinental ballistic missiles jumped from $14 million in 1954 to $1.4 billion in 1957. Spending on all missile programs more than doubled from 1954 to 1956 and doubled again by

1958.[23] By then, the furor over the Soviet Union's launch of Sputnik had created an entirely new round of spending pressures. The Army's response to Sputnik was to concoct a fifteen-year program to establish a base on the moon, justified by the timeless military axiom to "take the high ground." The Air Force invented the term aerospace to stake out its rhetorical claim to the space mission. Competing budget requests and program proposals followed. Eisenhower chose the Navy to launch an American response to Sputnik, but finally had to approve an Army launch on the controversial Jupiter missile when the Navy failed. When Lyndon Johnson, then Senate majority leader, convened hearings before a joint congressional committee, Eisenhower proposed the creation of the National Aeronautics and Space Administration; it was his best hope of avoiding the expensive and redundant missile and space initiatives advocated by the military services.[24]

Ironically, Eisenhower railed against the machinations of the military-industrial complex while himself moving comfortably amongst Mills's power elite. He appointed businessmen to his cabinet. He accepted advice from businessmen in his years as President of Columbia University, turning his salary and his military pension into a comfortable nest egg that allowed him to retire to his cherished farm at Gettysburg. On the golf course and in poker games, Ike relaxed in the company of like-minded men (almost never women) and told the stories that reinforced their shared worldview. In these circles he was performing the role that Mills ascribed to the power elite, shaping the broad consensus guiding America through the Cold War. Indeed, there is every reason to believe that he conceived of the power elite as a good thing, even while concluding that the military-industrial complex, which operated one or two tiers below the power elite, represented a serious threat to the nation.

The "scientific and technical elite" fell somewhere in between. Second only to businessmen in Ike's affection were the men he called "my scientists." After the shock of Sputnik in October 1957, Eisenhower grew increasingly dependent on science advisers, largely to help him resist the public and political pressure to launch a space race with the Soviet Union. He converted the old Office of Defense Mobilization into the President's Science Advisory Committee (PSAC) and moved it into the White House. He appointed a Presidential Science Adviser, who was chosen by the members of PSAC as their chairman. He created the Advanced Research Projects Agency, to develop America's nascent space program and to screen the crackpot schemes bubbling up in the Department of Defense.

Eisenhower told his military aide, General Andrew Goodpaster, that his happiest times in the White House were during his meetings with PSAC, for he felt himself in the presence of smart men who placed the country's interest above their own. It was they who laid out for him the blueprint of a national space policy that assigned human spaceflight to the National Aeronautics and Space Administration, and kept it out of the hands of the Pentagon.

THE TROPE

From the vantage point of the twenty-first century, in which the term military-industrial complex has become a commonplace, it is difficult to appreciate how little impact Eisenhower's warning had at first. The term circulated in some informed political circles, and the scientific community grumbled for years about the perceived affront in the epithet "scientific-technical elite." But for most of the 1960s, Eisenhower's warning achieved but small purchase on political discourse. Only in the rising rhetorical opposition to the Vietnam War late in the decade was the term revived and popularized. In the process, it was also redefined. Vietnam transformed "military-industrial complex" into a trope whose meaning was related to, but very different from, that intended by Eisenhower.

John F. Kennedy campaigned in 1960 against the image of Eisenhower as a disengaged, artless chief executive who had failed to keep America apace with the growing Soviet threat. If anything, Eisenhower's warning about the military-industrial complex suggested a President obsessed with the malfunctioning of American institutions, when—according to Kennedy—the real danger to the republic lay beyond its shores. Where Eisenhower saw the Cold War as a long-term struggle between economic and political systems, Kennedy saw it as a titanic struggle between military rivals, a struggle of freedom and democracy against a totalitarian state that had threatened to bury America. Kennedy vowed that Americans would pay any price to win that struggle. In his first months in office he proposed and then pushed through Congress the largest peacetime defense build-up in the history of the country. He cut taxes and accepted deficits in pursuit of greater national security, policies that Eisenhower had considered inimical the to country's security.

The public ignored the warning of their septuagenarian ex-president and embraced their combative and energetic new commander-in-chief.

A survey of *The New York Times* and *The Nation* for the years 1961 to 1990 reveals that the term military-industrial complex was little used in the early 1960s. In 1963, the year of Kennedy's assassination, the term did not appear at all in *The New York Times*. Far from worrying about a military-industrial complex, Americans followed their young, enthusiastic president into a confrontational escalation of the arms race.

Not until the Vietnam War escalated in the late 1960s did the "military-industrial complex" take firm hold on the public consciousness. (See figure 8.1.) In 1969, for example, the term appeared twenty-five times in *The Nation* and thirteen times in *The New York Times*. As the Vietnam War consumed more of America's soldiers, treasure, and attention, the antiwar movement appropriated the rhetoric of the military-industrial complex. And as the rhetoric grew more inflamed, the meaning of the term became less clear. Some claimed that the specific phenomena Eisenhower warned about were responsible for American involvement in Vietnam. Others equated the term to "the establishment," which historian Michael Sherry later characterized as encompassing "the entrenched machinery of racism, imperialism, militarism, and corporate capitalism."[25] "Military-industrial complex" became a club with which one bashed the government over failed policy in Vietnam; soon it was more closely associated in the public mind with Vietnam than with the Cold-War-induced political phenomenon it was invented to describe.

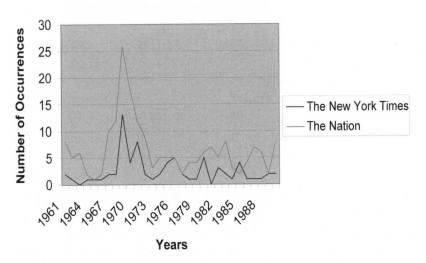

FIGURE 8.1. THE DISTRIBUTION OF THE TERM "MILITARY-INDUSTRIAL COMPLEX" IN SELECTED MEDIA

This tendency recurred in books and articles. Dozens of books on the military-industrial complex appeared in the early 1970s: inflamed polemics, whistle-blowing and muck-raking exposés, scholarly analyses, and political tracts.[26] At least one author defended what he called the MIC's "lonely warriors,"[27] while a few attempted detachment and scholarly rigor.[28] But most found the complex even more sinister and dangerous than the simple lobby that Eisenhower had experienced. Rather, they said, the military-industrial complex was symptomatic of a darker current in American life. Not only did it subvert public policy and undermine the constitutional powers of elected officials, but it also eroded the very principles for which the country stood and led to immoral and even illegal acts at home and abroad. Here in short was the culprit responsible for the debacle of Vietnam.

This new conceptualization of the military-industrial complex took two principal forms, both of them anticipated by Eisenhower's critique, but neither of them fully framed before Vietnam. The first was militarism.

MILITARISM

This pejorative, nineteenth-century term had long been associated with Karl von Clausewitz, the Napoleonic-era Prussian military philosopher often perceived as the architect and advocate of total war.[29] In Cold War America, militarism had been defined by Samuel P. Huntington's seminal *The Soldier and the State*. First published in 1957, it is an intellectual tour de force that has structured scholarly discussion of the topic for half a century.[30] Huntington's goal had been to identify a workable system of civil-military relations for the United States. The problem, as he saw it, was that military culture, of the kind needed by the United States to face the threat posed by the Soviet Union, was incompatible with America's dominant liberal culture. The United States valued individualism; its military forces required patriotism, loyalty, and service—subordination of the individual to the state. Liberals reconciled individualism and collectivism with civic militarism, the citizen soldier who took up arms in time of need.[31] This minuteman leavened the standing army with his democratic ideals and tempered the authoritarianism of the military establishment with his egalitarian values. When the crisis passed, he returned, Cincinnatus-like, to civilian life. Citizen-soldiers insulated the army from the temptation to meddle in the political process. No Junker aristocracy would force its policies on the American state.[32]

Huntington believed that the unique dangers posed by the Cold War swamped civic militarism. Liberal America would not have the will to face down the Soviets, and it would not give the army the resources it needed to do the job. As a remedy, he proposed what he called "objective control" of the military. In this social contract, society would allow the military great latitude and autonomy to provide for the country's national security in return for a commitment not to engage in politics. The bargain would permit democratically chosen civilian leaders to establish national policy without interference from the military while allowing the officer corps to carry out that policy without interference from the civilians. The military would remain a bastion of conservative, authoritarian, Hobbesian toughness swimming in and serving a liberal, individualistic, Rousseauan society. In this way, the discipline and selflessness of the military itself provided the best safeguard against militarism.

Huntington's analysis proved controversial, but his framing of the issue dominated scholarly discussion. The problem, he had seen, was having a military strong enough to meet the security threat but not so strong as to threaten democratic institutions. Was this not Eisenhower's complaint? Did he not warn of "an immense military establishment" reaching with the arms industry into "every city, every Statehouse, every office of the Federal government"? Was he not concerned about the circumvention of his authority as an elected official? Could it not be said that the military-industrial complex was really just a special form of militarism?

Indeed it could. The very specific sense Eisenhower intended when he used the term, the sense of a political lobby, evolved in some public rhetoric into a larger claim of militarism, or what Huntington called subjective civilian control. As historian Arthur Schlesinger Jr., put it, "the military-industrial complex was more a consequence than a cause of the problem," which "lay in the feebleness of civilian control of the military establishment."[33]

But the critics of the Vietnam War ignored the definitional niceties of Huntington's formulation and often used the term interchangeably with militarization. Richard Kaufman, for example, expounding on "the meaning of militarism," reported that the United States "was in the process of becoming militarized. . . . To prepare for its new role as guiding force of the American order, the military establishment," said Kaufman, had been "gradually reorganizing itself and taking on added responsibilities."[34] Perhaps the best exemplar of the phenomenon was NARMIC, the program for National Action/Research on the Military Industrial Complex. Established on September 2, 1969, as an arm of the American Friends Service

Committee, NARMIC promised its parent organization that it would "dramatize the need to demilitarize the American system through action-related research."[35] This goal comported with the Friends' avowed purpose: "to confront, non-violently, powerful institutions of violence, evil, oppression, and injustice."[36] NARMIC's first planned publication was to be *The Vietnam Profiteers*. In practice, however, NARMIC did not focus on the military-industrial complex. Instead it worked on a wide range of antiwar projects, ranging from foreign arms sales to the communist threat in Central America to South African apartheid. Its study of *Police on the Homefront*, for example, claimed that "in the last few years, the Military-Industrial Complex with its think-tanks and weaponry has joined with the Justice Department, and local police forces to construct a formidable and growing national police complex."[37] NARMIC's focus ranged across what it saw as a garrison state without ever defining, explaining, or highlighting the military-industrial complex. When NARMIC slipped from public view in the late 1980s, at the end of the Cold War, it had yet to publish *The Vietnam Profiteers*. But others made the connection NARMIC had envisioned, tying the evils of militarism to another oppressive force in American society: capitalism.

CAPITALISM

From the perspective of capitalism, the Vietnam-era arms industry was not primarily an instrument of militarization. Rather, the military was both a realm of capitalist enterprise and a vehicle of capitalist expansion. Analyses featured both traditional Marxist interpretations and more modern economic theory of the relationship between the economy and the state. Some raised the prospect that the United States was becoming a command economy, in the same sense that Lasswell and Eisenhower had dreaded.

The Marxist interpretation argued that American military and foreign policies were driven by an economic class concerned primarily with profits.[38] Weapons manufacture was attractive on several counts. The arms industry was an oligopoly; competition was limited to a small number of firms. They operated within a monopsony, but that single buyer, the government, was politically manipulable. Second, weapons were instruments of destruction, a capitalist's dream; they created their own demand. Third, at least in the context of the Cold War, weapons produced for the American government might be sold to other governments as soon as they became obsolescent, rather like the way television networks sell their reruns for syndication to various local stations or basic cable networks. Obsolescence therefore served two purposes, driving demand for new weapons while opening markets for the old ones.

From this perspective, the Vietnam War was good for America. It consumed existing weapons while generating demand for new ones.[39] Furthermore, constraints on profits, always weak in a market with few sellers, eroded further still in the rush to meet demand. War, in short, was good business, or so the critics claimed. Such critiques echoed the "merchants of death" hearings following World War I, Bruce Catton's *War Lords of Washington*,[40] and other more distant claims of war-profiteering throughout history. It mattered little in this analysis that war profiteering far predated capitalism.

The growth of the defense industry only reinforced this construction of the military-industrial complex. In the hothouse atmosphere of the Kennedy defense build-up, followed by the maw of Vietnam, defense contractors such as Lockheed, General Dynamics, McDonnell-Douglas rose on the *Forbes* magazine listing of the largest American corporations. The concentration of wealth in these firms and in the salaries of their leading executives contrasted with the static standard of living of the American laborer. The phenomenon paralleled the perception that working-class boys were going off to fight in Vietnam while the children of the power elite won deferments and safe appointments in the National Guard. Indeed, Vietnam as a capitalist project appeared to confirm classical Marxist theory that capitalism had to keep growing to survive, had to support imperialism in the constant search for new resources and new markets. Class as a category of analysis explained how the defense industry worked and why it found war lucrative and painless. A monied elite used war and preparation for war to gain control over a growing percentage of the nation's wealth.

Capitalism was also invoked in a more limited sense to describe the machinations of defense procurement. Seymour Melman's *Pentagon Capitalism* argued that President Kennedy and his Secretary of Defense, Robert McNamara, had actually addressed the problem posed in Eisenhower's farewell address. Succeeding where Eisenhower had failed, they had imposed civilian control on the military. McNamara, the industry executive turned government administrator, had brought from the private sector his own aides and his own style of rationalizing defense spending. McNamara resolved the missile mess and many other excesses of interservice rivalry. In the process, however, according to Melman, he introduced a new system of weapons procurement that posed greater danger to the Republic than the one it replaced. "Pentagon capitalism" installed "state-management," which "gathered into a very few hands the top economic, political, and military power in the United States." "State-management," claimed Melman, was not the same thing as the military-industrial complex, nor did it reprise the merchants of death. Rather, it "superseded" the military-industrial complex, submerging its market operations in "a closed-loop growth system" that integrated legislative power into the military-industrial nexus. In other words, it was more like Eisenhower's delta of power than it was like the complex he described in his farewell address. "State-management" transcended the garden-variety profiteering of the First World War because it operated across economic classes, representing a "vertical slice of society." It took on "something of the character of a 'garrison society'" because it blurred the "demarcation between military and civilian activity."[41] In other words, it did not really solve the problem of militarism as defined by Huntington; it just worsened "subjective control" of the military by politicizing the military and militarizing the civilians.[42]

"State-management," said Melman, was not "a necessary condition of industrial capitalism." West Germany and Japan, for example, enjoyed higher rates of growth than the United States while spending far less on the military. Still, Melman felt that the United States had to move decisively and soon lest it "become the guardian of a garrison-like society dominated by the Pentagon and its state-management."[43] The concluding chapter of his book asked if the United States would arrive at 1984 by 1974.

Melman answered his own question in the latter year in a new book entitled *The Permanent War Economy: American Capitalism in Decline*. Borrowing his title from a line in Mills's *Power Elite*, Melman claimed that state-management was leading the country into militarism. "Rather than an historically inevitable outcome of capitalist dynamics," he argued, "the American war economy . . . is the combined result of economic and political factors, with the latter finally determining the recourse to militarism."[44] Continuing his earlier argument, Melman claimed that the problem was state capitalism, an aberration of free market economics. The economy had grown so dependent on military spending that an outbreak of peace might send it spiraling into recession, even a return to the conditions of the Great Depression. Others echoed this surmise. One analysis in 1970 had concluded that

> the entire capitalist economy has a stake in militarism. For military spending is responsible for most of the economic growth the country

has experienced in the postwar period. Without militarism, the whole economy would return to the state of collapse from which it was rescued by the Second World War.[45]

The result was a command economy by indirection—state support of the war industry as an end in itself.

The dilemma was parodied in Leonard Lewin's originally anonymous hoax, *Report from Iron Mountain*.[46] Lewin presented the book as the work of a "Special Study Group," released without authorization by one of its members, known only as "John Doe." The group had supposedly been commissioned in 1963 to determine what would happen to the United States in the unlikely event that peace broke out. The members concluded that "an acceptable economic surrogate for the war system will require expenditure of resources for completely nonproductive purposes at a level comparable to that of the military expenditures."[47] Far from needing a moral equivalent of war, as William James had once recommended, America now needed an economic equivalent for war. Until the hoax was revealed, many reviewers and observers handled the book gingerly; it was just plausible enough to give them pause.

The rhetoric of the antiwar movement fed on that witches' brew of social evils: militarism, racism, imperialism, and corporate capitalism. In that litany, militarism and capitalism were the core evils. Imperialism was simply the logical result of mixing capitalism and militarism. Racism was a universal solvent that eroded human decency and revealed the profound injustice lurking beneath American pretensions to be a liberating and ennobling force in the world.

Two Prisms

With the end of the Cold War, the ground began to shift beneath the trope of the military-industrial complex. Militarism especially seemed far less threatening in America than it had at the height of the Cold War. Like Samuel P. Huntington, historian Richard H. Kohn worried about maintaining the right balance of powers in American civil–military relations, though Kohn focused more on firmly exerted civilian control of the military than on Huntington's "objective control."[48] His concerns found partial confirmation in the study he edited with Peter Feaver, *Soldiers and Civilians: The Civil-Military Gap and American National Security*.[49] They and their collaborators discerned an alarming politicization of the military and a penchant for military adventures among a generation of civilian leaders increasingly lacking military service experience. For his part, Feaver tended to treat the military as simply another corporate bureaucracy, responsive to traditional managerial incentives and disincentives.[50] Gone from his prescription was the worry of Huntington and Kohn that the military is *sui generis* in public life, the only large government bureaucracy capable of overthrowing the state and therefore requiring an exceptional social contract.

Meanwhile, the Marxist critique of Pentagon capitalism fell into complete disarray, driven both by the collapse of the Soviet Union and the perceived bankruptcy of Marxist theory. "Marxism is over," declared Ronald Aronson, a self-professed member of Marxism's "last generation."[51] Perry Anderson, founding editor of the *New Left Review*, confirmed the verdict in the first issue of a new series for the iconic journal. "Most of the corpus of Western Marxism has . . . gone out of general circulation," he lamented, and the few remaining practitioners had barricaded themselves in the academy, rejecting his call for "a lucid registration of historical defeat." Globalization emerged as the new face of neoliberal capitalism. As a consequence, wrote Anderson, "high forms" of leftist criticism "have fallen prey to tortuous routines of philosophical deconstruction, while popular forms have become the playground of 'cultural studies' of a sub-sociological type."[52]

As the old critiques lost their purchase in the late 1980s and 1990s, the term "military-industrial complex" also lost its salience. After the Reagan defense build-up peaked in 1986, national and world military spending began to decline. U.S. defense spending as a percentage of GDP shrank from 6.2 percent in 1986 to 2.9 percent in 2000. A steady stream of literature kept the military-industrial complex alive as a trope, but the reality looked far less ominous than it had in 1961. The popularity of the military in general, and such leaders as Colin Powell in particular, lessened the fear of militarism in the public consciousness. Marxist concerns about the capitalist project gave way to worries about globalization, a kinder, gentler vehicle of American hegemony. A cottage industry arose to argue about whether or not the United States was an empire, but the military and industry were no longer the villains portrayed at the height of the Cold War.

The changing landscape of Cold War historiography was reflected in the work of two scholars who undertook to reexamine the phenomenon of the military-industrial complex using frames of reference analogous to the lobby and the trope. Historian Michael Sherry published *In the Shadow of War* in 1995. Political Scientist Aaron Friedberg followed with *In the Shadow of the Garrison State* in 2000. Both books adopted imagery of a shadow hanging over the United States in the second half of the twentieth century. Both defined their shadows singularly, as militarization and statism, respectively. And both saw the dominant trends of the Cold War beginning during the Depression, in the policies of Franklin Roosevelt. But their styles of argument and analysis could not have been more different. Where Michael Sherry focused on public rhetoric, in almost a poststructuralist concentration on text, Friedberg examined the concrete evidence of budgets, force levels, weapons systems, research programs, institutions, and policies. Sherry focused on public discourse while Friedberg addressed the power and structure of the defense establishment, which so worried Eisenhower.

Sherry's magisterial history portrayed a constant pattern of militarization running from Roosevelt's New Deal to the post–Cold War policies of the Clinton administration. The military-industrial complex of the early Cold War was for him, as for Arthur Schlesinger, an effect, not a cause. The scale and intractability of the Great Depression moved Roosevelt to invoke military rhetoric, to enlist the citizenry in a war on economic conditions. His first inaugural address on March 4, 1933, promised to treat unemployment "as we would treat the emergency of a war." He called Americans to be "a trained and loyal army." He promised to seek, if necessary, "broad Executive power to wage a war against the emergency, as great as the power that would be given to me if we were in fact invaded by a foreign foe."[53] For Sherry this was tantamount to militarization, which he defined as "the process by which war and national security became consuming anxieties and provided the memories, models, and metaphors that shaped broad areas of national life."[54] He viewed militarization as a "broader term" than militarism, a "dynamic process" as opposed to a "static condition." Because he wanted to avoid the "politically charged" implications of militarism, he discounted the logical sequence that militarization breeds militarism. He did, however, allow that the country had flirted with militarism in the immediate aftermath of Vietnam.[55]

In the Shadow of War was a history of public rhetoric. It moved from one military metaphor to another, from the war on poverty to the war on cancer, from Richard Nixon's permanent state of war against his countless enemies, real and imagined, to the blatant militancy of some radical feminists. Popular culture swam in military metaphors, from the "remasculanization of America"[56] following Vietnam to the appeal of "Star

Wars"—the movie and the strategic defense system. If discourse was the medium of militarization, if "memories, models, and metaphors" are the measure of militarization, then the United States was surely a militarized society during the Cold War.

Sherry paid little specific attention to the military-industrial complex, treating it, like Schlesinger, as a symptom and not a disease. He notes that World War II "effected a partnership between big government and big business," though it appeared to Sherry to have been the partnership that Eisenhower was advocating during the Depression, not the one he encountered in office. Sherry lamented within the Air Force the "technological fanaticism" over strategic bombing that he had theorized in his earlier *The Rise of American Air Power: The Creation of Armageddon* (1987). And he believed that America's leaders set the country on the path to militarization before World War II had ended, fixing the trajectory by the time the Korean War began. During that time they

> sought to disseminate an ideology of preparedness, to forge a permanent military-industrial-scientific establishment, to reorganize the armed forces, to institute a permanent system of universal training, to acquire far-flung military bases, to occupy defeated enemies with American forces, to retain a monopoly of atomic weapons, and to create a high-tech Pax Aeronautica.[57]

His book, however, pursued none of these topics. He simply noted that scholars have been unable to agree on the origins or terminology of the phenomenon. Mills had called it a "permanent war economy"; others spoke of "military Keynesianism," "military-industrial complex," or "metropolitan-military complex," none of which Sherry defined or explored. He did note that intellectuals invoked the military-industrial complex in their opposition to the Vietnam War, but he concluded that the "intellectual" examinations of militarization were more the product of Vietnam-era crisis than its catalyst." The same, of course, was true of critiques of the military-industrial complex.[58]

In his *In the Shadow of the Garrison State* (2000), Aaron Friedberg posed an entirely different question for the same period of American history, although it covered much of the same ground. Did the United States succumb during the Cold War to the danger perceived by George Kennan in 1946? Did America become like the enemy? In William McNeill's terms, did the United States build a command economy?[59] Friedberg did not couch his question in terms of Michael Sherry's militarization, but he approximated Melman's "state-management." His touchstone was Harold Lasswell's garrison state, from which he took his title. His metric, his category of analysis, was not Lasswell's "socialization of danger," but "statism." By this he understood, in Weberian terms, an increase in "the size and strength of the executive branch of the federal government."[60] If there were a military-industrial complex, it would be administered and funded through the executive branch. The answer to his question would be found there.

Friedberg concluded that the United States resisted statism in the Cold War. Anti-statist forces deeply embedded in American ideas, institutions, and politics resisted the accretion of power in the executive branch. Exploring in turn strategy, funding, and military personnel levels, Friedberg found that the powerful statist tendencies impelled by the Cold War were arrested or contained at every turn. Devoting three chapters to industry, weapons systems, and technology—the constituents of the military-industrial complex—he arrived at the same conclusion in each case. A profit-seeking arms industry was more innovative and efficient than the Soviets and no more warmongering than an arsenal system staffed with government bureaucrats would have been. "The much bedeviled members of the 'military-industrial complex,'" he concluded, "did good by doing well."[61]

Judged by Friedberg's criteria, the military-industrial complex succeeded. The surprising result of the Cold War was not that the forces of statism swelled the executive branch of government so dangerously, but that they increased it so little. To have won the Cold War with so little damage to the nation's democratic principles and institutions was an outcome worthy of Dwight Eisenhower's relentless struggle against the statist tendencies of the military-industrial complex.

THE LOBBY

What, then, was the political entity Eisenhower warned about and how did it evolve through the remainder of the Cold War? A summary something like the following might capture at least its flavor, its benefits and risks, its achievements and crimes.

Dwight Eisenhower inherited from Harry Truman the Korean War, an accepted national policy of containment, and a reluctant and still inchoate commitment to maintain a standing military establishment in peacetime.

He ended the war, endorsed the policy, and fought like his predecessor to keep that military establishment within bounds. He introduced "The New Look" and then the "New, New Look" in an attempt to find a security policy the United States could afford. Political pressure, fueled by such developments as the discovery of a Soviet ICBM program, the so-called bomber gap, and the missile mess began to take the form of a campaign issue for 1960. When the Soviet Union launched Sputnik in 1957, the pressure mounted still further. If the Soviet Union had the technology to place a satellite in orbit, then it could place a nuclear weapon on New York. Furthermore, while air defenses offered at least partial protection from bomber attack, no known technology could intercept an intercontinental ballistic missile. The Soviet Union, hitherto seen as a backward and underdeveloped society, had produced two paired technologies that left the United States defenseless to devastating attack. In this circumstance, President Eisenhower found himself accused of allowing the nation to fall behind an avowed and dangerous foe.

In the wake of Sputnik, public fear bordering on paranoia, already manifest in the McCarthy panic of the early 1950s, broke over the Eisenhower administration. The military-industrial complex pushed public policy in the direction of more and better weapons, expansion of roles and missions, and mobilization of the civilian economy in the service of the state. The Army and the Air Force launched parallel development programs to field intermediate-range ballistic missiles.[62] The Navy and the Air Force raced each other to develop solid-fuel ballistic missiles, one to arm strategic submarines and the other to enhance the readiness of land-based ICBMs.[63] All the services proposed space activities to ensure for themselves a niche in this new realm of human activity. While the United States continued to fight the Cold War with diplomacy, propaganda, foreign aid, and other traditional tools of international relations, the race for new and better weapons defined the East-West struggle. Other activities of the federal government, such as intelligence, energy, and space flight became extensions of the Cold War by other means.

The argument over defense spending persisted throughout the Cold War under the banner "How Much Is Enough?"[64] Could the country afford to place an economic limit on its own security? Eisenhower argued strenuously that it could, indeed it must. He conceived a "great equation" that balanced military preparedness against sustainable economic growth. He expected the Cold War to be fought over "the long haul"; the winner would have to provide adequate security without bankrupting itself.[65]

This calculus helps to explain the defense expenditures of the Cold War and especially the nation's investment in research and development.

As Benjamin Fordham makes clear in his essay in this volume, the United States sustained unprecedented peacetime levels of defense spending through the Cold War and beyond. Yet contrary to Eisenhower's fears, these expenditures never crippled the economy. The unparalleled growth of the United States economy since World War II allowed the country to pay for a robust defense with a relatively small and declining percentage of GDP.[66]

Eisenhower's warning about a "scientific and technical elite" reflected his parallel fear that research and development might grow ruinously expensive; indeed such outlays quadrupled as a percentage of GDP during his presidency. While America's commitment to qualitative superiority in weapons did keep expenditures high throughout the Cold War and beyond, at least as a percentage of the federal budget, economic growth also absorbed the impact of this spending.[67]

Some segments of industry and academia evolved to match government spending. In 1958, thirty of the top fifty companies on the *Fortune* Five Hundred list of the largest industrial corporations also appeared on the list of the top one hundred defense contractors.[68] Government contracts—mostly defense related—to favored universities vaulted those institutions to national prominence. MIT, Stanford, and the Johns Hopkins University, for example, held perennial positions on the list of leading defense contractors.[69] Critics came to call it "the contract state."[70] Norman Mailer called it the "corporate state," a combination of the military-industrial complex, Mills's power elite, and John Kenneth Galbraith's *New Industrial State*.[71] Other economists joined Seymour Melman in warning that the country would sink into a "permanent war economy."[72]

Eisenhower's "delta of power" became an arena in which powerful political and economic forces contended for defense contracts. Would-be contractors lobbied their legislative representatives to pressure the Defense Department in favor of their bids. Legislators sought defense contracts on their own initiative, both to bring dollars to their district and to encourage campaign contributions from constituent contractors. The military services curried favor with legislative allies by placing contracts in their states and districts. Finally, the services realized that distributing contracts and subcontracts across a broad array of congressional districts provided political insulation against cancellation of their programs. The pork barrel of nineteenth-century American politics turned into a powerful, sophisticated, complex infrastructure that presidents from Eisenhower to Clinton often found irresistible. Even the end of the Cold War failed to extinguish this practice; the administration of President Clinton supported the construction of Seawolf submarines primarily as a jobs program for Groton, Connecticut, home of the manufacturer Electric Boat Company. This was by no means the first weapons system targeted at domestic politics and economics rather than a foreign adversary.

President Jimmy Carter, a former naval officer and a reform candidate for the presidency, discovered the power of the military-industrial complex in his fight over the B-1 bomber. Carter inherited from his predecessors a long-standing program to build a successor to the B-52, the workhorse of America's strategic bomber force and a mainstay of the air campaign in Vietnam. First proposed to President Eisenhower in 1957 as the B-70 Valkyrie, the airplane was repeatedly deferred or rejected either because its costs or capabilities were suspect or because the B-52 was still adequate. But Phoenix-like, the B-70 rose from the ashes, reinvented by the military-industrial complex as a cruise-missile-carrier, as a "Long Range Combat Aircraft," and as a "Strategic Weapons Launcher." President Carter thought he had terminated the program for good, but his successor, Ronald Reagan, especially sensitive to the aerospace industry in his home state of California, revived the airplane (now called the B-1) and put it into production in 1986. The last of the initial order of one hundred planes came off the assembly line in 1988, just in time for the end of the Cold War. At $280 million apiece, more than ten times the projected price of the B-70 proposed to Eisenhower (three times the price in constant dollars), the aircraft never approached the performance capabilities promised for it.[73] Furthermore, it would have been obsolescent at birth had not its successor, the B-2 Stealth Bomber, been even later in development and far more costly, rising finally to more than $2 billion per plane.

Stories such as this one illustrate two characteristics of Cold War technology. The first is the special form of obsolescence that gripped the arms industry. United States weapons systems often competed with themselves. Instead of measuring U.S. technology against the capabilities of the Soviet Union or other potential adversaries, the Department of Defense often gauged its needs against a projected wave of theoretical capability. The test of a weapons system was not its parity with the weapons systems of enemies or potential enemies, but rather parity with the next generation of weapons systems that industry could envision. The

United States had to develop the next generation because it could not run the risk that an adversary might steal a march. The system produced "requirements" to build weapons not because they were needed but because they were possible.

This criterion bred a kind of technological determinism, a second characteristic of Cold War weapons systems. The B-1, which journalist Nick Kotz called the "born again bomber," seemed to have a life of its own. Once proposed, it proved impervious to politics, economics, failures of performance, or even the waning of the Cold War. But it was not the technology as such that persisted and prevailed. Rather, the web of war, politics, economics, and technology formed a cocoon that made cancellation of a weapons program next to impossible, even in the face of lessening conflict, corrupt politics, bad economics, or failed technology. Weapons systems routinely came on line late, over cost, and under specifications. Promoters of military technology mastered the technique of "buying in," Washington jargon for inflated promises sustained until the sunk costs in a project made it too embarrassing for Congress to cut it off. The B-1 case was exceptional for its longevity and resilience, but it was hardly unique.

Perhaps the most salient characteristic of the military-industrial complex in its heyday was the stunning contrast between its marvels of technological achievement and its scandalous institutional excesses. The complex produced the arsenal that won the Cold War and contributed to the transformation of modern life. Reconnaissance satellites tracked the cars of Soviet officials on the streets of Moscow. The F-111 swing-wing attack bomber flew at two and a half times the speed of sound but landed slowly enough to stop on an aircraft carrier. Nuclear ballistic missile submarines eluded enemy detection for months on end while bristling with multi-warheaded missiles preprogrammed to deliver irresistible, cataclysmic retaliation against any attack on the vital interests of the United States. Ground-based ballistic missiles in the United States and around the world stood on constant alert to launch-on-warning still more retaliation with intercontinental accuracy measured in hundreds of meters. The Global Positioning Satellite system allowed American ground troops in the Gulf War of 1991 to navigate the pathless deserts of the Mesopotamian Valley with speed and accuracy that completely befuddled the indigenous soldiers and amazed America's coalition partners. Smart weapons allowed American soldiers to stand out of harm's way and launch strikes at room-size targets while minimizing collateral damage. Stealth technology degraded the power of radar, one of the decisive weapons of World War II, allowing American aircraft to fly with impunity through the enemy's electronic defenses. Developing effective ballistic missile defenses defied the best efforts of the military-industrial complex, but just the threat that the United States would attempt it contributed to the collapse of the Soviet Union. In the end, the military-industrial complex built up an arsenal of conventional weapons and capabilities almost as destructive and decisive as the nuclear arms with which the country began the Cold War.

But that same complex also bred political, social, and economic scandal. Defense contractors charged $435 for a hammer and $1,868 for a toilet seat cover.[74] And the military paid. The "missile mess" of the Eisenhower administration suggested services more interested in competing with one another than with the Soviet Union. Security classification routinely masked information from the American public that was well known to the Soviet government. The nation accrued a stockpile of 32,000 nuclear warheads, enough to destroy the Soviet Union many times over. A revolving door shuffled defense and industry executives back and forth despite the evident and egregious conflicts of interest. Defense industries received corporate welfare and insulation from market forces. Many of Eisenhower's scientific-technical elite served the complex in the name of serving national security. "Defense intellectuals" and "beltway bandits" (companies in the vicinity of the beltway surrounding Washington, D.C. that specialize in contracting for government) provided support services for the complex.

The good news is that the military-industrial complex won the Cold War. For better or for worse, it produced the arsenal that sustained deterrence long enough for the democratic, free-market system to prevail over the authoritarian, command economy of the Soviet Union. The bad news is that the complex exacted a high price. As Sovietologist George Kennan warned in 1946, the United States ran the risk in the Cold War of taking on the shape of the enemy, of becoming what it fought against. If the United States did not become a garrison state, as had seemed possible during the worst nights of the McCarthy era, it at least took on many of the aspects of a command economy, one driven not by market forces but by the imperative of state policy.[75]

This particular combination of forces in Cold War America made Eisenhower's military-industrial complex unique. All industrialized states in the twentieth century institutionalized some relationship between war and technology. Many states had developed this relationship in the nineteenth century or even earlier. It was only in the United States, however, that the concept of a military-industrial complex became part of the public debate. Born in World War II, energized in the McCarthy era, labeled by Eisenhower, made salient in the antiwar movement of the Vietnam era, and defused by the waning of the Cold War, the military-industrial complex cut a swath through American history unmatched by the experience of any other nation. No country claimed as much for its military technology or achieved as much. No country worried more about the militarization of its institutions. No country was shaped as forcefully by the science and technology of war.

The phenomenon transformed America in at least five ways.[76] First, it added a third dimension, industry, to the civil-military relationship as defined by Huntington. A president might demand allegiance to his policies within the military, but he had no comparable tool to keep industry in line. The military services and industry always wanted more and better arms, creating upward pressure on the defense budget from both within and without the executive branch of government. These pressures were tempered by divisions within the military-industrial alliance: some companies served more than one military service and some services bought from multiple suppliers. But there was honor among these raiders on the Treasury. Seldom did they promote their own project by attacking the projects of others.[77]

Second, the military-industrial complex transformed the relationship between the state and industry, drawing the government in some instances into the "state-management" perceived by Melman or the command economy feared by McNeill. Private vendors such as TRW and Haliburton received enormous contracts from the government to perform functions previously assigned to the military services or to conduct research previously undertaken in government arsenals. Skills and capabilities essential to national security came to reside exclusively in private firms. Defense contractors such as Lockheed Aircraft Corporation received generous deals and even bail-outs to ensure that their special capabilities were not lost to the nation. Pentagon capitalism became a synonym for poor work and high cost; the C-5A cargo plane was the classic exemplar of all that was wrong with the system.[78]

Third, the military-industrial complex changed the relationship among government agencies, exacerbating interservice rivalries within the Department of Defense and drawing nominally civilian agencies such as NASA and the Department of Energy into the military orbit. NASA was an artifact of the Cold War and a stepchild of the Department of Defense.

It imported military officers in times of crisis, as after the Apollo 204 fire of 1967 and the *Challenger* accident of 1986, and it provided the Air Force with below-cost shuttle flights in return for political help in saving the program. Similarly, weapons development was always the tail wagging the dog within the succession of government agencies created to oversee nuclear power. Commercial nuclear power in the United States could not escape the "nuclear fear" that Americans associated with the weaponry, not least because commercial reactors in the United States were based on military designs.[79] Other realms of national life, from intelligence gathering to environmental preservation, were similarly shaped by the imperatives of the military-industrial complex.

Fourth, the complex transformed American universities in much the way that Eisenhower had feared and profoundly reshaped the research agenda of the scientific and technical community. The scientific and technical elite that Eisenhower worried about remained housed primarily in the nation's universities, exploiting a model developed in World War II. The Department of Defense was the largest single supporter of science and technology in the Cold War. In 1984, 36 percent of MIT's engineering research budget came from the Department of Defense, as did 71 percent of the funding for its Laboratory for Computer Science, 62 percent for the Artificial Intelligence Laboratory, and 40 percent for the Research Laboratory of Electronics. Funding like this raised MIT and other universities to national and international prominence, but it also polarized campuses during the Vietnam era, introduced unprecedented and often unwelcome levels of secrecy to academic research, and in the minds of many critics corrupted the research agenda of the scientific community.[80]

Finally, the military-industrial complex stamped the relationship between science and technology with some of its most potent images. *Dr. Strangelove* personified the madness in MAD—mutual assured destruction. Vietnam came to be represented as "the electronic battlefield" and "the perfect war" because of American reliance on gee-whiz weaponry.[81] The press labeled President Reagan's Strategic Defense Initiative "Star Wars," a play on the science-fiction movie then filling theaters. The light and sound show over Baghdad in the two Iraq wars turned modern, high-tech war into theater. At the same time, Americans immersed themselves in the consumer electronics, computers, Jeeps, Hummers, and navigation systems that spun off from the military-industrial complex. As with everything else about the complex, the consequences were ambiguous.

The Present

The military-industrial complex–the lobby, not the trope—achieved all that Eisenhower had hoped for going back to his days at the Army War College: an alliance between the military and industry to give the United States the best tools of war in the world. But the denizens of the military-industrial complex also exaggerated the external threat, shaped national policies to suit their parochial interests, stoked the arms race with the Soviet Union, impelled the government toward unwise and unnecessary military acquisitions, and inflated the cost of defense through corruption, mismanagement, and cronyism. Because of America's unprecedented economic growth, these malignancies remained at tolerable levels, but they were malignancies nonetheless.

In the end, Eisenhower displayed a sure grasp of the concepts embodied in the military-industrial complex, both the lobby and the trope. Himself a member of the power elite, he tended to discount the threat it posed to democratic government. The garrison state worried him more, the subordination of democracy and free enterprise to a command economy born of fear. With George Kennan and William McNeill, he worried that the United States could end up like the Soviet Union, a victim of Aaron Friedberg's statism. Furthermore, Eisenhower parsed the trope of the military-industrial complex. He did not believe that the United States was becoming militarized in the sense understood by Michael Sherry, but he did fear the Huntingtonian militarism bred by the erosion of civilian control. He did not credit the Marxist critique of capitalism as a threat to freedom and a spur to empire, but he did worry about the Pentagon capitalism of Seymour Melman and its attendant state-management.

In the end, Eisenhower had it right, though his concerns were overtaken by events he failed to anticipate. The Cold War was a contest between political and economic systems. The United States won because it was stronger in both realms; it resisted the trap of the garrison state. Friedberg claims that the United States won because of deep-rooted institutional resistance to statism. Budget figures suggest the United States won because its economy grew far more rapidly than defense spending. In any case, it avoided the danger that worried Eisenhower most, drowning the economy in a wave of military spending. The military-industrial complex lives on as a lobby and a trope, but neither has the purchase on American politics that it knew at the height of the Cold War.

ACKNOWLEDGMENT

Portions of the essay are excerpted from Alex Roland, *The Military-Industrial Complex* (Washington: American Historical Association, 2001) with the permission of the American Historical Association. That essay, sponsored jointly by the AHA and the Society for the History of Technology, attempted to define what the military-industrial complex (MIC) was historically. This essay offers a reconceptualization of the topic. The goal here is to survey more fully the theoretical literature on the MIC and also to explore the gap between what my colleague Tami Davis Biddle calls the rhetoric and reality of this historical phenomenon. I am grateful to Andrew Bacevich, Malachi Hacohen, Richard Kohn, and Seymour Mauskopf for insightful readings of this essay in draft.

Notes

1. Tami Davis Biddle, *Rhetoric and Reality in Air Warfare: The Evolution of British and American Ideas about Strategic Bombing, 1914–1945* (Princeton: Princeton University Press, 2002).

2. Interview of General Andrew J. Goodpaster, Jr., by Eugene M. Emme and Alex Roland, the Pentagon, July 22, 1974, NASA Historical Reference Collection, File Number 13469.

3. Stephen J. Zempolich, "Dwight David Eisenhower and the Military-Industrial Complex: Advocacy to Opposition, 1928–1961," Senior Honors Thesis, Duke University, 1985.

4. Eisenhower appears to have had in mind what Herbert Hoover called an "associative state." See Ellis Hawley, "Herbert Hoover, the Commerce Secretariat and the Vision of an 'Associative State,' 1921–1928," *Journal of American History* 41 (June 1974): 116–40.

5. Dwight D. Eisenhower, Memorandum for Directors and Chiefs of War Department General and Special Staff Divisions and Bureaus and the Commanding Generals of the Major Commands, "Scientific and Technological Resources as Military Assets," quoted in Seymour Melman, *Pentagon Capitalism: The Political Economy of War* (New York: McGraw-Hill, 1970), 231–34, quote at 233.

6. Dwight D. Eisenhower, "Farewell Address," http://www.americanrhetoric .com/speeches/dwighteisenhowerfare~, accessed May 25, 2004.

7. The term "big science," which Eisenhower did not use, appears to have been introduced by Alvin Weinberg, "Impact of Large-Scale Science on the United States," *Science* 134 (July 21, 1961): 161–64.

8. James R. Killian, Jr., *Sputnik, Scientists, and Eisenhower: A Memoir of the First Special Assistant to the President for Science and Technology* (Cambridge: MIT Press, 1977), 237–39; George B. Kistiakowsky, *A Scientist at the White House: The Private Diary of President Eisenhower's Special Assistant for Science and Technology* (Cambridge: Harvard University Press, 1976), 424–25; see also Herbert F. York, *Race to Oblivion: A Participant's View of the Arms Race* (New York: Simon and Schuster, 1970), 9, at http://www.learnworld.com/ZNW/LWText. York.RaceToOblivion.html#index, accessed June 18, 2004.

9. Dana Adams Schmidt, "Eisenhower Talk Scored Moon Race," *The New York Times* (June 13, 1971), 67, quoted in Reita Priest, "The Military-Industrial Complex: A Content and Usage Analysis from 1961 to 1990," undergraduate research paper, Department of History, Duke University, April 21, 2004, 3.

10. Forrest C. Pogue, *George C. Marshall: Education of a General, 1880–1939* (New York: Viking Press, 1963), 280.

11. Joel Davidson, *The Unsinkable Fleet: The Politics of U.S. Naval Expansion in World War II* (Annapolis: U.S. Naval Institute Press, 1996), 176–78, *et passim*.

12. For example, in a radio address in May 1953, he said that "there is no such thing as maximum military security short of total mobilization of all our national resources. Such security would compel us to imitate the methods of the dictator." Dwight D. Eisenhower, "Radio Address to the American People on the National Security and Its Costs," http://www.presidency.ucsb.edu/site/docs/pppus.php? admin = 034&year = 1953&id = 82, accessed 10 August 2004. Kennan had ended his famous "long telegram" from Moscow in 1946 with the caution: "The greatest danger that can befall us in coping with this problem of Soviet communism, is that we shall allow ourselves to become like those with whom we are coping." Kennan to Secretary of State, February 22, 1946, http://www.gwu.edu/~nsarchiv/ coldwar/documents/episode-1/kennan.htm, accessed August 15, 2004

13. Alex Roland, "The Grim Paraphernalia: Eisenhower and the Garrison State," in Dennis Showalter, ed., *Forging the Shield: Eisenhower and National Security in the 21st Century* (Carson City, NV: Imprint Publications, 2005), 13–22.

14. Harold Lasswell, "The Garrison State," *The American Journal of Sociology* 46 (January 1941): 455–68, at 455.

15. Ibid., 458.

16. These were the conditions of subjective control of the military identified by Samuel P. Huntington in *The Soldier and the State: The Theory and Politics of Civil-Military Relations* (Cambridge: Belknap Press of Harvard University Press, 1957). See pp. 361–62.

17. Emmet John Hughes, *The Ordeal of Power: A Political Memoir of the Eisenhower Years* (New York: Atheneum, 1963), 250.

18. Dwight D. Eisenhower, "Address at the Annual Convention of the National Junior Chamber of Commerce, Minneapolis, Minnesota," June 10, 1953, http://

www.presidency.ucsb.edu/site/docs/pppus.php?admin = 034&year = 1953&id =, accessed August 9, 10, 2004.

19. Dwight D. Eisenhower, *The Public Papers of the President of the United States: Dwight D. Eisenhower, 1953* (Washington, DC: 1960), 182.

20. John C. Lonnquest, "The Face of Atlas: General Bernard Schriever and the Development of the Atlas Intercontinental Ballistic Missile, 1953-1960," PhD dissertation, Duke University, 1996, 92. The following account is drawn from Lonnquest and from H.L. Nieburg, *In the Name of Science* (Chicago: Quadrangle Books, 1966), 200–217.

21. United States, Congress, House, Committee on Government Operations, *Organization and Management of Missile Programs. Hearings before a Subcommittee of the Committee on Government Operations*, 86th Cong., 1st sess., February 4–March 20, 1959.

22. Michael Beschloss, *Mayday: The U-2 Affair* (New York: Harper & Row, 1987), 119–20, 149–50; Stephen I. Schwartz, "$4 Trillion and Counting," *Bulletin of the Atomic Scientists* 51 (Nov.–Dec. 1995): 32–51. Schwartz estimated that the United States spent $330 billion total on bomber defense during the Cold War.

23. Edmund Beard, *Developing the ICBM: A Study in Bureaucratic Politics* (New York: Columbia University Press, 1976), 206; Michael H. Armacost, *The Politics of Weapons Innovation: The Thor-Jupiter Controversy* (New York: Columbia University Press, 1969). Eisenhower said that if ballistic missiles were introduced, they should replace some other weapons system. Dwight D. Eisenhower, "The President's News Conference," November 5, 1958, http://www.presidency.ucsb.edu/site/docs/pppus.php?admin = 034&year = 1958&id = 310, accessed August 10, 2004.

24. Walter A. McDougall, . . . *the Heavens and the Earth: A Political History of the Space Age* (New York: Basic Books, 1985), 146–76.

25. Michael Sherry, *The Rise of American Air Power: The Creation of Armageddon* (New Haven: Yale University Press, 1987), 273.

26. Burton H. Klein, *The Economics of the Military-Industrial Complex* (S.I.: s.n., 1970); Sidney Lens, *The Military-Industrial Complex* (Philadelphia: Pilgrim Press, 1970); William Proxmire, *Report from Wasteland: America's Military-Industrial Complex* (New York: Praeger, 1970); Richard F. Kaufman, *The War Profiteers* (Indianapolis: Bobbs-Merrill, 1970); *War Incorporated: The Completed Picture of the Congressional, Military, Industrial, Academic Complex* (Berkeley: Student Research Facility, 1971); Richard Barnet, *The Economy of Death* (New York: Atheneum, 1971); Berkeley Rice, *The C-5A Scandal: An Inside Story of the Military-Industrial Complex* (Boston: Houghton-Mifflin, 1971); Sam Charles Sarkesian, *The Military-Industrial Complex: A Reassessment* (Beverly Hills: Sage Publications, 1972); Carroll W. Pursell, comp., *The Military-Industrial Complex* (New York: Harper & Row, 1972); Seymour Melman, *Pentagon*

Capitalism: The Political Economy of War (New York: McGraw Hill, 1970); John Kenneth Galbraith, *How To Control the Military* (Garden City, NY: Doubleday, 1969); H. L. Nieburg, *In the Name of Science* (Chicago: Quadrangle Books, 1966).

27. John Stanley Baumgartner, *The Lonely Warriors: The Case for the Military-Industrial Complex* (Los Angeles: Nash, 1970).

28. Paul A. C. Koistinen, *The "Industrial-Military Complex" in Historical Perspective: World War I* (Indianapolis: Bobbs-Merrill, 1970); Steven Rosen, ed., *Testing the Theory of the Military-Industrial Complex* (Lexington, MA: Lexington Books, 1973).

29. Alfred Vagts, *A History of Militarism: Romance and Realities of a Profession* (New York: Norton, 1937).

30. Huntington, *The Soldier and the State.*

31. Doyne Dawson, *The Origins of Western Warfare: Militarism and Morality in the Ancient World* (Boulder, CO: Westview Press, 1996), 4–8, 51–52, 101–7, 112–14, 159–62; Victor Davis Hanson, *Carnage and Culture: Landmark Battles in the Rise of Western Power* (New York: Doubleday, 2001), 46–59, 118–32, *et passim.*

32. Morris Janowitz, *The Professional Soldier: A Social and Political Portrait* (Glencoe, IL: Free Press, 1960).

33. Arthur Schlesinger, Jr., *A Thousand Days: John F. Kennedy in the White House* (Greenwich, CT: Fawcett Publications, 1965), 292.

34. Kaufman, *War Profiteers,* 171, 175.

35. Will Liles, "A Study of the National Action/Research on the Military Industrial Complex," seminar paper, Duke University, April 26, 2004.

36. http://www.afsc.org/about/mission.htm, accessed August 28, 2004.

37. Liles, "NARMIC," 12.

38. William Appleman Williams, *The Tragedy of American Diplomacy* (Cleveland: World, 1959); and *The Roots of Modern American Empire: A Study of the Growth and Shaping of Social Consciousness in a Marketplace Society* (New York: Random House, 1969).

39. Gabriel Kolko, *Anatomy of a War: Vietnam, the United States, and the Modern Historical Experience* (New York: Pantheon, 1985); James William Gibson, *The Perfect War: Technowar in Vietnam* (New York: Atlantic Monthly Press, 1986).

40. Bruce Catton, *The War Lords of Washington* (New York: Harcourt, Brace, 1948).

41. Melman, *Pentagon Capitalism,* 206, 219–20, 225, 216–17.

42. "It should be underscored . . . ," he said, "that the civilian officers controlling the military establishment, including the state-management, do not constitute what is termed elsewhere [i.e., in Huntington] 'civilian control over the

military.' This is because the crucial factor is the institution's nature, not the style of clothing worn by its top directors. The overwhelmingly military character of the state-management dominates the institution, not the personal professional identity of its chiefs." Ibid., 216.

43. Ibid., 207, 227.

44. Seymour Melman, *The Permanent War Economy: American Capitalism in Decline* (New York: Simon and Schuster, 1974), 260–261.

45. Michael Reich and David Finkelhor, "The Military Industrial Complex: No Way Out," in Tom Christoffel, David Finkelhor, and Dan Gilbarg, eds., *Up against the American Myth* (New York: Holt, Rinehart, Winston 1970), 82, quoted in Melman, *The Permanent War Economy*, 288.

46. *Report from Iron Mountain on the Possibility and Desirability of Peace* (New York: Dial Press, 1967).

47. *The Report from Iron Mountain*, section 7, at http://www.mega.nu:8080/ampp/ironmtn.html#sec.7, accessed June 19, 2004.

48. Richard H. Kohn, "Out of Control: The Crisis in Civil-Military Relations," *The National Interest*, no. 35 (Spring 1994): 3–17; "Erosion of Civilian Control of the Military in the United States Today," *Naval War College Review* 55 (Summer 2002): 8–59. See also Kohn's "How Democracies Control the Military," *Journal of Democracy* 8 (1997): 140–53.

49. Peter D. Feaver and Richard H. Kohn, eds., *Soldiers and Civilians: The Civil-Military Gap and American National Security* (Cambridge: MIT Press, 2001).

50. Peter D. Feaver, *Armed Servants: Agency, Oversight, and Civil-Military Relations* (Cambridge: Harvard University Press, 2003); see also Peter D. Feaver and Christopher Gelpi, *Choosing Your Battles: American Civil-Military Relations and the Use of Force* (Princeton: Princeton University Press, 2004).

51. Ronald Aronson, *After Marxism* (New York: Guildford Press, 1995), 1.

52. Perry Anderson, "Renewals," *New Left Review*, ns, 1 (January–February 2000), at http://www.newleftreview.net/NLR23501.shtml, accessed May 28, 2004, quotes at 10, 9, 12.

53. Michael Sherry, *In the Shadow of War: The United States since 1930* (New Haven: Yale University Press, 1995), 15.

54. Ibid., xi.

55. Ibid, xi, 340.

56. Susan Jeffords, *The Remasculanization of America: Gender and the Vietnam War* (Bloomington: Indiana University Press, 1989).

57. Sherry, *In the Shadow of War*, 125.

58. Sherry, *In the Shadow of War*, 72, 81, 125, 141, 271.

59. William H. McNeill, *The Pursuit of Power: Technology, Armed Force, and Society since A.D. 1000* (Chicago: University of Chicago Press, 1982); see especially chap. 8.

60. Aaron L. Friedberg, *In the Shadow of the Garrison State: America's Anti-Statism and Its Cold War Grand Strategy* (Princeton: Princeton University Press, 2000), 11.

61. Ibid., 345.

62. Armacost, *The Politics of Weapons Innovation.*

63. George A. Reed, "U.S. Defense Policy, U.S. Air Force Doctrine, and Strategic Nuclear Weapon Systems, 1958–1964: The Case of the Minuteman ICBM," PhD dissertation, Duke University, 1986.

64. Alain C. Enthoven and K. Wayne Smith, *How Much Is Enough?: Shaping the Defense Program, 1961–1969* (New York: Harper & Row, 1971).

65. Robert R. Bowie and Richard H. Immerman, *Waging Peace: How Eisenhower Shaped an Enduring Cold War Strategy* (New York: Oxford University Press, 1998), esp. 75, 96–108.

66. Benjamin O. Fordham, in this volume.

67. Alex Roland, *The Military-Industrial Complex* (Washington, DC: American Historical Association, 2001), 9–13.

68. "The Fortune Directory: The 500 Largest U.S. Industrial Corporations," *Fortune* (July 1959): 12–16; William Proxmire, "Retired High-Ranking Military Officers," in Pursell, ed., *Military Industrial Complex*, 260–62.

69. Stuart W. Leslie, *The Cold War and American Science: The Military-Industrial-Academic Complex at Stanford and MIT* (New York: Columbia University Press, 1993).

70. Nieburg, *In the Name of Science*, 184–99.

71. John Kenneth Galbraith, *The New Industrial State* (Boston: Houghton Mifflin, 1967).

72. Seymour Melman, *Pentagon Capitalism: The Political Economy of War* (New York: McGraw-Hill, 1970).

73. Nick Kotz, *Wild Blue Yonder: Money, Politics, and the B-1 Bomber* (New York: Pantheon Books, 1988).

74. James Barron, "High Cost of Military Parts," *New York Times*, September 1. 1983, 1, at http://web.lexis-nexis.com/universe/docu . . . zS&_md5 = 35633b59a4 9f57d22abb78c0a2ec4ee3, accessed March 9, 2000; and Mark Thompson, "Pliers Cost $999; New Spending Probe Urged," *The Record* (Washington), June 20, 1990, A01, at http://web/lexis-nexis.com/universe/docu . . . zS&_md5 = 96886e ab9a769b317eccbae65441a696. For a thoughtful discussion of such overruns, see Jacques Gansler, *Affording Defense* (Cambridge: MIT Press, 1991), 195–207.

75. McNeill, *Pursuit of Power*; see especially chap. 8.

76. Roland, *Military-Industrial Complex*, 19–45.

77. Andrew Stephens, "Cold Competition: A Study of Defense Contractors and their Role in Interservice Rivalry during the Cold War," seminar paper, Duke University, April 25, 2004.

78. Rice, *The C-5A Scandal*.

79. Spencer Weart, *Nuclear Fear: A History of Images* (Cambridge: Harvard University Press, 1988).

80. Paul Forman, "Behind Quantum Electronics: National Security as Basis for Physical Research in the United States, 1940–1960," *Historical Studies in the Physical Sciences*, 18 (1987): 149–229; and Forman and José M. Sánchez-Ron, eds., *National Military Establishments and the Advancement of Science and Technology: Studies in 20th Century History* (Dordrecht: Kluwer Academic Publishers, 1996).

81. Paul Dickson, *The Electronic Battlefield* (Bloomington: Indiana University Press, 1976); James William Gibson, *The Perfect War*.

9. PAYING FOR GLOBAL POWER
ASSESSING THE COSTS AND BENEFITS OF POSTWAR U.S. MILITARY SPENDING

BENJAMIN O. FORDHAM

Our overall policy at the present time may be described as one designed to foster a world environment in which the American system can survive and flourish. . . . This broad intention encompasses two subsidiary policies. One is a policy which we would probably pursue even if there were no Soviet threat. It is a policy of attempting to develop a healthy international community. The other is a policy of containing the Soviet system. —NSC 68[1]

In the summer and fall of 1950 the administration of President Harry S Truman entered into uncharted fiscal territory, committing the United States to very high levels of military spending on an open-ended basis. The rationale for this move was set forth in NSC 68, one of the foundational documents of U.S. postwar national security policy, completed just a few months before the start of the Korean War. In spite of the undeclared war in Korea, both military planners and their critics understood that the successive supplemental spending proposals that nearly quadrupled the fiscal 1951 military budget were not short-term emergency measures intended exclusively for that particular conflict. Instead, these increases reflected a fundamental shift in strategy. Henceforth, large military expenditures were to remain a fixture of U.S. policy, essential both for the long-term global struggle with the Soviet Union and, beyond that, for the effort to build and maintain "a healthy international community."

Given their understandable preoccupation with the Soviet Union, the senior administration officials who drafted NSC 68 did not spell out the military implications of policies "which we would probably pursue even if there were no Soviet threat." This aspect of the strategy, which included the construction of a world order open for American trade and investment, especially in economically important regions, was perhaps less salient at the time. Over the long run, however, it has proven more important. The need to contain the Soviet threat ended by 1990, with the end of the Cold War. Events since then suggest that the demands of developing a healthy international community—and the related high level of U.S. military spending—may never end.

In 1950, the prospect of maintaining relatively high levels of military spending for an indefinite period of time appeared daunting. Depending on their political orientation, observers worried either that the United States might spend too much on the Cold War, or that it might prove unwilling to spend enough. For critics on the right, permanent high levels of military spending carried the risk of transforming the country into a garrison state, its wealth consumed by the cost of its international commitments, and the political and economic freedoms of its citizens compromised by exigencies of permanent war, or at least what Senator Robert Taft (R-OH) called "semiwar."[2] On the other hand, national security policy planners like the authors of NSC 68 expressed concern about the nation's willingness to sustain the sacrifices required for a long struggle.

Because the United States had never before sought to maintain a large military force in peacetime, these concerns were understandable. They persisted throughout the Cold War. Policymakers and supporters of Cold War foreign policy never stopped worrying that cuts in spending might leave the United States or its allies vulnerable to attack or intimidation. Conversely, concerns about the implications of excessive military spending reemerged whenever the Pentagon budget rose, as it did during the wars in Korea and Vietnam, during the 1980s, and again after the terrorist attacks of September 11, 2001.

During the latter part of the Cold War, liberals replaced conservatives as the leading critics of military spending, but the critique itself did not change. The basic charge was this: by consuming an inordinate share of national resources, runaway military spending could damage the economy. It diverted investment away from more economically beneficial uses, and fueled inflation. It warped fiscal priorities, forcing tax increases or diverting funds from domestic priorities such as education, health care, and social welfare. Perhaps most importantly, permanent high levels of military spending promised to distort American politics and society, creating a constituency for militarism.

After more than fifty years of unprecedented levels of military spending, neither camp has seen its worst fears come to pass. The American people have not refused to pay the bill for global military engagement, nor has the country become a garrison state. Nevertheless, the fact that no nightmare scenario materialized does not mean that the concerns expressed by both camps were misplaced. The willingness of Americans to pay for national security policy did have real limits. Furthermore, these limits have left a lasting imprint on U.S. national security policies. Similarly, building and maintaining the force needed to carry out these policies had substantial political and economic effects, even if these effects fell short of causing economic collapse or a descent into military dictatorship. Understanding the patterns and the true implications of U.S. military spending since the end of World War II is essential for fully appreciating postwar national security policies.

PATTERNS OF MILITARY SPENDING AND AMERICAN POWER

Understanding what American military spending purchased in the postwar era requires an appreciation of two apparently contradictory facts. First, the scale of military spending since World War II has been massive and unprecedented. Second, that spending nevertheless had its limits, with important consequences for the character of the U.S. military. A review of several important trends underscores the importance of both these considerations.

When it comes to the aggregate level of military spending, NSC 68 and the Korean War were indeed watershed events. Ever since the large spending increases of the Korean War era, U.S. defense outlays have followed a recurring pattern. Figure 9.1 shows U.S. defense outlays in 2000 dollars between fiscal 1947 and fiscal 2005. As the graph suggests, American military spending had an inertial quality, consistently returning to its post-1950 mean after major buildups or cutbacks. The major fluctuations in the series can be attributed to the wars in Korea and Vietnam, the Reagan buildup, and the reaction to the September 11 terrorist attacks. Fears that the United States might not be able to sustain greatly increased levels of spending proved unfounded. Even during periods when there was little actual fighting, such as the 1950s (after Korea), the 1970s (after Vietnam), and the 1990s, the United States still allocated far more for defense than it had during the 1947–50 period. As the graph indicates, peacetime military spending during the 1954–2002 period averaged $317.7 billion in 2000 dollars, two and a half times the $124.6 billion spent annually during the 1947–50 period.

The inset table in Figure 9.1 offers several other historical comparisons. U.S. defense outlays since World War II have dwarfed not only prior American spending but also the military budgets of other major powers in the five years before each entered the Second World War.[3] The postwar peacetime average was nearly nine times what Germany spent annually as

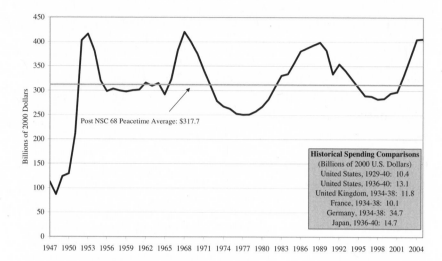

FIGURE 9.1. UNITED STATES DEFENSE OUTLAYS, 1947–2005

Source: *Office of Management and Budget; Correlates of War Project, National Military Capabilities Dataset*

it prepared to launch World War II. Although budgets do not translate directly into military power, and these comparisons are not exact, it is clear that when compared to the military outlays of great powers up to World War II, the scale of resources the United States has dedicated to its military since 1945 is historically unprecedented.

Of course, for most U.S. policymakers the demands of the Cold War had rendered historical comparisons with the 1930s irrelevant. In their view, the challenges facing the United States after 1945 were unique and the contemporary Soviet Union, not the record of earlier great powers or past American practice, provided the principal point of comparison. From this perspective, the key question was whether American military spending sufficed to maintain a force large enough to deter or, if necessary, defeat a Soviet attack on the United States or its allies. Raising and maintaining such a force formed only one aspect of this effort, of course, but it was an important aspect. If the Soviets outspent the United States for a long period of time, policymakers in Washington feared that the United States might slip into a position of pronounced military inferiority. At a minimum, compensating for such a disparity would have posed daunting diplomatic, military, and technological challenges. Using Soviet expenditures as a basis for comparison, U.S. defense outlays, while still impressive, look somewhat less extraordinary.

Figure 9.2 depicts the ratio of United States and NATO military spending to outlays by Soviet Union and the Warsaw Pact, respectively. (In the graph, a score of one indicates parity, while higher scores show an American or allied advantage.) The large jump in spending associated with NSC 68 and the Korean War gave the United States and its allies a substantial edge. Nevertheless, although American spending remained at very robust levels thereafter, the Soviet Union gradually eroded this edge, gaining a slight advantage over the United States during the 1970s, and maintaining it until the waning moments of the Cold War. As the graph indicates, the alliance system worked in favor of the United States, but did not greatly alter the overall East-West balance in Europe. Cuts in U.S. spending that followed the war in Vietnam allowed the Soviet Union to gain on the United States and its allies, a fact that helps explain growing concern among American policymakers and the general public that the United States was falling behind during the late 1970s and early 1980s.[4] Although the Soviet gains were real, it is important to keep them in perspective. Through an enormous effort, the Soviets gained little more than parity with the United States. In the long run, the costs of that effort to the Soviet system proved to be enormous.[5]

While U.S. defense outlays appear reasonable in the context of keeping pace with the Soviet Union, the end of the Cold War created a sudden

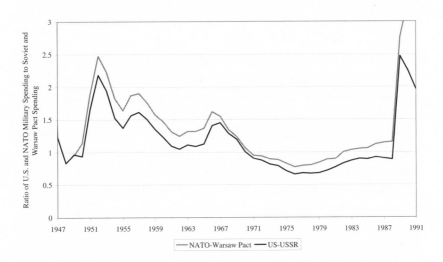

FIGURE 9.2. THE COLD WAR BALANCE IN MILITARY SPENDING

Source: National Military Capabilities data assembled by the Correlates of War Project

radical imbalance between the United States and all other potential military adversaries. Although some worried that China might soon emerge as a new "peer competitor," these concerns proved unfounded, at least in the near term. Chinese military spending did rise steadily during the 1990s. Even so, the $276.7 billion the United States spent in 2002 was nearly five times the $55.91 billion the Chinese allocated. Other states identified as potential threats were at an even greater disadvantage. According to CIA estimates, Iran spent $9.70 billion on its military in 2002. That same year, North Korea and Iraq spent $5.22 billion and $1.30 billion respectively. The military expenditures of major American allies in 2002, totaling some $247.36 billion, further increased the advantage enjoyed by the West.[6] These vast disparities in post–Cold War military spending reflected not conscious planning in Washington and allied capitals, but inertia. Although the sudden collapse of the Soviet Union and its empire transformed the international security environment, old spending habits persisted.

Accidental or not, the enormous edge in military spending had important implications for U.S. national security policy, permitting military actions that would have been unthinkable only a few years earlier. For post–Cold War administrations, the huge U.S. military advantage constituted a standing temptation—or opportunity, depending on one's point of view—to intervene militarily in international disputes or humanitarian disasters. Continued high levels of military spending purchased capabilities far beyond what was needed to defend the United States and its allies. Activists of many different political stripes, both in an out of government, clamored to put those capabilities to work.

Although the post-1950 U.S. military budget remained fairly consistent in terms of real dollars, it absorbed a declining share of the nation's overall wealth and of the federal budget. Figure 9.3 depicts the share of the gross domestic product and of total federal outlays allocated to the military. It shows that whereas the military consumed up to 70 percent of the federal budget during the Korean War, the Pentagon's share of the budget has remained below 20 percent since the end of the Cold War. It also shows that whereas the nation devoted more than 10 percent of GDP to military spending during the early part of the Cold War, this share trailed off to less than 4 percent after the Cold War ended.

It is important to be clear about what these figures mean. The declining Pentagon shares indicate not an erosion of military power but rather massive growth in both the federal budget and the overall U.S. economy.[7] However, the declining proportion of the economy or the budget spent on

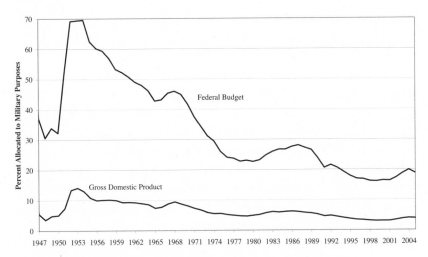

FIGURE 9.3. THE DEFENSE SHARE OF THE ECONOMY AND THE FEDERAL BUDGET
Source: Office of Management and Budget

the military does point to some important limits on what the American political system was willing to bear absent the impetus provided by an extreme national emergency. These limits required choices that successive postwar presidential administrations made in different ways.

The Korean War made it possible for the Truman administration to obtain the resources required by NSC 68. Senior officials in the Truman administration attributed greater importance to the security (and the economic recovery) of Western Europe and Japan than did their Republican opponents in Congress. The professional activities of many key administration figures before entering government service—mainly in Wall Street investment banks and law firms—had given them a lively appreciation of U.S. interests in Europe, and a corresponding determination to foster those interests. Men like Secretary of State Dean Acheson believed that security at home required the United States to defend its allies, even at the cost of maintaining large conventional forces overseas. Acheson and others in the Truman administration also expected the spending required to maintain these forces overseas to facilitate the economic recovery of Western Europe and Japan, another major goal of U.S. national security policy.[8]

The expanded military budgets for fiscal years 1951–53 produced the larger military force these Democrats wanted not only to fight the war in Korea but also to bolster the U.S. garrison in Europe. However, the buildup consumed nearly 15 percent of GDP and created a large budget deficit. For fiscal conservatives, including Truman himself, this was a bitter pill. Two groups within the administration collaborated in urging the president to swallow that pill: internationalists such as Acheson who wanted to expand U.S. military capabilities to meet its new obligations; and advocates of an expansionary fiscal policy, such as Leon Keyserling, who chaired the Council of Economic Advisers, determined to spur domestic economic growth.[9] The Truman administration's support for military spending reflected not only concerns about the Soviet threat but also a specific set of economic priorities. The principal economic concern of postwar Democrats was full employment. By contrast, their Republican counterparts worried more about balanced budgets and inflation. Given its economic implications—and even apart from the military crisis triggered by the Korean War—the Truman administration's national security policy may well have been one that only a Democratic administration could have adopted.[10]

This willingness to tolerate the economic consequences of very large military budgets ended when Dwight D. Eisenhower succeeded Truman as president in 1953. The Korean War era military build-up required wage and price controls, government intervention in the market for certain strategic raw materials, and higher taxes. To business leaders and conservatives more generally, these measures were anathema. For sound-dollar, low-tax Republicans, well-represented in the Eisenhower administration by the likes of budget director Joseph Dodge and Treasury Secretary George Humphrey, reining in government spending was imperative, even if it meant cuts in the Pentagon budget. Indeed, in spite of uniformed military predictions of dire consequences for U.S. national security, Humphrey and Dodge persuaded Eisenhower to implement substantial cuts in defense spending.[11] As figure 9.2 indicates, defense outlays dropped more than 25 percent between 1953 and 1956, and remained at that level throughout the remainder of the Eisenhower administration.

Beyond their budgetary concerns, many Republicans had been skeptical of the Truman administration's defense posture with its emphasis on conventional deterrence in Western Europe and Japan. By relying more heavily on strategic forces armed with nuclear weapons, the new administration's "New Look" promised to reduce military spending enough to bring national security policy into harmony with Republican economic policy priorities. Although Dwight Eisenhower was not among those in his party who viewed the U.S. commitment to Western Europe and Japan

as a temporary stopgap, he shared their fiscal preferences and was determined to subordinate the military budget to these concerns. For Eisenhower, the Cold War was as much an economic competition as a military
one. He continued to resist proposals to boost defense spending even
when the Joint Chiefs of Staff thought such increases were needed.[12]

The Eisenhower administration offered the first but by no means the
last instance of politics constraining postwar defense spending. In effect,
the peacetime average depicted in figure 9.1 acted as a baseline to which
successive administrations eventually returned. In the 1950s, conservatives concerned about the overall health of the economy returned the budget to this baseline. From the mid-1960s on, pressures to limit military
spending came mainly from liberals rather than conservatives, and arguments focused on domestic social programs rather than fiscal responsibility. Caught between the demands of the Vietnam War and his desire to
preserve his Great Society, Lyndon Johnson sought to limit or conceal any
military increases as long as possible.[13] When the Reagan administration
aggressively promoted increases in the military budget during the 1980s, it
siphoned off a relatively small share of the economy and the federal budget, a fact that almost certainly made the Reagan build-up less politically
controversial. Nevertheless, even this build-up had reached its limits well
before the end of the Cold War. Although total defense outlays grew
through 1989 because of previously budgeted spending, appropriations
began to fall in fiscal 1986.[14] The budget returned to its usual peacetime
baseline and remained there through the 1990s.

The political limits on American military spending affected not only
the aggregate size of the defense budget, but also decisions about the allocation of these funds within the Pentagon. Over time, technological advances made weapons not only more effective, but also more expensive.
During the several decades of the Cold War, the cost of individual aircraft,
tanks, and ships increased by several orders of magnitude. Bomber aircraft offer a good example. Throughout the postwar era, the unit cost of
each new generation of aircraft increased by roughly a factor of ten. The
venerable B-52, which became operational in the 1950s and continued in
service well into the next century, initially cost about $30 million each.
The unit cost of the B-1, which entered service in the 1980s, was about
$200 million. The B-2s, which began flying the 1990s, cost a staggering
$2.1 billion each.[15] Unfortunately, although not all weapons systems in-
creased in price at this rate, this pattern is not unusual. Commenting on
these increasing unit costs in the 1970s, one Pentagon official wrote (only

half jokingly) that the nation would one day be able to afford only "one plane, one tank, one ship."[16] Military personnel also cost more at the end of the Cold War than they did at the beginning. Commerce Department statistics indicate that the real wages of military personnel more than doubled over the postwar era, mainly in an effort to keep pace with rising civilian wages in recruiting an all-volunteer force after 1973.[17]

Strictly speaking, not all of these increases constituted inflation. Some of the higher costs bought superior equipment and paid for better-educated personnel. However, genuine price inflation—the cost of buying a roughly identical good or service—was also a serious problem. The price of military goods and services rose more rapidly than did the price of civilian government goods and services and prices in the economy as a whole.[18] As table 9.1 indicates, the prices of military services, as well as both durable and nondurable military goods, rose more rapidly than did civilian prices in all these categories. Over the thirty years covered in the table, the differences have been substantial. Military prices for nondurable goods rose 66 percent more than did civilian prices in this category. Durable goods prices rose 57 percent more. The military price of services rose 20 percent more than did the civilian price. In short, elevated rates of price inflation added to the cost of superior technology, making virtually everything the military budget purchased more expensive over time.

The fact that the unit costs of major weapons systems and the wages and benefits of military personnel rose steadily while the budget remained relatively constant had important structural implications. In essence, the

TABLE 9.1. THE RISE IN PRICES OF MILITARY AND CIVILIAN GOODS COMPARED

	DURABLE GOODS		NONDURABLE GOODS		SERVICES	
Year	Military	Civilian	Military	Civilian	Military	Civilian
1973	1.05%	1.01%	1.22%	1.08%	1.08%	1.05%
1978	1.60	1.37	2.53	1.56	1.57	1.52
1983	2.45	1.79	4.74	2.18	2.44	2.31
1988	2.58	1.94	4.00	2.43	3.34	2.90
1993	2.82	2.05	4.28	2.84	3.94	3.58
1998	2.85	1.98	4.11	2.99	4.52	4.09
2003	2.90	1.75	5.20	3.32	5.59	4.68

emphasis shifted from quantity to quality. Over time the U.S. military came to consist of fewer (but presumably more capable) weapons and personnel. In the 1990s, some observers began to argue that such a force could exploit emerging information technologies to gain a decisive military advantage, but the Pentagon's force structure was already moving in this direction well before such arguments made a virtue of this necessity.[19] For example, the number of navy ships at the peak of the Reagan buildup in fiscal 1987 stood at 594, falling to 337 by fiscal 2001. By comparison, the number of ships never fell below 812 during the budget-conscious Eisenhower administration, or below 523 during the 1970s, another trough in postwar military spending.[20] Because the costs associated with military personnel rose more rapidly than almost any other item in the budget, cuts in personnel strength became especially attractive to budget-conscious defense policymakers.[21] Increasingly, the Pentagon sought to substitute technology for personnel. Figure 9.4 illustrates this trend, showing dollars spent per man or woman in uniform. This figure rose steadily throughout the Cold War, accelerating after the end of the draft in 1973, and again during the post–Cold War era.

The capital-intensive force structure that has resulted from budgetary pressures has potentially important if uncertain implications for U.S. policy. If information technology is facilitating a "Revolution in Military Affairs," then the United States enjoyed a substantial head start in taking

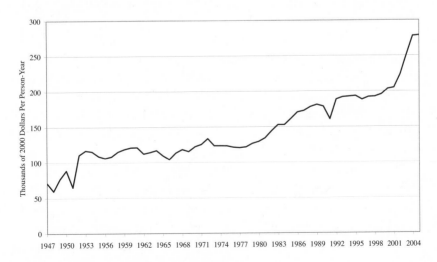

FIGURE 9.4. RATIO OF DEFENSE OUTLAYS TO PERSONNEL
Source: Department of Defense

advantage of this opportunity by the end of the Cold War. On the other hand, whatever the advantages of technological sophistication, a smaller force has its limits. Because even technologically superior forces cannot be in two places at once, small size limits the number of operations that can be conducted simultaneously. Moreover, some missions, such as peacekeeping, occupation, and counterinsurgency, are unavoidably labor-intensive, requiring the presence of large numbers of troops on the ground. If the United States cannot provide these troops, it will have to outsource this function, relying on mercenaries (in contemporary parlance, contractors) or allies to take up the slack. Yet mercenaries are expensive and less than fully reliable. And as the diplomatic wrangling over the war in Iraq suggested in 2002 and 2003, obtaining allied cooperation limits American freedom of action.

MILITARY SPENDING AND THE AMERICAN ECONOMY

What were the results of high military spending for the American economy? Cold War critics of the Pentagon budget worried that it might hurt overall economic performance, as well as channeling federal resources away from other desirable programs. There are indeed solid grounds for concern about the economic implications of military spending. Nevertheless, in the postwar United States, Pentagon spending did not have large or long-lasting adverse effects on the overall economy or even on the government's ability to support other priorities.

Economists have suggested two major avenues through which military spending might theoretically affect the economy: by influencing the allocation of resources in the economy as a whole, and through technological "spillovers" from military spending into the civilian economy.[22] The impact of defense spending on the allocation of resources within the economy could be either bad or good. When the economy is at or near full employment, diverting resources from civilian to military use will reduce economic growth. Resources used for military purposes, such as tanks or fighter jets, have fewer economic benefits than those employed to produce goods and services in the civilian sector, such as automobiles or airliners. Moreover, military demand for certain materials such as steel, electronic components, and the like, may drive up the prices of these items and contribute to inflation. On the other hand, when substantial unused economic capacity exists, devoting resources to military purposes would not draw them away from other uses. By using labor and capital that would otherwise be unemployed, defense spending could actually promote economic growth. The beginning of World War II demonstrated the positive effects of military spending, helping the United States recover from the Great Depression. The Vietnam War demonstrated the negative effects: because that conflict took place during the relatively prosperous 1960s, when the economy was much closer to full employment, increased military spending helped fuel inflation.

Economic conditions like those prevailing at the beginning of World War II or during the Vietnam era were not the norm. Across the entire postwar era, the impact of military spending through the allocation of resources was generally quite small. As some critics feared, there is evidence that military spending came partly at the expense of civilian investment.[23] On the other hand, military spending propped up some sectors of the economy at politically or economically propitious moments.[24] On balance, these conflicting dynamics did not add up to any clear effect on overall economic growth.[25]

The impact of spillovers from military spending into other economic activities has also been modest. Technologies developed for military use sometimes found civilian applications as well. Throughout the postwar era, many innovations in aviation, computers, and electronics—including the global positioning system and the Internet—got their start in military research and development programs. Similarly, many people received education and training in the military that they later put to use in civilian life. Not all the potential spillovers were beneficial, however. In spite of the success of some military technologies in civilian economy, military research was still less likely to produce useful civilian-sector applications than was civilian-sector research during the postwar era. In spite of well-known positive spinoffs like those just mentioned, the broader effects of military research on productivity have been small.[26]

Apart from its impact on the economy as a whole, many Cold War critics worried that high levels of military spending might force a tradeoff between "guns and butter" in the federal budget. In fact, military spending did not constrain the growth of civilian government spending during the Cold War era.[27] In practice, the United States generally incurred budget deficits in order to finance both military spending and social programs at times when the two priorities appeared to conflict. Confronted with an apparent need to choose guns or butter, the Congress typically opted for both, passing the bill on to future generations.

Although the overall pattern is clear, it requires some qualification. Even though there was no general tradeoff, military spending did influence funding for domestic social programs at particular points in time, most notably during the wars in Korea and Vietnam. The buildup associated with NSC 68 and the Korean War prompted the Truman administration to abandon the most ambitious social programs it had proposed, such as its national health insurance plan. Strictly speaking, there was no direct budgetary tradeoff, because nearly all the military spending was financed through borrowing and increased taxes. The cuts in non-defense programs, which amounted to only $550 million in the fiscal 1951 budget, came nowhere close to balancing the massive increase in military outlays, which totaled over $23 billion by the end of the fiscal year. However, the political necessities of rearmament certainly put an end to Harry Truman's "Fair Deal."[28]

The Vietnam War produced a similar result, forcing Lyndon Johnson to scale back his domestic social programs, but once again for political rather than strictly budgetary reasons. Through 1967, Johnson sought to finance both his "Great Society" and the war in Vietnam without higher taxes, an effort that ultimately proved futile. In the fall of 1967, Johnson tried to persuade congress to increase taxes but Wilbur Mills (D-AR), the powerful conservative chairman of the House Ways and Means Committee, refused to cooperate. Arguing that "I just do not believe that when we are in a war that is costing us $25 to $30 billion a year we can carry on as usual at home," Mills demanded cuts in Johnson's social programs, which he disliked in any case. Johnson held out against Mills until March 1968, when a financial crisis (also exacerbated by the overseas military spending associated with the war in Vietnam) forced him to give in.[29] As had been the case during the Korean War, the ensuing cuts in domestic spending did not compensate fully for the expenses associated with Vietnam, but the war's costs clearly undermined support for Johnson's domestic programs. Political realities proved more important than economic ones.

By the time the Cold War ended, the possibility that military spending could influence either the economy or overall government spending was becoming increasingly remote. The trends shown in figure 9.3 show why. Because military spending remained fairly constant in real terms while both the economy and the federal budget grew enormously, the economic and budgetary importance of military spending diminished. Even the large boost in military spending that followed the September 11 terrorist attacks, raising the military budget to levels comparable to the peak spending years of the Cold War, consumed less than 20 percent of the federal budget and less than 4 percent of gross domestic product, shares lower than those seen at any time since 1950. These facts help to explain why critics of the Bush administration's foreign and defense policies said relatively little about the size of the military budget. The major national debates about the need to choose "guns or butter" may well be a thing of the past. Future disagreements over national security policy are more likely to focus on issues where there is genuine scarcity. For example, while the supply of budgetary dollars is abundant, the supply of people is not. Recent military recruiting difficulties suggest that the limited number of citizens willing to volunteer for military service may constrain American policy in important ways. The potential solutions to a personnel shortage, ranging from a return to the draft to the acceptance of limits on overseas commitments, are all likely to spark controversy.

DISTRIBUTIVE IMPLICATIONS

Critics of postwar military spending worried a lot about its economic effects, but they were even more concerned about its political implications. During the early Cold War era, conservatives like Senator Taft and President Eisenhower feared that the United States might become a "garrison state."[30] Increased military spending entailed higher taxes, expanded bureaucracy, and a general growth in the power of the state, all of which seemed to threaten free enterprise and eventually to endanger democratic government.[31] Subsequently, liberal critics worried about the growth of militarism and a "military-industrial complex" that would undermine democratic control of foreign policy and promote war.[32] In both cases, the critics worried that constituencies benefiting most from military spending would sacrifice core political values in their quest for power and profit. Postwar military spending did not destroy American democracy or the free enterprise system, but it did have important political consequences. The changing identity of the domestic "winners" and "losers" from military spending tells a politically important story. Not surprisingly, the impact of military spending on different regions and socioeconomic classes helped shape the politics of national security policy.

Cold War military spending had major consequences for the regional distribution of manufacturing industries in the United States, contributing to the spread of these industries out of the Northeastern quadrant of the country and into the South and West. In 1939, the fourteen states from

Illinois east and from Pennsylvania north produced 71.1 percent of the country's manufacturing output, and contained 68.8 percent of its manufacturing jobs.[33] By 2001, the Northeast's share of national manufacturing output and employment had fallen to 39.7 and 40.2 percent, respectively.[34] Military spending was certainly not the only reason for this shift, but it was nevertheless an important contributing factor.[35]

The impact of military spending on the regional distribution of manufacturing began with the massive mobilization of the economy for World War II. Although the Northeast received the largest share of government contracts during World War II, new production facilities were set up outside established manufacturing centers. The need to supply the war in the Pacific, along with regulations prohibiting the construction of munitions plants within 200 miles of the coast, prompted the building of new facilities in areas that had previously had little manufacturing employment, such as Dallas and Oklahoma City. Labor shortages in traditional manufacturing centers also encouraged this practice: it was cheaper and easier to establish new plants in areas where labor was relatively abundant than to import workers from other parts of the country.

The legacy of the World War II mobilization proved important in two respects. First, the existence of manufacturing facilities in the South and West created expectations that these regions ought to receive a share of government contracts during the Cold War. Second, military investment in the South and West during World War II had emphasized the aircraft manufacturing and petroleum industries. During the postwar era, these industries grew especially rapidly, giving an important if unforeseen spur to the growth of manufacturing outside the Northeast.[36]

The contribution of military spending to the growth of manufacturing industry in the South and West also reflected partisan differences over the allocation of the military budget as well as the exigencies of the wars in Korea and Vietnam. The party differences that had developed during Truman and Eisenhower administrations persisted throughout the Cold War. The Democrats favored spending for conventional forces, although that commitment declined over time, and disappeared altogether under the Clinton administration in the 1990s. Republican administrations from Eisenhower through the younger Bush tended to favor strategic forces and to emphasize strategies that relied more heavily on technological advances. These preferences turned out to have important implications for the regional distribution of military spending, as well as for the content of the arsenal.[37]

The build-up that followed NSC 68 and the Korean War reflected the Democratic preference for conventional forces, a strategy that favored the predominantly Democratic states of the Northeastern manufacturing belt. The upper panel in figure 9.5 indicates the total per capita value of prime contracts issued by the Department of Defense during the three highest-spending fiscal years of the Korean War.[38] Although several states outside the Northeast, especially aircraft manufacturing centers like California, Washington, and Kansas, received substantial benefits from these prime

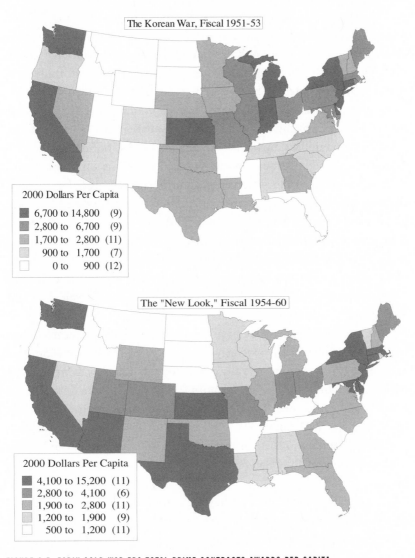

FIGURE 9.5. EARLY COLD WAR ERA TOTAL PRIME CONTRACTS AWARDS PER CAPITA

contracts, the Northeast received the lion's share. This regional concentration also reflects the fact that it was easier to convert factories from military to civilian use during the Korean War than it would be later. At the time, conventional war consumed huge quantities of manufactured goods that were similar to those produced for civilian use.[39] (As military hardware grew more technologically advanced in later years, the resemblance between military and civilian products diminished.) The Northeast, where most civilian manufacturing in the United States took place, was in the best position to meet these needs.

The Republicans who took office in 1953 had a different strategic vision and different spending priorities. As the lower panel in figure 9.5 indicates, Eisenhower's New Look geographically dispersed military spending across a wider range of states, and shifted it away from traditional manufacturing centers. The end of the Korean War and Eisenhower's more stringent fiscal policies greatly reduced military procurement, with the total value of prime contracts falling from an annual average of $176 billion in 2000 dollars during the Korean War to $87 billion between fiscal 1954 and 1960. Because of the reduced emphasis on conventional forces, the impact of this 51 percent decline in contracting fell most heavily on Northeastern manufacturing. Although New York and New England continued to receive a substantial per capita share of prime contracts, the Midwestern manufacturing belt suffered huge losses. States in the East North Central census region (Michigan, Wisconsin, Indiana, Ohio, and Illinois) lost an average of 82 percent of the value of their prime contracts. The declining military demand for motor vehicles made Michigan the biggest loser in the entire nation, with firms in the state losing 92 percent of the value of prime contracts they had received during the Korean War. By contrast, many states in the Rocky Mountain and Great Plains regions actually gained during the New Look, in spite of the overall drop in military spending. (The net winners were Florida, South Dakota, Arizona, New Mexico, Colorado, Montana, Wyoming, Utah, and North Dakota.) These states had produced fewer of the conventional manufactures most heavily cut after the end of the Korean War, and more of the relatively exotic high-technology items the New Look demanded.

The onset of the war in Vietnam once again required large quantities of materiel that could be produced by converted civilian industries. That meant more defense business for firms in the manufacturing belt. However, important differences between the Korea- and Vietnam-era buildups limited the flow of benefits to the Northeast during the Vietnam War. First, unlike the Truman administration, the Johnson administration did not couple its war effort with plans for maintaining a substantially larger military force after the war ended, and did not convert civilian industries to large-scale military production. Although the Johnson administration's efforts to contain the cost of the war were not successful, the Vietnam-era buildup in military procurement was still smaller than that associated with NSC 68 and Korea, lasting only from the 1966 through 1969 fiscal years. During this period, the value of prime contracts rose to $144 billion in 2000 dollars, a 66 percent increase over the New Look period, but smaller than the $176 billion annual average during the Korean War.

Second, in part because military industry had shifted away from the Northeast during the New Look, military contracting was also less geographically concentrated in the Northeast during the Vietnam War than it had been during the Korean War. This fact is evident in the upper panel of figure 9.6. Of the five East North Central states mentioned earlier, only Indiana and Wisconsin gained more than the national average in the value of prime contracts. Michigan gained 46 percent, but still received only $408 per capita in prime contracts during the Vietnam-era buildup compared to the $3,470 per capita firms in the state had received during the Korean War. The biggest geographic beneficiaries of Vietnam-era prime contracts compared to the New Look were located in the South. In Texas, Georgia, Mississippi, South Carolina, Arkansas, and Tennessee, for example, the annual average value of prime contracts all more than doubled. American manufacturing was still concentrated in the Northeast during the 1960s, but most of it continued producing civilian goods during the war. The benefits of Vietnam-era military contracts went mainly to defense contractors in other parts of the country.

The Reagan administration's military buildup differed from those associated with the wars in Korea and Vietnam in ways that further benefited the South and West rather than the Northeast. Because this buildup was not associated with a major war, it emphasized procurement rather than operations and maintenance. It was also sustained for a longer period of time than the Korean War or Vietnam War buildups, lasting from the 1981 through 1989 fiscal years before trailing off at the end of the Cold War. During this period, the value of prime contracts averaged $174

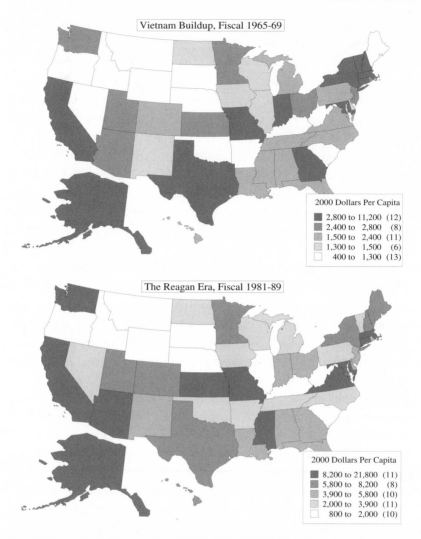

FIGURE 9.6. TOTAL PRIME CONTRACT AWARDS PER CAPITA IN 2000 DOLLARS

billion annually, roughly the same as during the Korean War. The Reagan administration's spending priorities resembled those of the Eisenhower administration, with its stress on strategic forces and advanced technology, more than those of the Democrats who had presided over the preceding military buildups.

A comparison between the regional beneficiaries of the 1951–53 and 1981–89 military buildups, shown in figures 9.5 and 9.6 respectively, reveals much about the evolution of military spending during the Cold

War. Leaders in aerospace like California, Washington, and Kansas still received relatively large per capita shares of prime contracts in both periods, but states in the old manufacturing belt received less during the 1980s in both absolute and relative terms. Of the fourteen New England, Mid-Atlantic, and East North Central states that had once dominated manufacturing and military industry in the United States, all but Massachusetts received a smaller annual per capita level of military prime contracts during the Reagan buildup than during the Korean War. In percentage terms, seven of the ten biggest losers were located in this region. As was the case during the New Look, Michigan was the biggest loser, suffering a 91 percent decline, almost exactly what it had experienced in the transition from the Korean War to the New Look.

The pattern of Democratic procurement favoring large conventional forces and Republican procurement favoring high-tech strategic forces ended with the Clinton administration in the 1990s. The Clinton administration abandoned the old Democratic commitment to a large conventional force, opting instead to continue Republican-style reliance on better technology and fewer personnel. This decision was a concession to new fiscal and technological realities. By the 1990s, standards for the technological sophistication of military equipment and the pay of military personnel were greater than ever, and the associated costs were much higher. Barring a return to a technologically simpler force—something no one contemplated—building a large conventional force in the 1990s would have been exceedingly expensive. Few in the Democratic Party were still willing to pay such a price.

In adopting Reagan-era spending priorities, the Clinton administration did not redirect military procurement back toward the "rustbelt." Instead, the "gunbelt" states that had received the largest share of prime contracts during the Reagan buildup continued to do so under the Clinton administration.[40] Of the ten states enjoying the greatest per capita success winning military contracts under the Reagan administration, eight remained in the Clinton-era top ten. Clinton made no effort to reverse the trend toward a more capital-intensive military, which accelerated during his last three years in office. The personnel strength of the force also fell by 18 percent between fiscal 1993 and 2001. As the shift toward a more technology-intensive force continued, firms in the Northeast continued to lose ground in prime contracting to firms in the South and West.

Defense contracting is not the only way military spending influenced the regional economies. Data on personal income from military sources gathered by the Department of Commerce offer a useful complement to the prime contracting data. These data reflect mainly military wages and salaries as well as some activities associated with military bases. They show an even more pronounced pattern favoring the South and West. The two maps in figure 9.7 depict the share of personal income derived from military spending in each state during the Korean War and the

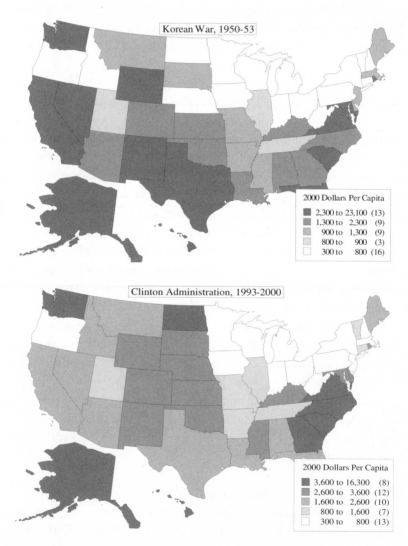

FIGURE 9.7. PERSONAL INCOME PER CAPITA FROM MILITARY SOURCES

Clinton administration. As the maps suggest, throughout the postwar era military spending accounted for a higher share of personal income in the South and West than it did in the Northeast. The fact that these regions always hosted more military bases than did the Northeast suggests that spending associated with these facilities canceled out much of the Northeast's advantage in prime contracting during the wars in Korea and Vietnam. The bottom line is that military spending since World War II redistributed income from the Northeast to the South and West. The regional disparities in income from military bases and salaries were clear throughout the postwar era, and amplified disparities in military contracting that grew over time.

As the regional beneficiaries of military spending became increasingly Southern and Western over time, they also became wealthier. Once again, a comparison of the major military build-ups of the Cold War era is instructive. Fighting wars in Korea and Vietnam required greater spending on operations and maintenance and on personnel. These types of expenditures tend to reduce poverty.[41] Much of this effect is due to the educational spinoffs from this type of spending. The relatively poor benefit more from military training and education than do the relatively wealthy because the poor have less education to begin with. Moreover, drafting relatively large numbers of people, especially from low-income groups, lowers unemployment by reducing the number of people looking for jobs.[42] Neither of these effects should generate enthusiasm for war as an anti-poverty program, but they are nevertheless quite real and relevant to understanding the impact of military spending during the first part of the Cold War.

Because it was not associated with a war, and reflected a different set of spending priorities than did earlier military buildups, Reagan-era spending lacked the poverty-reducing side effects of these earlier increases in the military budget. Indeed, increased peacetime military spending is correlated with increased poverty and inequality. Such a relationship is not surprising in view of the character of defense outlays during the 1980s. In spite of higher military spending, the number of men and women in uniform did not increase during the 1980s, limiting the education and training spillovers that have tended to help low-income groups. Moreover, the tightening of educational standards required of new recruits—in practical terms making most high school dropouts ineligible for military service—may also have had the unintended consequence of reducing these spillover effects. As military procurement focused on more specialized and exotic systems, and less on goods similar to those produced by civilian industry,

the workforce in defense industries also became wealthier and better educated. Overall, the increasingly capital-intensive force the United States
has established since the 1980s has fewer ancillary social benefits than did
the early Cold War era force.[43]

How did the changing identity of the winners and losers from military
spending affect politics? There is little evidence to support the proposition
that members of congress voted for military spending bills strictly based
on whether their constituents stood to gain as a result.[44] Nevertheless,
there is evidence to suggest that conservative or liberal support for military spending warmed or cooled depending on which constituencies benefited most from it. During the early Cold War era, congressional liberals
tended to support military spending and conservatives to oppose it. By the
early 1960s, these two factions had begun to switch their positions, a
transformation that was complete by the early 1970s, and persisted through
the rest of the Cold War. Figure 9.8 illustrates these trends, showing the
proportion of votes in support of maintaining or increasing military spending cast by the most liberal and most conservative senators. The shift in
both groups' behavior makes sense in terms of the changing distributive
implications of military spending.

Liberals were associated with the interests of organized labor and the urban Northeast. Indeed, one scholar has described liberals as "the northern

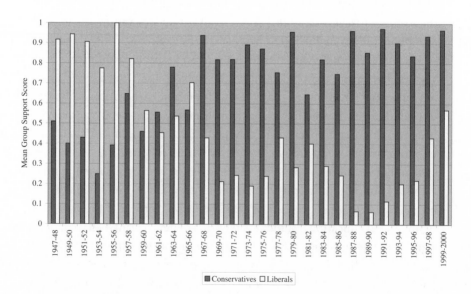

FIGURE 9.8. LIBERAL AND CONSERVATIVE SUPPORT FOR MILITARY SPENDING, 1947–2000

industrial wing of the Democratic party."[45] As we have seen, military spending during the early Cold War era tended to favor the interests of the industrial northeast. At the beginning of the Cold War, when manufacturing industries in the Northeast received the greatest share of prime contract from the Department of Defense, Northeastern congressional delegations were more likely than those from other regions to support military spending. Delegations from areas of the country that received a smaller share of the benefits were less so. By the 1970s, this situation had been reversed, with more conservative delegations from the South and West compiling more reliably pro-military voting records. The political complexion of the Northeastern congressional delegation remained relatively liberal, but that no longer implied enthusiastic support for military expenditures.[46]

Beyond the regional dynamics, the conservative shift from opposition to support for military spending also makes sense in terms of its changing economic implications. The relatively large share of the economy spent on the military during the early Cold War era required high taxes or large budget deficits, posed a serious risk of inflation, and often included substantial government intervention in the economy, all of which were anathema to conservatives, particularly those from Mountain states and areas of the Midwest outside the manufacturing belt.[47] Over time, however, the distributive implications of military spending became less of a barrier to conservative support. As defense outlays declined in terms of gross domestic product and the federal budget, their implications for taxes and inflation diminished.

Of course, the distributive implications of military spending do not entirely account for the politics of this issue. For one thing, liberals and conservatives also argued about the foreign policy objectives military spending supported, and these considerations probably had a greater effect on the positions they adopted than did the parochial benefits of defense outlays.[48] Neither the regional origins nor ideological orientation of members of congress or of other political actors fully explain all the positions they adopted. Nevertheless, despite many exceptions to the patterns discussed here, the changing identity of the economic winners and losers from military spending had important political implications.

CONCLUSION

Where has more than fifty years of elevated military spending left the United States? The evidence reviewed here suggests three major conclusions about postwar spending, each of which has important implications for the future of U.S. national security policy. First, military spending has not contributed to the decline of the United States as a world power by undermining its economy. Military expenditures have remained fairly consistent in real terms since 1950, but have consumed a steadily declining share of both the American economy and the federal budget. In contrast to the plight of the Soviet Union, which had a smaller economy and did not enjoy continuing economic growth, the United States saw the burden of fighting the Cold War ease the longer the struggle lasted. Since the end of the Cold War, the defense burden has become lighter still. The military spending increases that followed the September 11 terrorist attacks were as large as any undertaken during the Cold War, but consumed less than 4 percent of GDP and less than 20 percent of the federal budget. Both these figures are lower than those that prevailed at any point during the Cold War.

The adverse economic consequences of military spending have not been nearly so dire as critics feared during the early Cold War era. The effects of military spending on economic growth during the Cold War were mixed and generally small. Similarly, there was no systematic tradeoff between military and civilian spending in the federal budget, although the political implications of elevated military spending influenced funding for civilian programs at certain times, particularly during the Korean and Vietnam Wars. All the economic effects of military spending diminished as the military share of the economy and the federal budget declined. There may be many reasons for questioning contemporary U.S. national security policies, but the fiscal and economic consequences of military spending are not among them.

The absence of economic constraints on American military power is worth emphasizing both because it is historically unusual and because it has critical implications for the future of American foreign policy. Major powers have often been exhausted by their efforts to retain their position in the international system.[49] In view of the longstanding American effort to build and maintain a world order congenial to its economic and security interests—the "healthy international community" mentioned in the opening quotation from NSC 68—it is not surprising that the United States chose to maintain a relatively large military force after the end of the Cold War. What is surprising is that the United States has been able to maintain this force at such a low cost. The Cold War, in spite of the huge absolute expenditures it entailed, left the United States in a position to retain—and even to expand—its military advantage over all other states without seriously damaging its own economy. As the war in Iraq suggests, American military supremacy does not mean the nation can quickly defeat all possible opponents, but it does mean that other major powers will find it very difficult to seriously threaten the United States. This unprecedented situation is the cornerstone of American national security policy, and it has profound implications for other states as well. It may be the single most important fact about the contemporary international system.

Second, the economic implications of postwar military spending for different regions and groups within the country are more important than its effects on the economy as a whole. Pentagon expenditures benefited the South and West at the expense of the Northeast, particularly the Great Lakes manufacturing belt, and contributed to the geographic shift in manufacturing out of the Northeast. The Northeast consistently received a smaller share of the economic benefits of military bases, and wages and salaries.

The distributional effects of military spending were both a cause and a consequence of political divisions over national security policy. The Truman administration's preference for conventional forces in order to bolster the security of U.S. allies in Western Europe and Japan, as well as the need to fight the Korean War, tended to benefit the Northeast. The Eisenhower administration's search for a less costly alternative strategy resulted in an emphasis on strategic forces and nuclear weapons. It also tended to benefit the West and South. In both cases, the political constituencies these administrations represented set important limits on their strategic choices and corresponding decisions about the allocation of military spending. In this sense, politics drove spending decisions and determined their distributive consequences.

On the other hand, changing priorities in military spending also produced long-term (and probably unforeseen) changes in patterns of political support for it. Liberal support for defense outlays waned as the benefits of these outlays for heavily unionized industries in the Northeast and their poverty-reducing side effects diminished. At the same time, conservative support for military spending grew as its consequences for taxes, regulation, and government spending changed. The identity of the domestic winners and losers from military spending do not fully explain these political changes, but they were an important source of support and opposition to Cold War national security policy.

The distributive implications of military spending underscore the inescapably political nature of these policy choices. Even if all Americans could agree on national security policy goals in principle, the spending required to achieve these goals would still create domestic winners and losers. Although military spending is no longer as economically important as it was when it consumed ten or fifteen percent of GDP, it is still substantial enough to engender political conflict.

In view of the political character of military spending, the third conclusion follows from the second. Political considerations rather than economic realities have dictated the upper limit on what the United States has been willing to pay for defense. Even though the burden of defense fell steadily from the 1950s onward, the United States only episodically increased the absolute level of resources it allocated to the military. After each major buildup of the postwar era, military spending consistently reverted to a level very near its postwar peacetime average. This pattern continued even during the 1980s and 1990s, when military spending consumed a relatively small share of both the budget and the economy as a whole. The military budget was headed downward well before the fall of the Berlin Wall or the collapse of the Soviet Union, and it remained at typical postwar peacetime levels throughout the 1990s.

The political limits on military spending have important consequences for the future of American national security policy. The fairly consistent level of postwar spending did not buy the same military force across the entire period. In part because of the rising unit costs of high technology military equipment, the United States purchased a progressively smaller number of these (presumably) superior weapons systems and paired them with a declining number of relatively better-paid personnel. The United States military relied increasingly on technology as a substitute for personnel over the course of the Cold War, especially during its final decade. The budgets of the first fifteen years after the end of the Cold War give no indication that any change in this pattern is imminent.[50] The future of American power depends on part on whether this force is as effective for the missions assigned it in the future as it was in deterring the Soviet Union. Current events provide ample reasons for doubt. The irony of American military supremacy is that it makes the nation more likely to find itself involved in the unconventional wars for which its capital-intensive military force is least well-suited. Other states are unlikely to challenge the United States with conventional military forces, but guerrilla forces like those fighting in Iraq and Afghanistan are not so easy to deter. These conflicts suggest that technological superiority is not always a good substitute for more "boots on the ground," and that guerrilla forces can still do substantial damage to a technologically superior force. Finding a solution for this problem, whether it means restructuring American military forces or limiting the range of conflicts in which they are deployed, poses a major challenge for American policymakers.

Notes

1. Department of State, Historical Office, *Foreign Relations of the United States*, 1950, vol. 1 (Washington, DC: Government Printing Office, 1977), 252. The full text of NSC 68 is on pages 235–92.

2. Michael J. Hogan, *A Cross of Iron* (New York: Cambridge University Press, 1998), especially p. 363.

3. Current dollar spending figures for the other states are drawn from the National Military Capabilities data assembled by the Correlates of War II Project. It is available online at http://cow2.la.psu.edu/. They were converted into 2000 dollars using the military spending deflator computed by the U.S. Commerce Department's Bureau of Economic analysis for American military spending. It is available online at http://www.bea.doc.gov/beahome.html.

4. For discussions of the debate over military spending during the late 1970s and early 1980s, see Lawrence J. Korb, *The Fall and Rise of the Pentagon* (Westport, CT: Greenwood Press, 1979), and Daniel Wirls, *Buildup* (Ithaca: Cornell University Press, 1992). Concerning the effect of public opinion on the military budget, see Larry M. Bartels, "Constituency Opinion and Congressional Policy Making: the Reagan Defense Buildup." *American Political Science Review* 85, no. 2 (June 1991): 457–74.

5. On the role of military spending in the collapse of the Soviet Union, see Celeste Wallander, "Western Policy and the Demise of the Soviet Union," *Journal of Cold War Studies* 5, no. 4 (Fall 2003): 137–77.

6. The spending figures are published by the Central Intelligence Agency in its online *World Factbook* (http://www.cia.gov/cia/publications/factbook/index.html). The U.S. allies cited here, in descending order of the size of their military budgets, are France, Japan, Germany, the United Kingdom, Italy, South Korea, Australia, Israel, Spain, Turkey, Canada, the Netherlands, and Greece.

7. Among many tendentious uses of this index was Condeleeza Rice's comment that the Clinton administration "cut defense spending to its lowest point as a percentage of GDP since Pearl Harbor . . ." during the 2000 election campaign. (Condoleeza Rice, "Promoting the National Interest," *Foreign Affairs* 79, no. 1 (January–February 2000): 51.) In view of the American military spending advantage over all other states, the implication that the U.S. was militarily weak made little sense, except as campaign rhetoric.

8. On the concerns of Truman administration policy makers, see Benjamin O. Fordham, *Building the Cold War Consensus* (Ann Arbor: University of Michigan Press, 1998), 41–74; John Lewis Gaddis, *Strategies of Containment* (New

York: Oxford University Press, 1982), 89–126; and Melvyn Leffler, *A Preponder-ance of Power* (Stanford, CA: Stanford University Press, 1992), 355–60, 369–74.

9. Fordham, *Building the Cold War Consensus*, 35–36, 56–57; Gaddis, *Strategies of Containment*, 93–94.

10. Kevin Narizny, "Both Guns and Butter, or Neither: Class Interests in the Politi-cal Economy of Rearmament," *American Political Science Review* 97, no. 2 (May 2003): 203–20.

11. On the regulations required by Korean War mobilization, see Paul G. Pierpaoli Jr., *Truman and Korea* (Columbia: University of Missouri Press, 1999). On busi-ness opposition, see also Clarence Y. H. Lo, "Theories of the State and Business Opposition to Increased Military Spending," *Social Problems* 29, no. 4 (1982): 424–38. On the role of Dodge and Humphrey, see Hogan, *A Cross of Iron*, 370, 387–91.

12. Gaddis, *Strategies of Containment*, 355–56; Hogan, *A Cross of Iron*, 366–418; Richard A. Aliano, *American Defense Policy from Eisenhower to Kennedy* (Ath-ens: Ohio University Press, 1975), 26–31. On pressures for spending increases after 1957, see Robert P. Watson, *The History of the Office of the Secretary of De-fense*, vol. 4. (Washington: Historical Office, Office of the Secretary of Defense, 1997); and Peter J. Roman, *Eisenhower and the Missile Gap* (Ithaca: Cornell University Press, 1995).

13. On Johnson's concerns about the military spending increases associated with Vietnam, see Gaddis, *Strategies of Containment*, 270–73; Robert McNamara, *In Retrospect* (New York: Vintage, 1995), 204–6; and Robert Buzzanco, *Masters of War* (New York: Cambridge University Press, 1996), 237–41.

14. Daniel Wirls, *Buildup* (Ithaca: Cornell University Press, 1992), 207.

15. Unit costs are compiled by the Federation of American Scientists (http://www .fas.org/man/index.html).

16. Norman R. Augustine, "One Plane, One Tank, One Ship: Trend for the Fu-ture?," *Defense Management Journal* 2 (April 1975): 34–40.

17. Commerce Department, Bureau of Economic Analysis, *National Income and Product Accounts*, table 6.6 (http://www.bea.doc.gov/).

18. Benjamin O. Fordham, "The Political and Economic Sources of Inflation in the American Military Budget," *Journal of Conflict Resolution* 47, no. 5 (Octo-ber 2003): 574–93.

19. Concerning the "Revolution in Military Affairs," see for example Robert R. Tomes, "Boon or Threat? The Information Revolution and U.S. National Secu-rity," *Naval War College Review* 53, no. 3 (Summer 2000): 39–59.

20. Department of the Navy, Naval Historical Center. U.S. Navy Active Ship Force Levels, 1917-present. http://www.history.navy.mil/branches/org9–4.htm.

21. The price indices in the Commerce Department's National Income and Pro-duct Accounts (http://www.bea.doc.gov/beahome.html) indicate that since

1972, when the statistical series begins, the price index for the compensation of military employees has risen 438 percent, for civilian employees of the Department of Defense by 462 percent, and for personnel support by 527 percent. The only two items to exceed these rates of increase are petroleum products (up 616 percent) and "other equipment," which increased 676 percent.

22. For reviews, see Todd Sandler and Keith Hartley, *The Economics of Defense* (New York: Cambridge University Press, 1995), 200–220; and Steve Chan, "Grasping the Peace Dividend: Some Propositions on the Conversion of Swords into Plowshares," *Mershon International Studies Review* 39, supplement 1 (April 1995): 53–95.

23. See, for example, Alex Mintz and Chi Huang, "Defense Expenditures, Economic Growth, and the 'Peace Dividend,'" *American Political Science Review* vol. 84, no. 4 (December 1990): 1283–93, and Karen Rasler and William Thompson, "Defense Burdens, Capital Formation, and Economic Growth: The Systemic Leader Case," *Journal of Conflict Resolution* 32, no. 1 (March 1988): 61–86. For a conflicting view, see David Gold and Gordon Adams, "Defence Spending and the American Economy," *Defence Economics* 1, no. 1 (January 1990): 275–93.

24. Concerning the use of military spending to counter low economic growth, see Larry J. Griffin, Joel A. Devine, and Michael Wallace, "Monopoly Capital, Organized Labor, and Military Expenditures in the United States, 1949–1976," *American Journal of Sociology* 88 (1982 Supplement): S113–S153; and Alex Mintz and Alexander Hicks, "Military Keynesianism in the United States, 1949–1976: Disaggregating Military Expenditures and Their Determination," *American Journal of Sociology* 90, no. 2 (September 1984): 411–17. Concerning the election cycle, see Kenneth R. Mayer, *The Political Economy of Defense Contracting* (New Haven, CT: Yale University Press, 1992), 191–207.

25. Recent work suggesting a positive relationship between military spending and economic growth includes H. Sonmez Atesoglu, "Defense Spending Promotes Aggregate Output in the United States—Evidence from Cointegration Analysis," *Defence and Peace Economics* vol. 13, no. 1 (January 2002): 55–60. Those suggesting a negative relationship include Michael D. Ward and David R. Davis, "Sizing up the Peace Dividend: Economic Growth and Military Spending in the United States, 1948–1996," *American Political Science Review* 86, no. 3 (September 1992): 748–55. Recent work suggesting the absence of any consistent relationship includes Uk Heo, "The Defense-Growth Nexus in the United States Revisited," *American Politics Quarterly* 28, no. 1 (January 2000): 110–27.

26. Frank R. Lichtenberg, "Economics of Defense R&D," in Keith Hartley and Todd Sandler, eds., *Handbook of Defense Economics* (New York: Elsevier Science, 1995); David S. Saal, "The Impact of Procurement-Driven Technological Change on U.S. Manufacturing Productivity Growth," *Defence and Peace Economics* 12 (2001): 537–68.

27. William D. Berry and David Lowery, "An Alternative Approach to Under-standing Budgetary Trade-Offs," *American Journal of Political Science* 34, no. 3 (August 1990): 671–705; Tsai-Tsu Su, Mark S. Kamlet, and David C. Mowery, "Modeling U.S. Budgetary and Fiscal Policy Outcomes: A Disaggregated, Systemwide Perspective." *American Journal of Political Science* 37, no. 1 (February 1993): 213–45.

28. Fordham, *Building the Cold War Consensus*, 125–30.

29. Robert M. Collins, *More: The Politics of Growth in Postwar America* (New York: Oxford University Press, 2000), 68–97.

30. The positions liberals and conservatives have taken on foreign and defense policy issues have changed over the course of the postwar era. Conservatives of the early postwar era, such as Senator Robert Taft (R-OH) tended to oppose both high military budgets and overseas commitments. Since the 1970s, however, conservatives have worried less about these issues and more about the dangers of inadequate military preparations. During both periods, liberals have taken the opposite position. Some possible reasons for these changes will be discussed later in this chapter.

31. Aaron Friedberg, *In the Shadow of the Garrison State* (Princeton: Princeton University Press, 2000), esp. 40–61; Hogan, *A Cross of Iron*, esp. 5–9.

32. See, for example, Richard Barnet, *The Economy of Death* (New York: Atheneum, 1971).

33. U.S. Census Bureau, *Census of Manufactures, 1963: General Summary* (Washington, DC: Government Printing Office, 1964), 86–94. The Northeastern states are Maine, New Hampshire, Vermont, Massachusetts, Rhode Island, Connecticut, New York, New Jersey, Pennsylvania, Ohio, Indiana, Illinois, Michigan, and Wisconsin.

34. Department of Commerce, Bureau of the Census, *Annual Survey of Manufactures, 2002: Geographic Area Statistics* (Washington, DC: Government Printing Office, 2003), 1–4.

35. The regional implications of military spending were noted early in the Cold War. See, for example, Roger Bolton, *Defense Purchases and Regional Growth* (Washington, DC: Brookings Institution, 1966). Analyses of this phenomenon in later periods include Ann R. Markusen, Scott Campbell, Peter Hall, and Sabina Dietrich, *The Rise of the Gunbelt* (New York: Oxford University Press, 1991); and Gregory Hooks, "Military and Civilian Dimensions of America's Regional Policy, 1972–1994," *Armed Forces and Society* 29, no. 2 (Winter 2003): 227–51.

36. Gregory Hooks and Leonard E. Bloomquist, "The Legacy of World War II for Regional Growth and Decline: The Cumulative Effects of Wartime Investments on U.S. Manufacturing, 1947–72," *Social Forces* 71, no. 2 (December 1992): 303–37.

37. Party differences in the share of the budget allocated to strategic forces persisted throughout the Cold War. See Benjamin O. Fordham, "Domestic Politics, International Pressure, and the Allocation of American Cold War Military Spending," *Journal of Politics* 64, no. 1 (February 2002): 63–88. See also Alex Mintz, *The Politics of Resource Allocation in the U.S. Department of Defense* (Boulder, CO: Westview Press, 1988), esp. p. 115.

38. Data on prime contracts do not perfectly reflect the geographic location of military production. Prime contractors allot a substantial part of the business they receive from the Department of Defense to subcontractors, some of whom are based in different states. Moreover, the largest prime contractors have manufacturing operations in several states, not just the one in which they are headquartered. While these shortcomings are very important for some purposes, they do not obviate the regional patterns discussed here. For a discussion of these problems and a method for resolving them, see Bolton, *Defense Purchases and Regional Growth*, 54–81.

39. Hooks and Bloomquist, "The Legacy of World War II," 305.

40. The term "gunbelt" is borrowed from Markusen, et al., *Rise of the Gunbelt*.

41. Errol A. Henderson, "Military Spending and Poverty," *Journal of Politics* 60, no. 2 (May 1998): 503–20.

42. For a review of research on the implications of military service for the labor market and for the job skills of those who serve, see Sandler and Hartley, *The Economics of Defense*, 160–67.

43. Henderson, "Poverty and Military Spending"; John D. Abell, "Military Spending and Income Inequality," *Journal of Peace Research* 31, no. 1 (March 1994): 35–43. Henderson examines data from the 1959–1992 period, Abell from the 1972–1991 period.

44. For a review of the wide range of research on this question through the early 1990s, see James M. Lindsay and Randall B. Ripley, "Foreign and Defense Policy in Congress: A Research Agenda for the 1990s," *Legislative Studies Quarterly* 17, no. 3 (August 1992): 417–49. Exceptions to this generalization include Peter Trubowitz and Brian E. Roberts, "Regional Interests and the Reagan Military Buildup," *Regional Studies* 26, no. 6 (October 1992): 555–67.

45. Richard F. Bensel, *Sectionalism and American Political Development* (Madison: University of Wisconsin Press, 1984), 392.

46. Peter Trubowitz, *Defining the National Interest* (Chicago: University of Chicago Press, 1998), 169–234; Patrick Cronin and Benjamin O. Fordham, "Timeless Principles or Today's Fashion? Testing the Stability of the Linkage between Ideology and Foreign Policy in the Senate," *Journal of Politics* 61, no. 4 (November 1999): 967–98.

47. On conservative opposition to military spending during the early Cold War era, see Lynn Eden, "Capitalist Conflict and the State: The Making of United

States Military Policy in 1948," in Charles Bright and Susan Harding, eds., *Statemaking and Social Movements* (Ann Arbor: University of Michigan Press), 233–60; and Bruce Cumings, *The Origins of the Korean War* 2, (Princeton, NJ: Princeton University Press, 1990), 79–121.

48. On this point, see James M. Lindsay, "Testing the Parochial Hypothesis: Congress and the Strategic Defense Initiative." *Journal of Politics* 53, no. 3 (August 1991): 860–76; and Benjamin O. Fordham, "The Economic Origins of National Security Policy Preferences in the United States, 1947–2000," paper presented to the annual meeting of the American Political Science Association, Philadelphia, August 27–31, 2003.

49. See for example, Paul Kennedy, *The Rise and Fall of Great Powers* (New York: Random House, 1987); Karen A. Rasler and William R. Thompson, *War and Statemaking* (Boston: Unwin Hyman, 1989); and Robert Gilpin, *War and Change in World Politics* (New York: Cambridge University Press, 1983).

50. Office of the Undersecretary of Defense (Comptroller), *National Defense Budget Estimates for FY 2004* (Washington, DC: Department of Defense, 2003), 213. Available online at http://www.defenselink.mil/comptroller/defbudget/fy2004/fy2004_greenbook.pdf.

10. THE CHANGING MORAL CONTRACT FOR MILITARY SERVICE

JAMES BURK

Military service is sometimes thought of in instrumental terms. Service members receive the "king's shilling" and in exchange the state may use them as soldiers to fight wars. Once enrolled for pay, as Thomas Hobbes observed, soldiers are obliged to go into battle and not run away, at least not without the state's permission, no matter how much they may want to do so.[1] Put in the language of current social science, the instrumentalist view thinks about military service in terms of a "principal-agent" model, in which the state is the principal and those in the military are the principal's agents who (ideally) do exactly what the principal demands. It is a reasonable and sometimes useful view.[2] Nevertheless, it yields a limited understanding of the nature of the relationship that binds citizens who perform military service, the state that recruits them, and the society they serve. The explicit instrumental contract lays out only the material terms of exchange between the soldier and the state. Underneath it and supporting it—and so more important—is an often implicit moral contract. The moral contract embodies a set of values sustained by social practice that specify, among other things, the rights people must sacrifice when serving in the military, whether and when the state may compel military service, and how the state should treat people who risk combat in their society's defense.[3]

This chapter adopts the view that the terms of military service depend on and shape this moral relation between the citizen and the state. It defends the claim that after World War II, and in part owing to the experience of that war, the moral contract defining appropriate terms of military service expanded the rights, liberties, and opportunities of those who serve. The result effectively limited the power of the state over its citizens, and yet, for how long and how well remains to be seen. Paradoxically, with the advent of the all-volunteer force, the state began to reclaim its powers.

My assumption is that the terms of the moral contract are not fixed, but change over time, and for at least two related reasons. One is that the conduct of war changes, which affects the way people experience war. When warfare changes, original expectations about war go unmet and must be revised based on new experience. As a result, evaluations of the meaning and propriety of military practices are also revised, and this alters the terms of the moral contract.

The other reason for change is value pluralism.[4] In any complex society there are multiple practices and these will sometimes support values that are in conflict with one another. Understandably, especially in democratic societies, values embedded in the moral contract for military service sometimes contradict other social values. When they do, there will often be (perhaps on all sides) a sense of outrage at the violation of what some believe is right and good. At this point, political pressure builds up to reform either social or military practice or both. In short, when institutional practices, like the military's, accord with prevailing social values, there is little reason for change; the terms of the moral contract are left alone and largely taken for granted. Change is more likely when the terms of military service cannot be reconciled with prevailing social values, because either the military or the larger social practice with which it conflicts is thought to be out of step with society, an undesirable state.[5]

An illustration may help clarify how conflicting values lead to reform. In 1946, many soldiers who had served during World War II were returning home from Army posts all around the country.[6] Issac Woodard was one of these. He was a sergeant, having spent three years in the Army, serving fifteen months in the South Pacific. He was also African American. Now discharged, though still in uniform, he boarded a bus at Fort Gordon, Georgia, to go home to North Carolina. His trip, however, was neither uneventful nor joyous as it should have been. The bus driver became annoyed with Woodard at a bus stop in South Carolina. He thought Woodard took "too long" to use the "colored only" rest room. He cursed Woodard for his dereliction and when the bus stopped in the next town, the driver called for the sheriff to arrest Woodard, which the sheriff did, charging Woodard with drunkenness though he did not drink. While Woodard was in the sheriff's care, he was beaten with a blackjack and the blackjack was thrust into both of his eyes. He was given no medical care, but was locked in jail overnight. The next morning, he was found guilty of drunkenness and fined $50. By the time Woodard reached an Army hospital in Spartanburg, South Carolina, the doctors were unable to repair the damage done to his eyes. He was permanently blind.

What happened to Woodard was an example of the way African Americans were treated under the system of Jim Crow, a racially discriminatory social practice. The courts were already beginning to dismantle this system, years before the Supreme Court's famous 1954 decision in *Brown v. Board of Education* that overturned the "separate but equal" principle announced by *Plessy v. Ferguson* in 1898. But progress in this movement was not swift and blacks could not expect to be treated with ordinary decency. The bitter irony, of course, was that Woodard could serve his country in war, risking his life, and yet, when returning home, be denied the full laurels of citizenship and, worse, be subject to humiliation and assault. Because his maltreatment was extreme, the irony was difficult (though not impossible) for the dominant white majority to miss. The NAACP, knowing this, made sure that his plight was widely publicized, stirring the conscience of some. On hearing the news, President Truman reacted strongly in private, claiming that he "had no idea that it was as terrible as that" and that "we have to do something," which, as we shall see, he did. The Theatre Chapter of the American Veterans Committee held a theatrical benefit for Woodard in New York City. It called for 200 Army veterans to appear in uniform and act as ushers for the event.[7] Other fundraising was done on his behalf, enabling the NAACP to pay him a small pension. Still, justice was not done. Although the sheriff was brought to trial in a federal court in South Carolina, the federal prosecutor made no effort to present an effective case and the sheriff was acquitted.

What we have in this case is a conflict between the moral contract underlying military service and the social practice of racial oppression. The conflict was recognized at the time. In early December 1946, President Truman signed Executive Order 9808, creating the President's Committee on Civil Rights to study and report how civil rights might be more adequately protected. While the committee's report, *To Secure These Rights*, did not mention Woodard by name, it addressed his situation. It assumed the existence of a moral contract between one who serves in the military and the government served. The committee wrote that whoever performs military service surrenders "some of the rights and privileges that inhere in American citizenship." But in return the government "undertakes to protect his integrity as an individual and the dignity of the profession." This protection is what Woodard—and many others—were denied. The committee recognized that African American "servicemen are all too often treated with rudeness and discourtesy by civil authorities and the public." They are "forced to move to segregated cars on public carriers," "denied access to places of public accommodation and recreation," and "sometimes met with threats and even outright attacks." The committee, not mincing words, called these abuses. Failure to correct them, it said, was "morally indefensible."[8] It was a clear conflict between the moral contract for military service and the social practice of racial oppression. The next year, President Truman took a bold albeit partial step to resolve the conflict by ordering an end to segregation within the military.

We should not suppose that this conflict between the terms of military service and prevailing social mores was long standing. It arose during a period of transition in the social practices that sustained the value of military service during World War II. It was not that a well-established moral contract—whose terms were understood and widely accepted by most— was violated or neglected by a sheriff who was sadly ignorant of its requirements. On the contrary, the sheriff who beat Woodard knew and acted in accord with well-established and well-recognized prewar social practices. Prewar practices supported a more discriminatory understanding of the values found in the moral contract for military service than was found in the contract after World War II.[9] After the war, for reasons we consider later, the dominant interpretation of what practices could support the value of military service and, more broadly, the value of democratic citizenship no longer permitted disrespect for soldiers because of their race. While racial discrimination was still part of military practice, it had ceased to be an acceptable practice that defined the value of military service. In this case, the reasons underlying movements to reform the military's moral contract are fairly obvious and easy to interpret.

Unfortunately, that is not always so. Nonetheless, it is possible to see major patterns of change in the moral contract and the proximate causes pushing for reforms of one kind rather than another. This essay identifies three major trends that redefined the moral contract for military service as it evolved from the end of World War II to the beginning of this century. The first has to do with the rights of soldiers. Conscripted service during World War II and after facilitated a postwar expansion of the rights of citizens serving in the military or subject to military discipline. This expansion was part and parcel of the rights revolution that had its origins in World War I and proceeded more or less without interruption through the 1970s. Since then, the growth of rights has been impeded. The second trend explores the movement away from conscription, a form of compulsory military service, to the all-volunteer force established in the 1970s. At issue in this movement was whether or when the state could justly abridge the liberty of its citizens by requiring them to perform military service. This matter was hotly debated immediately after World War II and then again during the Vietnam War, with different judgments reached in each case about the value of compulsory service. While not hotly debated, this issue resurfaced as a simmering issue during the war in Iraq, which began in 2003. The third trend describes an emerging inclusiveness and expansion of equal opportunities for all those in the military, promoting the integration of minorities and women into the service. First steps in this direction were taken in the wake of World War II, but progress in this regard accelerated markedly in the 1970s pushed largely by the establishment of the all-volunteer force.

In what follows, I analyze these trends separately, to clarify the distinct character of change in each case. This strategy may be misleading as all three trends are empirically interrelated. To make amends for this, the concluding section will draw the trends together to identify unresolved issues they pose for understanding how the moral contract of military service might change in the twenty-first century.

Citizens' Rights in a Mass Military

The military raised to fight World War II was huge by any measure. In 1939, before mobilizing for the war, fewer than 340,000 Americans were in uniform. At its peak in 1945, over twelve million people were in uniform. Over six years, the military increased thirty-six times in size. In 1945, 8.6 percent of the population was in the service—the largest proportion in the nation's history. In World War I the comparable figure was only 2.8 percent, only slightly smaller than the 2.9 percent figure at the time of the Civil War.[10] It should be noted, however, that when armies equal more than one percent of the population they are usually considered large. For reasons of size alone all these armies are rightly called "mass armed forces." Yet, the term "mass army" does not refer to size alone. Raising a large military has political implications.

Mass armies first appeared in the American and French Revolutions in the late eighteenth century. They were armies of citizens mobilized to fight against the aristocratic and mercenary forces of Britain and

Europe. As Jacques van Doorn defined them, mass armies were not only large in size; they were also relatively homogeneous, which meant that the technological basis of the force was relatively simple, with the experience of the combat soldier being the predominant experience.[11] (In mass armies, increasing the army's size increased its might.) Most important was that mass armies required mass mobilization. To rely on mass armies for national security, as all belligerents in the world wars did, states depended on conscripted citizen soldiers for whom military service was not a full-time career. Professional soldiers were not enough. To legitimate this resort to coercion, softening its blow, states appealed to nationalism. As a result, the mass army was often thought of as a "nation in arms."[12]

Still, mass armies were not "cost free" to the political elites who raised them. Speaking about British experience in World War II, Richard Titmuss observed that "the war could not be won unless millions of ordinary people, in Britain and overseas, were convinced that we had something better to offer than had our enemies." That need led to "a call for social justice; for the abolition of privilege, for a more equitable distribution of income and wealth; for drastic changes in the economic and social life of the country."[13] The ordinary people, who were conscripted or related to those who were, increased their participation in and claims on society in response to their share in the fighting and dying. They gained political and social power relative to the state because their support was essential to win the war. British experience was not unique. Sociologists often argue that the rise of mass armies helped bring about fundamental democratization of Western societies and increased rights for their citizens.[14]

The argument underlying this claim is subtle and requires qualification to ensure it is not misunderstood. Mass mobilization of citizens for war does not invariably create democracy. The Prussian mass army that defeated France in 1870 belonged to the king (or rather to Bismarck and von Moltke) and was not subservient to the parliament. Prussia was a "monarchical-civil-service regime" and "the officer corps had its own direct representative at court and in the central organs of government."[15] In Russia, too, a conscript-based mass army supported "serflike [sic] sociopolitical relations"; it did not promote democratic development.[16] Similar observations could be made about the mass armies of Nazi Germany and the Soviet Union in the twentieth century. But, even in totalitarian societies, mass mobilization led states to moderate the use of state power against their citizens, to revise the moral contract for military service.[17] In open societies, movements to empower citizens, moderating state power, were more pronounced.

How does this moderating process work? As a rule, mobilizing citizen soldiers for military service has its greatest political effect when the fate of the country hangs in the balance or when the sacrifice required is high.[18] This condition was met in American history, for example, in the War for Independence and the Civil War. In these cases, citizen soldiers were not only or even primarily warriors (indeed, they need not have fought at all); but, because they served, they thought of themselves as defenders and bearers of the country's charisma. Subsequent generations endorsed that view. These veterans embodied what was at stake in that conflict, the meaning of which was articulated in the war's aims and the political ideology that supported those aims. Once the war was over, they (or others in their name) could and did use their charismatic prestige to reform the political order, to bring it as needed into closer conformity with the aims for which the war was fought. So the American Revolution resulted in the creation of a pluralistic republic in which sovereignty was widely (at first too widely) shared, while the Civil War resulted in a majoritarian republic that concentrated greater sovereignty in the hands of the central government than it had been, limiting the sovereignty of states (especially with respect to slavery and rights of secession).

World War II was another occasion when mobilizing citizen soldiers had a great political effect. Once more citizen soldiers were bearers of the country's charisma, embodying what was at stake in that conflict. When the war was won, in some cases even earlier, important reforms were made by (or on behalf of) those who fought. As before, the goal of the reformers was to bring America's political and social order into closer conformity with a society envisioned by the war aims and with the political ideology that supported them. The aims in this case focused on the protection and extension of democratic rights, succinctly outlined by President Franklin Delano Roosevelt in his address to Congress on January 6, 1941. In enumerating the "four freedoms" for which America fought, Roosevelt committed the United States to "the supremacy of human rights everywhere." A good society, he declared, was one that struggled, as he hoped America would, "to gain those rights and keep them."[19]

The reforms stemming from these aims helped to create the "rights revolution" that was so dominant in the decades immediately following World War II. By "rights revolution" I mean a radical liberalization in the stock of basic rights, liberties, and opportunities that members of society are able to enjoy. This happens when existing rights are redefined more broadly, new rights are created, or the set of people who are rights holders is made more inclusive. Revolutions of this kind do not occur without a political struggle. More precisely, they do not occur without legislatures and executives open to public pressure and sympathetic courts able and willing to uphold rights claims. Even then, as Charles R. Epp has shown, rights revolutions require strong support groups, like the NAACP or the American Civil Liberties Union, to state the case for rights.[20]

Our aim is to concentrate specifically on reformation of rights in the moral contract for military service. In the following section, we assess policies affecting the liberty rights of citizens versus the state's right to compel military service. Then we trace the expansion of rights to protect the equal opportunities of citizens who perform military service. But to begin, in this section, we examine efforts to secure the political rights of citizen soldiers. The political rights at issue are the right to vote, the right to a fair trial, and (a more disputed) right to conscientious dissent without losing one's standing as a citizen.

The right to vote is fundamental to democracy, and one might think that securing this right for citizen soldiers would long ago have been incorporated as a key clause in the moral contract for military service. In fact, efforts to secure the soldier's right to vote were not effectively institutionalized until late in World War II. Some reasons for this are relatively obvious. Members of the military frequently moved from one post to another and often could not fulfill state residency requirements for voting, which were stricter through the mid-twentieth century than they are today. If they were enlisted personnel, they may not have met the minimum age requirements for voting, which in most places required one to be twenty-one years old, until the voting age was lowered to eighteen by a constitutional amendment ratified in 1971.[21] Also, procedures to permit absentee voting were not well developed or commonly followed as they currently are. Finally, there was a less obvious, but important, normative barrier to voting by military officers that was strongly upheld at least through World War II. In that earlier period, Richard H. Kohn has argued, military officers long "abstained as a group from party politics, studiously avoiding any partisanship of word, deed, activity, or affiliation." There were exceptions, but they were exceptions, not the norm. The generation of officers who led the military in World War II believed that "partisan affiliation and voting conflicted with military professionalism."[22]

Rumblings for change were evident already during World War II, stirred by the approaching presidential election in 1944. With so many citizens in uniform, members of Congress (perhaps not entirely for disinterested reasons) hoped to provide some vehicle that would allow soldiers to vote. In April 1944, Congress passed the Serviceman Voting Act, establishing the War Ballot Commission, whose function was to assist those in uniform to complete forms required to vote by absentee ballot. In the end, 30 percent of the military voted in the election. It is hard to know how to measure the success of this effort. Nothing comparable had occurred—a presidential election with a large number of soldiers away at war—since the Civil War in 1864, when absentee ballots were used but the means of distribution and communication were far more primitive than in the 1940s. A more apt comparison is with the election of 1952, another presidential election year, with the country at war in Korea. In Korea, no organization existed to encourage voting, as the War Ballot Commission had done in 1944. (The War Ballot Commission was abolished in 1946.) As a result, in the 1952 election, only 15 percent of the military voted, half of the turnout recorded in 1944. In response to this experience, which seemed a backward step, Congress passed the Federal Voting Assistance Act in 1955, establishing the Federal Voting Assistance Program to facilitate absentee voting by military members in the presidential election and beyond. Rates of military voting increased to 35.2 percent in 1956, continued to rise throughout the 1960s and 1970s, so that by 1980 the military voting rate (49.7 percent) nearly equaled the civilian voting rate (52.6 percent). Since then the military voting rate has continued to increase, while the civilian voting rate has remained roughly the same, so that in the 2000 presidential election the military voting rate (69 percent) clearly exceeded the civilian voting rate (51.3 percent).[23]

This voting assistance program, it should be stressed, did not encourage or approve partisan activity. Rather, under it, military units designate a voting assistance officer who provides unit members information about registering to vote and ensures that they have the required absentee ballot to vote. The purpose is to safeguard what could not be counted on during World War II or (even more) during the Korean War—that those in uniform do not have to sacrifice but retain their right to vote. The program may have had the unintended consequence of eroding the norm that discouraged military officers from partisan affiliations and from voting. If so, this might, as Kohn thinks, make it more difficult to maintain a politically neutral military force. Yet it would not have been possible, given the aims of World War II, to advocate for a restricted military franchise; and it is hard to see how one might deprive citizen soldiers of their right to vote once that right has been secured. It is now part of the moral contract.

Another revision to the moral contract was made to grant citizen soldiers a right to a fair trial. Historically, the aim of military justice was to maintain "good discipline" and "military order" and it gave commanders broad powers to achieve these ends. It was not a system of law familiar to a democratic society. It punished acts that were not punishable under civilian law. Its punishment was swifter with no rights of appeal. And it was for civilians a procedural wonderland in which the commander who made the charge also selected and influenced the prosecutor, judge, and jury. After the trial, this same commander could suspend, modify, or approve the sentence meted out. During World War II, large numbers of citizen soldiers were for the first time subject to this peculiar form of justice. Jonathan Lurie reports that about 600,000 courts-martial per year were held when the war was at its height. In all, more than 1.7 million trials were held during the war. More than 100 servicemen were executed, and at war's end, 45,000 service members were still in prison.[24] Understandably, many thought this military justice system was too harsh and unfair, that it did not meet the minimum requirements for a fair trial. They brought pressure on the military and Congress to bring about reform.[25]

Between 1946 and 1950, Congressional committees and committees advising the Army and Navy generally agreed that two reforms were needed. One was to limit command influence over the conduct of trials and the other was to provide an appellate system to review matters of fact and law affecting the outcome of cases. Establishing an appellate system was particularly important. In early 1947, an advisory committee to the Navy argued that "this ultimate right of appeal [had to] be granted to every accused." It noted that accused Nazi saboteurs and Japanese generals had this right during the war, and their cases received prompt Supreme Court reviews; "we should be no less ready to grant similar privileges to our own military and naval personnel."[26] Nevertheless it proved difficult to balance the commander's need for discretion when using law to maintain order and discipline against the need of democratic societies to protect the rights of the accused to receive a fair trial. Unless this difficulty was overcome, members of the powerful Association of the Bar of the City of New York worried that "the opportunity to create a fair and impartial system of military justice" would be "frittered away."[27]

In July 1948, James Forrestal, the Secretary of Defense, appointed a civilian committee to work with representatives from all the services to draft a Uniform Code of Military Justice. Sensitive to the need to respect military tradition, the committee prepared a draft that retained the authority of commanders to select members of a court martial. But it also created an appellate court of military appeals that made "the military appeals process as similar as possible to its civilian counterpart."[28] This would provide protection against the worst abuses of command influence. Most important, Forrestal successfully prevented the various services from separately lobbying in Congress to preserve traditional practices that, if kept, would have undermined the proposed reform. Under these favorable circumstances, after hearings in 1949 and early 1950, Congress passed a bill to implement the new code, making no major changes in the Forrestal proposal (except to deny life tenure to the appeals court judges). President Truman signed it into law on May 6, 1950.

The result led to a significant extension in the procedural and substantive rights of military service members. As James B. Jacobs observed, the new Uniform Code of Military Justice had as an explicit objective "to civilianize and liberalize the military's criminal law and procedure, and to extend certain rights of citizenship to service personnel."[29] Article 31 of the code, for instance, required that service members be warned against making self-incriminating statements when they were suspected of an offense, even before they were held in custody. This was a more liberal standard than the *Miranda* rule, adopted by the Supreme Court sixteen years after the code.[30] No less important was the work of the Court of Military Appeals, now called the United States Court of Appeals for the Armed Forces.[31] Over the years, this court has made a "profound impact on military law," importing into military law "almost all the procedural protections available to civilian defendants."[32] These developments marked a sharp break with past practices, which were based on the idea that military justice served only to maintain good order and discipline within the armed forces. Now it was recognized that in addition to this purpose, a second purpose—to promote justice—was equally important. That meant military justice must respect "individual rights, due process, fairness, and impartiality."[33] In short, it guaranteed the right to a fair trial. Consequently, there was much less difference between military and civilian law after 1950 than there had been in World War II, with the rights of citizens in uniform far better protected.

The Supreme Court was also active in the postwar period to protect the rights of military members, their dependents, and civilians employed by the military. Most efforts were aimed at restricting the reach of military law in order to limit the jurisdiction of military courts. The Court, for instance, denied that civilians discharged from the military could be brought back into military service to be tried for a crime they might have committed while in the service.[34] It stopped Congress from stripping a citizen of citizenship as punishment for poor performance as a soldier.[35] It also restricted the use of courts martial to those who were in uniform. Neither civilian dependents of military members nor civilian employees working for the armed services overseas could be tried under the Uniform Code of Military Justice.[36] In what turned out to be a controversial ruling, *O'Callahan v. Parker* (1969), the Court went a step further and allowed military courts to hear criminal cases only if the alleged offense by the service member was "connected" with military service. Otherwise, members of the military (like everyone else) were subject to civilian law and its protections.

In addition to expanding the rights of citizens in uniform to a fair trial, the Supreme Court also moved to enlarge protections surrounding conscientious dissenters against military service, allowing dissent without risking the chance to become a citizen or being subject to punitive measures. The first of these decisions was made immediately after the end of the Second World War.[37] The question was whether aliens applying for citizenship must promise to bear arms in defense of the country. In this case, the applicant could not make that promise for religious reasons, but was willing to do noncombatant service. The Court noted that the government often made accommodations to respect the freedom of conscience of native-born citizens who opposed war and that Congress permitted expedited grants of citizenship for alien conscientious objectors who served during World War II, even though they served as noncombatants. Consequently, it saw no reason to make applicants for citizenship promise, against the claims of conscience, to bear arms in defense of the country. The decision overturned three previous decisions, the first of which had been made only seventeen years before.

Nineteen years later, during the Vietnam era, the Court again showed respect for the rights of conscience. It struck down language in the selective service law that required belief in a Supreme Being in order to qualify for classification as a conscientious objector. That requirement had been used in the selective service law since 1940, replacing less liberal language

from World War I that had required citizens to belong to a traditional pacifist denomination before being granted conscientious objector status. The
Court held it was enough if people demonstrated a sincere and meaningful religious belief that occupied a position parallel to belief in God.[38] Five
years later, it returned to this issue. Expanding its original ruling, the
Court now said that people could claim conscientious objector status so
long as they opposed all war. The beliefs underlying their opposition did
not have to be explicitly religious, but might be moral or ethical beliefs, so
long as they were sincerely held.[39] In these cases, we see a tilt to favor the
rights of citizens and their protected place in society over the responsibility to perform military service. The Court also prevented the government
from punishing people who protested against the Vietnam War. Before
this decision, the government punished protesters by increasing their liability to be drafted into military service whether by withdrawing their
otherwise legal draft exemptions or accelerating their induction.[40]

By the end of the Vietnam era, however, the rights revolution as it bore
on provisions of political rights seemed to have reached its limits. No new
fields were opened to expand the political rights of citizens in relation to
military service. Instead some signs were posted that said do not enter
here. The Supreme Court, for instance, was subject to a great deal of criticism for establishing the test that held a soldier subject to courts-martial
only if the alleged crime was "service connected."[41] Within two years after creating the test, the Court began to back away from it. First, it applied the test leniently; then it refused to apply it retroactively; next it
applied the test more leniently still; and finally it overturned the test altogether, restoring the military's original criminal jurisdiction over service
members.[42] The Court also set a limit on its protection of conscientious
dissent when it ruled that citizens could not refuse, without punishment,
to perform military service because they thought the war being fought
was unjust.[43]

Still, there was no wholesale retrenchment of the political rights of military personnel. As we have seen, the government has effectively encouraged exercise of the soldiers' right to vote from the mid-1950s to the
present. In addition, there has been a deepening commitment to the right
of appeal which helps guarantee the soldier's right to a fair trial. In 1984,
Congress amended the Uniform Code of Military Justice, permitting either party in certain cases to appeal the decision directly to the Supreme
Court. Furthermore, the Court of Appeals for the Armed Forces continues to embrace civilian standards in its review of military cases with the

effect of increasing reliance on civilian standards within military law.[44] Overall, the moral contract for military service has been substantially modified since the end of World War II to lessen the sacrifice of political rights that citizens make when they are in uniform or are otherwise subject to the claims of military service.

From Compulsory to Voluntary Service

Liberty is a basic right in democratic societies. It is the right freely to set and pursue ends of one's own choosing, compatible of course with a similar right held by others.[45] Yet even this right is not absolute. There are occasions when liberty is justly compromised so that other values can be achieved. The question is whether war and the defense of national security are (at least sometimes) among those occasions.

There are three general answers to the question. One has its roots in the civic republican tradition of Machiavelli and Rousseau. According to this tradition, the health of a democratic republic depends on the willingness of all citizens to subordinate their liberty to gain military training and actively to serve when called on to do so. It is a view that expects military training, like public education, to be compulsory for all citizens at a certain time in their life. In the United States, this idea commonly underwrites proposals for universal military training, a proposal first endorsed by George Washington for the new United States, and periodically revived by others since then. The proposal has never been adopted.

A second answer has its roots in the libertarian tradition and holds it is a contradiction to compel military service in defense of freedom. According to this view, state coercion is always suspect, even when used to defend its existence. If citizens are unwilling to volunteer (or adequately to support the recruitment of volunteers) to defend their freedom, that freedom must not be worth much and its disappearance would be no loss. Equally important, relying on volunteers rather than conscripts requires the government to have the people's support before going to war and prevents the government from undertaking "military adventures." This was the reason Congress, late in the War of 1812, refused to grant a request from the Secretary of War for authority to draft a larger force.[46] Congress feared the government might use drafted forces to expand the war into Canada. Both the republican and libertarian positions assume that the policy they recommend should be followed at all times.

A third approach adopts a pragmatic perspective. It does not assume that a single form of military service—compulsory or voluntary—will invariably meet the country's needs. Rather the nation should rely on whatever form of military recruitment meets the particular needs of a particular time. Sometimes war or threats of war might require a system of compulsory military service. Sometimes volunteer service will be enough. To decide which kind of recruitment is preferable, a prudential standard is employed. How many people are needed to create a military strong enough to defeat the threat? Given that answer, are these people more likely to be gained through compulsory service or volunteerism? When the United States has required mass armies, pragmatists have argued for some kind of conscription—usually a selective service through which citizens possessing required skills or capacities are drafted for a time into military service. This has not always worked. In the Civil War, conscription met with little success; citizens rioted rather than submit to it and found many ways to evade it. But during the world wars, conscription was widely accepted and proved to be a practical success.

With World War II drawing to a close, it was an open question whether to adopt a republican system of universal military training, create an all-volunteer force, or maintain the pragmatic system of selective service, in place since 1940. By 1950, the question was answered, with proposals for either universal military training or voluntary service rejected by an emerging consensus to continue selective service. This consensus lasted until the 1960s when, under pressure from the Vietnam War (and other factors), it unraveled. This created a political opportunity for libertarians to establish an all-volunteer force.

In 1945, President Truman (like Roosevelt before him) asked Congress to adopt a program of universal military training (UMT).[47] He had believed for thirty years that UMT was the best way to ensure military preparedness and build a strong citizenry. Addressing a joint session of Congress in October 1945 he outlined the principal features of his program, and asked Congress to approve it. The basic idea was to have all eighteen-year-old men, who were physically able, complete one year of military training.[48] They would not then go on "active duty," but would stand by for a period of time in the "general reserves," ready to be called up for active service should it be needed. Under this postwar plan, the country could maintain a relatively small active-duty force, with the National Guard and organized reserves serving as a first line of defense. Yet in case a large mass army were needed, as it was in World War II, there would be a supply of young men already trained and ready for service. UMT would provide the country "a well-trained and effectively organized citizen reserve to reinforce professional armed forces in times of danger." Truman also noted that "the latent strength of our untrained citizenry was no longer sufficient protection." Under the conditions of modern war, "we could never again count on the luxury of time with which to arm ourselves." We had to be trained already to repulse the enemy. There was no time, as there had been in prior wars, to raise and train a military force, as both a voluntary system and selective service required.[49] But even if unneeded for war, UMT was worth supporting. It would create good citizens. It would improve the health of those trained, provide them with moral and civic education, and make them more cosmopolitan as they met and learned to live with others unlike themselves.[50]

Truman's proposal, for which he lobbied repeatedly, did not receive a wildly enthusiastic response. The immediate postwar goal in Congress was drastically to reduce the size of the military as quickly as possible and to end compulsory military service.[51] Congress had no thoughts of adopting a new compulsory scheme for military training. In May 1945, while war still raged in the Pacific, it extended the draft for only one year. To the dismay of President Truman and General George C. Marshall, it required that draftees below nineteen years of age not be deployed overseas until they received six months training. Yet it was not acting arbitrarily; its actions reflected public sentiment. Congress was flooded with letters calling for demobilization. Troops stationed in Europe did not believe it was fair that, having fought the war, they should now remain in Europe as occupation forces; they thought occupation was a job for others. In August 1945, they "began rioting to get out." Troops stationed in the Pacific were of much the same mind; they rioted for their early release in January 1946.[52] Members of Congress knew that people were still needed to serve, but many hoped the military could rely on volunteers, not compulsory servers. As the historian George Q. Flynn tells us, "The public's position on the draft seemed clear: bring the troops home immediately and stop taking boys through the draft"; and he notes that "by VJ day leaders in both the House and Senate opposed continuing the draft."[53]

What followed was, in Truman's words, a "frenzied demobilization."[54] From its height of over twelve million active-duty personnel serving in 1945, the active duty force was reduced to just over three million in 1946. It reached a low of just under one and a half million in 1948, a low that would not be seen again until after the end of the Cold War in the late 1990s. This was a dramatic and rapid reduction in force size. Even so, at the low point in 1948, by American experience, the military was still large for a peacetime force; it was nearly four and a half times larger than the peacetime force of ten years before.[55] However frenzied, we cannot truly say demobilization went so far that the military was no longer a mass armed force. Although it may not have been entirely clear at the time, the central debate was not about whether to dismantle the mass army for some other kind of force structure. It was about how to raise the needed forces.

For five years, Truman lobbied for UMT while Congress hoped for an end to the draft. Congress held hearings to study Truman's proposal in 1945, 1946, 1947, and 1948, as it would also do in 1952, but nothing came from them, no matter which political party had the majority. It was not that bills for UMT were repeatedly put to a vote and defeated. Rather, bills were rarely reported out of committee. If a proposal for UMT ever did escape committee for a vote on the floor, the decision was to do nothing. This was the case on March 4, 1952, when the House voted to send the bill back to committee for further study.[56] UMT was never adopted. Congress, meanwhile, fared little better. The draft was ended briefly in 1947 and 1948, but it was not ended permanently. Neither Truman nor Congress got the policy it wanted. Instead, the country moved from confusion about how best to raise military forces to the consensus that the pragmatic alternative of selective service best met the country's needs. How is this outcome explained?

First, support for UMT was always mixed. When public opinion pollsters asked whether the public was for or against the program, which they did four times between 1947 and 1953, support for UMT was very high, ranging from 69 to 74 percent.[57] In particular, the proposal was popular among veterans groups, military reserve associations, chambers of commerce, and others. But the proposal also had strong detractors, including organized labor and education, church and peace groups, farmers, and the NAACP.[58] And public support was not as strong as it seemed. When pollsters asked in 1947 whether Congress had failed to do something it should have done, only 2 percent mentioned that it should have passed a UMT bill.[59] Support for UMT was high in principle, but the need for it did not seem pressing. In contrast, opponents of UMT were strongly against it. They thought the use of compulsion in peacetime, "whether for training or service, would militarize America, smother democracy, . . . contradict the principle of free conscience, and insult the memory of the millions who had fled conscript tyranny in Europe to find freedom and peace in the New World."[60] They wanted no part of this.

Second, there were practical reasons for choosing selective service even though as a matter of principle it was not a first choice. In 1945 and 1946, there was an immediate need for men to serve in the occupation forces. It was not clear whether enough people could be raised by voluntary means to do it. UMT was not a viable alternative, as it would take time to establish and was not designed to produce active duty forces. Only selective service, already in place, could meet the need. However reluctant Congress was to renew the draft, it was expedient to do so. In addition, by 1946, renewing the draft served as a signal of American resolve to counteract the new threat posed by the Soviet Union, which seemed to have expansionary ambitions in Eastern Europe and elsewhere. These ambitions were explained in George Kennan's famous "long telegram," sent from Russia in February 1946, and they led Kennan to advocate for a strong military to support what came to be called the policy of containment.[61] Fears of Soviet expansion, however, were not always enough to support the argument that conscription or some other form of compulsory service was needed to maintain military strength.

Third, the Truman administration was not consistent in making its case for UMT or any alternative policy. In his state of the union address of 1947, Truman claimed that the Army could not rely on volunteers to meet its manpower needs. Yet in the same month the War Department adopted a policy that seemed to contradict him. It decided no draftees were needed to meet its requirements between January and the end of March, when the draft was scheduled to expire. Under this circumstance, and with conscription opposed by two key Democratic Party constituencies (organized labor and African Americans), it would be hard to win support for extension of the draft. Truman told Congress he would not try. The mass army based on conscription was allowed to die and the case for compulsory UMT was considerably weakened.[62] Looking for a silver lining, Truman may have hoped to have an easier time building support for universal military training with conscription out of way. If he did, the hope was not long lived.

Lobbying for UMT continued. On March 2, 1948, just one week after the coup d'état in Czechoslovakia cast further doubts on the prospects for peace with the Soviet Union, George C. Marshall, now Secretary of State, met with members of the Senate Armed Forces Committee to promote Truman's UMT proposal. But, once again, contrary proposals being weighed within the administration pointed in a different direction. At the National Security Council meeting on February 12, 1948, Secretary of

Defense James Forrestal argued that conscription (not UMT) might be needed if the military were to meet its obligations to the United Nations and respond to developing security concerns in the Middle East. More pointedly, on March 14, the Joint Chiefs of Staff accepted a staff paper that said both voluntary enlistments and UMT were too slow to meet the military's manpower needs; it called for the "immediate reenactment of the draft." Three days later, Truman asked Congress to pass the European Recovery bill (the Marshall Plan), to reenact the draft "temporarily," and to enact a permanent program for UMT.[63] Congress passed the European Recovery Act on April 3, 1948. It reinstituted the draft on June 24, 1948.[64] But it only held hearings on UMT, ultimately to reject the measure.[65]

Finally, when considering whether to reinstate the draft, a central question dominating Congressional debate was whether the action was permanent or temporary, which in turn was to ask whether the threats justifying a mass army in peacetime were themselves permanent or temporary. There was of course no ready answer to the question. The next year, after the act was passed, fewer than 10,000 were inducted into the military. The measure must have seemed temporary and probably unnecessary. In January 1950, Truman asked Congress to renew the draft before it expired at the end of June, but it was not at all clear that Congress would agree. Once again the draft seemed destined to lapse. Then, on June 25, communist North Korea invaded South Korea and the outbreak of a war decisively turned the tables. Five days after the invasion, Congress passed and Truman signed what had been a languishing bill to continue the system of conscription.[66]

From this point until 1967, in the midst of the Vietnam War, the institution of selective service became a taken-for-granted and seemingly permanent part of the Cold War fabric of American life. There was some talk of returning to a volunteer force and some talk of promoting UMT. But neither alternative was seriously considered. Congress routinely renewed selective service legislation, referred to after 1951 as the Universal Military Training and Service Act (a title that was as close as the various UMT proposals ever got to being passed). In the 1950s through the early 1960s, there was consensus that a peacetime mass army was needed to deter the Soviet threat and that conscription was the best means to raise a mass army. After all, selective service had proven its effectiveness in two world wars and in the Korean War. In contrast, a volunteer system could not reliably provide sufficient numbers of volunteers to meet force requirements, especially when a surge of forces was required, and a program of universal military training was too slow and costly to implement and too demanding in its requirements for youth service to garner broad political support.

Why did this consensus about the need for a conscripted mass army break down by the early 1970s, over fifteen years before the collapse of the Soviet Empire and the end of the Cold War? The simplest answer is that popular protest against the Vietnam War spilled over to discredit it. There is truth to the claim, but it is incomplete and misleading as it stands.

While public support for the draft had been high through the 1950s and early 1960s, in retrospect we can say that support did not run deep. After all, the burden imposed by the draft was light. Since the end of the Korean War, the number of draft calls had been trending steadily downward and the rejection rate of draftees had risen from an average of 38.1 percent over the years 1948 to 1956 to 52.7 percent in 1961. More important, in 1963 and 1964 "more men were being deferred than conscripted."[67] In its annual report for fiscal year 1960, the Selective Service System noted that "delivery of manpower for induction into the Armed Forces [was] a collateral product of the System's operation." The System's other product, it claimed, were the millions of registrants it was "developing [into] more effective men in the national interest through channeling."[68] Channeling was the practice of offering draft deferments to encourage young men to continue with higher education—especially to become scientists, who were perceived to be in short supply—or else to enter into other kinds of employment that were necessary to maintain the nation's strength. It had its origins in the mid-1950s when fewer people were needed in the military at the same time draft-eligible youth cohorts were growing in size.[69] Despite this light burden, there were already protests against the draft, from the dramatic and destructive firebombing of Selective Service Headquarters in Wisconsin, a few weeks before President Kennedy was assassinated, to an anti-draft rally held on Armed Forces Day 1964, at which twelve young men burned their draft cards to the applause of 150 onlookers.[70]

President Lyndon Johnson tested the depths of public support for the draft when he decided in July 1965 to escalate American involvement in the Vietnam War. His aim was to avoid seeking Congressional approval for the escalation—beyond that already provided by the Tonkin Gulf Resolution of 1964—because it might risk support for his domestic Great Society programs. To do this, he decided to raise the troops by increasing draft calls and not calling up the National Guard or reserves as his military advisers had asked him to do. The decision was flawed. By failing to mobilize the reserves and instead opting for a strategy of gradual escalation, he withheld from the military the means and public support they thought were needed to wage a successful war. He also withheld from the public— and so from public debate—a full accounting of what he knew the war could cost in money, time, and lives, and of the reasons why at least some advisers thought the expected outcome was gloomy.[71] Although there were public warnings against American military involvement in Vietnam before the decision to escalate was made, the president did not anticipate how quickly escalation would generate strong protests against both the war and the draft.[72]

Ironically, the protesters came primarily from the ranks of the politically liberal, Johnson's natural constituency. They were college students associated with the New Left, veterans of the civil rights movement, leaders of liberal religious denominations, academics, and others who wished to emancipate individuals from the exercise of institutional authority. They offered various reasons for their opposition to the draft. They thought the draft was unjust because the war was unjust. Because it relied on compulsion, they thought the draft violated individual conscience, which free countries were pledged to respect. And they thought the draft operated inequitably, as it mobilized the less advantaged members of society while allowing the more advantaged to stay home, complete their educations, marry, and start families. Of all these reasons, the last, that the draft was inequitable, had the greatest currency. The draft's central problem was that it unfairly distributed the burdens of military service and that, in the absence of total mobilization as was required for World War II, it could not do otherwise. This irresolvable dilemma was conjured by the question: Who serves when not all serve?[73]

The apparent inequities in the draft had multiple sources. The major one was the demographic disparity between the large number of youth available to serve and the much smaller number required. The disparity was greater than it was for the Korean conflict, another limited war, because large numbers of the baby boomer generation came to military age during the Vietnam era.[74] This permitted continuing the practice of "channeling," which had the effect of excusing more advantaged youths from military service during a time of war. Another problem was that local draft boards were not representative of their communities, especially in urban areas, raising questions about whether their decisions to draft some and defer others were disinterested or biased. Moreover boards failed to implement draft regulations uniformly across the country so like cases were not treated alike. Resort to a lottery could help resolve these problems as could simplification (or elimination) of the system of deferments and exemptions that had grown complex since the end of the Korean War. Eventually, both steps were taken, yet not before the decision to end the draft was almost reached, and by then not everyone was convinced that even a reformed system was fairer. In 1966, for the first time since the question was asked, less than a majority (only 43 percent) believed that the draft was handled fairly in their community.[75]

The effects of popular protest alone, however, do not explain the decline of the mass army and the rise of the all-volunteer force. They were, at most, a "proximate cause," affecting the timing of the transition from one force to the other without being a fundamental cause. From a pragmatic perspective, far more important than popular protest was the changing technology of war. As Morris Janowitz put it, growth in the destructive capacity of modern weapons systems made mobilization of conscripts for a mass army virtually irrelevant to effective military organization.[76] This was partly a claim about how reliance on weapons of mass destruction might affect the utility of mass armies in battle. It was also a claim about growing complexity of the military division of labor. The effectiveness of the mass army was predicated on a relatively simple war technology that citizen soldiers could master with a minimum of training. But with more complex weapons systems and more complex ways of coordinating forces in battle, the need was greater for soldiers at all ranks to be highly versed in a specialized set of tasks. In this context, the citizen soldier was simply less useful than a professional soldier. This technological development was a general factor that did not affect the American military alone. Over the last third of the twentieth century, the militaries of all Western European countries tended away from conscripts and toward a reliance on professional volunteers.[77] When and how to they made this shift has varied, in no small part to accommodate values embedded in their domestic political cultures.[78] But all have moved away from the mass toward the professional army format.

In the American case, political support for transition to an all-volunteer force originated with conservative members of the Republican Party in the 1960s. They were "young Turks" who represented a rising tide of political conservatism, embracing a libertarian doctrine. The extent of their influence would not fully register in American politics until after Ronald Reagan's election as president in 1980. Nonetheless, they (unlike their Democratic opponents) had devised a solution to the inequities plaguing the draft, as early as 1964. They proposed to end the inequities by ending the draft itself and creating an all-volunteer force. The Republican Party platform drafted for that year's presidential election included a commitment to do just that. Nor were these Young Turks deterred when their candidate, Senator Barry Goldwater, lost in a landslide against the incumbent President Johnson. Theirs was a principled position. They opposed compulsory service. Although they wanted a strong defense, their larger aim was to preserve and protect individual freedom, and to rely on market forces to allocate benefits and burdens.

By 1966, at a famous conference on the draft held at the University of Chicago, the economists Walter Oi and Milton Friedman redefined the equity principles at stake in graphic material terms. The draft, they said, was like a tax unfairly levied. It fell heaviest on those who were forced to serve and were then poorly compensated for their service. The rest, meanwhile, got national security at cut rates. This inequity could be removed only if the people paid the going rate for military personnel, and that rate could be determined only if soldiers were recruited in the open market. In short, they advocated for an all-volunteer force. An influential group of Republicans promoted these ideas in their 1967 study on *How to End the Draft*.[79] This was the constituency to whom Richard Nixon appealed when he promised to end the draft in a major policy address broadcast over CBS on October 17, 1968, while he was running for the presidency. An all-volunteer force, he said, was demanded by the new technology of war, while the draft was unfair and unacceptable to a nation devoted to "liberty, justice and equality."[80] After the election was won, Nixon began to pay his campaign debts. In March 1969, he appointed a commission—led by Thomas Gates, who had served as Secretary of Defense in the Eisenhower administration—to study the feasibility of ending the draft.[81] While awaiting its report, he asked for and received authority from Congress to redress some of the draft's inequities by adopting a draft lottery, limiting the discretion of the local boards.[82]

The following February, the Gates Commission reported back to the president making what one scholar called, "the best case possible" for establishing an all-volunteer force.[83] On April 23, 1970, Nixon sent a message to Congress endorsing the Gates Commission report. At the same time he issued an executive order to end occupational, agricultural, and all future paternity deferments, and asked Congress for authority to end student deferments as well. In September, he hoped to make draft boards more representative of their communities by requiring that board members live in the county of the board's jurisdiction. These measures aimed to increase the fairness of the draft, and they were not unimportant, as Nixon also requested and received authority from Congress to continue the draft for another two years past its scheduled expiration in 1971. The additional time was needed to ensure a successful transition to a volunteer force. It allowed the government to wind down American involvement in the Vietnam War, reduce force size to meet fiscal restraints, and develop a recruiting plan that might work without compromising national defense. But ending the draft, not reforming it, was the primary objective. What proponents of the all-volunteer force within Nixon's administration sought was to revise the moral contract for military service. They rejected the idea that the government should compel people to perform military service.[84] On July 1, 1973, they got what they wanted; the draft was officially ended.

The first years of the all-volunteer force did not bode well for its long-term success. Serious questions were raised about the quality of the force. The proportion of enlisted recruits in the Army who had high school degrees dropped sharply from an average of 66.7 percent for the years 1967 to 1973 to an average of 56.6 percent for the years 1974 to 1979.[85] The proportion of recruits in the 1970s who scored in the lowest eligible category (CAT IV) on the Armed Forces Qualification Test soared from less than 20 percent in 1973 to nearly 50 percent in 1980.[86] Even when recruiting people who were only marginally qualified, the Army had trouble meeting its recruiting goals and on top of that fewer of its people were reenlisting.[87] Others worried that the volunteer force was not representative of the larger society. Morris Janowitz and Charles C. Moskos noted that, in its first five years, the all-volunteer force had become socially unrepresentative, with a disproportionately large number of African Americans. Before the all-volunteer force era, black enrollment in the military was roughly equal to the proportion of blacks in the total population (about 10 percent). By 1978, black representation had risen to nearly 20 percent within the enlisted ranks. There was wide variation by service, with the fewest blacks in the Navy (9.3 percent) and the highest in the Army (29.1 percent). This disproportion alarmed Janowitz and Moskos because, they believed, an unrepresentative force unfairly put a greater burden for national defense on the shoulders of minorities who were still subject to the disadvantages of racial discrimination. As a result, the military would have difficulty retaining its legitimacy within a democratic society.[88]

It is an important question to ask about the moral contract for military service, whether the burdens of service should weigh disproportionately on members of minority groups. How one answers it depends a great deal on whether the choice to enter the service is a genuinely free choice (as libertarians believe it is) or is an unfairly constrained choice resulting from discrimination in the larger society (as civic republicans, favoring universal service, suspect it might be). We have more to say on this issue in the next section. For now, it is enough to distinguish it from the problem of quality.

Through the 1980s, problems of quality were addressed. The various services learned how to market themselves in the youth labor market, and the appeal of military service was bolstered when President Jimmy Carter gained agreement from Congress substantially to increase military pay and enlistment bonuses over the next two fiscal years beginning in 1981.[89] President Carter asked for and received Congressional approval to reinstitute draft registration (for men only) in response to the Soviet Union's invasion of Afghanistan, but this was considered a matter of political signaling. It represented no serious move to resume the draft. When Ronald Reagan succeeded Carter as president, the volunteer force once again had a president who was ideologically committed to the free market ethos on which the all-volunteer force was based. Under his administration, the social representativeness of the force improved, in part by Congressional mandate, which required that virtually all new recruits into the military had to have a high school diploma.[90] In addition, in 1985, Congress passed the Montgomery G.I. Bill to provide substantial educational benefits to veterans of the volunteer force, making service more attractive to those with college aspirations.[91] The quality of the force was confirmed, nearly twenty years after it was formed, when it met and swiftly defeated the battle-tested army of Iraq in the Persian Gulf War in 1991. That confirmation has been ratified by the military's performance in the more recent wars in Afghanistan and Iraq, despite the deplorable and inexcusable practices of prisoner abuse during the subsequent occupations.

There are occasional calls to return to a conscript force, most recently in response to the War in Iraq. Even before that war began in March 2003, two members of Congress, Charles B. Rangel (D-NY) and John Conyers, Jr. (D-MI) supported reinstituting the draft to help ensure that "people of color and persons from low-income backgrounds" do not bear a disproportionate risk of death and injury when wars are fought. In Rep. Rangel's words they want to "give the rich a chance" to fight.[92] More recently some have considered a highly selective draft to supply the military with people who possess particularly needed skills, while others want a draft for additional forces to relieve a military currently overstretched by its fight against terrorism.[93] But these calls for a draft seem designed more to criticize the current composition and size of the all-volunteer force than to bid seriously for a return to a conscript-based mass army.

Support for selective service was always pragmatic, a contingent clause of the moral contract for military service. That support evaporated when President Johnson misused the draft to fight in Vietnam without leveling with the people about what sacrifice would be required. But this reason was not the only one at work. Support for selective service was already eroding because the changing technology of war favored a professional military over a conscripted one. With the new technology, it was not practical or necessary to continue the draft. For the same reasons, there was no strategic use for universal military training, despite continued calls for program of national service that emphasized its importance for civic education. In this setting, the libertarian case for a voluntary force was persuasive, although questions nag about whether the burden of national defense could be fairly shared or justly allocated by market forces.

Inclusiveness and Equal Opportunity

After the shift to an all-volunteer force in 1973, the most important revisions to the moral contract for military service dealt with inclusiveness and equal opportunity. On the surface, at stake was the social representativeness of the force. In part, questions about whether the composition of the military should mirror that of society in terms of class, ethnicity, and gender drove the debate. But underlying these questions was a deeper one, more challenging to the military and society. Should the opportunity to serve in the military be distributed fairly, in a nondiscriminatory way?[94] This question cannot be answered by ensuring that the proportion (say) of African Americans serving in the military—in each service or in every branch—is the same as their proportion in the larger society. What matters more is whether those who serve (or would like to serve) have a fair chance for an equal opportunity to compete for the social goods military service has to offer. Consider this. In World War II, black men served in the military at a rate roughly proportional to their presence in the total population, but they had no fair chance for equal opportunity in a segregated force within which they were largely restricted to combat support roles. In contrast, in the all-volunteer force, although blacks are over-represented relative to their presence in the total population, they have a much fairer chance for equal opportunity than their fathers and grand-fathers had in World War II. Rates of participation alone do not suffice as a measure of equal opportunity.

Some might dismiss this deeper question as simply rhetorical. Of course, we would say, the opportunity to serve in the military ought to be distributed fairly, in a nondiscriminatory way. But that glosses over diffi-culties. Not to distribute fairly, but to discriminate against one group or another, is an easy and common social practice, one that we often justify as wholly appropriate, when we do not belong to the group that is sub-jected to discrimination.

What needs to be examined, then, are the social deliberations under-taken, usually from unequal positions of power, to distinguish between fair and unfair kinds of discrimination. Often enough, as these delibera-tions relate to the moral contract for military service, they have institu-tionalized inequality among supposedly equal citizens.[95] But why should that be true? What determines the course these deliberations take? In our case, a general pattern is clear. The years from 1945 to 1973 were, as we have seen, characterized by a rapid growth of rights, but they recorded only halting progress by the military to increase inclusiveness and equal op-portunity within the ranks. In contrast, the history of the all-volunteer force is one of increasing inclusiveness and tearing down barriers to equal opportunity, but has not seen a rapid growth of political rights. To under-stand this curious reversal of trends, we have to consider what groups were likely beneficiaries of change and whether change was supported or re-sisted by prevailing social practices. Let's begin with the pursuit of equal opportunity by African Americans and women in World War II and the years following the end of that conflict up to the establishment of the all-volunteer force.

Like American society in general, the military was a segregated institu-tion before and throughout World War II. In World War I, states in the South drafted black men at a higher rate than white men. Then the mili-tary restricted blacks to service in menial occupations in segregated units. (Between the wars, the Navy allowed blacks to volunteer for service only in the kitchens.)[96] Not surprisingly, at the onset of World War II, African American leaders sought fairer treatment for African American men bound for military service or for employment in war-related industries. They knew that the country needed support from their community for the

war effort and they knew that the Democratic Party required their electoral support. They used this knowledge to good advantage. In 1940, while
Congress debated whether to establish a "peacetime" draft, they lobbied
President Roosevelt directly and gained his pledge that blacks would have
access to all branches, could serve as commissioned officers, and "would
be drafted only in proportion to their percentage in the population."[97] In
early 1941, A. Philip Randolph, president of the Brotherhood of Sleeping
Car Porters, threatened to organize a massive protest march on Washington unless President Roosevelt took action against racial discrimination in
defense plants. Roosevelt took action, "issuing an executive order banning
discrimination in defense plants and in government agencies" and establishing "the Fair Employment Practices Committee to implement the order." The committee later claimed that nearly two-thirds of the two
million blacks employed in war industry owed their jobs to its efforts.[98]

Promises were made, but not fully honored. Blacks were underrepresented in the military, making up roughly 8 percent of the Army and,
at the war's end, 4 percent of the Navy and 2.5 percent of the Marine
Corps. No service reached the planned for 10 percent quota. At the very
beginning of the war, the Navy and Marine Corps did not permit blacks to
volunteer, a restriction they relaxed in 1942. Eventually, they were ordered
to accept blacks who were drafted.[99] Not surprisingly, given years of Jim
Crow segregation that denied both basic liberties and opportunities for
blacks in civilian society, those who did enter the military were poorly educated when compared to whites (though they were better educated than
their fathers in World War I). Perhaps for this reason or perhaps because
the military reflected civilian practices of discrimination, black soldiers
were most often assigned to unskilled jobs. In 1942, 48 percent of the
blacks serving were assigned to the "service forces"—mainly to work in
engineer, quartermaster or transportation units. By 1945, 75 percent of
black soldiers serving were assigned to service units, which made up only
39 percent of the Army's strength.[100] Only toward the end of the war were
blacks given an opportunity to fight. When fighting as a segregated black
division, their combat performance was mixed at best, most likely due to
poor planning and training. But when fighting as segregated rifle platoons
beside white rifle platoons or as smaller all-black units such as fighter
squadrons or tank battalions, African American performance in combat
was distinguished.[101]

Blacks were acutely aware that they were fighting in a war for freedom
while they were subject to lynching and humiliating discrimination at

home. Yet they hoped, as a result of their service, to garner more rights and privileges than they had before.[102] As we saw at the beginning of the chapter, the "homecoming reception" that Issac Woodard received showed that these hopes were not quickly or easily fulfilled.

In 1948, when President Truman wanted to resume the draft, African Americans lobbied for more equal treatment, as they had in World War II. Once again A. Philip Randolph was a key leader applying pressure, calling on blacks to boycott the draft unless the military was racially integrated. But his bargaining position in peacetime, now not so great as it had been during war, left him unable to persuade Truman or Congress to integrate the military. The new draft law signed in June 1948 simply repeated the language of the 1940 draft law, which banned discrimination but not segregation. Unexpectedly, the prospects for change brightened when, in July, Southern Democrats bolted their party. Supporters of segregation, they left because the Democratic platform committee had, over their objection, embraced planks promising to protect blacks' voting rights and guarantee blacks equal opportunity. No longer needing to placate the racist wing of the party, Truman was freed politically to integrate the military, motivated in part by conviction and in part by his need for the black vote to win the upcoming election. On July 26, he issued Executive Order 9981 making it policy "that there shall be equality of treatment and opportunity for all persons in the Armed Forces." The order also established the President's Committee on Equality of Treatment and Opportunity, which was empowered to enforce the order. These were real turning points in the struggle for equal rights and opportunities for minorities. Still, the immediate results were disappointing. The military, in particular the Army, did not rush to implement the order.[103] Not until the Korean War broke out in 1950 did the Army move seriously to implement Truman's order.[104] It was October 1953 before the Army announced that 95 percent of African American soldiers were serving in integrated units and another year before there were no more all-black units.[105]

Even then, racial integration was far from complete, in part for understandable reasons, as American society at the time remained a highly segregated society. Evidence of racial prejudice and discrimination infecting American life would be easy to find in the military throughout the 1950s and 1960s.[106] Though, on some accounts, less intense than found in civilian society, racial frictions traveled with the military wherever it went, including Vietnam. Racial clashes were common throughout the military's presence there, though more often in the rear areas than in combat zones.

The race riot among prisoners in the Long Binh stockade following Martin Luther King's assassination in 1968 was only the most dramatic and violent of these. Other outbreaks of racial violence occurred elsewhere in the late 1960s and early 1970s, on board naval vessels and at home, and in each of the services.[107]

The situation for women in this period with respect to equal opportunity in the military was, if anything, worse than it was for African American men.[108] Women, of course, were mobilized into the military as they were mobilized into the workforce during World War II. Initially, the women who joined the Army had only an auxiliary status. As the need for their service grew, women were recruited into the Navy, Marines, and Coast Guard and given reserve military status. In the bidding for women's services, the Army soon gave full military status to those who joined its women's corps. By the time the war ended, about 350,000 women had served.[109] They hoped that their wartime service, not only in uniform but in defense industries as well, would justify passing an Equal Rights Amendment to the Constitution, as their service in World War I had justified passing the 19th Amendment, granting women's suffrage. President Truman was on record in favor of it as were thirty governors and Congress seriously considered it. But, in the end, support for the measure did not survive Congressional debate and it failed to pass.[110]

Congressional initiatives that did pass, designed to help veterans, turned out to be more generous and protective of male than of female veterans and a smaller percentage of women than men claimed the benefits they were due.[111] The number of women serving in the postwar military fell from its wartime peak of roughly 270,000 to 14,000, and the legislation authorizing them to serve at all was set to expire in 1948. To retain women's service, Congress passed the Women's Armed Service Integration Act. The act permitted women to serve both in the enlisted ranks and the officer corps. But their service was limited. By number, women in the enlisted ranks could total no more than 2 percent of the total enlisted force; and women in the officer corps could total no more than 10 percent of the females in the enlisted ranks (excluding nurses). The act also limited women's promotion opportunities and forbade their service on combat aircraft or combat navy ships.[112] But in practice, even these small proportions were not reached. When conscription was restored in 1948 to alleviate manpower shortages, the military's need for women in uniform decreased. For twenty years after the act was passed "the representation of women in the military, including nurses, never exceeded 1.5 percent."[113] In 1951 the

Department of Defense established the Defense Advisory Committee on Women in the Service (DACOWITS). Its purpose was to help the department recruit women but, in fact, it served for two decades mainly in a public relations role. There was no effort to create equal opportunities for women in the military, and this perfectly reflected the gender stereotypes of the era that cast women in an inferior position to men— stereotypes that were not seriously challenged until the women's movement gained force in the late 1960s.[114]

This is not to say that, in the aftermath of World War II, there was no interest in securing more opportunities for citizens in uniform. The Roosevelt administration was mindful of the dissatisfied veterans from World War I who, calling themselves the Bonus Army, marched on Washington in the early days of the Great Depression, seeking an early payment of bonuses due for their military service. It hoped to devise programs to make real the ideal that military service was a path toward full participation in the life of the community. Quite apart then from the movements (noted earlier) to expand political rights, the moral contract for military service was revised to expand equality of opportunity for those who served in the military and for those who would serve. This revision was written into the Servicemen's Readjustment Act—the GI Bill of Rights—signed into law on June 22, 1944. Spearheaded by the American Legion, the law authorized many benefits for veterans, the most important of which were low-cost loans to purchase a home or business and funds to pay for up to four years of education. At the signing ceremony President Roosevelt remarked that members of the armed forces—men and women—"have been compelled to make greater economic sacrifice, and every other kind of sacrifice, than the rest of us and are entitled to definite action to help take care of their special problems."[115] The entitlement was at least a compensation for service, to ensure that citizen soldiers, having performed their military service, had a fair chance at equal opportunities as they returned to their homes. It might be more. The Supreme Court thought veterans should be rewarded for their service, gaining "an advantage which the law withheld from those who stayed behind."[116]

However conceived, the entitlement program was quite successful. Over half of the veteran population—7.8 million—took advantage of the educational program alone at a cost of $14.5 billion. About one-fifth of the federal budget in 1948 went to pay for the whole range of veterans' benefits, from education and medical expenses to housing loans and job placement services. These programs were sufficiently popular that subsequent wars produced similar measures, one on July 16, 1952, to provide benefits for Korean War veterans, another on March 3, 1966, to provide benefits for Vietnam era veterans, and then another in 1985 to bolster recruiting into the all-volunteer force.[117] But successful as these have been, we should keep in mind that white male veterans and their families benefited disproportionately. The actual value of the GI Bill was much less for black veterans who were not as free to use educational benefits in a society that maintained a separate and unequal system of higher education or to use guarantees for home loans in a society that practiced residential segregation. The same was true for women veterans. When seeking job-placement assistance, they were directed to lower skilled (and lower paying) "women's jobs." Their dependents received lower levels of financial assistance than the dependents of male veterans; and if a woman veteran was married and disabled, her husband could not (as the wives of disabled male veterans could) be awarded her preference in civil service employment.[118]

Two factors undercut these discriminatory provisions in the moral contract for military service that disadvantaged women and African Americans and minorities more generally. One was the growing liberalism of American society with respect to civil and social rights, epitomized by the Civil Rights Movement and its success in dismantling Jim Crow in the 1950s and 1960s. But it was manifest more widely by increasing public support for civil liberties, women's rights, opposition to discrimination against homosexuals, and toleration of other kinds of differences. These trends remained robust well beyond the 1960s, continuing through the 1970s and beyond, despite a resurgence of political and economic conservatism in evidence since the Reagan administration.[119] But there was a second and more immediate factor: the creation of the all-volunteer force, which required the military to depend more on enlistments by minorities and women to meet its recruitment quotas. The two factors are related. As civilian society came increasingly to reject discriminatory practices that limited opportunities of minorities and women, it allowed the military to emphasize equal opportunity as a means of attracting recruits. Working against these factors, we shall see, was a conservative turn by the Supreme Court to slow—though it did not entirely stop—the expansion of military rights which had begun in the 1940s.

The need to reform discriminatory practices was evident in the early 1970s when military leaders began transition to the all-volunteer force. Racial tensions were high, as demonstrated by a number of dramatic incidents. In 1971, black airmen rioted at the Travis Air Force Base, protesting the failure of the base commander to declare a nearby apartment development off limits because it practiced racial discrimination. They also complained that blacks were unfairly fired from their jobs with on-base clubs.[120] Later that same year, a black enlisted soldier stationed in Europe was found not guilty for going AWOL because the racial climate of the Army was so poor that it excused his decision to escape, leading the commanding general of the army in Europe to work on improving that climate.[121] The next year brought a series of violent racial incidents on board three Navy ships.[122] Attempts by Admiral Elmo Zumwalt, the Chief of Naval Operations, to redress the matter by making "equal opportunity a reality and discrimination for any reason an unacceptable practice" met with resistance from his senior officers and some in Congress.[123] But he was joined by the Marine Corps Commandant, General Robert E. Cushman, who "declared that racial discrimination had no place in the corps" and showed that he meant it by banning "consideration of race" when assigning living quarters, selecting people for work details, or administering justice. Later that year, a task force reported that the administration of military justice was still plagued by systemic discrimination and recommended strong steps to overcome the problem—recommendations that the military was unready to accept.[124]

While unready to deal with systemic discrimination, the military was committed to reducing racial conflict, and that could be done only by curbing racial discrimination and offering training to promote better race relations.[125] The Army offered an example of how racial discrimination could be overcome, to provide a fair chance for equal opportunity, particularly for promotion in the ranks. As Charles Moskos and John Sibley Butler have shown, the Army did this by adopting three measures.[126] First, it established a policy of intolerance against any form of racial discrimination and allocated resources to give commanders tools to assess and improve the quality of race relations within their units. This work has been enhanced by the research and educational programs of the Defense Equal Opportunity Management Institute. Second, it maintained high performance standards for enlistments and promotions and adopted the goal of promoting minorities—and women—at the same rate as others. But there was no attempt to meet that goal if it could be met only by lowering standards. This helped ensure the success of the program. By not promoting unqualified people, the authority of minorities who were promoted was less likely to be questioned. Third, it made a significant commitment to establish training programs to help minorities and others with leadership potential acquire the education they needed to compete for advancement. The aim was to increase the pool of qualified people. Other services have followed a similar path.

As a result of such efforts, the military has offered a more attractive employment alternative than other venues for minorities seeking fair equality of opportunity. Minority service members are less subject to income discrimination than their counterparts in civilian society and, over the long run, minority veterans attain higher socioeconomic status than minorities who never served.[127] It is no wonder that blacks were disproportionately represented soon after the all-volunteer force was established and remain so to this day: Black rates of participation in the military were 19.2 percent in 1978; 23.2 percent in 1990, and 22.5 percent in 2001; the rates were highest in the Army at 29.1, 32.1, and 28.9 percent respectively. Over the whole period, almost twice the number of blacks served in the military as would be expected from the percent of blacks aged 18 to 44 in the civilian population.[128] Rather than indicating a problem with the all-volunteer force, this overrepresentation suggests the persistence of racial discrimination in the civilian labor force.

This is not to say, however, that the military has expunged all traces of racial prejudice or discrimination.[129] Even today blacks in the military, for instance, are more likely than whites to be charged, convicted, and sentenced within the military justice system.[130] This suggests a troubling persistence of systemic discrimination, despite the many efforts undertaken to ensure soldiers receive a fair trial. More generally, according to recent equal opportunity surveys, minorities in the military are significantly less likely than those in the majority to believe that problems of prejudice and discrimination have been overcome.[131] Further, whereas in civilian society, complaints of workplace discrimination can be brought before the courts for adjudication, that is difficult to do in the military. In *Chappell v. Wallace,* decided in 1983, the Supreme Court ruled that superior officers could not be sued by soldiers for practicing race discrimination even if their assignment, personnel evaluations, and punishments disproportionately harmed minorities.[132] (As we shall see, the right of women to redress equal opportunity complaints was also limited by the courts.)

A first step toward greater equality of opportunity for women in the military occurred in 1967, six years before the all-volunteer force was created. Responding to recommendations from a Defense Department task force and to public pressure organized by DACOWITS, Congress raised (without removing) the ceiling on promotion for female officers and

removed the 2 percent restriction on the number of female enlisted personnel, restrictions imposed by the Women's Integration Act of 1948.[133]
(Congress left untouched women's exclusion from certain combat roles.)
The immediate effect on increasing women's participation in the military
was limited, as the number of enlisted women on active duty was only 2.2
percent of the enlisted force when the all-volunteer force began. But the
action cleared the way for the increasingly higher rates of participation
which followed: 8.5 percent in 1980, 10.9 percent in 1990, 15.0 percent in
2002, and still rising.[134] Increases in women's participation were in part a
response to difficulties recruiting for an all-volunteer force. They were
also an anticipatory response by a majority in Congress who worked to
institute changes that might be required when the Equal Rights Amendment, approved by Congress in 1972, was ratified, as most at the time
thought it would be. (They were mistaken about this, as we shall see.)
Overcoming resistance in Congress and within the services, this majority
created a number of new opportunities for women in the military to enter the Reserve Officer Training Corps in 1972 and the service academies
in 1976, and to be assigned to noncombatant ships in 1978. In the same
year the Army moved toward greater gender integration by dissolving the
Women's Army Corps.[135]

The Supreme Court also found a constitutional basis for equal rights
for women. In 1971, it broke with a long line of precedent to rule that discrimination based on gender violated the equal protection clause of the
14th Amendment.[136] Two years later, the Court applied this logic to the
military, holding that spouses of women in the military were as entitled to
dependent's benefits as spouses of men in the military, reversing a discriminatory practice in place since World War II.[137] Yet, the Court did not
continue down this path, at least not with respect to the moral contract for
military service. Instead, under the influence of Justice (later Chief Justice) William H. Rehnquist, it followed a doctrine of "military deference."
The essence of this doctrine—first stated in *Parker v. Levy* (1974)—was
that the Constitution gave Congress, not the courts express powers to reg-
ulate the military, powers that the courts should respect. After all, as Justice Rehnquist wrote in the majority opinion, "the military is, by necessity,
a specialized society"; it is "a society apart from civilian society;" and
"while members of the military community enjoy many of the same
rights" as civilians, their rights are less.[138]

Adopting this doctrine allowed the Court to stand against further development of the rights revolution as it affected the terms of military

service. The doctrine stood behind the decision, *Chappell v. Wallace* (1983), that—as we earlier noted—denied service members the right to sue the military over acts they thought evidenced racial discrimination. It also stood behind decisions that thwarted the development of a strict equal rights approach toward men and women with respect to military service. In *Schlesinger v. Ballard* (1975), the Court ruled that the military could maintain different stricter promotion policies for men than for women, allowing women more time in rank before promotion, because there was a ceiling on the number of women's promotions. Instead, it might have asked what justified the ceiling. Four years later, it upheld the practice of giving veterans a lifetime preference over others for public employment, even though women had no equal right to join the military, thus putting them at a disadvantage in competing for this preference and for public employment.[139] Then, in *Rostker v. Goldberg*, the Court upheld the power of Congress to require only men to register for a possible draft into military service. At issue here was whether women shared equally with men the civic obligation to perform military service, even though their service was not in the combat arms. Those in dissent believed that the majority's decision unfairly discriminated against women in this regard, making them a kind of second-class citizen. The negative consequences of his decision, as we saw with respect to preferences for public employment, could last a lifetime.[140]

The role of women in the military was not only a topic for debate in the courts. It was also the central topic dividing supporters from opponents of the Equal Rights Amendment. Opponents of the amendment emphasized that, if passed, it would require sending women into combat, something that the public at that time was unwilling to support. (Public attitudes on this question changed markedly by the 1990s.) Proponents thought less about the pragmatic requirements of assuring its passage than about the principles at stake. They did not counter with a "deferential" interpretation of the amendment, holding that the military could decide how women in uniform should be employed. Rather, they stuck to a "strict egalitarian" interpretation that rejected any bars to sex-based discrimination. The political scientist Jane Mansbridge believes this was a crucial factor explaining why, in 1982, the amendment was defeated.[141]

A legacy of the debate, however, was to build a coalition between women within and outside the defense establishment to challenge restrictions on opportunities open to women in uniform. Higher ranking women officers and women working in the Defense Department's Equal Opportunity

Office encouraged the Women's Equity Action League and the National Federation of Business and Professional Women to challenge the classification of military jobs closed to women.[142] Women in uniform also created organizations (the Women's Officer Professional Association, for example) to promote their interests and to ally with organizations outside the military, like the Women's Rights Project of the ACLU.

In the 1980s and early 1990s, DACOWITS became an influential voice pushing for greater gender equality. This was nowhere more evident than in the campaign to repeal combat exclusion laws following the Persian Gulf War in 1991. DACOWITS passed a resolution urging the Secretary of Defense to support the repeal; the House voted to do so. But the measure stalled in the Senate, not least because the service chiefs opposed the repeal. They opposed it even if that meant—as the testimony of one chief confirmed—reducing military effectiveness. (This was an unusual twist, as opponents of gender integration usually contend that integration decreases effectiveness.) Despite the opposition of the chiefs, representatives of women's groups lobbied senators to pass the repeal. Beside them were uniformed officers, members of Women Military Aviators. Legally, these aviators could not lobby, but they were free to provide information based on their experience as military pilots. In part as a result of their efforts, the logjam in the Senate was broken. The National Defense Authorization Acts for 1992 and 1993 repealed the combat exclusion law. Further changes in law and policy opened more opportunities for women in the military throughout the 1990s. The prospects for change were further bolstered by strong support for equal opportunity from the Democratic administration of President William J. Clinton, which came to office in 1993.[143] Women are still barred from serving in ground combat units, but experience with the War in Iraq made clear (if it was unclear before) that women at war are exposed to the risks of combat.

Yet increased opportunities for minorities and women have not ensured their standing as equal members of the military community. We have already noted the persistence of systemic discrimination for minorities. To that we can add what appears to be deeply engrained gender discrimination as evidenced by sexual harassment scandals. The highly publicized Tailhook Association's meeting in 1991 suggested a pattern of degrading behavior toward women by naval aviators that was at least tacitly approved by senior military leaders. That perception was deepened in 1996 with disclosures of sexual harassment incidents in Army basic training camps.[144] In response to these scandals, the military instituted training programs to limit sexual harassment; from 1995 to 2002, surveys show, the number of incidents of sexual harassment declined substantially.[145] But in 2003, a new scandal broke, contradicting this impression. Journalists and congressional investigations revealed that well over 100 sexual assaults occurred over the previous decade at the Air Force Academy while those in command had done little to punish or prevent it. Nor were such problems confined to the academy. In 2004, the Air Force began investigating its response to allegations of sexual assaults throughout the service after learning about flaws in its handling of nearly 100 rape cases between 2001 and 2003.[146]

Finally, we should note, if only briefly, the failure of President Clinton's effort to rescind the ban on homosexuals openly serving in the military. Senior military officers adamantly opposed this proposal and they found substantial support in Congress. As a compromise measure, the military adopted a policy of "don't ask, don't tell." It prohibited "witch hunts" by the military against homosexuals in uniform and allowed homosexuals to serve, so long as they kept their sexual orientation private. The policy's effects are difficult to evaluate. The number of discharges for homosexuality actually increased after 1992, with women more likely than men to be discharged for this reason. As a percent of total military personnel, discharges rose from 0.04 percent in 1992 to 0.07 percent in 1997—and yet, this higher rate of discharge is lower than the rate for any year from 1980 to 1986 and roughly the same as rates for the years 1987 to 1991, before the policy was adopted.[147]

On balance, the shift to an all-volunteer force led to greater and more equal opportunities for women and African Americans to participate in the military in a fair, nondiscriminatory way. Since 1973, military participation rates by women rose from 2 percent to 15 percent, while participation rates by blacks rose from 10 to 22 percent. This represents a marked improvement for women, whose service opportunities were extremely limited during World War II and throughout the post-world war era up to 1973. It is also a marked improvement for blacks, whose service was limited by design to equal their proportion of the civilian population, until the all-volunteer force. Both women and blacks enjoy greater opportunities than they did in the postwar period before the all-volunteer force. Blatant racial discrimination leading to racial violence is now uncommon and programs are in place to ensure that blacks enjoy a fair chance to complete for military promotions. Similar programs are in place for women, and women are no longer excluded from most military jobs to shelter them from combat (though they are excluded from jobs in ground combat units). For blacks and for women, the volunteer military is an integrated, inclusive, equal opportunity force.

Nonetheless, worrisome evidence of continuing racial and gender discrimination cannot be overlooked. For blacks, the central issues have to do with a military justice system that is more punitive toward blacks than others at every step of the way, despite greater protections for a fair trial institutionalized over fifty years. Black perceptions that the military continues to discriminate cannot be ignored or dismissed so long as evidence of this kind exists. For women, the central issues have to do with weak institutional responses to sexual harassment, until the conduct becomes a public scandal. Could greater progress have been made? Counterfactual arguments are impossible to prove. Yet one might wonder if systemic discrimination against minorities would be so difficult to change had the Supreme Court—in *Chappell v. Wallace* (1983)—recognized that minorities had a right to sue the military to contest race-based assignments. In the same way, one might wonder if ratification of the Equal Rights Amendment would have increased the military's diligence to protect women in uniform from sexual harassment and assault. In any case, adequate protection of equal opportunities may require further revision of the moral contract for military service.

IMPLICATIONS

How, in the end, have changing terms of military service affected the development of American citizenship since the end of World War II? There is a great temptation to dodge the question because, as we have seen, an adequate answer requires many particular and qualified judgments. There is not likely to be one compelling answer to the question. Yet evasion on these grounds is no use. The issue at stake is too important. In American political culture, the normative ideal of the citizen soldier works to strengthen democratic citizenship when it employs mass armies. But does that mean democratic citizenship and so in some sense democracy itself is weakened when the mass army is traded for a volunteer force?

The question is not an idle one. As we have seen, the mass army raised to fight World War II and maintained through the end of the Vietnam era prepared the way for expanding citizens' rights, within the military and without. It also laid groundwork for a fairer equality of opportunities for the citizen soldiers who fought in the world war and for others, although this was less true for minorities and women than for others. This rights revolution came virtually to an end in the all-volunteer force era. In this period, there was no expansion of the rights of citizens in uniform to match what had come before; indeed, some retrenchment occurred. For pragmatic reasons, increasing equal opportunities for minorities and women received emphasis, to help meet the recruiting needs of the volunteer force. But even here the record was mixed, with significant achievements that promoted one's civic worth matched by continuing discrimination that undermined fair chances to serve as a free and equal citizen. The overall trend suggests that abandoning the ideal of the citizen soldier, conscripted into the mass army, curtailed the expansion of rights for citizens and soldiers who volunteered; and improvements in equal opportunities did not rest on a secure foundation of rights. What explains this trend?

As many have observed, the generation that fought in World War II had a unique and life-transforming experience. The political ideology justifying the war explained that they were fighting for the preservation of freedom itself, not just for themselves, but for all; and that freedom was realized through respect for human rights. When the war was done, those who fought and those who had stayed at home wished to secure those rights and worked to do so. Their efforts were successful in part because their numbers were so large, which counts in a democracy. But inevitably the influence of this generation began to wane; the freshness of its cause could not be sustained. It was not possible to transfer their political charisma to another generation. Yet the ideology of freedom justifying World War II could be passed on and was. Throughout the Cold War and beyond, that ideology occupied a central place in American political discourse. Still, its application to the Cold War proved to be more difficult, as was obvious in debates revolving around Vietnam and conflicts since then. More important, the number of people called to serve in the military steadily declined. Over 12 percent of the population was mobilized to fight in World War II, but only 4 percent to fight in Korea and Vietnam, only 1 percent in the Persian Gulf War, and far less than 1 percent are currently in uniform for the global war on terror. When only a small proportion of the population is called to serve, the political and social significance of the citizen soldier diminishes. As Max Weber argued, it is when the masses are under arms that they have political power.

Yet other countervailing factors need to be considered. Slowing the rights revolution was not entirely a product of the end of the mass army. We have seen that the movement to establish a volunteer force was led by a conservative movement within the Republican Party. The movement was based on a principled commitment to the justice of market-based solutions to public problems, like deciding who should serve in the military. Arguably, adherents of this movement accepted the vision of a rights-based society, but thought that those rights were better secured through market competition than through government compulsion and constitutional interpretation. They held an alternative vision of what was required to cultivate strong citizenship within a democratic society. The point is that while mass armies may make citizenship strong, there may be other means to accomplish that end.

Even if this conservative argument is not persuasive, the fact is that the military rights revolution occurred. Rights denied to citizens in uniform from the beginnings of the republic to 1945 are now well-established in military and constitutional law. This is not to imply that this establishment is without imperfections. The rights revolution did not lose momentum in the 1970s because there was no further need for reform. On the contrary: Our survey of the all-volunteer force era showed that minorities and women are not yet fully free and equal citizens, despite their military service. Yet the need for further reform does not deny the significant value of reforms already made.

On balance, changing terms of military service since 1945 expanded the rights of citizens and made citizenship more inclusive than it was. It stands as the accomplishment of a great generation. Slowed progress in this arena since the 1970s does not detract from the legacy. It defines a challenge citizens must face in generations to come.

Notes

1. Thomas Hobbes, *Leviathan*, ed. Richard Tuck (Cambridge: Cambridge University Press, 1991), 152. For a discussion of the rationale for Hobbes's instrumentalist views, see Everett Carl Dolman, "Obligations and the Citizen Soldier: Machiavellian Virtú Versus Hobbesian Order," *Journal of Political and Military Sociology* 23 (Winter 1995): 191–212.

2. For an excellent illustration of how the principal-agent model may be used to shed light on civil-military relations, see Peter D. Feaver, *Armed Servants* (Cambridge: Harvard University Press, 2003).

3. For a fuller discussion of the way values depend on or are sustained by social practice, see Joseph Raz, *The Practice of Value* (Oxford: Clarendon Press, 2003).

4. The term comes from Raz, *The Practice of Value*, 43.

5. Cf. *The Soldier and the State* (Cambridge: Harvard University Press, 1957), in which Samuel P. Huntington argues it is preferable that the military maintain values distinct from the larger society. He contends that a military somewhat alienated from society is better able to maintain its professional effectiveness. I am not persuaded that this is true.

6. Details for this story, unless otherwise noted, come from the account in Bernard C. Nalty, *Strength for the Fight: A History of Black Americans in the Military* (New York: Free Press, 1986), 204–6.

7. Truman is quoted in Nalty, *Strength for the Fight*, 205. Information about the theatrical benefit comes from "200 Veterans Wanted as Ushers," *New York Times* (August 14, 1946), 32. The article was only eight lines long. It was the only notice that the *New York Times* gave to the incident.

8. President's Committee on Civil Rights, *To Secure These Rights* (Washington, DC: Government Printing Office, 1947), 46.

9. As an example of how deeply racist was the moral contract for military service before World War II, notice that in the wake of World War I, the federal government paid the costs for war widows who visited the graves of their loved ones in Europe. All had sacrificed, but white war widows traveled aboard luxury liners, while black war widows were kept separate and sent on commercial steamers. See G. Kurt Piehler, "The War Dead and the Gold Star: American Commemoration of the First World War," in John R. Gillis, ed., *Commemorations: The Politics of National Identity* (Princeton: Princeton University Press, 1994), 169–85, esp. 178–80.

10. These figures are taken (with percentages calculated from) data found in Department of Defense, *Selected Manpower Statistics* (Washington, DC: Government Printing Office, 1997), table 2–11 and Bureau of the Census, *Historical Statistics of the United States: Colonial Times to 1970* (Washington, DC: Government Printing Office, 1975), table A6–8.

11. Jacques van Doorn, *The Soldier and Social Change* (Beverly Hills, CA: Sage, 1975).

12. On the connection between nationalism and mass armies, see Barry R. Posen, "Nationalism, the Mass Army and Military Power," *International Security* 18 (Fall 1993): 80–124 and Michael Howard, *War in European History* (Oxford: Oxford University Press, 1975). See also the classic work by Richard D. Challener, *The French Theory of the Nation in Arms, 1866–1939* (New York: Columbia University Press, 1955).

13. Titmuss, *Essays on 'The Welfare State'* (London: Allen & Unwin, 1958), 84.

14. Max Weber, *General Economic History* (New Brunswick, NJ: Transaction, 1981), 315–37; Janowitz, *Reconstruction of Patriotism* (Chicago: University of Chicago Press, 1983), 26–72; and Richard M. Titmuss, *Essays*, 75–87.

15. Morris Janowitz, *The Last Half-Century: Societal Change and Politics in America* (Chicago: University of Chicago Press, 1978), 176.

16. Morris Janowitz, *On Social Organization and Social Control*, ed. James Burk (Chicago: University of Chicago Press, 1991), 224.

17. Roger Reese, a Soviet scholar, has documented that Soviet citizens expected a softening in Stalin's regime as a result of their wartime service and their expectations were not disappointed, though of course the Soviet Union was no democracy. Personal communication.

18. James Burk, "The Citizen Soldier and Democratic Societies: A Comparative Analysis of America's Revolutionary and Civil Wars," *Citizenship Studies* 4 (Summer 2000), 149–65 and James Burk, "From Wars of Independence to Democratic Peace," in *Military, State, and Society in Israel* (New Brunswick: Transaction, 2001), 81–104. This argument has roots in the civic republican tradition, drawing on the ideas of Machiavelli and Rousseau, but it is not identical with that tradition.

19. The text of the speech can be found at http://www.americanrhetoric.com/speeches/fdrthefourfreedoms.htm; accessed 5/20/2004.

20. See Charles Epp, *The Rights Revolution: Lawyers, Activists and Supreme Courts in Comparative Perspective* (Chicago: University of Chicago Press, 1998). Note that emphasis on a rights revolution does not mean there were no countervailing movements occurring at the same time.

21. This was the twenty-sixth amendment. Congress had originally tried to lower the voting age by legislation passed in 1970 to extend the Voting Rights Act of 1965. The Supreme Court ruled that Congress could lower the voting age only for federal elections. A constitutional amendment to accomplish the purpose was quickly proposed by Congress in March 1971 and quickly ratified by the states in June 1971. One argument in favor of this amendment was that eighteen year-olds were being drafted to fight in Vietnam, but could not vote to support or oppose the war policy. But the amendment made little difference in military voting rates. See source cited in note 23 below.

22. Richard H. Kohn, "The Erosion of Civilian Control of the Military in the United States Today," *Naval War College Review* 55 (Summer 2002):27. See also sources cited there.

23. The data in this paragraph were taken from Brian David DuRant, "Military Suffrage: The Institutionalization of Political Participation by the American Military Since World War II," unpublished paper, Department of Sociology, Texas A&M University, April 2004.

24. Jonathan Lurie, *Arming Military Justice: The Origins of the United States Court of Military Appeals* (Princeton University Press, 1992), 128.

25. Diane H. Mazur, "Rehnquist's Vietnam: Constitutional Separatism and the Stealth Advance of Martial Law 77 *Indiana Law Review* (Fall 2002): 744–45.

26. Quoted in Lurie, *Arming Military Justice*, 145–146.

27. Quoted in ibid., 153.

28. Ibid., 218

29. James B. Jacobs, *The Socio-Legal Foundations of Civil-Military Relations* (New Brunswick: Transaction, 1986), 6.

30. William A. Moorman, "Fifty Years of Military Justice," *Air Force Law Review* 48 (2000): 189. When writing this article, Moorman was a major general and Judge Advocate General in the Air Force.

31. The National Defense Authorization Act for 1995 renamed the court, effective on October 5, 1994.

32. Jacobs, *Socio-Legal Foundations*, 7, 25.

33. Moorman, "Fifty Years of Military Justice," 188. As we shall see, it is not always clear that the principles he recognizes are observed in practice.

34. *Toth v. Quarles* (1955).

35. *Trop v. Dulles* (1958).

36. *Reid v. Covert* (1956); *McElroy v. Guagliardo* (1959).

37. *Girouard v. US* (1946).

38. *US v. Seeger* (1965).

39. *Welsh v. US* (1970).

40. *Oestereich v. Selective Service System Board* (1968); *Breen v. Selective Service System Local Board* (1970); and *Gutknecht v. US* (1970).

41. Eugene R. Fidell, "A World-Wide Perspective on Change in Military Justice," *Air Force Law Review* 48 (2000); 198; John F. O'Connor, "The Origins and Application of the Military Deference Doctrine," *Georgia Law Review* 35 (Fall 2000), 217.

42. *Relford v. US Disciplinary Commandant* (1971); *Goyas v. Mayden* (1973); *US v. Lockwood* (1983); and *Solorio v. US* (1987).

43. *Gillette v. US* (1971).

44. Eugene Fidell, "Going on Fifty: Evolution and Devolution in Military Justice," *Wake Forest Law Review* 32 (Winter 1997): 1213–31.

45. Arthur Ripstein, "Authority and Coercion," *Philosophy and Public Affairs* 32 (Winter 2004): 12.

46. Daniel Webster, "An Unpublished Speech," in Martin Anderson, ed., *The Military Draft: Selected Readings on Conscription* (Stanford: Hoover Institution Press, 1982), 633–45.

47. Eliot A. Cohen, *Citizens and Soldiers: The Dilemmas of Military Service* (Ithaca: Cornell University Press, 1985), 156–62.

48. UMT should not be confused with selective service. Under selective service, only some young men within a specified age range—not all—are liable to be

called and they are called to active duty service—not training only—for a period ranging usually from twenty-four months in peacetime to the duration in a war like World War II. After their active duty service is done, conscripts or draftees (the terms are interchangeable) are assigned to the reserves and subject to recall, as many veterans of World War II were recalled to fight in Korea.

49. This argument about the relative speed of mobilization with UMT only made sense if you assumed that UMT was in place, having already trained several cohorts of youth, while both selective service and raising a volunteer force had to start from scratch. If these conditions were met, had UMT been in place, Truman was "morally certain" that it would have deterred Soviet aggression in Eastern Europe and prevented the invasion of South Korea. Harry S. Truman, *Year of Decisions* (Garden City, NY: Doubleday, 1955), 511–12 and Margaret Truman, *Harry S. Truman* (William Morrow, 1973), 294.

50. Harry S. Truman, *Year of Decisions*, 510–11. See also Felix Belair Jr., "One-Year Military Training for Youth Asked By Truman; Congress Split on the Plan," *New York Times* (October 23, 1945), 1–2; "President Truman's Proposals for Year's Training of American Youth," *New York Times* (October 23, 1945), 3.

51. "Congress Divided on Training Plan," *New York Times* (October 24, 1945), 3. This was what Samuel P. Huntington called a policy of extirpation. See his *The Soldier and the State* (Cambridge: Harvard University Press, 1957), pp.155–56.

52. George Q. Flynn, *The Draft, 1940–1973* (Lawrence: University Press of Kansas, 1993), 91–92.

53. Ibid., 88–89. Officially VJ Day is September 2, 1945, the day the Japanese signed surrender papers. Unofficially, the war with Japan ended when President Truman announced on August 14, 1945 that the Japanese had agreed to an unconditional surrender.

54. Truman, *Year of Decisions*, 510.

55. Department of Defense, *Selected Manpower Statistics: Fiscal Year 2000* (Washington, DC: Government Printing Office, 2000), table 2–11.

56. Harold B. Hinton, "UMT Is Shelved in House, 236–162, as Coalition Wins," *New York Times* (March 5, 1952), 1, 10. The "coalition" was between Republicans and conservative Democrats, both of whom opposed the measure.

57. Poll data accessed through LexisNexis Academic from Roper Center, Public Opinion Online, Storrs, CT: University of Connecticut, question IDs USGALLUP.47–409, QK03E; USROPER.48–064, R11B; USGALLUP.436T, QT11A; and USGALLUP.021653, RK14B.

58. James M. Gerhardt, *The Draft and Public Policy: Issues in Military Manpower procurement, 1945–1970* (Columbus: Ohio State University Press, 1971), 15 and 53.

59. Poll data accessed through LexisNexis Academic from Roper Center, Public Opinion Online, Storrs, CT: University of Connecticut, question ID USGALLUP.47–401, QKT10D.

60. Gerhardt, *The Draft and Public Policy*, 22–23.

61. Warren I. Cohen, *America in the Age of Soviet Power, 1945–1991*, vol. 4 in *The Cambridge History of American Foreign Relations* (Cambridge: University of Cambridge Press, 1995), 32.

62. Flynn, *The Draft*, 98–100; Gerhardt, *The Draft and Public Policy*, 57–58.

63. Flynn, *The Draft*, 107; Gerhardt, *The Draft and Public Policy*, 83–87.

64. This was the same day that the Soviet Union imposed a blockade around West Berlin, halting all traffic into or out of the city. This led Truman to order a massive airlift of supplies into the city. After ten months, the Soviets admitted defeat and reopened the roads into the city. Cohen, *America in the Age of Soviet Power*, 45–46.

65. Gerhardt, *The Draft and Public Policy*, 104–5.

66. Flynn, *The Draft*, 108–10; Gerhardt, *The Draft and Public Policy*, 104–7.

67. Selective Service System, *Induction Statistics* (www.sss.gov/induct.htm-accessed 5/15/2004); George Q. Flynn, *Lewis B. Hershey, Mr. Selective Service* (Chapel Hill: University of North Carolina Press, 1985), 225, 228.

68. Quoted in Gerhardt, *The Draft and Public Policy*, 238. On the use of channeling as a means to avoid the draft, see Lawrence M. Baskir and William A Strauss, *Chance and Circumstance: The Draft, the War, and the Vietnam Generation* (New York: Knopf, 1978), 14–28.

69. Flynn, *Lewis B. Hershey*, 208–13.

70. Flynn, *The Draft*, 189; Charles DeBenedetti, *An American Ordeal: The Antiwar Movement of the Vietnam Era* (Syracuse: Syracuse University Press, 1990), 96.

71. On this decision to escalate the war in Vietnam, see Stanley Karnow, *Vietnam: A History* (New York: Viking Press, 1983), 435–73; Robert S. McNamara, *In Retrospect: The Tragedy and Lessons of Vietnam* (New York: Times Books, 1995), 169–206; and Mark Perry, *Four Stars* (Boston: Houghton Mifflin, 1989), 151–56.

72. In March 1965, Lewis Mumford wrote an open letter to the president that American involvement in Vietnam was morally indefensible and that the American people would oppose it. See James Burk, "How Vietnam Shaped the All-Volunteer Force," *Long Term View* 5 (Summer 2000): 53–54.

73. The question was the subtitle of the 1967 report submitted by the National Advisory Commission on Selective Service. The commission was appointed by President Johnson the year before to study the draft and make recommendations for its reform. The main title of the report, *In Pursuit of Equity*, told plainly enough what the goal was. For a general discussion of the importance of equity for the legitimacy of conscription see Eliot A. Cohen, *Citizens and Soldiers: The Dilemmas of Military Service* (Ithaca: Cornell University Press, 1985), 134–51.

74. Morris Janowitz, *The Reconstruction of Patriotism* (Chicago: University of Chicago Press, 1983), 59.

75. George H. Gallup, *The Gallup Poll: Public Opinion, 1935–1971* (New York: Random House, 1972), 3: 2017.

76. Janowitz, *Reconstruction of Patriotism*, 57.

77. Karl Haltiner has documented the effects of this factor for the fifteen nations in Western Europe that still retain some form of conscription. Overall, their dependence on conscripts has steadily declined, with the ratio of conscripts to total force size decreasing with increases in what he calls "the technical complexity of appliances and armed systems because conscripts serving on a short-term basis no longer meet the requirements regarding permanence in training and readiness for duty." See Karl W. Haltiner, "The Decline of the European Mass Armies," in Giuseppe Caforio, ed., *Handbook of the Sociology of the Military* (New York: Kluwer Academic/Plenum, 2003), 361–84, quoted at 373.

78. James Burk, "The Decline of Mass Armed Forces and Compulsory Military Service," *Defense Analysis* 8 (Spring 1992): 45–59.

79. Robert T. Stafford, Douglas L. Bailey, and Stephen E. Herbits, *How to End the Draft* (Washington, DC: National Press, 1967).

80. Quoted in Flynn, *The Draft*, 226; on Nixon's conversion to this view see also 225–26 and 235–36. Based on public opinion polls from early January 1969, which showed that the public preferred the draft (62 percent) over the all-volunteer force (31 percent), Flynn doubts that Nixon's stand on this issue was a major "vote getter" affecting his election.

81. Flynn, *The Draft*, 238; Gerhardt, *The Draft and Public Policy*, 340.

82. Flynn, *The Draft*, 245.

83. Gerhardt, *The Draft and Public Policy*, 341.

84. Flynn, *The Draft*, 251–58; Curtis W. Tarr, *By the Numbers: The Reform of the Selective Service System, 1970–1972* (Washington, DC: National Defense University, 1981).

85. Average calculated from data in Robert K. Griffith Jr., *The U.S. Army's Transition to the All-Volunteer Force, 1968–1974* (Washington, DC: U.S. Army Center of Military History, 1997), 288, table 7.

86. Gary R. Nelson, "The Supply and Quality of First-Term Enlistees Under the All-Volunteer Force," in William Bowman, Roger Little, and G. Thomas Sicilia, eds., *The All-Volunteer Force After a Decade* (Washington, DC: Pergamon-Brassey's, 1986), 33.

87. James Kitfield, *Prodigal Soldiers* (New York: Simon & Schuster, 1995), 207–8.

88. Morris Janowitz and Charles C. Moskos, "Five Years of the All-Volunteer Force: 1973–1978," *Armed Forces & Society* (Winter 1979): 171–218 and Department of Defense, *Population Representation in the Military Services, Fiscal Year 2001* (Washington, DC: Office of the Under Secretary of Defense, Personnel and Readiness, 2003), table D-17 (http://www.defenselink.mil/prhome/poprep2001/appendixd/d_17.htm; accessed 8/4/2004).

89. Kitfield, *Prodigal Soldiers*, 228.

90. Department of Defense, *Population Representation in the Military Services*, table D-11 (http://www.defenselink.mil/prhome/poprep/appendixd/d_11.htm; accessed 5/19/2004). These data show that the proportion of new recruits into the military with high school diplomas has exceeded the proportion among 18 to 24 year old civilian every year since 1982, and that from 1984 through 2001 (the last year of available data), the proportion of recruits with high school diplomas has been at least 90 percent, while the comparable proportion for civilians is about 80 percent.

91. Charles C. Moskos and John Sibley Butler, *All That We Can Be* (New York: Basic Books, 1996), 34. The historian Bernard C. Nalty notes that the act was "the only solution to black overrepresentation," as it made military service more attractive to whites—that and an economic downturn. Bernard C. Nalty, *Strength for the Fight: A History of Black Americans in the Military* (New York: Free Press, 1986), 347.

92. Darryl Fears, "2 Key Members of Black Caucus Support Military Draft," *Washington Post* (January 3, 2003), A8; Richard Sisk, "Pentagon Says No to a Draft," *New York Daily News* (January 8, 2003), 22.

93. Eric Rosenberg, "Military Draft Plan Drawn Up," *San Antonio Express-News* (March 14, 2004), 11A; Tom Bowman, "Stretched Forces Prompting Calls to Restore Draft," *Baltimore Sun* (April 23, 2004), 3A.

94. This way of putting the problem is taken from Amy Gutmann and Dennis Thompson, *Democracy and Disagreement* (Cambridge, MA: Belknap Press, 1996), 199–229, esp. 217.

95. See, for instance, Gretchen Ritter, "Of War and Virtue: Gender, American Citizenship, and Veteran's Benefits after World War II," *Comparative Social Research: The Comparative Study of Conscription in the Armed Forces* 20 (2002):201–26.

96. Flynn, *The Draft*, 15.

97. Ibid.

98. William J. Wilson, *Power, Racism, and Privilege* (New York: Free Press, 1973), 125.

99. Martin Binkin and Mark J. Eitelberg, *Blacks and the Military*, (Washington, DC: Brookings Institution, 1982), 20 and 24.

100. Samuel A. Stouffer, Edward A. Suchman, Leland C. DeVinney, Shirley A. Star, *The American Soldier: Adjustment During Army Life* (Princeton: Princeton University Press, 1949), 489–96, 527–30.

101. Binkin and Eitelberg, *Blacks in the Military*, 21–23.

102. Stouffer, et al., *The American Soldier*, 502–7, 514–15.

103. Flynn, *The Draft*, 102–3; Nalty, *Strength for the Fight*, 241–45; Moskos and Butler, *All That We Can Be*.

104. Nalty, *Strength for the Fight*, 255–69; Martin Binkin and Mark J. Eitelberg, *Blacks in the Military* (Washington, DC: Brookings Institution, 1982), 28–30.

105. Raymond H. Geselbracht, "The Truman Administration and the Desegregation of the Armed Forces" (posted on Truman Library website at http://www.trumanlibrary.ordg/deseg1.htm; accessed 5/22/2004); Segal, *Recruiting for Uncle Sam*, 109–10.

106. Nalty, *Strength for the Fight*, 282.

107. Ibid., 303–17, 333–51; Binkin and Eitelberg, *Blacks in the Military*, 30–38.

108. On the situation of black women in the military during World War II, see Brenda Moore, *To Serve My Country, To Serve My Race* (New York: New York University Press, 1996).

109. D'Ann Campbell, *Women at War with America* (Cambridge: Harvard University Press, 1984), 20 and Segal, *Recruiting for Uncle Sam*, 117.

110. Gretchen Ritter, "Of War and Virtue," 217–18.

111. Ibid, 219–24.

112. Campbell, *Women at War*, 20 and Segal, *Recruiting for Uncle Sam*, 117–19.

113. Segal, *Recruiting for Uncle Sam*, 119.

114. Mary Fainsod Katzenstein, *Faithful and Fearless: Moving Feminist Protest Inside the Church and Military* (Princeton: Princeton University Press, 1998), 58.

115. "Roosevelt on Rights Bill," *New York Times* (June 23, 1944), 32. See also "Roosevelt Signs 'G.I. Bill of Rights'," *New York Times* (June 23, 1944), 1, 32.

116. *Fishgold v. Sullivan* (1946) 328 US 275 at 284–85, quoted by Ritter, "Of War and Virtue," 221.

117. Department of Veterans Affairs, "GI Bill History" at http://www.gibill.va.gov/education/GI_Bill.htm (accessed 5/21/2004) See also, Segal, *Recruiting for Uncle Sam*, 87–89.

118. Ritter, "Of War and Virtue," 221–23.

119. For a brief summary of the data on the growing liberalism of American society, see Peter D. Feaver, *Armed Servants* (Cambridge: Harvard University Press, 2003), 27–28 and Benjamin I. Page and Robert Y. Shapiro, *The Rational Public* (Chicago: University of Chicago Press, 1992), 67–116.

120. Nalty, *Strength for the Fight*, 315–16.

121. Ibid, 327.

122. Ibid, 321–22.

123. Quoted by ibid, 324.

124. Ibid, 328–31.

125. Ibid, 316.

126. Charles C. Moskos and John Sibley Butler, *All that We Can Be: Black Leadership and Racial Integration the Army Way* (New York: Basic Books, 1996).

127. Robert L. Phillips, Paul J. Andrisani, Thomas N. Daymont, and Curtis L. Gilroy, "The Economic Returns to Military Service: Race-Ethnic Differences," *Social Science Quarterly* 73 (June 1992): 340–59; Yu Xie, "The Socio-Economic Status of Young Male Veterans, 1964–1984," *Social Science Quarterly*

454

73 (June 1992): 379–96; Binkin and Eitelberg, *Blacks in the Military*, 65–75.

128. *Population Representation in the Military Services, Fiscal Year 2002*, table D-17 (http://www.defenselink.mil/prhome/poprep/appendixd/d_17.htm; accessed 5/26/2004). Table D-18 from the same report shows that Hispanics are underrepresented in the military relative to the percent of Hispanics aged 18 to 44 in the civilian population.

129. Jacquelyn Scarville, Scott B. Burton, Jack E. Edwards, Anita R. Lancaster, and Timothy W. Elg, *Armed Forces Equal Opportunity Survey* (Arlington, VA: Defense Manpower Data Center, 1997); Sheila Nataraj Kirby, Margaret C. Herrell, and Jennifer Sloan, "Why Don't Minorities Join Special Forces?" *Armed Forces & Society* 26 (Summer 2000), 523–45.

130. Dan Landis, Mickey R. Dansby, and Michael Hoyle, "The Effects of Race on Procedural Justice: The Case of the Uniform Code of Military Justice," *Armed Forces & Society* 24 (Winter 1997): 183–219; Binkin and Eitelberg, *Blacks in the Military*, 52–55.

131. Scarville et al, *Equal Opportunity Survey*.

132. *Chappell et al v. Wallace et al* (1983), 462 US 296.

133. Katzenstein, *Faithful and Fearless*, 45, 58 and Segal, *Recruiting for Uncle Sam*, 119–20.

134. *Population Representation in the Military Services, Fiscal Year 2002*, table D-19 (http://www.defenselink.mil/prhome/poprep/appendixd/d_19.htm; accessed 5/26/2004).

135. Margaret C. Harrell, Megan K. Beckett, Chiaying Sandy Chien, and Jerry M. Sollinger, *The Status of Gender Integration in the Military* (Santa Monica: Rand, 2002), 2; Katzenstein, *Faithful and Fearless*, 58. Not every member of Congress nor every military leader embraced these as positive changes. See, for example, Linda Charlton, "Bill to Open Military Academies to Women Is Passed by Senate," *New York Times* (June 7, 1975), 22 and James Feron, "Integrated West Point Prepares for First Women Cadets," *New York Times* (September 22, 1975), 70.

136. *Reed v. Reed* (1971), 404 US 71. Kermit L. Hall, *The Oxford Companion to the Supreme Court of the United States* (New York: Oxford University Press, 1992), 713–14.

137. *Frontiero v. Richardson* (1973), 411 US 677.

138. 417 US 733 (1974), at 743–44; John F. O'Connor, "The Origins and Application of the Military Deference Doctrine," *Georgia Law Review* 35 (Fall 2000), 229–30; and Diane H. Mazur, "Rehnquist's Vietnam," 745–48.

139. *Personnel Administrator of Massachusetts v. Fenny* (1979), 442 US 256.

140. 453 US 57 (1981).

141. Jane J. Mansbridge, *Why We Lost the ERA* (Chicago: University of Chicago Press, 1986), 68–84 and Clyde Wilcox, "Race, Gender, and Support for Women in the Military," *Social Science Quarterly* 73 (June 1992): 310–23.

142. Mansbridge, *Why We Lost*, 71–76.

143. Katzenstein, *Faithful and Fearless*, 47–54; Segal and Hansen, "Value Rationales in Policy Debates on Women in the Military," *Social Science Quarterly* 73 (June 1992): 296–309; Harrell et al, *Status of Gender Integration*, 2–4. Margaret C. Harrell and Laura L. Miller, *New Opportunities for Military Women* (Santa Monica: RAND, 1997), 11–12.

144. William H. McMichael, *The Mother of All Hooks: The Story of the US Navy's Tailhook Scandal* (New Brunswick, NJ: Transaction, 1997); Charles C. Moskos, "Toward a Postmodern Military: The United States as a Paradigm," in Charles C. Moskos, John Allen Williams, and David R. Segal, eds., *The Postmodern Military* (New York: Oxford University Press, 2000), 22–23.

145. Rachel N. Lipari and Anita R. Lancaster, *Armed Forces 2002 Sexual Harassment Survey* (Arlington, VA: Defense Manpower Data Center, 2003).

146. Bradley Graham, "Panel Faults Air Force Brass for Response to Assaults," *Washington Post* (September 23, 2003), A02; R. Jeffery Smith, "Air Force to Study Rape Complaints," *Washington Post* (March 10, 2004), A03.

147. Moskos, "Toward a Postmodern Military," 23–24; James Burk, "Power, Morals and Military Uniqueness," *Society* 31 (December 1993): 29–36; and Office of the Under Secretary of Defense (Personnel and Readiness), *Report to the Secretary of Defense: Review of the Effectiveness of the Application and Enforcement of the Department's Policy on Homosexual Conduct in the Military* (April 1998) found at http://www.defenselink.mil/pubs/rpto40798.html; accessed 7/17/2004.

11. AMERICAN INSECURITY
DISSENT FROM THE "LONG WAR"

CHARLES CHATFIELD

American leaders have always prided themselves on seeing the United States as a beacon to civilization. Early in their experience, however, Americans came down from their City on a Hill and pressed across the continent, then beyond the seas and around the globe. Relentlessly they carried forward the distinctive forms of political democracy and market economy with which they rationalized their achievement and elevated it to a Cause, imbued with liberty and justice for all.

Interest and principle have ever been entwined in U.S. policy and rhetoric. Foreign policy has been both advanced and challenged on practical and principled grounds; often the one obscures the other. Accordingly, wars and prospective wars have provided flashpoints, occasions when dissent turned into organized protest. This essay examines the rhythmic relationship of dissent and protest to national security policy from the 1940s through 2004.

Foreign policy evolved quickly after World War II under a Cold War paradigm that in the next twenty years would produce a strategy of militarized containment—a massive arms race and intervention abroad, including military engagement in East Asia. Dissent in those years modified the extent of military mobilization, but for the most part without frontally challenging Cold War policy. Between 1965 and 1975, though, a powerful protest movement helped to reverse military intervention in Indochina and, with other events, eroded the Cold War worldview.

In the decade 1979 to 1989 the administration of Ronald Reagan sponsored a resurgent nuclear arms race and intervention in Central America under the guise of containment. Each was modified, even contained, by a combination of domestic protest movements and external events. Then, in the 1990s, with U.S. foreign policy entering uncharted waters in the wake of Cold War, issues of global economic justice generated a fresh transnational social movement, while early in the new century U.S. war in Iraq provoked broad and intense protest in America and overseas.

Across this entire period, recurrent dissent and organized protest was an undulating counterpoint to official policy—two parts of the single, complex process of policymaking that involves the interplay of private and public interests, all framed in competing paradigms. Thus, dissent has been part of the process of building consensus and, once built, of challenging it—in foreign as well as domestic affairs.

In recounting this process during the post–World War II era, this essay raises several questions. Were there common patterns, motifs of protest, and to what extent was dissent and protest a function of historic American traditions? Were there common mechanisms and instruments of protest, and in what respects was dissent and protest a function of our political system? To what extent did dissent and protest affect policy?

The Terms and Dynamics of Protest: Their Historic Base

The historically dominant themes of foreign policy dissent and protest have reflected five major dilemmas facing policymakers.[1]

1. What global responsibilities and what forms of power are consonant with U.S. national interests (the realist dilemma)?
2. What global responsibilities and what forms of power are consonant with American values (the idealist dilemma)?
3. Is an expanding world role for America best served by unilateralism or by some degree of multilateralism (the internationalist dilemma)?
4. How can an expansionist military policy in the "shadow of war"[2] be reconciled with traditional limits on government authority (the federal dilemma)?
5. How can there be meaningful constraints on economic institutions that are increasingly global and concentrated (the populist dilemma)?

Foreign policy is subject to constant critique, of course. Some criticism comes from the foreign policy establishment of senior professionals and politicians in government, academia, and independent "think tanks," the prestige press, and lobbyists representing powerful private interests. These "insider" critics target tactics, and they help decisionmakers fine-tune policy, reconcile competing concepts and interests, and adapt to new situations and information. "Dissent," as used in this essay, implies something more fundamental. Dissenters target strategy; they question the basic assumptions of applied policy.

Although dissent does arise within governing administrations, it is usually *organized* through select nongovernmental organizations (NGOs). The Chamber of Commerce provides one example; labor unions and peace societies are others. Many of these NGOs have international connections, and when seeking to influence U.S. national policy (and even international institutions) they act as transnational social movement organizations.[3] Domestically, NGOs become catalysts for organized public protest. When an issue is especially salient or compelling, a coalition of NGOs forms around it to mobilize public constituencies into a broad social movement.

DISSENTING THEMES AND PLAYERS: THE 1920S

The themes, process, and politics of transposing dissent into organized protest predate the Cold War, indeed they were largely forged in the foreign policy debates of 1920–1945, and drew upon even earlier traditions.

The policies that predominated in the 1920s employed diplomacy and sometimes military force to back the overseas expansion of U.S. commerce and ideology (usually defined as Christian and democratic civilization). Informally and somewhat reluctantly, the United States cooperated with the League of Nations insofar as doing so involved no enduring obligations. The foreign policy leadership (Secretary of State Frank Kellogg, for example) also welcomed international law insofar as it did not involve enforcement. In the eyes of its architects, U.S. policy in the 1920s was benign and unobjectionable.

In fact, though, these policies attracted substantial dissent. Several Republican senators, aptly called "peace progressives" by historian Robert Johnson,[4] stood in opposition, chief among them Robert La Follette (R-WI) and William Borah (R-ID) whose critique of U.S. policy extended back to the presidencies of William Howard Taft and Woodrow Wilson. Now in the 1920s they were joined by other dissenters, agrarian progressives all, who developed a coherent critique of U.S. foreign relations.

The "peace progressives" evoked the tradition of anti-imperialism, which dated from the Republic's beginning and was reasserted in opposition to the Philippine War (1898–1901). They believed in economic expansion, but theirs was an economy of small-scale production and open trade, not of large-scale corporate control. They attacked corporatism and the economic subjugation of weak countries. In this respect they added a *populist motif* to anti-imperialism as they addressed the foreign policy dilemma of constraining large-scale economic expansion abroad.

They argued that territorial and even informal economic empire was neither in America's interest nor in accord with her principles. They opposed the mandate system of Wilson's League of Nations (a kind of disguised imperialism, they thought) as well as military interventions in Latin America. They probed the modern problem of how to respect the legitimacy of rising small nations while incorporating them in an international system consonant with U.S. interests. They argued that it was more important for leaders in developing countries to reflect the interests of their people than to copy U.S. institutions. In these respects, as Johnson noted, the "peace progressives" offered a "self-conscious left-wing alternative" to Wilsonianism.[5]

Those politicians absorbed two other long-established American traditions: antimilitarism and restrictions on executive power. Warning that militarism was an arm of imperialism, they had challenged Wilson's 1916 Preparedness Program, and in the 1920s they continued to fight peacetime conscription and military spending. They had opposed intervening in the European war of 1914, and subsequently fought any semblance of military ties to European powers. In addition, they had objected to the abuse of civil liberties during World War I and to the Red Scare afterward. Worrying about expanding presidential power, they checked executive interventions in Nicaragua, Mexico, and elsewhere in Latin America.

In all these respects, the "peace progressives" anticipated major themes in twentieth-century foreign policy debate. Like the conservative establishment, they believed in economic and cultural expansion and in military security so long as it did not involve open-ended commitments to other nations. Unlike conservatives, though, the progressives sought to constrain the imperialist impulse of their own government and corporations. Both wings were grounded in traditional unilateralism—independence from any international obligations except economic treaties.

Multinationalism, on the other hand, was mainly cultivated by NGOs that aspired to influence foreign policy. Between 1915 and 1929 the modern American peace movement became fully articulated, along with a nascent liberal internationalism.[6] Intellectuals like editor Hamilton Holt, and

Presidents William Howard Taft and Woodrow Wilson, believed that national security was threatened by an increasingly armed and competitive world, and they promoted a multinational organization capable of deterring aggression and invoking the rule of law. In itself, this was a conservative version of internationalism, a condition of order compatible with unfettered economic interplay and unilateral sovereignty.

There were, however, some who aimed beyond stability to "institutionalize managerial controls over the fragile interdependence of modern industrial civilization."[7] These were distinctly liberal internationalists, often social scientists and social workers, commentators, and religious activists who represented the cutting edge of progressive reform. Initially they counted on a new League of Nations system with U.S. leadership to provide the instruments of a progressive world order.

Their hopes were dashed. With internationalists split by questions of American unilateralism and sovereignty, the Senate rejected the League. Out of that defeat emerged several internationalist organizations of political import.[8] The League of Nations Non-Partisan Association (LNNPA, founded in 1922), subsequently League of Nations Association (LNA, 1929), quietly courted support for the League, becoming politically significant in the 1930s. The National Council for Prevention of War (NCPW, 1921), on the other hand, was a coalition for arms limitation. It acted as a foreign policy lobby for groups as disparate as the Farm Bureau Federation and the League of Women Voters, often working with the "peace progressives" on Capitol Hill.

The NCPW projected into the politics of foreign policy a distinctively pacifist wing of liberal internationalists who had emerged during the vigorous 1915–1917 public campaign against U.S. intervention in European war. They combined an activist reform mentality with their personal rejection of warfare. For them, the sacredness of life was a motivating personal ideal as well as a social value, so that these pacifists could abjure warfare as individuals on grounds of absolute principle while opposing it in relative, pragmatic terms as an issue of social realism. Progressive pacifists were part of an American reform tradition that ranged from the moral crusades of the 1840s to the modern civil rights movement, an orientation they made relevant to the *realist-idealist dilemma* in foreign policy.

Pacifists acted politically through organizations that emerged during and after World War I—among them the Fellowship of Reconciliation (FOR, 1915), the American Friends Service Committee (AFSC, 1917), the Women's International League for Peace and Freedom (WILPF, 1919), and the War Resisters League (WRL, 1921). Two characteristics of these groups contributed to their political role. One was their transnationalism. Associating with people abroad who had shared the horrendous experience of modern war, and later of Nazism and Soviet communism, they built upon a sense of solidarity beyond the nation state. A second defining characteristic was their rejection of warfare as an instrument of social change. Leading pacifists like social evangelist Kirby Page, journalist Devere Allen, and socialist leader Norman Thomas popularized the view that war is an extension of injustice, notably in the form of imperialism and militarism. Conversely, they insisted, social justice is a precondition for peace.

Thus, in the 1920s there emerged several dissenting players on foreign policy: a core of "peace progressives" in Congress, as well as liberal internationalist NGOs and progressive pacifist ones. Those groupings advocated alternative approaches to foreign policy and brought distinctive ways of thinking into the post–World War II era.

THE PROCESS OF MOBILIZING PROTEST: THE 1930S

When coalitions of NGOs can engage substantial public constituencies, they can turn dissent into an advocacy or protest *movement*. Throughout the twenties the NGOs oriented to peace and internationalism tried to mobilize the public against military spending and in support of world disarmament, U.S. admission to the World Court, and the outlawry of war. They had limited success, but they lacked an overarching mobilizing issue. In the 1930s, however, Americans felt increasingly insecure. The question of whether or not the United States should employ or even pledge military force abroad for so-called collective security emerged as a politically salient issue stemming from real crises abroad, especially Japanese expansionism in Asia and the rise of Hitler in Europe.

The security issue transformed dissent into organized protest.[9] From 1934 on progressive pacifists helped to crystallize public fear of being drawn into another war. They were instrumental in setting up and staffing a committee chaired by Senator Gerald P. Nye (R-ND) to investigate the role of the munitions industry in World War I, and they popularized its disclosures in support of strict neutrality. The NCPW coalition largely planned and operated the subsequent campaign for neutrality revision in coordination with congressional "peace progressives," resulting in the Neutrality Act of 1935, which required an impartial embargo of all nations declared to be belligerents.

Liberal internationalists like historian James T. Shotwell of the League of Nations Association organized a coalition to rally popular support for internationalism bordering on collective security. At the same time, progressive pacifists from the FOR, AFSC, WILPF, and NCPW formed an Emergency Peace Campaign that endorsed stronger League and international economic cooperation, but basically pressed to keep the United States from going to war and lobbied against presidential discretion in applying neutrality legislation.

It was an immense undertaking that opened dramatically in April 1936, burgeoned early the next year, but played itself out in the spring of 1938 when the so-called Ludlow Amendment, which would have required a national referendum before a declaration of war except in the case of invasion, was turned back in the House by only twenty-one votes. With the internationalist coalition split over the critical issue of intervening in war, liberal internationalists in the LNA now explicitly advocated collective security and organized the Committee to Defend America by Aiding the Allies (1940).

Politically active pacifists became allied with the Keep America Out of War Congress (1938) initiated by Norman Thomas and the Socialist Party. Within a year or so, however, pacifists began to withdraw from politics in order to prepare their communities for war. In 1940 Thomas reluctantly allied himself with the conservative America First Committee (1940), based strongly in the Midwest and Plains states and disproportionately among farmers, industrialists, students, and some ethnic groups.

The anti-interventionists purveyed a variety of arguments. Some of them, including historians Eric F. Goldman and Harry Elmer Barnes, interpreted overseas wars as conflicts among imperial hegemonies. They asked, with former Roosevelt adviser Raymond Moley: "Are we going to be a nation or an empire?"[10] Other lines of argument were to deny that any real military threat existed or to design U.S. defense on hemispheric lines. Building on accumulated resistance to the New Deal, anti-interventionists vigorously opposed further expansion of the president's discretionary authority. The common denominators of all forms of anti-interventionism were unilateralism and popular antipathy to another foreign war.

Surging violence in both Europe and Asia eroded antiwar protest in the fall of 1941, although not to the point of allowing Roosevelt a free hand in ratcheting up military aid to Britain. Anti-interventionism decreased in intellectual substance as well as in political strength. The case for a comprehensive alternative to imperial corporatism, collective security, and an expanding and militarized state was shelved for the duration.

FROM DISSENT TO ADVOCACY, 1941–1945

Dissent from World War II was pointed, if muted. Leading pacifists sharply criticized the arbitrary internment of Japanese-Americans, the handling of conscientious objectors (COs), and indiscriminate bombing of cities, including Hiroshima and Nagasaki. Some COs experimented with Gandhi-like nonviolent direction action, thus expanding the repertoire of tactics that would figure in postwar protest.[11]

Political influence had shifted to those liberal internationalists who had begun by dissenting against the traditional U.S. policy of unilateral expansion and intervention in the 1920s and then had advocated multilateral cooperation and collective security. Shortly after the outbreak of European war in 1939, James T. Shotwell and Clark Eichelberger of the LNA formed a public commission that worked with the State Department on postwar planning and generated a well-funded coalition to rally public support for a world organization. By 1941 they had become part of the Roosevelt foreign policy establishment. From that vantage point and through the United Nations Association, which they created in 1943, they helped to sell the United Nations Organization to the American public.[12] Thanks in part to their mobilization of public support, NGOs won official status in the international body, and they helped to ensure that its Charter explicitly protected human rights.[13]

The United Nations, created in 1945, was a collective security organization, of course. But the larger UN system reflected liberal internationalist aspirations. With the creation of various UNO councils and independent though UNO-related international organizations such as UNRRA for relief programs, WHO to deal with health, and UNESCO to foster cultural and scientific cooperation, along with the independent World Monetary Fund (IMF) and International Bank for Reconstruction and Development (World Bank), and the General Agreement on Trade and Tariffs (the GATT), a liberal international order had arrived.

CHALLENGING MILITARIZED CONTAINMENT: 1945–1963

The end of the Second World War opened what historian Wesley T. Wooley has called a brief window of "unusual fluidity in the history of American diplomatic thought." It was an era when unilateralism had been discredited but the direction of internationalism was unclear.[14] That window closed abruptly when the Korean War locked the nation into a militarized version of containment, including a massive arms buildup and military intervention.

Overnight many liberal internationalists embraced so-called Cold War realism. The new Cold Warriors subscribed to a paradigm of insecurity that would dominate policymaking for over a generation. They assumed a division between totalitarian communism and the "free world" that even accommodated the rise of postcolonial, developing nations by labeling them the "Third World"—an area at once peripheral to the central players and the field for which they contested. Containment, the grand strategy of the Cold War, aimed not merely to limit an expansive Russia but to thwart the presumed Soviet goal of imposing its communist ideology throughout the world. This grand strategy did not go unchallenged. Indeed, it evoked public opposition. Despite being confronted with anticommunist extremism at home, dissent and public protest played a crucial role in preventing the rise of a full-fledged American "garrison state."[15]

CONTAINMENT PREEMPTS WORLD
FEDERALISM, 1945–1950

U.S. leaders easily transferred the rationale for collective security from the "Axis" of World War II to postwar Soviet communism. Indeed, the Soviet Union had often been bracketed with the totalitarian states threatening Western democracy before it became a wartime ally. Then conflicts of American and Russian national interests were subordinated to the war effort and, under Roosevelt, to an accommodating peacetime agenda. That changed quickly. Although Truman at first treated Josef Stalin like a stubborn political rival, the president and his foreign policy advisers came to view the Russians as not only intractable but also ideological and aggressive (a mirror image of the way the Soviets viewed them). By January 1946 Truman was determined to stop "babying the Soviets."[16] The following month Stalin himself declared that conflict with the capitalist West was "inevitable."[17] In March Winston Churchill pronounced Europe was now divided by an "Iron Curtain."

Events through 1950 institutionalized the Cold War paradigm. Applied first in Europe, containment was soon extended globally and would involve America in two major wars. In the process the strategic doctrine became ever more militarized. Whereas initially it envisioned a potential security threat in an indefinite future, to be met by the capacity for limited warfare on the Soviet perimeter, containment came to provide for military responses on the Soviet-Chinese perimeter plus capability for fighting full-scale war. As envisioned in NSC 68 (spring 1950), that meant an enlarged and modernized Air Force and Navy, a stronger Army, a Central Intelligence Agency that supplemented intelligence with covert force, a hydrogen bomb, the rearmament of West Germany within NATO, and of course a deficit budget to pay for it all.

The transformation of collective security into containment was greatly facilitated by a core of internationalist intellectuals—so-called "Realists" such as commentator Walter Lippmann, diplomat George Kennan, political scientist Hans Morgenthau, and theologian Reinhold Niebuhr. They blamed pacifist idealism for the failure to confront totalitarian power in the 1930s, arguing that social ethics required leaders to weigh both values and interests in a calculation of power. Niebuhr and Kennan especially combined a sophisticated relativism in political and ethical calculations with a Manichean polarization of social forces along a moral axis (thus Niebuhr's titles, *Moral Man and Immoral Society, Children of Light and . . . Darkness*). Accordingly, their realism could be adapted both to containment understood as a flexible response to threats that were relatively political, ideological, and economic, and also as to the Cold War paradigm of contending good and evil.

From the outset of Cold War, policymakers and the public were faced by the reality of atomic insecurity. Within days of the Hiroshima and Nagasaki bombings radio commentator Edward R. Murrow observed, "Seldom, if ever, has a war ended leaving the victors with such a . . . realization that the future is obscure and that survival is not assured." "Modern Man is Obsolete," wrote Norman Cousins in the *Saturday Review* he edited: Hiroshima "marked the violent death of one stage in man's history and the beginning of another."[18] John Hershey's *Hiroshima* vividly recounted the horror experienced by the victims for a large public. Atomic scientists, many of whom had expressed reservations about the bomb's use, spoke out publicly for international control of nuclear weapons. Joining them were pacifists (who had condemned the bombings), church groups, and others for whom anxiety over atomic warfare drove a transnational movement for world federalism.

Cord Meyer was a marine wounded in the Pacific and an astute political commentator. He concluded after observing the formation of the UNO in San Francisco that "the death agony of nationalism will be prolonged beyond our lifetime."[19] Skeptical of the USSR and convinced that the veto vitiated cooperation, he campaigned for UN revision and international control of nuclear weapons. In 1947 Meyer became president of the United World Federalists, a coalition of world government groups. Within two years its paid membership had grown from 17,000 to 40,000, organized into hundreds of local chapters and affiliated with a worldwide network. World federalism found support in principle with 56 percent of Americans, 21 state legislatures, and congressional resolutions with some 150 cosponsors.[20]

In 1949–50, however, the world government movement collapsed with the "dramatic suddenness" of the Korean War.[21] It never regained its popular appeal, even though most of the public gradually accepted UN institutions within the Cold War paradigm. In that context nuclear anxiety became directed toward the USSR, notably in the Eisenhower doctrine of "massive retaliation," and it reinforced the militarization of containment. Cord Meyer was one of many liberal internationalists who turned Cold Warrior: he was converted to containment and joined the CIA in 1951. [22]

ANTICOMMUNISM REPRESSES LEFT-WING DISSENT

During the brief, "unusual fluidity" of strategic policy in Truman's first term, Henry A. Wallace epitomized prewar liberal internationalism and humanitarianism along with the egalitarianism and anti-imperialism of the populist motif. Two-term secretary of agriculture under Roosevelt and then vice president in FDR's third term, Wallace was given to speaking his mind. During World War II he headed the Board of Economic Warfare, where he lobbied aggressively for postwar planning that would treat the world as "an economic unit," promote free trade, and break free from both tariffs and monopolies. [23] Displaced as vice president by Truman on FDR's ticket in 1944, Wallace got the position of secretary of commerce, from which he worked for full employment at home and an economically united human community.

As the Cold War took shape, Wallace was the most important voice of dissent within government. His vision for the postwar world was predicated open negotiations and accommodation with Russia. He believed that a realistic policy should take into account Soviet interests in securing and socializing Eastern Europe, even as U.S. interests lay in fostering democratic institutions and a market economy throughout the West.

Accommodating such spheres of influence was perfectly consonant with trade between them and with the "peaceful competition" of the two systems, he argued; and a unified Germany was "absolutely essential to any lasting European settlement." Without idealizing the Soviet Union, Wallace rejected the emerging Cold War paradigm: "The real peace treaty we need now," he said, "is between the United States and Russia."[24] Ever outspoken, the secretary challenged the policies of Truman and Secretary of State James Byrnes in public, and he was finally forced to resign in the fall of 1946. At that point Wallace became a focal point for left-liberal popular dissent and idealistic rhetoric—and for intense anticommunist opposition.

Anticommunism encompassed a wide range of political positions. On one hand it pitted liberal Cold Warriors against the remnant of communists and their Popular Front allies who opposed containment, either accepting direction from the Soviet Union or independently rejecting the Cold War paradigm. On the other hand, anticommunism also came in an extreme right wing variant that charged Truman and Cold War liberals with being soft on communism at home and abroad. Thus historian George Nash identified a "militant, evangelistic anti-Communism, shaped decisively by a number of influential ex-radicals of the 1930s" like Whittaker Chambers and James Burnham. They were supplemented by émigrés from communist Europe. To members of this group destiny dictated that the world would either become an American bastion of freedom or succumb to the totalitarian, atheistic communism of Russia. According to James Burnham, "the only alternative to the communist World Empire is an American Empire which will be, if not literally world-wide in formal boundaries, capable of exercising decisive world control. . . . "[25]

There were two corollaries for these anticommunists. First, they pushed an aggressive policy abroad. For Chambers and others the nation had a religious calling to move "beyond containment to liberation," to roll back the Soviet empire.[26] The second corollary was to condemn liberals for tolerating and even embracing "communist" inroads in U.S. government and culture. The trial of Alger Hiss dramatized the right-wing anticommunists' conviction that New Dealers were naïve if not treasonous. Reports from House and Senate investigating committees seemed to further legitimate anticommunism, and J. Edgar Hoover institutionalized it within the FBI. In the hands of the radical right, as on the left and for mixed motives, anticommunism became a tool with which to marginalize ideological opponents.

Henry Wallace plunged inadvertently into this conflict when he left the administration in 1946. He helped to form a new Progressive Party and ran as its 1948 presidential candidate in order to promote New Deal priorities and also peaceful coexistence as an alternative to military confrontation. At that time communists and their Popular Front allies enlisted in the Progressive crusade in an attempt to use it as a base for their confrontation with Cold War liberals, despite the fact that Wallace was openly critical of Stalinism. Because he naively accepted their endorsement, "communists and fellow travelers ended up playing a central role in the Progressive Party, as other potential supporters seemed to back off in proportion to communist enthusiasm for the campaign."[27]

This left Wallace extremely vulnerable. The administration exploited his weakness, attacking him through the Americans for Democratic Action (ADA, 1947), while Republicans and independent anticommunists were merciless. In the 1948 presidential election, Wallace won only 2.37 percent of the total vote. In the campaign's wake he recanted his former association with communists, and by time war erupted in Korea he endorsed military containment. Even so, the Wallace of 1948 became a mythic hero to progressives who needed to believe that there had been an alternative to the national security state and Cold War.

The 1948 elections left American communism so weak that only its image remained as a viable object of attack. Yet even this sufficed to stage the virulent form of anticommunism known as "McCarthyism" after Senator Joseph McCarthy (R-WI). The senator wielded innuendo, distortion, and lies to attack people in the government and civil service as communist dupes and spies. The House Un-American Activities Committee (HUAC) and its Senate counterpart had already anticipated his techniques. HUAC, evolving from the feverish exaggeration of a Nazi threat during World War II, transferred its attentions to communism after the war, encouraging a "widespread witch-hunting spirit both in government and in private life" that peaked in McCarthyism. Large numbers of people were intimated and harassed; thousands lost jobs, had their careers aborted, and lived in fear.[28] Some encountered violence.

Anticommunism targeted established pacifist groups like the FOR, AFSC, and WILPF. Although these groups rejected association with communists and criticized Soviet totalitarianism and militarism, they also challenged U.S. national security policy, including the Korean War and especially the H-bomb.[29] They attributed international polarization to both Soviet *and* U.S. intransigence, each provoking the other in a spiraling conflict of interests that became a test of will and force. Trying to break into that spiral, peace advocates in Europe and America advocated policies not aligned with either Cold War power, notably nuclear disarmament. They spoke of a Third Way.

Anticommunist critics manipulated pacifist statements so as to associate peace advocates with the World Peace Congress, launched in the late 1940s by communist leaders and aligned with the Soviet position on disarmament. Even world federalists were labeled subversive by citizens' groups and congressional "loyalty investigators" alike. Attacks accelerated into the Eisenhower years. Not only were liberal pacifists defamed in public; they also divided among themselves over whether or not to exclude peace advocates with prior communist associations. Some worried about what Norman Cousins called "Communist infiltration or [even the] taint" of communist association.[30] In 1960, Cousins himself disrupted the Committee for a Sane Nuclear Policy by dropping a staff member accused of having had communist associations, thereby compromising freedom of association for the sake of public legitimacy.

By that time, extremist anticommunism as an organized movement had lost its force. The Senate had censured McCarthy in 1954 and the House had reined in HUAC. The Eisenhower administration seemed to have tamed right-wing extremism within the Republican Party. Nonetheless, McCarthyism haunted the collective memory of peace and antiwar groups, and the issue of communist association was still dividing them in the mid-1960s as they organized against war in Vietnam.

The capitulation of world federalists, the defeat of Wallace progressives, the wave of McCarthyism, even the marginalizing of progressive pacifists—all of these figured in establishing a national consensus on the Cold War premise that the United States, defender of the free world, was challenged by the ideological and military threat of a monolithic, aggressive communist power centered in the totalitarian Soviet Union. The centrality of that premise dominated policymaking and the national culture as well, putting pacifist critics on the fringe.

Dissent Within the Paradigm

Yet dissent persisted, some of it coming from the right. Conservative dissent together with economic considerations restrained national security policy in the formative period of the Cold War. Sometimes executive prerogative was directly attacked in Congress. A few Senate conservatives, for example, tried in vain to require congressional approval for sending U.S. troops abroad under NATO; Robert Taft (R-OH) called Truman's intervention in Korea "an absolute usurpation of authority by the President"; and early in the Eisenhower administration Senator John Bricker (R-OH) proposed a constitutional amendment to limit the president's treaty-making power.[31]

Although these conservatives echoed the warnings of earlier "peace progressives," they drew their inspiration from distinctly conservative sources. George H. Nash identified one group of conservative intellectuals with Friedrich Heyek, who pitted a libertarian version of classical liberalism against the threat of "statism," which was the conservative take on socialism. Nash called a second group "traditionalists." This group included people like Peter Viereck and Russell Kirk, for whom a return to traditional, absolute social values was a necessary antidote to a relativist, mass culture run amuck.[32] Both groups feared the consequences of putting the country on an indefinite wartime footing (which advocate James Forrestal and critic Robert Taft each called "*semiwar*"[33]). Conservative dissent thus flowed from an apprehension of what Harold D. Lasswell called the "Garrison State."[34]

For the most part, congressional challenges were directed at the practical aspects of the national security state: economic planning and military budgets, tax policies, deficit spending, manpower proposals, military reorganization and consolidation (including intelligence), and government influence in science, technology, and culture.

However pragmatic those debates, they revealed a dissenting minority of Republicans who criticized military containment on a global scale as overly ambitions. Robert Taft was the leader and spokesman of this group. In some large measure he accepted the Cold War paradigm of a struggle between democratic and communist-totalitarian forces. But he regarded the contest as essentially ideological and resisted its militarization. Taft warned against overextending U.S. capacity through military alliances. Moreover, he sensed in the Truman Doctrine, Marshall Plan, and NATO "a tendency to interfere in the affairs of other nations, to assume that we are a kind of demigod and Santa Claus to solve the problems of the world, [an attitude] more and more likely to involve us in disputes where our liberty is not in fact concerned." Returning to an old populist and anti-empire theme, Taft added: "It is easy to skip into an attitude of imperialism where war becomes an instrument of public policy rather than its last resort."[35]

Ironically, Republicans also charged the administration with failure to resist communism in China or to roll it back in Europe. Lamenting the so-called "loss of China" and promoting the "liberation" of Eastern Europe became major GOP themes during the 1952 presidential campaign.[36] Although an early favorite to win his party's presidential nomination that year, Taft was outmaneuvered by Eisenhower, who cemented a bipartisan consensus for a military-oriented and global version of containment. To some extent, Taft fell victim to his own inconsistency, especially during the Korean War. In part that reflected a Realist's dilemma: not unlike diplomat George Kennan, Taft tried to challenge an emerging NSC 68 consensus for militarized containment while still affirming the Cold War policy premise. The two proved inseparable.

Universal Military Training (UMT) provided an issue where dissent within the Cold War paradigm proved successful. Proposed twice during the period between the First World War and the Second, UMT was introduced in the House again in 1944 and won Roosevelt's endorsement the following year. The idea also found favor with Truman who saw it as a way to offset demobilization and provide a manpower base for "semiwar." His staff mobilized support through a Presidential Advisory Commission and hearings in the House, 1946–47. The next year UMT went to Congress as part of a comprehensive manpower package. By that time Senator Taft and the conservative bloc were challenging the administration's foreign policy and military strategy, criticizing the economic costs and raising the specter of a garrison state. In the public arena a strong liberal coalition echoed Taft's arguments.[37] UMT became a focal point for bipartisan resistance.

The Friends [Quakers] Committee on National Legislation (FCNL 1943) engineered the liberal anti-UMT movement. Founded in order to deal with wartime conscription and extended to oppose peacetime militarization, the FCNL was the first full-time Protestant lobby.[38] It mobilized religious bodies, educational associations, labor unions, women's organizations, farmers, social workers, and similar constituencies. Most FCNL supporters insisted that the cost of UMT would degrade social welfare, and argued that indefinite militarization would weaken American values and liberties. Even though public opinion polls showed generalized public support for UMT, the intense lobbying of the conservative-liberal coalition repeatedly swayed Congress. Here was a politically viable issue that related foreign to domestic policy in ways that touched a plethora of public constituencies.[39] UMT had been the "centerpiece" of Truman's legislative program that year, selective service only a short-term measure. When it became clear that UMT was headed for defeat, the draft emerged as a successful compromise position, in part because it could be rationalized as an emergency measure and administered by local draft boards.[40] Conscription remained in force into the Vietnam War. The defeat of UMT thus modified the administration's containment program but, ironically, contributed to its political viability.

The Test-Ban Campaign repeated that phenomenon in a far more dramatic way from 1957 to 1963, and it rejuvenated the peace movement. The salient issue was radioactive fallout.[41] Postwar expressions of alarm from nuclear scientists had become muted by 1954 as the Cold War paradigm and arms race enlisted elements of academia, industry, and the military. That spring the government tested its H-bomb at Bikini atoll. Radioactive fallout contaminated inhabitants of the Marshall Islands and hospitalized fishermen who had been aboard a Japanese trawler, *The Lucky Dragon,* one of whom died. It also affected the fish supply of Japan, where opposition to nuclear testing mushroomed. U.S. scientists challenged their government's assurances of safety. British mathematician and philosopher Bertrand Russell, Albert Einstein, Joseph Rotblat and other distinguished scientists appealed to the world "to think in a new way" about war, in which there could no longer be meaningful victory. Scientists became increasingly active and organized.

Testing was the wedge that activist scientists hoped would open up a larger debate over war. Three years after the *Lucky Dragon* incident Norman Cousins persuaded Albert Schweitzer to issue his own appeal, and the renowned humanitarian captured the focus of rapidly gelling transnational protest. For practical reasons "the place to take hold is with the matter of nuclear testing," he told Cousins. Given a ban on testing, "the stage can be set for other and broader measures related to peace." Schweitzer's reasoning mirrored that of the Federation of American Scientists, the established peace groups, and leading citizens such as the 1952 and 1956 Democratic presidential candidate, former Governor Adlai Stevenson of Illinois.[42]

In April 1957, the day before Schweitzer's declaration was broadcast, American liberal peace advocates and pacifists agreed on a campaign for a comprehensive test-ban treaty. Its core sponsors—the AFSC, FCNL, FOR, and WILPF—valued the test ban issue for opening a critique of military containment itself, but they understood that the politically viable issues were radioactivity and disingenuous government assessments of the hazards posed by fallout. They would focus on "nuclear testing as the first step towards disarmament."[43] Their coalition encompassed a range of tactics. Its main effort was on education and advocacy, coordinated through the Committee for a Sane Nuclear Policy (SANE, 1958), while a loose network of activists experimented with direct action and civil disobedience under the aegis of the Committee for Non-Violent Action (CNVA, 1958).

Direct Action included vigils, demonstrations, forced entry at atomic test sites, sailing into Pacific H-bomb testing waters, and boarding Polaris nuclear submarines. Some of those actions involved openly illegal activity in order to challenge law or the policy it protected (like nuclear testing). By this means CNVA activists could at least be witness to their beliefs. Beyond that, they tried to raise public awareness of the arms race itself and of multiple social justice issues. They were openly challenging the basic premise of Cold War containment. Moreover, and in the context of the Civil Rights movement, they were also publicizing the repertory and philosophy of Gandhi-like nonviolent direct action.

Concurrently, SANE concentrated on the single issue of a multilateral ban on atmospheric atomic testing, linking its efforts to an impressive transnational movement with especially strong centers in England, Germany, Japan, and nonaligned Third World states like India.[44] Public response in the United States was so forthcoming that it transformed SANE from a coordinating committee into a membership organization (25,000 in its first year) with an executive director and a staff that grew to twenty. It facilitated a growing coalition of pacifists, scientists, and citizen association. Its constituency was broadly liberal, so much so that even mainstream organizations like the ADA signed on to the test ban campaign.

The coalition advertised in newspapers and magazines, and organized public forums and assemblies. It petitioned and lobbied Congress, where Senator Hubert Humphrey (D-MN) emerged as the leading proponent of a test ban. From the late 1950s and into the 1960s the test ban coalition waged a constant battle against the Atomic Energy Commission (AEC) claim that radioactive fallout was relatively harmless. The AEC retaliated by charging that the campaign was communist-inspired.[45]

Eisenhower initially regarded testing as necessary for "massive retaliation," his deterrent alternative to an expensive full fighting force. But he and Secretary of State John Foster Dulles were also sensitive to public opinion, especially world opinion. When scientific advisers, notably James R. Killian, president of the Massachusetts Institute of Technology, assured

Eisenhower that a test ban was technically verifiable, he began to shift the administration's position, even before the Soviets announced a unilateral moratorium upon ending a testing series in March 1958. In August of that year Eisenhower explained that "the new thermonuclear weapons are tremendously powerful; however, they are not . . . as powerful as is world opinion today in obliging the United States to follow certain lines of policy."[46] After the U.S. test series that month and overriding AEC and Defense Department objections, he placed a moratorium on atmospheric testing, pending negotiations on a permanent ban.

Events dashed the hopes of any such ban. In the midst of the crisis over Berlin and the Wall, the Soviets resumed testing in August 1961. President John F. Kennedy followed suit with underground tests and, the next spring, atmospheric ones. Anxiety about radioactive fallout became a staple of popular culture in this period. Nevil Shute's *On the Beach*, a novel about fallout from an atomic war ending life on earth, was widely read and serialized in forty newspapers. A full-page newspaper ad, reproduced around the world, showed the nation's most widely followed pediatrician looking down upon a child: "Dr. Spock Is Worried," the caption read, about Strotium-90 in the nation's milk supply. Similar ads and scientific testimonials popularized his worry.

As Cold War tensions mounted the fallout threat became identified with the possibility of nuclear war, and the test ban campaign expanded beyond its single-issue approach. SANE publicly addressed the Berlin crisis in 1961, suggesting that Germany be reunified under international auspices. It also mobilized public support for creation of a U.S. Arms Control and Disarmament Agency as proposed by Senator Humphrey. The coalition welcomed new constituencies, often with counterparts abroad—national religious bodies and Physicians for Social Responsibility, for instance, Women Strike for Peace, and the Student Peace Union. Indeed, American students attending a massive nuclear disarmament demonstration in England brought back its logo (lines representing the semaphore signals for N and D, superimposed on one another within a circle), which soon became the universally recognized symbol for peace.

Coalition leaders were encouraged by President Kennedy's 1961 invitation to the USSR to open a quest for peace. They accepted Humphrey's suggestion that they "encourage, support, and needle the administration" to offset the conservatives within it. SANE, now directed by Sanford Gottlieb, established a Washington office for political action and moved into electoral politics. By 1963 it could count a small constituency of Democratic senators who mirrored the former "peace progressives" on foreign policy. They in turn joined conservatives in both parties to challenge military spending.[47]

Just before the 1962 election, the Cuban Missile Crisis sharpened the threat of nuclear war, which left President John F. Kennedy and Premier Nikita Khrushchev all the more receptive to a compromise on testing. Norman Cousins met with Kennedy in November 1962 before leaving on a trip to Russia. The president authorized him to convey to Khrushchev his readiness to make a test-ban treaty a means of improving relations between their countries. The Russian leader, who already regarded the test-ban movement as a measurable shift in Western opinion, was cautiously responsive to Cousins, who continued to act as a trusted intermediary in the following months. He even helped to craft Kennedy's breakthrough American University speech of June 10, 1963. In that speech the president called for a reexamination of the USSR and the Cold War, and revealed that negotiations for a test ban were underway. When diplomacy produced the limited test-ban treaty, Kennedy turned to Cousins and SANE for what his press secretary Pierre Salinger called "a whirlwind campaign for educating and mobilizing public opinion" in support of Senate ratification. The coalition coordinated its efforts with the White House and its Senate supporters. The treaty, although initially behind in polls, was overwhelming adopted on September 24, 1963.

As it moved from dissent to protest, the test ban campaign of 1957–1963 created the constituent base and much of the repertory of modern peace activism. It won greater accountability from the AEC. It mobilized public insecurity about radioactive fallout and war as part of a worldwide movement. The intensity of public concern varied with the political salience of the fallout issue; as the coalition gave a political focus to popular and informed opinion, it contributed to a moratorium on testing and then to the atmospheric test-ban treaty of 1963. This was a notable success.

Yet that success was a limited one. "By the time the Kennedy administration began to take the prospect of cooperation with Khrushchev seriously," as historian Matthew Evangelista observed, "it was too late."[48] The president was assassinated in November 1963 and the Russian leader was ousted in October 1964. Moreover, stopping atmospheric tests did not itself dampen Kennedy's program of expanded military presence and "flexible response" abroad.

Nor did the test-ban treaty lead to disarmament, as peace advocates had fervently hoped. It became an instrument of arms control, like the Arms Control and Disarmament Agency that SANE also supported. Thus, ironically the campaign helped to introduce measures of control that tempered an accelerating nuclear arms race, but in doing so enhanced the political viability of nuclear deterrence. Rather than leading to the abolition of nuclear weapons, the test-ban movement helped to make them more palatable.

At the same time, however, the campaign inclined some establishment leaders to reevaluate the threat of Soviet aggression in the context of a prospective nuclear war. What was the utility of nuclear force? What constituted a meaningful victory? What if national survival required coexistence with the Soviet Union? Reinhold Niebuhr, among others, concluded that nuclear deterrence was dangerously unrealistic, a "time bomb under our vaunted security."[49] In this regard the test-ban campaign provoked an initial discussion of the realist and idealist dilemmas of military containment in a nuclear era.

The Crux of the Matter: Antiwar Protest in the Vietnam Era, 1965–1975

An extraordinary array of public constituencies transformed dissent into a massive protest against the war in Vietnam. The antiwar movement was a loose, shifting coalition divided over principles, tactics, and in-group politics; but it was driven by an overwhelming belief that the war was a moral and political tragedy, a growing sense that the public was withdrawing its support from the war, and a gnawing frustration that nonetheless protest could not reverse national policy. The movement contributed to public opposition and renewed anti-imperialism in the context of America's role as a superpower. Although antiwar leaders divided over many things, their central disagreement concerned the breadth of their critique of interventionist containment. Should antiwar protest repudiate the Cold War paradigm altogether? Or should it concentrate on opposing the Vietnam War?

During the war and for a decade thereafter, antiwar protest was stereotyped as essentially radical, youthful, and countercultural. Recent scholarship reveals a far more broad and inclusive movement that predated the

"Americanization" of the Vietnam War and extended beyond the end of U.S. military engagement.[50]

BASIC MOTIFS

A full-fledged organized antiwar movement coalesced after President Johnson launched a sustained air assault on North Vietnam in February 1965. Before that, however, a few senators, academics, commentators, foreign correspondents, and the core groups in the Test Ban coalition had already begun to criticize U.S. policy in Indochina.[51] Those early dissenters returned to several themes that long had characterized foreign policy dissent, themes that now carried over into a decade of protest.

Antiwar Realists such as Kennan, Niebuhr, or Morgenthau believed that the United States could not expect to impose a democratic, responsible Vietnamese government from the outside, or to sustain the drain of combat on its own resources. These views echoed the anti-imperialism of the earlier "peace progressives." In geopolitical terms, the Realists said, Indochina did not warrant the cost: South Vietnam was "not worth the life of one American boy," as Senator Ernest Gruening (D-AK) bluntly put it.[52]

For their part, liberal internationalists were anxious lest armed intervention militarize containment all the more and reinforce Ho Chi Minh's dependence on China, thus further polarizing the world and risking an expanded war. They added that to support dictatorial regimes in Vietnam was counterproductive in practice and wrong on principle, thus echoing the challenge from dissenting senators to the policy of aiding friendly dictatorships in Latin America and Africa. When the Senate defeated a resolution by Frank Church (D-ID) to withhold all aid from South Vietnam's autocratic ruler, Ngo Dinh Diem, George McGovern (D-SD) complained, "we find our money and our arms used to suppress the very liberties we went in to defend in southeast Asia."[53]

Dissenting idealists passionately agreed. They also insisted that communist rule would be less destructive to Vietnam than all-out war, and that expending Vietnamese lives for essentially American interests was immoral. Antiwar idealists elevated the personal quality of protest into what historian Charles DeBenedetti called the "Nuremberg syndrome"— the ideal that individuals must renounce immoral government policy and be governed instead by the higher laws of humanity.[54]

Such themes as these mingled in protest rhetoric. The issue of excessive executive power was a common denominator in all protest. Even before full-scale war, congressional dissenters worried about the extent of executive discretion in foreign affairs. Democratic Senators Gruening, Eugene McCarthy (MN), Stephen Young (OH), and Wayne Morse (OR) especially insisted on tighter oversight of the CIA. In 1964, Morse and Gruening voted against the Tonkin Gulf Resolution, which they warned was a blank check for war. Popular protest groups, moreover, accused the administrations of Lyndon Johnson and then Richard Nixon of acting arbitrarily and (at least in Nixon's case) repressively.

Protest themes were rounded out when the newly emerging radical left expanded on traditional anti-imperialism at the first major demonstration of the war, sponsored in April 1965 by Students for a Democratic Society (SDS, 1960). Young Paul Potter demanded of a crowd of some 20,000 people: "What kind of system" would lead to such a war?[55] The implicit answer was "capitalism," but it might as well have been "imperialism" or "corporatism," language that SDS had borrowed especially from historian William Appleton Williams of the University of Wisconsin.

Williams and other members of the so-called Wisconsin School" were updating the anti-imperialism of the earlier "peace progressives" and *their* historian, Charles Beard. Capital expansion was the essence of America's history and political economy, they argued. It required an Open Door foreign policy of accessibility abroad, to be imposed if necessary. U.S. policy meant aligning dominant, even dictatorial elites abroad with U.S. capital interests in an informal, nonterritorial form of empire. Long the established pattern in Latin America, these revisionists argued, that policy had more recently contributed to the Cold War. Williams left an indelible imprint on his students and field, even if few 1960s activists actually troubled to master his analyses. They claimed his authority, though, and borrowed his depiction of empire as the tragic American trajectory that led inexorably to Vietnam.[56]

Beyond Indochina, Williams' analysis opened a critique of the essential Cold War premise that was appropriated by what came to be called the New Left. It was an illusive, changing term: a 1960s version of populism in the sense that its leaders regarded the "concentration of power, in whatever hands, as the main threat" to themselves and American society. Unlike the nineteenth-century rural Populists, however, New Left leaders challenged not business monopolies but rather the interaction of economic and government elites whose power was cushioned, they thought, by the welfare state and a culture of complacent conformity: "the history of modern society [whether capitalist or communist] may be readily understood as . . . the enlargement and the centralization of the means of power in economic, in political, and in military institutions."[57] New Left ideology drew heavily upon Williams and other authors of the 1950s—C. Wright Mills, Paul Goodman, and Herbert Marcuse, for example. It was initially synthesized for SDS in Tom Hayden's 1962 "Port Huron Statement."

But how could "corporate liberalism" be challenged? This was a critical question, for those within the New Left, especially young people, felt a moral and very personal imperative to act. Their initial answer was to "empower the powerless"—the whole spectrum of groups "repressed" by gender, age, ethnic background, economic class, political position. This affirmative side of the New Left ethic led Hayden and his colleagues to organize community self-help groups among the urban poor. Another approach was to challenge the legitimacy of established institutions and culture ("Resist!" "All Power to the People"). This led to the confrontation of mass demonstrations, nonviolent direct action, war resistance, and by the end of the decade even street fighting as epitomized by the Weathermen. New Left ideology confronted a more pragmatic and political approach to mobilizing opposition to the war.

Each dissenting theme noted above engaged its own specific public constituencies, so that the political salience of the war became expanded into a set of issues. What is more, other currents of change and conflict swirled through the 1960s. Critics like Williams challenged the view fostered by 1950s liberal intellectuals that the country had found a "vital center" within a stable pluralist culture: a civil rights movement spread from South to North, challenging ever more forms of injustice, and giving rise to demands for "black power"; New Left reformers pointed to a crisis of class injustice and urban life that generated calls for "empowerment" and "participatory democracy"; activist feminism grew, as did environmentalism. A revolution in dress, drugs, music, sex, and attitudes toward authority flouted mainstream social mores. In colleges and universities, demands for change focused on curricula, *in loco parentis* regulations, the status of women, and campus governance.

In short, the war became enmeshed with and reinforced wide-ranging demands for change. Antiwar protest linked advocates of various changes into what they called "The Movement." For activists the war made many kinds of change seem all the more urgent; for many Americans the totality of activist demands felt the more threatening.

GATHERING CONSTITUENCIES

A series of teach-ins on Vietnam began at the University of Wisconsin in April 1965 and eventually involved some 120 campuses and national television. The teach-ins legitimated debate on the war and gave exposure to authoritative dissenters. Protest expanded throughout the year as Johnson continued to increase the number of U.S. troops in Vietnam.

With the formation of antiwar coalitions, differences appeared between liberal and radical approaches. For a time they divided over the old issue of excluding communists, for somewhat longer over whether to demand immediate and unconditional, or negotiated withdrawal from Vietnam. More fundamentally, for antiwar liberals the salient issue was the war itself, whereas New Left–oriented radicals tended to view the war as an issue with which to mobilize aggrieved people and reconstruct society. Pacifist groups like the FOR and AFSC included leaders of both persuasions. They, with remnants of the Old Left like the Socialist Workers Party (SWP), were instrumental in forming tenuous alliances of liberal and radical constituencies.

On the left, by 1966 SDS became loosely linked to some 250 chapters in colleges and universities, even though activists were a tiny fraction of students (perhaps two percent). Conscription created a constituency of draft-age men. African American leaders claimed angrily that their men were drafted more readily than whites. While that is disputable, blacks did suffer a disproportionate number of combat deaths through 1966 and were hardly represented on draft boards.[58] In the mood of the time, the fact that draftees were mostly the poorer and less educated men, made the Selective Service system vulnerable to attack. Draft resisters and their supporters, mostly better educated and middle class, challenged conscription through public rallies and civil disobedience (while local draft boards and volunteer counselors began to cripple the system from within). Meanwhile, elements of the counterculture, colorful if small in number, were attracted to large street demonstrations, where they were highlighted by the media, thus helping to stereotype the antiwar movement as radical and extremist.

Meanwhile, altogether conventional Americans were gathering in liberal protest. In early 1966 Senator William Fulbright (D-AR) organized televised hearings of the Foreign Relations Committee to critically examine the war. Administration leaders like Secretary of State Dean Rusk met with sharp questioning while East Asia experts critical of the war received a sympathetic hearing. The Fulbright hearings helped legitimate congressional and

popular dissent. Antiwar constituencies came to include physicians, enter-
tainers, authors, labor unions, former Peace Corps workers, the Federation
of American Scientists, and Business Executives Move for a Vietnam Peace.
Clergy and Laymen Concerned About Vietnam (CALCAV, 1965) became a
powerful conduit for religious protest. Another Mother for Peace was added
to women's organizations such as WSP and WILPF. Martin Luther King Jr.
brought his civil rights associations to the movement. He helped to bridge
its liberal and radical wings, as did the FOR, AFSC, and Vietnam Veterans
Against the War (1967). SANE also played a prominent role, coordinating
the efforts of liberal antiwar groups, especially with respect to demonstrations and congressional lobbying.

By the fall of 1967, dissent was spreading within the administration,
underlined by Robert McNamara's resignation as Secretary of Defense.
The Democratic Party roiled with disaffection, as did the ADA. Allard
Lowenstein, lawyer, political consultant, and later congressman (NY,
1969–71), assiduously cultivated that dissent and enrolled dissident Senator Eugene McCarthy to challenge Johnson for the 1968 Democratic presidential nomination.

PROTEST MARGINALIZED AND MAINSTREAMED

The Tet Offensive in the winter of 1968 provoked a sharp reaction to the
president's overly rosy picture of war prospects. It revealed Democratic
Party fissures and a loss of public support for war on Johnson's terms. The
president withdrew from the electoral race. Almost immediately the assassination of Martin Luther King threw the nation into turmoil. A sense
of crisis pervaded the presidential contest, in which virtually the whole
liberal antiwar movement was enlisted. Generalized public anxiety intensified with the assassination of Robert Kennedy in June and the violence-
ridden Democratic convention held in Chicago that August.

Eventually, a divided Democratic Party nominated Hubert Humphrey
while the Republicans chose Richard Nixon as their nominee. Both promised to end the war but neither was specific about how; the fact that differences between them on this central issue were narrow underscored both a
popular consensus for peace and the ambiguity of translating it into policy. Nixon's victory in November served to solidify antiwar dissent among
congressional Democrats, now freed from political loyalty to the executive
branch. In that regard, by the time of Nixon's inauguration in January
1969, liberal antiwar opposition had gone mainstream.

One result was to marginalize the radical wing of the movement. Various of its constituencies, feminists and blacks for example, increasingly pursued their own agendas, while SDS itself disintegrated in factional disputes during 1968–69. Tom Hayden, among others, dropped out of the movement after the Chicago convention, and when he did return, in 1972, it was as a liberal activist. Others split off into ever more rigid Marxist or anarchist ideologies. A small faction of Weathermen went underground and turned to apparently nihilistic violence. By 1970 the "New Left was in complete disarray," as historian Irwin Unger observed, both organizationally and ideologically. When its leaders began to look back, Unger added, they were "appalled to see what an enormous gap had opened between [themselves] and the great mass of the American people."[59] Radicals were equally distanced from the rest of the peace movement.

The movement's new configuration was illustrated in 1969 when former Kennedy and McCarthy campaigners like Sam Brown organized a decentralized October "Moratorium" that enlisted deeply patriotic *local* appeals for peace from a quarter of a million people in cities and towns across the country. Participants were less angry than distressed. Twenty-four Democratic senators endorsed the Moratorium. The media covered it fully and appreciatively. Observed commentator Walter Cronkite: "Never before had so many demonstrated their hope for peace."[60] Nixon and his advisers were appalled, and the president later recalled that the Moratorium had "undercut" his plan to confront North Vietnam with a military ultimatum.[61] In November a broad antiwar coalition staged a "Mobilization" in Washington and San Francisco to demand immediate withdrawal from Vietnam. Liberals in pacifist groups like the AFSC and FOR reclaimed leadership and accommodated civil disobedience on controlled terms so that the Mobilization was a relatively controlled, poignant demonstration by a half million people in the capital alone. Liberal activists then moved into the off year elections of 1970.

Nixon meanwhile pursued a policy of Vietnamization, withdrawing U.S. troops and leaving the fighting to the South Vietnamese. In some measure that weakened the salience of the war issue at home, but it also contributed to the disillusionment of combat troops abroad and to the growth of the Vietnam Veterans Against the War, which reached its political zenith in 1971 (when John Kerry left its leadership for a political venue). By this time the media had lost sight of the "street protest" antiwar stereotype they had created and concluded that the movement itself had disappeared.

This perception was wrong: in fact, liberal protest was now being channeled into the political system, where SANE took a leading role.

That organization had maintained a tenuous relationship with the rest of the antiwar movement in the mid-1960s. It had been slow to press for unilateral withdrawal from Vietnam and was uncomfortable with radical tactics. Although SANE supported mass demonstrations that were disciplined and focused (the 1969 Moratorium, for instance, and the 1971 March on Washington), its heart was in public information, lobbying, and electoral politics. It helped to bring together liberal Democratic leaders in conversations about new national priorities, addressing the Cold War institutions and assumptions from which the Vietnam War was a logical outcome. Beyond SANE, the weight of liberal constituencies in the movement increased after 1968, manifest in several new coalitions and in the tactics of persuasion and legislative pressure. Congress rescinded the Tonkin Gulf Resolution and cut funding for U.S. military operations in Cambodia in 1970, pressed the president to "set the date" for withdrawal, threatened to stop funding the war, and passed the War Powers Act (1973).

When Nixon finally extricated the nation from military engagement in Vietnam, in January 1973, the salient political issue had shifted from the war to his abuse of executive power, leading to his resignation in August 1974. Pressed by a still active, liberal peace movement, Congress resisted the entreaties of President Gerald Ford to fund further military assistance in South Vietnam. War ended there in the spring of 1975.

Had the antiwar movement succeeded only in prolonging it, as some have charged? Nixon, determined to control the nation's memory of the Vietnam War, argued that it had. The charge stands up only if ephemeral demonstrations had actually preempted military or diplomatic options that could have been decisive. The nearest example would have been Nixon's own Duck Hook operation. That was a projected campaign to crush North Vietnam by bombing even Hanoi and mining the Haiphong harbor. Its purpose was to force the North to negotiate an end to the war on Nixon's terms. But the president had concluded even before the 1969 Moratorium that he could not effectively ratchet up the war within boundaries acceptable to the public. Antiwar demonstrations only confirmed that. Rather, Nixon himself prolonged the war by pursuing the elusive goal of South Vietnamese sovereignty. The peace movement neither prolonged nor stopped the Vietnam War.

The movement did force the issue, though, in at least three ways. It generated alternative sources of authority on Vietnam policy and provoked critical political and ethical analysis among elites and the general public. Second, as the movement engendered controversy, it also increased the war's social cost. Third, the movement gave a political focus to generalized discontent with the war, mobilizing enough opposition to limit its scope. In part that was a function of the ever-larger demonstrations of the era: they confronted the administrations and public with evidence of opposition even as they dramatized the movement to itself (although mass mobilizations drew scarce resources from local and political work). In part, too, the liberal wing helped to set the perimeters of presidential action by recruiting mainstream constituencies for antiwar information, electoral work, and lobbying activity.

Antiwar activism changed the peace movement. National groups finessed the issue of including former communists by relegating it to the local level. New tactics, from street theater to draft resistance, expanded the repertory of protest. Mass demonstrations came to be managed with discipline and attention to the media. National symbols were appropriated to identify protest as *loyal* opposition. Electoral politics became a field of peace activism. Networking began to supplant the directive style of earlier campaigns.

The war itself, and withdrawal from it, was the urgent *raison d'être* for the antiwar movement. On one hand the war engaged all the major motifs of U.S. foreign policy dissent. In another sense, however, the attention paid to military withdrawal preempted systematic, focused debate on the crux of the matter: the Cold War paradigm that had produced U.S. military intervention in the first place. Nonetheless, the war and protest against it prompted leaders of the foreign policy establishment—even presidents—to question some key Cold War assumptions. Two questions in particular demanded attention. First, given the experience of Vietnam, what was the utility of military force? And second, if the communist threat was, in fact, not monolithic, then what remained of a strategy of containment?

COLD WAR ARMS RACE AND MILITARY INTERVENTION REVERSED: 1975–1989

The Nixon administration had framed its own answers to those questions even before the end of the fighting in Vietnam. The president's "Vietnamization" policy and his "Nixon Doctrine," calling on allies to

defend themselves, acknowledged that military intervention had exceeded
the bounds of feasibility and public support. His negotiation of nuclear
weapons limitations with the USSR (SALT I) recognized the mutual advantage of arms control; conceding that communism was not monolithic
modified the Cold War paradigm in order to leverage the differing interests of Russians, Chinese, and Vietnamese. Tentatively at least, pragma-
tism trumped ideology.

Succeeding Nixon as president, Gerald Ford was equally realistic in foreign policy, but he dropped the language of détente in recognition of a
hardening Cold War orientation within his own Republican Party. Jimmy
Carter, Ford's Democratic successor, campaigned on a platform that included moderating the nuclear threat and substituting human rights for
anticommunism as a criterion for U.S. support abroad. Carter also strongly
endorsed the UN and multinationalism.

This flexibility did not last. Soviet leadership under Leonid Brezhnev
concluded a START II arms control treaty, but undermined it by deploying a new generation of SS-20 intermediate range nuclear-armed missiles
in Europe and, late in 1979, invading Afghanistan. Carter increased U.S.
military spending, authorized preparation for protracted nuclear war, and
tried to negotiate from strength. Republicans, notably those in the Ronald
Reagan wing, pressed for an even tougher approach. When Reagan took
office, the stage was set for a revival of Cold War confrontation and, by extension, for fresh protest.

In particular, Reagan's initial weapons policy galvanized the Nuclear
Weapons Freeze Campaign (NWFC, 1980), and his intervention in Central America generated the Solidarity Movement. These two social movements built upon earlier challenges to militarized containment. They
interacted with the internal politics of the United States, Europe, and the
USSR, and with the diplomatic relationship between Reagan and Mikhail
Gorbachev to shatter the Cold War paradigm.

The Reagan administration represents the last chapter of the Cold War
story, of course, but the Freeze and Solidarity movements that it elicited by
no means were the concluding chapter in resistance to the national security state. On the contrary, those campaigns opened a whole new vein of
protest that continues long after the Cold War has become history. The
Freeze and Solidarity ought to considered along with two subsequent organized protests—the opposition to so-called economic "globalization"
during the George H.W. Bush and Bill Clinton administrations, and the
challenge to President George W. Bush's Iraq War—as inaugurating a new

variant of protest. Each of the four movements had a distinctly salient issue and context, organization, and political impact. Still there were common denominators that distinguished all four protest movements from earlier campaigns.

1. They increasingly employed *a networking style* of organization in contrast to a directive one.
2. They intentionally *avoided ideological confrontations* but encountered practical ones.
3. They appealed to *middle class values and patriotism.*
4. They continued to experiment with *nonviolent action.*
5. They were ever more *transnational* in scope.
6. They increasingly moved beyond the Cold War paradigm to challenge new cases of militarization, imperialism, and unilateral intervention.

THE NUCLEAR WEAPONS FREEZE CAMPAIGN

Although controversy over the arms race dated from the nuclear test ban years, during Reagan's first term in office issues related to nuclear weapons achieved greater than ever salience.[62] As the revolution in destructive power was succeeded by a revolution in the striking capacity of weapons, an arms control regime had evolved to negotiate ceilings on specified delivery systems. The point was to maintain a rough balance of proliferating new weapons while deterring a first strike: arms control was a "loose harness for a runaway horse that could not be stopped."[63] This process was institutionalized in international agreements, a small bureaucracy in the Arms Control and Disarmament Agency, and the doctrine of minimum deterrence. The revived Cold War, whether attributable to Soviet recklessness or Reaganesque ideological fervor—or both—put all of this in jeopardy.

Even in the 1970s, core peace groups, together with the Union of Concerned Scientists (UCS) had lobbied for measures like nuclear nonproliferation and prohibition of nuclear weapons on sea beds, and they had fought the antiballistic missile system, the B-1 bomber, and the MX mobile missile with some success. The Mobilization for Survival (1978) aligned those opponents of nuclear arms with a strong environmental coalition against atomic power, but it did not have a viable focus. That changed with Russia's Afghan invasion and NATO's two-track decision to deploy a new family of nuclear missiles to Europe, which raised urgent concerns there and in America. In December 1979 defense analyst Randall

Forsberg proposed that the peace coalition advocate a negotiated bilateral freeze on deployment and development of nuclear weapons. Core peace groups agreed and began to organize a single-issue coalition, while the AFSC moved the freeze idea into the 1980 election. The Nuclear Weapons Freeze Campaign was under way, but it was galvanized by Ronald Reagan's militant Cold War presidential campaign.

As president, Reagan departed from Carter's weapons policy: with belligerently anti-Soviet language, and seeming almost cavalier on nuclear war, he replaced arms experts in the Arms Control and Disarmament Agency (and elsewhere) with people from the Committee on the Present Danger (1978) who, like Eugene Rostow, disdained the idea of mutual self-restraints.[64] Reagan's action created a political focus for the Freeze Campaign even as his rhetoric energized it.

The campaign was intentionally decentralized and driven by local initiatives. As in the Test Ban Campaign, broad public response led to the formation of a national organization, the NWFC, that linked local groups and enlisted new constituencies. Within a year the Freeze Campaign expanded to a rank-and-file force of 20,000 activists in 40 states. Despite generally unsympathetic news coverage, it garnered attention as a result of reports of massive European demonstrations, nonviolent direct action against U.S. weapons manufacturers, Jonathan Schell's best-selling *Fate of the Earth,* independent theater projects, periodical articles, and a TV dramatization of *The Day After* a nuclear attack. (That show was censored and hamstrung as part of a massive administration and right-wing counterattack, which included labeling the NWFC as a communist dupe).[65] Perhaps a million Americans marched through New York City in June 1982, while the UN General Assembly was holding its second of three Special Sessions on Disarmament. A large transnational movement spawned simultaneous demonstrations in cities abroad and lobbied at the UN. American-European cooperation was not cohesive, however, owing to the differing national priorities of activists as well as the diverse political contexts and cultures in Europe.[66]

From the outset the campaign was intended to embody a powerful movement capable of rethinking and ultimately reversing the nuclear arms race. The same goal motivated activists in Europe and the USSR, although they used different tactics. In America the campaign focused on electoral politics and a congressional effort to pass Freeze legislation. During the winter of 1982 Edward Markey (D-MA) introduced a resolution in the House, as did Edward Kennedy (D-MA) and Mark Hatfield (R-OR) in the Senate. Establishment supporters valued the Freeze as a tool to save the arms control regime or otherwise constrain the administration. As its political focus attracted new constituencies and significant funding, the Freeze became essentially a legislative campaign.[67] Its leaders consciously avoided extrapolitical tactics like nonviolent direct action, which in turn caused dissension with pacifist groups. There were other rifts over practical and policy matters. In May 1983 the House of Representatives passed Freeze legislation that had been weakened by amendments, but the Senate defeated it in October (it won 40 votes). Although the Freeze Campaign continued beyond the 1984 election, it faded with the deployment of Euro missiles, the failure of Freeze legislation, and a new plateau in defense spending. The Freeze did survive as an organization, eventually merging with SANE in 1986 even as its networks dissipated or shifted their attention to other issues (the name SANE/FREEZE, Campaign for Global Security was adopted in 1989).

What did the Freeze Campaign accomplish? It provided a political platform in defense of negotiated arms control, which it may have saved. Although the priority of gaining congressional support precluded the Campaign from explicitly challenging Cold War assumptions, it almost certainly contributed to Reagan's shift to an internationally more accommodating, peace-oriented profile in 1982. "A nuclear war cannot be won and must never be fought," the president declared in April that year. It was as though he projected himself, *Le Monde* observed, "as the leader of the peace movement."[68] Reagan's rhetorical reorientation, his negotiation of nuclear disarmament with Mikhail Gorbachev, and the changes in the USSR under Gorbachev: all began to displace the Cold War paradigm nearly without debate.

THE U.S. SOLIDARITY MOVEMENT

The controversy provoked by the Reagan administration's interventions in Central America gave rise to the U.S. Solidarity Movement. It was arguably "the most conspicuously protracted and volatile political struggle of the decade."[69] In a sense, the episode revived a long record of U.S. intervention and anti-imperialist criticism. President Carter had modified the policy of regional hegemony by making support for Central American elites conditional on their human rights records. But Reagan abrogated that formula, his administration viewing the region in Cold War terms. It explained away popular resistance to adversity and exploitation

as Soviet and Cuban machinations. To sustain elitist regimes in Guatemala, Costa Rica, and El Salvador, Reagan employed not only economic
and diplomatic pressure, but also military aid and training, supplemented
by CIA covert action. He sponsored Contra attacks on the revolutionary
Sandinista government in Nicaragua, which he called a "communist
reign of terror."[70] He sustained Salvadoran governments dependent on
right-wing military force.

All of this induced surging protest in the United States. A liberal Democratic bloc in the House resisted Reagan's intervention. The president
moderated his approach as necessary to maintain a supportive alliance of
southern Democrats and Republicans there, and to keep the Republican-
dominated Senate in line. When that failed, the administration ignored
Congressional restrictions on military aid, most blatantly in the Iran-
Contra affair of 1986–87. Congressional dissent, to the extent that it was
effective, was grounded in solidly anti-interventionist public opinion.
Given historic popular indifference to Central America, organization was
required to cultivate dissent and give it a political focus. "Solidarity" was
that movement.[71]

The mechanism of structured protest, Solidarity evolved as an informal coalition of over 150 national groups and "tens of thousands" of activists.[72] Organizationally it involved grass-roots initiatives and extensive
networking among church and "affinity" groups with like concerns (a
structure imported from the Freeze campaign). What held the "loosely
knit, widely scattered activist" network together, according to historian
Christian Smith, was "AT&T [the phone], the personal computer [to generate data and mailing lists] and the U.S. Postal Service."[73]

Solidarity drew on preexisting political action groups, especially from
the Freeze campaign, and it had an especially strong religious dimension.
In part that reflected the involvement of U.S.-based churches in Central
America, not least through some 2,234 missionaries there.[74] The Catholic
Church in Central America was, moreover, directly linked to its U.S.
counterparts, which reacted strongly to the 1980 murders of Archbishop
Oscar Romero and of U.S. churchwomen in El Salvador. A third religious
aspect combined "liberation theology," which aligned Latin and North
American church leaders on justice causes, and the tactics of nonviolent
action with which Latins were linked to the Fellowship of Reconciliation,
the oldest of U.S. core pacifist groups.[75] And fourth, Central America became a cause célèbre because it energized a well-staffed, essentially church-
based human rights lobby in Washington. Solidarity was essentially a

middle-class movement, animated less by politics than by a combination of religious and humanitarian instincts.

For example, when the Immigration and Naturalization Service in 1987 tried to repatriate Salvadoran refugees back to El Salvador (where right-wing death squads awaited them), some four hundred churches across the United States constituted a faith-based network of sanctuaries. [76] Similarly, after witnessing the results of a Contra attack on the Nicaraguan village of El Porvenir in April 1983, a cadre of North Carolinians helped forge a national program that placed two hundred U.S. citizens in Nicaragua, both to deter Contra attacks and to coordinate short-term village tours for some four thousand fellow citizens. Most of those Americans returned home if not as activists then at least as informed and emotionally charged interpreters. Witness for Peace evolved to coordinate this program and became a credible source of field-based information for its forty thousand newsletter readers and over a thousand congressional and media contacts. [77]

Meanwhile, the Pledge of Resistance was formed to coordinate multiple efforts to sign up people who would pledge to oppose a U.S. invasion of Nicaragua. Over forty thousand resisters signed on, half of whom promised civil disobedience.[78] As the prospect of invasion yielded to the reality of Contra attacks, pledge signers were repeatedly solicited to lobby against congressional aid to the Contras. On another line, a group called Quest for Peace matched congressional military grants to the Contras with over $327 million in humanitarian aid to Nicaragua.[79] Such forms of protest as these linked innumerable local groups to national peace organizations with the Committee in Solidarity with the People of El Salvador (CISPES, 1980), each of which had its own base of activists and local chapters.

A coalition lobby evolved into the Central America Working Group (created in 1987), seizing the opportunity offered by rising Democratic opposition in Congress and widespread popular misgivings. For most of the decade it fought Reagan's budget requests to arm the Contras and sustain its client government in El Salvador.

Necessarily, Solidarity contested the administration for public support. It challenged Reagan's Cold War framework for Central America and argued that his military, win-lose approach was distorting the economic and political modernization in the region. Echoing the "peace progressives" of the interwar years, movement leaders argued that American policy should support people everywhere in their aspirations for "life, liberty, and the pursuit of happiness," but that the administration's intervention contributed instead to paramilitary death squads, repression, and poverty in the region. Solidarity's arguments contained some echoes of New-Left anti-imperialism, but those were muted: the movement ascribed oppression in Central America to a "wayward" administration more readily than to the logic of U.S. political culture.[80]

The result was something of a standoff. Public opinion consistently opposed intervention in Nicaragua and El Salvador, but Congress never quite prevented it. Voting on military and (ostensibly) humanitarian aid to the Contras and the Salvadoran regime vacillated throughout the period. In 1982 Congress passed a resolution prohibiting CIA or Defense funds from being used to overthrow the government of Nicaragua. The bill was sponsored by Edward Boland (D-MA) but initiated by Solidarity.[81] The following year the Senate emasculated an even stronger version of the Boland legislation. When it could not prevent congressional prohibitions the administration simply ignored them, as in its Iran-Contra operation.

The Iran-Contra scandal of 1986–87 led many Solidarity activists to expect that Congress might finally curtail Reagan's war. It didn't. What did end the war was a process of negotiation and compromise sponsored in 1987 by the governments of Costa Rica, Honduras, El Salvador, and Guatemala. The Sandinistas cooperated in the process, which resulted in election of a centrist government friendly to the United States. The Contras were disbanded. The civil war in El Salvador also ended through negotiation and compromise.

Officials in the Reagan administration claimed victory, since the Sandinistas lost in Nicaragua and a friendly government was sustained in El Salvador. That claim rested on the Cold War paradigm of externally fomented communist rebellion that simply did not fit the facts in Central America. In reality Central American heads of state and not the U.S.-sponsored Contras resolved the situation in Nicaragua. U.S. authorities acceded only reluctantly. Sandinistas vindicated their claim to democratic aspirations and shared power in the new government, which retained its mixed economy and social welfare. And Salvadoran rebels succeeded in integrating tactical force with an essentially political strategy, to which a new government acceded (whereas the United States had hardened the resistance to rebels, it now endorsed accommodation with them). Such victory as there was belonged to Central Americans who determined, in the words of Costa Rican president Oscar Arias, "to take the fate of our region into our hands."[82]

Solidarity limited the intensity of warfare in Nicaragua by its pressure on a vacillating Congress, obliged Reagan to expend enormous political capital when he illegally circumvented the legislature, and helped force El Salvador to curb death-squads and blatant violence by bringing public opinion to bear on that issue. The movement did not altogether reverse U.S. policy, but it did almost certainly constrain it.

TRADITIONAL DILEMMAS AND THEMES IN UNCHARTED WATERS, 1989–2004

When Communist regimes crashed in Europe in 1989 and in Russia the next year, the Cold War paradigm lost its salience, along with the issue of nuclear weapons. One result was to open up space for a social justice framework that long had accompanied antiwar protest (and research into the conditions for peace) but had not been in the forefront. Solidarity focused its action on the direct U.S. intervention in Central America, for instance, but it interpreted the crisis there in terms of economic deprivation and class oppression. As the issue of direct intervention in civil wars faded, issues of systemic economic and social justice claimed increasing attention. Framed as "economic globalization," those issues generated a worldwide protest movement.

AN ECONOMIC JUSTICE MOVEMENT: GLOBALIZATION AND PROTEST

The phrase "Globalization and Protest" suggests at least the worldwide interdependence that links disparate issues and institutions, dissenters, and protest movements in increasingly dense relationships across national boundaries. In another sense, however, the word "globalization" conveys "that loose combination of free-trade agreements, the Internet, and the integration of financial markets that is erasing borders and uniting the world into a single, *lucrative*, but *brutally competitive* marketplace." This view carries the assumption that the United States, or more broadly the North, dominates international economics "while weaker states fall into line."[83] Although a world economy has benefited even the developing world in some respects, the so-called free-trade, or "neoliberal" model of economic globalization that rose to prominence in the wake of the Cold War became the target of a strong, if somewhat inchoate, global justice movement.

The dominant institutions in this globalizing economy no longer belong to a single great power such as the United States but are international in their composition. The principal international economic agencies are the International Monetary Fund (IMF) and the World Bank, as well as the World Trade Organization (WTO), which in 1994 replaced the GATT and claimed enhanced enforcement capability. Following World War II, the IMF and World Bank had helped stabilize and expand the global economy for the mutual benefit of nations. The United States had preponderant power in these agencies, whereas in the UN General Assembly it faced a bloc of Third World, developing nations that nearly doubled between 1955 and 1975. U.S. hostility to UN and regional development programs culminated during the Reagan free-trade era;[84] concurrently the World Bank began operating on an increasingly rigid neoliberal, free trade ideology and its partner agencies followed suit.

For rich countries and elites the result was "lucrative," but for much of the developing world it was a "brutally competitive marketplace" that accelerated poverty, plunged living standards, and renewed instability. Insistence on devaluation triggered inflation; retiring debts cut resources for development and social welfare; constraints on land reform prevented the redistribution of resources (and incentives); emphasis on growth investment curtailed education in educational and social infrastructure. The population living in poverty increased by nearly 100 million people in the 1990s, even as total world income grew at an annual average of 2.5 percent.[85] The unrestrained market favored the already strong, among and within nations. In Latin America, just emerging from a cycle of civil war, rising expectations were frustrated. One result was increased political opportunity for NGOs that helped to transform frustration into protest. These circumstances also affected protest in the United States.

Witness for Peace was a case in point. It was reassessing its mission in the wake of the Contra war when early in 1994 Zapatista rebels in poverty stricken Chiapas, Mexico, denounced their government's economic policies and its participation in the North American Free Trade Agreement (NAFTA), which they insisted hurt indigenous people. Witness for Peace was listening. By the end of the year it promised solidarity with Latin Americans trying to deal with the underlying causes of poverty, economic instability, and oppression. The organization increasingly located those problems in economic globalization.[86] As local protesters everywhere encountered the plethora of transnational social movements, they expanded their understanding of issues: from their land rights to their environment, for example, from "international environmental challenges to World Bank lending policies."[87]

Other U.S. public interest groups shared that broadening orientation, as did the largely faith-based "Jubilee 2000" campaign for Third World debt relief. In turn, they became allied with organizations having vested interests in international economic policy, like labor and environmental organizations. Establishment dissenters like Joseph E. Stiglitz buttressed their understanding.[89] The political difficulty was that economic globalization never became a really salient public issue in the United States (by contrast with Latin America). Even the debate over NAFTA engaged mainly issue-specific constituencies like unions. It did, on the other hand, align U.S. groups like the Mobilization for Development with Canadian and Mexican counterparts, for whom NAFTA *was* a viable political cause. In fact, American activists increasingly aligned with dissenters around the world, some of them joining protest rallies at annual meetings of the meetings of the World Bank, the IMF, and the Group of Seven (G7, the advanced industrial powers—now G8). As never before, American dissent was becoming internationalized.

This development formed the background for the so-called 1999 "Battle of Seattle" at the third ministerial conference of the World Trade Organization. Thousands of protesters informed the public, witnessed to their values, demonstrated their outrage, put the WTO under siege, and conducted nonviolent direct action (accompanied by some anarchist violence to shops and large-scale police riot control operations). The scale and comprehensive organization caught governments and especially the Clinton administration by surprise, although protests had been in the planning stage for months. The event brought together some 50,000 activists, about half from Seattle and Washington state, another large bloc from elsewhere in the United States, 3,000–5,000 from Canada, and up to 3,000 from abroad. Of the protesters, 66 percent were from organized labor, 11 percent were environmental activists, 2 percent advocates of economic justice, together with human rights and peace activists and some anarchists.[90] Of course, many of those people addressed multiple issues. The WTO consultation was ineffective, not only because of the protest outside the conference room but also because of disaffection inside from developing nations and regions. [91]

The Battle of Seattle represented a dramatic step in the process of organizing diverse, sometimes conflicting, forms of protest against neoliberal economic globalization.[92] It was preceded by demonstrations at multinational economic meetings around the world over five years. It was accompanied by protests in London, Geneva, India, France, the Philippines, and

Mexico City. Further actions were staged in Washington, Prague, Quebec, and Genoa, but that template of protest became less important than the Social Justice Forums that brought the movement together on regional and global scales beginning in 2001. In essence, the populist motif became globalized. Meanwhile, the political environment changed dramatically for American activists on September 11, 2001.

THE IRAQ WAR: DISSENT AND PROTEST

Following the devastating 9/11 attack on the United States, President George W. Bush assembled a strong multinational coalition with which to unseat al-Qaeda and its patron Taliban government in Afghanistan, just as a decade earlier his father had mobilized a powerful coalition against Iraq in the Gulf War. Subsequently, and unlike his father, George W. Bush defied the UN Security Council in March 2003, when he launched war on Saddam Hussein with a coalition that represented neither NATO nor the UN. Bush argued that invasion was justified by the threat from Iraqi weapons of mass destruction (WMD) and links to al-Qaeda. Whatever combination of strategy, erroneous intelligence, moral principle, and mendacity motivated the attack, the president's call for war generated massive protest.

Immediately after 9/11, peace activists coordinated by the Fourth Freedom Fund and some four thousand religious leaders appealed for a national response that emphasized cooperative law enforcement rather than indiscriminate warfare: the Twin Towers tragedy was a horrendous crime, they said, but not an act of war. New communications networks were formed, including movement newspaper *War Times,* to which seventy thousand subscribed in its first week, and an Internet website that evolved into a powerful organizing tool. Demonstrations were organized by a multi-issue coalition, Act Now to Stop War and End Racism (ANSWER). Even the invasion of Afghanistan in November 2001 was not a salient, contestable public issue, however, and no major antiwar coalition emerged until early fall 2002, when the administration began to cultivate support for its preplanned war on Iraq.

At one level the issue was Saddam Hussein, described by Bush as a compelling threat because of his weapons of mass destruction and connection to al-Qaeda. At another level the issue was much broader: in post-9/11 speeches, most notably his speech at West Point in June 2002, Bush had begun to assert an absolute prerogative to initiate a preemptory (preventive[93])

unilateral attack on any nation that constituted a threat to the United
States. This emerging doctrine of preventive war fired congressional debate
and several bills that would have required UN Security Council approval
for the use of force on Iraq. But those legislative efforts came to nothing.
Instead, on October 10, 2002, Congress passed a resolution that gave the
president considerable discretion in deciding how to deal with Iraq. In the
House the vote was 296 to 133, in the Senate 77 to 23. Congressional deference to the president over a substantial minority made the war issue salient
and stimulated rapid antiwar mobilization.[94] From the outset, then, the federal motif of expansive executive authority was linked to the anti-imperial
issue of an expansive, interventionist U.S. role.

In three months organizers raised public opposition to levels not seen
since the Vietnam era. They were especially effective in using the Internet.
With MoveOn they built networks of communication and education
around the country and abroad, channeled thousands of messages to
members of Congress, organized and coordinated hundreds of local meetings, and raised money for peace-oriented legislators (notably Senator
Paul Wellstone, D-MN).[95] They also raised funds with which to use the
traditional media. With Ben Cohen's TrueMajority they reached out to
constituencies like those of Business Leaders for Sensible Priorities and
the National Council of Churches. Founded in June 2002, the TrueMajority site had 350,000 subscribers by the end of 2003.[96]

Two new coalitions were formed by organizations uncomfortable with
the New Left tone of ANSWER. United for Peace and Justice was designed
mainly to organize protest demonstrations through grassroots activism. It
was sponsored by core peace groups like Peace Action (SANE-Freeze),
AFSC, FOR, WRL, Sojourners, together with the Women's Action for
New Directions (WAND), global justice groups like Global Exchange, the
Internet-based groups, and constituency organizations. Some of its leaders aligned major constituencies—religious organizations, environmen-
talists, physicians, the NAACP—in Win Without War, with an emphasis
on the media. This antiwar coalition had a greater capacity for raising
funds and mobilizing support than previous ones, in large measure because of its decentralized, networking style of organization and its extensive use of Internet communication.

As alarm grew in the winter of 2002–2003, antiwar protest became "the
largest transnational antiwar movement" ever undertaken," truly a "global
phenomenon."[97] On February 15 Americans cooperated in a wave of demonstrations that were reported in over six hundred cities worldwide, and

were accompanied by innumerable resolutions and petitions. Estimates of participants ran to ten million, perhaps four hundred thousand of them in the bitterly cold streets of New York.[98] Organized dissent reinforced official disaffection among key allies including Germany, Turkey, and South Korea. Even Bush's major ally, Great Britain, experienced the largest demonstration of its history as a million protested in London. Coordinated worldwide vigils followed in March.

Meanwhile, Bush sought support in the UN Security Council for his plan to disarm Iraq forcibly. But the protest movement opposed him there, and it had the advantage of being transnational. It took public opinion directly to the world body, as when movement leaders delivered a million-person petition to UN representatives in March. "A creative dialectic developed between the Security Council and global civil society," observed scholar-activist David Cortright. "The public opposition to war hinged on the lack of UN authorization. The objection of the UN in turn depended on the strength of antiwar opposition . . . in the United States, Germany, France, Mexico, and other countries. . . . "[99]

None of this mattered to the administration. In an immediate sense, the protest movement's effort to prevent the Iraq War failed. The president authorized an invasion, preempting the Security Council process of bringing Saddam Hussein to account, disregarding the sharp division in American public opinion, and arguably violating the spirit of the Constitution. When WMD failed to materialize after the Hussein regime was demolished, the president justified the war for liberating Iraq. That was America's world role, he averred: to liberate and democratize. And, as a half century before at the beginning of the Cold War, this expansive vision of U.S. mission was placed in the context of a dichotomous paradigm of the world; only this time communism was replaced by terrorism.

The Iraq War was unusually intentional; it represented a choice more than a response to attack—the words of Robert Taft, "an instrument of public policy rather than its last resort." And it occasioned a distinctly broad-based opposition. Liberal internationalists objected to the revolutionary unilateral character of the choice, especially in the context of available multinational options and objections. Realists agreed and worried about the consequences for American diplomacy, and the potential for spreading terrorism. Humanitarians rued the sacrifice of Americans and Iraqis even considering the ruthlessness of Hussein. Large numbers of activists from the global social justice movement joined antiwar protest. They conceded that terrorism was a threat, but they added that it was aggravated by injustice resulting from the neoliberal economic regime imposed on the Third World. Many of them concluded, "Militarization was just the other arm of the corporate agenda."[100] Author Noam Chomsky updated a New Left critique in *Hegemony or Survival: America's Quest for Global Dominance,* while Libertarian conservatives restated the case against righteous imperialism and national security state even more sharply than had their predecessors in the early years of expansive containment: a spate of books carried evocative titles like *The Sorrows of Empire,* and *The Crisis of Democracy and the Quest for Empire.*[101] On all sides there was anxiety about the expansion of executive power and lack of accountability.

The Bush administration expended enormous political capital to defy a powerful wave of opposition to war at home and abroad. Protest continued long after the actual invasion of Iraq, inspired in part by the fact that a war intended to be brief and decisive turned out to be long and inconclusive. Dissent took the form of campaigns against U.S. occupation, of overtures to support American troops by "bringing them home," and of humanitarian and informational actions in Iraq once it *was* occupied. Increasingly protestors faulted the president for falsifying the WMD threat. Quite deliberately the movement's major resources—a large network of local activists, Internet capacity to raise funds, and media savvy—were fed into the political process, where they targeted the nation's mainstream. This process culminated in the spectacular presidential primary campaign of Howard Dean, former governor of Vermont. The Democratic Party, apparently assuming that it could count on antiwar votes in any case, nominated the far more centrist Senator John Kerry (D-MA) to challenge Bush.

Late in September, after months of hesitation, Kerry made the war issue fully integral to his campaign. It was "the wrong war in the wrong place at the wrong time." he insisted. In particular, he faulted the president for misleading the public about his reasons for war, isolating the country from major allies, failing to plan for effective regime change, and for the extensive U.S. casualties after Hussein's fall. Kerry insisted on a multilateral approach to the future of Iraq, but like Bush he advocated staying the course there, differing mainly on what constituted an effective use of force.

For his part, the president deftly turned aside objections to the way he had initiated and conducted the Iraq War. Bush did not argue those issues so much as he framed the current fighting as part of a worldwide March of Democracy and War on Terrorism. A paradigm of Terror threatened to succeed the Cold War premise: as the "trustee of global stability," the United States faces an implacable foe in a war on terrorism from a militant

and radical fundamentalist Muslim fringe.[102] If preventive war and unilateral policy were part of the administration's comprehensive, global strategy to deal with terrorism, they did not emerge in the presidential campaign.
Rather, foreign policy issues were dominated by the *rhetoric* of terror during
the election. Kerry attacked the president's record, but he did not seriously
challenge the incumbent's premise. The paradigm won by default.

Not only foreign policy issues but also major domestic policy choices were
obfuscated by a cloud of attacks on each candidate's character and military
record, and also by cultural controversies such as abortion and marriage between homosexuals. Although Bush was narrowly reelected with Republican
majorities in the House and Senate, his victory left a very large core of embittered opposition that remained organized and formally independent of the
Democratic Party, although potentially in alignment with it.

This phenomenon was a result of the antiwar movement. Organized
opposition had failed to prevent the Iraq War: it was mobilized too late
and, in any case, its mounting political influence was preempted by the
administration's unilateral invasion. In turn, the movement had become
politicized, carrying the war issue into the 2004 presidential campaign.
The war issue did not dominate the Democratic campaign, as Howard
Dean and others had hoped it would, and the election was not specifically
a referendum on foreign policy; but antiwar sentiment became a rallying
point for disaffected citizens who resented Bush's record on a range of domestic and international issues.

In that process, and spurred by disillusionment with the election results, antiwar organizations such as MoveOn and TrueMajority broadened into a multi-issue network with a common orientation to progressive
social and political reform. They retained their Internet capacity to mobilize resistance to renewed strategic aggression abroad or extremely partisan
domestic programs. This political restraint on administration priorities was
compounded by a federal deficit of over seven trillion dollars. Constraints
on the national security state still operated in America, therefore, even
within a newly dichotomous global paradigm.

DISSENT AND PROTEST ON NATIONAL SECURITY, 1957–2006

Three things at least remained constant from the consolidation of militarized containment in the 1940s and 1950s, through the shattering of the

Cold War and into the remobilization of America under a paradigm of global terrorism. They were: the premise that America should maintain dominant military power consonant with its preeminent role as "trustee of global stability," the insecurity of Americans faced with a plethora of real and politicized threats, and the recurrence of organized dissent and protest over the appropriate kind and application of power.

The Dynamics of Dissent: The Instruments and Political Function of Protest

At the *organizational core* of protest were enduring groups for which broad issues of peace and justice were related. Fresh associations were added with each new campaign. Some, like Solidarity in the 1980s, were informal networks of program-specific groups. Others began as single-issue coalitions but broadened their programs and endured beyond the crisis that called them into being, as SANE did, for example, and the Freeze (they merged in 1987 and eventually became Peace Action), Witness for Peace, Physicians for Social Responsibility, and MoveOn, among others. Thus the base of protest expanded and diversified, enabling successive coalitions to reach more constituencies. This expansion was not linear, however, because the overall movement expanded and contracted sharply with the public salience of security issues.

Peace and antiwar activists in the last quarter century intentionally combined grass-roots *mobilization*, often locally initiated and recently facilitated by the Internet, with the sophisticated *management* of protest resources (e.g., information, funds, lobbying and media skills). This combination was uneven and should not be romanticized. It is still evolving in MoveOn, for example, and among opponents of neoliberal economic globalization. The latter, the global justice movement, has not yet developed an overall organizational structure; it remains a transnational *network* of diverse groups with a common "search for collective solutions."[103]

Not surprisingly, each campaign refined tactics proven during previous protests, while adding new ones. To preserve and transmit the tactical repertoire has been a movement function for enduring, multi-issue groups like the AFSC, FOR, WRL, SANE, and PEACE ACTION, and now MoveOn. To create and experiment with new tactics (most recently the Internet) has been the role of successive single-issue groups. Broadly speaking, these efforts have produced two different approaches: *confrontational* and *participatory*.

Confrontation occurred when dissenters felt excluded from the decision-making process or harassed by authorities, as especially during the Vietnam War. It occurred, too, when protesters felt driven to challenge the fundamental premise of foreign policy more than strategic or tactical issues. That was the case of CNVA during the test ban campaign, of New Left pacifists in the 1960s and 1980s, and of some elements opposing the war in Iraq. In those cases, as in the Civil Rights movement, nonviolent direct action and civil disobedience were understood to be a symbolic language that dramatized a gap between national values and political behavior. It was also a way for individuals to witness to their moral convictions and anguish.

Confrontational protest was overwhelmingly nonviolent. The relatively few incidents of violence occurred on the movement's periphery and were counterproductive to its goals, as in the case of the Weathermen of the Vietnam era. By contrast, the peace and Civil Rights movements of the 1950s and 1960s helped to establish nonviolence as a contending *political culture* in America.[104] Nonviolent direct action, even civil disobedience, became legally protected and widely understood as a protest tactic. Draft resistance was widespread during the Vietnam War, for instance. Direct action against nuclear weapons was undertaken and protected by the courts by CNVA in the 1950s and by Daniel and Philip Berrigan during the Freeze. Civil disobedience was basic to the Sanctuary movement, Witness for Peace, and Pledge of Resistance, and it was a part of training for the Seattle protests. The FOR sent peace witness teams to Iraq. Nonviolent direct action has become institutionalized, both in training for confrontational protests and in the way that authorities deal with demonstrators. The larger philosophical frames of nonviolence have been exemplified from India to Poland and South Africa, the American South to the Philippines.

The second line of protest has emphasized participation in the political process. Tactics have included public information and education, endorsements from respected elites like scientists and physicians, academic authorities and journalists, religious leaders, cultural and entertainment figures. In the Iraq War crisis public outreach (and fund raising) extended to the Internet. While they mobilized public opinion, movements lobbied Congress and became involved in both local and national elections, most notably in 1968 and 1972, 1980 and 1982, and 2004. Participatory protest was most effective when the political system was open to organized dissent, and it also helped to open up that process.

Participatory and confrontational protest often worked in tandem to dramatize issues. The combination raised the political costs of nuclear testing, weapons production, and deployment. It also raised the social costs of intervention in Vietnam and Central America. Modern protesters learned from the Vietnam War. They sought influence in the political center, helped by the fact that by the mid-1970s the former counterculture had become passé, along with New Left extremism. Since Vietnam, dissent has been explicitly associated with national symbols and portrayed as patriotic. Thus opponents of the Iraq War emphasized support for the troops there. Moreover, painful memories of movement conflicts in the 1960s helped subsequent leaders to keep their differences in balance and their focus on whatever national security issue was viable. Lessons from the past? The Solidarity movement warned, "El Salvador is Spanish for Vietnam."[105]

Organization and tactics were only as effective as there were *political opportunities* to mobilize dissent. A case in point was the nuclear weapons debate of the 1980s. Europe's two-track option both raised the salience of INF deployment and legitimated a zero-sum alternative. Public awareness of the issue was heightened by Reagan's militant rhetoric, his call for a neutron bomb, and then his Strategic Defense Initiative. Concurrently a strong bloc of Democrats defended arms control on principle and saw it as an issue with which to challenge the president. Reagan reduced the viability of the nuclear weapons issue when he accommodated arms control and disarmament, but his covert support of the Contras created political opportunity for the Solidarity activists. In turn, as then deputy director of the CIA Robert Gates observed, the uproar over Iran-Contra convinced "Reagan, his wife, and his closest White House advisors that the stain of the scandal could only be . . . diminished, by the President becoming a peacemaker, by his achievement of a historic breakthrough with the Soviet Union."[106]

In the case of Iraq, political opportunity for organized dissent occurred when Congress legitimated public debate but failed to decisively limit the president. The opportunity to move the war issue into electoral politics derived from the volatility of Iraq after Bush declared it occupied, together with mounting evidence that the WMD rationale had been contrived. Although the world movement resisting economic globalization has not yet generated sustained public protest in the United States, there may yet be a political opportunity, given the growing focus on American jobs displaced overseas.

One further dimension of dissent and protest in this half century is its growing *transnationalism*.[107] In the 1980s the Freeze Campaign was part of

a worldwide social movement that penetrated and influenced even the Soviet Union.[108] Europeans contributed to the multinational pressures on
U.S. policy then, and even more effectively before the Iraq War. In another
case, the Solidarity movement's connection with Central American peoples personalized transnational protest, deepened grass-roots commitment, and made its lobbying more credible. In the campaign against a
neoliberal economic regime, transnational groups are addressing international institutions, and they are linked to other transnational movements.
Indeed, plans for the worldwide antiwar protests of February 15, 2003,
were initiated in a European Social Forum, a regional conference of the
global justice movement. Those plans were refined in Copenhagen and fi-
nalized at the World Social Forum of January in Porto Allegre, Brazil.
Boundaries mean less and less for popular pressures on foreign policy, collaboration ever more.

THE POLITICS AND CONSEQUENCES OF PROTEST

Organized peace advocates initiated some significant modifications of
policy, like arms control and test ban treaties. Mostly they generated constraints on policy, as in the case of weapons development and deployment,
intervention in Central America, and quite possibly in future global economics. In the case of the Vietnam War peace advocates were the catalyst
and driving force for withdrawal—a fundamental redirection of policy.
With few exceptions (like Norman Cousins on the test ban), protest movements engaged the executive branch indirectly.

There were two paths to political influence, and both required that dissenters mobilize public opinion, using the organization, tactics, and political opportunities described above. One path led from an aroused public
directly to the executive branch, where it took the form of constraints that
administrations imposed on themselves—restraints they regarded as acceptable, even useful modifications of their own policies. Examples of this
path would include Eisenhower's moratorium on nuclear testing, Kennedy's
partial test ban, Nixon's Vietnamization, Reagan's INF policy, and his endorsement of the Arias plan for Central America. Presidents even used
peace movements to strengthen their hands politically, Roosevelt to promote the UNO for example, Kennedy for his test ban, and Carter when he
attempted to check some arms developments.

In all these cases presidents factored public opinion into the political
costs and benefits of policy modification. Lyndon Johnson, in the most

extreme instance, must have made a similar calculation on behalf of his party and overall priorities when he withdrew from the 1968 election campaign. Moreover, even presidential decisions to challenge a protest movement (or in Nixon's case to harass it) involved a calculation of political risk and advantage. Organized dissent thus has been an integral factor in national security policy management, and increasingly that calculus has included the influence of transnational movements on other governments.

A second path to influence led through congressional and party politics. In this approach an aroused public empowered a party organization like ADA or a congressional bloc, which in turn negotiated with the executive branch. In the process, issues became framed in tactical, program-specific terms. That happened when antiwar sentiment was mainstreamed in the Vietnam War, and in the cases of the Freeze and Central America debates under Reagan. It was the story of the Dean and Kerry campaigns of 2004. It was the story in 2006 when unhappiness with Bush's war enabled Democrats to regain control of Congress.

When a protest movement took this path it risked having its cause co-opted by conventional politics; in effect, it traded some loss of control and focus in hopes of political gains. Thus the Freeze campaign saw a friendly congressional bloc metamorphose its proposal into arms control; Solidarity relied on friends in the House who were strong enough to check but not to overturn administration policy; and antiwar activists found themselves disappointed and dispersed when Kerry lost the election. To the extent that an executive branch internalized constraint or a congressional bloc imposed it, peace and antiwar movements did make limited gains. In that measure, however, the mobilizing issue was defused. That was, after all, the calculation of accepting constraint. Coalitions waned as supportive public constituencies returned to their usual concerns. Core organizations and networks of dissent remained, to be mobilized again around another salient issue.

Incremental gains have value in the American system; there is no balance without checks. Still, it seemed to frustrated movement activists in various campaigns that their effort was all out of proportion to the results. Yet the larger significance of mobilizing the public lies in the effort itself insofar as it modifies the very terms of public discourse. That seems to have happened with respect to nuclear weapons development. It may have happened regarding intervention abroad, given the exceptional public opposition to the Bush Doctrine of preventive war, his reelection not

withstanding. The question of long-term influence leads us to the underlying themes of organized protest to national security policy.

MOTIFS OF DISSENT IN RELATION TO HISTORIC AMERICAN TRADITIONS

Insecure "in the shadow of war" since 1939, the United States rejected a
Fortress America approach to security and, instead, reached outward.
Expansion on the nation's periphery produced an aggregation of power at
the center, especially in the executive branch, where political, economic,
and military decisionmaking converges. Recurrent dissent from national
security policy became public protest when events generated sufficient insecurity about policy to mobilize constituencies in the public sector.

The characteristic themes of organized dissent were anticipated in the
questions asked of the national security state: what is most important to
secure, and how best is security attained? Those very questions revealed
the insecurity of Americans in the so-called "American Century."

The populist motif of limiting the concentration of economic power has
been a constant in American history. It arose with nineteenth-century
agrarian anxieties about corporate control and was extended in the reforming mentality of the Progressive Era. Its form changed as sources of
economic insecurity altered, but it has recurred in fears of "bigness" and
the concentration of economic decisionmaking. Conservative protesters
in the 1930s and 1940s applied the populist motif against government regulation and Keynesian finance. Since the 1980s protesters have wielded it
on behalf of the world's most vulnerable. They assume that an unre-
stricted market ideology is the instrument of predatory corporate power
intent on avoiding social controls. Neoliberal globalization carries inherent
contradictions, they argue, between concentrated capital and "popular-
democratic and parliamentary control over crucial economic, social and
ecological policies."[109] Neopopulist protesters echo the historian Walter
LaFeber: "The American Century . . . has especially been a century shaped
by U.S. policies demanding that the world be made safe and [accessible]
for the American economic system."[110] Thus has the populist theme
been raised to the level of global, systemic analysis—in some cases to an
ideology.

The anti-imperialist motif characterized opposition to U.S. expansion
that once was territorial but shifted to political, economic, and military
hegemony. Dissidents have insisted that America compromises its own

principle of self-determination by imposing U.S. norms and institutions on other nations and cultures. This critique has complemented the populist motif where it appeared that compromising the universal value of self-governance served vested economic and political interests, as in the case of Banana Republic diplomacy.

The *federal motif*, or the principle of distributing authority and responsibility, has been at issue throughout the construction of a national security state in America. Often the salient political issue shifted from a specific policy to excessive executive discretion, as in the cases of Johnson and Tonkin Gulf, Nixon and Watergate, Reagan and Iran-Contra, or Bush and preemptive war. Domestic authority also has been at issue, as in the Patriot Act, and foreign policy has sometimes been the lightning rod for resentment over enlarged government roles, as it was under Franklin Roosevelt.

The federal principle has also been applied to the international system, notably in the cases of global neoliberalism and intervention in Central America and Iraq: at issue has been the appropriate extent and role of U.S. power abroad. Realists recognized that international realities limit U.S. options. But transnational protest movements also constrained foreign policy. On occasion they reinforced the independence of other nations and strengthened domestic protest (as in the cases of the Nuclear Weapons Freeze, Central America, economic globalization, and the Iraq War). Transnational social movements herald a global civil society that aspires to share authority and responsibility with international institutions and states.[111] Underlying much recent American protest there has been a strong sense that unilateralism, insofar as it is pursued in an increasingly integrated world as ours, is itself a symptom of insecurity.

National interests and values have been employed both to justify and to oppose the course of the national security state. On one level, foreign policy has been contested in terms of the flag and other symbols of national identity. On another, it has involved alternative calculations of interest. Self-designated realists like Kennan and Morgenthau endorsed containment but then objected to its use as a rationale for a nuclear arms race and military intervention in Vietnam. At stake in the Cold War discourse was a calculation of different *forms* of power. Thus Reagan argued that U.S. military spending destabilized the Soviet Union and softened its hard line; but his claim excluded other forces of change, such as the ineptness of the communist economy, the drain of its empire, and even the connections between transnational networks and Russian dissenters from the

Cold War. Similarly, U.S. opponents contested Bush's Iraq War on the grounds that whatever the real merits of Saddam Hussein's threat, a preemptive strike was likely to isolate the United States as a "feet-and-Fahrenheit power in a metric world."[112] They insisted that unilateral warfare in defiance of the UN and major NATO allies was counterproductive to U.S. national interests *and* values. Protest organized against the Iraq War depicted it as both immoral and fraught with disaster in very practical terms, counter both to relative national interests and to fundamental values. Even setting aside the normative issues involved, the war was held to be misguided on pragmatic grounds.

Still, the enduring core of organized protest is rooted in normative considerations that strongly reflected the principles of progressive pacifism. A deep, personal commitment to abjure violence has formed the benchmark value against which public interests are assessed; justice and peace were assumed to be concomitant, violence antithetical to either. In the public arena, though, when it comes to organizing dissent and coalitions, protest has been mobilized by relating national interests to national values. Solidarity, for example, challenged Reagan's intervention in Central America as both counterproductive to long-term stability in the region and contrary to the principle of self-determination. Earlier the "body bags" of the Vietnam era became poignant symbols of not only loss but also waste—sacrifice without compensating value. They were symbols that carried the bitter irony of an officer's explanation for leveling the town of Ben Tre: it was necessary, he said, "to destroy the town in order to save it."[113]

Motifs of organized dissent? Who is likely to take to the streets for a motif? Who will jeopardize their personal security and challenge national policy for the sake of a scholar's paradigm? It costs a lot to swim upstream, after all. Why do it?

Many Americans who engaged in dissent did so to witness to their deep-seated religious principles or moral outrage. Some were anguished at the policy costs in death and destruction, to other peoples or their own. Others responded to specific opportunities to make a difference, to the fear that precious American qualities were at risk, or to their unease about the national security state and its direction. Doubtless some just followed the crowd. Often dissidents and protesters concentrated on finite political issues that obscured their larger Cause. Whatever their motives though, and win or lose, they helped to define America, its state, and its world roles. They have been integral to that process. The obverse of any act of protest is, after all, an affirmation. Since the creation of the national security state after World War II, many Americans have judged that national security policy has yielded an increased sense of insecurity; insofar as they challenged it in active dissent or organized protest, they have affirmed themselves and what they valued most of their nation. They have also affirmed the existence of alternatives to the policy choices that both stemmed from and contributed to national insecurity.

ACKNOWLEDGMENT

This essay owes much to Andrew Bacevich's insightful reading of various versions of it and his editing of the final one.

Notes

1.   Here I use "realist" to connote the priority of calculating forces and interests, and "idealist" as the priority of values; these are not necessarily mutually exclusive. I suggest by "internationalist" the view that national interest is appropriately pursued as one in a community of states; by "federal" the legitimate distribution of and constraints on power; and by "populist" the values attached to cooperatively empowering individuals in the face of controls imposed by concentrated finance capitalism.

2.   I use Michael Sherry's apt phrase as he did, referring to America's constant war footing. Sherry, *In the Shadow of War: The United States Since the 1930s* (New Haven: Yale University Press, 1995).

3.   See Akira Iriye, "A Century of NGOs," in Michael J. Hogan, ed., *An Ambiguous Legacy: U.S. Foreign Relations in the "American Century"* (New York: Cambridge University Press, 1999), 416–36. Arguably, the main catalyst for this innovation before 1945 was the work of peace-advocating INGOs. See also Louis Kriesberg, "Social Movements and Global Transformation" and Charles Chatfield, "Intergovernmental and Nongovernmental Associations to 1945," in Jackie Smith, Charles Chatfield, and Ron Pagnucco, eds., *Transnational Social Movements and Global Politics: Solidarity Beyond the State* (Syracuse: Syracuse University Press, 1997), 3–18, 419–41.

4.   Robert David Johnson, *The Peace Progressives and American Foreign Relations* (Cambridge: Harvard University Press, 1995).

5.   Ibid., 314.

6.   The basic work is Charles DeBenedetti, *Origins of the Modern American Peace Movement, 1915–1929* (Millwood, NY: KTO Press, 1978).

7.   Ibid., 8.

8. The most enduring of them, the Foreign Policy Association (FPA, founded in 1921) was unwilling to sacrifice its cohesion for political activism; it pursued an educational agenda. (In these notes and in the text, dates following the names or initials of organizations indicate their founding.)

9. This account is drawn largely from Charles Chatfield, *The American Peace Movement: Ideals and Activism* (New York: Twayne, 1992), 62–73, and the fuller treatment in Chatfield, *For Peace and Justice: Pacifism in America, 1914–1941* (Knoxville: University of Tennessee Press, 1971), 256–86.

10. Justus D. Doenecke, *The Battle Against Intervention, 1939–1941* (Malabar, FL: Krieger Publishing, 1997), 25.

11. Regarding Gandhian pacifism among COs see Lawrence Wittner, *Rebels Against War* (New York: Columbia University Press, 1969; revised, Philadelphia: Temple University Press, 1984), and Scott H. Bennett, *Radical Pacifism: The War Resisters League and Gandhian Nonviolence in America, 1915–1963* (Syracuse: Syracuse University Press, 2003), 98–133.

12. The standard history of this movement is Robert A. Divine, *Second Chance: The Triumph of Internationalism in America During World War II* (New York: Atheneum, 1967).

13. Christy Jo Snider argues that inclusion of NGOs in the UNO structure was a result also of their increasingly active role in international affairs in the 1930s. Snider, "The Influence of Transnational Peace Groups on U.S. Foreign Policy Decision-Makers during the 1930s: Incorporating NGOs into the UN," *Diplomatic History* 27, no. 3 (June 2003): 377–404.

14. Wesley T. Wooley, "Finding a Usable Past: The Success of American World Federalism in the 1940s," *Peace and Change* 24, no. 3 (July 1999): 333. This article, part of a "World Federalism Forum," encapsulates Wooley's basic history of the movement, *Alternatives to Anarchy: American Supranationalism Since World War II* (Bloomington: Indiana University Press, 1988), quote at p. 59.

15. Organized public protest thus joined other countervailing forces that constrained the development of a garrison state, as argued by Michael J. Hogan and Aaron L. Friedberg. See Hogan, *A Cross of Iron: Harry S. Truman and the Origins of the National Security State, 1945–1954* (New York: Cambridge University Press, 1998) and for a longer span of time Friedberg, *In the Shadow of the Garrison State: America's Anti-Statism and Its Cold War Strategy* (Princeton: Princeton University Press, 2000).

16. Phrase quoted from Robert J. Donovan in Hogan, *A Cross of Iron*, 29.

17. Walter L. Hixon, *George F. Kennan: Cold War Iconoclast* (New York: Columbia University Press, 1989), 29.

18. Murrow quoted in Lawrence S. Wittner, *One World or None*, vol. 1 of *A History of the World Nuclear Disarmament Movement* (Stanford, CA: Stanford

University Press, 1993), 58; Norman Cousins, *Modern Man Is Obsolete* (New York: Viking Press, 1945), 10.

19. Cord Meyer, "A Service Man Looks at the Peace," *Atlantic Monthly*, (September 1945), 43–48, quoted in Meyer, *Facing Reality: From World Federalism to the CIA* (New York: Harper & Row, 1980).

20. Wesley T. Wooley, "Finding a Usable Past," 329. Lawrence S. Wittner treats world federalism in a global context in *One World or None*.

21. Quotation from Wooley, ibid., 333, and *Alternatives to Anarchy*, 59.

22. For an explicit treatment of this theme see Mark G. Toulouse, *The Transformation of John Foster Dulles: From Prophet of Realism to Priest of Nationalism* (Macon, GA: Mercer University Press, 1985).

23. Quoted in Graham White and John Maze, *Henry A. Wallace: His Search for a New World Order* (Chapel Hill: University of North Carolina Press, 1995), 154.

24. Quotations from ibid., 227–28.

25. Quoted in George H. Nash, *The Conservative Intellectual Movement in America Since 1945* (New York: Basic Books Inc., 1976), 93.

26. The phrase was the title of a 1951 article by Bogdan Raditsa, in part replicated in William Chamberlain's 1953 *Beyond Containment*, and quoted in ibid., 90.

27. Robbie Lieberman, *The Strangest Dream: Communism, Anticommunism, and the U.S. Peace Movement, 1945–1963* (Syracuse: Syracuse University Press, 2000), 45. "Communist" is capitalized in the original.

28. Quotation from Robert K. Carr, *The House Committee on Un-American Activities: 1945–1950* (Ithaca: Cornell University Press, 1952); Ellen Schrecker, estimates 10,000 jobs lost at a bare minimum, perhaps 200 imprisoned, and countless persons harassed, in *Many Are the Crimes: McCarthyism in America* (Boston: Little, Brown, 1998), 362–63. She acknowledges the anti-fascist origins of anticommunist extremism, but John E. Haynes develops them more fully in *Red Scare or Red Menace: American Communism and Anticommunism in the Cold War Era* (Chicago: Ivan R. Dee, 1996).

29. The WRL did not deny membership because of communist affiliation, but its principles were clearly noncommunist. See Bennett, *Radical Pacifism*.

30. Quoted in Milton S. Katz, *Ban the Bomb: A History of SANE, the Committee for a Sane Nuclear Policy, 1957–1985* (New York: Greenwood Press, 1986), 47.

31. Taft speech of March 29, 1951, quoted in Ronald Radosh, *Prophets on the Right: Profiles of Conservative Critics of American Globalism* (New York: Simon and Schuster, 1975), 185.

32. Nash, *The Conservative Intellectual Movement in America Since 1945*, xiii and *passim*.

33. Hogan, *A Cross of Iron*, 74, 363 (my italics).

34. Friedberg, *In the Shadow of the Garrison State*, 57.

35. Taft speech of January 28, 1949, quoted in ibid., 168.

36. For cameo studies of a wide range of dissenters see Radosh, *Prophets on the Right;* and Thomas G. Paterson, ed., *Cold War Critics: Alternatives to American Foreign Policy in the Truman Years* (Chicago: Quadrangle Books, 1971).

37. The coalition and its contending positions, although not the organization of its liberal wing, are analyzed in Hogan, *A Cross of Iron,* 119–58, 318–22.

38. E. Raymond Wilson, *Uphill for Peace: Quaker Impact on Congress* (Richmond, IN: Friends United Press, 1975), 14. For the anti-UNT campaign see 190–204.

39. Hogan, *A Cross of Iron,* 133.

40. Ibid., 155–56.

41. This account draws upon Chatfield, *The American Peace Movement,* 100–116. For fuller treatments see Robert Divine, *Blowing on the Wind: The Nuclear Test Ban Debate, 1954–1960* (New York: Oxford University Press, 1978); Katz, *Ban the Bomb;* and Robert Kleidman, *Organizing for Peace: Neutrality, the Test Ban, and the Freeze* (Syracuse: Syracuse University Press, 1993).

42. Lawrence S. Wittner, *Resisting the Bomb: A History of the World Nuclear Disarmament Movement, 1954–1970,* vol. 2 (Stanford, CA: Stanford University Press, 1997), 31, 11.

43. Katz, *Ban the Bomb,* 22.

44. For a thorough account of the worldwide campaign for a comprehensive test ban and nuclear weapons control and of government attempts to undercut it, see Wittner, *Resisting the Bomb.*

45. On government confrontation of the campaign see ibid., 125–59.

46. Quoted from the minutes of a meeting of August 12, 1958 in ibid., 182.

47. Quotation from Katz, *Ban the Bomb,* 65. The dissenting minority included Senators Humphrey, George McGovern (SD), Frank Church (ID), Eugene McCarthy (MN), Albert Gore, (TN), Gaylord Nelson (WI), Stephen Young (OH), Ernest Gruening (AK), Wayne Morse (OR), and Edmund Muskie (ME). Their role is recounted in Robert David Johnson, "The Origins of Dissent: Senate Liberals and Vietnam, 1959–1964," *Pacific Historical Review,* 65 (May 1996): 249–75.

48. Matthew Evangelista, *Unarmed Forces: The Transnational Movement to End the Cold War* (Ithaca: Cornell University Press, 1999), 121. Cousins' role is recounted in Wittner, *Resisting the Bomb,* 416–28, and in Norman Cousins, *The Improbable Triumvirate: John F. Kennedy, Pope John, Nikita Khrushchev* (New York: Norton, 1972). The test ban diplomacy is treated in Glenn T. Seaborg with Benjamin S. Loeb, *Kennedy, Khrushchev, and the Test Ban* (Berkeley: University California Press, 1981).

49. Niebuhr, Foreword to Harrison Brown and James Real, *Community of Fear* (Santa Barbara, CA: Center for the Study of Democratic Institutions, 1960), 5.

50. This section is based on works referenced in the interpretive bibliography by Charles Chatfield, "At the Hands of Historians: The Antiwar Movement of the Vietnam Era," *Peace and Change* 29, nos. 3/4 (July 2004): 483–526, and on

Charles DeBenedetti and Charles Chatfield, *An American Ordeal: The Antiwar Movement of the Vietnam Era* (Syracuse, NY: Syracuse University Press, 1990).

51. The role of early academic and journalistic dissent is covered in most thorough histories of the war, the role of the peace societies in DeBenedetti and Chatfield, *An American Ordeal*, 9–102. The congressional core is analyzed in Robert David Johnson, "The Origins of Dissent: Senate Liberals and Vietnam, 1959–1964," *Pacific Historical Review*, 65 (May 1996): 249–75.

52. Quoted in ibid., 272.

53. Quoted in ibid., 270.

54. Charles DeBenedetti, "On the Significance of Citizen Peace Activism: America, 1961–1975," *Peace and Change* 9, nos. 2/3 (Summer 1983): 13–17.

55. Quoted in Tom Wells, *The War Within: America's Battle Over Vietnam* (Berkeley: University of California Press, 1994), 24.

56. Paul M. Buhle and Edward Rice-Maximin, *William Appleman Williams: The Tragedy of Empire* (New York: Routledge, 1995. The most influential of Williams' histories for the 1960s generation was *The Tragedy of American Diplomacy* (Cleveland: World Publishing Co., 1959).

57. Quotations from Anatol Rapaport and Barton J. Bernstein in Matthew Stolz, *Politics of the New Left* (Beverly Hills, CA: Glencoe Press, 1971), vii, x. The New Left is the subject of a large literature, but it remains especially accessible in Irwin Unger, *The Movement: A History of The American New Left 1959–1972* (New York: Dodd, Mead, 1974).

58. David Coffey, "African American Personnel in U.S. Forces in Vietnam," in Spencer C. Tucker, ed., *Encyclopedia of the Vietnam War: A Political, Social, and Military History* (New York: Oxford University Press, 1998).

59. Unger, *The Movement*, 188.

60. Quoted in Wells, *The War Within*, 375.

61. See ibid., 377–79, and Jeffrey P. Kimball's fuller, more nuanced assessment in *Nixon's Vietnam War* (Lawrence: University Press of Kansas, 1998), 158–76.

62. Regarding the U.S. Freeze movement see especially David S. Meyer, *A Winter of Discontent: The Nuclear Freeze and American Politics* (New York: Praeger, 1990), Frances B. McCrea and Gerald E. Markle, *Minutes to Midnight: Nuclear Weapons Protest in America* (Newbury Park, CA: Sage, 1989), and Kleidman, *Organizing for Peace*.

63. Chatfield, *The American Peace Movement*, 140.

64. Rostow was a co-founder of the CPD, typical of what David S. Meyer calls the "war winners" who for the first time "dominated an administration's strategic planning," in *A Winter of Discontent*, 39.

65. On the media see Lawrence S. Wittner, *Toward Nuclear Abolition: A History of the World Nuclear Disarmament Movement: 1971 to the Present*, vol. 3 (Stanford, CA: Stanford University Press, 2003), 186–90, 255–64.

66. David Cortright and Ron Pagnucco, "Limits to Transnationalism: The 1980s Freeze Campaign," in Jackie Smith, et al., *Transnational Social Movements and Global Politics: Solidarity Beyond the State* (Syracuse: Syracuse University Press, 1997), 159–74. For the transnational story see Wittner, *Toward Nuclear Abolition*.

67. Kleidman, *Organizing for Peace.* 160.

68. Quotations and interpretation in Wittner, *Toward Nuclear Abolition,* 264–65.

69. Christian Smith, *Resisting Reagan: The U.S. Central America Peace Movement* (Chicago: University of Chicago Press, 1996), xvii.

70. Quoted in John E. Findling, *Close Neighbors, Distant Friends: United States–Central American Relations* (New York: Greenwood Press, 1987), 165.

71. "Solidarity" was the descriptive title given to the heterogeneous movement; it was not an organizational title.

72. Figures from David Cortright, *Peace Works: The Citizen's Role in Ending the Cold War* (Boulder, CO: Westview Press, 1993), 227. They are reaffirmed in Christian Smith, *Resisting Reagan*. My understanding of Solidarity is heavily indebted to Smith's sophisticated analysis.

73. Ibid., 121.

74. Ibid., 141.

75. This connection was organizational: the American FOR was an active part of the network through which nonviolent revolution was popularized in the Latin American church and connected with liberation theology. See Ron Pagnucco, "Transnational Strategies of the Service of Peace and Justice in Latin America," in Jackie Smith, *Transnational Social Movements,* 123–38.

76. Christian Smith, *Resisting Reagan,* 70.

77. Figures from ibid., 77–78. David Cortright estimates that during the decade 70,000 Americans visited Nicaragua in various capacities. Cortright, *Peace Works,* 219.

78. Chrstian Smith, *Resisting Reagan.,* 81–82.

79. Cortright, *Peace Works,* 225. This figure includes the value of donated labor and services along with actual aid. David Cortright to author, September 9, 2004.

80. For a discussion of how the public discourse was framed on both sides see Christian Smith, *Resisting Reagan,* 231–79; regarding the administration's "harassment and repression" of Solidarity, see ibid., 280–324.

81. Cortright, *Peace Works,* 228.

82. Arias quoted in Smith, *Resisting Reagan,* 352.

83. Tom Friedman, "Revolt of the Wannabees" (my italics in text), quoted by Sidney Tarrow in "From Lumping to Splitting: Specifying Globalization and Resistance," Jackie Smith and Hank Johnston, eds., *Globalization and Resistance: Transnational Dimensions of Social Movements* (New York: Rowman & Littlefield, 2002), 235.

84. Joseph E. Stiglitz, *Globalization and Its Discontents* (New York: Norton, 2002), 10–13 and throughout; Gary B. Ostrower, *The United Nations and the United States* (New York: Twayne, 1998), 125, 149–58.

85. Figures from Stiglitz, *Globalization and Resistance*, 5; examples throughout.

86. Virginia Williams, "Grassroots Movements and Witnesses for Peace: Challenging U.S. Policies in Latin America in the Post-Cold War Era," *Peace & Change*, 29 3/4 (July 2004): 42–44.

87. Jackie Smith and Hank Johnston, "Globalization and Resistance: An Introduction," Smith and Johnston, *Globalization and Resistance*, 5. See also Smith, "Globalizing Resistance," ibid., 209–10, and Smith, "The World Social Forum and the Challenges of Global Democracy," *Global Networks* 4 (October 2004): 3. A good case study of this process is Franklin Daniel Rothman and Pamela E. Oliver, "From Local to Global: The Anti-Dam Movement in Southern Brazil, 1979–1992," in Smith and Johnston, *Globalization and Resistance.*, 115–32.

88. Stiglitz, cited above, was awarded the Nobel Prize for economics in 2001, and served on President Clinton's Council of Economic Advisors, and as chief economist at the World Bank. The discourse of activists in the global social justice movement reflects "academic criticisms of multinational economic institutions" and "debate about economic development." See Mark Irving Lichbach, "Global Order and Local Resistance: Structure, Culture, and Rationality in the Battle of Seattle," (preliminary draft, January 25, 2002), 40.

89. Jeffrey M. Ayres, *Defying Conventional Wisdom: Political Movements and Popular Contention against North American Free Trade* (Toronto: University of Toronto Press, 1998), 125–26. Ayres's point here relates to a specific event, the International Citizen's Forum at Zacatecas, Mexico, October 1991, but it is central to his analysis of the contention of NAFTA in Canada.

90. Lichbach, "Global Order . . . in the Battle of Seattle," 54, 27.

91. Stephen Gill, *Power and Resistance in the New World Order* (New York: Palgrave Macmillan, 2003), 212–14, 216–17; and see Jackie Smith, "Globalizing Resistance: The Battle of Seattle and the Future of Social Movements," in Smith and Johnston, *Globalization and Resistance*, 207–27.

92. This is the richly developed thesis of Lichbach, "Global Order . . . in the Battle of Seattle."

93. This pivotal distinction is drawn in Ivo H. Daalder and James M. Lindsay, *America Unbound: The Bush Revolution in Foreign Policy* (Washington: Brookings Institution, 2003), 127.

94. The votes were 77–23 in the Senate, 296–133 in the House.

95. See http://MoveOn.org/about.html for Internet contact and background. The organization claimed 3.3 million members in 2005, when it had evolved into a "family" of organizations under two umbrellas, MoveOn.org Civic Action (formerly

MoveOn.org) for education, advocacy and public service, and MoveOn.org Political Action (formerly MoveOn PAC) for lobbying and electoral campaiging.

96. Cortright, *A Peaceful Superpower: The Movement against War in Iraq* (Goshen, IN: Fourth Freedom Forum, 2004), 22. See also http://truemajority.org/who/.

97. Quotations from Barbara Epstein and Cortright in ibid., ix and 29.

98. Ibid., ix and footnote 2 on p. xii.

99. Ibid., 98–99.

100. Activist Leslie Cagen, quoted in ibid., 5.

101. Chomsky, *Hegemony or Survival: America's Quest for Global Dominance* (New York: Metropolitan Books, 2003); Chalmers Johnson, *The Sorrows of Empire: Militarism, Secrecy, and the End of the Republic* (New York: Metropolitan Books, 2004); Claes G. Ryn, *America the Virtuous: The Crisis of Democracy and the Quest for Empire* (New Brunswick, NJ: Transaction Publishers, 2003).

102. The phrase "trustee of global stability" is Henry Kissinger's in his "America's Assignment," *Newsweek*, (November 8, 2004), 33. I quote him to show the pervasiveness of the premise; Kissinger shared it with the Bush administration even though he recommended a more internationalist applied policy.

103. Stephen Gill, *Power and Resistance*, 219, but see also Jackie Smith, "Globalizing Resistance: The Battle of Seattle and the Future of Social Movements."

104. Peter Ackerman and Jack Duvall illustrate the world context of nonviolence as a contending political culture in *A Force More Powerful: A Century of Nonviolent Conflict* (New York: St. Martin's, 2000), a book also made into a three-hour 1999 PBS documentary film (for availability contact Miriam Zimmerman mzimmerman@yorkzim.com). A recent case study is Sean Chabot, "Transnational Diffusion and the African-American Reinvention of the Gandhian Repertoire," in Smith and Johnston, *Globalization and Resistance*, 97–114.

105. Raymond Bonner quoted in Christian Smith, *Resisting Reagan*, 93.

106. Robert M. Gates, *From the Shadows*. New York: Simon & Schuster, 1996, 421 (quoted in Wittner, *Toward Nuclear Abolition*, 396). "President" is capitalized in the original.

107. Thomas Risse-Kappen defined transnational relations as "regular interactions across national boundaries when at least one actor is a non-state agent or does not operate on behalf of a national government or an intergovernmental organization." Risse-Kappen, ed., *Bringing Transnational Relations Back In: Non-State Actors, Domestic Structures and International Institutions* (New York: Cambridge University Press, 1995), 3. Among the several works to follow up this approach, see Donatella della Porta, et al, *Social Movements in a Globalizing World* (New York: St. Martin's Press, 1999) and especially Jackie Smith, "Characteristics of the Modern Transnational Social Movement Sector," and "Social Movements and World Politics . . . " in Jackie Smith, et al, eds., *Transnational Social Movements and Global Policies*, 42–77.

108. This is the documented thesis of Evangelista, *Unarmed Forces*. The world nuclear disarmament movement from 1971 is woven together in Wittner, *Toward Nuclear Abolition*.
109. Stephen Gill, *Power and Resistance*, 215.
110. Walter LaFeber, "The Tension between Democracy and Capitalism during the American Century," in Michael J. Hogan, *The Ambiguous Legacy*, 182.
111. Gary Ostrower, *The United Nations and the United States*, 222–27.
112. Columnist Bill Keller quoted in Daadler and Lindsay, *America Unbound*, 189.
113. Quoted in "The Slaughter Goes On," *New Republic*, (February 24, 1968), 13.

12. THE "GOOD" WAR
NATIONAL SECURITY AND AMERICAN CULTURE

William L. O'Neill

I

This essay is concerned mainly with how the mass media—and especially film and television—treat war and the military. Although popular music and fiction have exercised considerable influence, no song, however widely played, and no book, regardless of sales, has anything like the reach and impact of the moving image. War movies have been an important genre since 1942, when Hollywood signed up for the duration, and became ubiquitous with the advent of cable television. TV shows on World War II, especially service comedies, are almost as old as the medium itself. Since cable channels began multiplying in the 1990s, their desperate need for product has led them to air repeatedly almost every "A" movie made since the inception of talkies, and plenty of "B" movies as well. Inevitably, combat films, including those made during World War II, are part of this surging flood. Further, technology keeps widening the viewers' range of choices. Almost every film and TV series mentioned in this essay is now available on videotape and/or DVD. The more successful war films, and some TV shows, notably the omnipresent *M*A*S*H*, are played and replayed around the clock on cable. Since World War II and Korean War veterans are passing away, the number of Americans who have experienced combat is shrinking fast, while the number whose knowledge of war is derived solely from the media is constantly expanding. That fact alone justifies taking a closer look at what it is Americans are learning about war, and, by extension, the national security state.

The combat film as we know it is a product of World War II. Until December 7, 1941, Hollywood had been intimidated by the public's revulsion against American entry into the First World War, which started developing soon after the Armistice in 1918. During the 1930s, as the Axis powers grew stronger and more threatening, antiwar sentiment became even more intense. *All Quiet on the Western Front* (1930), an antiwar film based on the experience of German soldiers as rendered by a German novelist, passed muster. Otherwise, war films tended to be historical. The major exception was air combat during World War I, which audiences seemed to like because of its aerial duels and seemingly chivalrous standards. William Wellman's *Wings* (1927) is the prototype of this genre. It won the first Oscar given for Best Picture, and inspired others films such as *Dawn Patrol* (1938) starring Errol Flynn, who in picture after picture ran up one of the highest cinematic body counts of any contemporary actor.

The first major film to deal seriously (if implicitly) with World War II as an issue is *Sergeant York* (1941), which came out before Pearl Harbor and relates the story of a real American hero of World War I. The message, however, is timely and specific. Gary Cooper portrays York as a religious pacifist who overcomes his scruples to fight for freedom and win imperishable glory. *Sergeant York* was aimed directly at the isolationists who were successfully working to keep America neutral. The great popularity of this Warner Bros. film, which required some bravery to release since polls showed a majority of Americans still opposed entering World War II, established the war movie as a genre. After December 7, 1941, the gloves came off. Hollywood threw itself into the war effort to the mutual benefit of both. As the film historian Thomas Doherty puts it in his masterful *Projections of War* (1993): "The unique, unprecedented alliance between Washington and Hollywood generated not only new kinds of movies but a new attitude toward them. Hereafter, popular art and cultural meaning, mass communications and national politics would be intimately aligned and commonly acknowledged in American culture."[1]

World War II put movies at the very center of American popular culture, and Hollywood gave its all to help win the war. The studios did so not only because it was expected of them and to make money, but also out of conviction. Almost everyone in the industry had family members or relatives in the military. More than 16 million men and women, out of a total population numbering 140 million in 1945, served in the armed forces during World War II, making it the most personally felt American war of the twentieth century. A few figures reveal the importance of Hollywood to national morale. In 1944 the Commerce Department estimated that 80 cents of every dollar spent on the category "spectator amusement," which included sports, theater, and films, went to the movies. Exhibitors sold an average of 90 million tickets a week. Only radio, to which everyone listened, and newspapers, with a daily circulation of about 46 million, reached a larger audience. But neither of these had anything like the emotional power of moving pictures.

From the outset, Hollywood had the will; finding the way proved to be harder. Studios eagerly cooperated with the War and Navy Departments, since combat films could not be made without the equipment, weaponry, and (sometimes) manpower that only the services could provide. The Army and Navy did not want to see themselves depicted unflatteringly, but as Hollywood had no intention of doing so, relations with the armed services usually went smoothly. The Bureau of Motion Pictures, a branch of the Office of War Information established in 1942, proved far more troublesome. BMP bureaucrats had their own agenda. They wanted films that featured liberal values and promoted the idea of a "people's war," a vague concept that had to do with promoting democracy and uniting the public behind desirable social changes. Since opinion polls showed that the American people actually wanted to come out of the war pretty much as they had entered it—plus full employment—Hollywood mostly resisted efforts to propagandize for anything except the war effort. As BMP officials knew little about making pictures but pushed their agenda aggressively, they were thorns in the sides of producers until 1943, when Congressional cutbacks forced OWI to close the Bureau. The Office of Censorship, which certified films for import and export, never went away. It refused to license for export films, as an instance, that depicted foreigners, except for the enemy, in comic, sinister, or other undesirable ways. This deprived the industry of many negative alien stereotypes at no cost to creativity.

The biggest problem for filmmakers was how to define the genre, which took time to solidify. One solution appears to have been arrived at by unspoken consent. World War II films would be about the combat team, not the lonely hero, *Sergeant York*, a pre-Pearl Harbor film in any case, being the exception that proves the rule. In the quintessential genre movie *Air Force* (1943), probably Howard Hawks's worst film, there is one rebel (John Garfield), but Pearl Harbor serves as an epiphany, and he bonds with the other nine men in his B-17 heavy bomber crew. This is a common theme. America would win the war through teamwork on the factory floor and the battlefield. Further, except for blacks, who served in segregated units, the team would be diverse and representative in terms of religion, ethnicity, and place of origin. Hollywood even worked in black characters where possible, along with Asian Americans and Hispanics.

In this respect movies were considerably ahead of the rest of the country. Doherty notes that the melting pot is what combat films are always about. He cites *Gung Ho* (1943), a rather viciously anti-Japanese film that includes not only the usual ethnic and regional diversity but also an outspoken attack on prejudice. Based on the actual exploits of Marine raiders, the film goes out of its way to moralize. In order to achieve maximum efficiency Colonel Carlson (Randolph Scott) orders his soldiers to "cast out all prejudices—racial, religious, and every other kind."

Through trial and error Hollywood learned the line that would be followed in most war movies. "It said that war is a serious business where people you love die, where you sacrifice your personal desires for the nation's good, where the enemy is deadly not dumb, where there is true glory but where victory exacts a price."[2] Examples of this are the immortal *Casablanca* (1943), and *Sahara* (1943) also starring Bogart; in this film he is one of a band of soldiers fighting their way across North Africa. An otherwise unremarkable combat film, *Sahara* portrays Italians (still part of the Axis when the film was made) in a sympathetic light while a Negro character beats up a typically arrogant German. The Hollywood formula applies mostly to films where Germans are the enemy. In films about the Pacific War, racial themes often figure. Many, including *Gung Ho,* use racist invective, a function both of racism itself and the particularly virulent hatred of Japan by Americans owing to the surprise attack on Pearl Harbor and the subsequent brutal mistreatment of American POWs by the Japanese. Opinion polls revealed that most Americans hated Imperial Japan far more than Nazi Germany until fairly late in the war. Being part of the public, Hollywood exhibited rather less sensitivity in depicting the Pacific War than it did the war in Europe.

Few films made during the war have stood the test of time. The most durable are not combat films as a rule. Generally they portray civilians, *Casablanca*, of course, and Alfred Hitchcock's unforgettable *Lifeboat* (1944), which includes Tallulah Bankhead's finest work. The best combat film, still deeply moving after all these years, is *The Story of G.I. Joe* (1945), based on the work of war correspondent Ernie Pyle, a favorite of the troops, who was killed on Okinawa shortly before VJ-Day. A true story, it depicts the suffering of the infantry and the death of a beloved company commander (Robert Mitchum) in Italy.

For our purposes the important feature of combat films made during World War II is that they are the font from which most subsequent war films have flowed. More broadly, Hollywood's immediate response to this one war defined the frame of reference within which American culture thereafter interpreted the phenomenon of war. After Japan's surrender, studios no longer required filmmakers to abide by the unwritten code of the war years. Yet by and large, the terms of that code continued to prevail. "Sacrifice, obedience, choral contribution, moral clarity in battle, due respect for the enemy, and the other wartime tropes endured in postwar Hollywood cinema—but as remembered and embroidered myth, not as clear and present necessity."[3] Film makers could loosen up, in short, but as a rule World War II combat films, even those made long after the war, seldom stray far from the conventions established during wartime. Doherty thinks they never will because of the Holocaust. Another reason is that World War II remains the "Good War" in everyone's mind since the enemy was unambiguously evil, the end intensely desired, and the sacrifices seen as eminently worth making. No subsequent war has combined these qualities in anything like the same measure. The term is a misnomer obviously, since wars by definition cannot be good. When Studs Terkel used it in the title of his book *"The Good War" An Oral History of World War Two* (1984) he enclosed it in quotation marks to underscore the irony. Now the term usually appears without quotation marks as the irony has been lost. Even some veterans, their memories having been softened by time, think of the conflict as the Good War. Hollywood almost always does, and has from the beginning.

Since the World War II combat genre film remains so central it follows that combat films rarely deal with the relationship between battle and the national security state. During World War II Americans had no idea that they were living in one. People assumed that all the changes going on around them would end when the war did. They would last only for "the duration," as everyone called it. Afterward conditions would return to normal, that is, the state of affairs prevailing *ante bellum*, with two exceptions. First, Americans hoped to avoid a return to the Great Depression. Second, thanks to copious propaganda, they accepted that the United States would have to play the role of world leader. They never expected the wartime military-industrial complex, a term that did not even exist until President Eisenhower coined it in his farewell address, to become permanent. That most Americans take it for granted today is partially owing to the force of events, but also because from World War II onward films and television have conditioned Americans to see the military not as a huge, anonymous institution headquartered in the Pentagon, but as individuals and small groups. Consequently, every American major war effort since 1941 has worn a human face. With the obvious exception of Vietnam, most service comedies and combat films strengthen the national security state by ignoring historical background and discounting political issues while keeping a tight focus on the small picture.

After something of a postwar lull, World War II combat films poured out of the major studios in 1949. Among them were *Battleground, Command Decision, Home of the Brave, Task Force, Fighter Squadron, Tokyo Joe, Twelve O'Clock High*, and *Sands of Iwo Jima*. With the exception of *Home of the Brave*, all followed the conventions established in wartime. That one exception was Hollywood's boldest attack on racism in the military to that date. In *Home of the Brave* a black soldier sent on a secret mission to the South Pacific must contend not only with the Japanese but also with his fellow soldiers who discriminate against him and bombard him with racial slurs. The film is a direct assault on the segregated military of World War II, and, implicitly, on the segregated military of the day, because little had actually changed since President Harry Truman ordered the armed services to desegregate in 1948.

Although the quality of these films varies, most echo official positions taken during the war. *Twelve O'Clock High* and *Command Decision* dramatize the strategic bombing of Germany. Both support the Air Force doctrine that attacking German (and Japanese) cities had been essential to victory. With all respect to the brave crewmen who flew these missions, strategic bombing—in theory precision attacks on vital enemy military installations—in practice consisted largely of burning down entire cities and killing civilians by the hundreds of thousands. It remains the worst blot on America's war record and has never been questioned by Hollywood. From *Air Force* to *Memphis Belle* (1990), strategic bombing films all concern themselves with the bomber crews, never with the victims of bombing. They perpetuate the myth of precision bombing, which thanks to the available technology, was seldom very accurate. In addition, bad weather over Germany usually forced Americans to bomb blindly through the undercast, cities being the smallest targets that airborne radar could identify. By the time *Memphis Belle* was filmed a number of historians had criticized strategic bombing for just that reason.[4] Yet the film, while perpetuating wartime falsehoods, actually goes them one better. On its twenty-fifth and final mission, the B-17 leads its combat wing over the target twice to make certain that a nearby school escapes destruction. In the entire history of the air war over Germany no main bomber force ever performed such an unbelievably dangerous maneuver for humanitarian reasons.

The prototypical ground combat film is *Sands of Iwo Jima*, which bloodlessly celebrates what actually cost the Marine Corps more casualties than any other battle in World War II. It differs from movies made during the war in only one respect, namely in portraying John Wayne's Sergeant Stryker as a somewhat dubious character, alcoholic, divorced, disobedient, and forbidding. At first resented, Stryker becomes a hero to his men for teaching them how to survive in combat. Having nothing to lose he takes absurd risks, but is killed, almost accidentally, by a sniper. Despite its failings, *Sands of Iwo Jima* was a big hit and made Wayne the number one box office attraction for the first time in his career. *Sands of Iwo Jima* also deviates from the choral tradition in that while it focuses on the combat squad, both the squad and the picture are dominated by Wayne's Stryker. The lone hero, long a staple of popular culture, becomes part of the Good War package. This is true of some of the others as well. In *Command Decision* and *Twelve O'Clock High,* Clark Gable and Gregory Peck demonstrate how lonely it is at the top.

Even when a World War II movie seems to be casting a service, or an officer, in a bad light, it usually ends up putting the blame elsewhere. A classic of its kind is *The Caine Mutiny* (1954), based on Herman Wouk's popular novel. The *USS Caine* is a destroyer-minesweeper captained by Lieutenant Commander Philip Francis Queeg (Humphrey Bogart). Apart from the hard-nosed and eccentric Queeg, the remainder of the *Caine's* officers all hold temporary commissions. He is a professional. They are citizen-sailors. Yet under the stress of wartime service, it is Queeg who begins to fall apart, handling the ship so badly in a storm that his executive officer, Lieutenant Steve Maryk (Van Johnson) relieves Queeg of command. At the subsequent court martial Maryk and another officer are represented by Lieutenant Barney Greenwald (Jose Ferrer). Greenwald breaks Queeg on the stand and the two officers are acquitted. But at the victory party thrown by the *Caine's* officers Greenwald dresses them down for failing to offer Queeq the loyalty and support to which he was entitled, and which if extended might have saved his sanity. Further, he reminds them that while they were enjoying civilian life, unappreciated regulars like Queeg were faithfully guarding this country. Thus, even the collapse of a man like Queeg vindicates the Navy.

Documentaries have done much to form the public's opinions on war and the military, especially the many documentaries of World War II.

Victory at Sea, the father of them all, deserves special mention. This twenty-six episode series, which aired weekly on NBC from October 1952 through May 1953, was a big gamble at a time when there was yet no precedent for such an ambitious enterprise. Each thirty-minute episode consists largely of footage filmed by the American, British, German, and Japanese navies. This reduced production costs, but the budget still ran to half a million dollars, a large sum of money at the time. NBC gambled that it would make a profit because the series could be syndicated and marketed in various ways. To improve its prospects NBC hired Richard Rodgers, the famous Broadway composer known for his collaborations with Lorenz Hart and later Oscar Hammerstein, to write the musical score. NBC had an abundance of riches to work from, as its crew assembled 60 million feet of film, which was edited down to 61,000 feet.[5]

Rarely has a commercial venture paid off so handsomely. A critical success, the winner of a Peabody and a special Emmy among other awards, *Victory at Sea* attracted a huge audience. Syndication began in 1953 and continues on cable to this day. Recut as a ninety-minute feature, the film played in theaters and was broadcast by NBC in prime time at least twice during the 1960s. The series played in forty foreign markets, and for the first ten years of its syndication earned back its production costs annually. The recording of Rodgers' score alone had earned $4 million by 1963. The series was all the more effective for being true, so far as it went. Like most subsequent war documentaries *Victory at Sea* glosses over mistakes, like the failure to defend Pearl Harbor against Japan's surprise attack (which local commanders ought to have anticipated, but did not owing to bad peacetime habits) and the dubious wartime command arrangements in the Pacific theater. With neither the Army nor the Navy willing to concede primacy in the Pacific to the other service, U.S. forces waged competing wars against the Japanese. Throughout the Pacific War each service vied for scarce resources instead of mounting a unified effort. Thus, while documentaries like *Victory at Sea* are valuable educationally, they almost never ask the hard questions that would show the national security apparatus in a less than flattering light.

II

In some respects Korean War movies follow the well-worn tracks laid down during World War II, focusing still on the squad and the small picture. With Korea coming hard on the heels of World War II, uniforms, equipment, and weapons had not changed much, giving both wars a similar look. Because racial integration was now actually beginning to take place, the combat squad could include blacks and Asian Americans. But because the Korean War was unpopular, Hollywood had more artistic freedom. An early film, *The Steel Helmet* (1951) centers on a patched-together group that includes two medics, one black and the other a conscientious objector, a Korean boy, a Japanese American soldier, and a mute. Instead of glorifying the cause or the military, this film has a dark, fatalistic tone. Nearly everyone dies, including a North Korean POW, and, rather crudely, a political note is sounded. Film scholar Norman Kagan says the film, "is shaped around a great theme of the Korean decade—America's bitter, reluctant taking on of the role of world policeman, in a world now without laws or remorse. The survivors of the platoon . . . have accepted their burden."[6] Other scholars take a narrower view of *The Steel Helmet*, seeing it simply as an antiwar film owing to the pervasive chaos, cynicism, and doom that mark the picture. In the event, its darkness contrasts with previous combat films and foreshadows those about Vietnam.

The best film about the Korean War is *Pork Chop Hill* (1959), in which a war-weary Lieutenant, Gregory Peck, holds an intrinsically useless piece of real estate against repeated Chinese onslaughts. While peace talks drag on, Peck's unit beats off wave after wave of enemy soldiers, their assaults being punctuated by Chinese loudspeakers drawing attention to the war's lack of purpose. Four days after the truce Pork Chop Hill becomes part of the demilitarized zone or DMZ. An antiwar film, *Pork Chop Hill* by implication does criticize the national security state for one of its major blunders. This was not the commitment of U.S. troops in June 1950 to repel North Korea's invasion of South Korea, an act of aggression that had to be stopped, but rather the subsequent decision to continue attacking after the North Koreans had been driven out. The U.S.-led invasion of North Korea brought China into the war, turning a swift Allied victory into a prolonged stalemate. For two solid years, from July 1951 to July 1953, the Korean War mixed peace talks with static warfare reminiscent of the Western Front in World War I. The great majority of Allied casualties occurred after South Korea had been liberated in September 1950. This botched war poisoned American politics. Whether considering President Harry Truman and his advisers in Washington or General of the Army Douglas MacArthur and his staff in the Far East, it also showed the national security elite at its worst. Without inquiring into its causes or without provoking from viewers much in the way of reflection, *Pork Chop Hill* illustrates the effects of governmental and military hubris.

III

Most Americans are too young to remember the Korean War and what little knowledge they have of it comes from viewing TV's *M*A*S*H*. But long before that series appeared, the service comedy had been a staple of films and TV. The service comedy is a peculiar genre, especially during wartime, when tragic events serve as the background for humorous antics. It predates World War II, going back at least as far as 1926 when *Behind the Front* was a big hit for Wallace Beery. Others followed, the French Foreign Legion being a favorite subject for comedies as well as action films. Most service comedies are eminently forgettable, an exception being Preston Sturges' *Miracle of Morgan's Creek* (1944), about the misadventures of a floozy who gets pregnant with sextuplets after fooling around with soldiers. Another is *The Americanization of Emily* (1964), in which James Garner, a naval officer who has maneuvered himself into a cushy job as an admiral's aide, discovers that he may have to become the first casualty of D-Day as part of a public relations stunt. Although set in the Good War this black comedy overflows with the antiwar cynicism of the 1960s and bears little relation to the typical service picture. The most recent picture in this vein is *Good Morning Vietnam* (1987). Loosely based on the experiences of an actual disk jockey in Vietnam the picture features Robin Williams at his most outrageous. It transpires that even the Vietnam War had its funny side if you dig deeply enough.

Service comedies flourished on television as well. *You'll Never Get Rich*, commonly known as the Phil Silvers show after its star, or as the Sergeant Bilko show, after its lead character, had a four season run from 1955 to 1959. It benefited from the comedic gifts of Silvers, who played a larcenous motor pool chief, and from the country being at peace. The Bilko show paid a backhanded tribute to the classic squad-as-melting-pot theme while also subverting it, since the only cause to which Silvers and his sidekicks devote themselves are avoiding duty and greasing their own palms. (*Sgt. Bilko*, a 1996 film starring Steve Martin, quickly died a merciful death.)

If Sergeant Bilko qualifies in some respects as subversive, the next generation of service comedies is merely sophomoric. Despite the escalating war in Vietnam, or maybe because of it, several of these shows did very well in the sixties. Josh Ozersky describes one of the most popular as follows: "*Gomer Pyle, U.S.M.C.* (1964–1970), in which a mentally challenged gas station attendant from Andy Griffith's hometown, inducted into the Marines, clashes week after week with his crusty but benevolent drill instructor and a swell bunch of barrack mates who have never heard of Vietnam. . . ."[7] In *McHale's Navy* (1965–1971) the fun-loving crew of a PT Boat outwit their skipper during the Pacific War. *The Wackiest Ship in the Army* (1965–1966) likewise features the zany crew of a two-masted schooner in World War II who suspend their hijinks at intervals to gun down the enemy.

Far and away the oddest offering in this group is *Hogan's Heroes* (1965–1971). It took a real leap of faith to imagine that having American prisoners of war outsmart a bunch of goofy prison guards would keep viewers glued to their seats. Set in a German camp for American POWs during World War II, it portrays the officers and men guarding the POWs as cretins and worse. Colonel Robert E. Hogan, played by Bob Crane, runs rings around the brain dead commandant Colonel Klink and his lackeys to further an ongoing program of espionage, sabotage, and slapstick. The humor could hardly have been broader—or more elusive. An exchange that one of the web sites devoted to this moronic show finds especially funny goes as follows.

> COLONEL KLINK: In to the cooler they go. Throw away the key.
> CARTER: Don't we get a trial or anything?
> COLONEL KLINK: This is Germany. Although I do appreciate your sense
>   of humor.

Three of these service farces aired during the darkest days of the Vietnam War, the years 1967 through 1969. Total losses for this period amounted to 40,000 of the 46,000 Americans killed in action during the entire war. Is it only a coincidence that the most recent of these shows ended in 1971, when the number of men killed in action fell to 1,381? Perhaps. But it remains striking that with the end of heavy combat in Vietnam the genre ceased to be popular. It is hard to avoid concluding that service comedies—leaving out *M*A*S*H*—played a vital role in helping people avoid thinking about the realities of combat during wartime. In this sense they may have been therapeutic on some deeply buried level. Otherwise, they performed the mass media's usual role of diverting attention from what the national security state had actually wrought.

The ultimate TV service comedy remains, of course, *M*A*S*H*. Based on a book by a doctor who served in Korea, and by an enormously successful 1970 movie with the same title, *M*A*S*H* portrays the life and times of a not very Mobile Army Surgical Hospital during the Korean War. The show premiered in late 1972 and ended, with its popularity undiminished, early in 1983. Its total of 251 episodes plus the pilot were shot over ten and a half years, more than three times as long as the Korean War lasted. It still airs frequently on cable, and perhaps always will. Robert Altman, who directed the movie, said it was not antiwar, but rather against movies "or any form of entertainment that made war seem acceptable because the people involved were able to be such good sports about it."[8] In contrast, Larry Gelbart, who created the TV series, describes his purpose as explicitly antiwar.

Because the film and series were conceived during the Vietnam War years their ethos is blatantly that of the sixties, not the fifties, most notably distrust of authority, hostility toward the military, and an absolute lack of reverence for just about everything except the dreadfulness of war. In fact, neither the film nor the series realized Altman's hopes. Both are comedies with entertaining characters who do take the edge off war by being good sports. The movie is wilder and raunchier than the TV series because by 1970 moviemakers could do pretty much as they pleased, while broadcast networks allowed far less room for maneuver. According to Gelbart, CBS censors, members of the euphemistically named Department of Program Practices, were always complaining to *M*A*S*H* producers about sexual references and the like, but never once tried to censor the show's political content. They never had to: *M*A*S*H* sounds exactly one political note, opposition to the nominally Korean, but actually Vietnam, War. Since most Americans had turned against the Vietnam War by 1972, *M*A*S*H* hardly went against the grain. It is a funny and at times moving series, far superior to other sitcoms. Even today, more than three decades after it premiered, *M*A*S*H* remains impressive for a half-hour show minus 5 minutes and 40 seconds of commercials. Still, given its mandate to amuse, *M*A*S*H* is anything but deep.

At least two films do a much more effective job of skewering Cold War–era preoccupations with national security. The brilliant *Dr. Strangelove or: How I Learned to Stop Worrying and Love the Bomb* (1964) is a work of dark comic genius made by Stanley Kubrick at the height of his powers. Its superb cast includes George C. Scott and Peter Sellers, who scored a tour de force by playing three parts, including the title role. *Dr. Strangelove* exposes the deranged and self-serving aspects of nuclear deterrence by stripping away its veneer of rationality. The end of the world begins when General Jack D. Ripper sends his B-52 bomber wing to attack the USSR with nuclear weapons. Ripper intends to touch off nuclear strikes by both sides, an exchange the United States is certain to win. Destruction of the Soviet Union will prevent any further contamination of the West's "Pure Bodily Essences." Unbeknownst to Ripper, or anyone else, however, the Russians have created a doomsday device that will automatically destroy the world if nuclear weapons are employed against Soviet targets. Self-evidently, this is the ultimate deterrent. It is also criminally insane, and would still be so even if the Soviets had revealed their doomsday scenario before Ripper launched his B-52s. A long, frantic, sometimes funny effort to recall the wing, or shoot the planes down if necessary, ensues. One determined B-52 crew delivers its payload and the world goes up in flames. Though broadly satiric, *Dr. Strangelove* exposes the real truth about nations that stockpile enough weapons to literally destroy the world in the name of self-defense.

Catch-22 (1970) is a less accomplished film despite numerous advantages: an all-star cast, the gifted director Mike Nichols, and a script based on Joseph Heller's much admired 1961 novel. To be sure, the challenge was daunting; Heller's black comedy is a classic and had sold millions of copies by 1970. Further, Heller's book is not just antiwar, but takes as its specific target the Good War, which Hollywood venerates. Parts of the film do suggest that greatness was within its reach. The characters are beautifully rendered, from the avaricious Lieutenant Milo Minderbinder (Jon Voight), who stands capitalism on its head, to the despotic General Dreedle (Orson Welles). Captain Yossarian (Alan Arkin) tries to get himself out of piloting B-25 medium bombers against German targets in Italy, but is foiled by Catch-22. Doc Daneeka (Jack Gilford) explains to Yossarian that since only a madman would fly in combat Yossarian is therefore in his right mind and cannot be grounded by reason of insanity. "That's some catch, that Catch-22," Yossarian says. "The best there is," Daneeka agrees. After Minderbinder arranges for the Luftwaffe to bomb their base in Corsica in payment for a botched trade, Yossarian climbs into a tiny lifeboat and starts paddling for neutral Sweden. Although the film sags at points, and, like the novel, is extremely complex, no viewer can fail to grasp its message— that wars are run by lunatics and profiteers. Yet *Catch-22*, like *Dr. Strangelove*, did poorly at the box office, suggesting that satirizing matters of national security has little popular appeal.

By coincidence 1970 was also the year of *Patton*, magnificently played by George C. Scott, which destroys Good War conventions from a war lover's perspective. No film could fully capture the complexities of General George S. Patton Jr., athlete and soldier, skilled trainer of troops and organizer, immensely gifted commander impelled by a mystical sense of his own destiny as a great warrior. Yet Scott comes close, portraying his subject as the complete professional soldier who is at the very least emotionally unbalanced, if not slightly mad. *Patton* is important, quality aside, because it violates just about every rule in the Good War manual. It focuses on one man, not the combat squad; and the big picture, not the small. War is not hell but something that Patton loves in the film, as he did in life. He makes no sacrifices, is no more obedient than he has to be, lacks moral clarity, and does not play well with others. *Patton* treats the Germans with respect but not the British, especially Patton's rival Field Marshal Montgomery. During World War II it was unthinkable to criticize an ally, especially Great Britain, upon which so much depended. Good War movies like *The Longest Day* (1962) continue that tradition, which *Patton* defies.

The makers of this film apparently did not set out to glorify war or subvert the Good War canon, but they stuck closely to the known facts about Patton's life and views and personality, thereby dictating the outcome. Everyone loved the film, which won seven Oscars and earned over $28 million in its first year. It still sells today and pops up regularly on cable. By comparison Catch-22 grossed a mere $12.5 and Dr. Strangelove only a pitiful $5 million, despite its brilliance. *Patton* is the exception that proves the rule. It is the only war movie not set in Vietnam to have trampled all over Good War conventions and still make money. Its uniqueness shows how hard it is to pull this thing off, and *Patton* is *sui generis* by accident. There was simply no honest way to depict the real Patton's life in a Good War context.

IV

The only big-budget feature film on Vietnam made during the war is *The Green Berets* (1968), featuring John Wayne. With Wayne also co-directing, the movie premiered during the worst year of the war, when over 20,000 American servicemen lost their lives. On one level *The Green Berets* is just another war movie of the type Wayne had starred in many times before. On another, it is an earnest work of propaganda meant to convince an increasingly skeptical public that the "Commies" had to be beaten for the sake of mom, apple pie, and world freedom. Released at the peak of the antiwar sixties, it earned a measly $11 million, partly because moviegoers sometimes had to walk through picket lines, while soldiers in Vietnam were convulsed with laughter owing to the implausible battle scenes and hapless efforts to justify the war. Outdated even before its release, *The Green Berets* probably failed to change anyone's mind.

Wayne's real impact on Vietnam derived from the fact that young soldiers who served there had grown up watching his movies, especially *Sands of Iwo Jima*. Many writers who fought in Vietnam—Larry Heinemann, Philip Caputo, Ron Kovic—have testified that Wayne's iconic Sergeant Stryker was the soldier they hoped to be. Katherine Kinney, an English professor and film scholar, points out that in "scores, if not hundreds of novels, memoirs, poems, films, plays, and works of criticism about the Vietnam War, John Wayne is parodied, debunked, reviled, rejected, and metaphorically and sometimes literally shot dead. But somehow he always returns. . . ."[9] In Wayne's case particularly, but with movies set in the Good War generally, the remembered moving image trumps actual experience. The striking aspect of combat films to this day is the gravitational pull exerted by film conventions established in the 1940s as well as by John Wayne, who is indeed born again in picture after picture. The Good War is Hollywood's black hole, sucking in every war filmmaker not alive to the dangers.

Only in the seventies and eighties did serious films about Vietnam break with tradition. There are several explanations for this. First, the Vietnam War was much more heavily documented on film than any previous conflict. Camera footage often aired on the evening news a day or two after it had been shot. Some of the best Vietnam movies have the TV look, as if they had been made in the field and quickly edited without planning or polish. They seem more authentic than previous war pictures. Second, as censorship had virtually ended, Vietnam films are more realistic in that they portray blood, guts, and flying body parts, unlike traditional Good War movies in which the fallen have clean deaths. Third, advances in film technology generated astonishing special effects both visually and by reproducing the noise of battle.

As the Vietnam War remains controversial even today, films about the war sometimes fed into the ongoing political debate. Four ambitious combat pictures came out in 1978–79, ending the drought that followed *The Green Berets*. They are *The Boys in Company C* (1978), *Go Tell The Spartans* (1978), *The Deer Hunter* (1978), *Apocalypse Now* (1979), and a domestic recovery film *Coming Home* (1978). A second wave began with Oliver Stone's *Platoon* (1986) and includes Stanley Kubrick's *Full Metal Jacket* (1987), John Irvin's *Hamburger Hill* (1987), and Brian De Palma's *Casualties of War* (1989).

From combat pictures to service comedies, more than thirty movies on Vietnam and its aftereffects have appeared to date. Yet this seemingly impressive figure shrinks to insignificance compared to the number of films about World War II. By the end of the 1980s, the peak of Hollywood's interest in Vietnam had passed, even as its appetite for subjects related to World War II remained strong. There are many reasons for this. To begin with, thus far at least, Vietnam has retained its singular status as the war we lost. Korea, broadly perceived as a draw, was bad enough. But, as America is not supposed to lose wars, the memory of Vietnam still festers. Furthermore, unlike World War II (but as with every other conflict in which the United States has engaged since 1945), Vietnam directly touched relatively few Americans. Taxes increased only marginally. The National Guard and military reserves were not called to active duty. Sustaining the war effort did not entail huge demographic shifts or challenge established social relationships, for example, by sweeping women into defense industries as replacements for drafted men. A considerable number of Americans experienced Vietnam directly, but the people collectively did not.

The draft calls themselves were not large by World War II standards, and many draftees ended up in Germany and other countries outside Southeast Asia. Of some 9 million men who served in uniform during the period, about 2.5 million were stationed in South Vietnam at one time or another. Most of these did not engage directly in combat, although, since no place in the country was entirely safe, some of them became casualties as well. Just over 58,000 died of all causes, while another 150,000 had to be hospitalized. In 1972, when the last American died in Vietnam, the United States had a total population of 210 million persons grouped into about 66 million households, of which no more than 200,000 suffered direct losses in Vietnam.

In a broadly political sense, these figures are misleading. The Vietnam War may have been small by Good War standards, but it seemed very large at the time. No contemporary issue—with the possible exception of civil rights—divided the nation as profoundly as the Vietnam War did. No war of the twentieth century was so bitterly debated at the time, and for so long afterward. No war produced so many large demonstrations and such violent protests. A Vietnam combat film, *We Were Soldiers* with Mel Gibson, premiered as recently as 2002, and is probably not the last of its kind, as Vietnam is the war that never quite goes away. Another reason for the intensity of feelings, beyond the war's outcome, is that Vietnam was our longest war. The armed forces began to take serious casualties in 1965 and the losses continued through 1972. The following year was the first in which no Americans were KIA, and not until 1975, when Saigon fell, did the debate shift from what should be done to what went wrong and who is responsible, questions that have yet to be answered, and probably never will be—at least to general satisfaction. All these features, the length and scale of the war, the furious resistance to it, and America's failure there, make Vietnam unique and unforgettable.

Many Vietnam films are imbued with raw feelings engendered by powerful controversies still much in evidence. The troops are often portrayed negatively, a sharp break with Hollywood tradition. In *Casualties of War* the squad rapes and murders a young Vietnamese woman. In most Vietnam movies the natives are hardly noticed, except when they turn out to be Viet Cong guerrillas, victims of American atrocities, or are officers in the Army of the Republic of Vietnam (ARVN), always depicted as incompetent, venal, and eager to avoid fighting. This was often the case, as attested to by Colonel David Hackworth, the Army's most decorated Vietnam-era soldier, who was a battalion commander in Vietnam. He writes in *About Face* (1989), which includes his riveting personal account of the war, that he never allowed any native, ARVN or civilian, inside his compound for security reasons.[10] *Go Tell the Spartans* takes a similar view of ARVN, but also makes clear that America betrayed South Vietnam. Corruption, moral confusion, and bitterness are staples of Vietnam films, as they were of the war itself. Graham Greene's novel *The Quiet American* captures the arrogance, moral ambiguities, and perverted logic of the American presence in Vietnam so well that two movies have been made of it. The first *Quiet American* (1958) failed, deliberately, to replicate Greene's book, turning his anti-American novel into a pro-Yankee tract. The second appeared in 2002 and starred Michael Caine as a British journalist taken in by the quiet American. He turns out to be CIA and a terrorist who is secretly waging war against both the French and the Communists. Set in 1952 this version does justice to Greene's fears that American overconfidence and recklessness would devastate Vietnam.

The major problem for anyone, whether pro or anti, is that the very nature of the Vietnam War makes it almost impossible for artists to create a plausible narrative. Tony Williams, a film scholar, maintains that what Toby G. Herzog has written about literature applies to movies as well.

"Vietnam with its fragmentation, complexity and illogic presents special problems for an author attempting to order the chaos in a meaningful way. The novelist's disadvantage is that this was a war with no center, no decisive battles; it was all circumference and it is therefore difficult to filter the thing through unified plot and point of view."[11] The striking feature of Vietnam films is that they usually don't make sense. This is true of a big, sprawling epic like *Apocalypse Now* as well as more tightly focused movies like *Platoon*.

The principal exception to this rule is the 2002 film *We Were Soldiers,* based on a memoir by Lieutenant General Harold G. Moore, *We Were Soldiers Once . . . and Young* published in 1992. The movie depicts portions of a real event, the battle of the Ia Drang Valley in 1965, the first major engagement between American troops and those of North Vietnam.[12] Helicopters inserted Moore, then a lieutenant colonel, and his under-strength battalion, numbering some four hundred men, in the middle of what turned out to be about two thousand North Vietnamese Army (NVA) regulars. The battalion fought almost continuously for two straight days before being relieved. Except for a few moving scenes of officer's wives receiving telegrams announcing their husbands' deaths, the film is devoted mainly to combat.

As in virtually every film about ground warfare American soldiers do a lot of running around, and, near the end charge the enemy fully erect and drive him back. This climactic counterattack is a Hollywood staple very much at odds with the way that U.S. troops are trained to advance—on their hands and knees, or in short rushes, taking cover wherever they can. But "fire and maneuver," as this technique is called, is not cinematic. In the real battle Moore sensed that the enemy was going to attack at dawn. Accordingly, he ordered a "Mad Minute"—every weapon in the battalion opening up and firing at everything in front of them for a specified interval. Perfectly timed, the wave of fire caught an NVA company in the open and cut it down—this, rather than an epic American charge, marked the pivotal moment in the battle.

We Were Soldiers ends with the withdrawal of Moore's surviving troops, although the real battle lasted a week, the replacement battalions taking heavy casualties also. After the NVA withdrew from Ia Drang, General William Westmoreland, Commander, U.S. Military Assistance Command, Vietnam, called the battle an "unprecedented victory." However, *We Were Soldiers* contradicts Westmoreland and is quite explicit about the real meaning of the battle. A victory in the narrowest sense—NVA forces took many more casualties and then retreated—the battle of the Ia Drang Valley foreshadowed America's ultimate defeat. *We Were Soldiers* demonstrates the willingness of NVA commanders to expend lives in order to counter America's enormous advantage in mobility and firepower.

In subsequent years America won every battle, but lost the war of attrition that Westmoreland had deliberately waged. Following every "defeat," as after Ia Drang, when the Americans moved on, the Communists moved back in. *We Were Soldiers* looks like many other Vietnam combat films, but takes advantage of nearly thirty years of hindsight to deliver a powerful statement. Critics usually missed the point, pigeon-holing it as just another example of the genre. Wrong as to details, the movie is right on target with its message: as long as the North Vietnamese were willing to continue dying, fortune would eventually favor their cause, whatever the material advantages enjoyed by U.S. forces. In other respects, *We Were Soldiers* is right out of the Good War playbook with Mel Gibson playing the John Wayne role.

We Were Soldiers is not the only Vietnam film with a message. In the eighties two films, *Hamburger Hill* (1987) and *The Hanoi Hilton* (1987), deviated from Hollywood's normally liberal line. They make the point, long held by conservatives and by many military officers, that the media lost the war by falsely portraying events on the ground and poisoning public opinion at home. *Hamburger Hill* treats newsmen with contempt. *Hanoi Hilton* presents them as silent allies of North Vietnam. A handful of Vietnam War films do lay the blame for failure on someone or something. In *Casualties of War* a character tells his men that corporate America regards the war as a money-loser and wants to pull the plug. Usually, though, there is very little in the way of analysis. Good War movies have an enormous built-in advantage. They don't have to explain World War II or offer reasons for fighting it. Everyone knows that Nazi Germany and Imperial Japan had to be stopped. No such certainty is associated with the Vietnam War and this lack of consensus means that the majority of films about it take place in a political and ideological vacuum.

This lack of focus and agreed-upon values leads to the lack of commonality in Vietnam movies. They share the same setting, usually depict the horrors of war, and, as a rule, are about the combat squad and the small picture. Otherwise they differ more than might be supposed. At one end of the spectrum Oliver Stone's *Platoon* treats the war as completely dehumanizing for all concerned. His protagonist Chris Taylor (Charlie Sheen) is loosely based on Stone, who is a Vietnam veteran. Taylor left college to join the army out of some dim sense of obligation. Soon after arriving in Vietnam he discovers that the platoon's two leaders, Sergeant Barnes (Tom Berenger) and Sergeant Elias (Willem Dafoe) are at odds over how to treat civilians. When the platoon believes a village is supporting the enemy Barnes commits, and endorses, atrocious acts against unarmed natives. The slaughter is stopped only when Elias assaults Barnes. Thereafter the platoon is divided between pro and anti-atrocity factions. Since Elias has threatened to report Barnes when they get back to camp Barnes takes the first opportunity to shoot Elias in cold blood. During the movie's final battle the platoon and its parent company are nearly wiped out. Then it is the wounded Barnes's turn to be murdered by Taylor in retaliation for having killed Elias. Apart from Elias, who is something of a Christ figure, there are no good guys in this picture. The enemy and the Americans are equally brutal, and by slaying Barnes Taylor sinks to his level. John Wayne is nowhere to be seen. Actually, Barnes is the anti-Stryker, insane and immoral. Stone stands the Good War on its head, the only Vietnam War filmmaker to do so with complete success.

Most other Vietnam War movies fall somewhere in between *Platoon* and *We Were Soldiers*. Brian De Palma's *Casualties of War* resembles *Platoon* as the squad rapes and murders a Vietnamese girl. But De Palma's protagonist Private Eriksson (Michael J. Fox) remains good throughout, and eventually, despite much opposition the evil sergeant (Sean Penn) and his fellow rapists are brought to justice. The Good War is not much in evidence here, but goodness and justice prevails so *Casualties of War* never achieves the bleakness of *Platoon*. At the other end of the spectrum *Hamburger Hill* has many Good War elements. It trashes the news media and wrestles a bit with the war's unpopularity, but most of the film is devoted to a real event, the 101st Airborne's attack on Hill 937 in 1969, which launched eleven days of savage combat, at the end of which the featured platoon had lost 70 percent of its men. This is Good War material, and there is even a Sergeant Stryker, played in a somewhat lower key than John Wayne by the then unknown Dylan McDermott.

A unique post-Vietnam movie is *Twilight's Last Gleaming* (1977), which according to film critic Tony Williams "presents the whole military and government establishment as collectively responsible. It failed at the box office, however, ignored by a public that preferred the well-worn truisms. The whole American democratic system, this film insists, is irredeemably corrupt, making any attempt at political and individual heroism ineffective."[13] Ex-general Burt Lancaster, unjustly imprisoned for trying to make the truth about Vietnam public, breaks out of the joint with a band of fellow malcontents. They seize control of nine Titan intercontinental ballistic missiles, which they threaten to launch unless government authorities agree to open all the files on Vietnam. The problem with *Twilight's Last Gleaming* is its utter nihilism, which goes beyond even that of *Platoon*. The only people brave enough to take on the national security state turn out to be certifiably insane.

Film scholars are fascinated by the Rambo films, which, in spite of, or maybe because of, their cartoonish quality, offer plenty of room for interpretation. There are actually three Rambo pictures, but *Rambo III* (1988) takes place in Soviet-occupied Afghanistan and nobody liked it, including the public—it cost $63 million to make and earned $28.5. In contrast, *First Blood* (1982) and especially *Rambo: First Blood, Part II* (1985) made money and have inspired a surprising amount of critical thought. Reviewers often saw the two films as anti-Communist parables, typical of the Reagan era, or as a celebration of Reaganite right-wing values. Yet English professor John Hellmann overturns the received wisdom. Of the first two Rambo films he writes:

> In contrast to the stab-in-the-back theory, Rambo's fury is not aimed at a minority group or an ideology it would be possible to punish or to exclude but rather at the dominant majority, with its "mainstream" pieties and tendencies—that is, at the moviegoing public itself. A former Green Beret, Rambo aligns himself with nature against the city, with a victimized black comrade against a careless white society, and with a liberated woman warrior against exploitative men. He thus signifies the liberal aspirations of the Kennedy era, driven to desperate, and ludicrous, outlaw status in the aftermath of the disillusionment with the New Frontier, including the complacent and money-driven Reagan era.[14]

As Rambo tends to grunt more than speak, some stretching is required to view him as an embodiment of New Frontier aspirations, by which Hellman means initiatives like the Peace Corps and Kennedy's famous call to public service when he urged Americans not to ask what the country could do for them but rather what they could do for their country. The Rambo movies do in fact indict society as whole for turning on Vietnam veterans and abandoning the MIAs, and they paint a pretty dark picture of Reagan's America, as of the entire national security apparatus. Alas, Hellmann notwithstanding, few viewers seem to have noticed their scathing subtext. At the same time Rambo accuses society of betraying its heritage he recalls the Good War, notably by asking, after being ordered to rescue POWs still held in Vietnam, if this time "we get to win?" Rambo is not a Good War hero but the yearning for victory is a Good War theme, made all the more haunting by America's actual defeat in Vietnam.

Considering the Vietnam War's profound effects upon the United States, and given the efforts of some filmmakers to break with Good War conventions in the 1970s and 1980s, it might be expected that combat films would never be the same again. But they have failed to change much, partly because none of the Vietnam combat films are good enough. Some are very powerful, but none reach the level of greatness achieved by, say, Steven Spielberg's masterpiece *Schindler's List* (1993). It is not a combat film to be sure, but it proves that out of horror can come art. Or, it might be that the combat film as a genre is too constricting to reach the level of art. This is always a problem with genre pictures where particular conventions have to be observed. Yet there are striking exceptions like John Houston's *The Maltese Falcon* (1941). Considered to be the first *film noir*, it may not be high art but is certainly a great motion picture. Strikingly, unlike Good War movies where everything is perfectly clear, *The Maltese Falcon* is riddled with moral ambiguities and paradoxes, beginning with the "hero" Sam Spade (Humphrey Bogart) who does not always play by the rules although he has his own code of honor. *The Maltese Falcon* is in the hard-boiled detective tradition but also above it, whereas, except for *The Story of G.I. Joe*, combat films never transcend their genre. *Patton* does, but it is not a combat movie; it did not actually require battle scenes, although it has some rather unconvincing ones.

V

The 1990s brought a distinctive crop of set of war movies reflecting a range of post-Vietnam sensibilities. Triumphant in the Cold War and (seemingly) triumphant in the Persian Gulf War of 1990–1991—the first major conflict of the post-Cold War era—the United States regained some of the self-confidence and self-assertiveness lost in Vietnam. Hollywood's treatment of war tended to reflect this cultural trend, although not without exceptions.

Independence Day (1996), nominally set in the near future when alien marauders attack earth, actually, political scientist Michael Rogin speculates, "re-fights World War II as virtual reality. Bringing up to date the Cold War liberal, military, post-industrial, infotainment complex and using bodily invasion to electrify the body politic, *Independence Day* is the defining motion picture of Bill Clinton's America."[15] The film does incorporate just about every World War II cliché, together with a host of others. Although the aliens destroy the world's largest cities and drive governments into hiding, they are defeated by the surviving fighter pilots of many air forces, led by a plucky band of politically correct and multicultural Americans. President Bill Pullman, himself an ex-fighter pilot, heroically returns to the cockpit. The alien mother ship is destroyed by Captain Will Smith and computer genius Jeff Goldblum. Smith flies an alien space ship which the government found in Roswell, New Mexico, just after World War II and has been hiding ever since (a favorite theme of science-minded conspiracy theorists), and Goldblum gets them in and out of the belly of the beast with his notebook computer. *Independence Day* borrows from a host of other films, including *Top Gun* (1986) in which flyboy machismo and advanced technology replace democratic values as the military's strong suit.

Even critics liked this silly, feel-good picture, and the public loved it. *Independence Day* grossed over $300 million. President Clinton screened it in the White House with some of the film's makers, including Pullman, who sat next to his real life counterpart. Afterward Clinton recommended *Independence Day* to viewers. Bob Dole, Clinton's opponent in the presidential election then underway, did so too, belatedly, although he had been vigorously attacking the film industry for turning out "nightmares of depravity." Despite having the establishment stamp of approval, and even though it glorifies fighter pilots and the presidency, *Independence Day* is so inclusive that as propaganda it fails to send a coherent message. What it does do, despite all the screen carnage, is reflect the cocky triumphalism of post–Cold War America in which the ghost of Vietnam has been exorcised—or so it appeared at the time.

The most harrowing combat film ever made is Stephen Spielberg's *Saving Private Ryan*, the highest grossing film of 1998 (over $200 million) and the winner of seven Academy Awards, including Best Direction. The acclaim stems primarily from the film's twenty-four-minute introduction in which we follow Tom Hanks as a U.S. Army captain leading a band of intrepid rangers during the D-Day assault on the beaches of Normandy. The sequence follows Hanks from the stern of his racing landing craft as it approaches Omaha Beach until his unit secures its objective on high ground

overlooking the landing area. Veterans hailed the authenticity of this sequence and viewers were overwhelmed by the blood, gore, and mutila-
tions, as by the remarkable sound track. Amid the roaring explosions and
automatic weapons fire it is possible to distinguish small noises, like
rounds bouncing off metal and even the pings spent M1 rifle clips make
when ejected from the weapon. Never before had any sound track achieved
this level of technical virtuosity.

Few observers noticed that after this astounding scene the picture
gradually slides into the familiar grooves of Hollywood's World War II
genre movies. The plot device, based on a true story, has the War Department discover that three of the Ryan family's four sons have been killed in
action. The sole survivor is a paratrooper dropped behind enemy lines in
Normandy. In the film Captain John Miller (Tom Hanks) and a squad are
ordered to bring him back alive. By casting Hanks, Spielberg made another Good War statement. In World War II it was not superman but ev-
eryman who won the victory.

But Ryan declines to be rescued until he and handful of lightly armed
men complete their mission, to defend a bridge against a much stronger
German force. This being Hollywood, Miller agrees to lead the defense
employing only small arms and improvised explosives. It is a suicidal decision, Miller himself receiving a fatal wound when he stands fully erect in
the face of enemy fire. At the last minute, while Miller lies dying, American fighter-bombers and reinforcements arrive to save the day. A Hollywood ending, to be sure, with a touch of the maudlin thrown in when
Miller tells Ryan to "earn this," as if Ryan had not already proven himself
in battle. *Saving Private Ryan* does not glorify war, since no sane viewer
would want to have been among the men who assaulted Omaha Beach.
But it does reinforce Good War stereotypes. Indeed, apart from the spectacular effects and strong performances by individual cast members, reviewers particularly liked being reminded of the war that had to be fought,
unlike the more or less elective wars that have perpetuated the national security state. This seems to have blinded them to the film's lapse into Good
War clichés.

Later, perhaps out of remorse, Spielberg and Hanks joined forces again
as executive producers to make *Band Of Brothers* (2001) for HBO, perhaps
the most historically accurate rendering of combat ever shown on the big
or small screen. In ten episodes *Band of Brothers* follows E Company,
506th Regiment, 101st Airborne from its training camps to VE-Day in
Germany. It helps that the writers stuck closely to Steven Ambrose's book,

which is based on lengthy interviews with veterans of Easy Company. *Band of Brothers* is the anti-*Private Ryan*, realistic to be sure, but with genuine heroism replacing the heroics. Apart from necessary conventions, the combat squad and the small picture, most Good War tropes have been omitted and patriotic themes are notably absent. Since the paratroopers were all volunteers, certain fine qualities can be inferred but are not stated. Leadership is good, bad, or indifferent, as in life. *Band of Brothers* depicts the real war in Europe, not the Good War of altered memory and myth.

An incident illustrates the difference. *Band of Brothers* is an ensemble work, but one figure stands out. Dick Winters joined the company in training as a lieutenant, rose to become company commander, and ended the war as a major in command of the battalion. Late in the war the regiment's commander ordered Easy to send a patrol across a river at night to take German prisoners. Easy accomplished its mission but lost a man in the process. The regiment's commander, who is treated respectfully in both the book and the series, was so elated that he ordered Easy to take more prisoners. This was a very bad decision, since he already had the prisoners he wanted, and, in any case, the Germans would be ready for a raid, unlike the previous night when they had been caught by surprise. Major Winters quietly told Easy's commander to ignore the order and file a report in the morning saying that the company attempted to take prisoners but failed owing to heavy German resistance. No fuss, no muss, no casualties. That is what happened in the real war. A Good War version of this same incident would not have missed the opportunity to showboat the incident by having someone, probably Winters, stand up to the regimental commander at the risk of his job, displaying nobility and an utter lack of common sense.

Juxtaposed against *Independence Day* and *Saving Private Ryan* as the third culturally significant war movie of the 1990s is *Three Kings* (1999). It makes the boldest attempt yet to break free from the Good War's clutches. *Three Kings* is set in 1991 in the immediate aftermath of Operation Desert Storm, when the cease-fire between Iraq and Coalition forces has just taken effect. George Clooney plays a disaffected career officer who agrees to lead two, and eventually three, enlisted men in their search for a hidden cache of gold stolen from Kuwait by the Iraqis. Although not a great hit at the box office *Three Kings* impressed many critics. Roger Ebert called it a weird masterpiece (see his review at suntimes.com) for its original combination of humor and action. Unlike most films in this genre *Three Kings* makes a point, it being that while President George Bush I called upon the people to rise up against Saddam Hussein he failed to back them when they did. After witnessing atrocities committed by Iraqi troops, Clooney pulls a Bogart; he and his men lead a group of refugees to Iran and safety. They are pursued by Iraqi soldiers and by American troops as well for having disobeyed standing orders. Critics liked the film's look, its pace, its way of turning clichés upside down, and its emphasis upon character as well as action. This is one film that does not support the national security state but rather brings out the moral and political complexities of postcolonial wars.

The film is different in other ways also. It is a war movie that takes place after the war is technically over but chaos and violence still reign supreme. Eerily it foreshadows President Bush II's invasion of Iraq, after which lawlessness and disorder became a way of life for Iraqis. Unlike Vietnam War movies, the Iraqi soldiers and civilians are not a mysterious or neglected "other" but actual people. While President Bush I made the mistake of comparing Saddam Hussein to Hitler and tried to represent the First Gulf War as another World War II, *Three Kings* says it was all about loot, Kuwaiti gold standing in for oil, the real wealth of the region. One day we may regard this film as a masterpiece unappreciated in its time, much as we now view *Dr. Strangelove*.

VI

By far the most important way in which films and television really criticize the national security state is by promoting conspiracy storylines. Conspiracy theories go back a long way, but after World War II a kind of theory explosion took place. The atomic bomb had a great deal to do with this proliferation as it demonstrated that the United States could build something like a doomsday machine without the public having a clue. Indeed, ever since World War II, the executive branch has insisted that keeping Americans (and their elected representatives) in the dark about a wide range of activities is imperative. Not knowing what goes on behind close doors encourages suspicion that what is unknown might also be evil. Hollywood has relentlessly cashed in on such suspicions.

We will be concerned chiefly with government and/or military conspiracies that have been the subject of film and TV dramas. There is even a film entitled *Conspiracy Theory* (1997) that covers every base. Mel Gibson, the star of *Conspiracy Theory*, plays a seemingly addled New York cab driver who believes in all known conspiracy theories. He even publishes his own newsletter that sums everything up and has a grand total of five subscribers. Then he is abducted and beaten by CIA agents, absolute proof that a conspiracy is afoot. His problem is that Gibson has no idea which of the many CIA-related conspiracies wants him out of the way. Eventually he learns the truth in a film that both mocks conspiracy theorists and suggests that sometimes they are right.

Some of the better conspiracy movies were released in the 1970s, inspired probably by Watergate, a real conspiracy. Director Alan J. Pakula's *The Parallax View* (1974) begins with the assassination of a United States senator in the Seattle Space Needle. Although a government commission concludes that a single killer was to blame, witnesses to the crime keep turning up missing, including journalist Warren Beatty's girlfriend. Beatty traces the crime to the little known but apparently omnipotent Parallax Corporation, which he infiltrates. Dark even by conspiracy standards, *The Parallax View* failed commercially.

Not so Sydney Pollack's *Three Days of the Condor*, one of the top grossing films of 1975. CIA analyst Robert Redford comes back from lunch to his small office in New York only to find that all of his coworkers have been slaughtered. When he reports to his boss someone tries to kill him as well. On the run, he holes up with Faye Dunaway in hopes to getting his story to the *New York Times*. It transpires that everyone with power is corrupt. But, low on the totem pole as he is, Redford manages to outwit the conspirators, a cheering end to a film about government conspiracies in the Watergate era.

The best of these films is about that very same conspiracy. *All the President's Men* (1976) stars Redford again, this time as the reporter Bob Woodward, who together with Carl Bernstein (Dustin Hoffman), broke the Watergate story. Sensing there was more to the burglarizing of Democratic Party headquarters than simple theft, and with the support of *Washington Post* editor Ben Bradlee (Jason Robards), Woodward and Bernstein establish a link between the crime and the Nixon White House. With invaluable hints provided by a mysterious informant, Deep Throat, Woodward and Bernstein "follow the money." It takes them all the way to the top. The film does not claim that President Nixon authorized, or knew about, the Watergate break-in, a covert political operation not a burglary. But in the film, as in life, the two reporters find a host of crimes and irregularities. Even though we know the ending, *All the President's Men* is an exciting, fast paced movie that entertains even as it instructs. In the film, as in life again, the guilty are punished, high officials go to

jail, and Nixon resigns his office. This happy ending is all the more satisfactory for being true. The picture made money and won critical acclaim,
although, as so often happens, it lost the Oscar for best picture.

The Blob (1988) is one of the most neglected movies in this genre.
Loosely based on a 1958 science fiction film with the same title, *The Blob*
updates the basic plot for a more cynical era. In the original, the Blob is an
alien entity from outer space, which grows exponentially as it absorbs
people. The remake turns the alien into a biological weapon manufactured by the usual secret government agency. No sooner does the Blob arrive than soldiers and scientists turn up in protective suits. They herd the
townspeople together, and everyone is then nearly devoured by the out of
control Blob. A plucky girl and her unlikely sidekick, the town's resident
juvenile delinquent, save them, in a nice change from the original. A low
budget picture with a cast of unknowns, the film whipped through theaters in a flash but survives on cable, video, and DVD. Apart from adding
its bit to government conspiracy lore, *The Blob* is amusing and does not
take itself too seriously.

The most controversial conspiracy picture is Oliver Stone's *JFK* (1991).
President Kennedy's assassination has been a favorite subject of conspiracy
buffs ever since it took place, and the report of the blue ribbon Warren
Commission, which found Lee Harvey Oswald to have been a lone gun-
man, did nothing to discourage the many Americans, millions perhaps,
who are always ready to believe the worst about their government. *The
Warren Report* is big and boring, and, while *JFK* at 189 minutes running
time is big as well, no one can call it boring. Conspiracy theorists have
blamed Kennedy's murder on everyone from Lyndon Baines Johnson to
organized crime. Stone chose to base his interpretation on the accusations
of New Orleans District Attorney Jim Garrison (Kevin Costner). A hero to
some and an opportunistic glory hound to many more, Garrison, after
making numerous unsupported allegations, indicts a local businessman
Clay Shaw (Tommy Lee Jones). In real life a jury cleared Shaw of the base-
less charges brought against him. Indeed, no concrete evidence supports
any of the wild charges made in this movie. Historians detest the film,
which was popular all the same, grossing over $70 million domestically in
its first year. By this time American box office receipts often ended up being less than half the total earned by a film. Foreign rights have become
more important, as also video sales and rentals, and, latterly DVDs. A film
like *JFK* could easily earn hundreds of millions over the years. But, while
JFK garnered eight Oscar nominations it won only two, for photography

and editing, the Motion Picture Academy coming down on the side of taste and accuracy, for a change.

A film that mocks the genre, Barry Levinson's *Wag the Dog* (1997), is just about perfect. Shortly before his reelection a Clinton-like president is accused of having sex with a girl scout in the Oval Office. Political consultant Robert De Niro is brought in to spin the incident. He persuades movie producer Dustin Hoffman to distract the public by creating an imaginary war with Albania, confident that the public does not know where, or even what, Albania is. Hoffman, in a brilliant comic performance, produces the war on a sound stage with a direct link to CNN. The war has its own song and logo and a champion, Woody Harrelson, nominally a rescued pilot, actually a crazed military prisoner. The phony war works and the president is reelected, although Hoffman gets too caught up in the enterprise for his own good. The novel on which *Wag the Dog* is dimly based, *American Hero* (1993) by Larry Beinhart, depicts the First Persian Gulf War in a similar light, with President George Bush and Sadaam Hussein as the co-conspirators.

The mother lode of television conspiracy stories is *The X-Files*. It premiered in September 1993 and by the time its long run ended in May 2002 *The X-Files* had served up to viewers an extraordinary number of paranormal events. To critic Joyce Millman it was the defining TV series of the nineties because it "hauntingly captured the cultural moment when paranoid distrust of government spilled over from the political fringes to the mainstream, aided by the conspiracy-theory-disseminating capability of the Internet. With its high-level cover-ups, Deep Throats and adherence to the watchwords "Trust no one," "The X-Files" tapped into still-fresh memories of Iran-contra and Watergate, not to mention Ruby Ridge and Waco."[16] The series turns on two FBI agents, Mulder (David Duchovny) and Scully (Gillian Anderson), who receive all the cases for which no rational explanation can be found. Mulder had once been a rising star in the Bureau, but aliens abducted his sister in childhood and gradually his obsession with her disappearance broadened to include practically everything in the conspiracy theory handbook—hence his banishment to a remote sub-basement of the J. Edgar Hoover Building. Scully, both an agent and a physician, is assigned to rein in Mulder, her hard, science-based skepticism offsetting his unhealthy open mindedness.

Although many episodes are free standing, the main conspiracies involve aliens who are seeking to take over the planet, the government's conspiracy to keep the public from learning the truth, and also a secret effort involving leaders of the private and public sectors to create a race of supermen who can defeat the aliens. The show began as a cult hit, but loyal supporters, who called themselves X-philes, generated so much buzz on the Internet that it became a real success. As the writers made little effort to keep the various story lines on track, or sometimes even intelligible, watching *The X-Files* can be a bewildering experience. Like most long series the show eventually ran out of steam. Duchovny lost interest in his role and mostly absented himself for its last two seasons. By then, however, *The X-Files* had pretty much achieved its goal of bringing to the small screen all the national obsessions, and then some, that had for so long been movie staples.

What are we to make of this genre as a whole? Apart from films made strictly for their entertainment value such as *Conspiracy Theory* and *The Blob*, they would seem to fall into two categories, films about real conspiracies, notably *All the President's Men*, and films that give a conspiratorial interpretation to actual events such as *JFK*. *Wag The Dog* inhabits a third category unique to itself in which a fictional conspiracy is so convincing that it seems to predict the future. *Wag The Dog* came out in 1997 and in 1999 President Clinton bombed Serbia for 11 weeks, some critics claiming that he did so to distract public attention from the Monica Lewinsky case, which was all over the news then. Conversely it might explain the past, as when President Nixon put the military on high alert during the 1973 Arab-Israeli war to drag people's minds away from Watergate. Both accusations now seem unfounded, but *Wag The Dog* remains a classic cautionary tale all the same.

All conspiracy films blur the line between the real and the unreal. And they all encourage the public to distrust government, the better the film the more effectively it promotes suspicion. In this sense they all, even those with nothing more than entertainment value, subvert the national security apparatus to greater or lesser degrees. The drawback is that because conspiracy films always have villains, the viewer is freed from the need to look for deeper, more structural explanations of governmental misbehavior. This negates the genre's usefulness.

Conspiracy films and TV series, along with the exceptions already noted, do little to weaken the rule that Hollywood and television legitimize, or obscure the existence of, the national security state. Films made during World War II, which were consciously meant to support the war effort, show these effects in their purest forms. But the overwhelming majority of serious combat films focus on a small group of mostly good men, doing a hard, risky, and distasteful job as best they can. This clearly has little to do with politics, since liberals who do not consciously serve as flacks for the Pentagon make most Hollywood films. For the most part, combat films reinforce Good War stereotypes that work in the military's favor. The World War II combat film, even after all these years, has an overpowering attraction. War movies almost invariably gravitate toward it and, as we have seen, even *Saving Private Ryan*, the most spectacular combat film ever made, begins with savage realism but ends in a welter of genre clichés.

The media, including print and TV journalism, want every war to be the Good War, and so does every war leader. President George Bush I tried to make the First Gulf War seem like World War II all over again and President George Bush II encored his father during and after the Second Gulf War. Journalists attempted, against heavy odds, to find Good War features in both conflicts. Life even imitated art when the military made its own picture, "Saving Private Lynch." in 2003. To her everlasting credit, Private Jessica Lynch insisted that she had not fought off her captors until she ran out of ammunition. She had been well treated by her Iraqi doctors and nurses and was in no danger when American troops stormed the undefended hospital to "rescue" her. But the film—that is, the storm of publicity aroused by her capture and return—eclipsed the truth and Private Lynch became a hero despite herself.

The farther we get from World War II the more we seem to want it back. The desire is not literal, in the sense of taking heavy casualties and making sacrifices at home. No one wishes to see 400,000 Americans die for their country again. Even after 9/11 and the onset of a conflict that some have likened to another world war, there is no clamor for a draft, or high taxes, or rationing, or any of the real hardships that marked the last war effort we ever had that engaged the entire population. But we yearn for the unity and remembered purpose of those years, the authentic patriotism, the sharp division between good and evil, and the combat squad—that little melting pot emblematic of the nation at arms. Beginning with Vietnam and continuing through the Gulf Wars, efforts to recapture the Good War have become increasingly hollow. Often they amount to little more than attacking critics as traitors and saying that everyone must "support our troops," meaning keep them in harm's way for the sake of political agendas, when obviously nothing would help the troops more than bringing them home unscathed. It is the apparent mission of popular culture to add to this confusion by helping people see what they want to see, or at least by distracting them from uncomfortable truths.

This is true of the news media as well. Some documentaries and newspaper stories explore the big issues raised by America's seizure of Iraq. But overwhelmingly the news media concern themselves with suicide bombings, human-interest stories, and the small picture. In the First Gulf War news reporting was notoriously bad because military leaders, believing they had been burned by the media in Vietnam, kept reporters out of the field and provided them only with information that the authorities wanted people to have. After numerous complaints the second time around reporters were assigned to, "embedded in" as they say, combat units. But owing to self-censorship and the desire of news agencies to entertain their audiences the reporting did not get any better. The line between news and entertainment having disappeared, news organizations increasingly are just another arm of show business.

So the national security state forges ahead, protected by images of the Good War, endlessly repeated and recast by the mass media, and by print and broadcast journalism's instinctive desire to make every war a Good War. Like F. Scott Fitzgerald's boats beating against the current, we are borne back ceaselessly into the past, and not even the real past but an ever more idealized version of what never was and never shall be.

Notes

1.   Thomas Doherty, *Projections of War: Hollywood, American Culture, and World War II* (New York: Columbia University Press, 1993), 5.

2.   Ibid., 133.

3.   Ibid., 272.

4.   Michael S. Sherry, *The Rise of American Air Power: The Creation of Armageddon* (New Haven: Yale University Press, 1987).

5.   William Bluem, *Documentary in American Television* (New York: Hastings, 1965).

6.   Norman Kagan, *The War Film* (New York: Pyramid, 1974), 76.

7.   Josh Ozersky, *Archie Bunker's America: TV in an Era of Change* (Carbondale: Southern Illinois University Press, 2003), 12.

8.   Larry Gelbart, *Laughing Matters: On Writing M*A*S*H, Tootsie, Oh God!, and a Few Other Funny Things* (New York: Random House, 1998), 32.

9.   Katherine Kinney, *Friendly Fire: American Images of the Vietnam War* (New York: Oxford University Press, 2000), 12.

10. Colonel David H. Hackworth and Julie Sherman and *About Face: The Odyssey of an American Warrior* (New York: Touchstone, 1989).

11. Tony Williams, "Narrative Patterns and Mythic Trajectories in Mid'1980's Vietnam Movies," in Michael Anderegg, ed., *Inventing Vietnam* (Philadelphia: Temple University Press, 1991), 118.

12. Harold G. Moore and Joseph L. Galloway, *We Were Soldiers Once . . . and Young: Ia Drang—The Battle That Changed The War in Vietnam* (New York: Random House, 1992).

13. Williams, *Narrative Patterns.*, 126.

14. John Hellmann, "Rambo's Vietnam and Kennedy's New Frontier" in Anderegg, ed., *Inventing Vietnam*, 141.

15. Michael Rogin, *Independence Day, or How I Learned to Stop Worrying and Love the Enola Gay* (London: British Film Institute, 1998), 13.

16. Joyce Millman, "The X'Files' Finds the Truth: Its Time Is Past," *New York Times* (May 19, 2002), AR34.

CONTRIBUTORS

ANDREW J. BACEVICH is professor of history and international relations at Boston University. A graduate of the U.S. Military Academy, he received his Ph.D. in American diplomatic history from Princeton. He is the author most recently of *The New American Militarism: How Americans Are Seduced by War* (2005).

TAMI DAVIS BIDDLE is the George C. Marshall Chair of Military Studies in the Department of National Security and Strategy at the U.S. Army War College in Carlisle, PA, where she teaches national security strategy and military history. Dr. Biddle received her Ph.D. from Yale. Her book, *Rhetoric and Reality in Air Warfare: The Evolution of British and American Ideas about Strategic Bombing, 1914–1945* (2002), was a *Choice* outstanding academic book.

JAMES BURK is professor of sociology at Texas A&M University and former editor of the journal *Armed Forces & Society*. He received his Ph.D. from the University of Chicago and studies the relationships between war, morality, and democracy. His essays have appeared in *Armed Forces & Society, Citizenship Studies, The Journal of Military Ethics*, and *Social Forces* among other publications.

CHARLES CHATFIELD is H.O. Hirt Professor of History Emeritus of Wittenberg University. He earned his Ph.D. at Vanderbilt University, and has interpreted historic U.S. peace and antiwar movements. His books include *The American Peace Movement* (1992) and, with Charles DeBenedetti, *An American Ordeal: The Antiwar Movement of the Vietnam Era* (1990).

Benjamin O. Fordham is associate professor of political science at Binghamton University (SUNY). His research focuses on the influence of domestic political and economic considerations on foreign policy choices, particularly those concerning military spending and the use of force. He has essays in *International Studies Quarterly, International Organization, The Journal of Conflict Resolution, The Journal of Politics,* and elsewhere.

James Kurth is Claude Smith Professor of Political Science at Swarthmore College, where he teaches international politics and U.S. defense and foreign policy. He received his Ph.D. in political science from Harvard University and has been a visiting professor of strategy at the U.S. Naval War College. He is the author of more than ninety professional articles on international and military affairs.

Anna Kasten Nelson is the Distinguished Historian in Residence at American University where she teaches courses on American foreign policy. She has published on a wide variety of subjects while concentrating on the evolution of the national security process during the first decades of the Cold War. Among the journals where her articles can be found are *Diplomatic History, The Journal of American History, Political Science Quarterly, The Journal of Military History,* and *Cuban Studies.*

Arnold A. Offner is Cornelia F. Hugel Professor of History at Lafayette College. A graduate of Columbia University, he received his Ph.D. in American History from Indiana University. His most recent book is *Another Such Victory: President Truman and the Cold War, 1945–1953* (2002).

William L. O'Neill is a professor emeritus of history at Rutgers University. He received his Ph.D. from the University of California at Berkeley. His latest book, *Tabloid Nation*, a history of the United States in the 1990s, is due to appear in the fall of 2007.

John Prados, a senior fellow with the National Security Archive in Washington, DC, graduated from Columbia College in history and holds a Ph.D. in international relations from Columbia University. The author of many works on national security, intelligence, diplomatic and military history, and foreign policy, his most recent book is *Safe for Democracy: The Secret Wars of the CIA* (2006).

GEORGE QUESTER is a professor of government and politics at the University of Maryland, where he teaches courses on international security, American foreign policy, and international relations. He has taught also at Harvard and Cornell Universities, UCLA, the National War College and the United States Naval Academy. His most recent book is *Nuclear First Strike: Consequences of a Broken Taboo* (2006).

ALEX ROLAND is professor of history at Duke University, where he teaches military history and the history of technology. A graduate of the U.S. Naval Academy, he took his Ph.D. at Duke. He is the author most recently of *The Military-Industrial Complex* (2001) and, with Philip Shiman, *Strategic Computing: DARPA and the Quest for Machine Intelligence, 1983–1993* (2002).

INDEX

model, 37–38; Four Freedoms, 3–4; Guam Doctrine, 21–22; Kennedy administration, 18–20, 22; lessons of history, 37–38, 41; liberation politics, 31–32; Marshall Plan, 9–10; nation-building doctrine, 39; neoconservatism, 23–24; Nixon administration, 21–23; oil interests and, 31; political-economic systems, 37–38; radical changes in U.S. policy, 41–42; Reagan administration, 26–29; realism, 22–24; Roosevelt administration, 2–4; "The National Security Policy of the United States," 1–2; Truman administration, 4–14; Truman Doctrine, 7–10; universality, rhetoric of, 34, 37; U.S. military superiority, 37–38; Vietnam era, 15–16; war against terrorism, 37, 498–99; Wilsonianism, 2–3. *see also* Cold War ideology; containment; National Security Document 68; "National Security Strategy" (Bush NSS, 2002); preemption/preventive war

Immigration and Naturalization Service, 489

imperialism, 13, 142, 456, 458–59

Independence Day (movie), 538–39

individualism, 346

Indochina, 66, 456. *see also* Vietnam War

industry: defense contractors, 357–61; regional distribution of manufacturing, 385–95, *387, 390*; war as industrial enterprise, 211–12

INF (intermediate range nuclear weapons treaty), 29, 177, 183–84, 502

information technology, 124–25, 195, 295

intelligence, 266–67; 1945–1947 era, 304–5; 1950–1952 era, 304–5, 305; 1992–1995 era, 307; accuracy of, 86; analytic element, 316–23; as ancillary form of military action, 302–3, 305; budgets, 307–8; Bush, George H. W. administration and, 313; Bush, George W. administration and, 311–12; career advancement,

320; clandestine services vs. technical collection, 323–32; Clinton administration and, 314, 331; Cold War factor, 304–5; collection capability, 308; cryptography, 305; disciplines, 316–17; Eisenhower administration and, 324–25; eras of, 304–5; estimates, 317–19; external influences on, 304–5, 308; fusion concept, 308–9, 331; Intel-Link computer network, 322–23; internal expectations, 304–5; Iran-Contra affair and, 310–11, 330; Kennedy administration and, 327; Korean War and, 272, 305, 318, 325; military, 274, 303, 306–7, 317–18; origins of, 302–3; overhead photography, 305, 321; patterns, 304–12; Pearl Harbor factor, 302, 303, 305, 307; political actions, 325; post-Cold War reductions, 307–8; presidential findings, 310–11; product, 317; Reagan administration and, 310–11, 313, 331; reductions reconsidered, 312–16; relationship between analysts and managers, 317, 320; scientific, 305; September 11, 2001 attacks and, 307–8, 311, 331; strategic forces and, 155–56; studies, 315–16; technology and, 305, 322–23; Truman administration and, 323–24; war on terrorism and, 331. *see also* Central Intelligence Agency; covert operations; Defense Intelligence Agency; National Security Council; national security state; *individual agencies*

Intelligence Advisory Board, 275

Intelligence Advisory Committee (IAC), 318

intelligence community: charter proposal, 310; controversies within, 320; oversight, patterns of, 309–12; White House monitoring of, 309

Intelligence Community Staff, 307

Intelligence Identities Protection Act, 310

Intelligence Oversight Act of 1980, 311

Intel-Link, 322–23